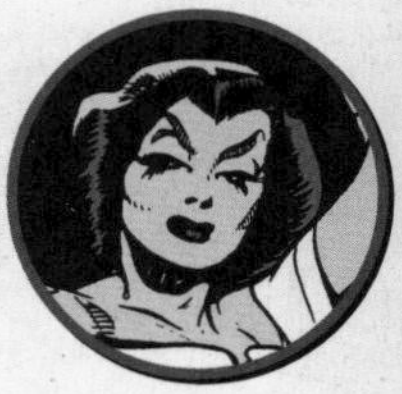

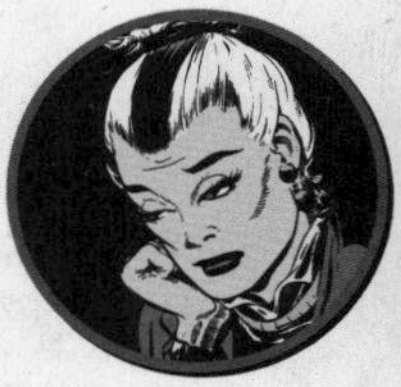

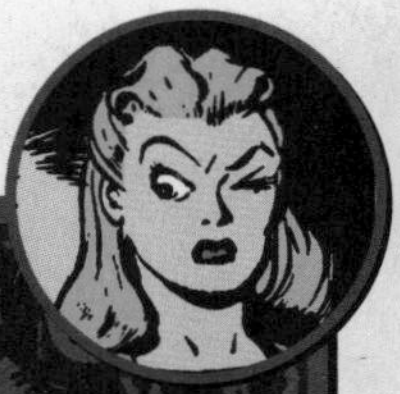

Denny ... ung criminologist,
believe... ost his life in a fight against crime,
was bur... tate of suspended animation.

He awoke o... in Wildwood Cemetery,
determined ... ry on his struggle...
his true identit... known only to Police Commissioner Dolan.

He is feared b... riminals of all stripes as the SPIRIT!

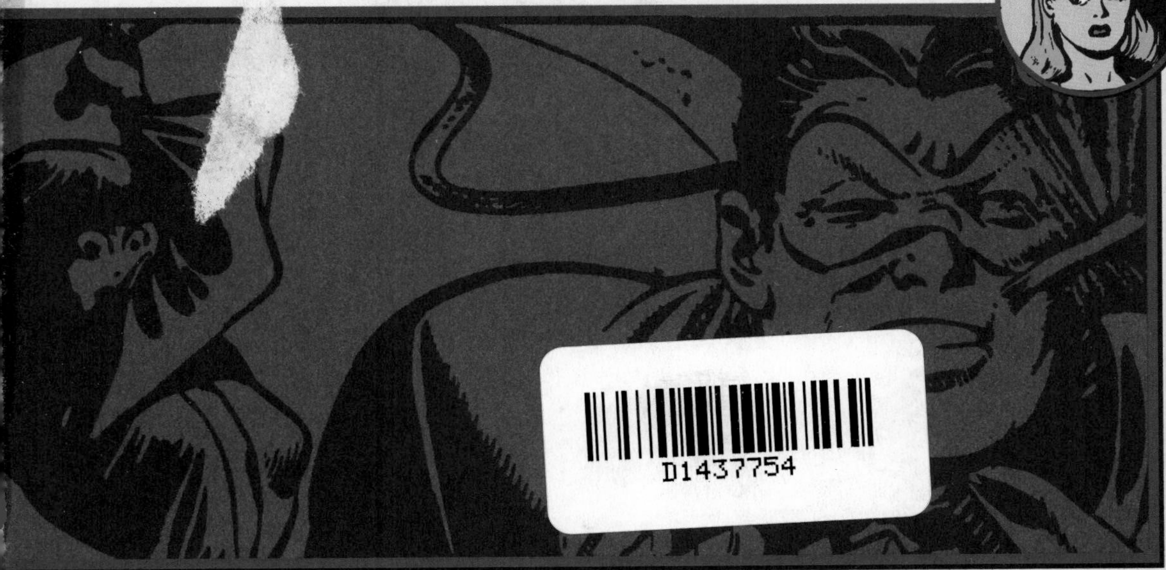

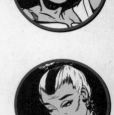

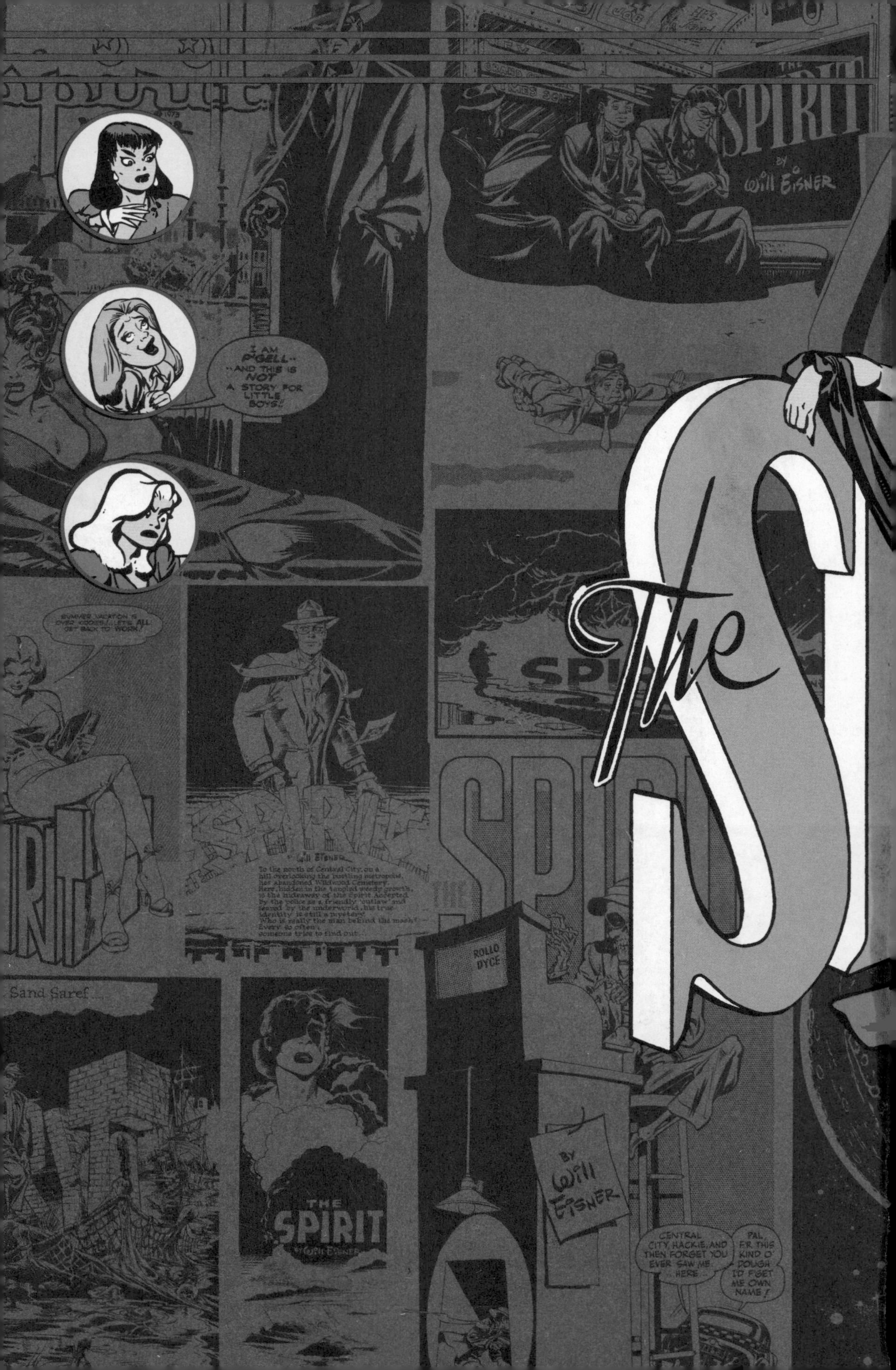

THE SPIRIT
BY Will Eisner
I AM P'GELL.. ..AND THIS IS NOT A STORY FOR LITTLE BOYS!
SUMMER VACATION IS OVER KIDDIES... LET'S ALL GET BACK TO WORK!
SPIRIT
SPIRIT
Will Eisner
To the north of Central City, on a hill overlooking the bustling metropolis, lies abandoned Wildwood Cemetery. Here, hidden in the tangled weedy growth, is the hideaway of the Spirit. Accepted by the police as a friendly 'outlaw' and feared by the underworld, his true identity is still a mystery. Who is really the man behind the mask? Every so often, someone tries to find out...
SPIRIT
THE SPIRIT
The S
ROLLO DYCE
Sand Saref...
THE SPIRIT
BY Will Eisner
CENTRAL CITY, HACKIE, AND THEN FORGET YOU EVER SAW ME. HERE
PAL, FR THIS KIND O' DOUGH I'D F'GET ME OWN NAME!

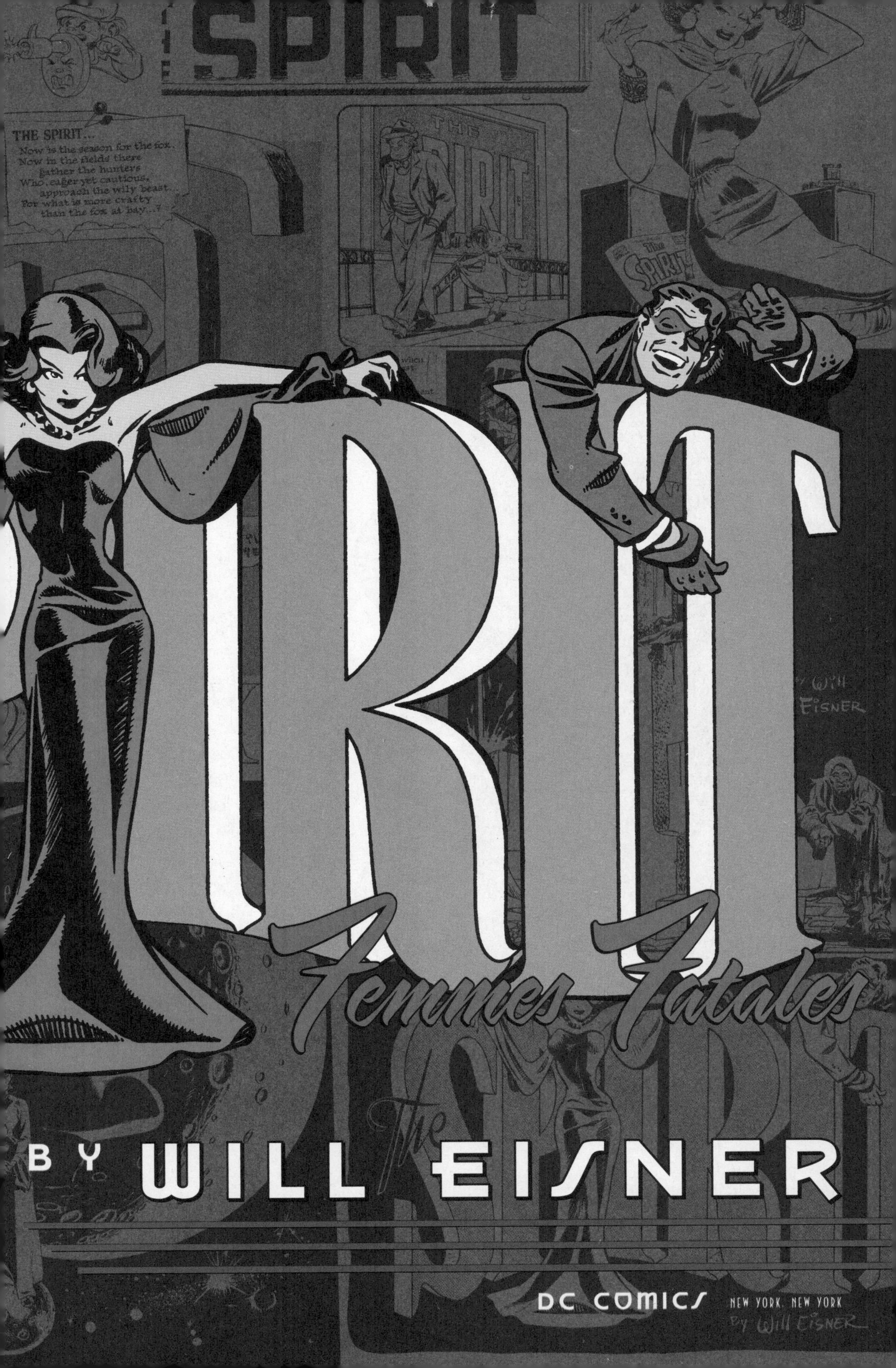
SPIRIT
THE SPIRIT...
Now is the season for the fox.
Now in the fields there
gather the hunters
Who, eager yet cautious,
approach the wily beast...
For what is more crafty
than the fox at bay...?
The SPIRIT
Femmes Fatales
The SPIRIT
BY WILL EISNER
DC COMICS NEW YORK, NEW YORK
By Will Eisner

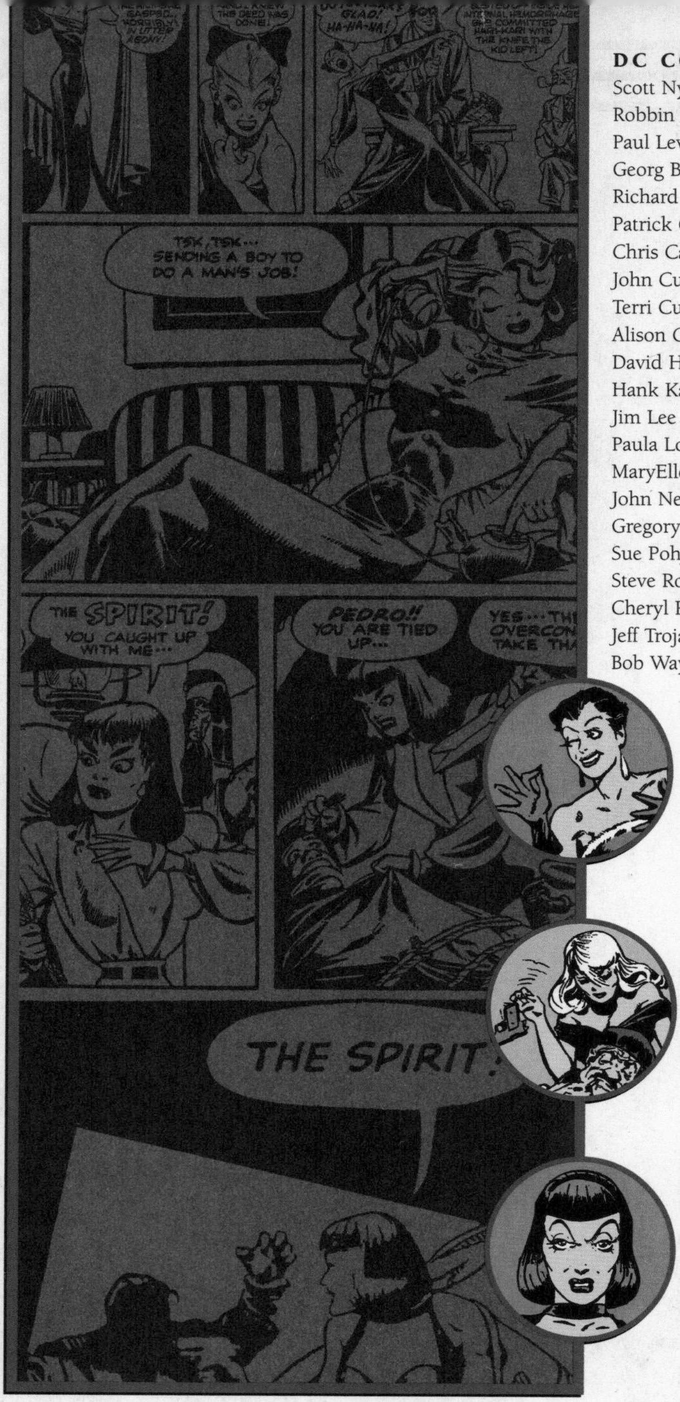

TSK, TSK...
SENDING A BOY TO
DO A MAN'S JOB!
THE SPIRIT!
YOU CAUGHT UP
WITH ME...
PEDRO!!
YOU ARE TIED
UP...
THE SPIRIT!

Throughout the run of The Spirit, *Will Eisner was assisted by many talented individuals, among them John Belfi, Phillip (Tex) Blaisdell, Chris Christiansen, Jack Cole, Martin DeMuth, Jim Dixon, Jules Feiffer, Dick French, Lou Fine, Jerry Grandenetti, Abe Kaenegson, Jack Keller, Robin King, Alex Kotzky, Joe Kubert, Andre LeBlanc, Marilyn Mercer, Klaus Nordling, Ben Oda, Bob Palmer, Don Perlin, Bob Powell, Sam Rosen, Aldo Rubano, Sam Schwartz, John Spranger, Manny Stallman, Manly Wade Wellman, Al Wenzel, Wallace Wood, and Bill Woolfolk.*

The Author and publisher wish to thank them for their vital contributions.

Cover illustrations by Will Eisner.
Cover color and interior color reconstruction by Jamison.
Special thanks to Bill Blackbeard, Director of the San Francisco Academy of Comic Art, Diamond International Galleries *and* Denis Kitchen *for loan of source material.*
Publication design by Amie Brockway-Metcalf.

DC Comics, 1700 Broadway, New York, NY 10019. A Warner Bros. Entertainment Company
Printed in Canada. First Printing. ISBN: 978-1-4012-1973-4.

TABLE OF CONTENTS

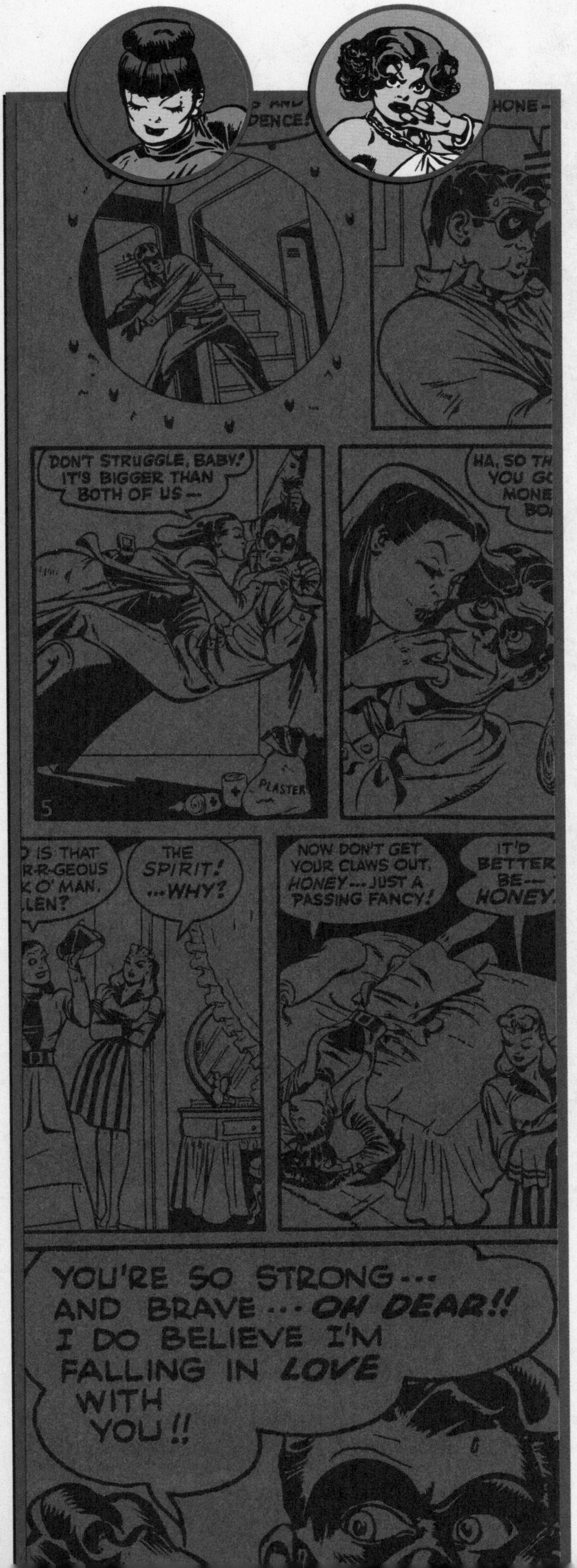
DON'T STRUGGLE, BABY! IT'S BIGGER THAN BOTH OF US—
PLASTER
THE SPIRIT! ...WHY?
NOW DON'T GET YOUR CLAWS OUT, HONEY— JUST A PASSING FANCY!
YOU'RE SO STRONG... AND BRAVE... OH DEAR!! I DO BELIEVE I'M FALLING IN LOVE WITH YOU!!

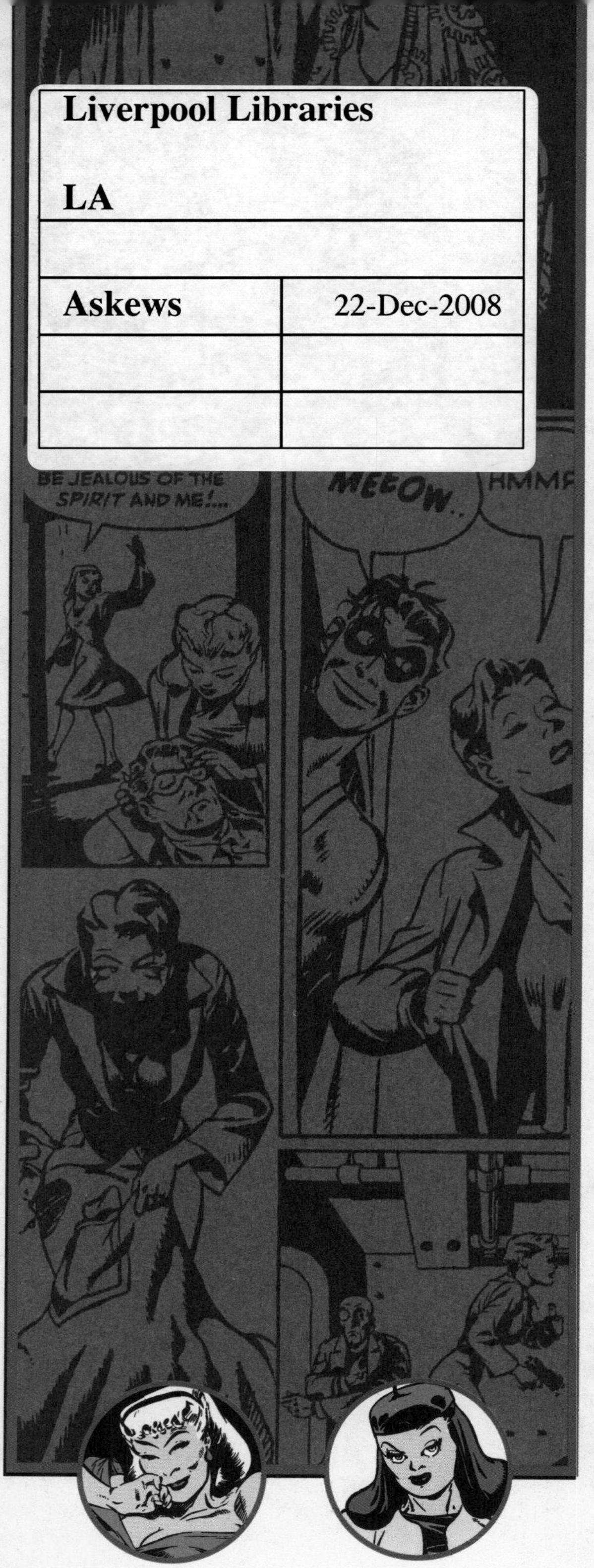
BE JEALOUS OF THE SPIRIT AND ME!...
MEEOW..

THE SPIRIT: *Cherchez La Femme!*

No one ever taught me what *femme fatale* meant during four years of high school French classes. Will Eisner, however, taught me in the pages of *The Spirit*. Inspired by the Dragon Lady and Burma from the newspaper comic strip *Terry and the Pirates*, and by the greatest actresses of the golden age of Hollywood (Joan Crawford, Veronica Lake, Mary Astor, Katharine Hepburn, Lauren Bacall, Rita Hayworth, Barbara Stanwyck, Loretta Young, Lana Turner and so many more), Will Eisner took his villainesses seriously — deadly seriously. In Will's own words:

> "Exotic female villainesses were not new. I had grown up on [Milton] Caniff's Dragon Lady and those who often inhabited the way-out pulps. 'The Kiss of Death' [the first story in this collection, published on November 10, 1940, five months after the launch of *The Spirit*] was an effort, the first of many, to produce an interesting (and sexy) female villain. 'The Black Queen' was compounded of all the fantasies that I thought would stir my readers. Irony and mysticism are a very good combination. Perhaps the only thing that I 'introduced' was the actual physical struggle between the Spirit and the Queen. I had 'Sheena, Queen of the Jungle,' which I had created for the Fiction House line a few years earlier, do a lot of man-handling. This was the same in reverse. The ending was, of course, the kind of finale that I felt belonged in *The Spirit*. This was 'strong stuff' in 1940."

Drenched in *film noir* cinematic techniques of lighting, mood, character, dialogue and pacing, and influenced by Alfred Hitchcock's work as well as other great directors of the era, Will Eisner brought to life a formidable stable of murderesses, husband killers, blackmailers, extortionists, thieves, assassins and sirens, all cloaked in alluring faces, voluptuous bodies and entrancing hair. Pied Pipers to a city of testosterone-filled lunks, they could mesmerize any man on Earth. Resistance was futile — *except* for a guy called the Spirit.

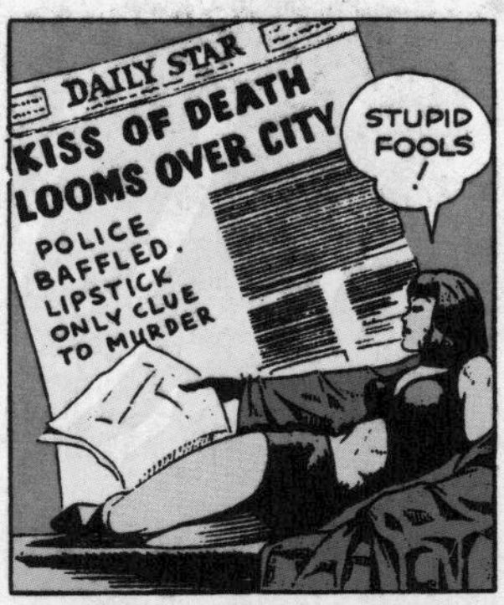
DAILY STAR
KISS OF DEATH LOOMS OVER CITY
POLICE BAFFLED. LIPSTICK ONLY CLUE TO MURDER
STUPID FOOLS !

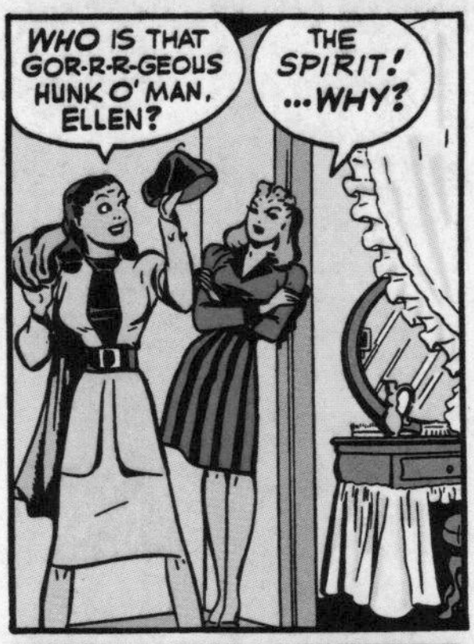
WHO IS THAT GOR-R-R-GEOUS HUNK O' MAN, ELLEN?
THE SPIRIT! ...WHY?

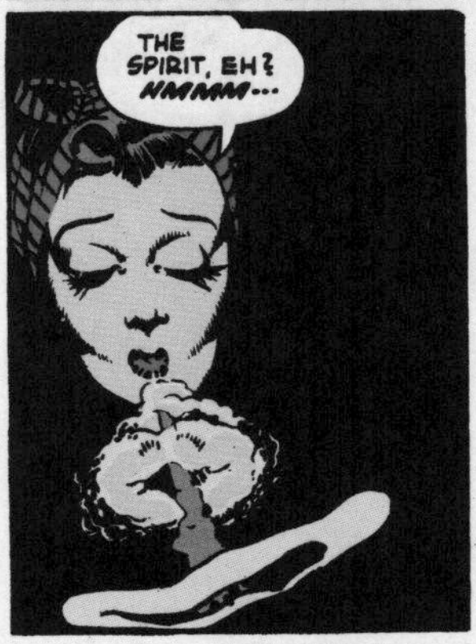
THE SPIRIT, EH? HMMMM...

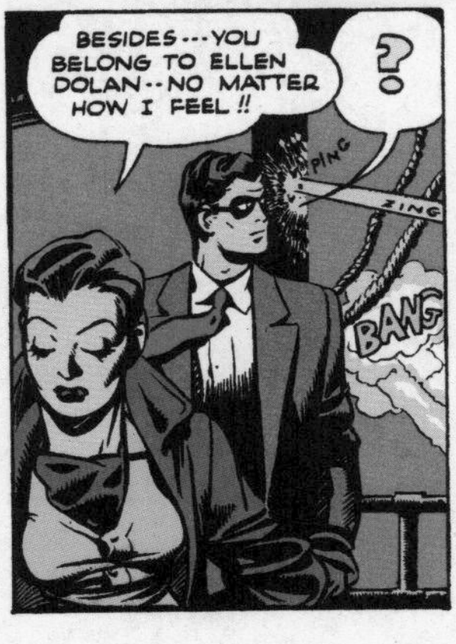
BESIDES---YOU BELONG TO ELLEN DOLAN--NO MATTER HOW I FEEL!!
?
PING
ZING
BANG

In this very special collection we'll meet many of the Spirit's most captivating female adversaries — each as smart, clever, powerful, complex and sexy as the next.

The aforementioned story "Kiss of Death," featuring a Phantom Lady look-alike, sets the pace for Eisner's *femmes fatales* to come: by page five we have the Spirit's first kiss with his sexy nemesis, and by page seven she is already slapping him.

The following tale, "Introducing Silk Satin," is a seminal story in our hero's history. Her name is Sylvia Satin, but everyone knows her as "Silk." She's a bad girl — but not *all* bad. Bad enough to be intriguing to the Spirit, but good enough to let him know she's his equal (Eisner often referred to the character as his female Spirit). A somewhat reformed criminal, Silk winds up working as a spy for the British government in the dark days of World War II — a life whose gray shadows challenge the Spirit's black-and-white perceptions of right and wrong. The palpable sexual tension between the two of them is on full display every time she returns to bewitch, bother and bewilder our Spirit.

Amid all the exotic and erotic bad girls slinking their way through these pages, you'll also find the commanding presence of Ellen Dolan, the Police Commissioner's daughter and the Spirit's true love. She's Betty to Satin's Veronica... the girl next door... the kind you bring home to meet the parents... the kind you marry (eventually). Check out Ellen in the story "Women!" as well as her classic, defining moment in the last few panels of "Thorne Strand and The Spirit." Clearly, she's his link to the real world and to any eventual chance for a normal life.

Before that can happen, though, there's plenty of competition for the Spirit's attention. Silk Satin returns in "Sphinx & Satin," and suffice it to say that by page four she's locked in her ship's stateroom with the masked crimefighter. On the other hand, in "Madame Minx" it takes a whole five pages before the Loretta Young look-alike admits to the Spirit she's madly in love with him (male readers could only bemoan their inability to find women like this in the real world). It's a mere four pages into "Aunt Mathilda" before a busybody tricks the Spirit into marriage, while in "Satin Returns" it's seven pages before Silk and Ellen are trading insults over our hero. In "Nylon Rose," five pages pass before the titular antagonist attempts to sexually assault the Spirit, and it's seven whole pages in "Dulcet Tone" before the women finally get into a catfight over him.

You get the picture. So now let's meet... P'gell!

The splash page of P'gell's introductory story may be the most famous, most reprinted image of all of the original comic's run. It would be easy to ramble on for a page or two of this introduction trying to explain and define P'gell, but truly in this case one picture is worth a thousand words, so I will let the splash speak for itself. P'gell's importance as the Spirit's chief *femme fatale* is demonstrated by the fact that this is merely the first of five P'gell stories gracing this collection. Savor them.

Pantha Stalk, the villainess in "Caramba!" is no P'gell, but she does seem to have a superpower — her amazing ability to hold her plunging (make that "dive-bombing") blouse in place. Far more fascinating is the wonderful Eisner creation named Silken Floss. First introduced in the Spirit adventure published a week prior to the episode reprinted herein, she is a beautiful nuclear physicist with an IQ somewhere between the stratosphere and the ionosphere. In this episode she is also suddenly the world's greatest surgeon. What a learning curve this lady has! And a heart of gold as well. Perfectly played by Scarlett Johansson in Frank Miller's *The Spirit* feature film, Silken reappears in the original comic on just one other occasion (to help the Spirit when he is blinded). Mysteriously under utilized by Eisner, her full back story has only recently come to light in DC's current comic book featuring the Spirit.

"The Name Is Powder," featuring a *Kiss of the Spider Woman*-style logo, is the tale of one of the genuinely bad girls inhabiting the Spirit's world. And if Powder Pouf is a violent dame straight out of some 1930s Warner Bros. crime film, then Wild Rice is a villainess fallen into sheer madness. Parts of her story echo future real events involving actress Frances Farmer and heiress Patty Hearst.

Two of the Spirit's most unforgettable characters are found in the stories "Lorelei Rox" and "Plaster of Paris," both featuring ultra-famous splash pages that showcase Eisner's cinematic techniques and introduce their characters in memorable ways. Who is Lorelei, really? A siren? A witch? A ghost? A war bride with a captivating voice? Eisner never got specific. In Miller's film (where she is played by Jaime King), those questions expand and deepen, raising the possibility of her being some sort of

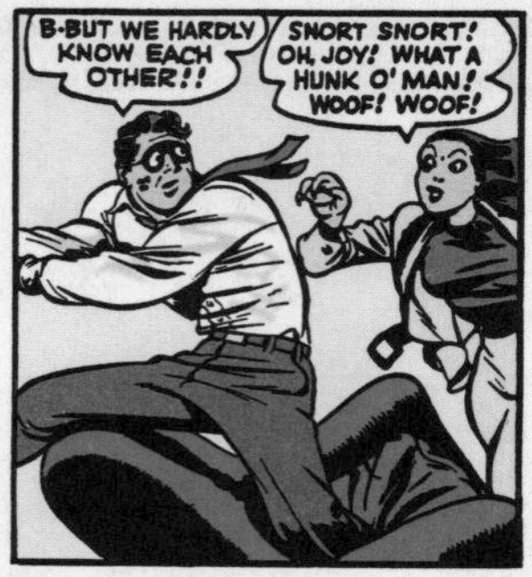
B-BUT WE HARDLY KNOW EACH OTHER!!
SNORT SNORT! OH, JOY! WHAT A HUNK O' MAN! WOOF! WOOF!

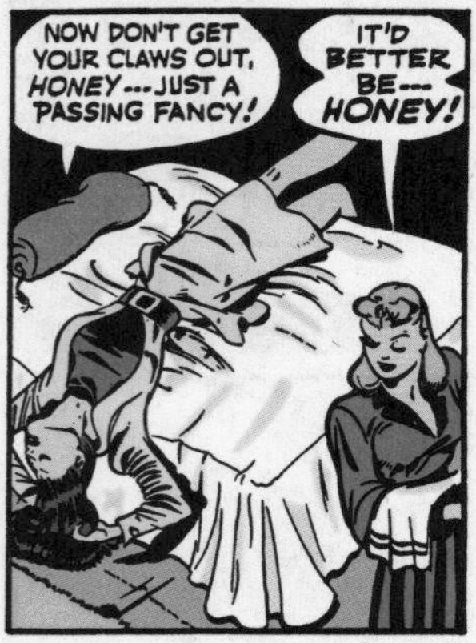
NOW DON'T GET YOUR CLAWS OUT, HONEY--- JUST A PASSING FANCY!
IT'D BETTER BE--- HONEY!

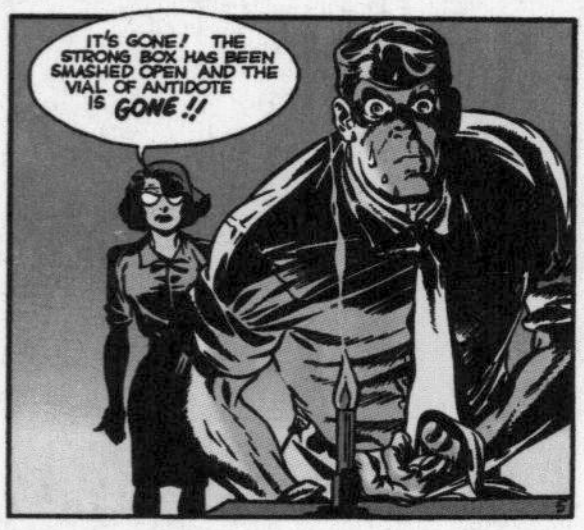
IT'S GONE! THE STRONG BOX HAS BEEN SMASHED OPEN AND THE VIAL OF ANTIDOTE IS GONE!!

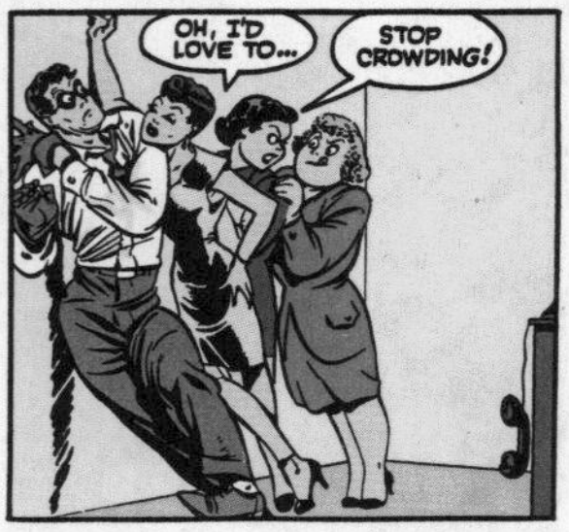
OH, I'D LOVE TO...
STOP CROWDING!

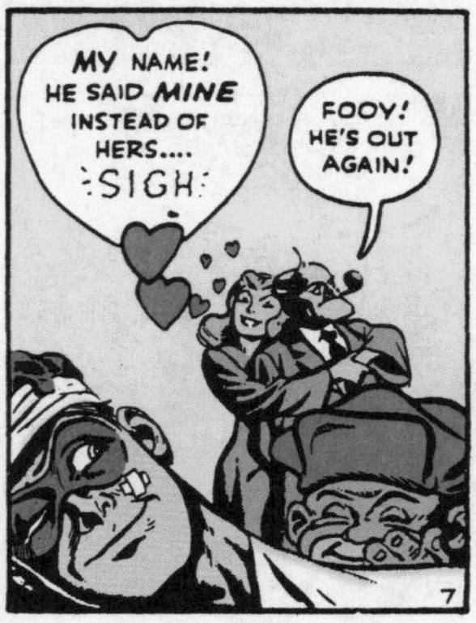
MY NAME! HE SAID MINE INSTEAD OF HERS.... SIGH
FOOY! HE'S OUT AGAIN!
7

modern-day Valkyrie, carting off slain warriors to Valhalla. Or maybe she's a dream, or a figment of Denny Colt's imagination. Again, it's in the ongoing DC title THE SPIRIT that more of her backstory comes to light.

Plaster of Paris is revealed on a page that moves like the finest striptease (Frank Miller was determined to capture the grace of Will's art for this opening in his film, using a heated dance performed around our hero by the already hot Paz Vega in the role of Plaster). Eisner hints in this tale that Plaster and the Spirit have some history together, but once more it's only in the current DC series that we finally learn just how these two met and the nature of their past "adventure" together.

This collection concludes with the villainess Thorne Strand and the slinky adventuress Autumn Mews, as well as with another iconic Eisner splash page. There are so many more great *femmes fatales* in *The Spirit* that one can only hope that the comic book gods will someday permit a second volume of their stories to be released. (One adversary who deserves her own volume is Sand Saref, played in the movie by the beyond-stunning Eva Mendes. Her ties to the Spirit's hidden past place her in a category all by herself.)

Stan Lee always said that a great hero is defined by his villains. Though the vamps and seductresses you're about to meet aren't all evil, they certainly do their part to bring the Spirit into the realm of greatness — each in their own unique, enthralling, maddening way.

–MICHAEL USLAN
2008

Michael Uslan is a producer of Frank Miller's film The Spirit *and an executive producer of the films* Batman Begins *and* The Dark Knight. *He has also written, with F.J. DeSanto, some of the current adventures of Will Eisner's creation in DC Comics' ongoing title THE SPIRIT.*

THE KISS OF DEATH

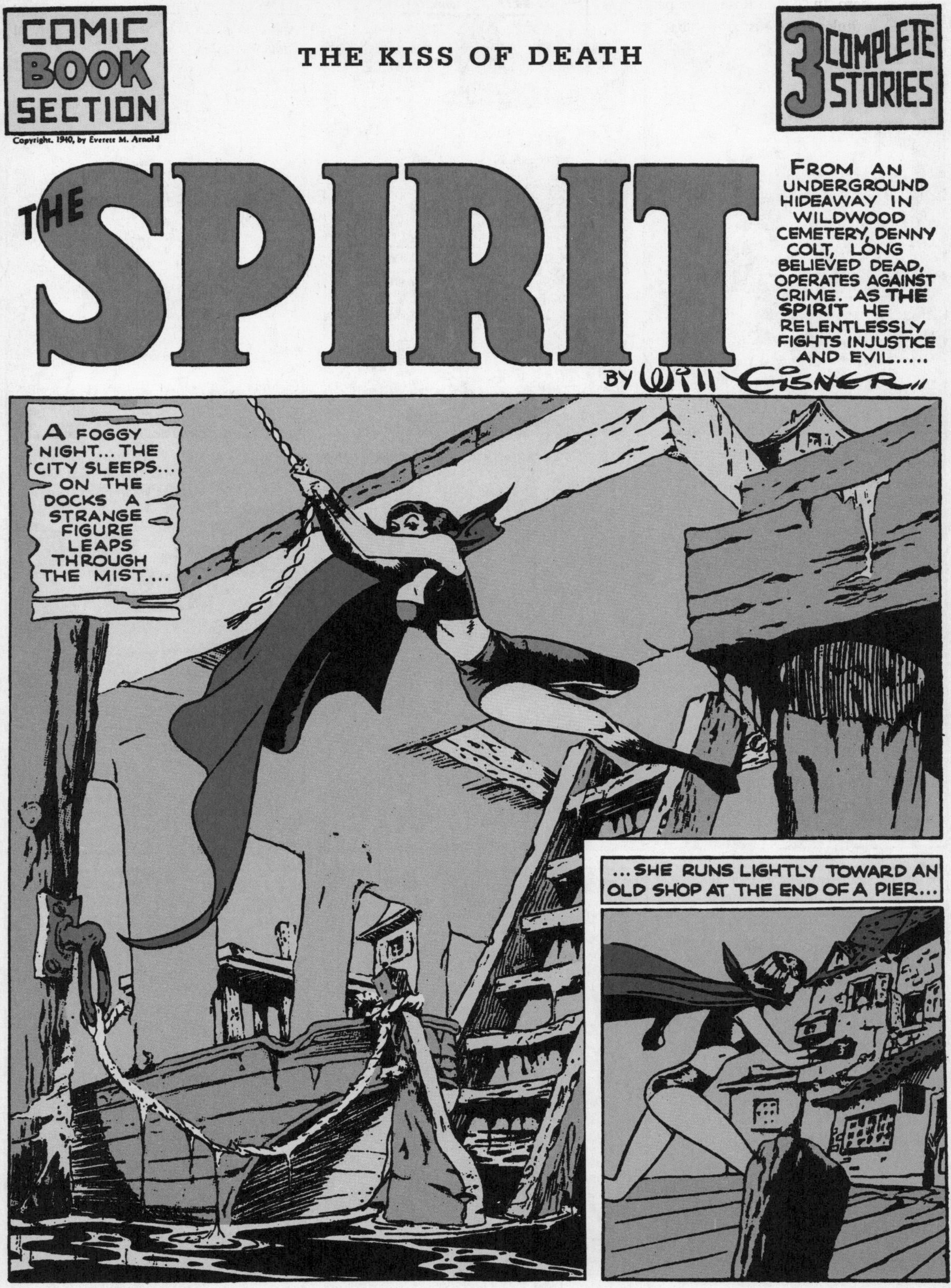
COMIC BOOK SECTION
Copyright, 1940, by Everett M. Arnold
3 COMPLETE STORIES
THE SPIRIT
FROM AN UNDERGROUND HIDEAWAY IN WILDWOOD CEMETERY, DENNY COLT, LONG BELIEVED DEAD, OPERATES AGAINST CRIME. AS THE SPIRIT HE RELENTLESSLY FIGHTS INJUSTICE AND EVIL.....
BY WILL EISNER
A FOGGY NIGHT... THE CITY SLEEPS... ON THE DOCKS A STRANGE FIGURE LEAPS THROUGH THE MIST....
...SHE RUNS LIGHTLY TOWARD AN OLD SHOP AT THE END OF A PIER...

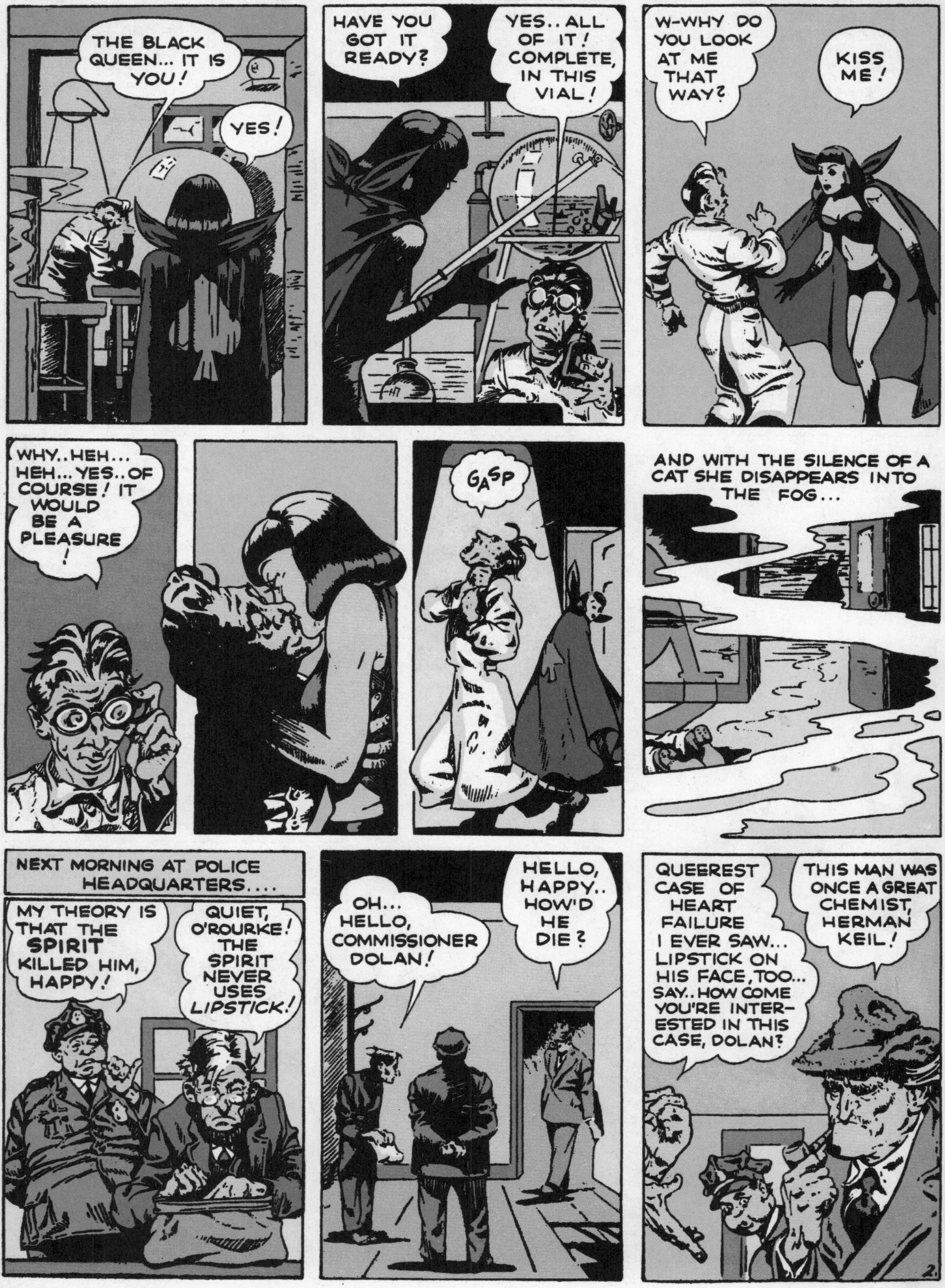

THE BLACK QUEEN... IT IS YOU!
YES!
HAVE YOU GOT IT READY?
YES.. ALL OF IT! COMPLETE, IN THIS VIAL!
W-WHY DO YOU LOOK AT ME THAT WAY?
KISS ME!
WHY.. HEH... HEH... YES.. OF COURSE! IT WOULD BE A PLEASURE!
GASP
AND WITH THE SILENCE OF A CAT SHE DISAPPEARS INTO THE FOG...
NEXT MORNING AT POLICE HEADQUARTERS....
MY THEORY IS THAT THE SPIRIT KILLED HIM, HAPPY!
QUIET, O'ROURKE! THE SPIRIT NEVER USES LIPSTICK!
OH... HELLO, COMMISSIONER DOLAN!
HELLO, HAPPY.. HOW'D HE DIE?
QUEEREST CASE OF HEART FAILURE I EVER SAW... LIPSTICK ON HIS FACE, TOO... SAY.. HOW COME YOU'RE INTERESTED IN THIS CASE, DOLAN?
THIS MAN WAS ONCE A GREAT CHEMIST, HERMAN KEIL!
2.

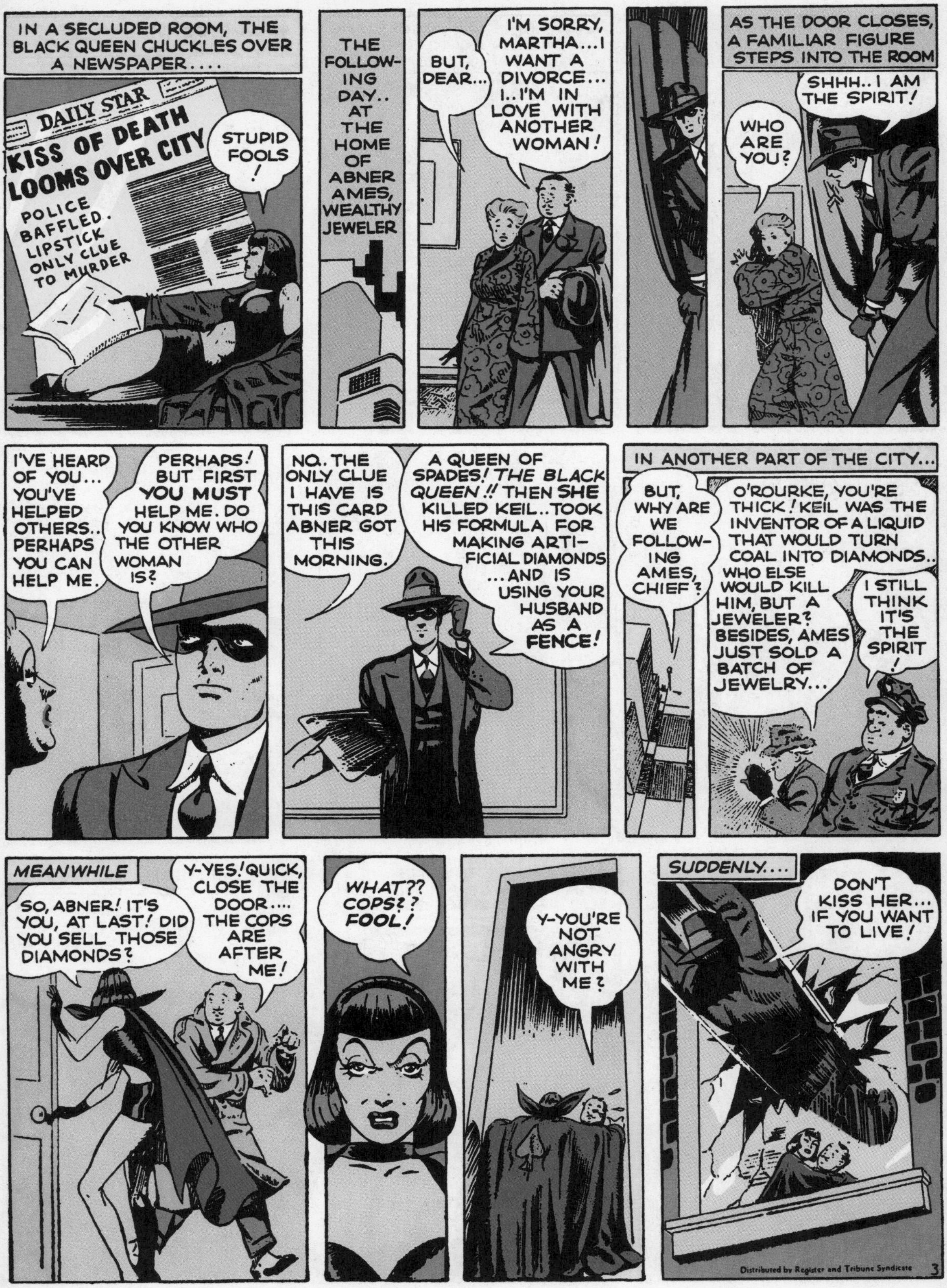
IN A SECLUDED ROOM, THE BLACK QUEEN CHUCKLES OVER A NEWSPAPER....
DAILY STAR
KISS OF DEATH LOOMS OVER CITY
POLICE BAFFLED. LIPSTICK ONLY CLUE TO MURDER
STUPID FOOLS!
THE FOLLOWING DAY.. AT THE HOME OF ABNER AMES, WEALTHY JEWELER
I'M SORRY, MARTHA...I WANT A DIVORCE... I..I'M IN LOVE WITH ANOTHER WOMAN!
BUT, DEAR...
AS THE DOOR CLOSES, A FAMILIAR FIGURE STEPS INTO THE ROOM
WHO ARE YOU?
SHHH.. I AM THE SPIRIT!
I'VE HEARD OF YOU... YOU'VE HELPED OTHERS.. PERHAPS YOU CAN HELP ME.
PERHAPS! BUT FIRST YOU MUST HELP ME. DO YOU KNOW WHO THE OTHER WOMAN IS?
NO. THE ONLY CLUE I HAVE IS THIS CARD ABNER GOT THIS MORNING.
A QUEEN OF SPADES! THE BLACK QUEEN!! THEN SHE KILLED KEIL..TOOK HIS FORMULA FOR MAKING ARTIFICIAL DIAMONDS ...AND IS USING YOUR HUSBAND AS A FENCE!
IN ANOTHER PART OF THE CITY...
BUT, WHY ARE WE FOLLOWING AMES, CHIEF?
O'ROURKE, YOU'RE THICK! KEIL WAS THE INVENTOR OF A LIQUID THAT WOULD TURN COAL INTO DIAMONDS.. WHO ELSE WOULD KILL HIM, BUT A JEWELER? BESIDES, AMES JUST SOLD A BATCH OF JEWELRY...
I STILL THINK IT'S THE SPIRIT!
MEANWHILE
SO, ABNER! IT'S YOU, AT LAST! DID YOU SELL THOSE DIAMONDS?
Y-YES! QUICK, CLOSE THE DOOR.... THE COPS ARE AFTER ME!
WHAT?? COPS?? FOOL!
Y-YOU'RE NOT ANGRY WITH ME?
SUDDENLY....
DON'T KISS HER... IF YOU WANT TO LIVE!
Distributed by Register and Tribune Syndicate
3

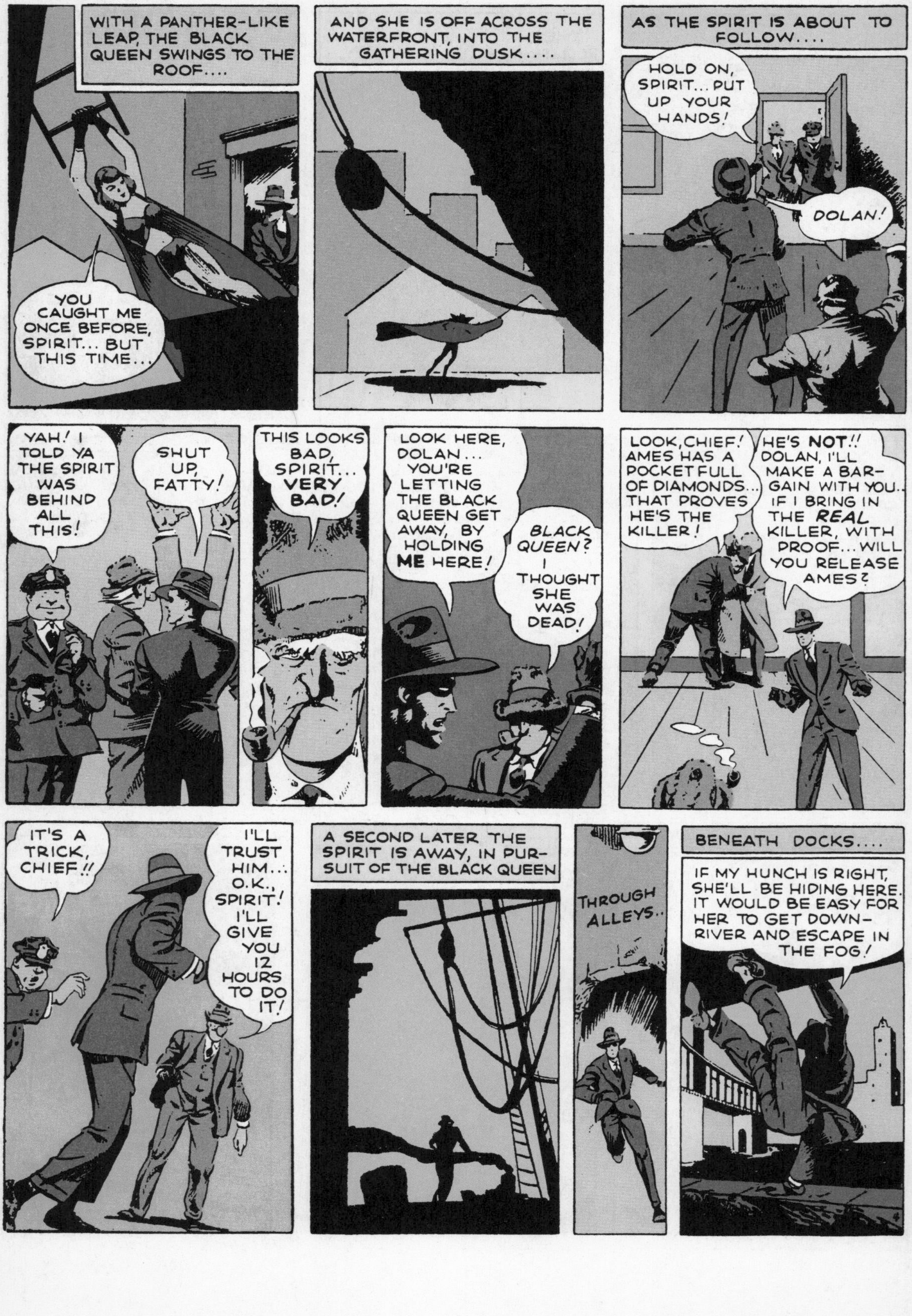

WITH A PANTHER-LIKE LEAP, THE BLACK QUEEN SWINGS TO THE ROOF....
YOU CAUGHT ME ONCE BEFORE, SPIRIT... BUT THIS TIME...
AND SHE IS OFF ACROSS THE WATERFRONT, INTO THE GATHERING DUSK....
AS THE SPIRIT IS ABOUT TO FOLLOW....
HOLD ON, SPIRIT... PUT UP YOUR HANDS!
DOLAN!
YAH! I TOLD YA THE SPIRIT WAS BEHIND ALL THIS!
SHUT UP, FATTY!
THIS LOOKS BAD, SPIRIT... VERY BAD!
LOOK HERE, DOLAN... YOU'RE LETTING THE BLACK QUEEN GET AWAY, BY HOLDING ME HERE!
BLACK QUEEN? I THOUGHT SHE WAS DEAD!
LOOK, CHIEF! AMES HAS A POCKET FULL OF DIAMONDS... THAT PROVES HE'S THE KILLER!
HE'S NOT!! DOLAN, I'LL MAKE A BAR-GAIN WITH YOU.. IF I BRING IN THE REAL KILLER, WITH PROOF... WILL YOU RELEASE AMES?
IT'S A TRICK, CHIEF!!
I'LL TRUST HIM... O.K., SPIRIT! I'LL GIVE YOU 12 HOURS TO DO IT!
A SECOND LATER THE SPIRIT IS AWAY, IN PUR-SUIT OF THE BLACK QUEEN
THROUGH ALLEYS..
BENEATH DOCKS....
IF MY HUNCH IS RIGHT, SHE'LL BE HIDING HERE. IT WOULD BE EASY FOR HER TO GET DOWN-RIVER AND ESCAPE IN THE FOG!

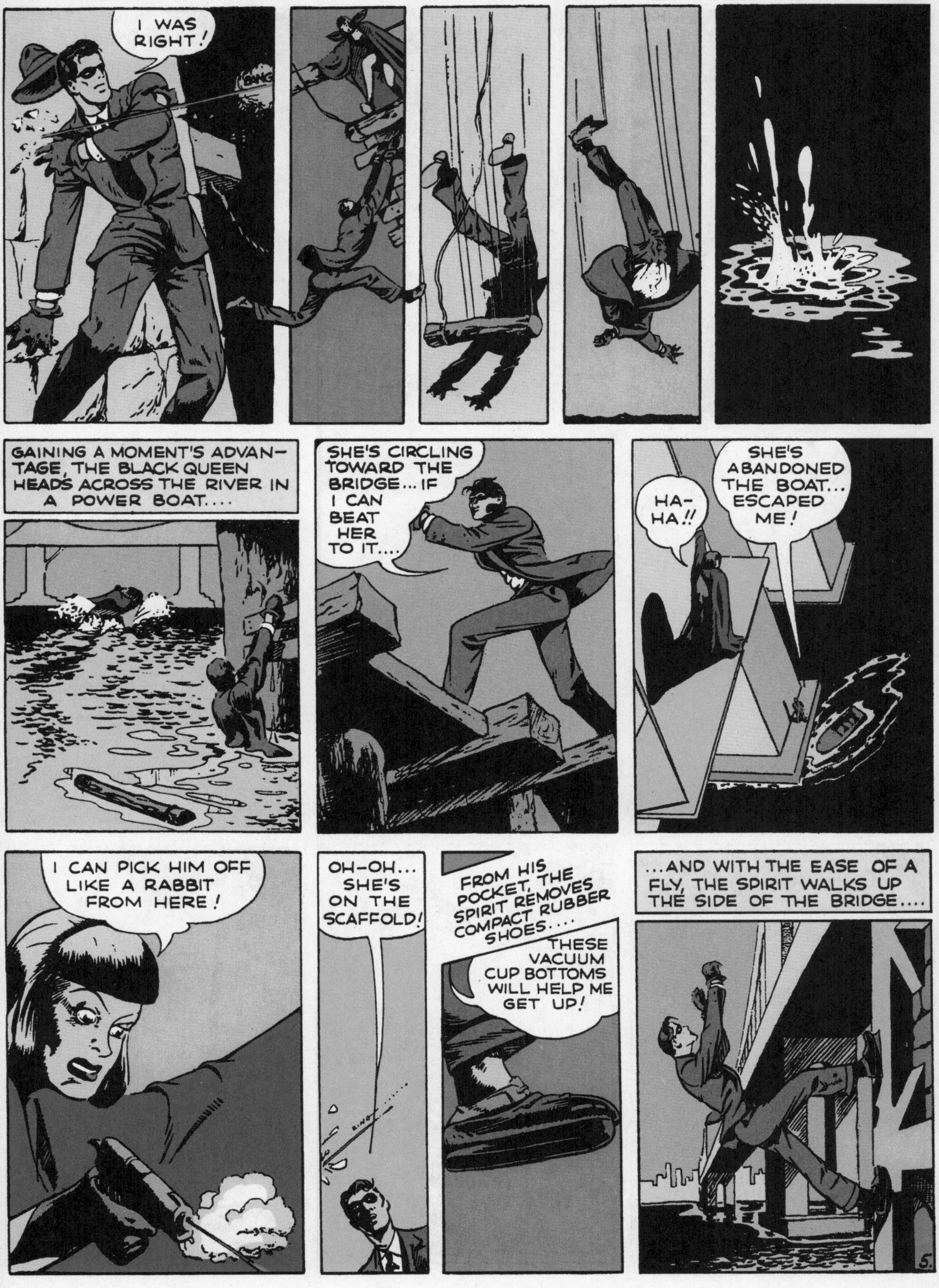
I WAS RIGHT!
BANG
GAINING A MOMENT'S ADVANTAGE, THE BLACK QUEEN HEADS ACROSS THE RIVER IN A POWER BOAT....
SHE'S CIRCLING TOWARD THE BRIDGE... IF I CAN BEAT HER TO IT....
HA-HA!!
SHE'S ABANDONED THE BOAT... ESCAPED ME!
I CAN PICK HIM OFF LIKE A RABBIT FROM HERE!
OH-OH... SHE'S ON THE SCAFFOLD!
FROM HIS POCKET, THE SPIRIT REMOVES COMPACT RUBBER SHOES....
THESE VACUUM CUP BOTTOMS WILL HELP ME GET UP!
...AND WITH THE EASE OF A FLY, THE SPIRIT WALKS UP THE SIDE OF THE BRIDGE....
5.

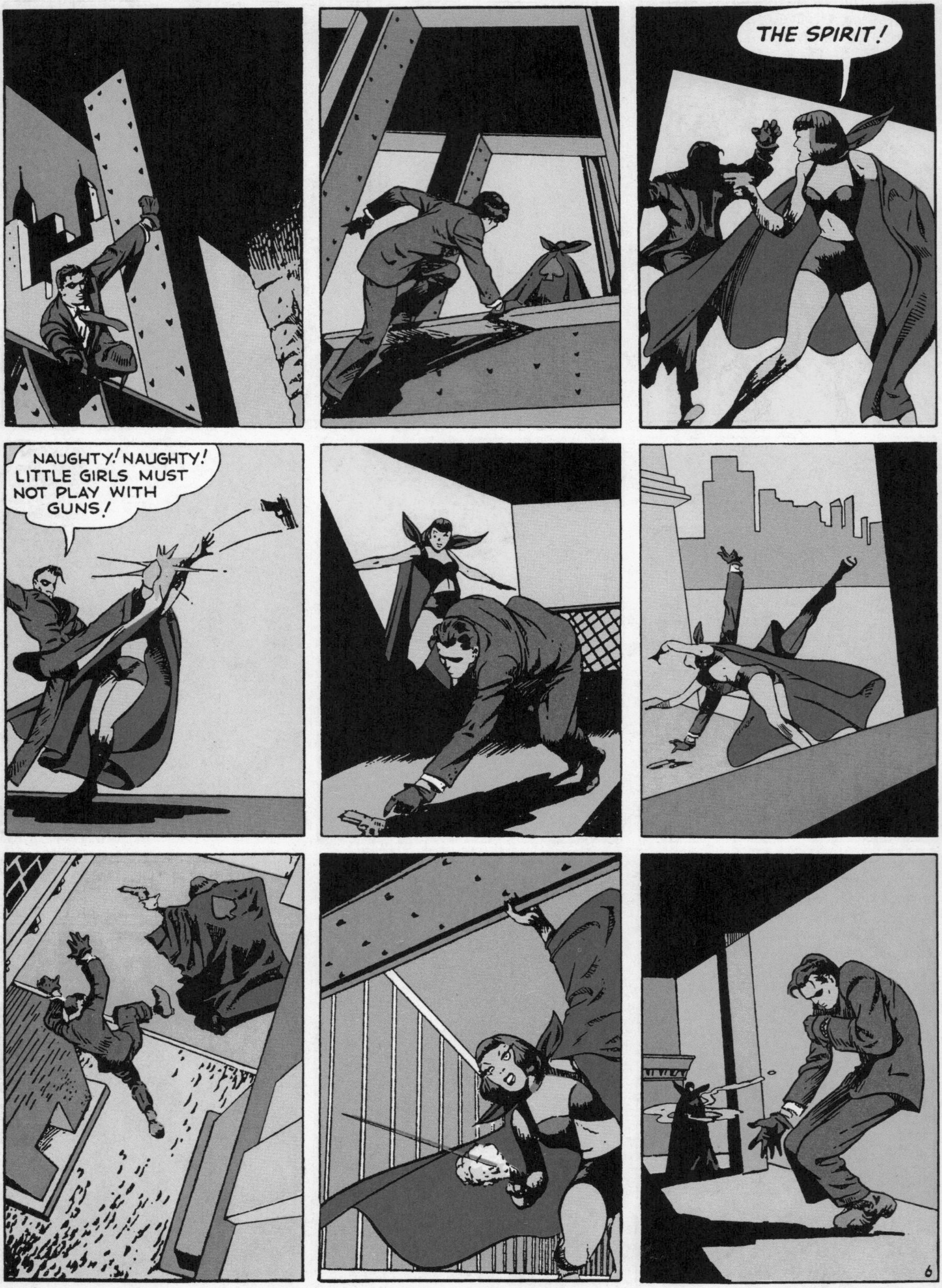
THE SPIRIT!
NAUGHTY! NAUGHTY! LITTLE GIRLS MUST NOT PLAY WITH GUNS!
6

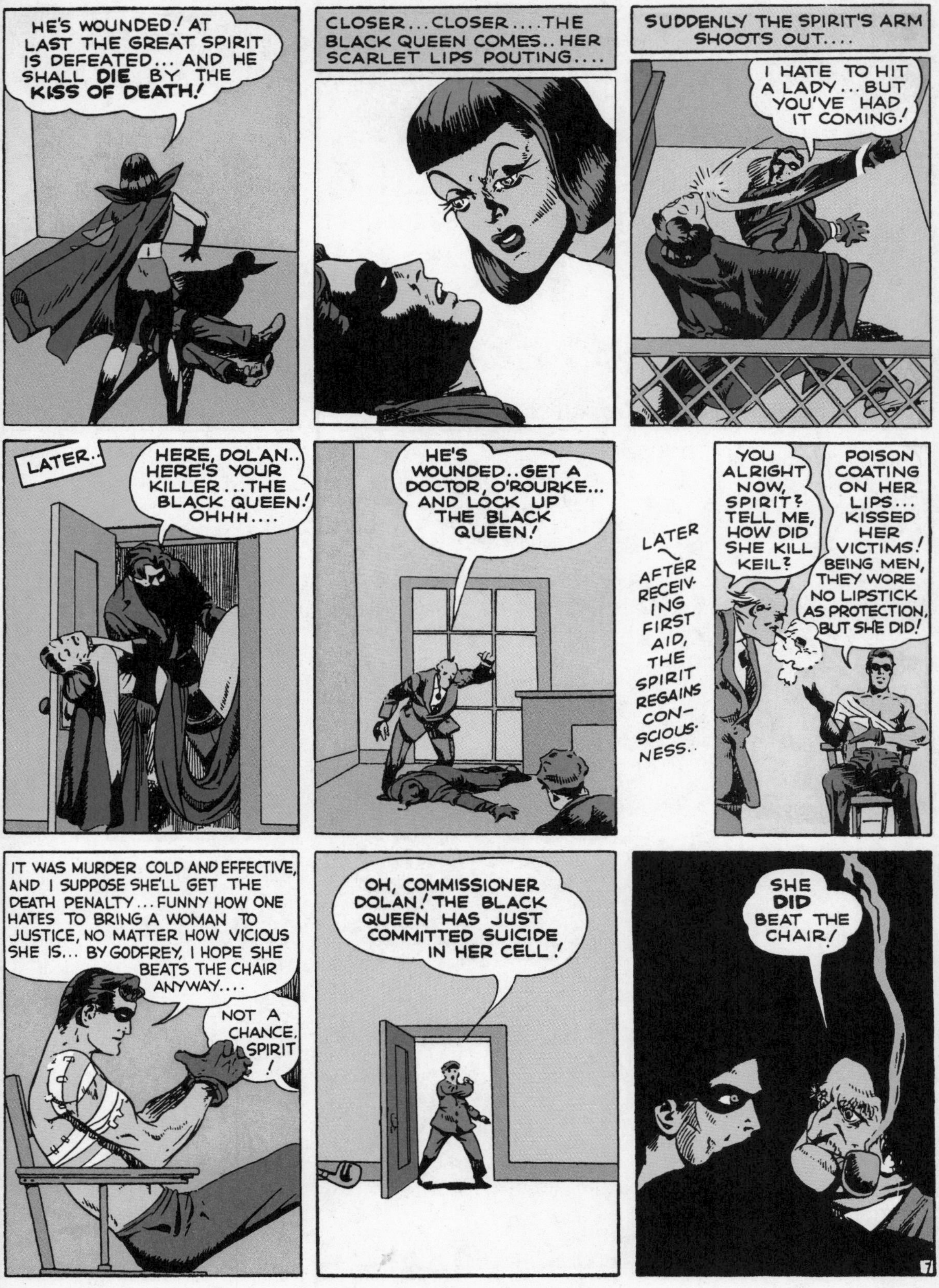
HE'S WOUNDED! AT LAST THE GREAT SPIRIT IS DEFEATED... AND HE SHALL **DIE** BY THE **KISS OF DEATH!**
CLOSER... CLOSER.... THE BLACK QUEEN COMES.. HER SCARLET LIPS POUTING....
SUDDENLY THE SPIRIT'S ARM SHOOTS OUT....
I HATE TO HIT A LADY... BUT YOU'VE HAD IT COMING!
LATER..
HERE, DOLAN.. HERE'S YOUR KILLER... THE BLACK QUEEN! OHHH....
HE'S WOUNDED..GET A DOCTOR, O'ROURKE... AND LOCK UP THE BLACK QUEEN!
LATER ~ AFTER RECEIV-ING FIRST AID, THE SPIRIT REGAINS CON-SCIOUS-NESS..
YOU ALRIGHT NOW, SPIRIT? TELL ME, HOW DID SHE KILL KEIL?
POISON COATING ON HER LIPS... KISSED HER VICTIMS! BEING MEN, THEY WORE NO LIPSTICK AS PROTECTION, BUT SHE DID!
IT WAS MURDER COLD AND EFFECTIVE, AND I SUPPOSE SHE'LL GET THE DEATH PENALTY... FUNNY HOW ONE HATES TO BRING A WOMAN TO JUSTICE, NO MATTER HOW VICIOUS SHE IS... BY GODFREY, I HOPE SHE BEATS THE CHAIR ANYWAY....
NOT A CHANCE, SPIRIT!
OH, COMMISSIONER DOLAN! THE BLACK QUEEN HAS JUST COMMITTED SUICIDE IN HER CELL!
SHE **DID** BEAT THE CHAIR!
7

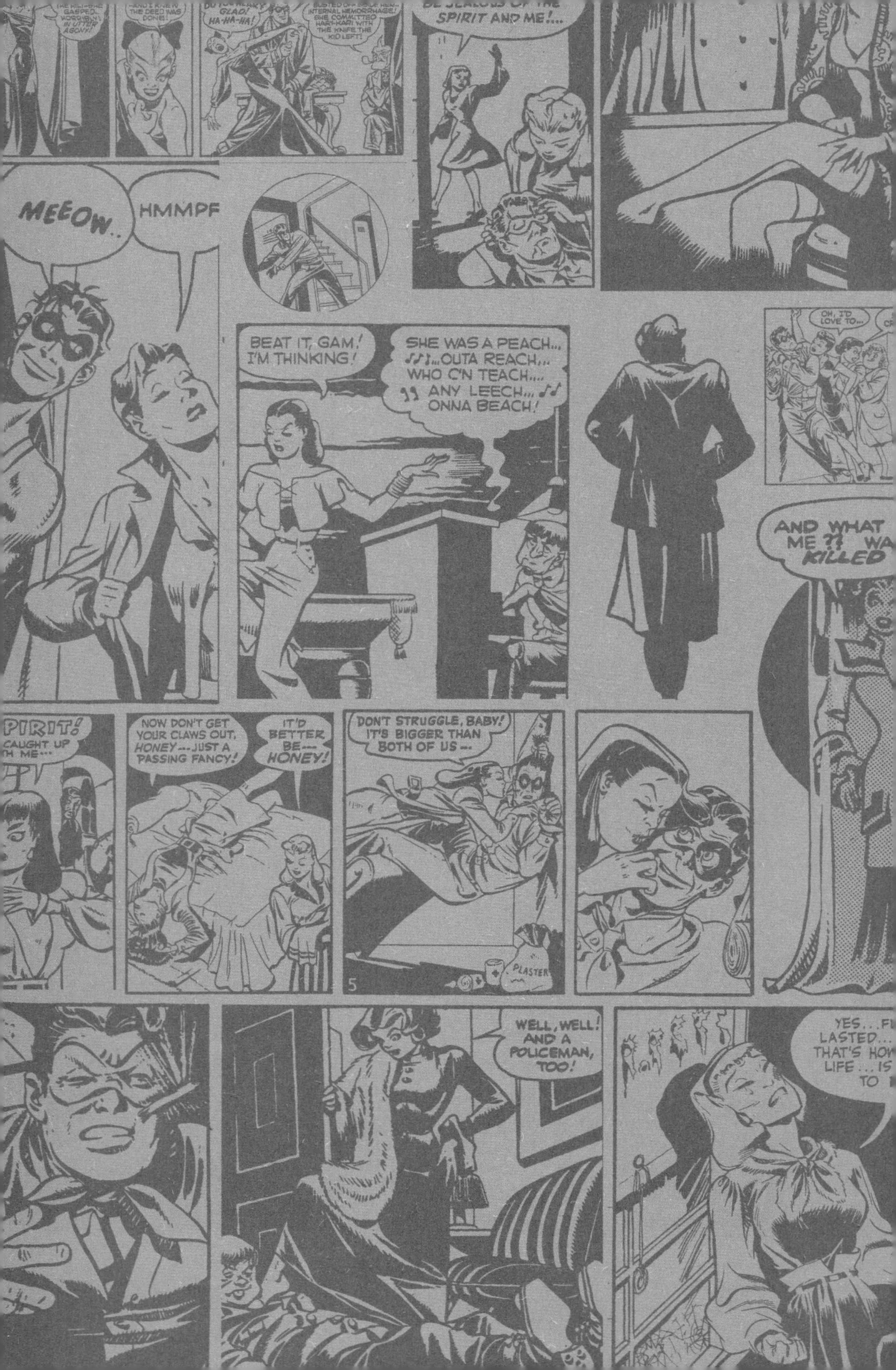

SPIRIT AND ME!...
MEEOW..
HMMPF
BEAT IT, GAM! I'M THINKING!
SHE WAS A PEACH... ♪♪...OUTA REACH... WHO C'N TEACH.... ANY LEECH... ♪♪ ONNA BEACH!
OH, I'D LOVE TO...
AND WHAT ME ?? WA KILLED
NOW DON'T GET YOUR CLAWS OUT, HONEY--- JUST A PASSING FANCY!
IT'D BETTER BE--- HONEY!
DON'T STRUGGLE, BABY! IT'S BIGGER THAN BOTH OF US--
PLASTER
WELL, WELL! AND A POLICEMAN, TOO!
YES... LASTED... THAT'S HOW LIFE... IS TO

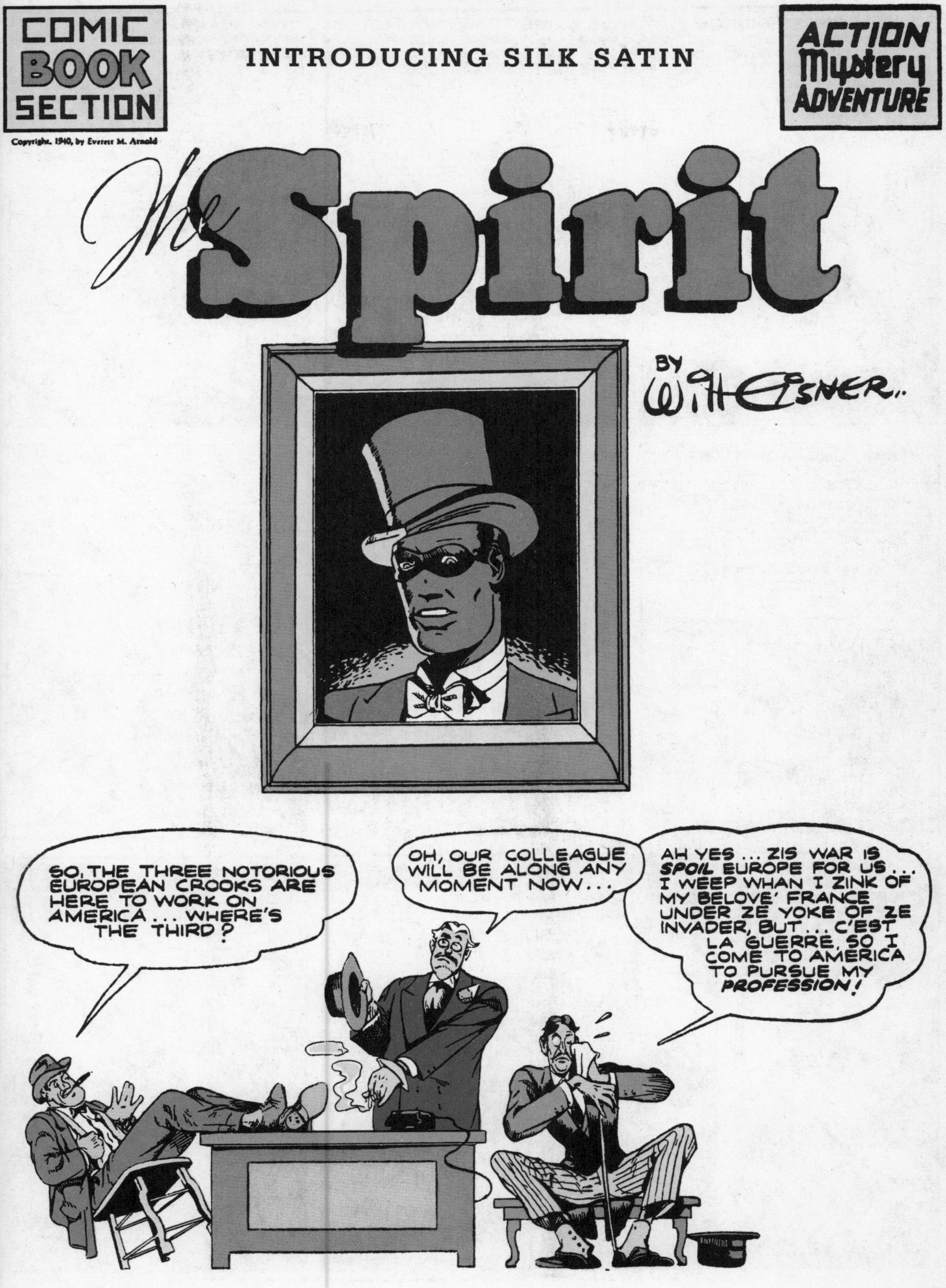
COMIC BOOK SECTION
INTRODUCING SILK SATIN
ACTION Mystery ADVENTURE
Copyright, 1940, by Everett M. Arnold
The Spirit
BY Will Eisner
SO, THE THREE NOTORIOUS EUROPEAN CROOKS ARE HERE TO WORK ON AMERICA ... WHERE'S THE THIRD?
OH, OUR COLLEAGUE WILL BE ALONG ANY MOMENT NOW...
AH YES ... ZIS WAR IS *SPOIL* EUROPE FOR US ... I WEEP WHAN I ZINK OF MY BELOVE' FRANCE UNDER ZE YOKE OF ZE INVADER, BUT ... C'EST LA GUERRE, SO I COME TO AMERICA TO PURSUE MY *PROFESSION*!

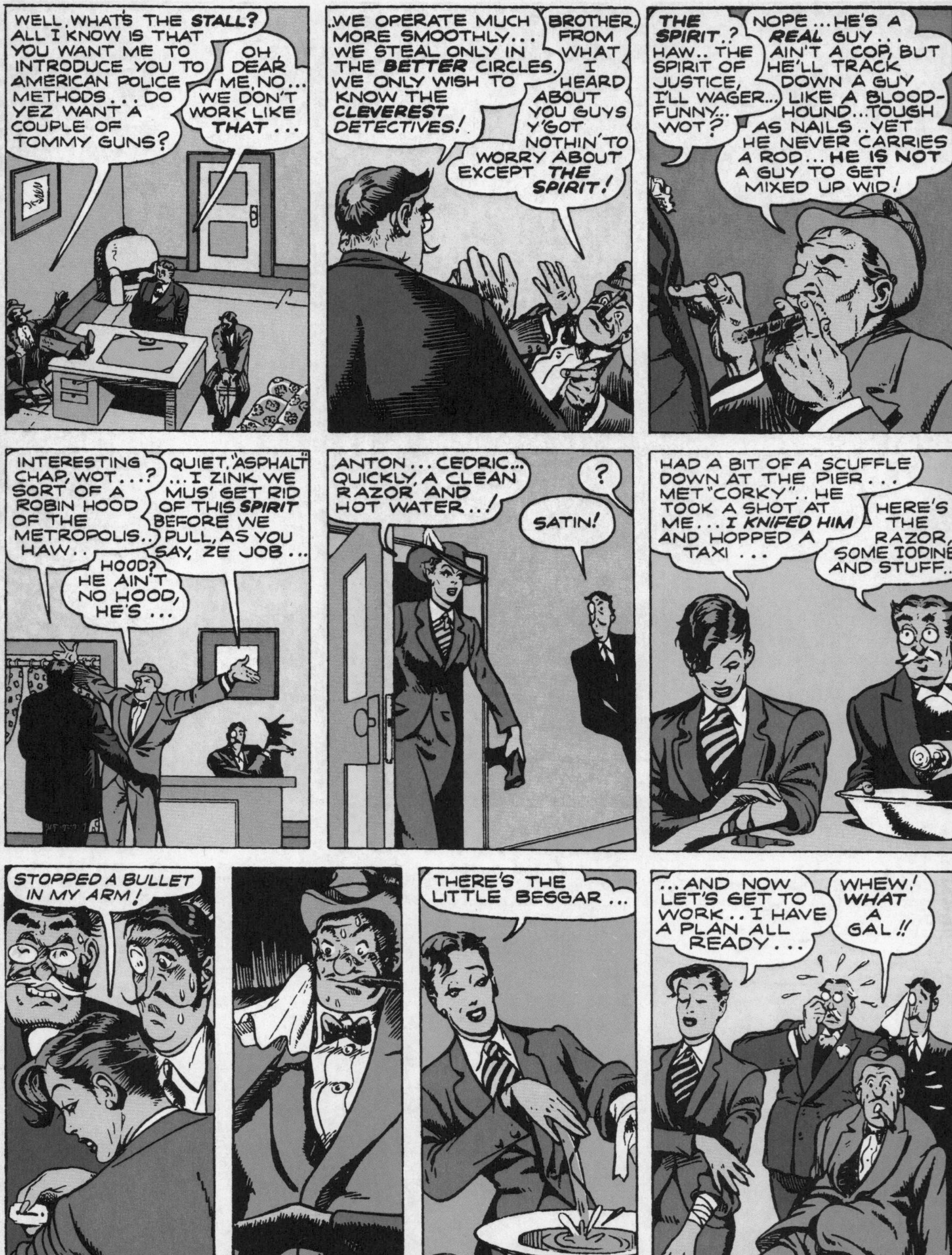
WELL, WHAT'S THE STALL? ALL I KNOW IS THAT YOU WANT ME TO INTRODUCE YOU TO AMERICAN POLICE METHODS... DO YEZ WANT A COUPLE OF TOMMY GUNS?
OH, DEAR ME, NO... WE DON'T WORK LIKE THAT...
..WE OPERATE MUCH MORE SMOOTHLY... WE STEAL ONLY IN THE BETTER CIRCLES. WE ONLY WISH TO KNOW THE CLEVEREST DETECTIVES!
BROTHER, FROM WHAT I HEARD ABOUT YOU GUYS Y'GOT NOTHIN' TO WORRY ABOUT EXCEPT THE SPIRIT!
THE SPIRIT..? HAW.. THE SPIRIT OF JUSTICE, I'LL WAGER... FUNNY... WOT?
NOPE... HE'S A REAL GUY... AIN'T A COP, BUT HE'LL TRACK DOWN A GUY LIKE A BLOOD-HOUND...TOUGH AS NAILS..YET HE NEVER CARRIES A ROD... HE IS NOT A GUY TO GET MIXED UP WID!
INTERESTING CHAP, WOT...? SORT OF A ROBIN HOOD OF THE METROPOLIS.. HAW..
QUIET, "ASPHALT" ...I ZINK WE MUS' GET RID OF THIS SPIRIT BEFORE WE PULL, AS YOU SAY, ZE JOB...
HOOD? HE AIN'T NO HOOD, HE'S...
ANTON... CEDRIC... QUICKLY, A CLEAN RAZOR AND HOT WATER...!
?
SATIN!
HAD A BIT OF A SCUFFLE DOWN AT THE PIER... MET "CORKY".. HE TOOK A SHOT AT ME... I KNIFED HIM AND HOPPED A TAXI...
HERE'S THE RAZOR, SOME IODINE AND STUFF...
STOPPED A BULLET IN MY ARM!
THERE'S THE LITTLE BEGGAR...
...AND NOW LET'S GET TO WORK.. I HAVE A PLAN ALL READY...
WHEW! WHAT A GAL!!
2

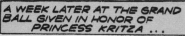

A WEEK LATER AT THE GRAND BALL GIVEN IN HONOR OF PRINCESS KRITZA...

THE DUKE AND DUCHESS OF MERZ COLONEL DRAKE... CAPTAIN MOFFET...

THE BARON AND BARONESS OF BAGDOVIA...

THAT'S COUNT GAZOFF... HAVE YOU GOT THE PHONEY MEDAL ??...

RIGHT-HO... YOU SHALL HAVE THE NEXT DANCE..

A FEW MINUTES LATER ...

AH, MY DEAR BARONESS... IT WAS VERY KIND OF SIR CEDRIC TO INTRODUCE US ...

YES INDEED.. IT ISN'T OFTEN I HAVE THE PLEASURE OF DANCING WITH THE OWNER OF THE MALBRO MEDAL..

TUT..TUT.. M'DEAR, YOU ARE VERY BEAUTIFUL ..

OOH COUNT.. HOW YOU FLATTER!

AHH ..THE WALTZ .. IT ENDED SO SOON!

GOOD HEAVENS! MY MEDALLION IS GONE!!

AT THAT MOMENT CEDRIC STEPS FORWARD AND BENDS DOWN BEFORE THE IRATE COUNT ...

I SAY, ISN'T THIS IT ON THE FLOOR?

CLINK   CLINK

A PHONEY OR COPY DROPS FROM HIS SLEEVE

OH.. HEH, HEH.. HOW SILLY OF ME.. THANKS AWFULLY.. Y'SEE IT'S WORTH AT LEAST 10,000 DOLLARS AND I'D SO HATE TO LOSE IT !!

QUITE, COUNT GAZOFF..

OH WELL, COME ALONG, SIR CEDRIC AND WE'LL HAVE A SPOT O' PUNCH ... AFTER ALL, YOU FOUND MY MEDAL..

RIGHT-HO, COUNT ...

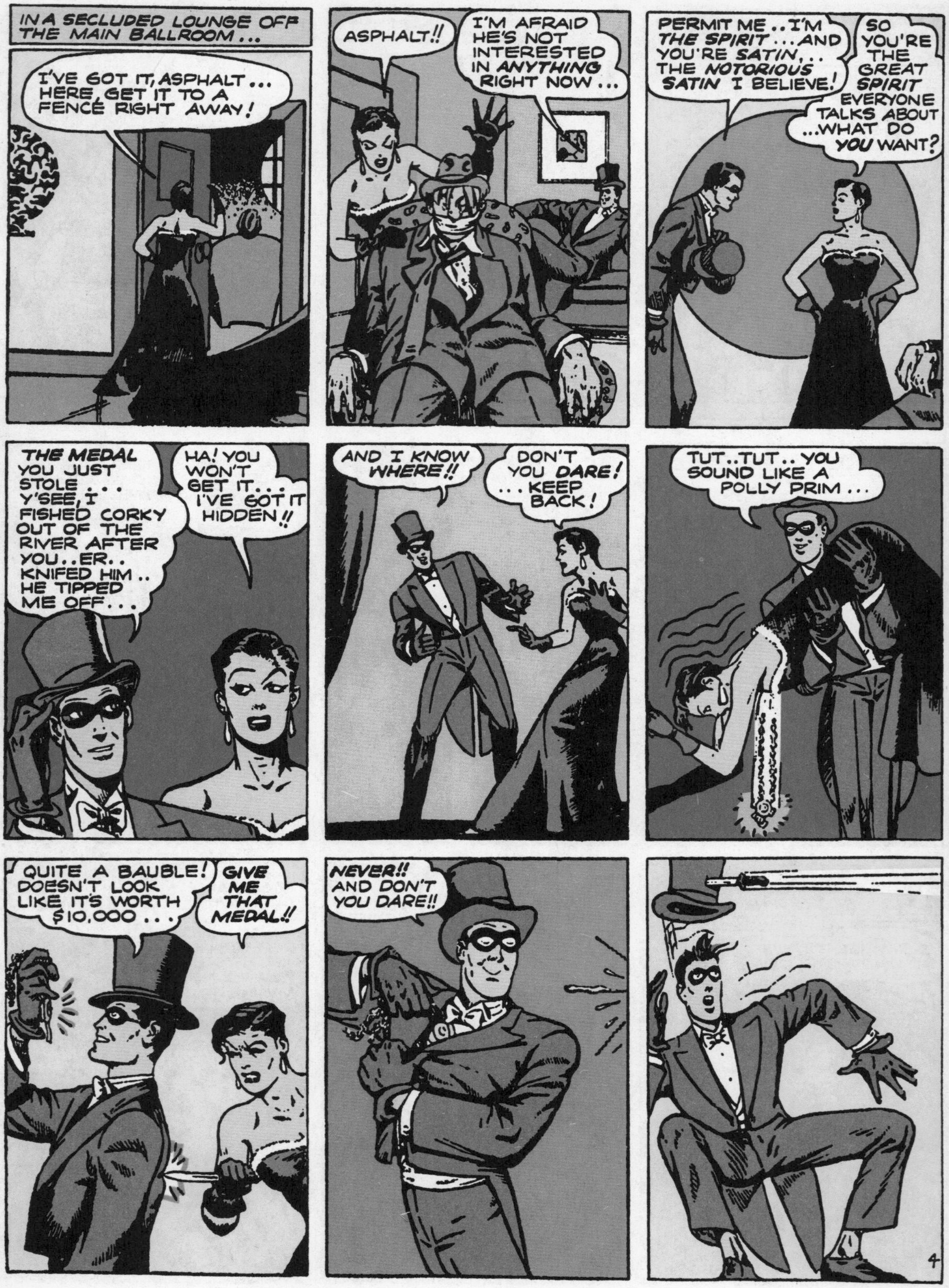
IN A SECLUDED LOUNGE OFF THE MAIN BALLROOM...
I'VE GOT IT, ASPHALT... HERE, GET IT TO A FENCE RIGHT AWAY!
ASPHALT!!
I'M AFRAID HE'S NOT INTERESTED IN ANYTHING RIGHT NOW...
PERMIT ME.. I'M THE SPIRIT... AND YOU'RE SATIN,.. THE NOTORIOUS SATIN I BELIEVE!
SO YOU'RE THE GREAT SPIRIT EVERYONE TALKS ABOUT ...WHAT DO YOU WANT?
THE MEDAL YOU JUST STOLE... Y'SEE, I FISHED CORKY OUT OF THE RIVER AFTER YOU..ER.. KNIFED HIM.. HE TIPPED ME OFF...
HA! YOU WON'T GET IT... I'VE GOT IT HIDDEN!!
AND I KNOW WHERE!!
DON'T YOU DARE! ...KEEP BACK!
TUT..TUT.. YOU SOUND LIKE A POLLY PRIM...
QUITE A BAUBLE! DOESN'T LOOK LIKE IT'S WORTH $10,000...
GIVE ME THAT MEDAL!!
NEVER!! AND DON'T YOU DARE!!
4

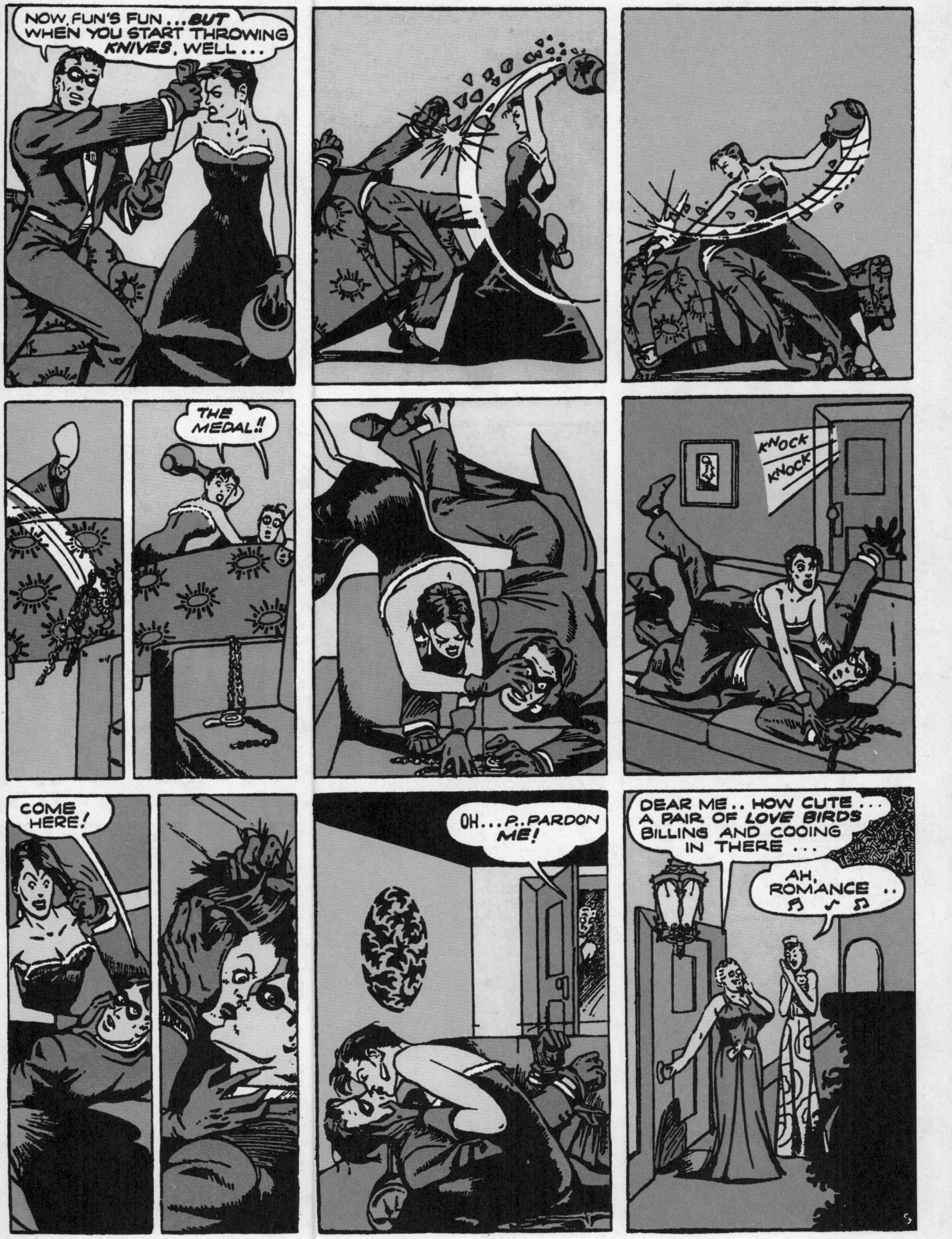
NOW, FUN'S FUN ... BUT WHEN YOU START THROWING KNIVES, WELL ...
THE MEDAL!!
KNOCK
KNOCK
COME HERE!
OH ... P..PARDON ME!
DEAR ME .. HOW CUTE ... A PAIR OF LOVE BIRDS BILLING AND COOING IN THERE ...
AH, ROMANCE ..

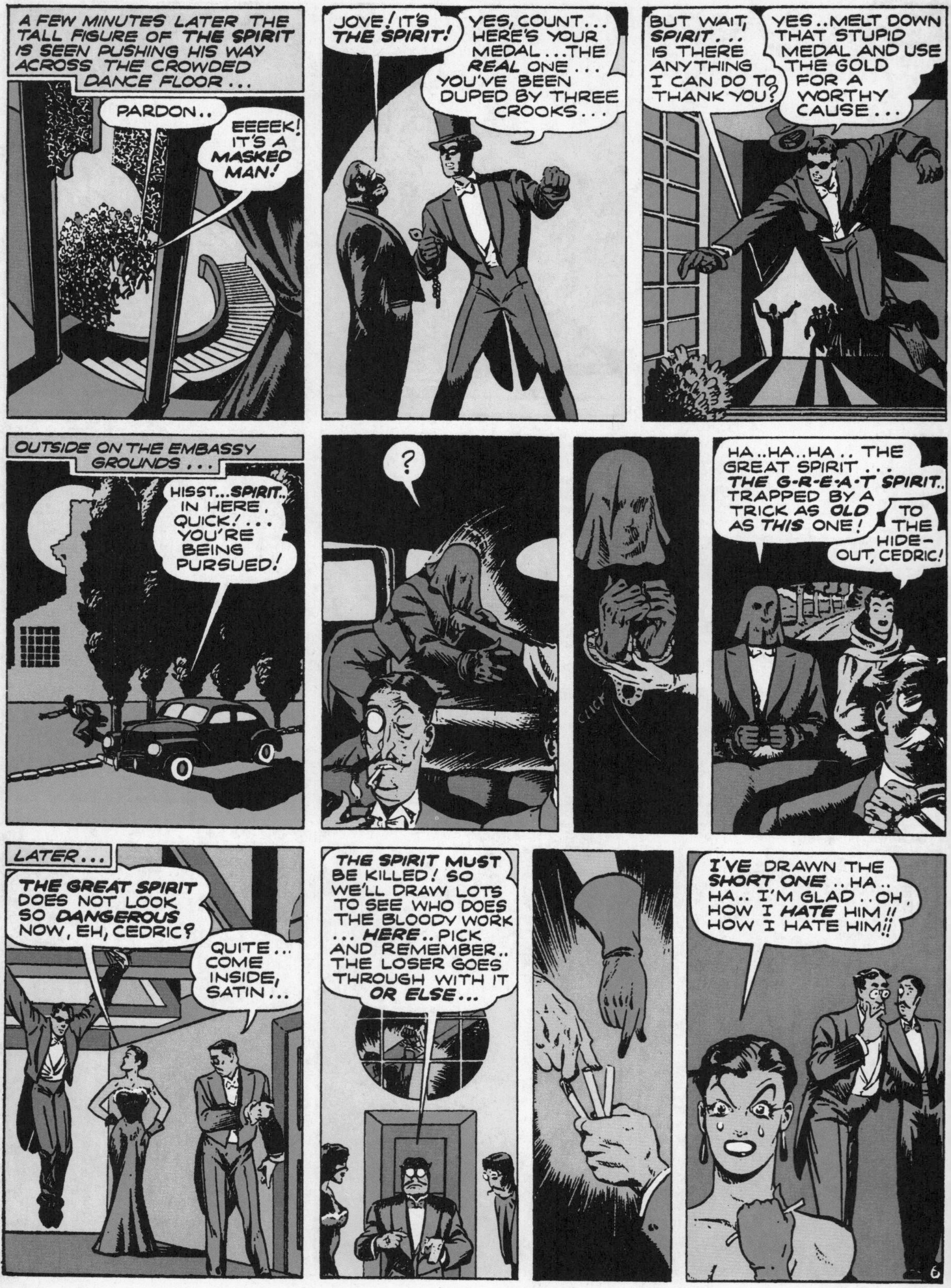

A FEW MINUTES LATER THE TALL FIGURE OF THE SPIRIT IS SEEN PUSHING HIS WAY ACROSS THE CROWDED DANCE FLOOR...
PARDON..
EEEEK! IT'S A MASKED MAN!
JOVE! IT'S THE SPIRIT!
YES, COUNT... HERE'S YOUR MEDAL...THE REAL ONE... YOU'VE BEEN DUPED BY THREE CROOKS...
BUT WAIT, SPIRIT... IS THERE ANYTHING I CAN DO TO THANK YOU?
YES..MELT DOWN THAT STUPID MEDAL AND USE THE GOLD FOR A WORTHY CAUSE...
OUTSIDE ON THE EMBASSY GROUNDS...
HISST...SPIRIT.. IN HERE, QUICK!... YOU'RE BEING PURSUED!
?
CLICK
HA..HA..HA.. THE GREAT SPIRIT... THE G-R-E-A-T SPIRIT.. TRAPPED BY A TRICK AS OLD AS THIS ONE!
TO THE HIDE-OUT, CEDRIC!
LATER...
THE GREAT SPIRIT DOES NOT LOOK SO DANGEROUS NOW, EH, CEDRIC?
QUITE... COME INSIDE, SATIN...
THE SPIRIT MUST BE KILLED! SO WE'LL DRAW LOTS TO SEE WHO DOES THE BLOODY WORK ... HERE.. PICK AND REMEMBER.. THE LOSER GOES THROUGH WITH IT OR ELSE...
I'VE DRAWN THE SHORT ONE..HA.. HA.. I'M GLAD..OH, HOW I HATE HIM!! HOW I HATE HIM!!
6

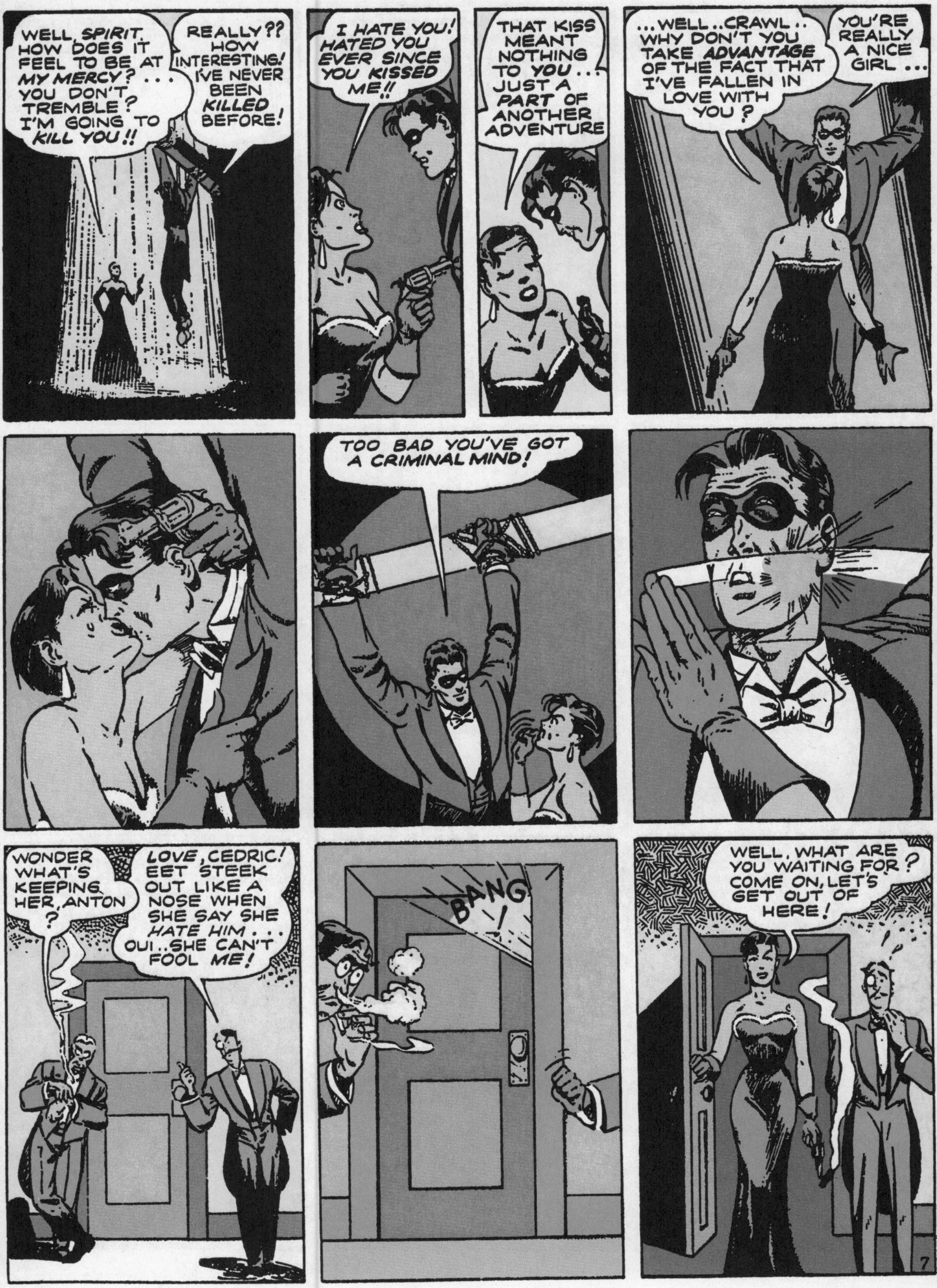
WELL, SPIRIT, HOW DOES IT FEEL TO BE AT MY MERCY? . . YOU DON'T TREMBLE? I'M GOING TO KILL YOU!!
REALLY?? HOW INTERESTING! I'VE NEVER BEEN KILLED BEFORE!
I HATE YOU! HATED YOU EVER SINCE YOU KISSED ME!!
THAT KISS MEANT NOTHING TO YOU . . . JUST A PART OF ANOTHER ADVENTURE
. . . WELL . . CRAWL . . WHY DON'T YOU TAKE ADVANTAGE OF THE FACT THAT I'VE FALLEN IN LOVE WITH YOU?
YOU'RE REALLY A NICE GIRL . . .
TOO BAD YOU'VE GOT A CRIMINAL MIND!
WONDER WHAT'S KEEPING HER, ANTON?
LOVE, CEDRIC! EET STEEK OUT LIKE A NOSE WHEN SHE SAY SHE HATE HIM . . . OUI . . SHE CAN'T FOOL ME!
BANG!
WELL, WHAT ARE YOU WAITING FOR? COME ON, LET'S GET OUT OF HERE!
7

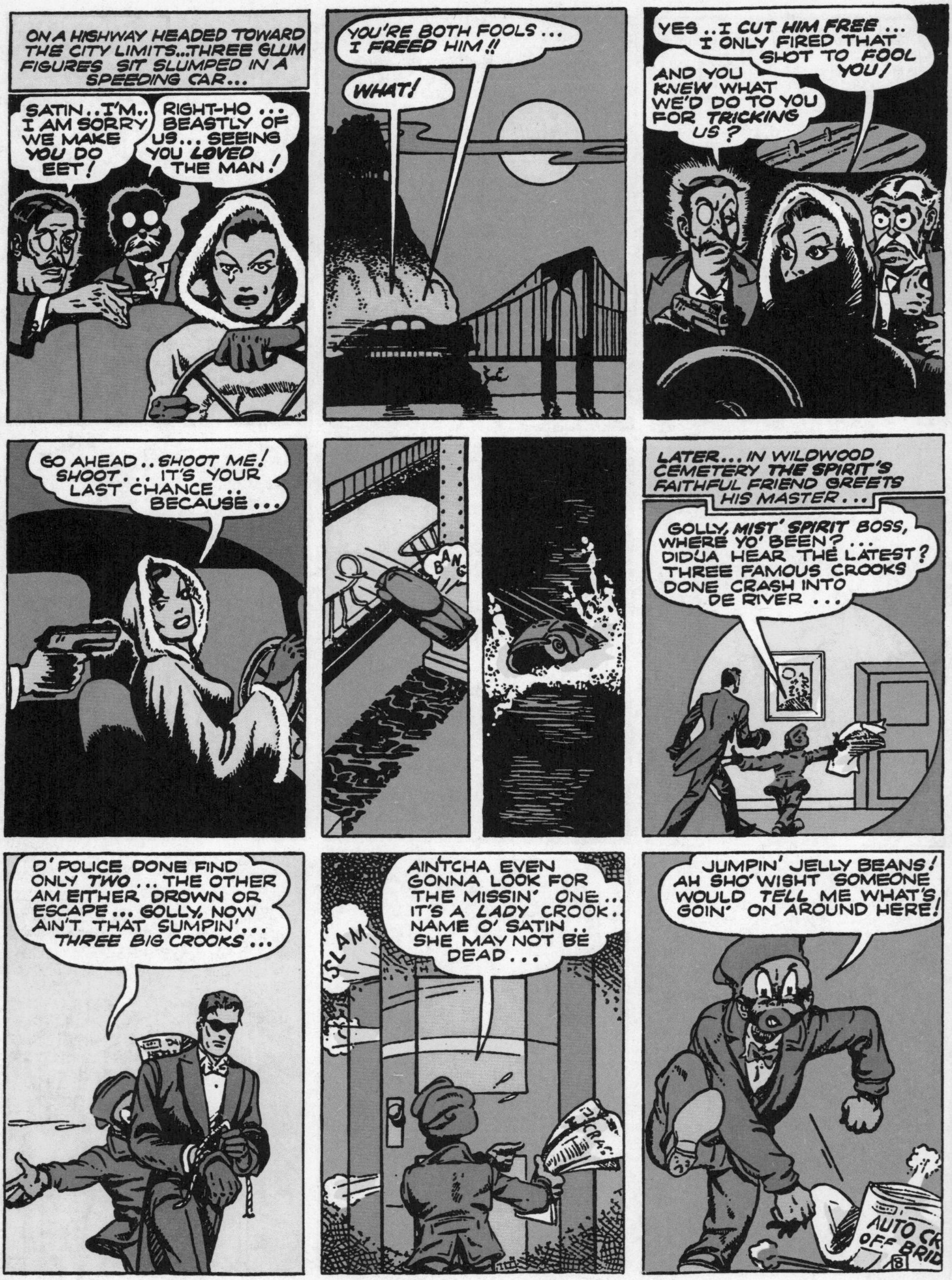
ON A HIGHWAY HEADED TOWARD THE CITY LIMITS...THREE GLUM FIGURES SIT SLUMPED IN A SPEEDING CAR...
SATIN..I'M.. I AM SORRY WE MAKE YOU DO EET!
RIGHT-HO ... BEASTLY OF US... SEEING YOU LOVED THE MAN!
YOU'RE BOTH FOOLS ... I FREED HIM!!
WHAT!
YES..I CUT HIM FREE ... I ONLY FIRED THAT SHOT TO FOOL YOU!
AND YOU KNEW WHAT WE'D DO TO YOU FOR TRICKING US?
GO AHEAD..SHOOT ME! SHOOT... IT'S YOUR LAST CHANCE .. BECAUSE...
BANG
LATER... IN WILDWOOD CEMETERY THE SPIRIT'S FAITHFUL FRIEND GREETS HIS MASTER...
GOLLY, MIST' SPIRIT BOSS, WHERE YO' BEEN? ... DIDJA HEAR THE LATEST? THREE FAMOUS CROOKS DONE CRASH INTO DE RIVER ...
D' POLICE DONE FIND ONLY TWO... THE OTHER AM EITHER DROWN OR ESCAPE... GOLLY, NOW AIN'T THAT SUMPIN'... THREE BIG CROOKS...
SLAM
AIN'TCHA EVEN GONNA LOOK FOR THE MISSIN' ONE... IT'S A LADY CROOK.. NAME O' SATIN.. SHE MAY NOT BE DEAD...
JUMPIN' JELLY BEANS! AH SHO' WISHT SOMEONE WOULD TELL ME WHAT'S GOIN' ON AROUND HERE!

COMIC BOOK SECTION

WOMEN!

ACTION Mystery ADVENTURE

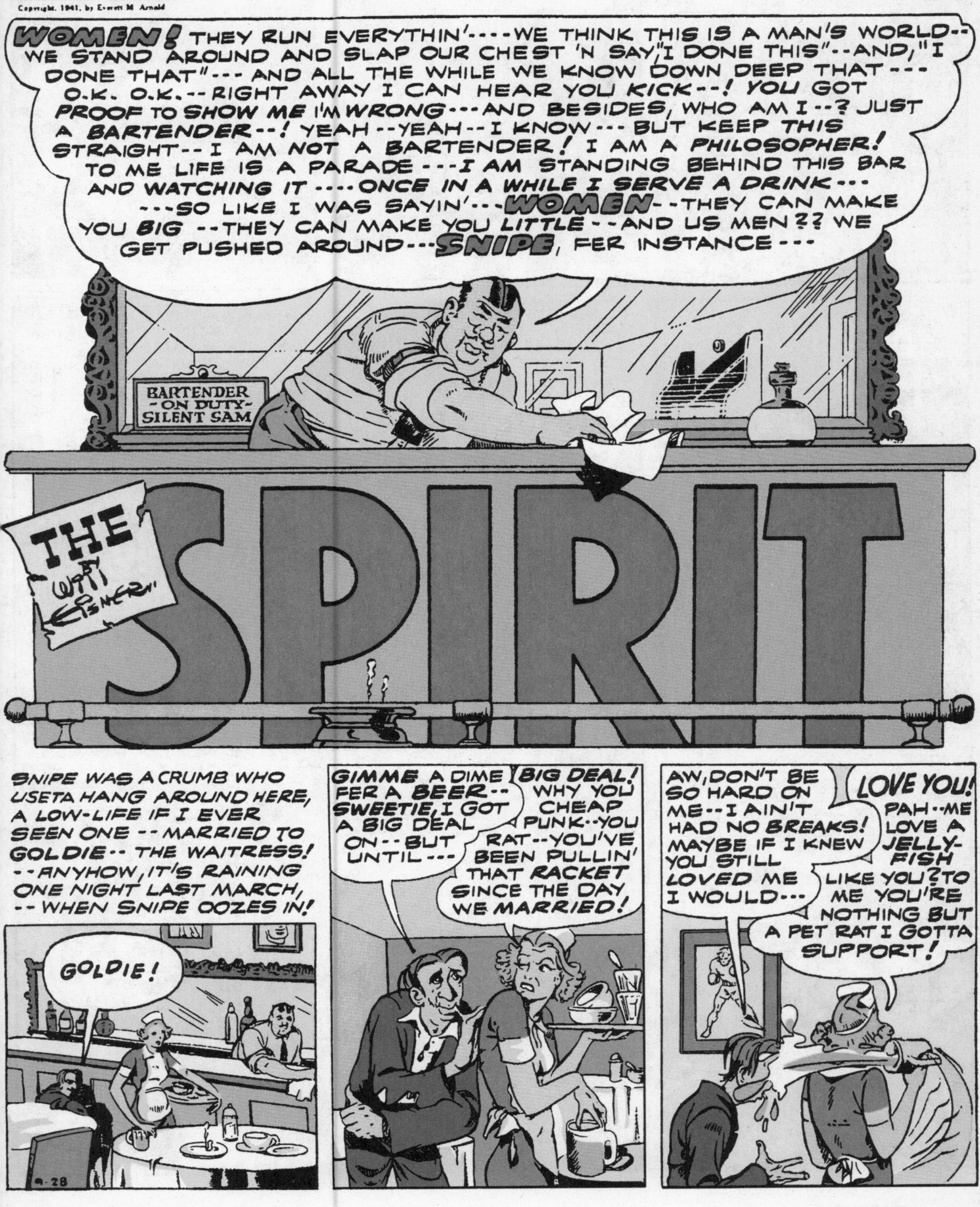
WOMEN! THEY RUN EVERYTHIN'----WE THINK THIS IS A MAN'S WORLD--WE STAND AROUND AND SLAP OUR CHEST 'N SAY,"I DONE THIS"--AND,"I DONE THAT"---AND ALL THE WHILE WE KNOW DOWN DEEP THAT---O.K. O.K.--RIGHT AWAY I CAN HEAR YOU KICK--! YOU GOT PROOF TO SHOW ME I'M WRONG---AND BESIDES, WHO AM I--? JUST A BARTENDER--! YEAH--YEAH--I KNOW---BUT KEEP THIS STRAIGHT--I AM NOT A BARTENDER! I AM A PHILOSOPHER! TO ME LIFE IS A PARADE---I AM STANDING BEHIND THIS BAR AND WATCHING IT----ONCE IN A WHILE I SERVE A DRINK---
---SO LIKE I WAS SAYIN'---WOMEN--THEY CAN MAKE YOU BIG--THEY CAN MAKE YOU LITTLE--AND US MEN?? WE GET PUSHED AROUND---SNIPE, FER INSTANCE---
BARTENDER -ON DUTY- SILENT SAM
THE SPIRIT
SNIPE WAS A CRUMB WHO USETA HANG AROUND HERE, A LOW-LIFE IF I EVER SEEN ONE--MARRIED TO GOLDIE--THE WAITRESS! --ANYHOW, IT'S RAINING ONE NIGHT LAST MARCH, --WHEN SNIPE OOZES IN!
GOLDIE!
GIMME A DIME FER A BEER--SWEETIE, I GOT A BIG DEAL ON--BUT UNTIL---
BIG DEAL! WHY YOU CHEAP PUNK--YOU RAT--YOU'VE BEEN PULLIN' THAT RACKET SINCE THE DAY WE MARRIED!
AW, DON'T BE SO HARD ON ME--I AIN'T HAD NO BREAKS! MAYBE IF I KNEW YOU STILL LOVED ME I WOULD---
LOVE YOU! PAH--ME LOVE A JELLY-FISH LIKE YOU? TO ME YOU'RE NOTHING BUT A PET RAT I GOTTA SUPPORT!

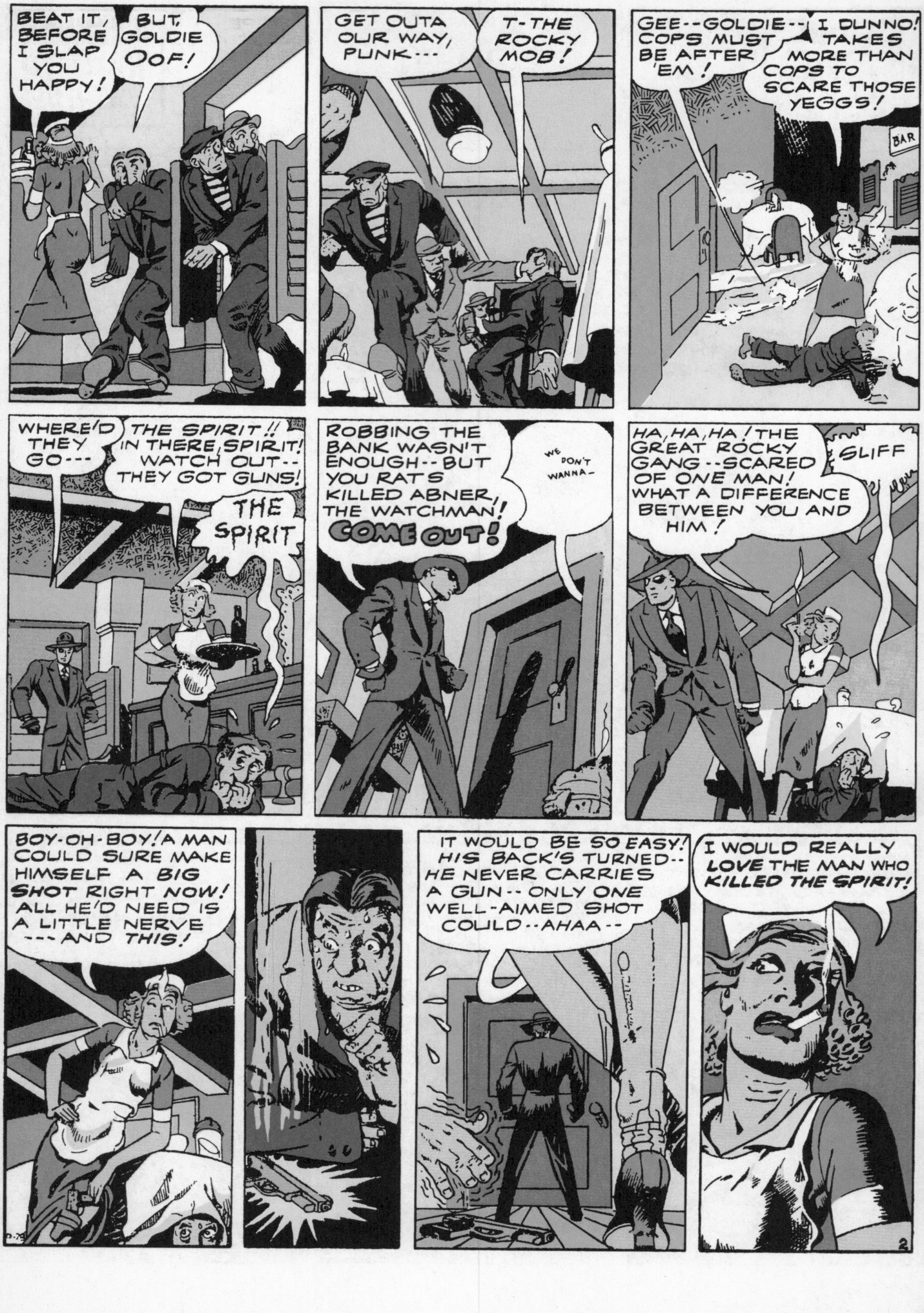
BEAT IT, BEFORE I SLAP YOU HAPPY!
BUT, GOLDIE OOF!
GET OUTA OUR WAY, PUNK---
T-THE ROCKY MOB!
GEE--GOLDIE--COPS MUST BE AFTER 'EM!
I DUNNO! TAKES MORE THAN COPS TO SCARE THOSE YEGGS!
BAR
WHERE'D THEY GO---
THE SPIRIT!! IN THERE, SPIRIT! WATCH OUT-- THEY GOT GUNS!
THE SPIRIT
ROBBING THE BANK WASN'T ENOUGH--BUT YOU RATS KILLED ABNER, THE WATCHMAN! COME OUT!
WE DON'T WANNA-
HA,HA,HA! THE GREAT ROCKY GANG--SCARED OF ONE MAN! WHAT A DIFFERENCE BETWEEN YOU AND HIM!
SLIFF
BOY-OH-BOY! A MAN COULD SURE MAKE HIMSELF A BIG SHOT RIGHT NOW! ALL HE'D NEED IS A LITTLE NERVE ---AND THIS!
IT WOULD BE SO EASY! HIS BACK'S TURNED-- HE NEVER CARRIES A GUN-- ONLY ONE WELL-AIMED SHOT COULD--AHAA--
I WOULD REALLY LOVE THE MAN WHO KILLED THE SPIRIT!

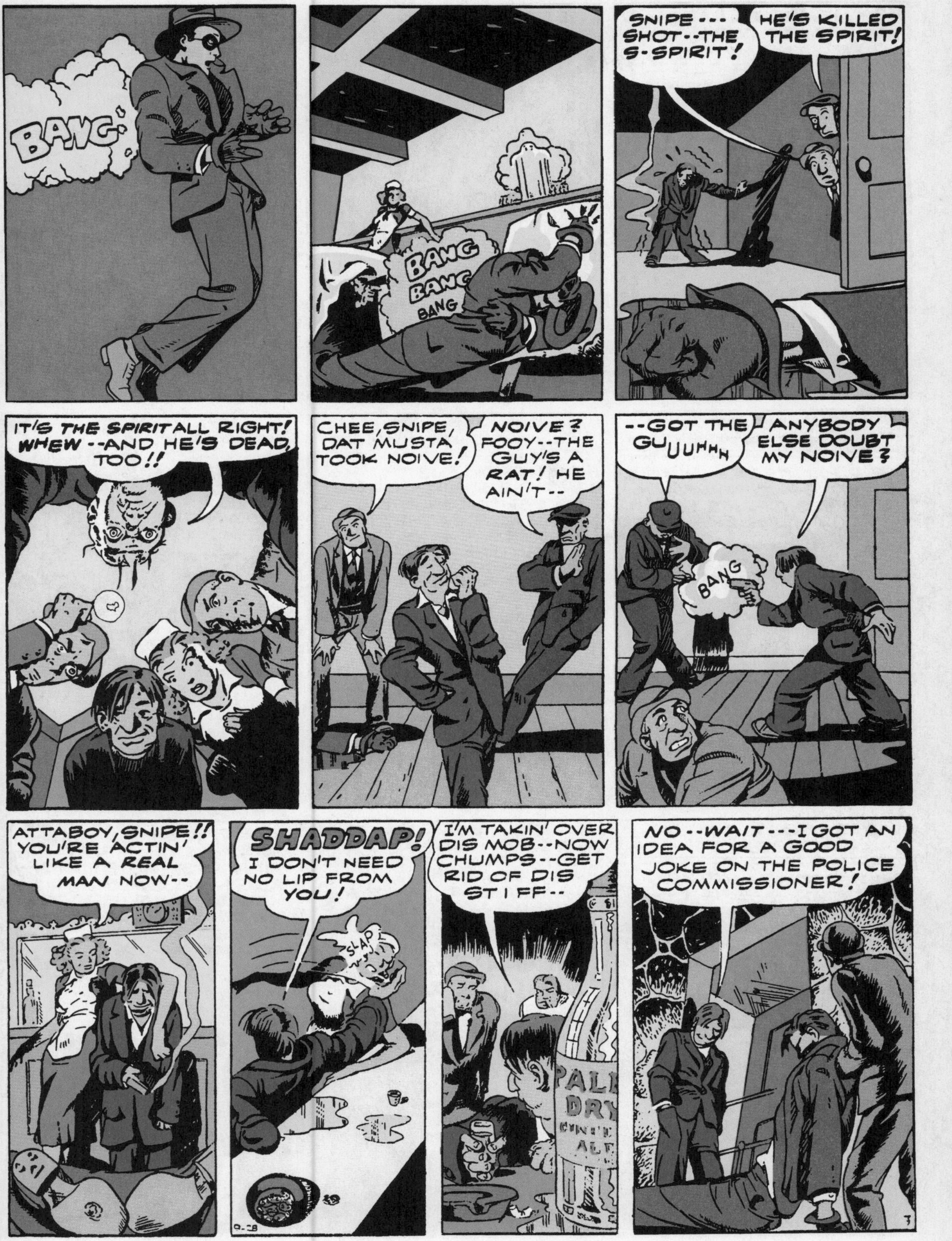

BANG!
BANG
BANG
BANG
SNIPE --- SHOT--THE S-SPIRIT!
HE'S KILLED THE SPIRIT!
IT'S THE SPIRIT ALL RIGHT! WHEW --AND HE'S DEAD, TOO!!
CHEE, SNIPE, DAT MUSTA TOOK NOIVE!
NOIVE? FOOY--THE GUY'S A RAT! HE AIN'T--
--GOT THE GUUUHHH
ANYBODY ELSE DOUBT MY NOIVE?
BANG
ATTABOY, SNIPE!! YOU'RE ACTIN' LIKE A REAL MAN NOW--
SHADDAP! I DON'T NEED NO LIP FROM YOU!
SLAP
I'M TAKIN' OVER DIS MOB--NOW CHUMPS--GET RID OF DIS STIFF--
PALE DRY
NO--WAIT---I GOT AN IDEA FOR A GOOD JOKE ON THE POLICE COMMISSIONER!

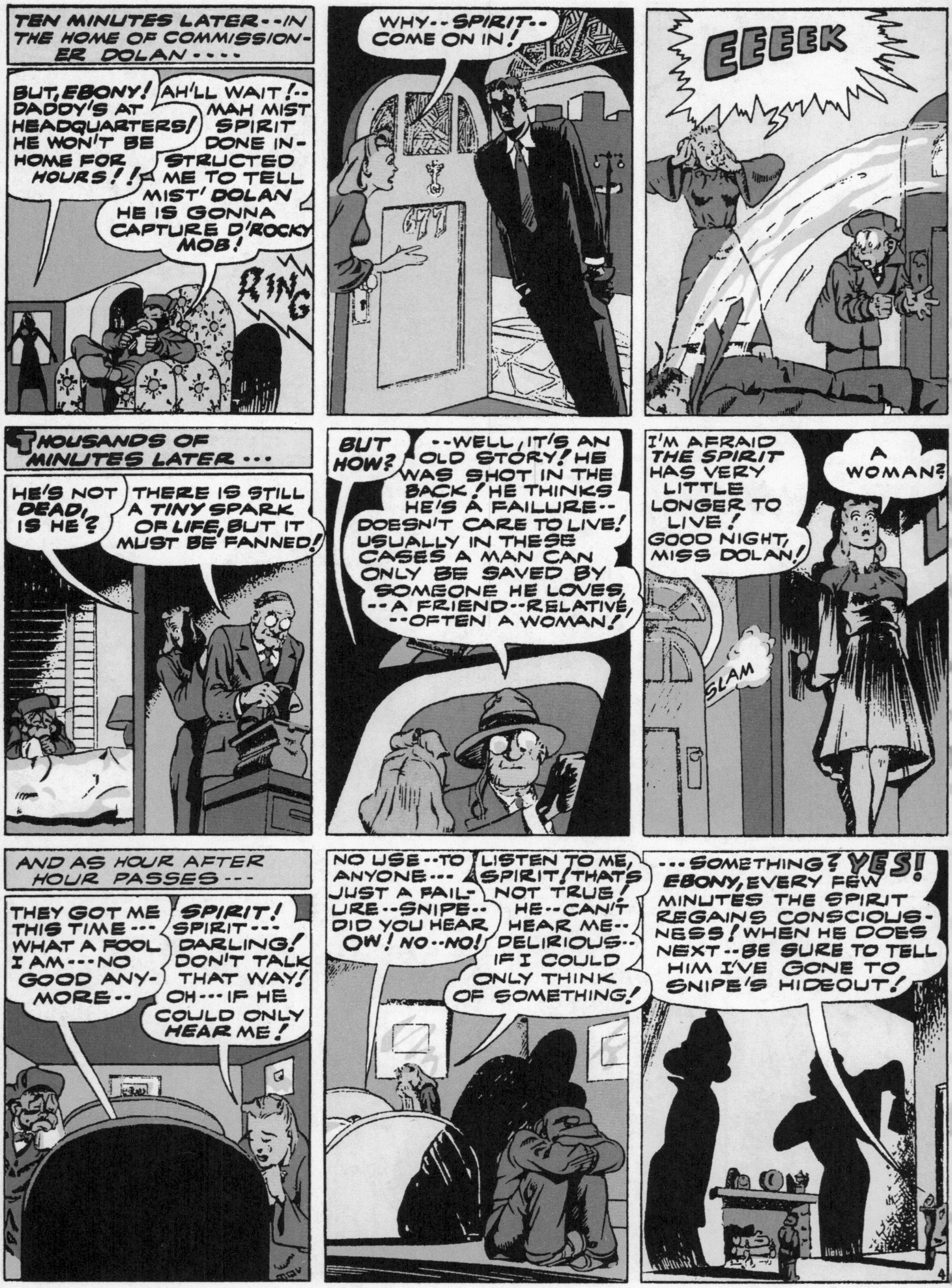
TEN MINUTES LATER--IN THE HOME OF COMMISSIONER DOLAN....
BUT, EBONY! DADDY'S AT HEADQUARTERS! HE WON'T BE HOME FOR HOURS!!
AH'LL WAIT!-- MAH MIST SPIRIT DONE INSTRUCTED ME TO TELL MIST' DOLAN HE IS GONNA CAPTURE D'ROCKY MOB!
RING
WHY--SPIRIT-- COME ON IN!
EEEEK
THOUSANDS OF MINUTES LATER...
HE'S NOT DEAD, IS HE?
THERE IS STILL A TINY SPARK OF LIFE, BUT IT MUST BE FANNED!
BUT HOW?
--WELL, IT'S AN OLD STORY! HE WAS SHOT IN THE BACK! HE THINKS HE'S A FAILURE-- DOESN'T CARE TO LIVE! USUALLY IN THESE CASES A MAN CAN ONLY BE SAVED BY SOMEONE HE LOVES, --A FRIEND--RELATIVE, --OFTEN A WOMAN!
I'M AFRAID THE SPIRIT HAS VERY LITTLE LONGER TO LIVE! GOOD NIGHT, MISS DOLAN!
A WOMAN?
SLAM
AND AS HOUR AFTER HOUR PASSES---
THEY GOT ME THIS TIME--- WHAT A FOOL I AM---NO GOOD ANYMORE--
SPIRIT! SPIRIT--- DARLING! DON'T TALK THAT WAY! OH---IF HE COULD ONLY HEAR ME!
NO USE--TO ANYONE--- JUST A FAILURE--SNIPE-- DID YOU HEAR OW! NO--NO!
LISTEN TO ME, SPIRIT! THAT'S NOT TRUE! HE--CAN'T HEAR ME-- DELIRIOUS-- IF I COULD ONLY THINK OF SOMETHING!
---SOMETHING? YES! EBONY, EVERY FEW MINUTES THE SPIRIT REGAINS CONSCIOUSNESS! WHEN HE DOES NEXT--BE SURE TO TELL HIM I'VE GONE TO SNIPE'S HIDEOUT!
4

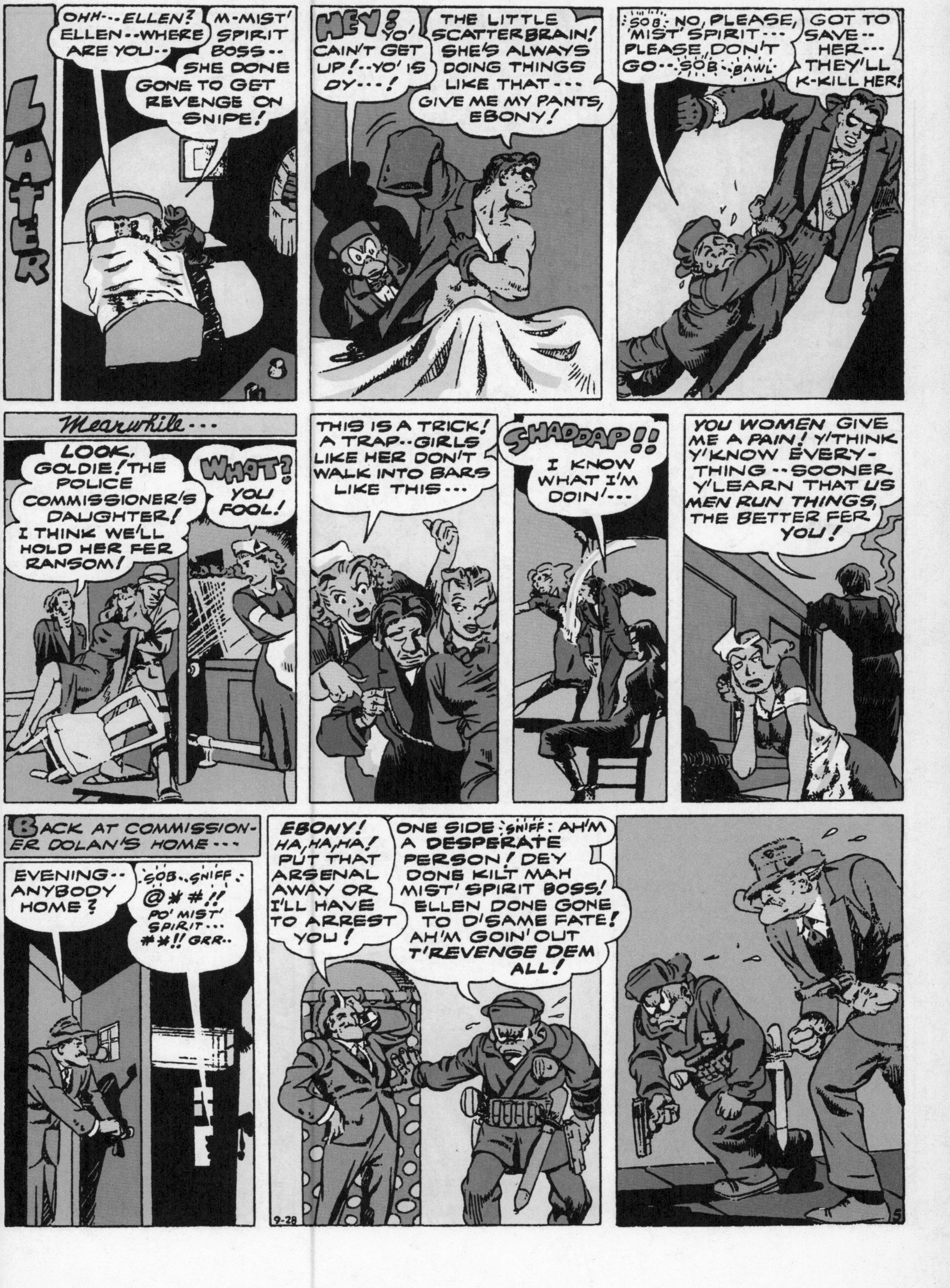
LATER
OHH--ELLEN? ELLEN--WHERE ARE YOU--
M-MIST' SPIRIT BOSS-- SHE DONE GONE TO GET REVENGE ON SNIPE!
HEY! YO' CAIN'T GET UP!--YO' IS DY---!
THE LITTLE SCATTERBRAIN! SHE'S ALWAYS DOING THINGS LIKE THAT--- GIVE ME MY PANTS, EBONY!
SOB-NO, PLEASE, MIST' SPIRIT--- PLEASE, DON'T GO---SOB--BAWL
GOT TO SAVE-- HER--- THEY'LL K-KILL HER!
Meanwhile...
LOOK, GOLDIE! THE POLICE COMMISSIONER'S DAUGHTER! I THINK WE'LL HOLD HER FER RANSOM!
WHAT? YOU FOOL!
THIS IS A TRICK! A TRAP--GIRLS LIKE HER DON'T WALK INTO BARS LIKE THIS---
SHADDAP!!
I KNOW WHAT I'M DOIN'---
YOU WOMEN GIVE ME A PAIN! Y'THINK Y'KNOW EVERY-THING--SOONER Y'LEARN THAT US MEN RUN THINGS, THE BETTER FER YOU!
BACK AT COMMISSION-ER DOLAN'S HOME---
EVENING-- ANYBODY HOME?
SOB--SNIFF @*#!! PO' MIST' SPIRIT--- *#!! GRR--
EBONY! HA, HA, HA! PUT THAT ARSENAL AWAY OR I'LL HAVE TO ARREST YOU!
ONE SIDE SNIFF AH'M A DESPERATE PERSON! DEY DONE KILT MAH MIST' SPIRIT BOSS! ELLEN DONE GONE TO D'SAME FATE! AH'M GOIN' OUT T'REVENGE DEM ALL!
9-28
5

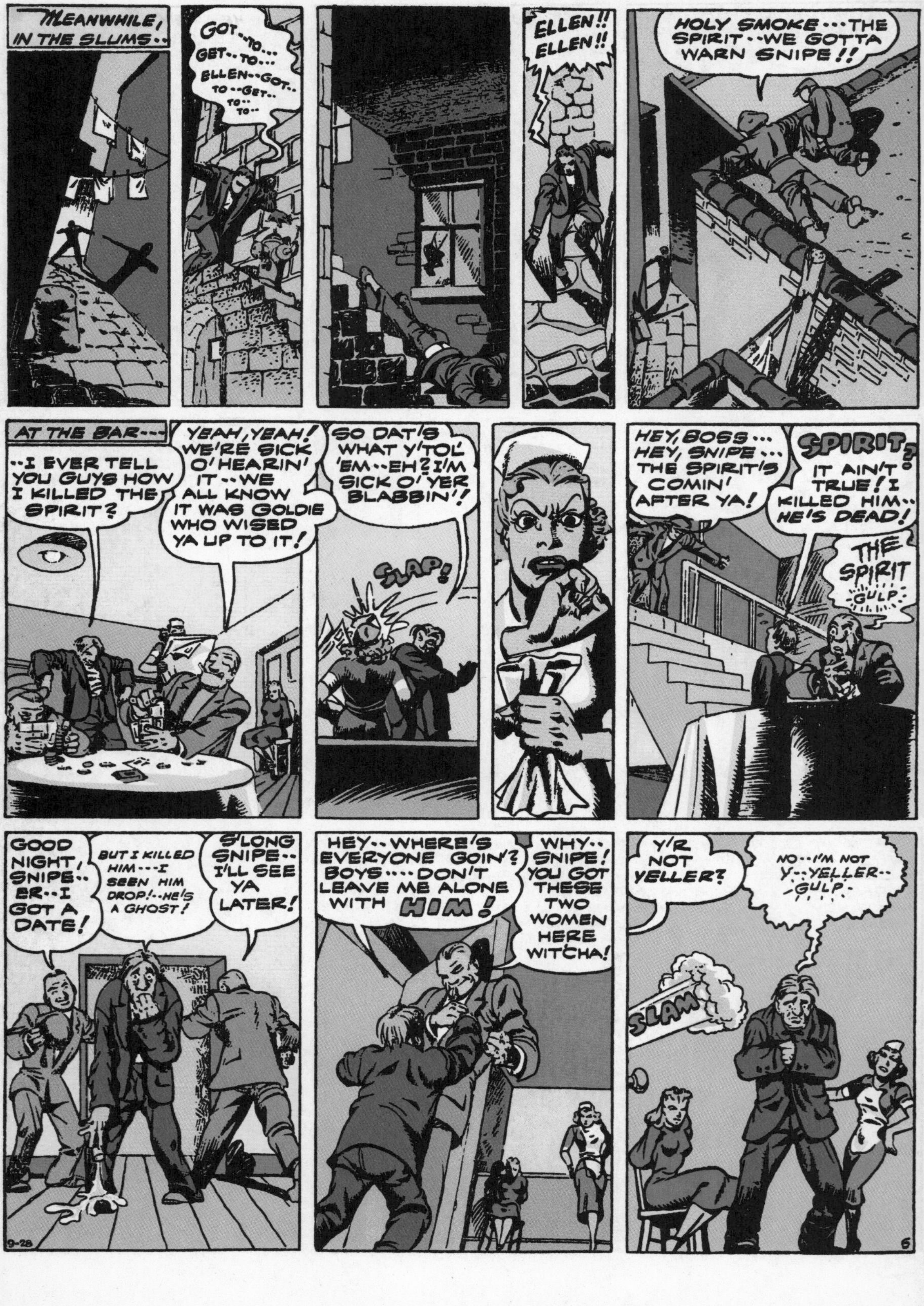
MEANWHILE, IN THE SLUMS..
GOT...TO... GET..TO... ELLEN..GOT.. TO..GET.. TO.. TO..
ELLEN!! ELLEN!!
HOLY SMOKE...THE SPIRIT..WE GOTTA WARN SNIPE!!
AT THE BAR...
..I EVER TELL YOU GUYS HOW I KILLED THE SPIRIT?
YEAH, YEAH! WE'RE SICK O' HEARIN' IT..WE ALL KNOW IT WAS GOLDIE WHO WISED YA UP TO IT!
SO DAT'S WHAT Y'TOL' 'EM..EH? I'M SICK O' YER BLABBIN'!
SLAP!
HEY, BOSS... HEY, SNIPE... THE SPIRIT'S COMIN' AFTER YA!
SPIRIT? IT AIN'T TRUE! I KILLED HIM.. HE'S DEAD!
THE SPIRIT -GULP-
GOOD NIGHT, SNIPE.. ER..I GOT A DATE!
BUT I KILLED HIM...I SEEN HIM DROP!..HE'S A GHOST!
S'LONG SNIPE.. I'LL SEE YA LATER!
HEY..WHERE'S EVERYONE GOIN'? BOYS....DON'T LEAVE ME ALONE WITH HIM!
WHY.. SNIPE! YOU GOT THESE TWO WOMEN HERE WITCHA!
Y'R NOT YELLER?
NO..I'M NOT Y..YELLER.. -GULP-
SLAM
9-28
6

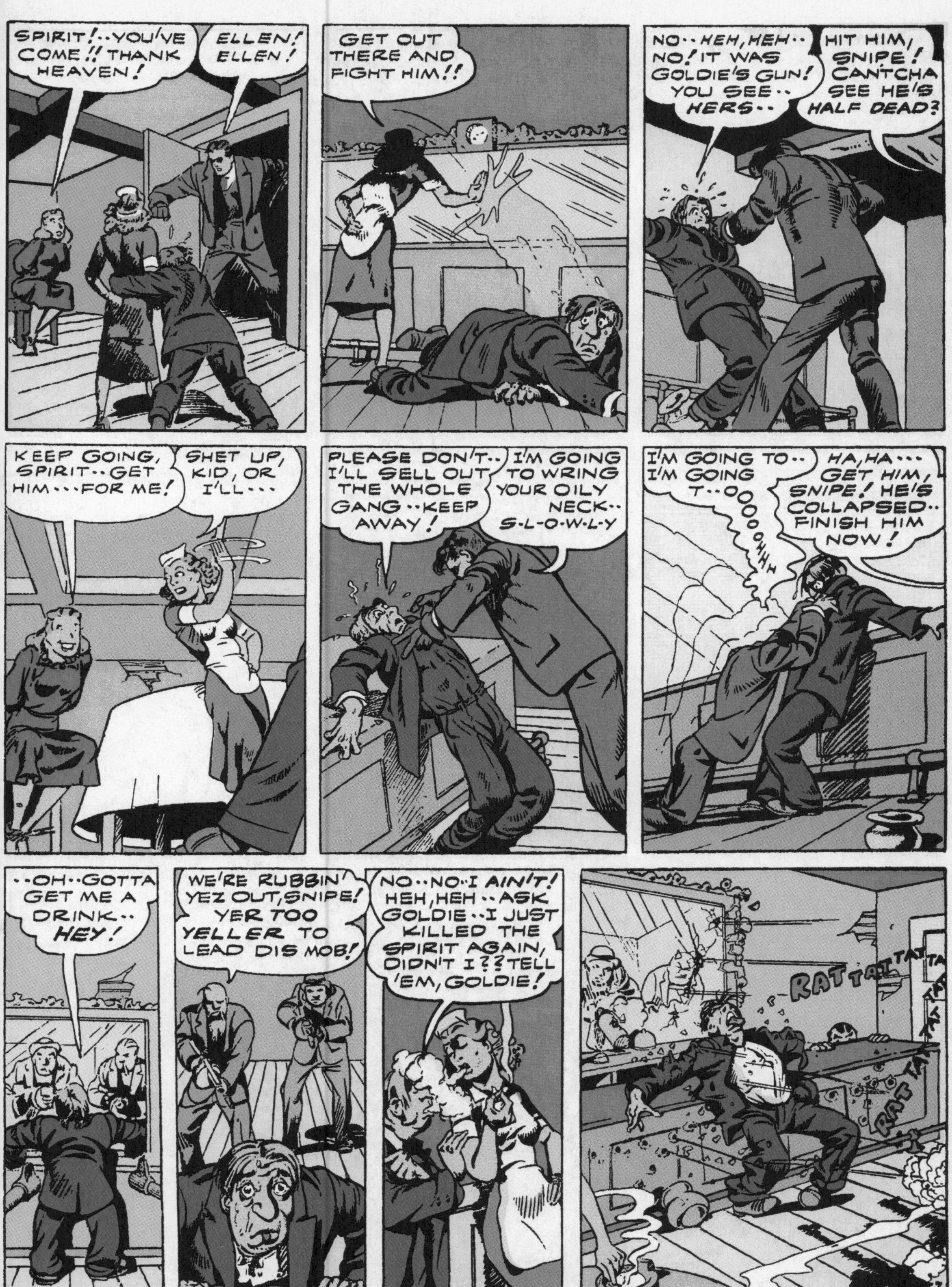
SPIRIT!..YOU'VE COME!! THANK HEAVEN!
ELLEN! ELLEN!
GET OUT THERE AND FIGHT HIM!!
NO..HEH, HEH.. NO! IT WAS GOLDIE'S GUN! YOU SEE.. HERS..
HIT HIM, SNIPE! CAN'TCHA SEE HE'S HALF DEAD?
KEEP GOING, SPIRIT..GET HIM...FOR ME!
SHET UP, KID, OR I'LL...
PLEASE DON'T.. I'LL SELL OUT THE WHOLE GANG..KEEP AWAY!
I'M GOING TO WRING YOUR OILY NECK.. S-L-O-W-L-Y
I'M GOING TO.. I'M GOING T..OOOOOOHHH
HA, HA... GET HIM, SNIPE! HE'S COLLAPSED.. FINISH HIM NOW!
..OH..GOTTA GET ME A DRINK.. HEY!
WE'RE RUBBIN' YEZ OUT, SNIPE! YER TOO YELLER TO LEAD DIS MOB!
NO..NO..I AIN'T! HEH, HEH..ASK GOLDIE..I JUST KILLED THE SPIRIT AGAIN, DIDN'T I?? TELL 'EM, GOLDIE!
RAT TAT TAT TAT
RAT TAT TAT

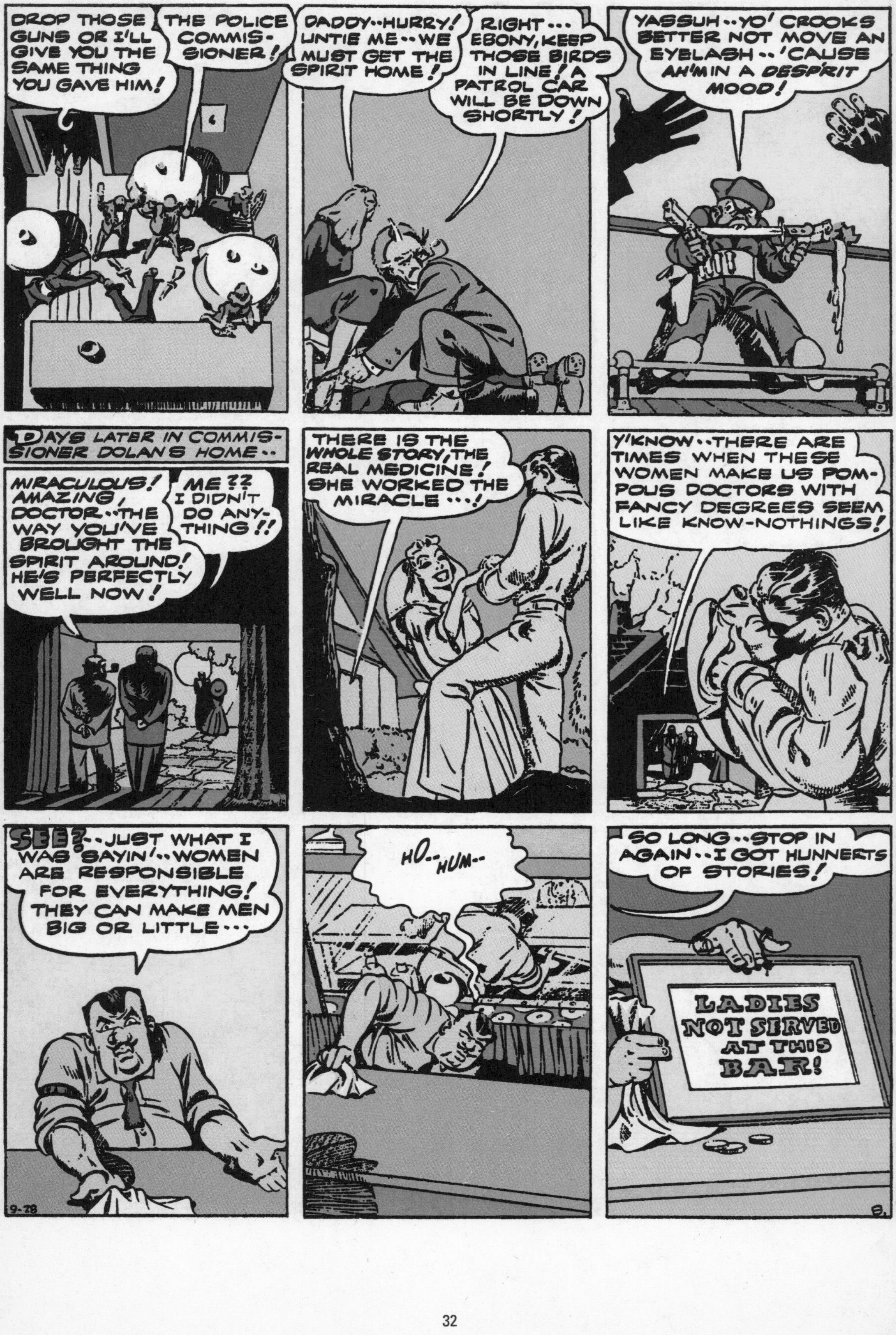
DROP THOSE GUNS OR I'LL GIVE YOU THE SAME THING YOU GAVE HIM!
THE POLICE COMMIS-SIONER!
DADDY--HURRY! UNTIE ME--WE MUST GET THE SPIRIT HOME!
RIGHT... EBONY, KEEP THOSE BIRDS IN LINE! A PATROL CAR WILL BE DOWN SHORTLY!
YASSUH--YO' CROOKS BETTER NOT MOVE AN EYELASH--'CAUSE AH'M IN A DESP'RIT MOOD!
DAYS LATER IN COMMIS-SIONER DOLAN'S HOME--
MIRACULOUS! AMAZING, DOCTOR--THE WAY YOU'VE BROUGHT THE SPIRIT AROUND! HE'S PERFECTLY WELL NOW!
ME?? I DIDN'T DO ANY-THING!!
THERE IS THE WHOLE STORY, THE REAL MEDICINE! SHE WORKED THE MIRACLE...!
Y'KNOW--THERE ARE TIMES WHEN THESE WOMEN MAKE US POM-POUS DOCTORS WITH FANCY DEGREES SEEM LIKE KNOW-NOTHINGS!
SEE?--JUST WHAT I WAS SAYIN'--WOMEN ARE RESPONSIBLE FOR EVERYTHING! THEY CAN MAKE MEN BIG OR LITTLE...
HO--HUM--
SO LONG--STOP IN AGAIN--I GOT HUNNERTS OF STORIES!
LADIES NOT SIRVED AT THIS BAR!
9-28
8.

COMIC BOOK SECTION

SPHINX & SATIN

ACTION Mystery ADVENTURE

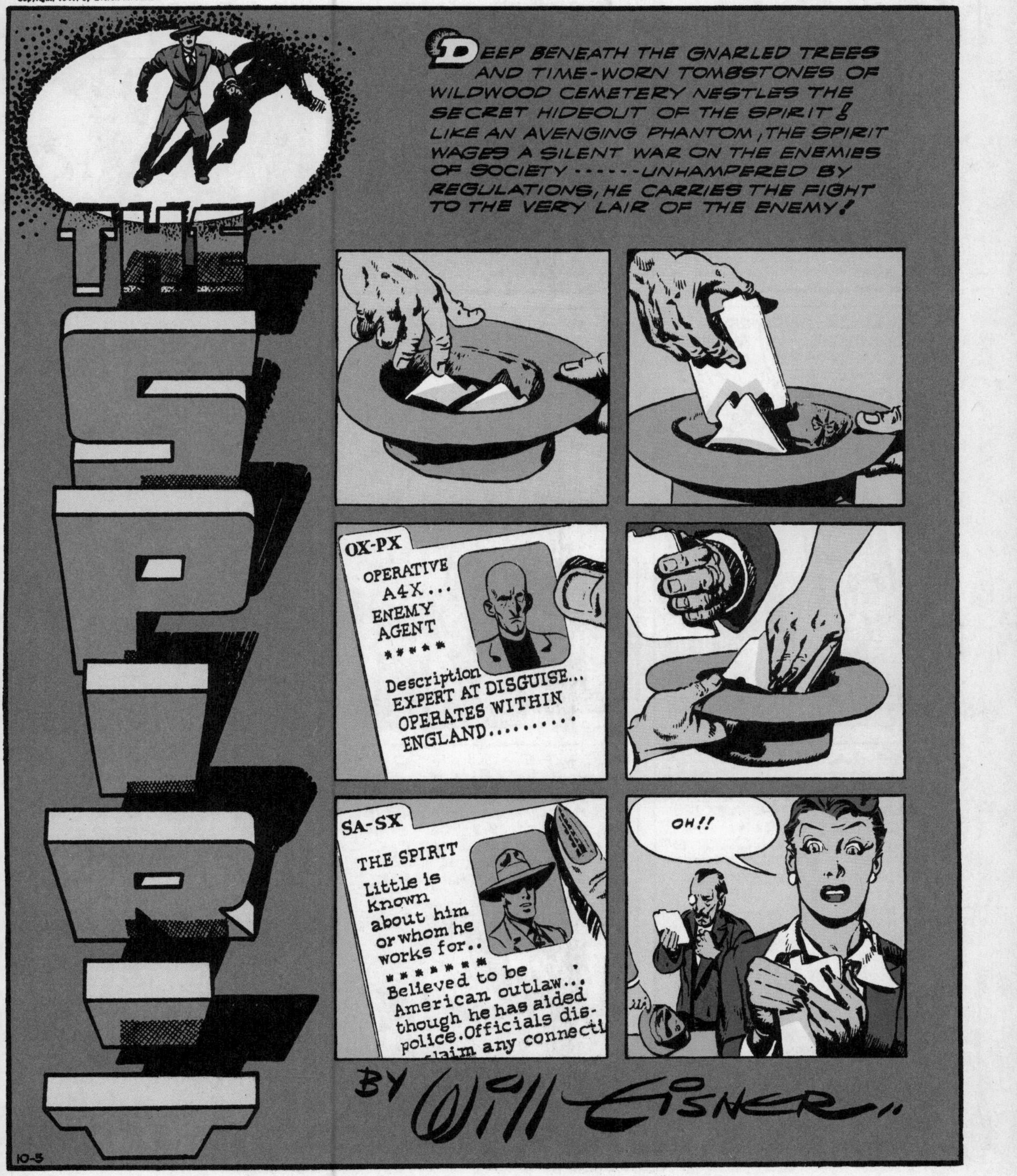
THE SPIRIT
DEEP BENEATH THE GNARLED TREES AND TIME-WORN TOMBSTONES OF WILDWOOD CEMETERY NESTLES THE SECRET HIDEOUT OF THE SPIRIT! LIKE AN AVENGING PHANTOM, THE SPIRIT WAGES A SILENT WAR ON THE ENEMIES OF SOCIETY ------UNHAMPERED BY REGULATIONS, HE CARRIES THE FIGHT TO THE VERY LAIR OF THE ENEMY!
OX-PX
OPERATIVE A4X... ENEMY AGENT *****
Description EXPERT AT DISGUISE... OPERATES WITHIN ENGLAND..........
SA-SX
THE SPIRIT
Little is known about him or whom he works for..
******* Believed to be American outlaw... though he has aided police. Officials dis-
OH!!
BY Will Eisner
10-5

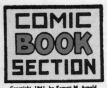

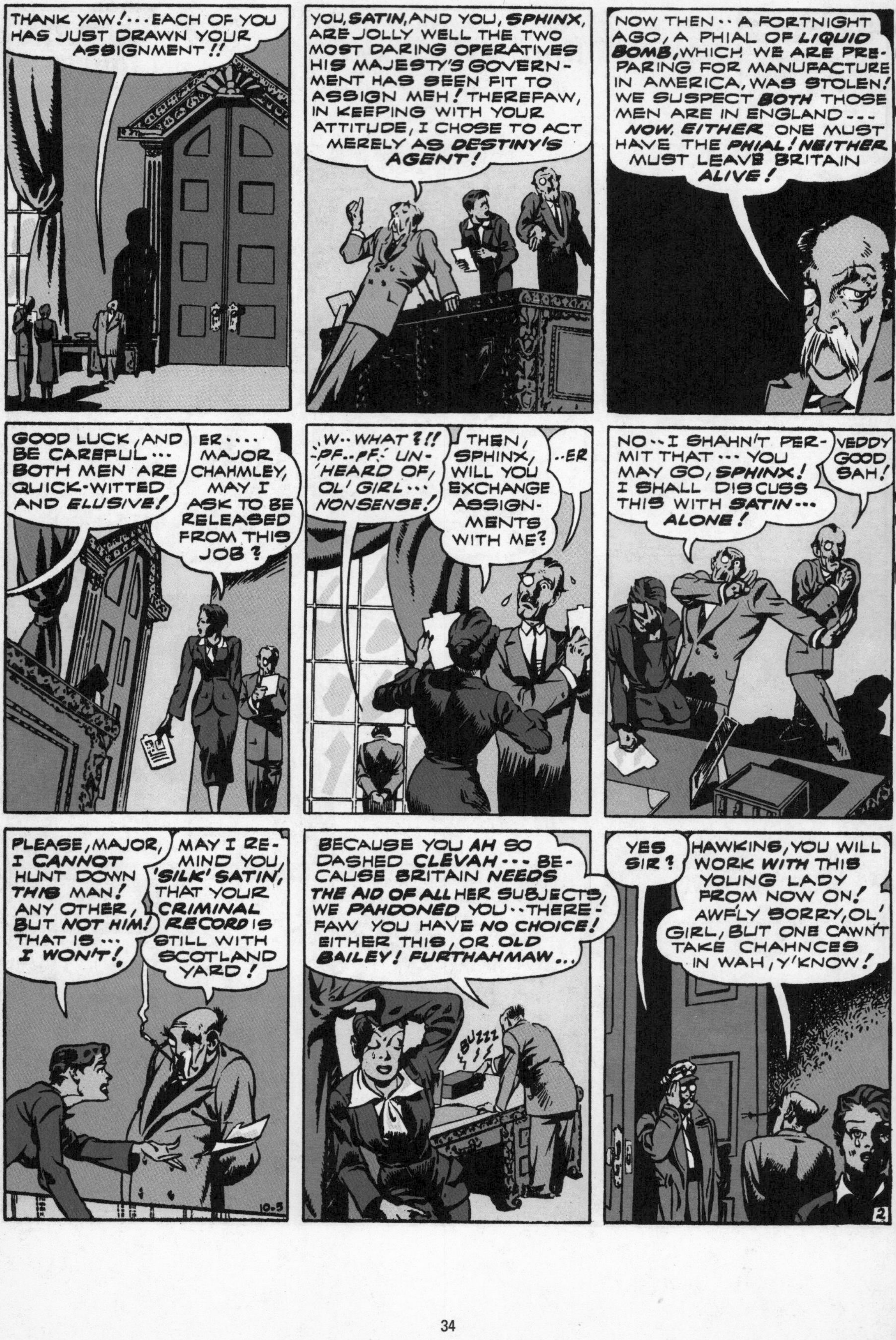

THANK YAW!... EACH OF YOU HAS JUST DRAWN YOUR ASSIGNMENT!!
YOU, SATIN, AND YOU, SPHINX, ARE JOLLY WELL THE TWO MOST DARING OPERATIVES HIS MAJESTY'S GOVERNMENT HAS SEEN FIT TO ASSIGN MEH! THEREFAW, IN KEEPING WITH YOUR ATTITUDE, I CHOSE TO ACT MERELY AS DESTINY'S AGENT!
NOW THEN.. A FORTNIGHT AGO, A PHIAL OF LIQUID BOMB, WHICH WE ARE PREPARING FOR MANUFACTURE IN AMERICA, WAS STOLEN! WE SUSPECT BOTH THOSE MEN ARE IN ENGLAND... NOW, EITHER ONE MUST HAVE THE PHIAL! NEITHER MUST LEAVE BRITAIN ALIVE!
GOOD LUCK, AND BE CAREFUL... BOTH MEN ARE QUICK-WITTED AND ELUSIVE!
ER.... MAJOR CHAHMLEY, MAY I ASK TO BE RELEASED FROM THIS JOB?
W.. WHAT?!! PF..PF.. UNHEARD OF, OL' GIRL... NONSENSE!
THEN, SPHINX, WILL YOU EXCHANGE ASSIGNMENTS WITH ME?
..ER
NO.. I SHAHN'T PERMIT THAT... YOU MAY GO, SPHINX! I SHALL DISCUSS THIS WITH SATIN... ALONE!
VEDDY GOOD SAH!
PLEASE, MAJOR, I CANNOT HUNT DOWN THIS MAN! ANY OTHER, BUT NOT HIM! THAT IS... I WON'T!
MAY I REMIND YOU, 'SILK' SATIN, THAT YOUR CRIMINAL RECORD IS STILL WITH SCOTLAND YARD!
BECAUSE YOU AH SO DASHED CLEVAH... BECAUSE BRITAIN NEEDS THE AID OF ALL HER SUBJECTS, WE PAHDONED YOU.. THEREFAW YOU HAVE NO CHOICE! EITHER THIS, OR OLD BAILEY! FURTHAHMAW...
BUZZZ
YES SIR?
HAWKINS, YOU WILL WORK WITH THIS YOUNG LADY FROM NOW ON! AWFLY SORRY, OL' GIRL, BUT ONE CAWN'T TAKE CHAHNCES IN WAH, Y'KNOW!
2

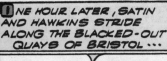

ONE HOUR LATER, SATIN AND HAWKINS STRIDE ALONG THE BLACKED-OUT QUAYS OF BRISTOL...

BLIMEY, MISS SATIN...Y'AIN'T SAID A WORD FOR AN HOUR! WHAT'S UP?

HAWKINS, IF YOU WERE ASSIGNED TO KILL SOMEONE YOU LOVED FOR THE SAKE OF ENGLAND, WHAT WOULD YOU DO?

'OW...THAT'S AN UNFAIR QUESTION, BUT I'D SAY IT WOULD DEPEND ON WHO I LOVED MOST AND HOW MUCH WAS AT STAKE...POOR GIRL, YOU 'AVE GOT A BIT OF A PROBLEM, WOT?

YOU'VE GIVEN ME THE ANSWER, HAWKINS! ...I'M GOING AFTER THE SPIRIT IN EARNEST!

MEANWHILE, BACK AT MAJOR CHAHMLEY'S OFFICES...

WE FOUND POOR OL' 'AWKINS JUST LYKE THIS, 'ERE HIN A CLOSET!

THEN THE SPIRIT IS NOW WITH SATIN...POSING AS HAWKINS!

...AND BACK IN BRISTOL...

NOW, HERE'S OUR PLAN...THE SPIRIT WILL SURELY HEAD FOR AMERICA AT THE FIRST CHANCE...I'VE SUPPLIED THAT CHANCE...BY NOW THE WATERFRONT WILL KNOW THAT THE TANKER "YAKK" IS SAILING AT DAWN!

DEUCEDLY CUTE, MISS SATIN...'E COMES ABOARD, AND WE NABS THE BLIGHTER!

RIGHT!!

AND PRAY HEAVEN WE DON'T HAVE TO HURT HIM...

WELL...GOODNIGHT, MISS SATIN! GOT TO FILE A REPORT!

'NIGHT, HAWKINS! I'M GOING UP TO BED!

...IN A FEW LIGHT BOUNDS, HAWKINS IS ON THE PIER...SCALES SLIME-RUSTED SIDES...

...AND DROPS LIGHTLY ON THE DECK OF THE "YAKK"!

SATIN!

'EVENING, HAWKINS! I EXPECTED YOU!

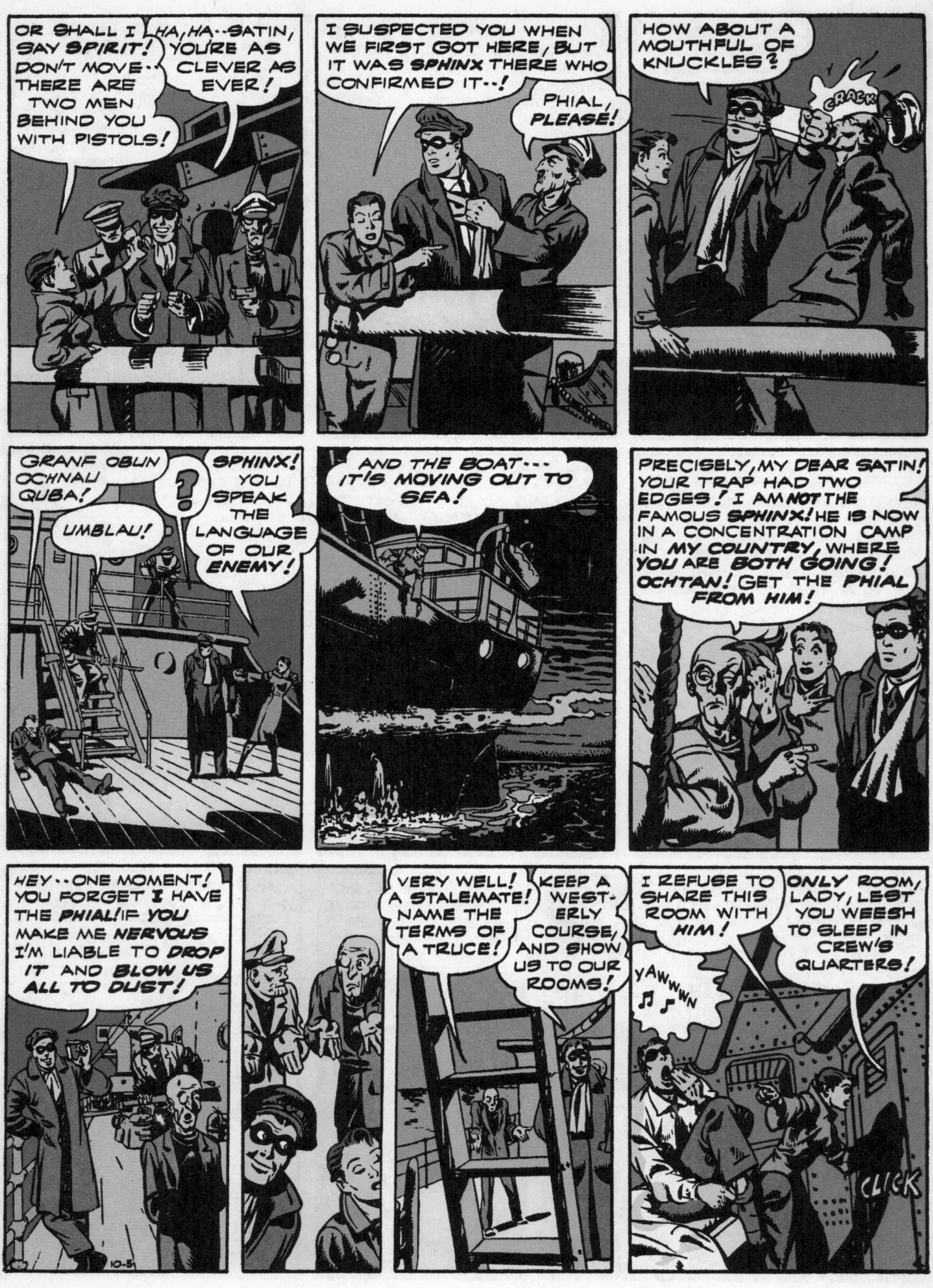

OR SHALL I SAY SPIRIT! DON'T MOVE.. THERE ARE TWO MEN BEHIND YOU WITH PISTOLS!
HA, HA..SATIN, YOU'RE AS CLEVER AS EVER!
I SUSPECTED YOU WHEN WE FIRST GOT HERE, BUT IT WAS SPHINX THERE WHO CONFIRMED IT..!
PHIAL, PLEASE!
HOW ABOUT A MOUTHFUL OF KNUCKLES?
CRACK
GRANF OBUN OCHNAU QUBA!
UMBLAU!
?
SPHINX! YOU SPEAK THE LANGUAGE OF OUR ENEMY!
AND THE BOAT... IT'S MOVING OUT TO SEA!
PRECISELY, MY DEAR SATIN! YOUR TRAP HAD TWO EDGES! I AM NOT THE FAMOUS SPHINX! HE IS NOW IN A CONCENTRATION CAMP IN MY COUNTRY, WHERE YOU ARE BOTH GOING! OCHTAN! GET THE PHIAL FROM HIM!
HEY..ONE MOMENT! YOU FORGET I HAVE THE PHIAL! IF YOU MAKE ME NERVOUS I'M LIABLE TO DROP IT AND BLOW US ALL TO DUST!
10-5
VERY WELL! A STALEMATE! NAME THE TERMS OF A TRUCE!
KEEP A WEST-ERLY COURSE, AND SHOW US TO OUR ROOMS!
I REFUSE TO SHARE THIS ROOM WITH HIM!
ONLY ROOM, LADY, LEST YOU WEESH TO SLEEP IN CREW'S QUARTERS!
YAWWWN
CLICK

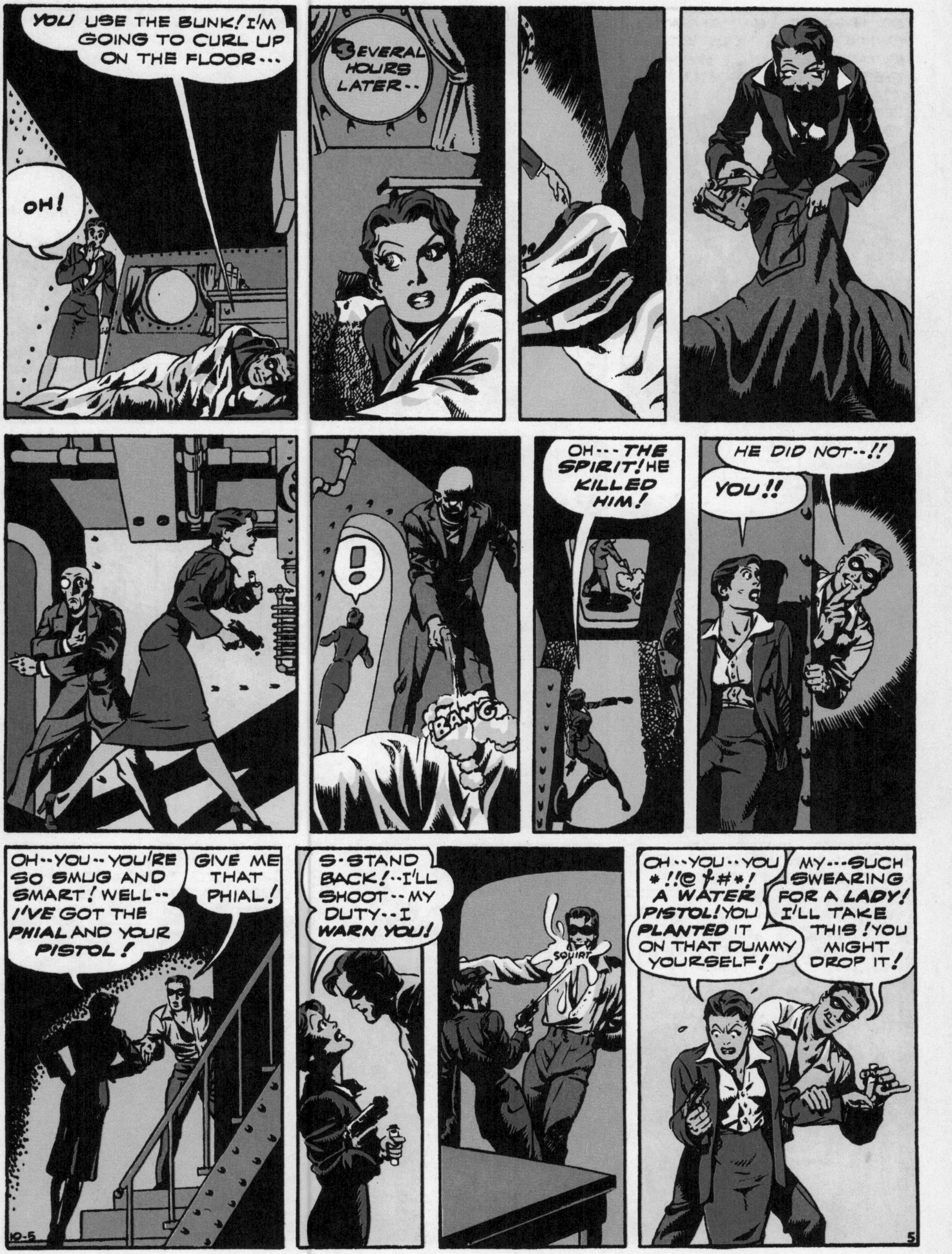
YOU USE THE BUNK! I'M GOING TO CURL UP ON THE FLOOR...
OH!
SEVERAL HOURS LATER..
!
BANG
OH--- THE SPIRIT! HE KILLED HIM!
HE DID NOT--!!
YOU!!
OH--YOU--YOU'RE SO SMUG AND SMART! WELL-- I'VE GOT THE PHIAL AND YOUR PISTOL!
GIVE ME THAT PHIAL!
S-STAND BACK!--I'LL SHOOT--MY DUTY--I WARN YOU!
SQUIRT
OH--YOU--YOU *!!@‡#*! A WATER PISTOL! YOU PLANTED IT ON THAT DUMMY YOURSELF!
MY---SUCH SWEARING FOR A LADY! I'LL TAKE THIS! YOU MIGHT DROP IT!
10-5
5

LOOK HERE, SATIN! WE'RE IN THIS TOGETHER! LET'S CALL AN ARMISTICE TILL *WE* GET CONTROL!

VERY WELL, I'LL WORK *WITH* YOU FOR NOW!

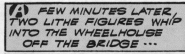

A FEW MINUTES LATER, TWO LITHE FIGURES WHIP INTO THE WHEELHOUSE OFF THE BRIDGE...

HAVE ONE, SATIN!

THANK YAW! BINGO, OL' CHAP!

THERE'S A FEW MORE BELOW DECKS! I'LL POLISH THEM OFF... MEANWHILE *YOU* WIRELESS FOR AN *AMERICAN* PATROL TO STAND BY!

O.K.

SLAM

SATIN A1 CALLING PATROL--CALLING BRITISH PATROL!! HAVE CAPTURED SPIRIT WITH PHIAL!!

...AND NOW!

DOWN IN THE HOLD, THE SPIRIT BATTLES HEAVY ODDS...

KEEP HIM BUSY WHILE I GET THE PHIAL!

10-5

AH!

WITH THE PRECIOUS TUBE CLUTCHED TIGHTLY, THE ENEMY AGENT RACES TO SAFETY----

6

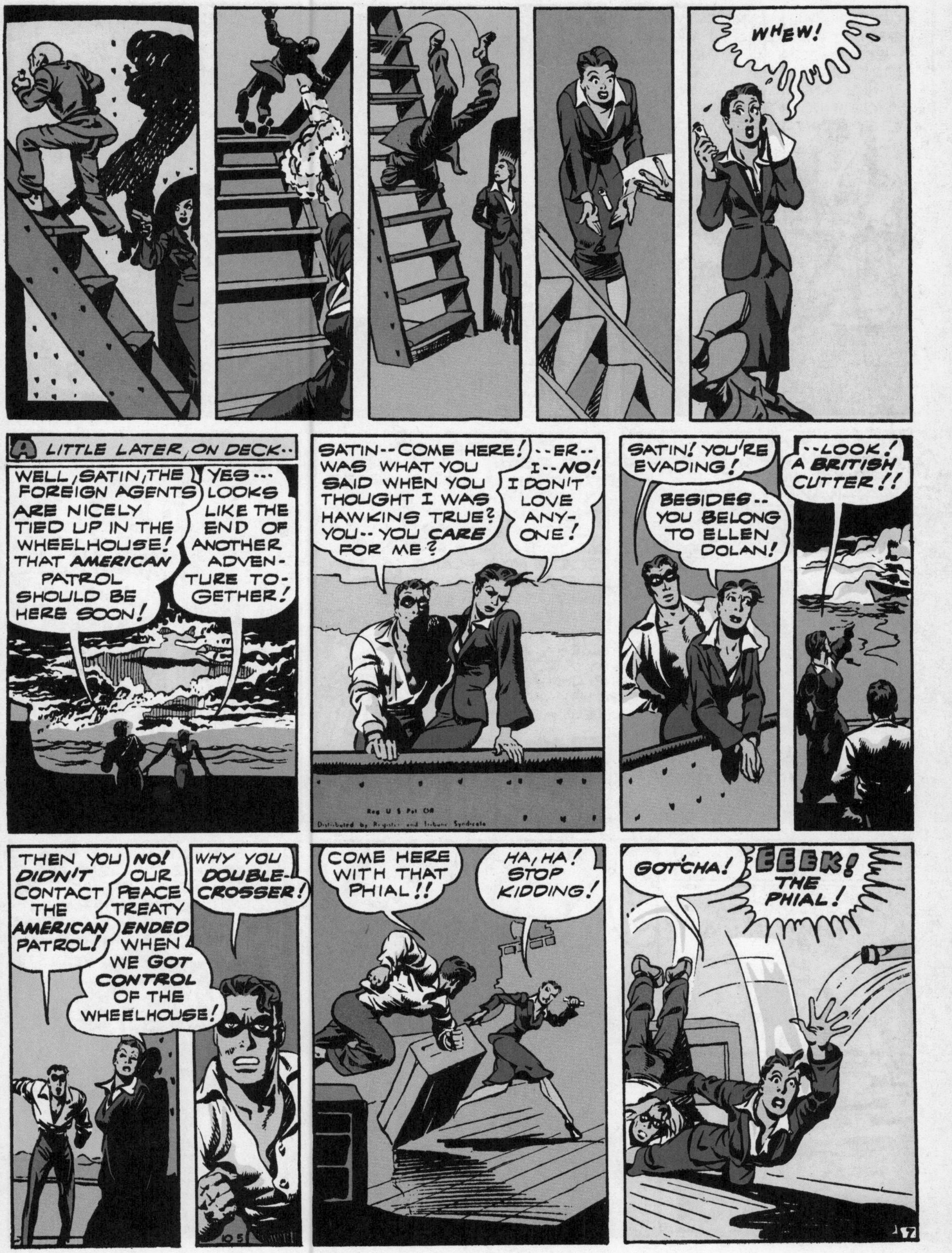
WHEW!
A LITTLE LATER, ON DECK..
WELL, SATIN, THE FOREIGN AGENTS ARE NICELY TIED UP IN THE WHEELHOUSE! THAT AMERICAN PATROL SHOULD BE HERE SOON!
YES... LOOKS LIKE THE END OF ANOTHER ADVENTURE TOGETHER!
SATIN--COME HERE! WAS WHAT YOU SAID WHEN YOU THOUGHT I WAS HAWKINS TRUE? YOU--YOU CARE FOR ME?
--ER-- I--NO! I DON'T LOVE ANYONE!
SATIN! YOU'RE EVADING!
BESIDES-- YOU BELONG TO ELLEN DOLAN!
--LOOK! A BRITISH CUTTER!!
THEN YOU DIDN'T CONTACT THE AMERICAN PATROL!
NO! OUR PEACE TREATY ENDED WHEN WE GOT CONTROL OF THE WHEELHOUSE!
WHY YOU DOUBLE-CROSSER!
COME HERE WITH THAT PHIAL!!
HA, HA! STOP KIDDING!
GOT'CHA!
EEEK! THE PHIAL!

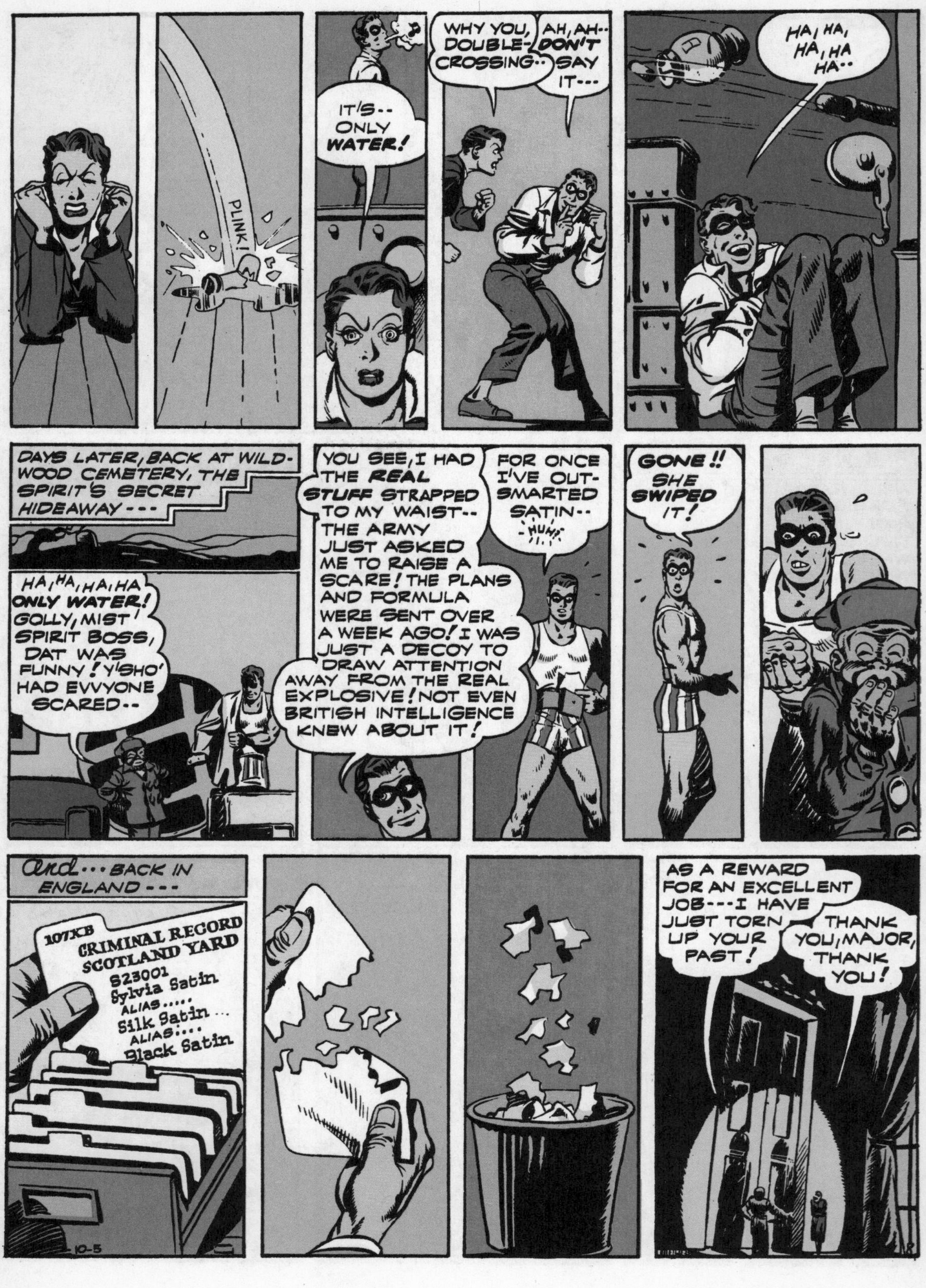
PLINK!
IT'S-- ONLY WATER!
WHY YOU, DOUBLE-CROSSING--
AH, AH--DON'T SAY IT---
HA, HA, HA, HA HA--
DAYS LATER, BACK AT WILDWOOD CEMETERY, THE SPIRIT'S SECRET HIDEAWAY---
HA, HA, HA, HA ONLY WATER! GOLLY, MIST' SPIRIT BOSS, DAT WAS FUNNY! Y'SHO' HAD EVVYONE SCARED--
YOU SEE, I HAD THE REAL STUFF STRAPPED TO MY WAIST-- THE ARMY JUST ASKED ME TO RAISE A SCARE! THE PLANS AND FORMULA WERE SENT OVER A WEEK AGO! I WAS JUST A DECOY TO DRAW ATTENTION AWAY FROM THE REAL EXPLOSIVE! NOT EVEN BRITISH INTELLIGENCE KNEW ABOUT IT!
FOR ONCE I'VE OUTSMARTED SATIN--
-HUH!
GONE!! SHE SWIPED IT!
and--- BACK IN ENGLAND---
107KB
CRIMINAL RECORD SCOTLAND YARD
823001
Sylvia Satin
ALIAS.....
Silk Satin ...
ALIAS:...
Black Satin
10-5
AS A REWARD FOR AN EXCELLENT JOB---I HAVE JUST TORN UP YOUR PAST!
THANK YOU, MAJOR, THANK YOU!

MADAM MINX

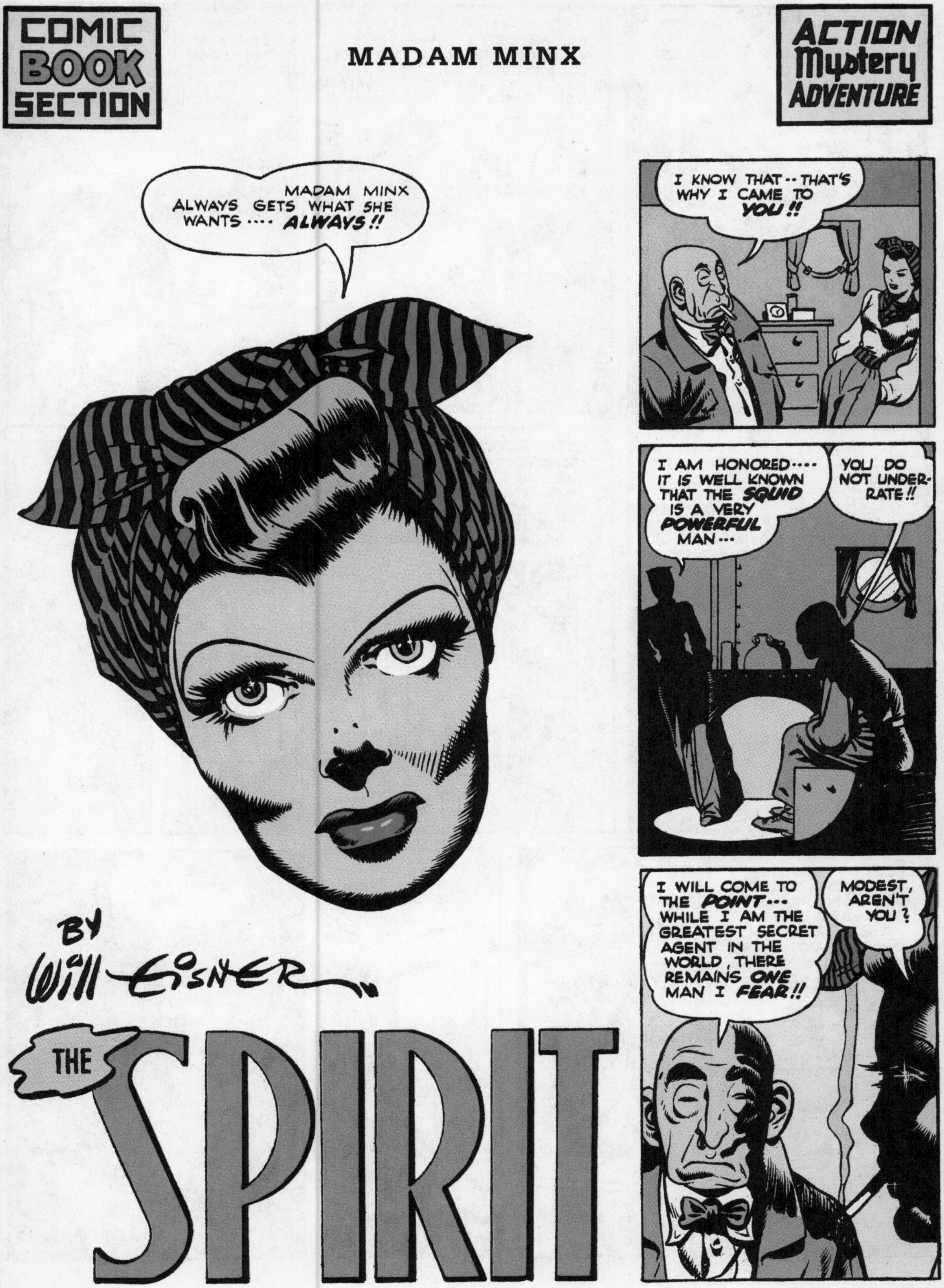
COMIC BOOK SECTION
ACTION Mystery ADVENTURE
MADAM MINX ALWAYS GETS WHAT SHE WANTS .... ALWAYS!!
BY Will Eisner
THE SPIRIT
I KNOW THAT -- THAT'S WHY I CAME TO YOU!!
I AM HONORED.... IT IS WELL KNOWN THAT THE SQUID IS A VERY POWERFUL MAN...
YOU DO NOT UNDER-RATE!!
I WILL COME TO THE POINT... WHILE I AM THE GREATEST SECRET AGENT IN THE WORLD, THERE REMAINS ONE MAN I FEAR!!
MODEST, AREN'T YOU?

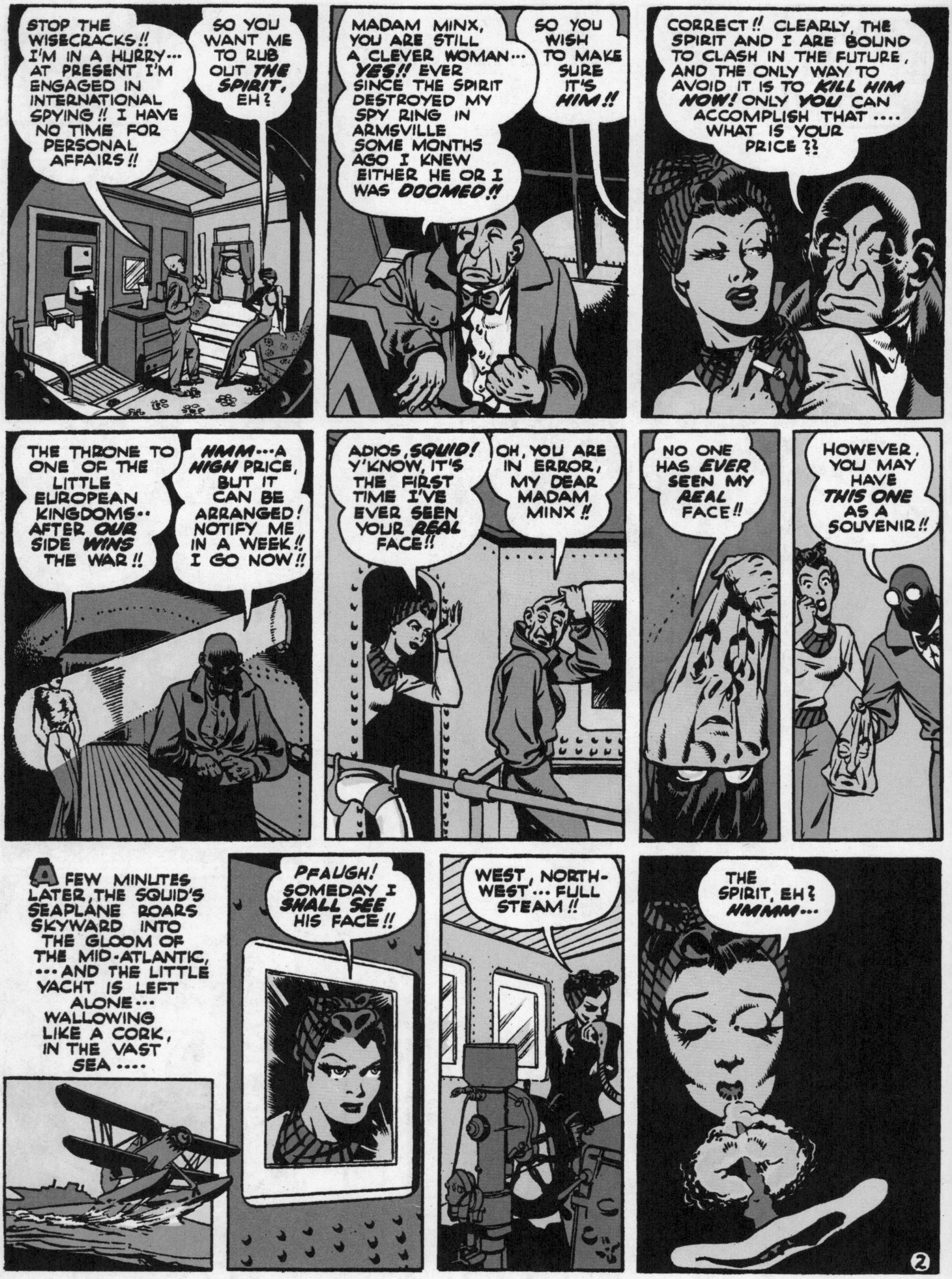
STOP THE WISECRACKS!! I'M IN A HURRY... AT PRESENT I'M ENGAGED IN INTERNATIONAL SPYING!! I HAVE NO TIME FOR PERSONAL AFFAIRS!!
SO YOU WANT ME TO RUB OUT THE SPIRIT, EH?
MADAM MINX, YOU ARE STILL A CLEVER WOMAN... YES!! EVER SINCE THE SPIRIT DESTROYED MY SPY RING IN ARMSVILLE SOME MONTHS AGO I KNEW EITHER HE OR I WAS DOOMED!!
SO YOU WISH TO MAKE SURE IT'S HIM!!
CORRECT!! CLEARLY, THE SPIRIT AND I ARE BOUND TO CLASH IN THE FUTURE, AND THE ONLY WAY TO AVOID IT IS TO KILL HIM NOW! ONLY YOU CAN ACCOMPLISH THAT.... WHAT IS YOUR PRICE??
THE THRONE TO ONE OF THE LITTLE EUROPEAN KINGDOMS.. AFTER OUR SIDE WINS THE WAR!!
HMM...A HIGH PRICE, BUT IT CAN BE ARRANGED! NOTIFY ME IN A WEEK!! I GO NOW!!
ADIOS, SQUID! Y'KNOW, IT'S THE FIRST TIME I'VE EVER SEEN YOUR REAL FACE!!
OH, YOU ARE IN ERROR, MY DEAR MADAM MINX!!
NO ONE HAS EVER SEEN MY REAL FACE!!
HOWEVER, YOU MAY HAVE THIS ONE AS A SOUVENIR!!
A FEW MINUTES LATER, THE SQUID'S SEAPLANE ROARS SKYWARD INTO THE GLOOM OF THE MID-ATLANTIC, ...AND THE LITTLE YACHT IS LEFT ALONE... WALLOWING LIKE A CORK, IN THE VAST SEA....
PFAUGH! SOMEDAY I SHALL SEE HIS FACE!!
WEST, NORTH-WEST... FULL STEAM!!
THE SPIRIT, EH? HMMM...
2

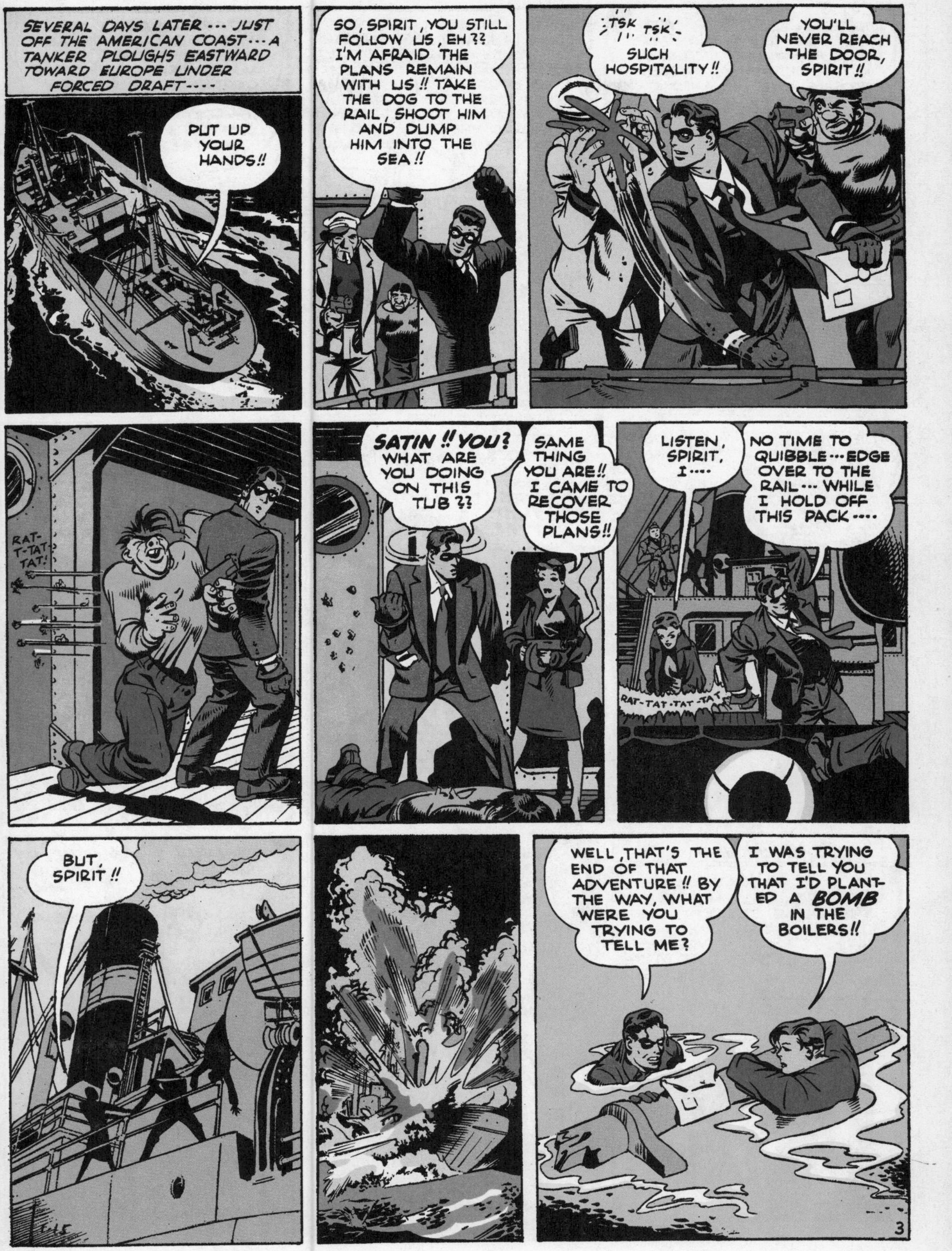

SEVERAL DAYS LATER --- JUST OFF THE AMERICAN COAST --- A TANKER PLOUGHS EASTWARD TOWARD EUROPE UNDER FORCED DRAFT ----
PUT UP YOUR HANDS!!
SO, SPIRIT, YOU STILL FOLLOW US, EH?? I'M AFRAID THE PLANS REMAIN WITH US!! TAKE THE DOG TO THE RAIL, SHOOT HIM AND DUMP HIM INTO THE SEA!!
TSK TSK
SUCH HOSPITALITY!!
YOU'LL NEVER REACH THE DOOR, SPIRIT!!
RAT-T-TAT-TAT!
SATIN!! YOU? WHAT ARE YOU DOING ON THIS TUB??
SAME THING YOU ARE!! I CAME TO RECOVER THOSE PLANS!!
LISTEN, SPIRIT, I ----
NO TIME TO QUIBBLE --- EDGE OVER TO THE RAIL --- WHILE I HOLD OFF THIS PACK ----
RAT-TAT-TAT-TAT
BUT, SPIRIT!!
WELL, THAT'S THE END OF THAT ADVENTURE!! BY THE WAY, WHAT WERE YOU TRYING TO TELL ME?
I WAS TRYING TO TELL YOU THAT I'D PLANT-ED A BOMB IN THE BOILERS!!
3

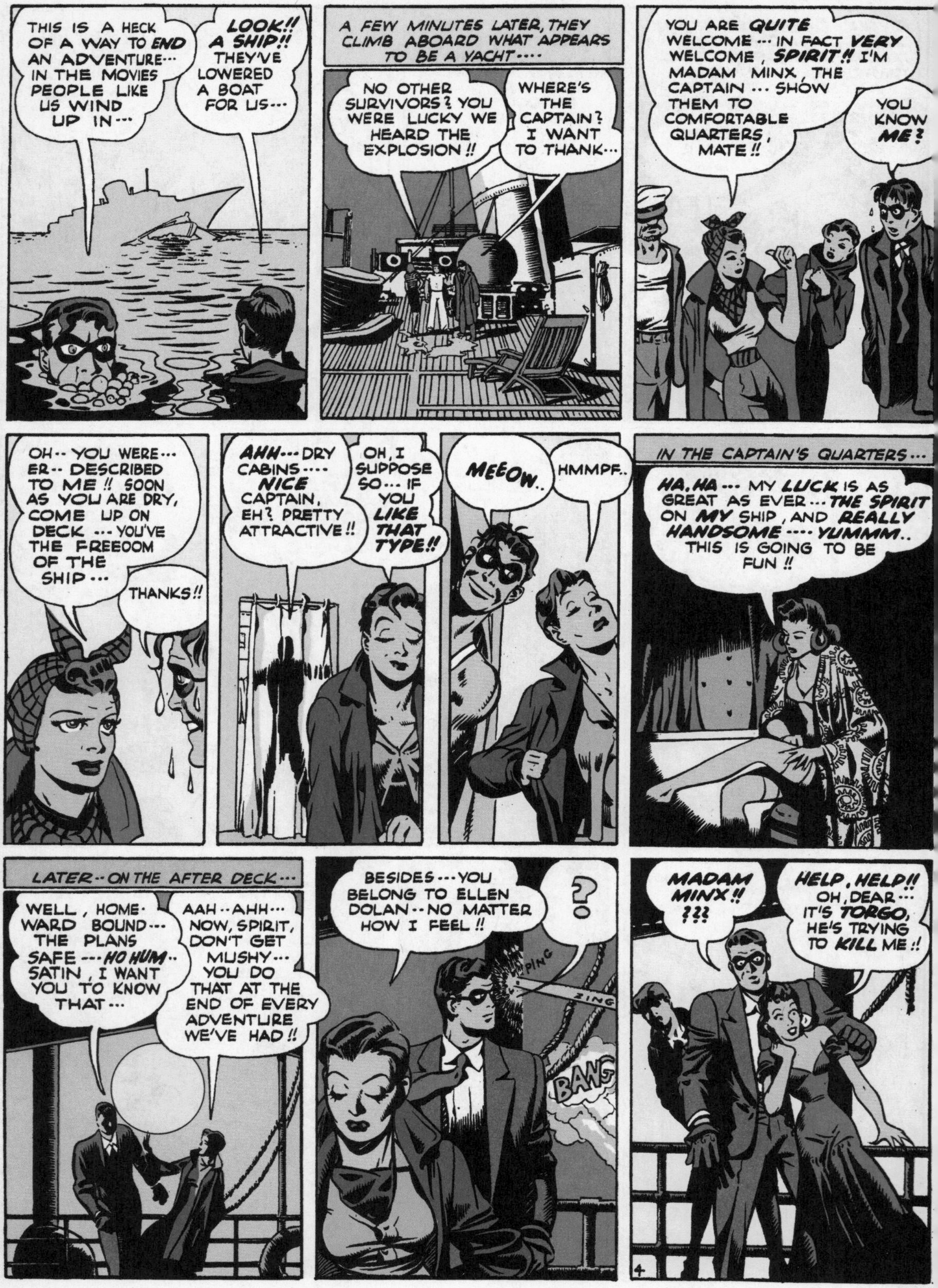
THIS IS A HECK OF A WAY TO END AN ADVENTURE... IN THE MOVIES PEOPLE LIKE US WIND UP IN...
LOOK!! A SHIP!! THEY'VE LOWERED A BOAT FOR US...
A FEW MINUTES LATER, THEY CLIMB ABOARD WHAT APPEARS TO BE A YACHT....
NO OTHER SURVIVORS? YOU WERE LUCKY WE HEARD THE EXPLOSION!!
WHERE'S THE CAPTAIN? I WANT TO THANK...
YOU ARE QUITE WELCOME... IN FACT VERY WELCOME, SPIRIT!! I'M MADAM MINX, THE CAPTAIN... SHOW THEM TO COMFORTABLE QUARTERS, MATE!!
YOU KNOW ME?
OH-- YOU WERE... ER-- DESCRIBED TO ME!! SOON AS YOU ARE DRY, COME UP ON DECK ... YOU'VE THE FREEDOM OF THE SHIP...
THANKS!!
AHH... DRY CABINS.... NICE CAPTAIN, EH? PRETTY ATTRACTIVE!!
OH, I SUPPOSE SO... IF YOU LIKE THAT TYPE!!
MEEOW..
HMMPF..
IN THE CAPTAIN'S QUARTERS...
HA, HA... MY LUCK IS AS GREAT AS EVER... THE SPIRIT ON MY SHIP, AND REALLY HANDSOME.... YUMMM.. THIS IS GOING TO BE FUN!!
LATER-- ON THE AFTER DECK...
WELL, HOME-WARD BOUND... THE PLANS SAFE... HO HUM.. SATIN, I WANT YOU TO KNOW THAT...
AAH-- AHH... NOW, SPIRIT, DON'T GET MUSHY... YOU DO THAT AT THE END OF EVERY ADVENTURE WE'VE HAD!!
BESIDES... YOU BELONG TO ELLEN DOLAN-- NO MATTER HOW I FEEL!!
?
PING
ZING
BANG
MADAM MINX!! ???
HELP, HELP!! OH, DEAR... IT'S TORGO, HE'S TRYING TO KILL ME!!
4

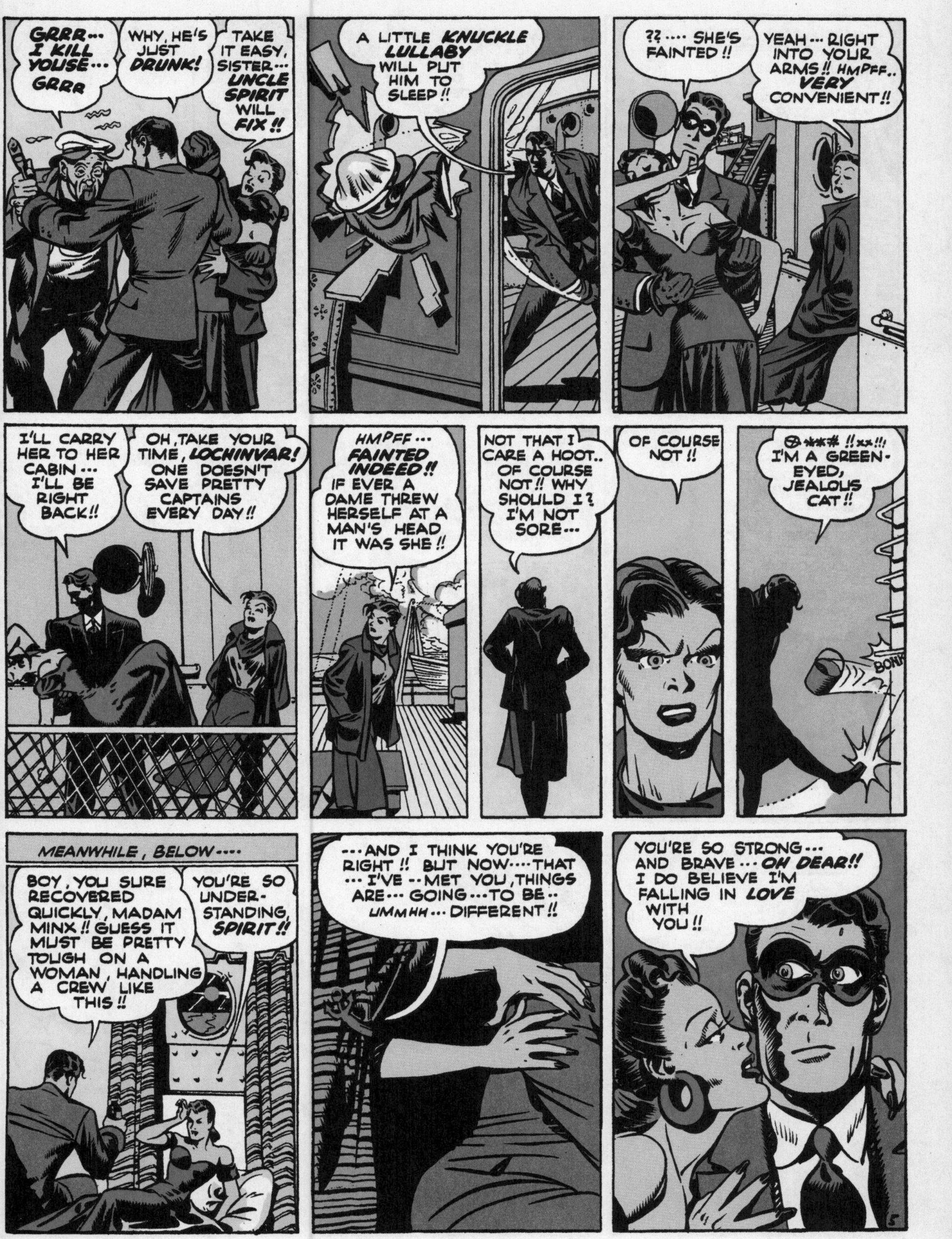
GRRR... I KILL YOUSE... GRRR
WHY, HE'S JUST DRUNK!
TAKE IT EASY, SISTER... UNCLE SPIRIT WILL FIX!!
A LITTLE KNUCKLE LULLABY WILL PUT HIM TO SLEEP!!
??.... SHE'S FAINTED!!
YEAH... RIGHT INTO YOUR ARMS!! HMPFF.. VERY CONVENIENT!!
I'LL CARRY HER TO HER CABIN... I'LL BE RIGHT BACK!!
OH, TAKE YOUR TIME, LOCHINVAR! ONE DOESN'T SAVE PRETTY CAPTAINS EVERY DAY!!
HMPFF... FAINTED INDEED!! IF EVER A DAME THREW HERSELF AT A MAN'S HEAD IT WAS SHE!!
NOT THAT I CARE A HOOT.. OF COURSE NOT!! WHY SHOULD I? I'M NOT SORE...
OF COURSE NOT!!
@***# !!xx!!! I'M A GREEN-EYED, JEALOUS CAT!!
BONK
MEANWHILE, BELOW....
BOY, YOU SURE RECOVERED QUICKLY, MADAM MINX!! GUESS IT MUST BE PRETTY TOUGH ON A WOMAN, HANDLING A CREW LIKE THIS!!
YOU'RE SO UNDER-STANDING, SPIRIT!!
...AND I THINK YOU'RE RIGHT!! BUT NOW....THAT ...I'VE --MET YOU, THINGS ARE... GOING ...TO BE.. UMMHH... DIFFERENT!!
YOU'RE SO STRONG... AND BRAVE... OH DEAR!! I DO BELIEVE I'M FALLING IN LOVE WITH YOU!!
5

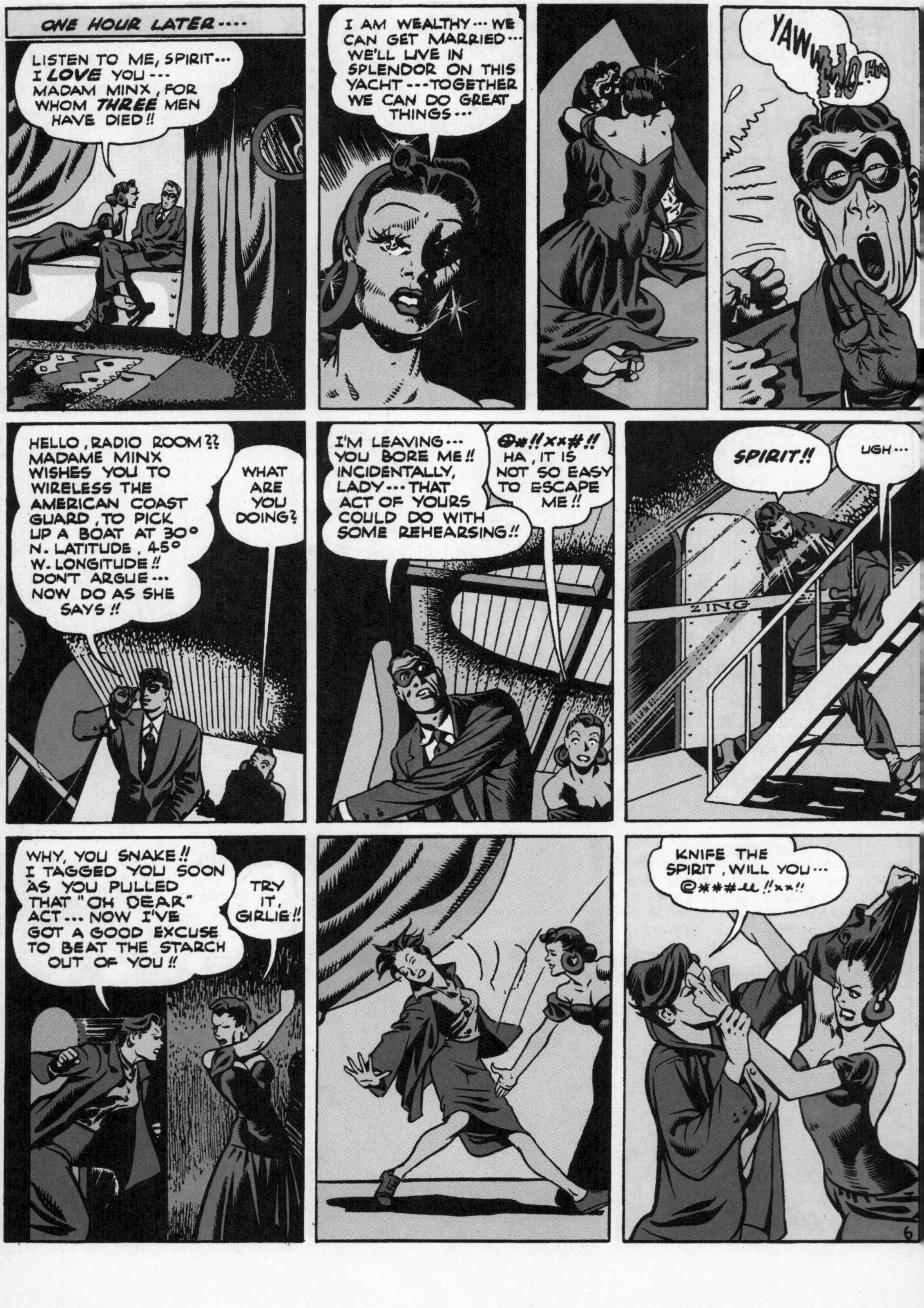

ONE HOUR LATER....
LISTEN TO ME, SPIRIT... I LOVE YOU--- MADAM MINX, FOR WHOM THREE MEN HAVE DIED!!
I AM WEALTHY... WE CAN GET MARRIED... WE'LL LIVE IN SPLENDOR ON THIS YACHT---TOGETHER WE CAN DO GREAT THINGS...
YAWWHO HM
HELLO, RADIO ROOM?? MADAME MINX WISHES YOU TO WIRELESS THE AMERICAN COAST GUARD, TO PICK UP A BOAT AT 30° N. LATITUDE, 45° W. LONGITUDE!! DON'T ARGUE... NOW DO AS SHE SAYS!!
WHAT ARE YOU DOING?
I'M LEAVING... YOU BORE ME!! INCIDENTALLY, LADY---THAT ACT OF YOURS COULD DO WITH SOME REHEARSING!!
@*!!××#!! HA, IT IS NOT SO EASY TO ESCAPE ME!!
SPIRIT!!
UGH...
ZING
WHY, YOU SNAKE!! I TAGGED YOU SOON AS YOU PULLED THAT "OH DEAR" ACT... NOW I'VE GOT A GOOD EXCUSE TO BEAT THE STARCH OUT OF YOU!!
TRY IT, GIRLIE!!
KNIFE THE SPIRIT, WILL YOU... @***!!××!!
6

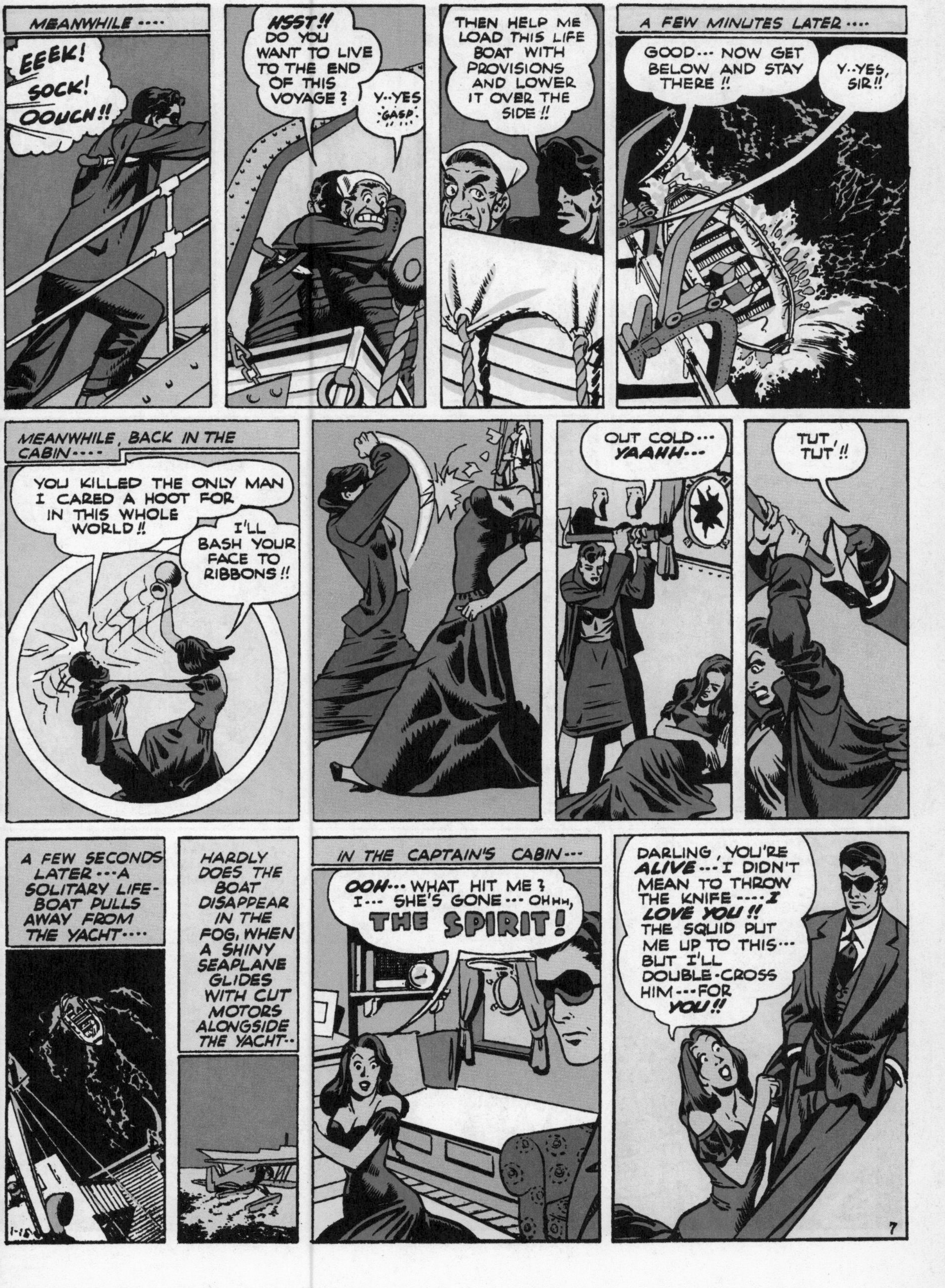
MEANWHILE ····
EEEK!
SOCK!
OOUCH!!
HSST!! DO YOU WANT TO LIVE TO THE END OF THIS VOYAGE ?
Y··YES GASP
THEN HELP ME LOAD THIS LIFE BOAT WITH PROVISIONS AND LOWER IT OVER THE SIDE !!
A FEW MINUTES LATER ····
GOOD··· NOW GET BELOW AND STAY THERE !!
Y··YES, SIR!!
MEANWHILE, BACK IN THE CABIN····
YOU KILLED THE ONLY MAN I CARED A HOOT FOR IN THIS WHOLE WORLD!!
I'LL BASH YOUR FACE TO RIBBONS!!
OUT COLD··· YAAHH···
TUT, TUT!!
A FEW SECONDS LATER···A SOLITARY LIFE-BOAT PULLS AWAY FROM THE YACHT····
HARDLY DOES THE BOAT DISAPPEAR IN THE FOG, WHEN A SHINY SEAPLANE GLIDES WITH CUT MOTORS ALONGSIDE THE YACHT··
IN THE CAPTAIN'S CABIN···
OOH··· WHAT HIT ME ? I··· SHE'S GONE··· OHHH, THE SPIRIT!
DARLING, YOU'RE ALIVE··· I DIDN'T MEAN TO THROW THE KNIFE ····I LOVE YOU !! THE SQUID PUT ME UP TO THIS··· BUT I'LL DOUBLE-CROSS HIM···FOR YOU!!
1-15
7

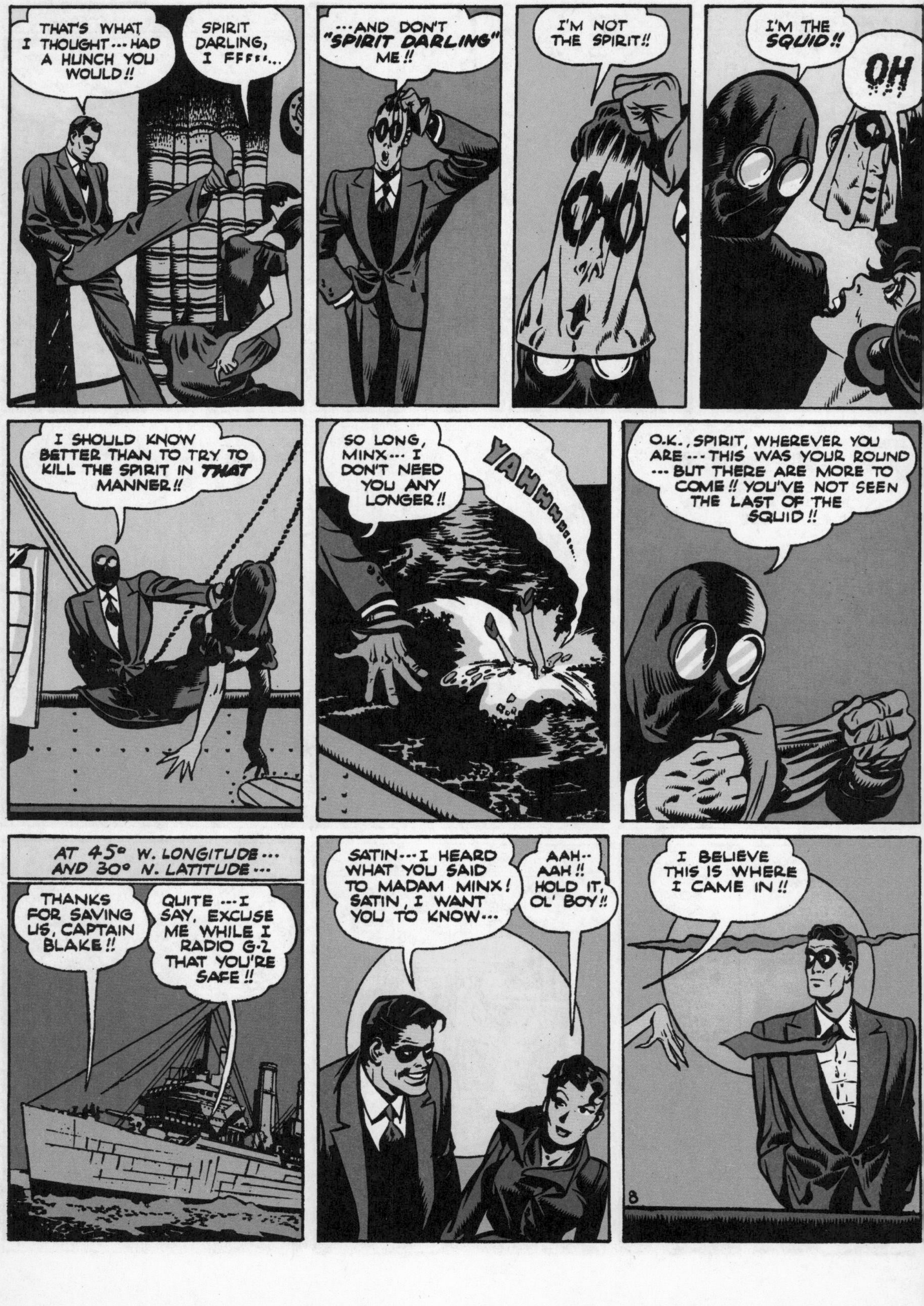
THAT'S WHAT I THOUGHT --- HAD A HUNCH YOU WOULD!!
SPIRIT DARLING, I FFF...
---AND DON'T "SPIRIT DARLING" ME!!
I'M NOT THE SPIRIT!!
I'M THE SQUID!!
OH
I SHOULD KNOW BETTER THAN TO TRY TO KILL THE SPIRIT IN THAT MANNER!!
SO LONG, MINX--- I DON'T NEED YOU ANY LONGER!!
YAHHH.......
O.K., SPIRIT, WHEREVER YOU ARE --- THIS WAS YOUR ROUND --- BUT THERE ARE MORE TO COME!! YOU'VE NOT SEEN THE LAST OF THE SQUID!!
AT 45° W. LONGITUDE --- AND 30° N. LATITUDE ---
THANKS FOR SAVING US, CAPTAIN BLAKE!!
QUITE --- I SAY, EXCUSE ME WHILE I RADIO G-2 THAT YOU'RE SAFE!!
SATIN --- I HEARD WHAT YOU SAID TO MADAM MINX! SATIN, I WANT YOU TO KNOW---
AAH-- AAH!! HOLD IT, OL' BOY!!
I BELIEVE THIS IS WHERE I CAME IN!!
8

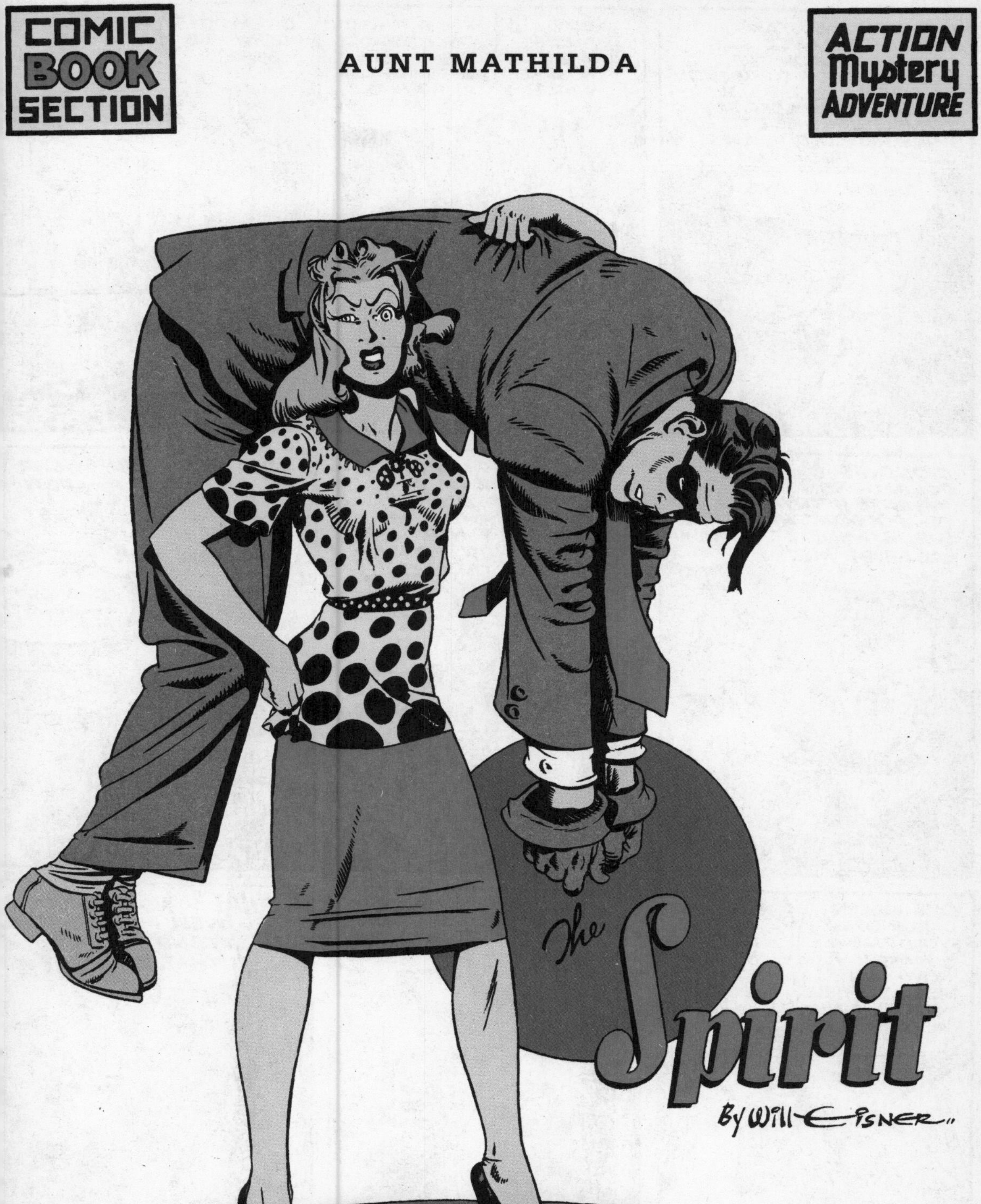
COMIC BOOK SECTION
AUNT MATHILDA
ACTION Mystery ADVENTURE
The Spirit
By Will Eisner

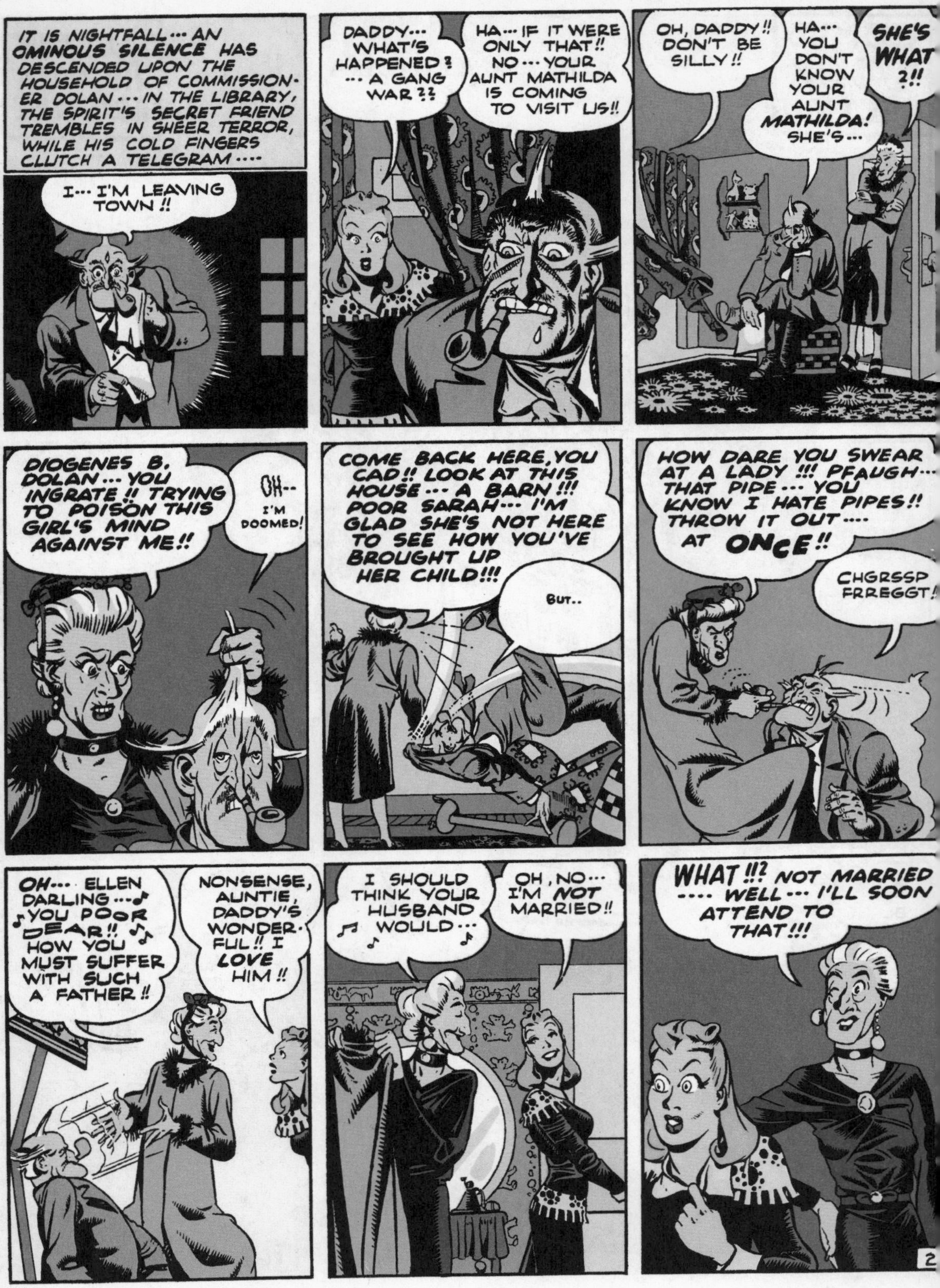
IT IS NIGHTFALL... AN OMINOUS SILENCE HAS DESCENDED UPON THE HOUSEHOLD OF COMMISSIONER DOLAN... IN THE LIBRARY, THE SPIRIT'S SECRET FRIEND TREMBLES IN SHEER TERROR, WHILE HIS COLD FINGERS CLUTCH A TELEGRAM....
I... I'M LEAVING TOWN!!
DADDY... WHAT'S HAPPENED?... A GANG WAR??
HA... IF IT WERE ONLY THAT!! NO... YOUR AUNT MATHILDA IS COMING TO VISIT US!!
OH, DADDY!! DON'T BE SILLY!!
HA... YOU DON'T KNOW YOUR AUNT MATHILDA! SHE'S...
SHE'S WHAT?!!
DIOGENES B. DOLAN... YOU INGRATE!! TRYING TO POISON THIS GIRL'S MIND AGAINST ME!!
OH-- I'M DOOMED!
COME BACK HERE, YOU CAD!! LOOK AT THIS HOUSE... A BARN!!! POOR SARAH... I'M GLAD SHE'S NOT HERE TO SEE HOW YOU'VE BROUGHT UP HER CHILD!!!
BUT..
HOW DARE YOU SWEAR AT A LADY!!! PFAUGH... THAT PIPE... YOU KNOW I HATE PIPES!! THROW IT OUT.... AT ONCE!!
CHGRSSP FRREGGT!
OH... ELLEN DARLING... YOU POOR DEAR!! HOW YOU MUST SUFFER WITH SUCH A FATHER!!
NONSENSE, AUNTIE, DADDY'S WONDERFUL!! I LOVE HIM!!
I SHOULD THINK YOUR HUSBAND WOULD...
OH, NO... I'M NOT MARRIED!!
WHAT!!? NOT MARRIED.... WELL... I'LL SOON ATTEND TO THAT!!!
2

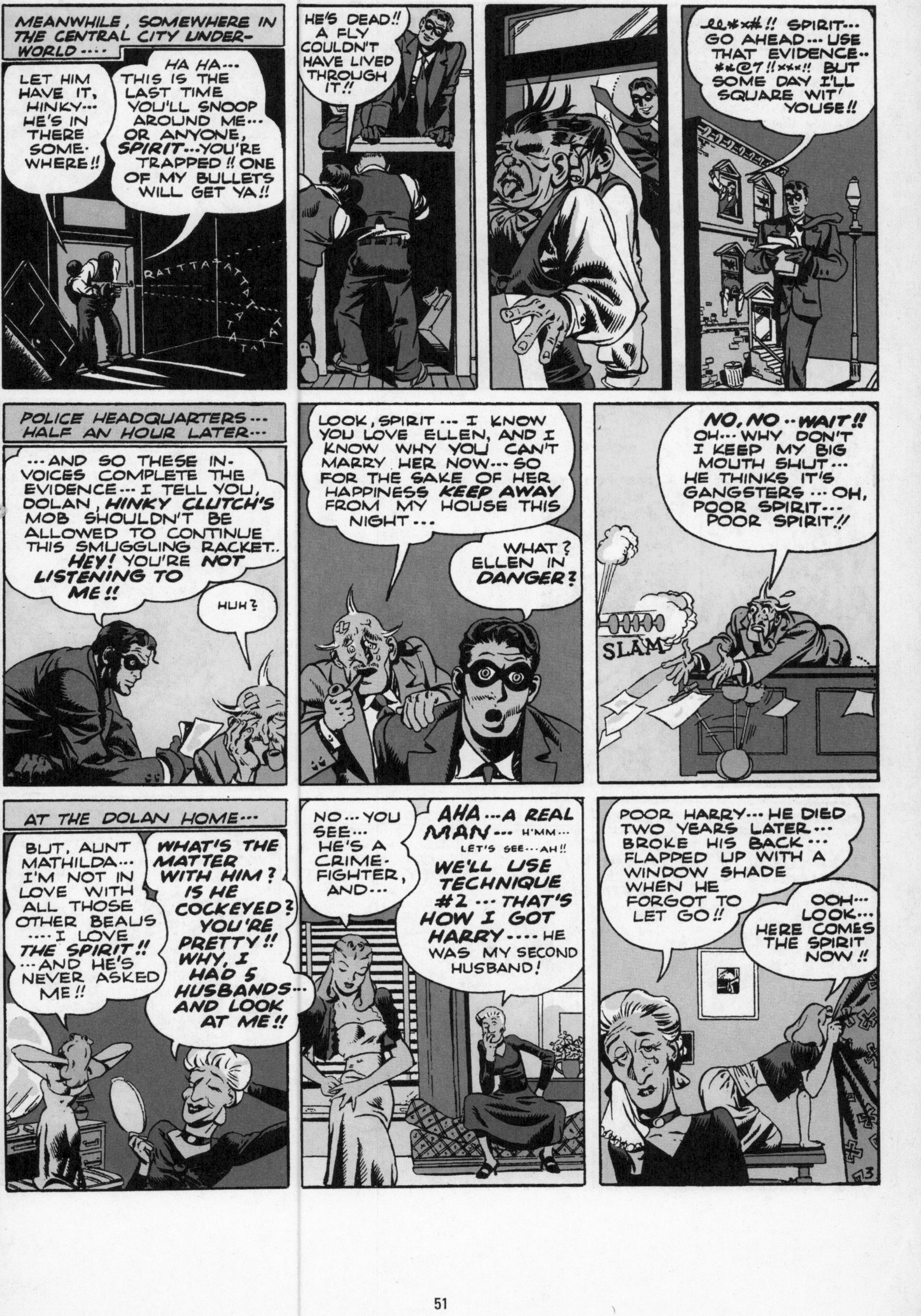

MEANWHILE, SOMEWHERE IN THE CENTRAL CITY UNDERWORLD····
LET HIM HAVE IT, HINKY··· HE'S IN THERE SOMEWHERE!!
HA HA··· THIS IS THE LAST TIME YOU'LL SNOOP AROUND ME··· OR ANYONE, SPIRIT···YOU'RE TRAPPED!! ONE OF MY BULLETS WILL GET YA!!
RATTTATATTATATATATATAT
HE'S DEAD!! A FLY COULDN'T HAVE LIVED THROUGH IT!!
SPIRIT··· GO AHEAD··· USE THAT EVIDENCE·· **@?!!xxx!! BUT SOME DAY I'LL SQUARE WIT' YOUSE!!
POLICE HEADQUARTERS··· HALF AN HOUR LATER···
···AND SO THESE INVOICES COMPLETE THE EVIDENCE··· I TELL YOU, DOLAN, HINKY CLUTCH'S MOB SHOULDN'T BE ALLOWED TO CONTINUE THIS SMUGGLING RACKET.. HEY! YOU'RE NOT LISTENING TO ME!!
HUH?
LOOK, SPIRIT··· I KNOW YOU LOVE ELLEN, AND I KNOW WHY YOU CAN'T MARRY HER NOW··· SO FOR THE SAKE OF HER HAPPINESS KEEP AWAY FROM MY HOUSE THIS NIGHT···
WHAT? ELLEN IN DANGER?
NO, NO··WAIT!! OH··· WHY DON'T I KEEP MY BIG MOUTH SHUT··· HE THINKS IT'S GANGSTERS··· OH, POOR SPIRIT··· POOR SPIRIT!!
SLAM
AT THE DOLAN HOME···
BUT, AUNT MATHILDA··· I'M NOT IN LOVE WITH ALL THOSE OTHER BEAUS ····I LOVE THE SPIRIT!! ···AND HE'S NEVER ASKED ME!!
WHAT'S THE MATTER WITH HIM? IS HE COCKEYED? YOU'RE PRETTY!! WHY, I HAD 5 HUSBANDS··· AND LOOK AT ME!!
NO··· YOU SEE··· HE'S A CRIMEFIGHTER, AND···
AHA···A REAL MAN··· H'MM··· LET'S SEE···AH!! WE'LL USE TECHNIQUE #2 ··· THAT'S HOW I GOT HARRY···· HE WAS MY SECOND HUSBAND!
POOR HARRY··· HE DIED TWO YEARS LATER··· BROKE HIS BACK··· FLAPPED UP WITH A WINDOW SHADE WHEN HE FORGOT TO LET GO!!
OOH··· LOOK··· HERE COMES THE SPIRIT NOW!!
3

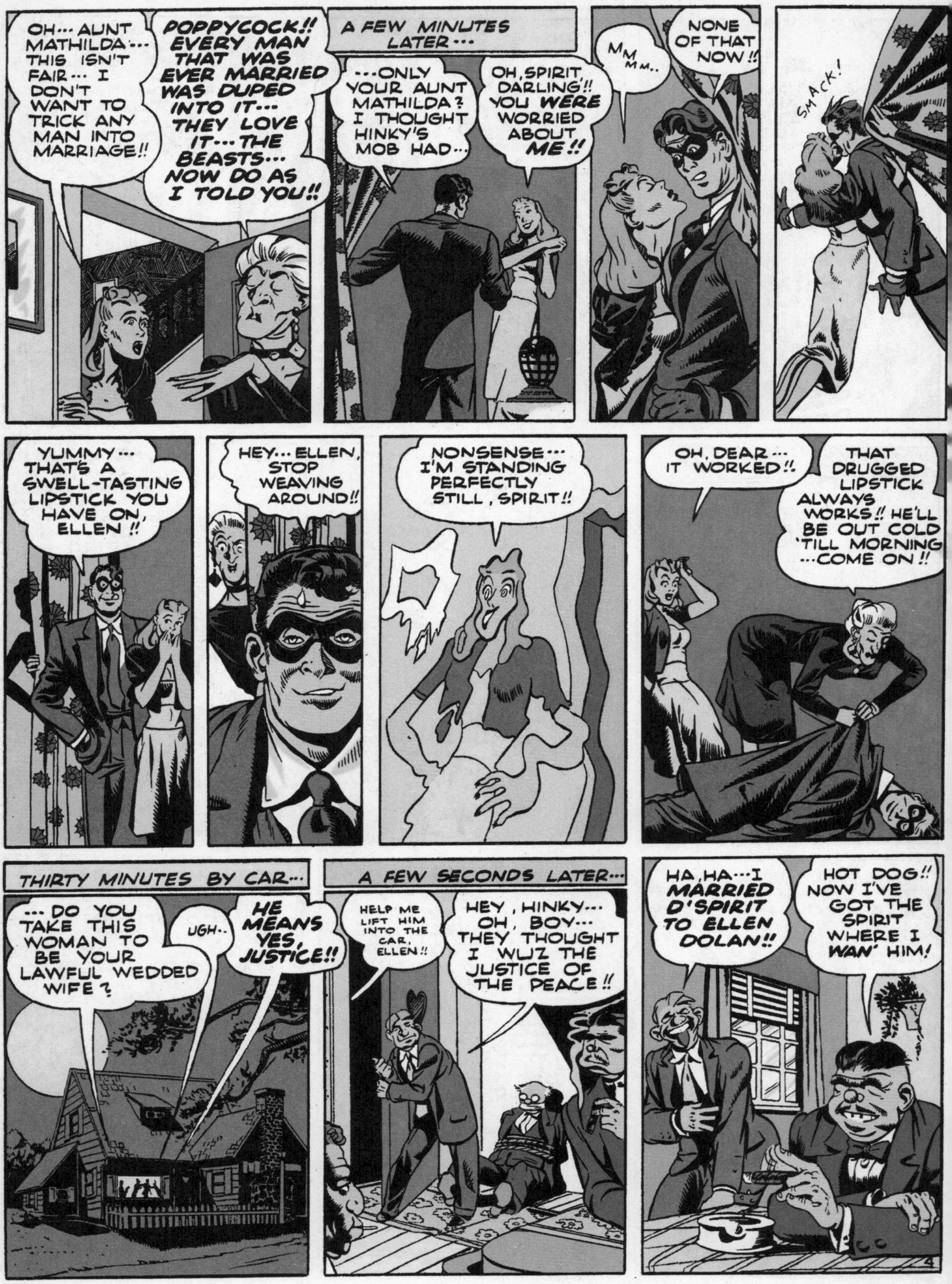

OH... AUNT MATHILDA... THIS ISN'T FAIR... I DON'T WANT TO TRICK ANY MAN INTO MARRIAGE!!
POPPYCOCK!! EVERY MAN THAT WAS EVER MARRIED WAS DUPED INTO IT... THEY LOVE IT... THE BEASTS... NOW DO AS I TOLD YOU!!
A FEW MINUTES LATER...
...ONLY YOUR AUNT MATHILDA? I THOUGHT HINKY'S MOB HAD...
OH, SPIRIT, DARLING!! YOU WERE WORRIED ABOUT ME!!
MMMM..
NONE OF THAT NOW!!
SMACK!
YUMMY... THAT'S A SWELL-TASTING LIPSTICK YOU HAVE ON, ELLEN!!
HEY... ELLEN, STOP WEAVING AROUND!!
NONSENSE... I'M STANDING PERFECTLY STILL, SPIRIT!!
OH, DEAR... IT WORKED!!
THAT DRUGGED LIPSTICK ALWAYS WORKS!! HE'LL BE OUT COLD 'TILL MORNING ...COME ON!!
THIRTY MINUTES BY CAR...
...DO YOU TAKE THIS WOMAN TO BE YOUR LAWFUL WEDDED WIFE?
UGH..
HE MEANS YES, JUSTICE!!
A FEW SECONDS LATER...
HELP ME LIFT HIM INTO THE CAR, ELLEN!!
HEY, HINKY... OH, BOY... THEY THOUGHT I WUZ THE JUSTICE OF THE PEACE!!
HA, HA... I MARRIED D'SPIRIT TO ELLEN DOLAN!!
HOT DOG!! NOW I'VE GOT THE SPIRIT WHERE I WAN' HIM!
4

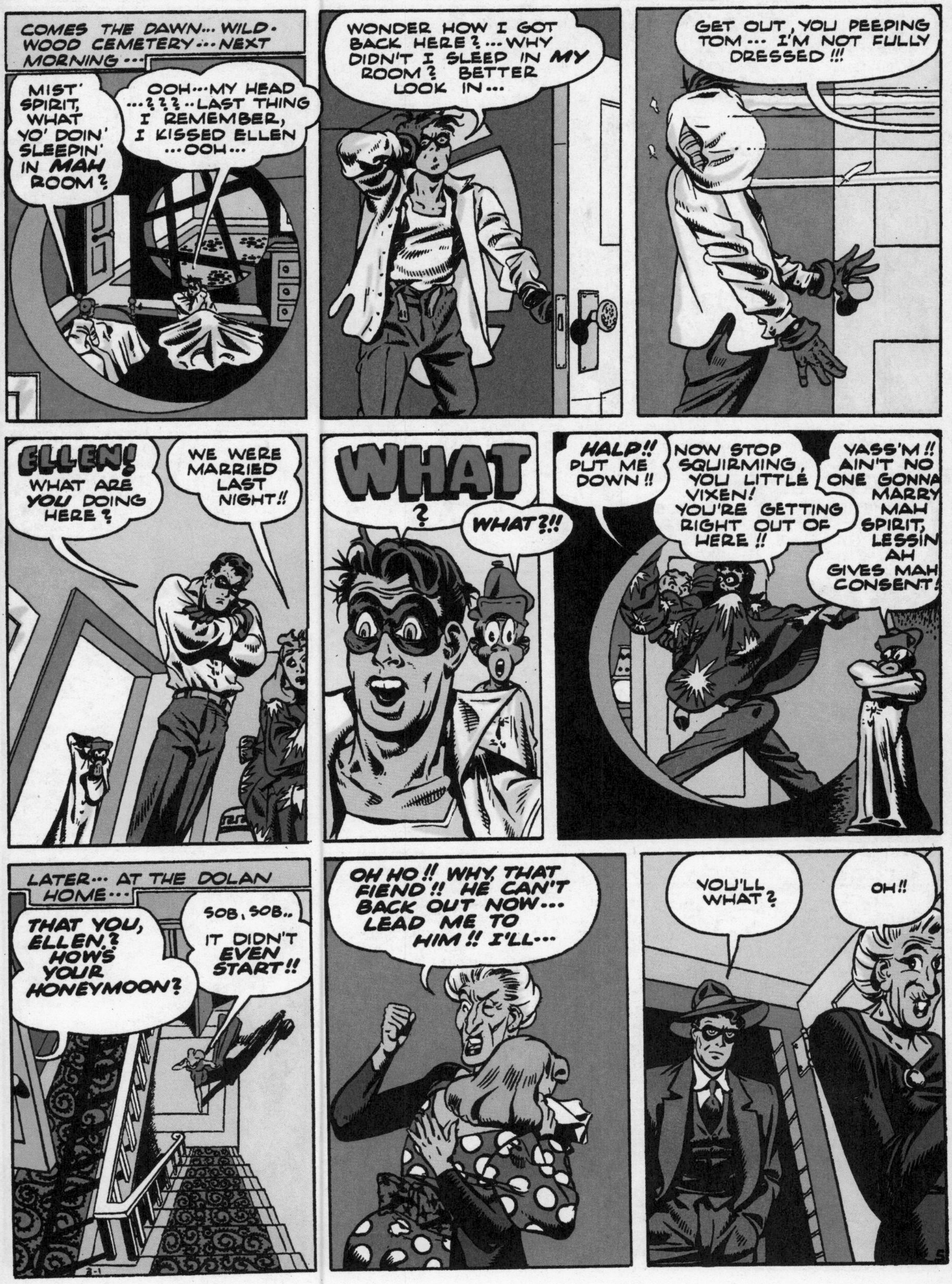
COMES THE DAWN... WILD-WOOD CEMETERY... NEXT MORNING...
MIST' SPIRIT, WHAT YO' DOIN' SLEEPIN' IN MAH ROOM?
OOH... MY HEAD ...???.. LAST THING I REMEMBER, I KISSED ELLEN ...OOH...
WONDER HOW I GOT BACK HERE?... WHY DIDN'T I SLEEP IN MY ROOM? BETTER LOOK IN...
GET OUT, YOU PEEPING TOM... I'M NOT FULLY DRESSED!!!
ELLEN! WHAT ARE YOU DOING HERE?
WE WERE MARRIED LAST NIGHT!!
WHAT ?
WHAT?!!
HALP!! PUT ME DOWN!!
NOW STOP SQUIRMING, YOU LITTLE VIXEN! YOU'RE GETTING RIGHT OUT OF HERE!!
YASS'M!! AIN'T NO ONE GONNA MARRY MAH SPIRIT, LESSIN AH GIVES MAH CONSENT!
LATER... AT THE DOLAN HOME...
THAT YOU, ELLEN? HOW'S YOUR HONEYMOON?
SOB, SOB.. IT DIDN'T EVEN START!!
OH HO!! WHY, THAT FIEND!! HE CAN'T BACK OUT NOW... LEAD ME TO HIM!! I'LL...
YOU'LL WHAT?
OH!!

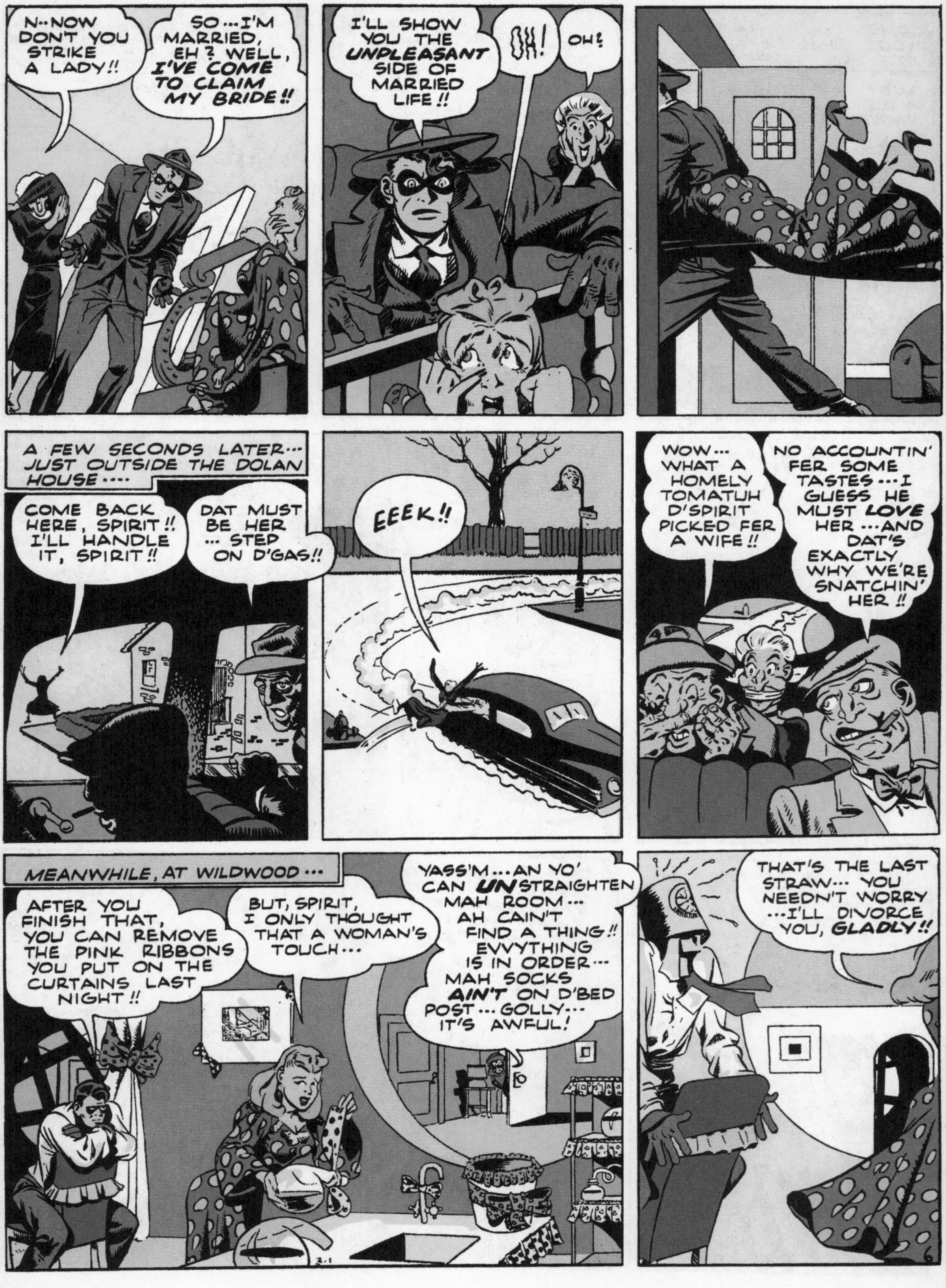
N--NOW DON'T YOU STRIKE A LADY!!
SO...I'M MARRIED, EH? WELL, I'VE COME TO CLAIM MY BRIDE!!
I'LL SHOW YOU THE UNPLEASANT SIDE OF MARRIED LIFE!!
OH!
OH?
A FEW SECONDS LATER... JUST OUTSIDE THE DOLAN HOUSE....
COME BACK HERE, SPIRIT!! I'LL HANDLE IT, SPIRIT!!
DAT MUST BE HER ... STEP ON D'GAS!!
EEEK!!
WOW... WHAT A HOMELY TOMATUH D'SPIRIT PICKED FER A WIFE!!
NO ACCOUNTIN' FER SOME TASTES...I GUESS HE MUST LOVE HER...AND DAT'S EXACTLY WHY WE'RE SNATCHIN' HER!!
MEANWHILE, AT WILDWOOD...
AFTER YOU FINISH THAT, YOU CAN REMOVE THE PINK RIBBONS YOU PUT ON THE CURTAINS LAST NIGHT!!
BUT, SPIRIT, I ONLY THOUGHT THAT A WOMAN'S TOUCH...
YASS'M...AN YO' CAN UNSTRAIGHTEN MAH ROOM... AH CAIN'T FIND A THING!! EVVYTHING IS IN ORDER... MAH SOCKS AIN'T ON D'BED POST... GOLLY... IT'S AWFUL!
THAT'S THE LAST STRAW... YOU NEEDN'T WORRY ...I'LL DIVORCE YOU, GLADLY!!

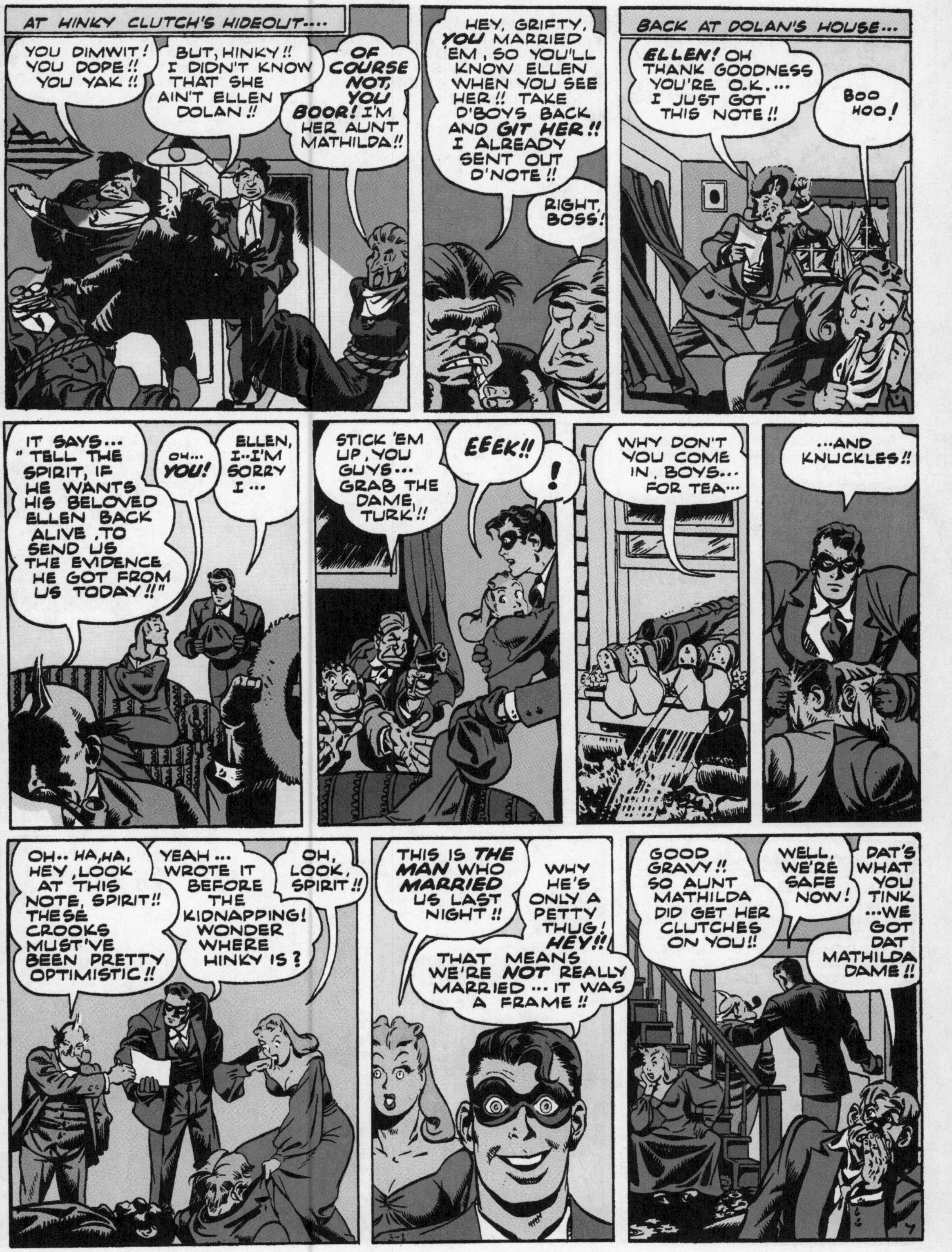
AT HINKY CLUTCH'S HIDEOUT....
YOU DIMWIT! YOU DOPE!! YOU YAK!!
BUT, HINKY!! I DIDN'T KNOW THAT SHE AIN'T ELLEN DOLAN!!
OF COURSE NOT, YOU BOOR! I'M HER AUNT MATHILDA!!
HEY, GRIFTY, YOU MARRIED 'EM, SO YOU'LL KNOW ELLEN WHEN YOU SEE HER!! TAKE D'BOYS BACK AND GIT HER!! I ALREADY SENT OUT D'NOTE!!
RIGHT, BOSS!
BACK AT DOLAN'S HOUSE...
ELLEN! OH THANK GOODNESS YOU'RE O.K.... I JUST GOT THIS NOTE!!
BOO HOO!
IT SAYS... "TELL THE SPIRIT, IF HE WANTS HIS BELOVED ELLEN BACK ALIVE, TO SEND US THE EVIDENCE HE GOT FROM US TODAY!!"
OH... YOU!
ELLEN, I..I'M SORRY I...
STICK 'EM UP, YOU GUYS... GRAB THE DAME, TURK!!
EEEK!!
!
WHY DON'T YOU COME IN, BOYS... FOR TEA...
...AND KNUCKLES!!
OH.. HA,HA, HEY, LOOK AT THIS NOTE, SPIRIT!! THESE CROOKS MUST'VE BEEN PRETTY OPTIMISTIC!!
YEAH... WROTE IT BEFORE THE KIDNAPPING! WONDER WHERE HINKY IS?
OH, LOOK, SPIRIT!!
THIS IS THE MAN WHO MARRIED US LAST NIGHT!!
WHY HE'S ONLY A PETTY THUG! HEY!!
THAT MEANS WE'RE NOT REALLY MARRIED ... IT WAS A FRAME!!
GOOD GRAVY!! SO AUNT MATHILDA DID GET HER CLUTCHES ON YOU!!
WELL, WE'RE SAFE NOW!
DAT'S WHAT YOU TINK ...WE GOT DAT MATHILDA DAME!!

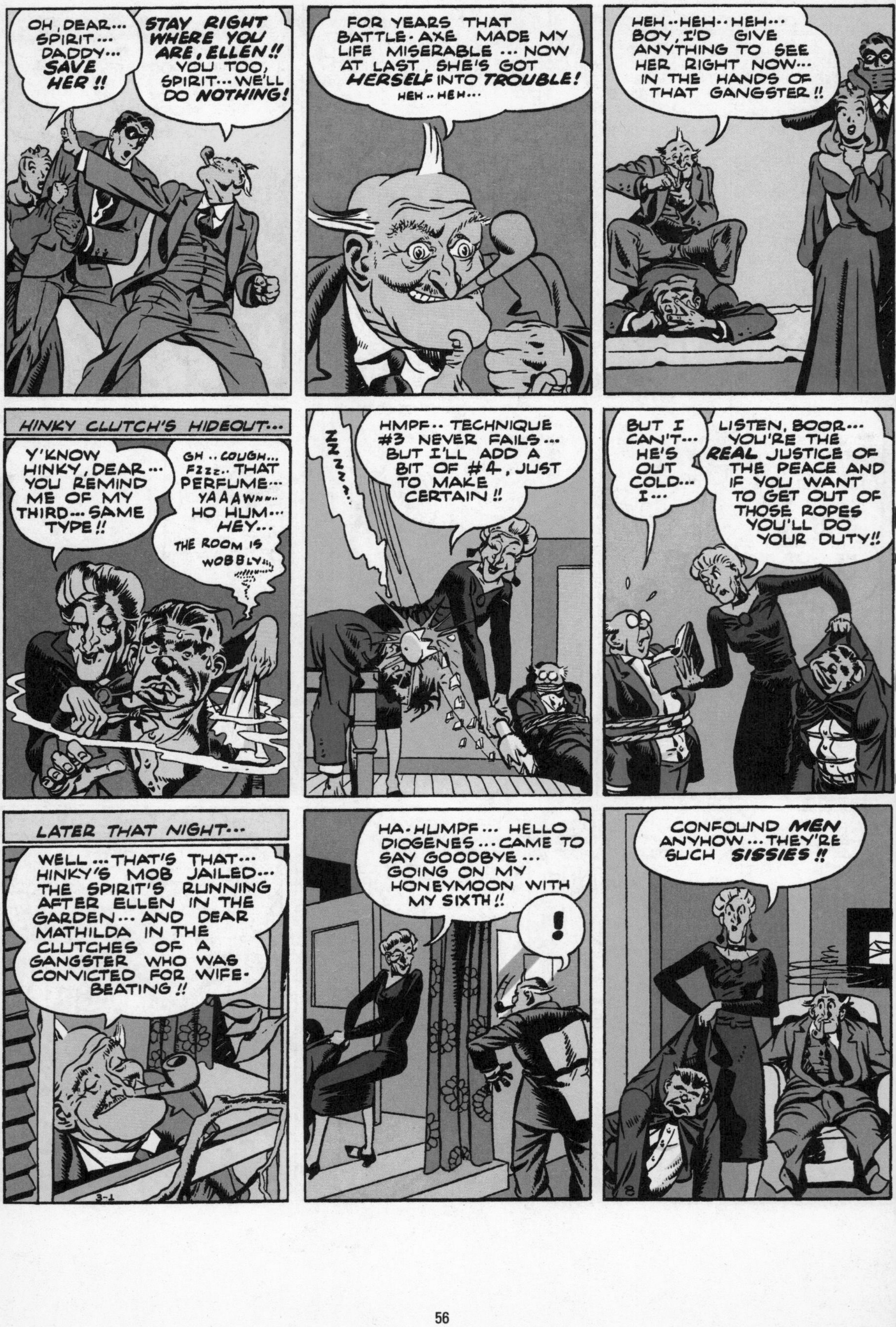

OH, DEAR... SPIRIT... DADDY... SAVE HER !!
STAY RIGHT WHERE YOU ARE, ELLEN !! YOU TOO, SPIRIT... WE'LL DO NOTHING!
FOR YEARS THAT BATTLE-AXE MADE MY LIFE MISERABLE ... NOW AT LAST, SHE'S GOT HERSELF INTO TROUBLE! HEH .. HEH...
HEH .. HEH .. HEH... BOY, I'D GIVE ANYTHING TO SEE HER RIGHT NOW... IN THE HANDS OF THAT GANGSTER !!
HINKY CLUTCH'S HIDEOUT...
Y'KNOW HINKY, DEAR... YOU REMIND ME OF MY THIRD... SAME TYPE !!
GH .. COUGH... FZZZ.. THAT PERFUME... YAAAWN... HO HUM... HEY... THE ROOM IS WOBBLY...
ZZZz...
HMPF.. TECHNIQUE #3 NEVER FAILS... BUT I'LL ADD A BIT OF #4, JUST TO MAKE CERTAIN !!
BUT I CAN'T... HE'S OUT COLD... I...
LISTEN, BOOR... YOU'RE THE REAL JUSTICE OF THE PEACE AND IF YOU WANT TO GET OUT OF THOSE ROPES YOU'LL DO YOUR DUTY !!
LATER THAT NIGHT...
WELL ... THAT'S THAT... HINKY'S MOB JAILED... THE SPIRIT'S RUNNING AFTER ELLEN IN THE GARDEN... AND DEAR MATHILDA IN THE CLUTCHES OF A GANGSTER WHO WAS CONVICTED FOR WIFE-BEATING !!
HA-HUMPF... HELLO DIOGENES... CAME TO SAY GOODBYE... GOING ON MY HONEYMOON WITH MY SIXTH !!
!
CONFOUND MEN ANYHOW ... THEY'RE SUCH SISSIES !!

COMIC BOOK SECTION

SATIN RETURNS

ACTION Mystery ADVENTURE

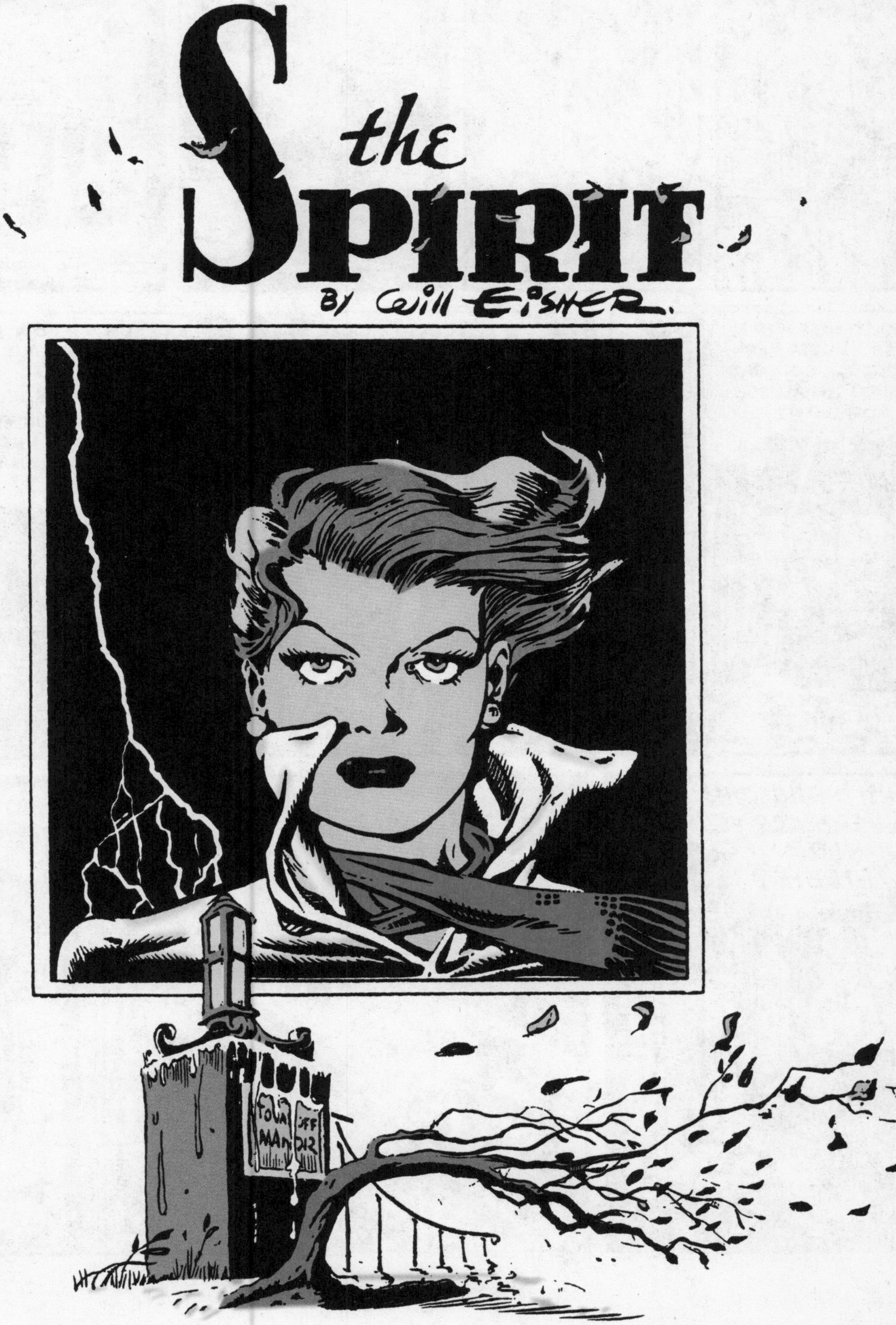
the SPIRIT
BY Will Eisner

CRACKLE!!
CRACKLE!

CRASH!

OVAROFF
ANOR

BRRR! WHAT A NIGHT FOR A MURDER!

BANG.

CRASH!

GOLLY, MISS HILDIE, IT SHO MUSTA BEEN RUGGED IN COLOGNE WHEN THE ALLIES BOMBED IT!

YES, I'M GLAD I CAME TO AMERICA, EVEN IF I HAD TO *SNEAK* IN WITH HOODLUMS.

AH KNOW Y'R DOIN' SWELL AT THAT SCHOOL MISS DOLAN IS SENDIN' YO' TO.... 'CAUSE MIST' *SPIRIT* WAS TELLIN' ME THAT YO'RE GITTIN' PERMOTED NEX' WEEK! Y' KNOW US CRIME FIGHTERS SHO'... HEY?!

HILDIE, HILDIE! WHERE ARE YO' HIDIN', HILDIE?

HILDIE!

HILDIE!

HILDIE!

2

GOLLY, SHE'S GONE!

CRASH

58

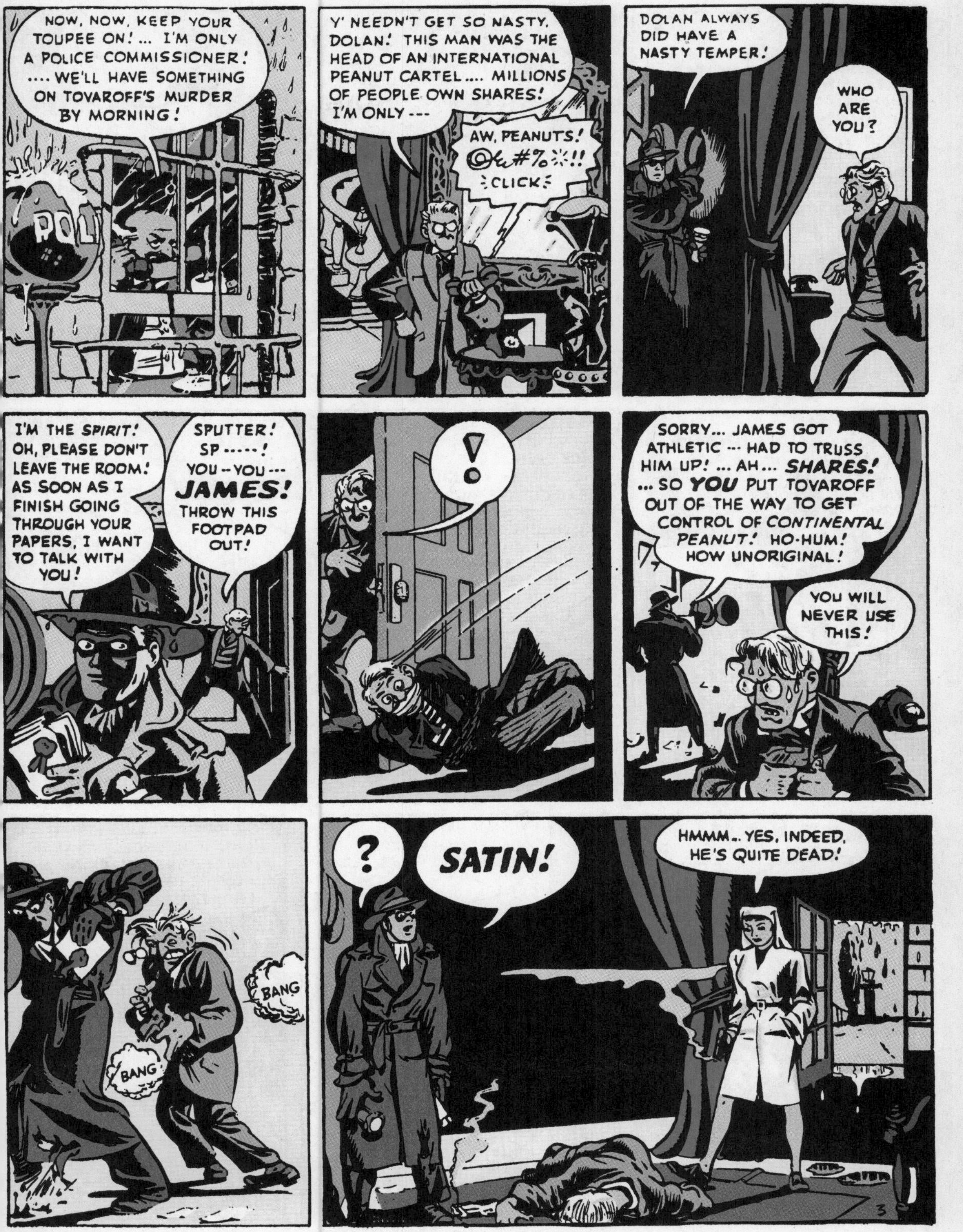
NOW, NOW, KEEP YOUR TOUPEE ON! ... I'M ONLY A POLICE COMMISSIONER! .... WE'LL HAVE SOMETHING ON TOVAROFF'S MURDER BY MORNING!
POLI
Y' NEEDN'T GET SO NASTY, DOLAN! THIS MAN WAS THE HEAD OF AN INTERNATIONAL PEANUT CARTEL.... MILLIONS OF PEOPLE OWN SHARES! I'M ONLY ---
AW, PEANUTS! @&#%*!! CLICK
DOLAN ALWAYS DID HAVE A NASTY TEMPER!
WHO ARE YOU?
I'M THE SPIRIT! OH, PLEASE DON'T LEAVE THE ROOM! AS SOON AS I FINISH GOING THROUGH YOUR PAPERS, I WANT TO TALK WITH YOU!
SPUTTER! SP-----! YOU--YOU--- JAMES! THROW THIS FOOTPAD OUT!
!
SORRY... JAMES GOT ATHLETIC --- HAD TO TRUSS HIM UP! ... AH... SHARES! ... SO YOU PUT TOVAROFF OUT OF THE WAY TO GET CONTROL OF CONTINENTAL PEANUT! HO-HUM! HOW UNORIGINAL!
YOU WILL NEVER USE THIS!
BANG
BANG
?
SATIN!
HMMM.. YES, INDEED, HE'S QUITE DEAD!
3

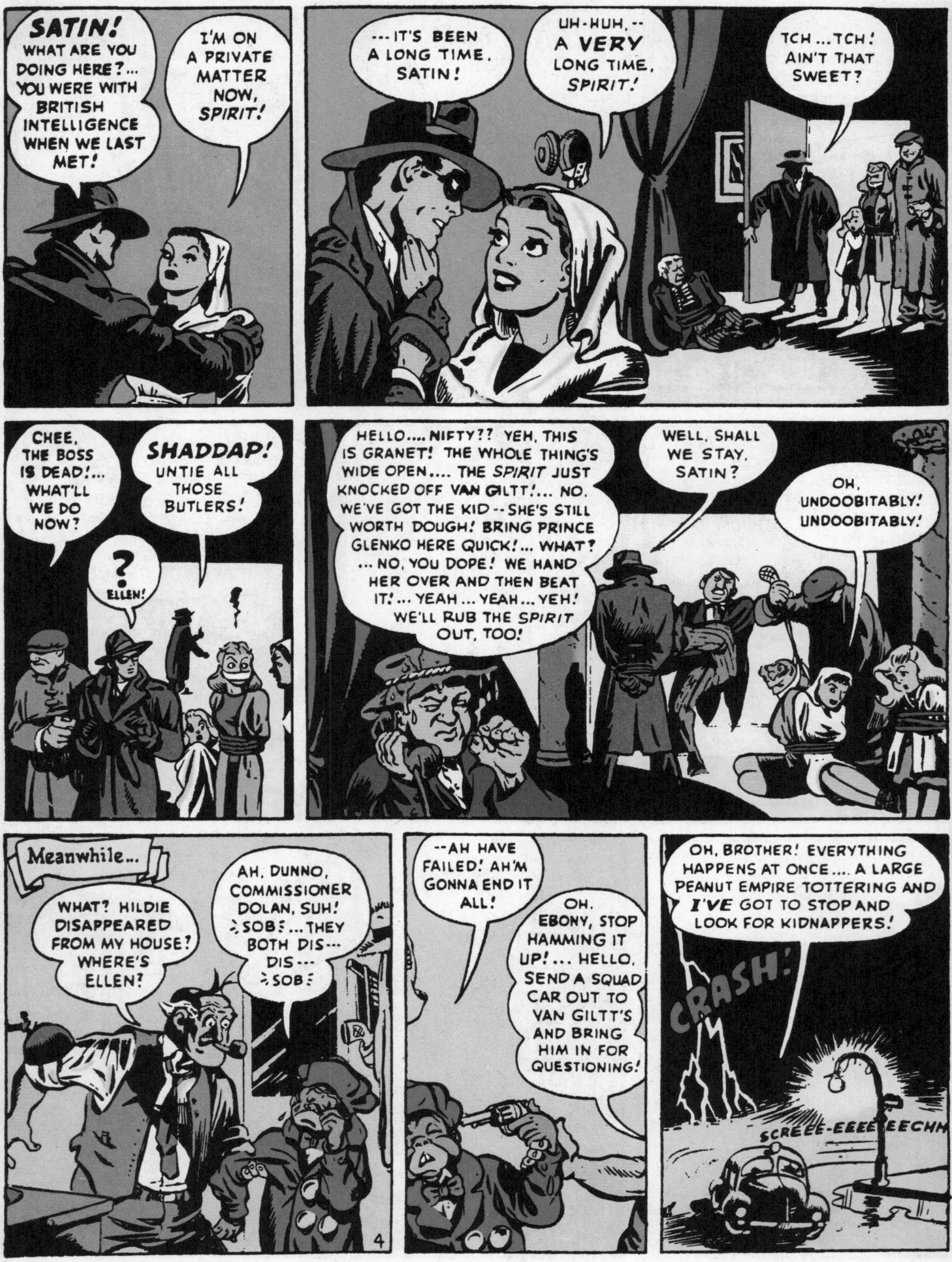
SATIN! WHAT ARE YOU DOING HERE?... YOU WERE WITH BRITISH INTELLIGENCE WHEN WE LAST MET!
I'M ON A PRIVATE MATTER NOW, SPIRIT!
---IT'S BEEN A LONG TIME, SATIN!
UH-HUH, -- A VERY LONG TIME, SPIRIT!
TCH...TCH! AIN'T THAT SWEET?
CHEE, THE BOSS IS DEAD!... WHAT'LL WE DO NOW?
SHADDAP! UNTIE ALL THOSE BUTLERS!
? ELLEN!
HELLO.... NIFTY?? YEH, THIS IS GRANET! THE WHOLE THING'S WIDE OPEN.... THE SPIRIT JUST KNOCKED OFF VAN GILTT!... NO, WE'VE GOT THE KID--SHE'S STILL WORTH DOUGH! BRING PRINCE GLENKO HERE QUICK!... WHAT? ... NO, YOU DOPE! WE HAND HER OVER AND THEN BEAT IT!... YEAH... YEAH... YEH! WE'LL RUB THE SPIRIT OUT, TOO!
WELL, SHALL WE STAY, SATIN?
OH, UNDOOBITABLY! UNDOOBITABLY!
Meanwhile...
WHAT? HILDIE DISAPPEARED FROM MY HOUSE? WHERE'S ELLEN?
AH, DUNNO, COMMISSIONER DOLAN, SUH! SOB ...THEY BOTH DIS--- DIS--- SOB
4
--AH HAVE FAILED! AH'M GONNA END IT ALL!
OH, EBONY, STOP HAMMING IT UP!... HELLO, SEND A SQUAD CAR OUT TO VAN GILTT'S AND BRING HIM IN FOR QUESTIONING!
OH, BROTHER! EVERYTHING HAPPENS AT ONCE.... A LARGE PEANUT EMPIRE TOTTERING AND I'VE GOT TO STOP AND LOOK FOR KIDNAPPERS!
CRASH!
SCREEE-EEEEEEECHH

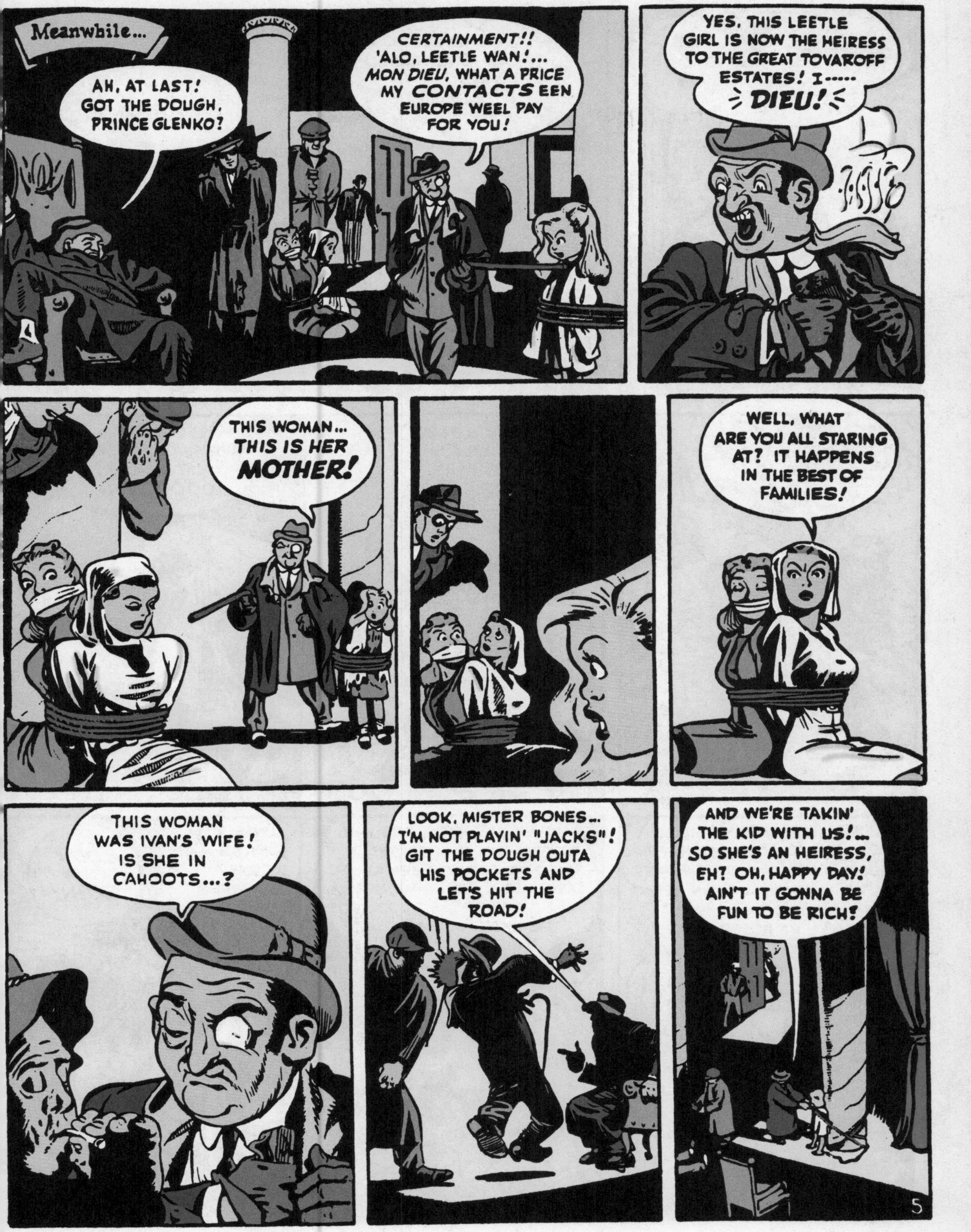
Meanwhile...
AH, AT LAST! GOT THE DOUGH, PRINCE GLENKO?
CERTAINMENT!! 'ALO, LEETLE WAN!... MON DIEU, WHAT A PRICE MY CONTACTS EEN EUROPE WEEL PAY FOR YOU!
YES, THIS LEETLE GIRL IS NOW THE HEIRESS TO THE GREAT TOVAROFF ESTATES! I-----
DIEU!
THIS WOMAN... THIS IS HER MOTHER!
WELL, WHAT ARE YOU ALL STARING AT? IT HAPPENS IN THE BEST OF FAMILIES!
THIS WOMAN WAS IVAN'S WIFE! IS SHE IN CAHOOTS...?
LOOK, MISTER BONES... I'M NOT PLAYIN' "JACKS"! GIT THE DOUGH OUTA HIS POCKETS AND LET'S HIT THE ROAD!
AND WE'RE TAKIN' THE KID WITH US!... SO SHE'S AN HEIRESS, EH? OH, HAPPY DAY! AIN'T IT GONNA BE FUN TO BE RICH!
5

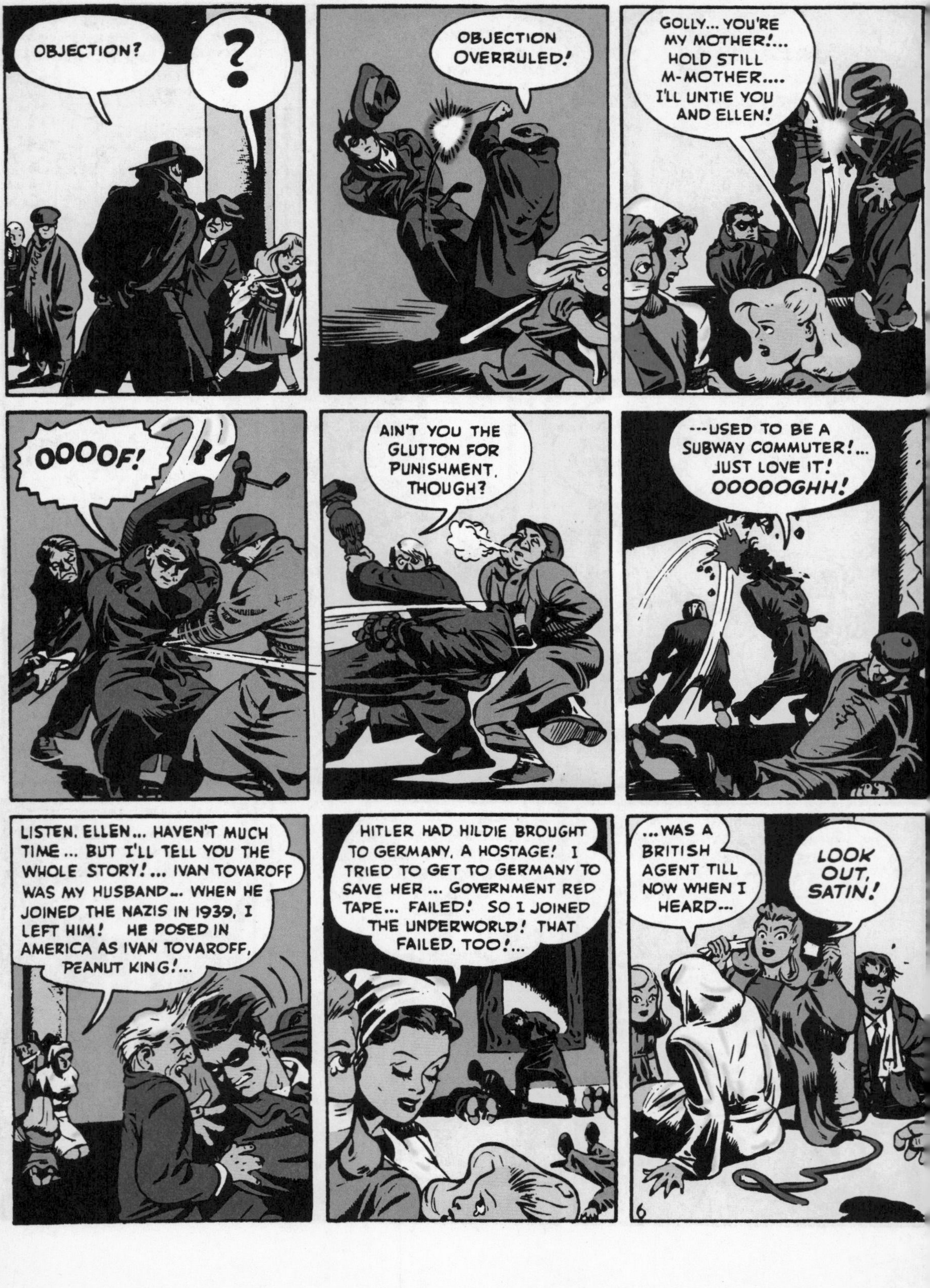
OBJECTION?
?
OBJECTION OVERRULED!
GOLLY... YOU'RE MY MOTHER!... HOLD STILL M-MOTHER.... I'LL UNTIE YOU AND ELLEN!
OOOOF!
AIN'T YOU THE GLUTTON FOR PUNISHMENT, THOUGH?
---USED TO BE A SUBWAY COMMUTER!... JUST LOVE IT! OOOOOGHH!
LISTEN, ELLEN... HAVEN'T MUCH TIME... BUT I'LL TELL YOU THE WHOLE STORY!... IVAN TOVAROFF WAS MY HUSBAND... WHEN HE JOINED THE NAZIS IN 1939, I LEFT HIM! HE POSED IN AMERICA AS IVAN TOVAROFF, PEANUT KING!...
HITLER HAD HILDIE BROUGHT TO GERMANY, A HOSTAGE! I TRIED TO GET TO GERMANY TO SAVE HER... GOVERNMENT RED TAPE... FAILED! SO I JOINED THE UNDERWORLD! THAT FAILED, TOO!...
...WAS A BRITISH AGENT TILL NOW WHEN I HEARD---
LOOK OUT, SATIN!
6

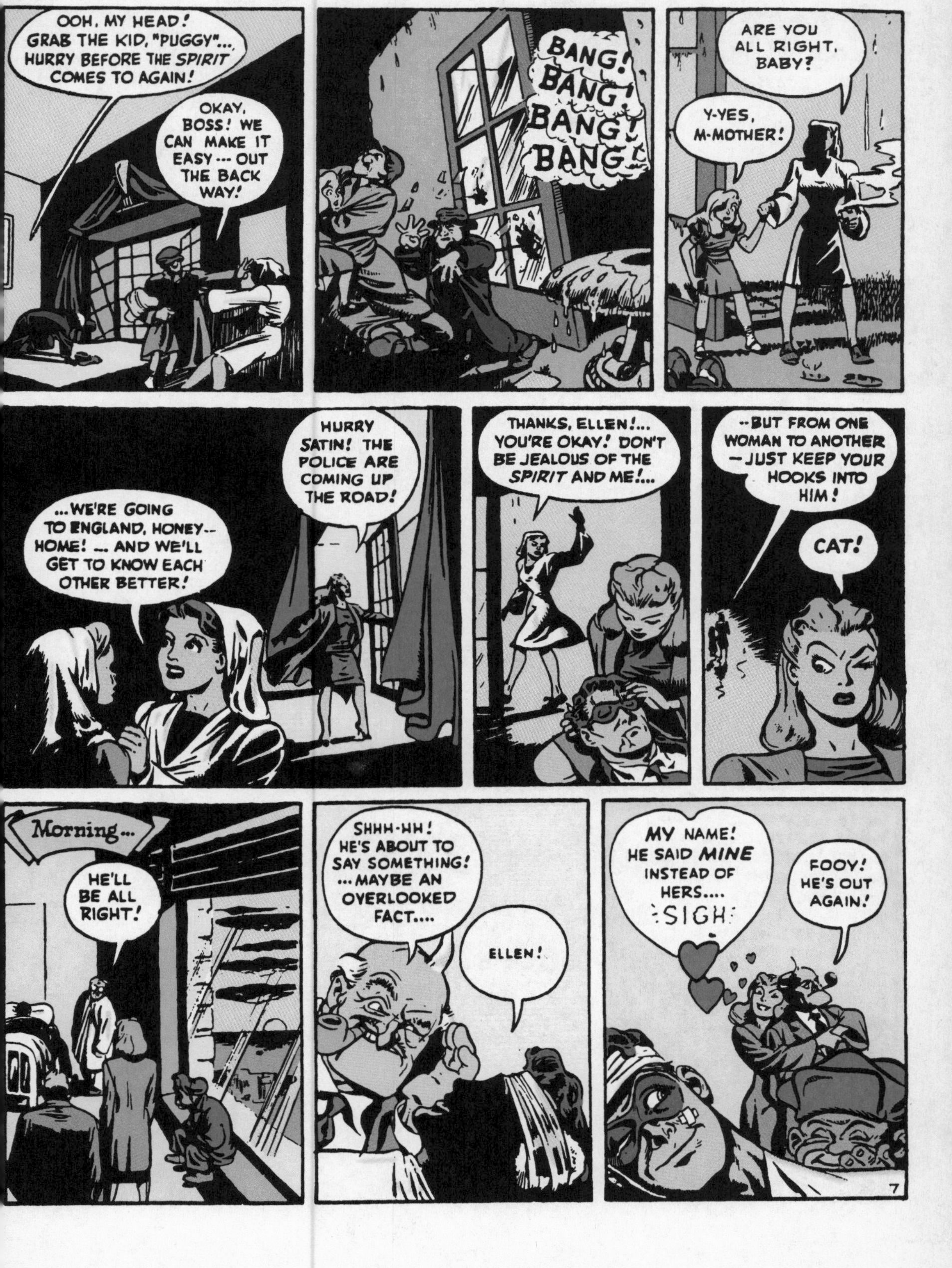

OOH, MY HEAD! GRAB THE KID, "PUGGY"..., HURRY BEFORE THE SPIRIT COMES TO AGAIN!
OKAY, BOSS! WE CAN MAKE IT EASY --- OUT THE BACK WAY!
BANG! BANG! BANG! BANG!
ARE YOU ALL RIGHT, BABY?
Y-YES, M-MOTHER!
...WE'RE GOING TO ENGLAND, HONEY-- HOME! ... AND WE'LL GET TO KNOW EACH OTHER BETTER!
HURRY SATIN! THE POLICE ARE COMING UP THE ROAD!
THANKS, ELLEN!... YOU'RE OKAY! DON'T BE JEALOUS OF THE SPIRIT AND ME!...
--BUT FROM ONE WOMAN TO ANOTHER --JUST KEEP YOUR HOOKS INTO HIM!
CAT!
Morning...
HE'LL BE ALL RIGHT!
SHHH-HH! HE'S ABOUT TO SAY SOMETHING! ...MAYBE AN OVERLOOKED FACT....
ELLEN!
MY NAME! HE SAID MINE INSTEAD OF HERS.... SIGH
FOOY! HE'S OUT AGAIN!
7

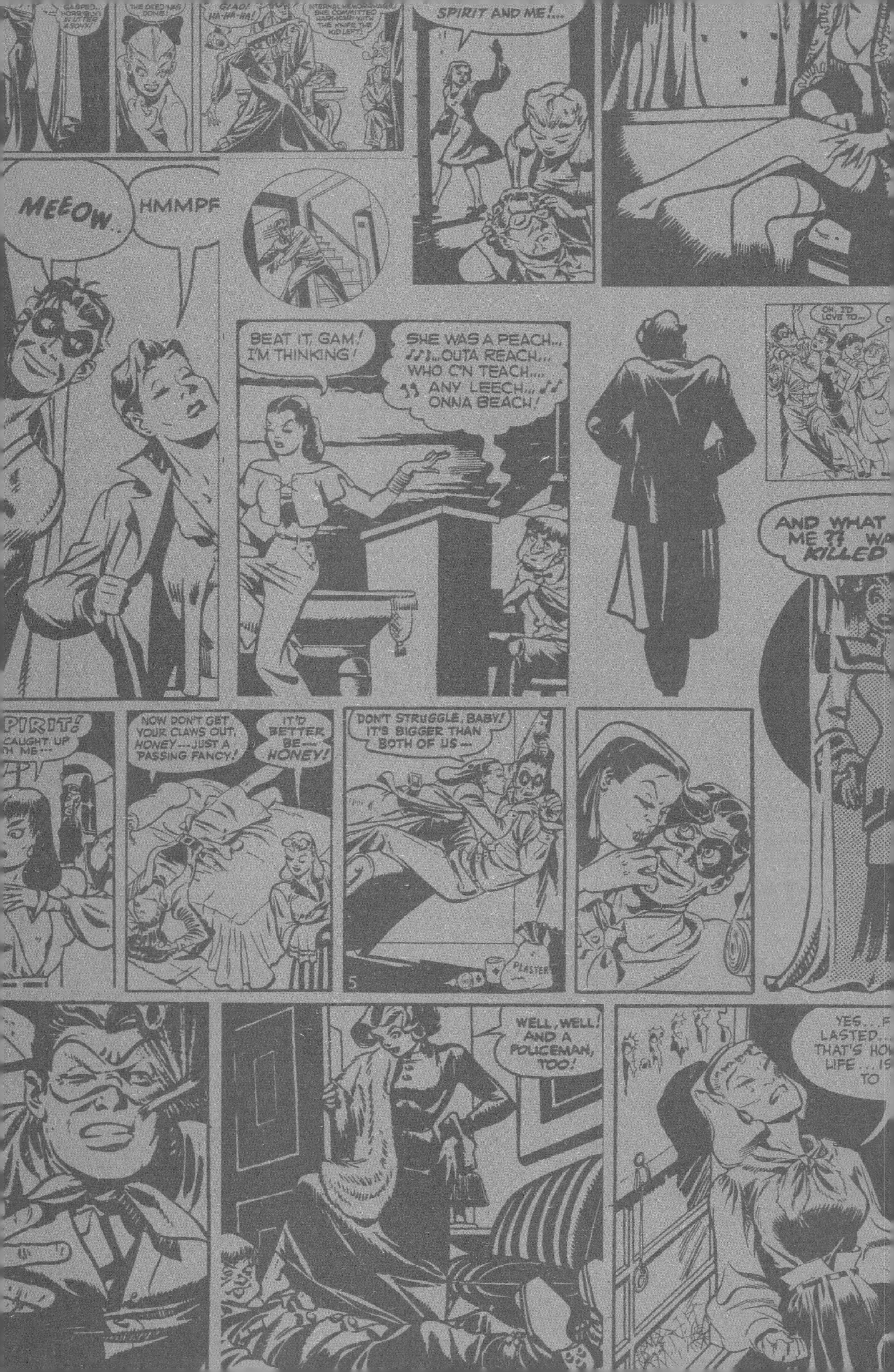
THE DEED WAS DONE!
HA-HA-HA!
INTERNAL HEMORRHAGE! SHE COMMITTED HARI-KARI WITH THE KNIFE THE KID LEFT!
SPIRIT AND ME!...
MEEOW..
HMMPF
BEAT IT, GAM! I'M THINKING!
SHE WAS A PEACH... ♫♪...OUTA REACH... WHO C'N TEACH.... ♫ ANY LEECH... ♫ ONNA BEACH!
OH, I'D LOVE TO...
NOW DON'T GET YOUR CLAWS OUT, HONEY... JUST A PASSING FANCY!
IT'D BETTER BE--- HONEY!
DON'T STRUGGLE, BABY! IT'S BIGGER THAN BOTH OF US---
PLASTER
WELL, WELL! AND A POLICEMAN, TOO!

NYLON ROSE

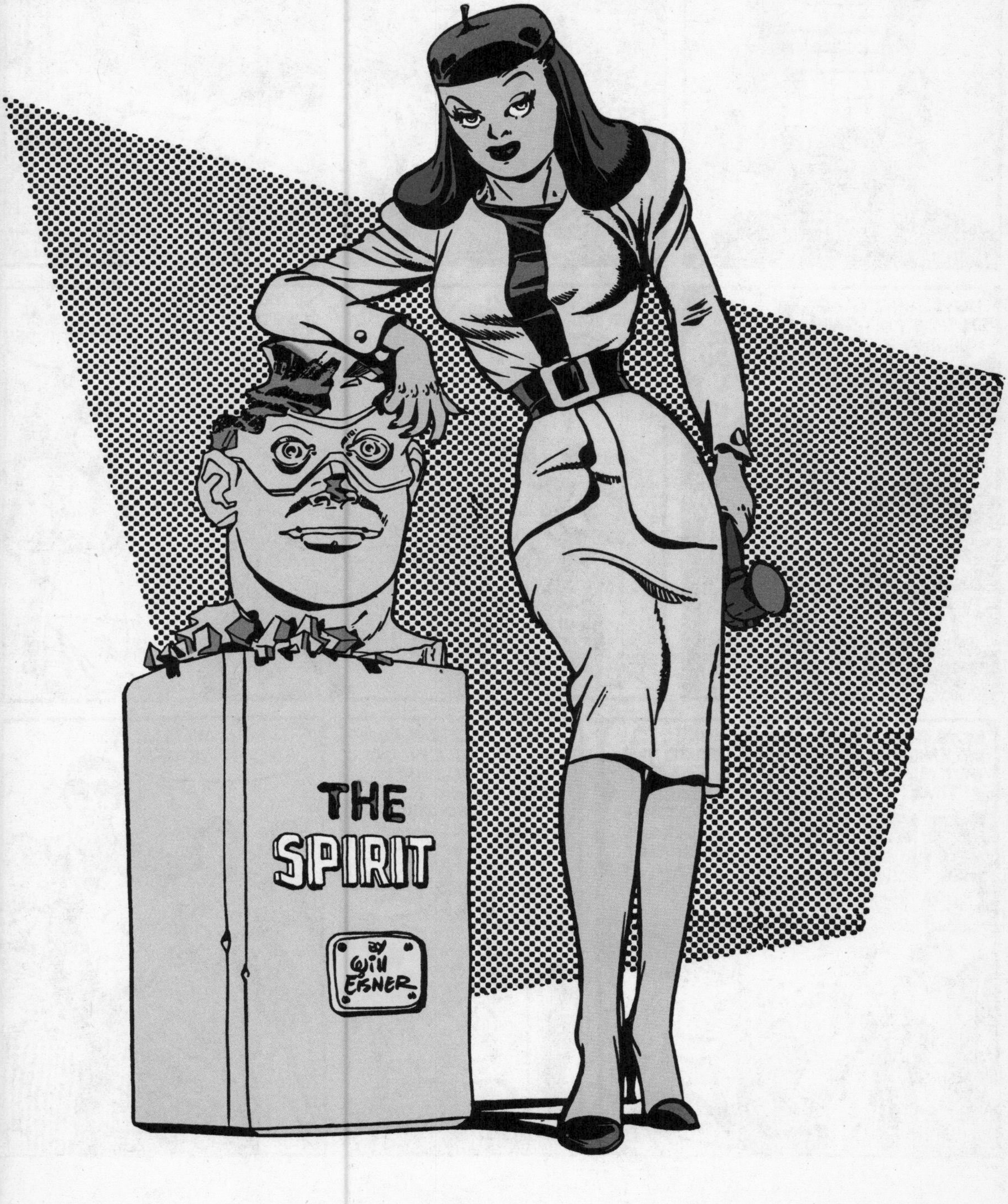
THE SPIRIT
BY Will Eisner

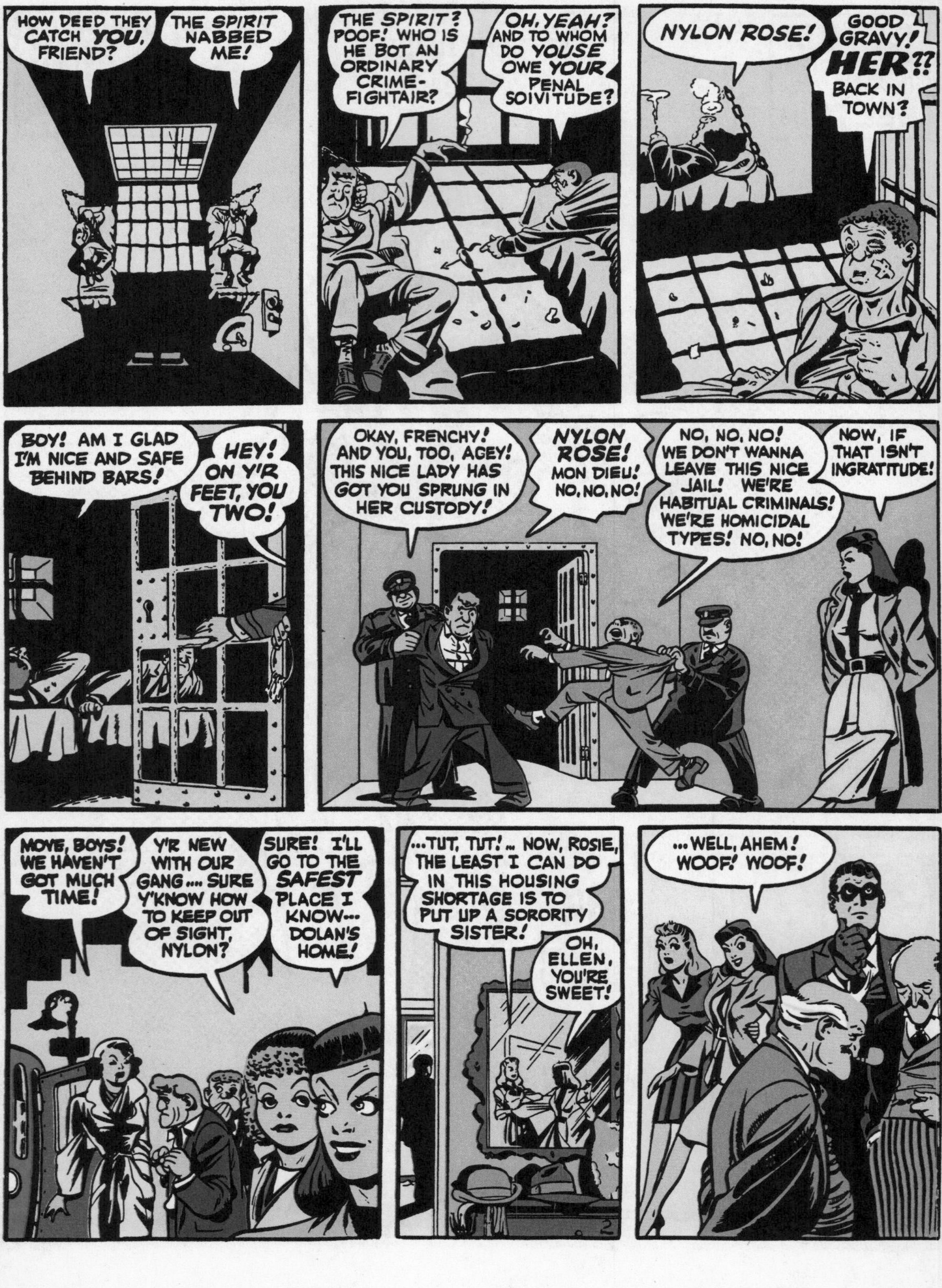
HOW DEED THEY CATCH YOU, FRIEND?
THE SPIRIT NABBED ME!
THE SPIRIT? POOF! WHO IS HE BOT AN ORDINARY CRIME-FIGHTAIR?
OH, YEAH? AND TO WHOM DO YOUSE OWE YOUR PENAL SOIVITUDE?
NYLON ROSE!
GOOD GRAVY! HER?? BACK IN TOWN?
BOY! AM I GLAD I'M NICE AND SAFE BEHIND BARS!
HEY! ON Y'R FEET, YOU TWO!
OKAY, FRENCHY! AND YOU, TOO, AGEY! THIS NICE LADY HAS GOT YOU SPRUNG IN HER CUSTODY!
NYLON ROSE! MON DIEU! NO, NO, NO!
NO, NO, NO! WE DON'T WANNA LEAVE THIS NICE JAIL! WE'RE HABITUAL CRIMINALS! WE'RE HOMICIDAL TYPES! NO, NO!
NOW, IF THAT ISN'T INGRATITUDE!
MOVE, BOYS! WE HAVEN'T GOT MUCH TIME!
Y'R NEW WITH OUR GANG.... SURE Y'KNOW HOW TO KEEP OUT OF SIGHT, NYLON?
SURE! I'LL GO TO THE SAFEST PLACE I KNOW... DOLAN'S HOME!
...TUT, TUT! .. NOW, ROSIE, THE LEAST I CAN DO IN THIS HOUSING SHORTAGE IS TO PUT UP A SORORITY SISTER!
OH, ELLEN, YOU'RE SWEET!
...WELL, AHEM! WOOF! WOOF!

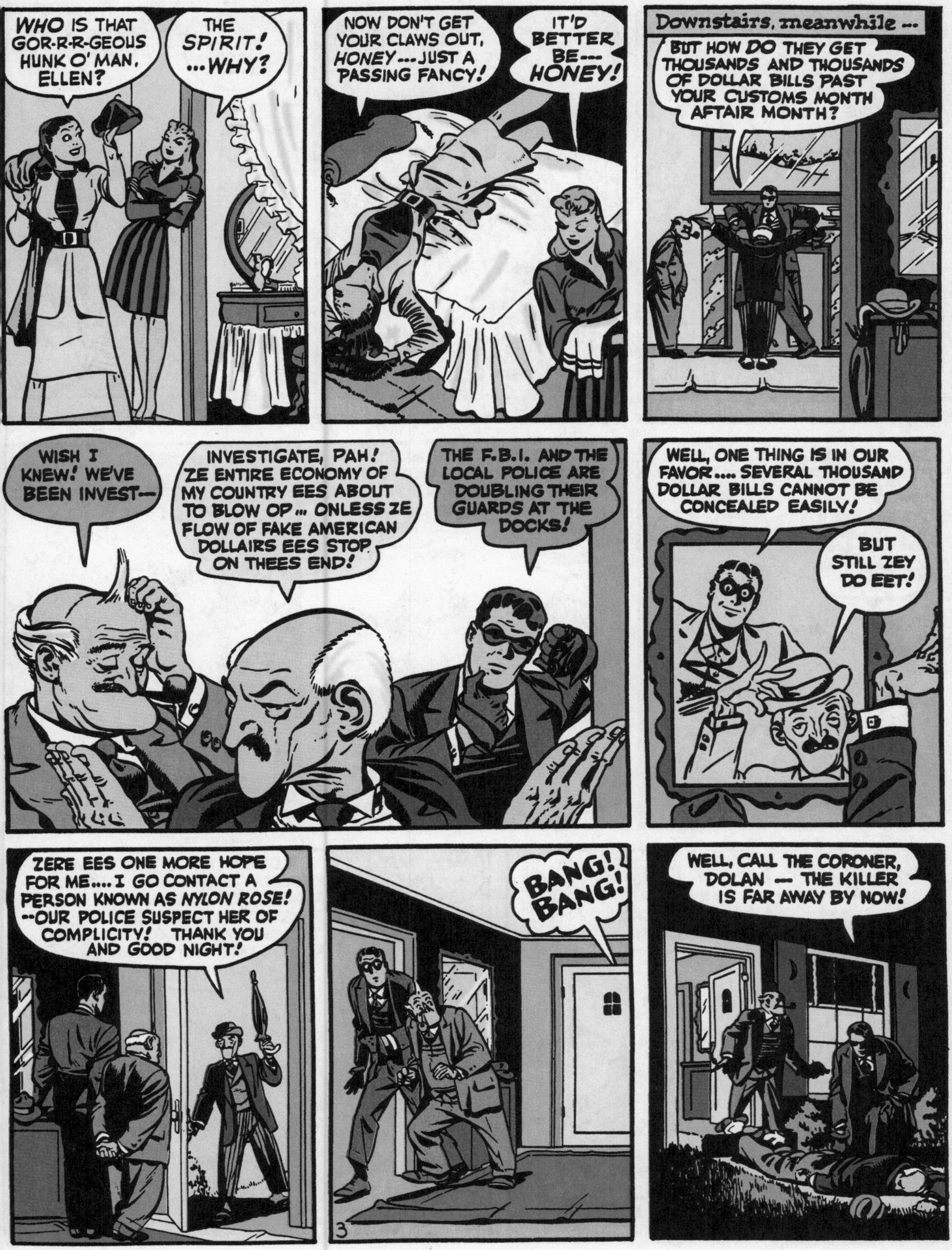
WHO IS THAT GOR-R-R-GEOUS HUNK O' MAN, ELLEN?
THE SPIRIT! ...WHY?
NOW DON'T GET YOUR CLAWS OUT, HONEY --- JUST A PASSING FANCY!
IT'D BETTER BE--- HONEY!
Downstairs, meanwhile --
BUT HOW DO THEY GET THOUSANDS AND THOUSANDS OF DOLLAR BILLS PAST YOUR CUSTOMS MONTH AFTAIR MONTH?
WISH I KNEW! WE'VE BEEN INVEST---
INVESTIGATE, PAH! ZE ENTIRE ECONOMY OF MY COUNTRY EES ABOUT TO BLOW OP... ONLESS ZE FLOW OF FAKE AMERICAN DOLLAIRS EES STOP ON THEES END!
THE F.B.I. AND THE LOCAL POLICE ARE DOUBLING THEIR GUARDS AT THE DOCKS!
WELL, ONE THING IS IN OUR FAVOR.... SEVERAL THOUSAND DOLLAR BILLS CANNOT BE CONCEALED EASILY!
BUT STILL ZEY DO EET!
ZERE EES ONE MORE HOPE FOR ME.... I GO CONTACT A PERSON KNOWN AS NYLON ROSE! --OUR POLICE SUSPECT HER OF COMPLICITY! THANK YOU AND GOOD NIGHT!
BANG! BANG!
3
WELL, CALL THE CORONER, DOLAN -- THE KILLER IS FAR AWAY BY NOW!

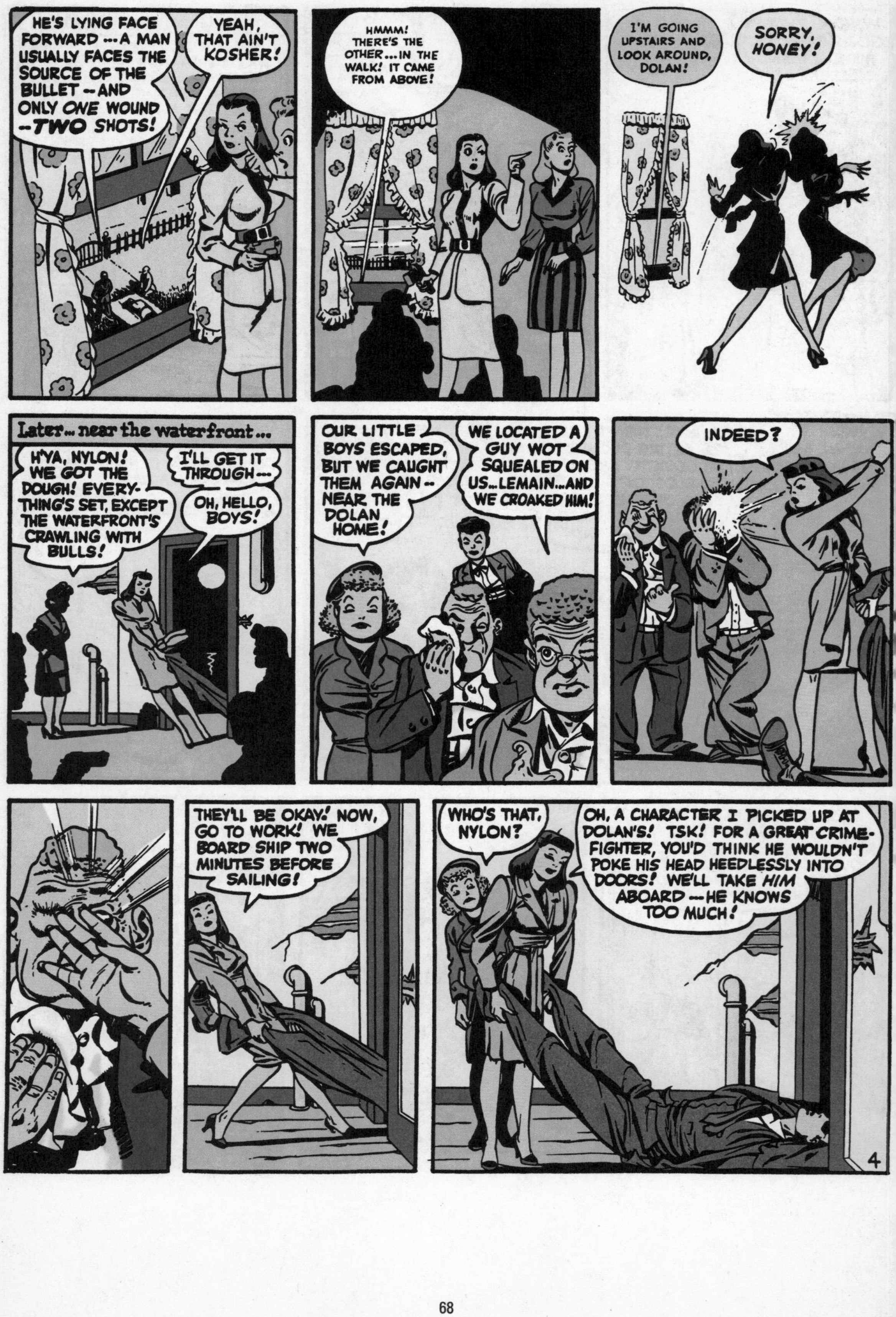
HE'S LYING FACE FORWARD --- A MAN USUALLY FACES THE SOURCE OF THE BULLET -- AND ONLY ONE WOUND -- TWO SHOTS!
YEAH, THAT AIN'T KOSHER!
HMMM! THERE'S THE OTHER... IN THE WALK! IT CAME FROM ABOVE!
I'M GOING UPSTAIRS AND LOOK AROUND, DOLAN!
SORRY, HONEY!
Later... near the waterfront...
H'YA, NYLON! WE GOT THE DOUGH! EVERYTHING'S SET, EXCEPT THE WATERFRONT'S CRAWLING WITH BULLS!
I'LL GET IT THROUGH ---
OH, HELLO, BOYS!
OUR LITTLE BOYS ESCAPED, BUT WE CAUGHT THEM AGAIN -- NEAR THE DOLAN HOME!
WE LOCATED A GUY WOT SQUEALED ON US... LEMAIN... AND WE CROAKED HIM!
INDEED?
THEY'LL BE OKAY! NOW, GO TO WORK! WE BOARD SHIP TWO MINUTES BEFORE SAILING!
WHO'S THAT, NYLON?
OH, A CHARACTER I PICKED UP AT DOLAN'S! TSK! FOR A GREAT CRIME-FIGHTER, YOU'D THINK HE WOULDN'T POKE HIS HEAD HEEDLESSLY INTO DOORS! WE'LL TAKE HIM ABOARD --- HE KNOWS TOO MUCH!
4

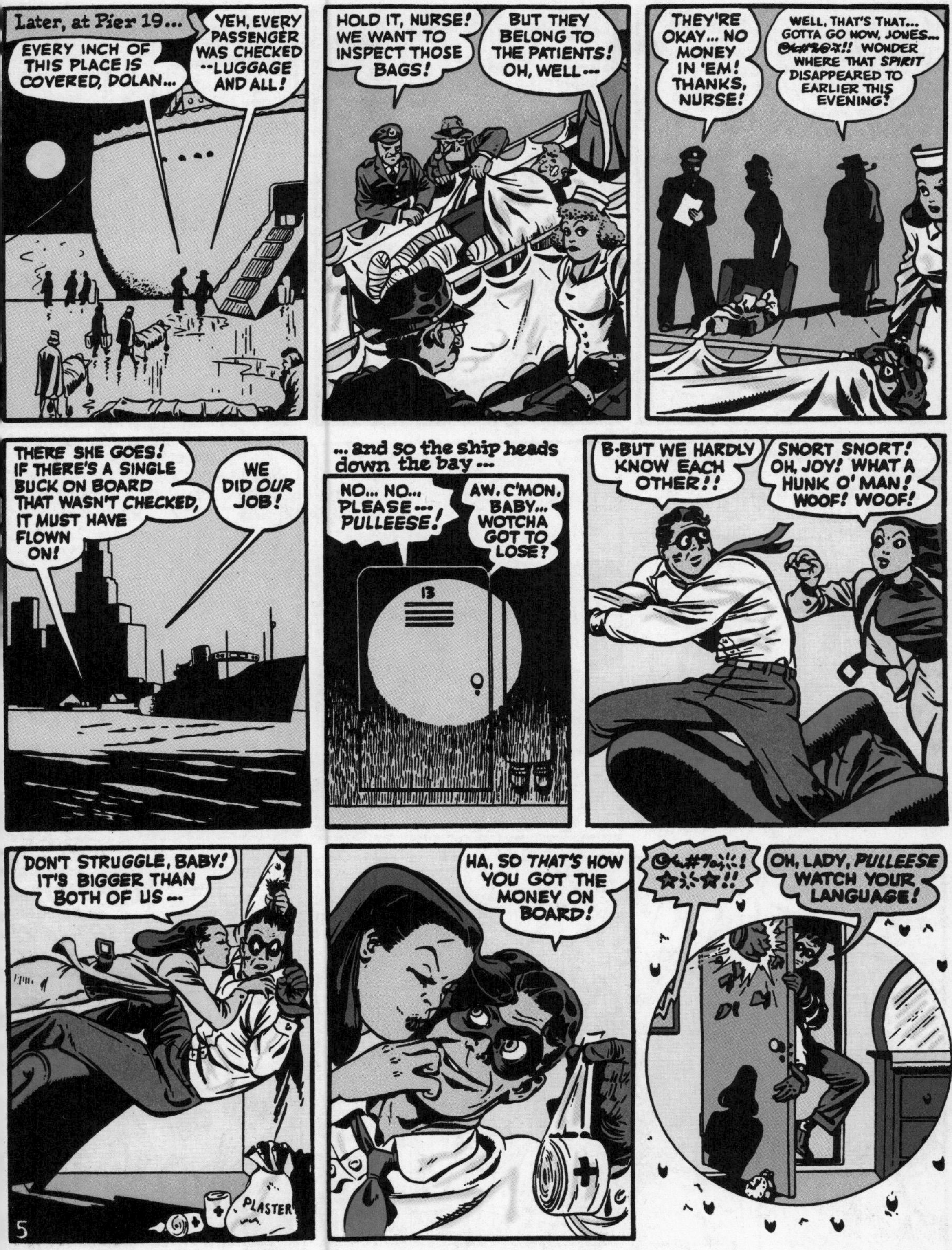
Later, at Pier 19...
EVERY INCH OF THIS PLACE IS COVERED, DOLAN...
YEH, EVERY PASSENGER WAS CHECKED --LUGGAGE AND ALL!
HOLD IT, NURSE! WE WANT TO INSPECT THOSE BAGS!
BUT THEY BELONG TO THE PATIENTS! OH, WELL---
THEY'RE OKAY... NO MONEY IN 'EM! THANKS, NURSE!
WELL, THAT'S THAT... GOTTA GO NOW, JONES... WONDER WHERE THAT SPIRIT DISAPPEARED TO EARLIER THIS EVENING?
THERE SHE GOES! IF THERE'S A SINGLE BUCK ON BOARD THAT WASN'T CHECKED, IT MUST HAVE FLOWN ON!
WE DID OUR JOB!
... and so the ship heads down the bay ---
NO... NO... PLEASE--- PULLEESE!
AW, C'MON, BABY... WOTCHA GOT TO LOSE?
13
B-BUT WE HARDLY KNOW EACH OTHER!!
SNORT SNORT! OH, JOY! WHAT A HUNK O' MAN! WOOF! WOOF!
DON'T STRUGGLE, BABY! IT'S BIGGER THAN BOTH OF US ---
PLASTER
5
HA, SO THAT'S HOW YOU GOT THE MONEY ON BOARD!
OH, LADY, PULLEESE WATCH YOUR LANGUAGE!

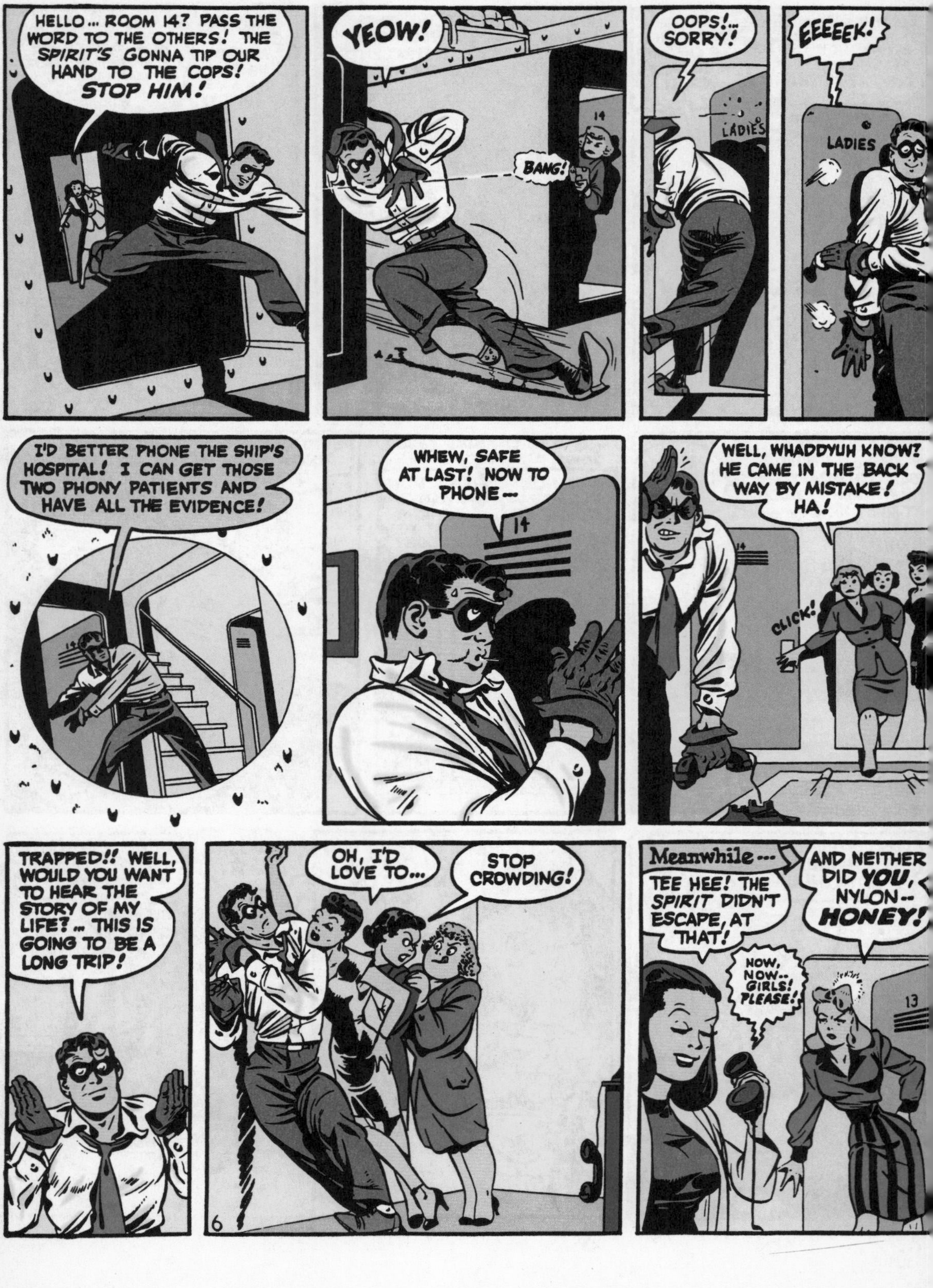
HELLO... ROOM 14? PASS THE WORD TO THE OTHERS! THE SPIRIT'S GONNA TIP OUR HAND TO THE COPS! STOP HIM!
YEOW!
BANG!
14
OOPS!.. SORRY!
LADIES
EEEEEK!
LADIES
I'D BETTER PHONE THE SHIP'S HOSPITAL! I CAN GET THOSE TWO PHONY PATIENTS AND HAVE ALL THE EVIDENCE!
14
WHEW, SAFE AT LAST! NOW TO PHONE—
14
WELL, WHADDYUH KNOW? HE CAME IN THE BACK WAY BY MISTAKE! HA!
14
CLICK!
TRAPPED!! WELL, WOULD YOU WANT TO HEAR THE STORY OF MY LIFE?... THIS IS GOING TO BE A LONG TRIP!
OH, I'D LOVE TO...
STOP CROWDING!
6
Meanwhile ...
TEE HEE! THE SPIRIT DIDN'T ESCAPE, AT THAT!
AND NEITHER DID YOU, NYLON-- HONEY!
NOW, NOW.. GIRLS! PLEASE!
13

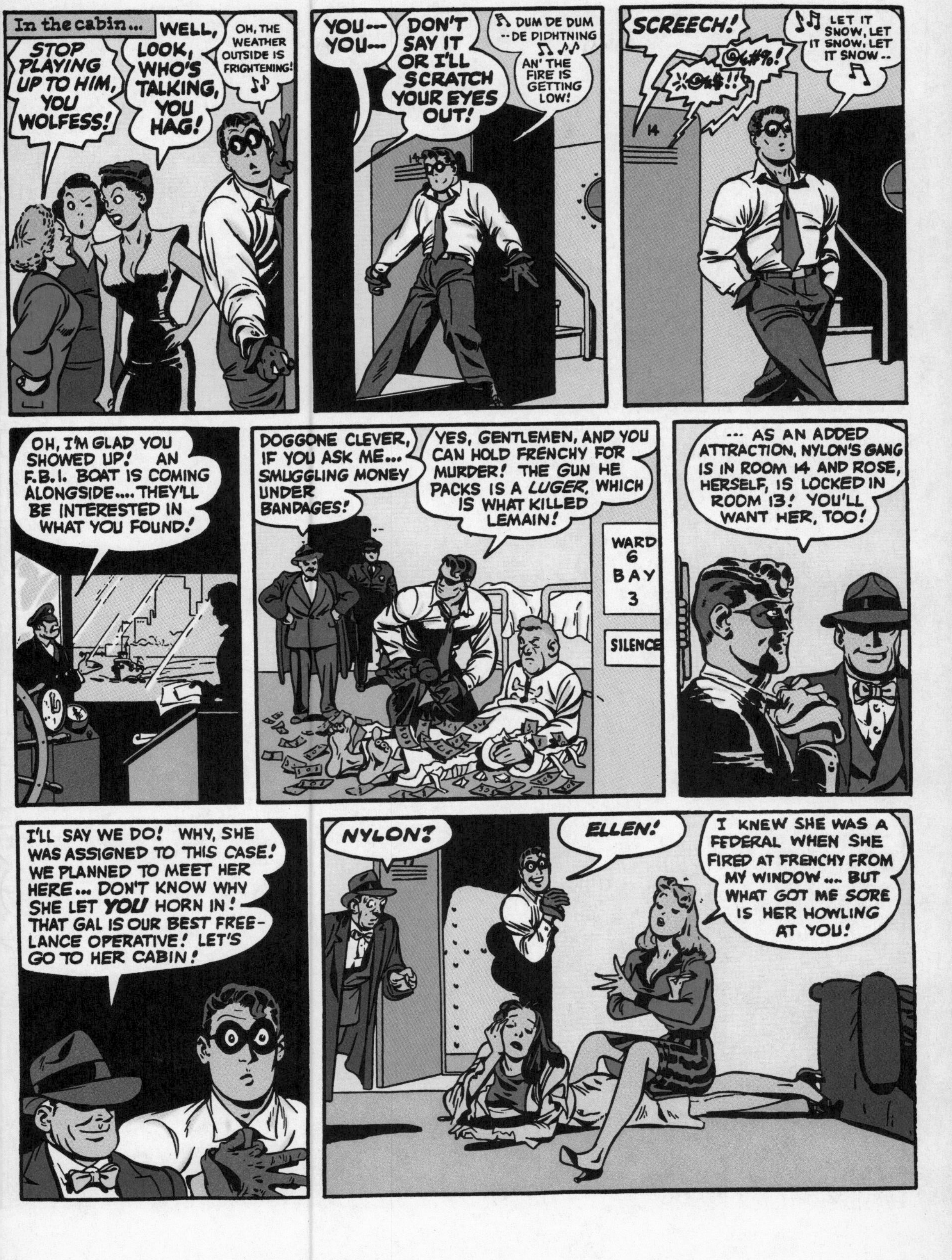
In the cabin...
STOP PLAYING UP TO HIM, YOU WOLFESS!
WELL, LOOK, WHO'S TALKING, YOU HAG!
OH, THE WEATHER OUTSIDE IS FRIGHTENING!
YOU--- YOU---
DON'T SAY IT OR I'LL SCRATCH YOUR EYES OUT!
DUM DE DUM --DE DIDHTNING AN' THE FIRE IS GETTING LOW!
SCREECH!
LET IT SNOW, LET IT SNOW, LET IT SNOW --
OH, I'M GLAD YOU SHOWED UP! AN F.B.I. BOAT IS COMING ALONGSIDE.... THEY'LL BE INTERESTED IN WHAT YOU FOUND!
DOGGONE CLEVER, IF YOU ASK ME... SMUGGLING MONEY UNDER BANDAGES!
YES, GENTLEMEN, AND YOU CAN HOLD FRENCHY FOR MURDER! THE GUN HE PACKS IS A LUGER, WHICH IS WHAT KILLED LEMAIN!
WARD 6 BAY 3
SILENCE
... AS AN ADDED ATTRACTION, NYLON'S GANG IS IN ROOM 14 AND ROSE, HERSELF, IS LOCKED IN ROOM 13! YOU'LL WANT HER, TOO!
I'LL SAY WE DO! WHY, SHE WAS ASSIGNED TO THIS CASE! WE PLANNED TO MEET HER HERE... DON'T KNOW WHY SHE LET YOU HORN IN! THAT GAL IS OUR BEST FREE-LANCE OPERATIVE! LET'S GO TO HER CABIN!
NYLON?
ELLEN!
I KNEW SHE WAS A FEDERAL WHEN SHE FIRED AT FRENCHY FROM MY WINDOW .... BUT WHAT GOT ME SORE IS HER HOWLING AT YOU!

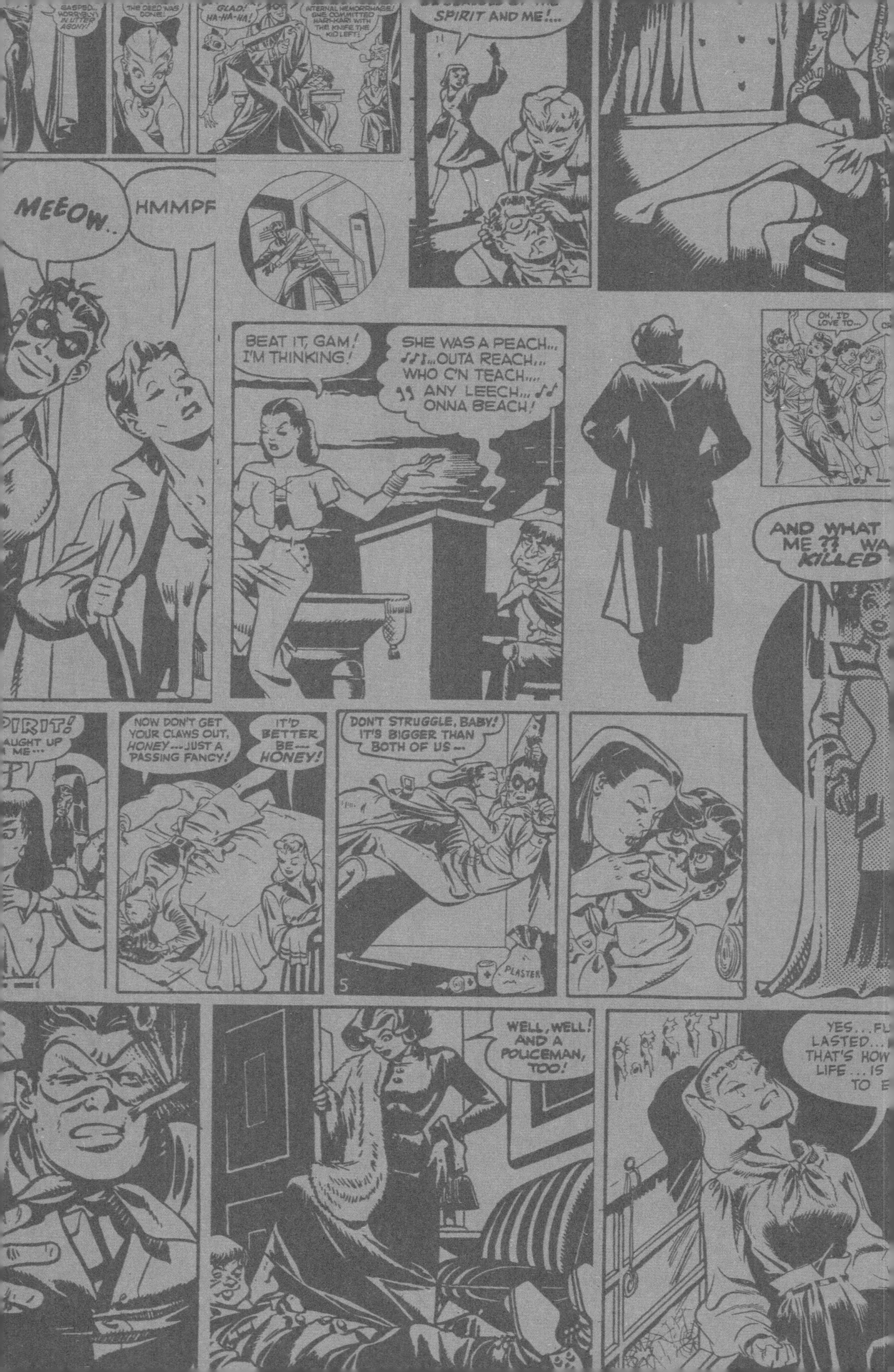
GASPED... HORRIBLY! IN UTTER AGONY!
THE DEED WAS DONE!
GLAD! HA-HA-HA!
INTERNAL HEMORRHAGE! SHE COMMITTED HARI-KARI WITH THE KNIFE THE KID LEFT!
SPIRIT AND ME!...
MEEOW..
HMMPF
BEAT IT, GAM! I'M THINKING!
SHE WAS A PEACH... ♪♪♪...OUTA REACH... WHO C'N TEACH.... ♪♪ ANY LEECH... ♪♪ ONNA BEACH!
OH, I'D LOVE TO...
NOW DON'T GET YOUR CLAWS OUT, HONEY--- JUST A PASSING FANCY!
IT'D BETTER BE--- HONEY!
DON'T STRUGGLE, BABY! IT'S BIGGER THAN BOTH OF US---
5
PLASTER
WELL, WELL! AND A POLICEMAN, TOO!

COMIC BOOK SECTION

DULCET TONE

ACTION Mystery ADVENTURE

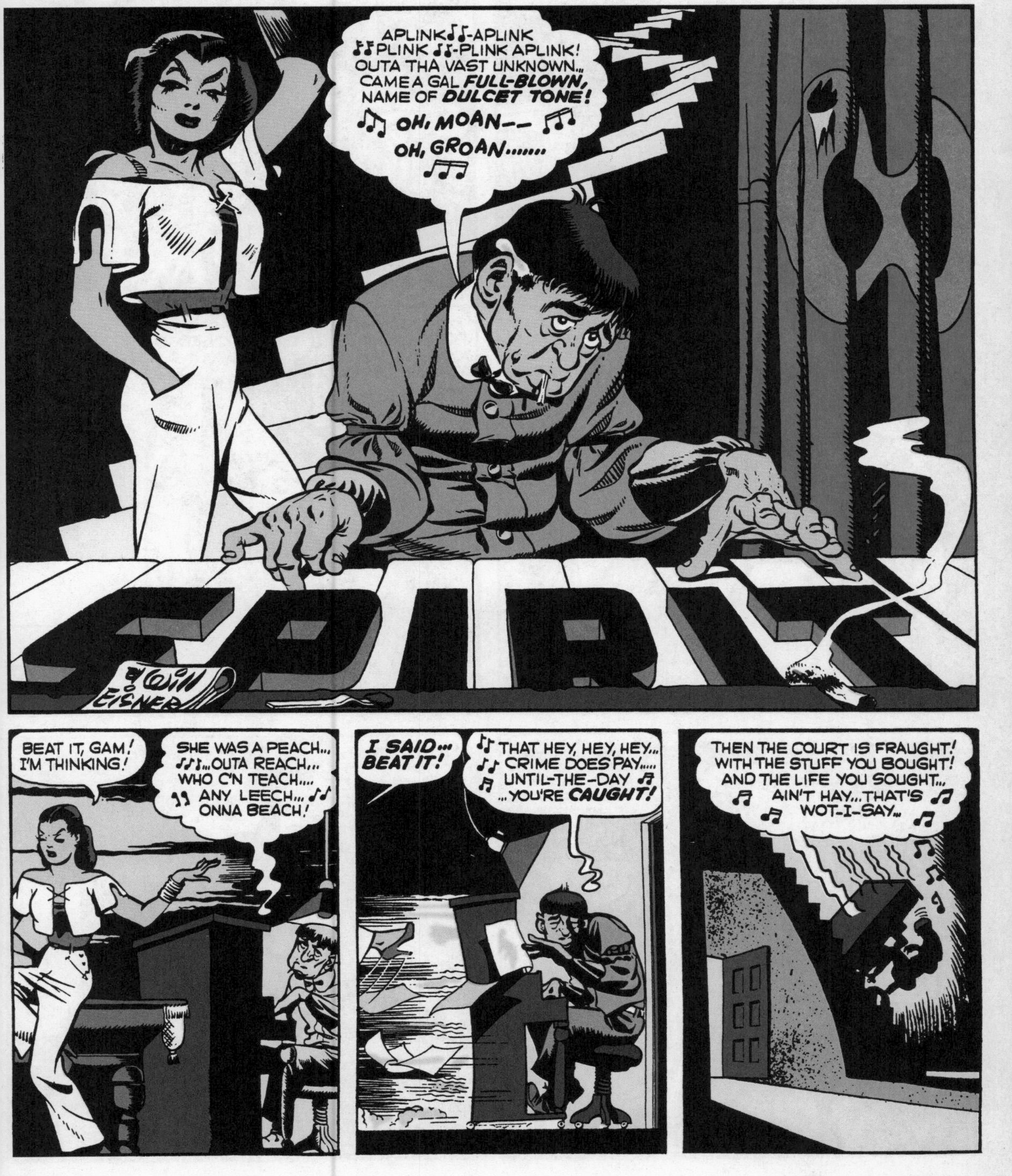
APLINK♫-APLINK ♫PLINK ♫-PLINK APLINK! OUTA THA VAST UNKNOWN... CAME A GAL FULL-BLOWN, NAME OF DULCET TONE! ♫ OH, MOAN-- ♫ OH, GROAN....... ♫
Will Eisner
SPIRIT
BEAT IT, GAM! I'M THINKING!
SHE WAS A PEACH... ♫...OUTA REACH... WHO C'N TEACH.... ♫ ANY LEECH... ♫ ONNA BEACH!
I SAID... BEAT IT!
♫ THAT HEY, HEY, HEY... ♫ CRIME DOES PAY..... ♫ UNTIL-THE-DAY ♫ ...YOU'RE CAUGHT!
THEN THE COURT IS FRAUGHT! WITH THE STUFF YOU BOUGHT! AND THE LIFE YOU SOUGHT... ♫ AIN'T HAY...THAT'S ♫ WOT-I-SAY... ♫

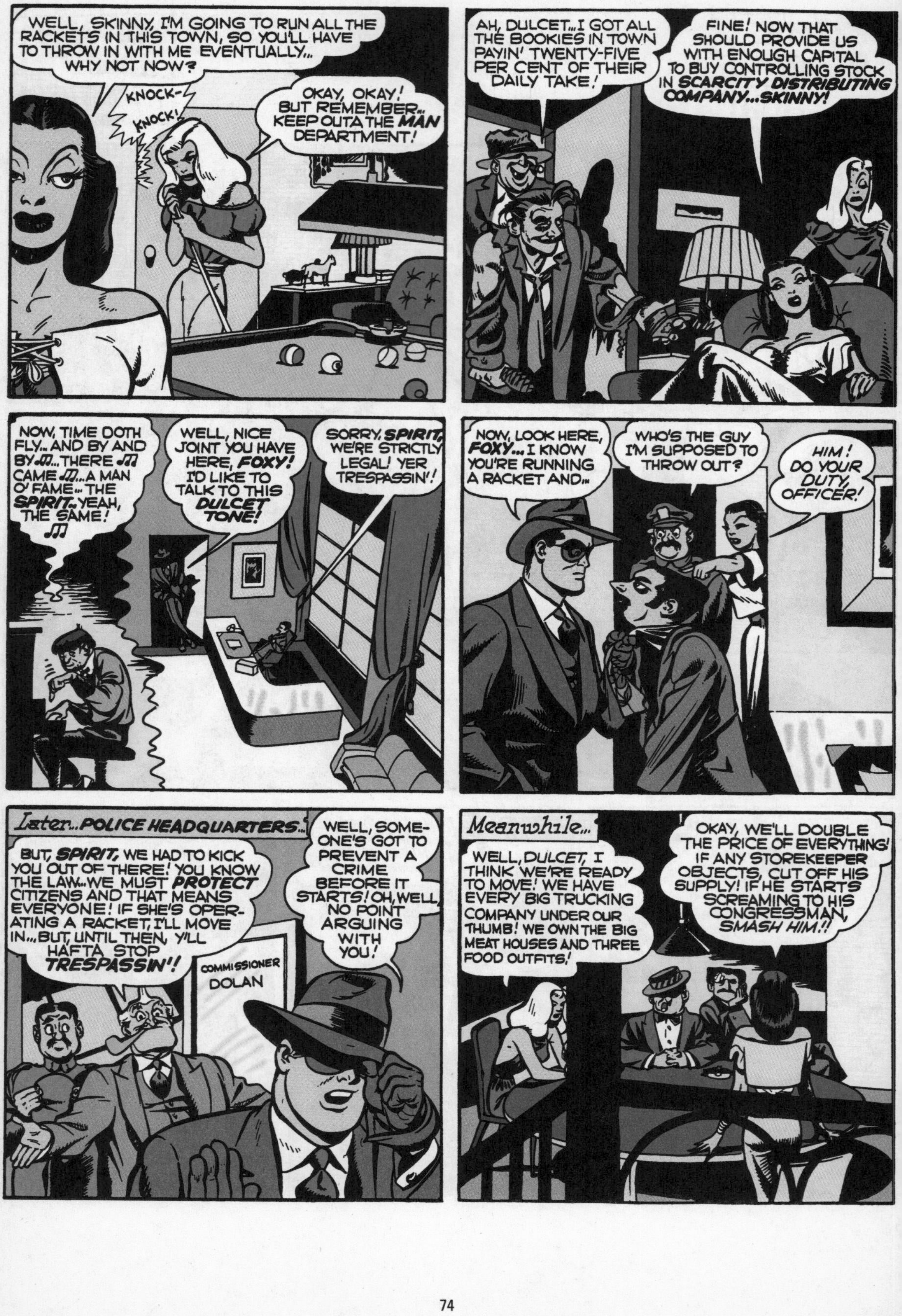
WELL, SKINNY, I'M GOING TO RUN ALL THE RACKETS IN THIS TOWN, SO YOU'LL HAVE TO THROW IN WITH ME EVENTUALLY... WHY NOT NOW?
KNOCK-
KNOCK!
OKAY, OKAY! BUT REMEMBER... KEEP OUTA THE MAN DEPARTMENT!
AH, DULCET... I GOT ALL THE BOOKIES IN TOWN PAYIN' TWENTY-FIVE PER CENT OF THEIR DAILY TAKE!
FINE! NOW THAT SHOULD PROVIDE US WITH ENOUGH CAPITAL TO BUY CONTROLLING STOCK IN SCARCITY DISTRIBUTING COMPANY... SKINNY!
NOW, TIME DOTH FLY... AND BY AND BY... THERE CAME... A MAN O' FAME... THE SPIRIT... YEAH, THE SAME!
WELL, NICE JOINT YOU HAVE HERE, FOXY! I'D LIKE TO TALK TO THIS DULCET TONE!
SORRY, SPIRIT, WE'RE STRICTLY LEGAL! YER TRESPASSIN'!
NOW, LOOK HERE, FOXY... I KNOW YOU'RE RUNNING A RACKET AND...
WHO'S THE GUY I'M SUPPOSED TO THROW OUT?
HIM! DO YOUR DUTY, OFFICER!
Later... POLICE HEADQUARTERS...
BUT, SPIRIT, WE HAD TO KICK YOU OUT OF THERE! YOU KNOW THE LAW... WE MUST PROTECT CITIZENS AND THAT MEANS EVERYONE! IF SHE'S OPERATING A RACKET, I'LL MOVE IN... BUT, UNTIL THEN, Y'LL HAFTA STOP TRESPASSIN'!
WELL, SOMEONE'S GOT TO PREVENT A CRIME BEFORE IT STARTS! OH, WELL, NO POINT ARGUING WITH YOU!
COMMISSIONER DOLAN
Meanwhile...
WELL, DULCET, I THINK WE'RE READY TO MOVE! WE HAVE EVERY BIG TRUCKING COMPANY UNDER OUR THUMB! WE OWN THE BIG MEAT HOUSES AND THREE FOOD OUTFITS!
OKAY, WE'LL DOUBLE THE PRICE OF EVERYTHING! IF ANY STOREKEEPER OBJECTS, CUT OFF HIS SUPPLY! IF HE STARTS SCREAMING TO HIS CONGRESSMAN, SMASH HIM!!

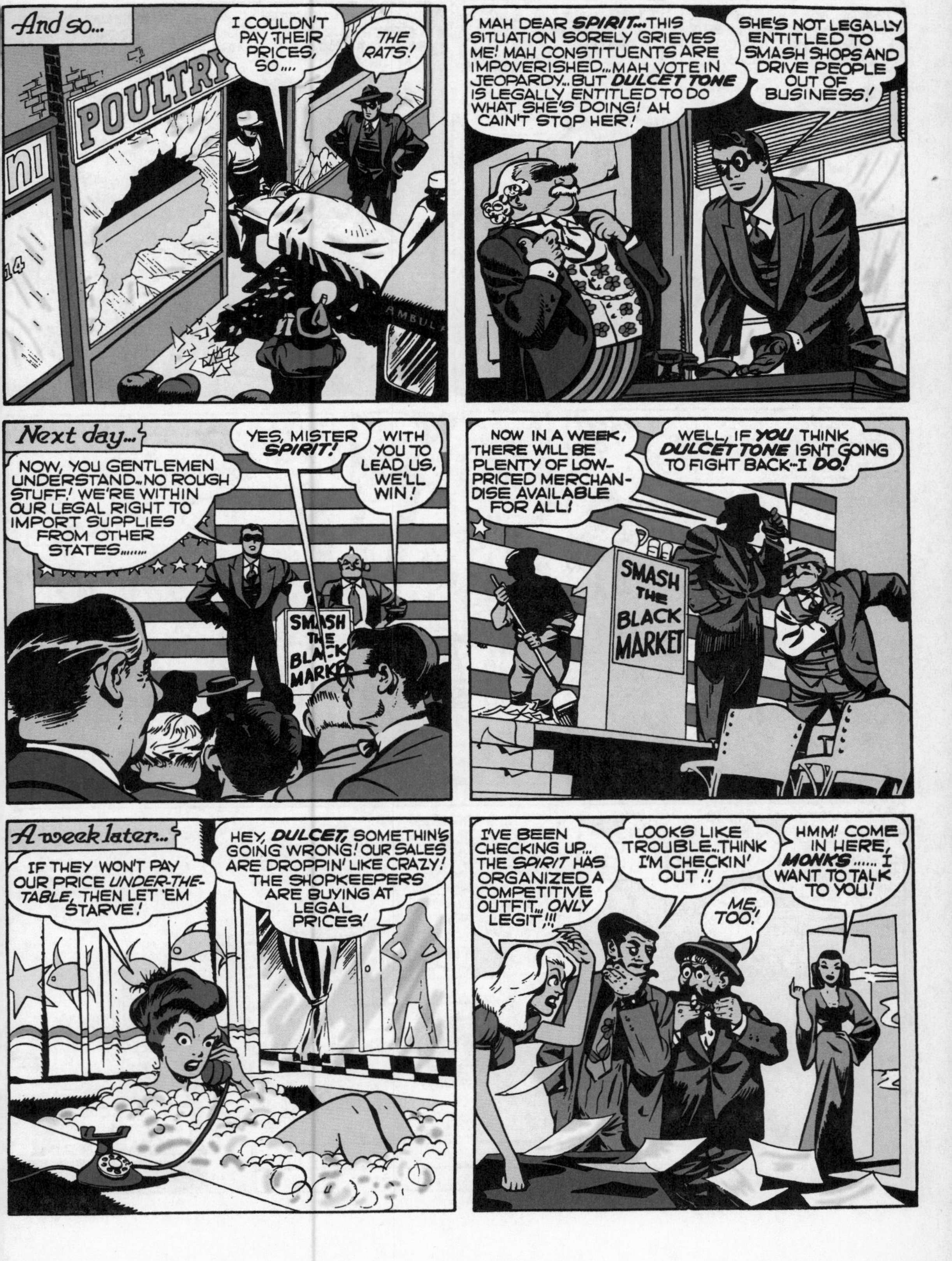
And so...
I COULDN'T PAY THEIR PRICES, SO....
THE RATS!
POULTRY
MAH DEAR SPIRIT... THIS SITUATION SORELY GRIEVES ME! MAH CONSTITUENTS ARE IMPOVERISHED... MAH VOTE IN JEOPARDY... BUT DULCET TONE IS LEGALLY ENTITLED TO DO WHAT SHE'S DOING! AH CAIN'T STOP HER!
SHE'S NOT LEGALLY ENTITLED TO SMASH SHOPS AND DRIVE PEOPLE OUT OF BUSINESS!
Next day...
NOW, YOU GENTLEMEN UNDERSTAND... NO ROUGH STUFF! WE'RE WITHIN OUR LEGAL RIGHT TO IMPORT SUPPLIES FROM OTHER STATES.......
YES, MISTER SPIRIT!
WITH YOU TO LEAD US, WE'LL WIN!
NOW IN A WEEK, THERE WILL BE PLENTY OF LOW-PRICED MERCHANDISE AVAILABLE FOR ALL!
WELL, IF YOU THINK DULCET TONE ISN'T GOING TO FIGHT BACK--I DO!
SMASH THE BLACK MARKET
A week later...
IF THEY WON'T PAY OUR PRICE UNDER-THE-TABLE, THEN LET 'EM STARVE!
HEY, DULCET, SOMETHIN'S GOING WRONG! OUR SALES ARE DROPPIN' LIKE CRAZY! THE SHOPKEEPERS ARE BUYING AT LEGAL PRICES!
I'VE BEEN CHECKING UP... THE SPIRIT HAS ORGANIZED A COMPETITIVE OUTFIT... ONLY LEGIT!!!
LOOKS LIKE TROUBLE... THINK I'M CHECKIN' OUT!!
ME, TOO!
HMM! COME IN HERE, MONKS...... I WANT TO TALK TO YOU!

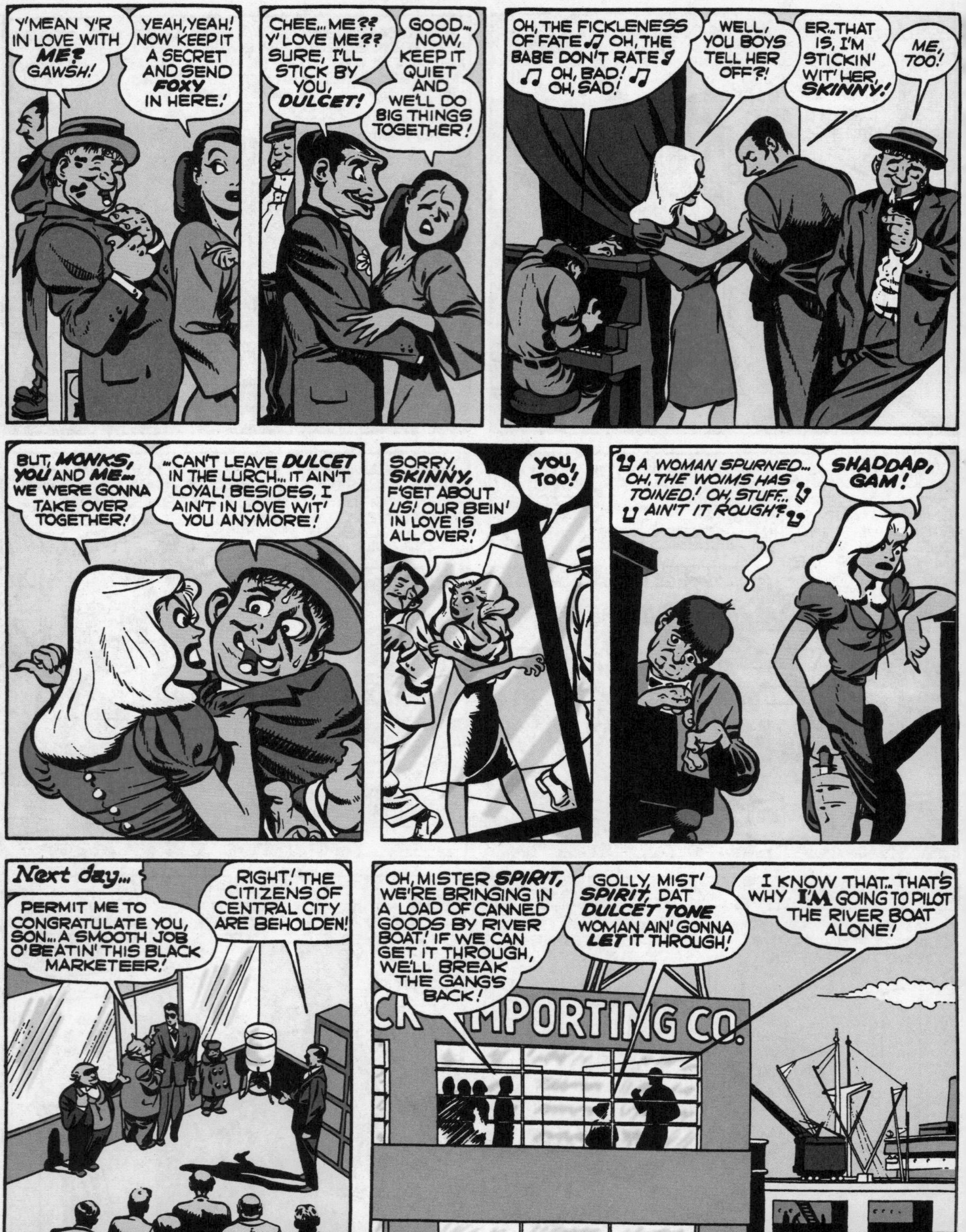

Y'MEAN Y'R IN LOVE WITH ME? GAWSH!
YEAH, YEAH! NOW KEEP IT A SECRET AND SEND FOXY IN HERE!
CHEE... ME?? Y' LOVE ME?? SURE, I'LL STICK BY YOU, DULCET!
GOOD... NOW, KEEP IT QUIET AND WE'LL DO BIG THINGS TOGETHER!
OH, THE FICKLENESS OF FATE OH, THE BABE DON'T RATE OH, BAD! OH, SAD!
WELL, YOU BOYS TELL HER OFF?!
ER.. THAT IS, I'M STICKIN' WIT' HER, SKINNY!
ME, TOO!
BUT, MONKS, YOU AND ME... WE WERE GONNA TAKE OVER TOGETHER!
...CAN'T LEAVE DULCET IN THE LURCH... IT AIN'T LOYAL! BESIDES, I AIN'T IN LOVE WIT' YOU ANYMORE!
SORRY, SKINNY, F'GET ABOUT US! OUR BEIN' IN LOVE IS ALL OVER!
YOU, TOO!
A WOMAN SPURNED... OH, THE WOIMS HAS TOINED! OH, STUFF... AIN'T IT ROUGH?
SHADDAP, GAM!
Next day...
PERMIT ME TO CONGRATULATE YOU, SON... A SMOOTH JOB O'BEATIN' THIS BLACK MARKETEER!
RIGHT! THE CITIZENS OF CENTRAL CITY ARE BEHOLDEN!
OH, MISTER SPIRIT, WE'RE BRINGING IN A LOAD OF CANNED GOODS BY RIVER BOAT! IF WE CAN GET IT THROUGH, WE'LL BREAK THE GANG'S BACK!
GOLLY, MIST' SPIRIT, DAT DULCET TONE WOMAN AIN' GONNA LET IT THROUGH!
I KNOW THAT.. THAT'S WHY I'M GOING TO PILOT THE RIVER BOAT ALONE!
IMPORTING CO.

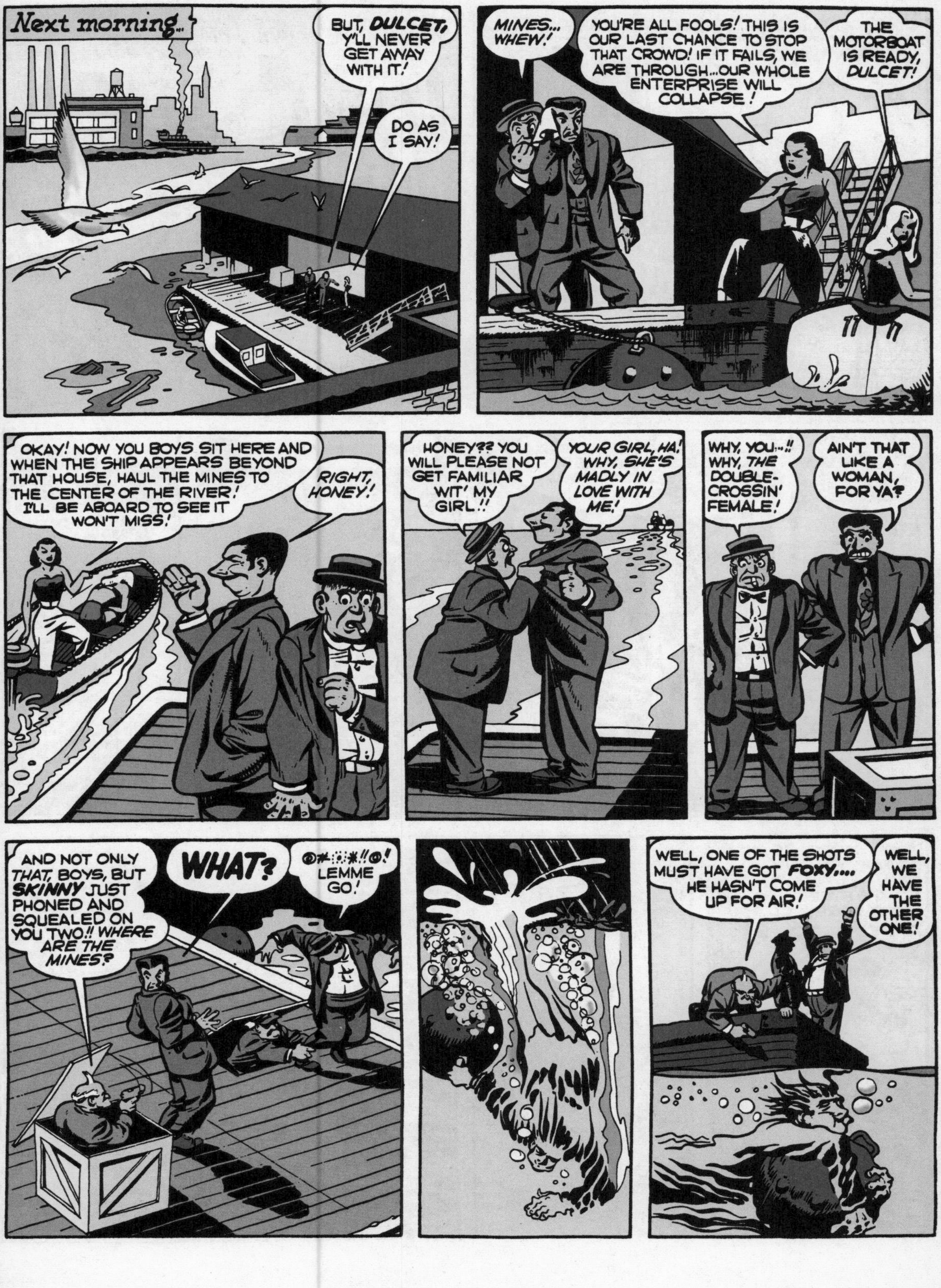

Next morning...
BUT, DULCET, Y'LL NEVER GET AWAY WITH IT!
DO AS I SAY!
MINES... WHEW!
YOU'RE ALL FOOLS! THIS IS OUR LAST CHANCE TO STOP THAT CROWD! IF IT FAILS, WE ARE THROUGH...OUR WHOLE ENTERPRISE WILL COLLAPSE!
THE MOTORBOAT IS READY, DULCET!
OKAY! NOW YOU BOYS SIT HERE AND WHEN THE SHIP APPEARS BEYOND THAT HOUSE, HAUL THE MINES TO THE CENTER OF THE RIVER! I'LL BE ABOARD TO SEE IT WON'T MISS!
RIGHT, HONEY!
HONEY?? YOU WILL PLEASE NOT GET FAMILIAR WIT' MY GIRL!!
YOUR GIRL, HA! WHY, SHE'S MADLY IN LOVE WITH ME!
WHY, YOU--!! WHY, THE DOUBLE-CROSSIN' FEMALE!
AIN'T THAT LIKE A WOMAN, FOR YA?
AND NOT ONLY THAT, BOYS, BUT SKINNY JUST PHONED AND SQUEALED ON YOU TWO!! WHERE ARE THE MINES?
WHAT?
@#*!!@! LEMME GO!
WELL, ONE OF THE SHOTS MUST HAVE GOT FOXY.... HE HASN'T COME UP FOR AIR!
WELL, WE HAVE THE OTHER ONE!

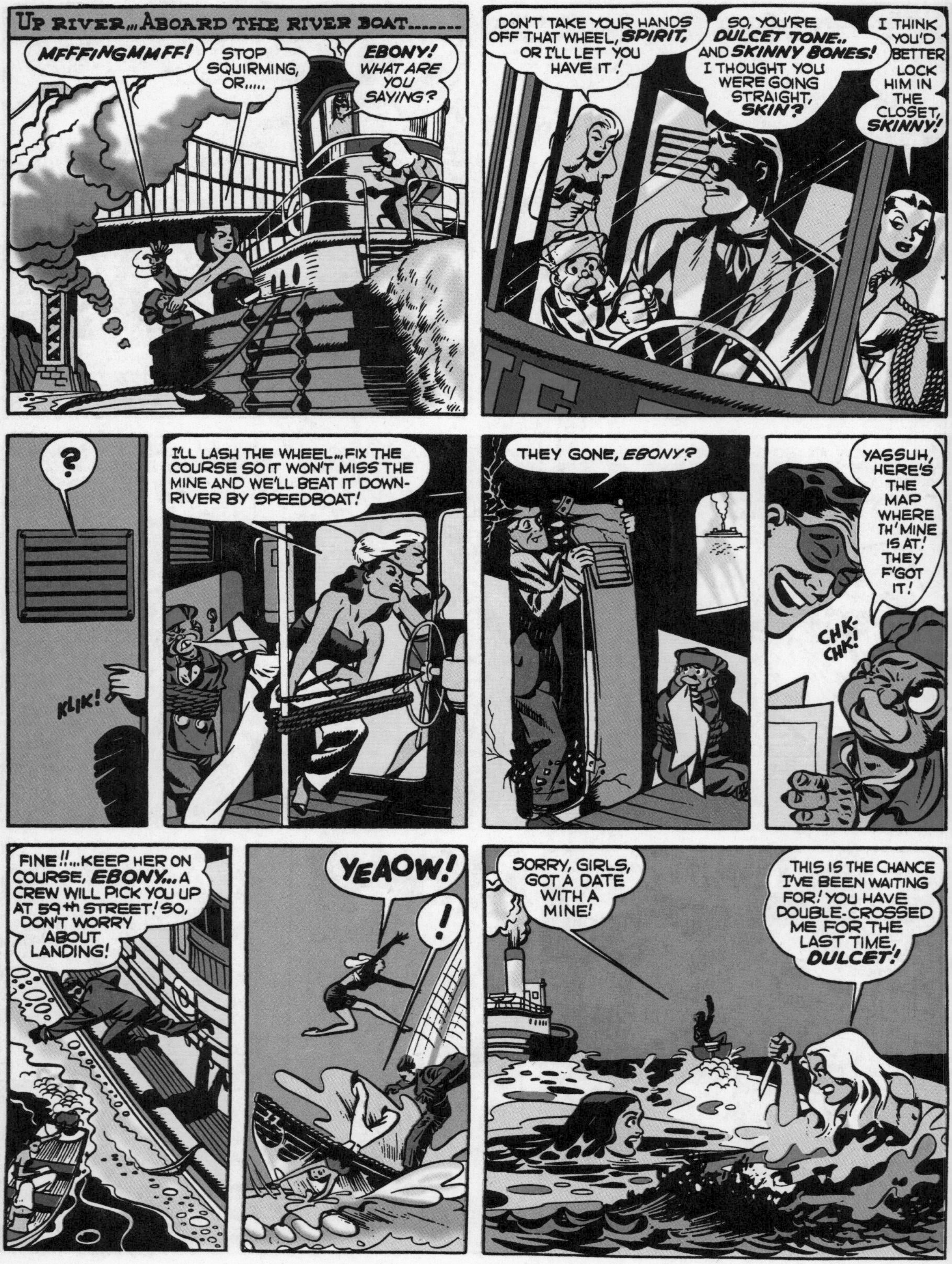

UP RIVER... ABOARD THE RIVER BOAT........
MFFFINGMMFF!
STOP SQUIRMING, OR.....
EBONY! WHAT ARE YOU SAYING?
DON'T TAKE YOUR HANDS OFF THAT WHEEL, SPIRIT, OR I'LL LET YOU HAVE IT!
SO, YOU'RE DULCET TONE.. AND SKINNY BONES! I THOUGHT YOU WERE GOING STRAIGHT, SKIN?
I THINK YOU'D BETTER LOCK HIM IN THE CLOSET, SKINNY!
?
KLIK!
I'LL LASH THE WHEEL... FIX THE COURSE SO IT WON'T MISS THE MINE AND WE'LL BEAT IT DOWN-RIVER BY SPEEDBOAT!
THEY GONE, EBONY?
YASSUH, HERE'S THE MAP WHERE TH' MINE IS AT! THEY F'GOT IT!
CHK-CHK!
FINE!!... KEEP HER ON COURSE, EBONY... A CREW WILL PICK YOU UP AT 59th STREET! SO, DON'T WORRY ABOUT LANDING!
YEAOW!
!
SORRY, GIRLS, GOT A DATE WITH A MINE!
THIS IS THE CHANCE I'VE BEEN WAITING FOR! YOU HAVE DOUBLE-CROSSED ME FOR THE LAST TIME, DULCET!

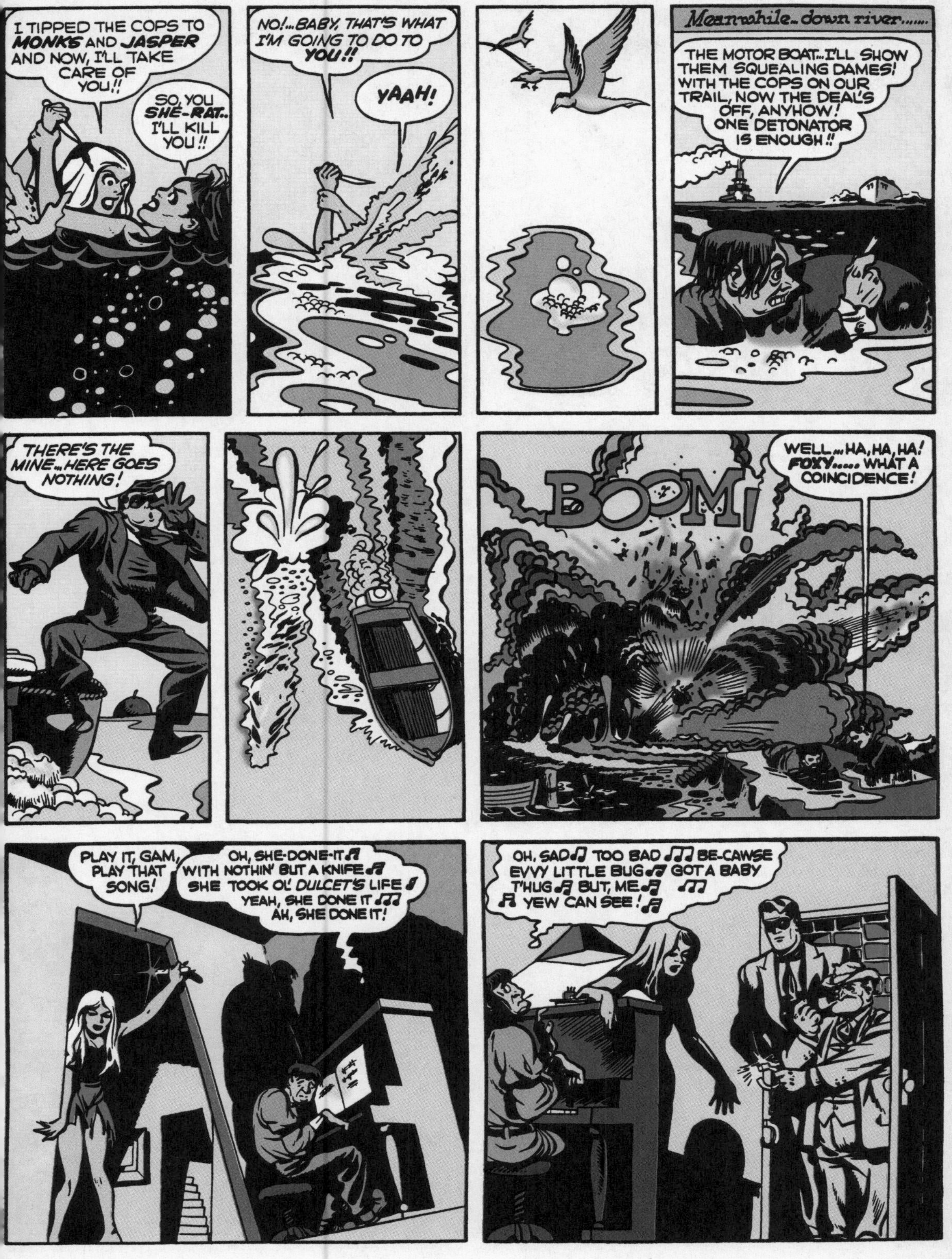
I TIPPED THE COPS TO MONKS AND JASPER AND NOW, I'LL TAKE CARE OF YOU!!
SO, YOU SHE-RAT.. I'LL KILL YOU!!
NO!...BABY, THAT'S WHAT I'M GOING TO DO TO YOU!!
YAAH!
Meanwhile.. down river.......
THE MOTOR BOAT...I'LL SHOW THEM SQUEALING DAMES! WITH THE COPS ON OUR TRAIL, NOW THE DEAL'S OFF, ANYHOW! ONE DETONATOR IS ENOUGH!!
THERE'S THE MINE...HERE GOES NOTHING!
BOOM!
WELL...HA, HA, HA! FOXY..... WHAT A COINCIDENCE!
PLAY IT, GAM, PLAY THAT SONG!
OH, SHE-DONE-IT WITH NOTHIN' BUT A KNIFE SHE TOOK OL' DULCET'S LIFE YEAH, SHE DONE IT AH, SHE DONE IT!
OH, SAD TOO BAD BE-CAWSE EVVY LITTLE BUG GOT A BABY T'HUG BUT, ME YEW CAN SEE!

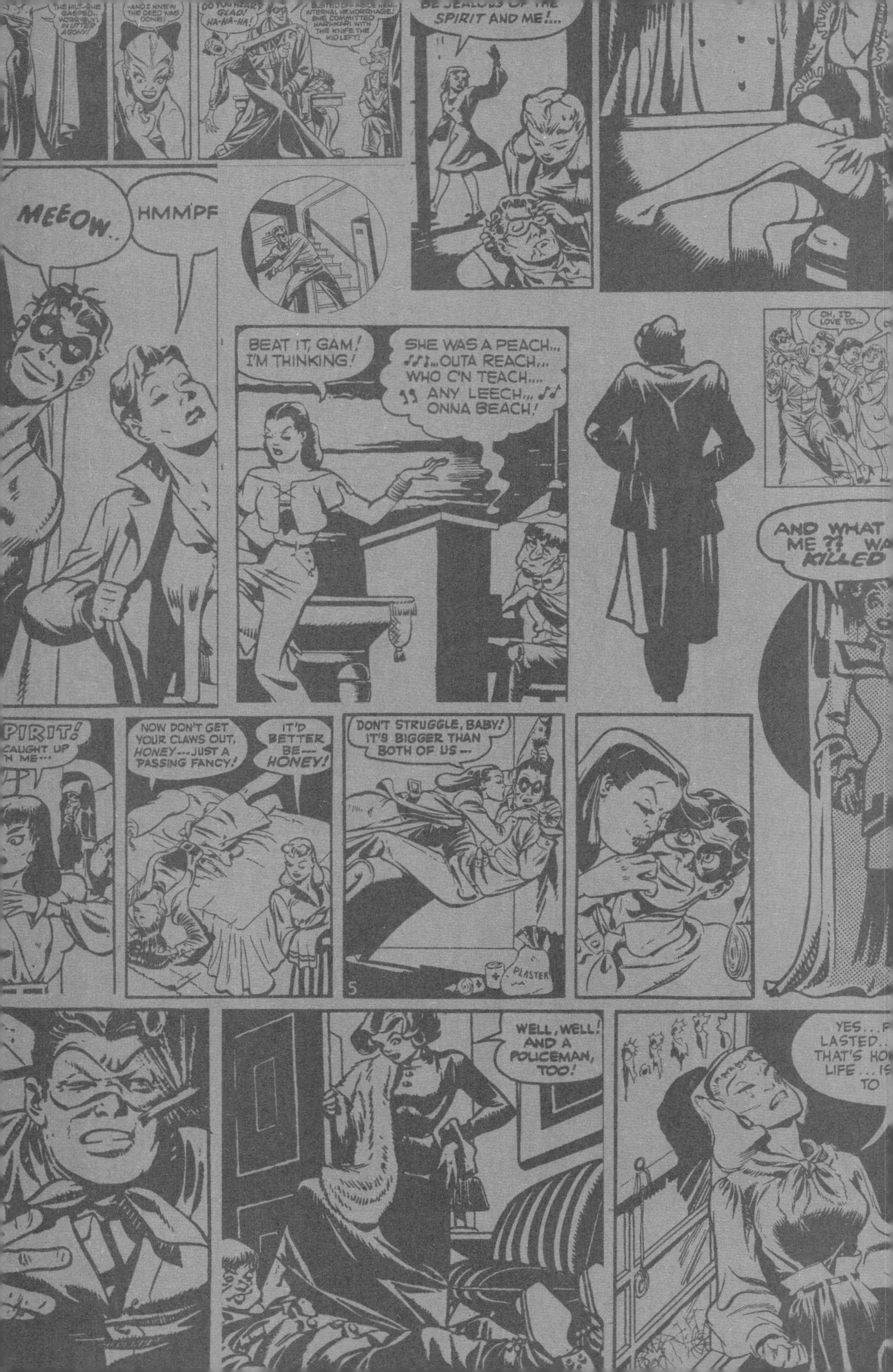
THE HILT-SHE GASPED.. HORRIBLY IN UTTER AGONY!
-AND I KNEW THE DEED WAS DONE!
GLAD! HA-HA-HA!
INTERNAL HEMORRHAGE! SHE COMMITTED HARI-KARI WITH THE KNIFE THE KID LEFT!
SPIRIT AND ME!...
MEEOW..
HMMPF
BEAT IT, GAM! I'M THINKING!
SHE WAS A PEACH... OUTA REACH... WHO C'N TEACH.... ANY LEECH... ONNA BEACH!
OH, I'D LOVE TO...
AND WHAT
ME ?? WA
KILLED
PIRIT!
CAUGHT UP
H ME...
NOW DON'T GET YOUR CLAWS OUT, HONEY--- JUST A PASSING FANCY!
IT'D BETTER BE--- HONEY!
DON'T STRUGGLE, BABY! IT'S BIGGER THAN BOTH OF US--
PLASTER
WELL, WELL! AND A POLICEMAN, TOO!
YES...
LASTED...
THAT'S HO
LIFE ... IS
TO

COMIC BOOK SECTION

MEET P'GELL

ACTION Mystery ADVENTURE

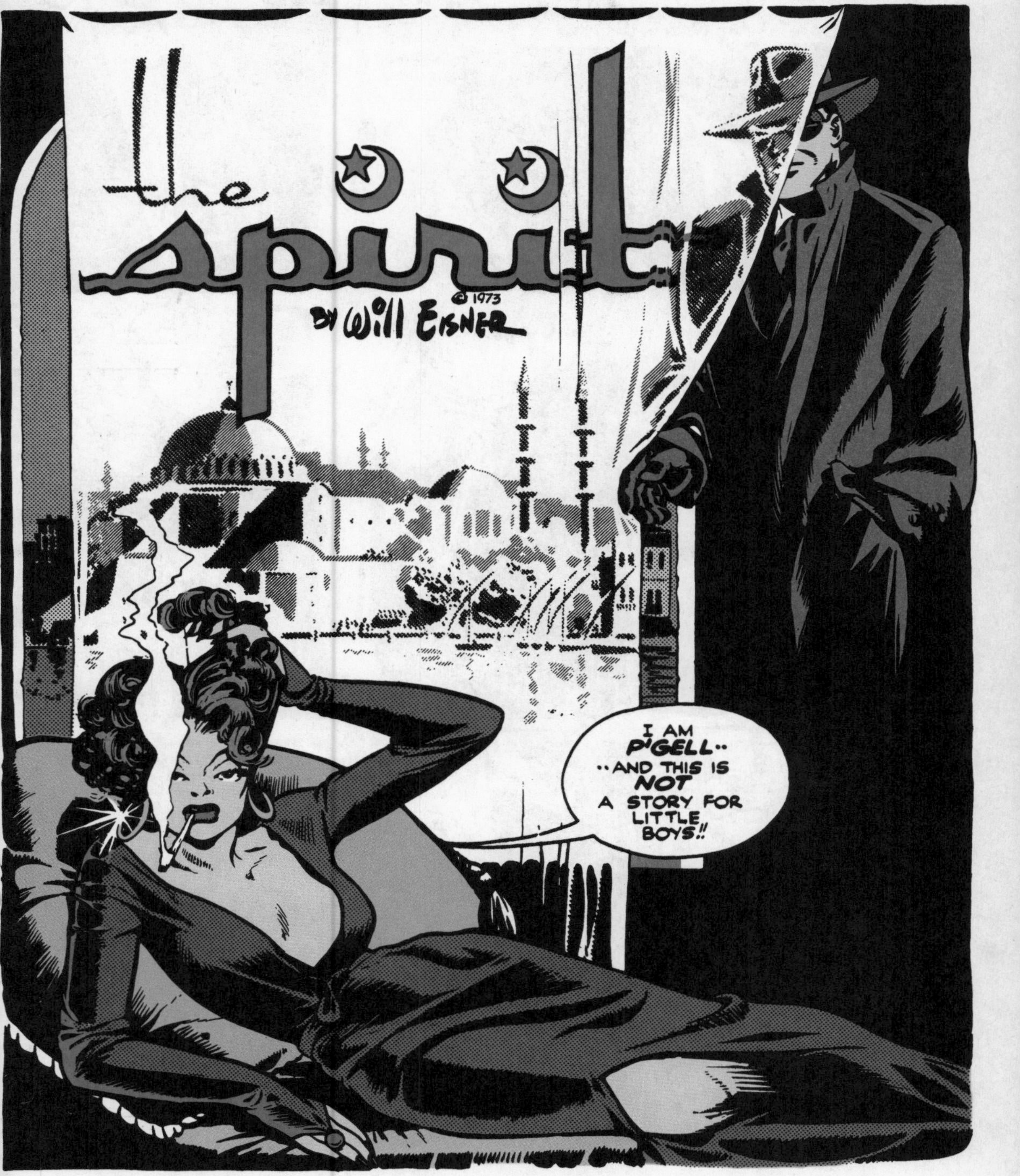
the spirit
© 1973
BY Will Eisner
I AM P'GELL.. ..AND THIS IS NOT A STORY FOR LITTLE BOYS!!

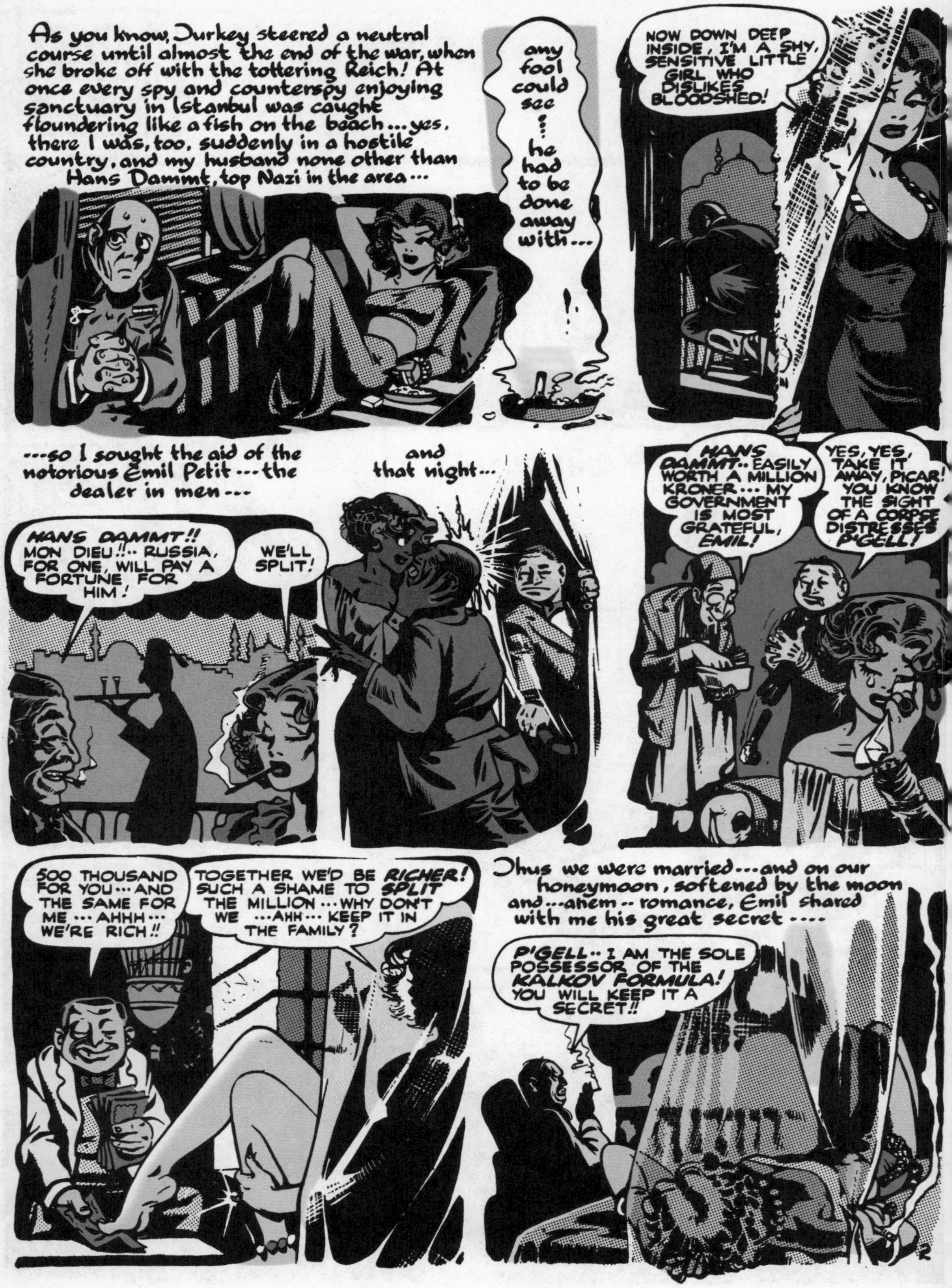
As you know, Turkey steered a neutral course until almost the end of the war, when she broke off with the tottering Reich! At once every spy and counterspy enjoying sanctuary in Istanbul was caught floundering like a fish on the beach ... yes, there I was, too, suddenly in a hostile country, and my husband none other than Hans Dammt, top Nazi in the area ...
any fool could see ... he had to be done away with ...
NOW DOWN DEEP INSIDE, I'M A SHY, SENSITIVE LITTLE GIRL WHO DISLIKES BLOODSHED!
... so I sought the aid of the notorious Emil Petit ... the dealer in men ...
HANS DAMMT!! MON DIEU!! .. RUSSIA, FOR ONE, WILL PAY A FORTUNE FOR HIM!
WE'LL SPLIT!
and that night ...
HANS DAMMT .. EASILY WORTH A MILLION KRONER ... MY GOVERNMENT IS MOST GRATEFUL, EMIL!
YES, YES, TAKE IT AWAY, PICAR! YOU KNOW THE SIGHT OF A CORPSE DISTRESSES P'GELL!
500 THOUSAND FOR YOU ... AND THE SAME FOR ME ... AHHH!! WE'RE RICH!!
TOGETHER WE'D BE RICHER! SUCH A SHAME TO SPLIT THE MILLION ... WHY DON'T WE ... AHH ... KEEP IT IN THE FAMILY?
Thus we were married ... and on our honeymoon, softened by the moon and ... ahem .. romance, Emil shared with me his great secret ....
P'GELL .. I AM THE SOLE POSSESSOR OF THE KALKOV FORMULA! YOU WILL KEEP IT A SECRET!!

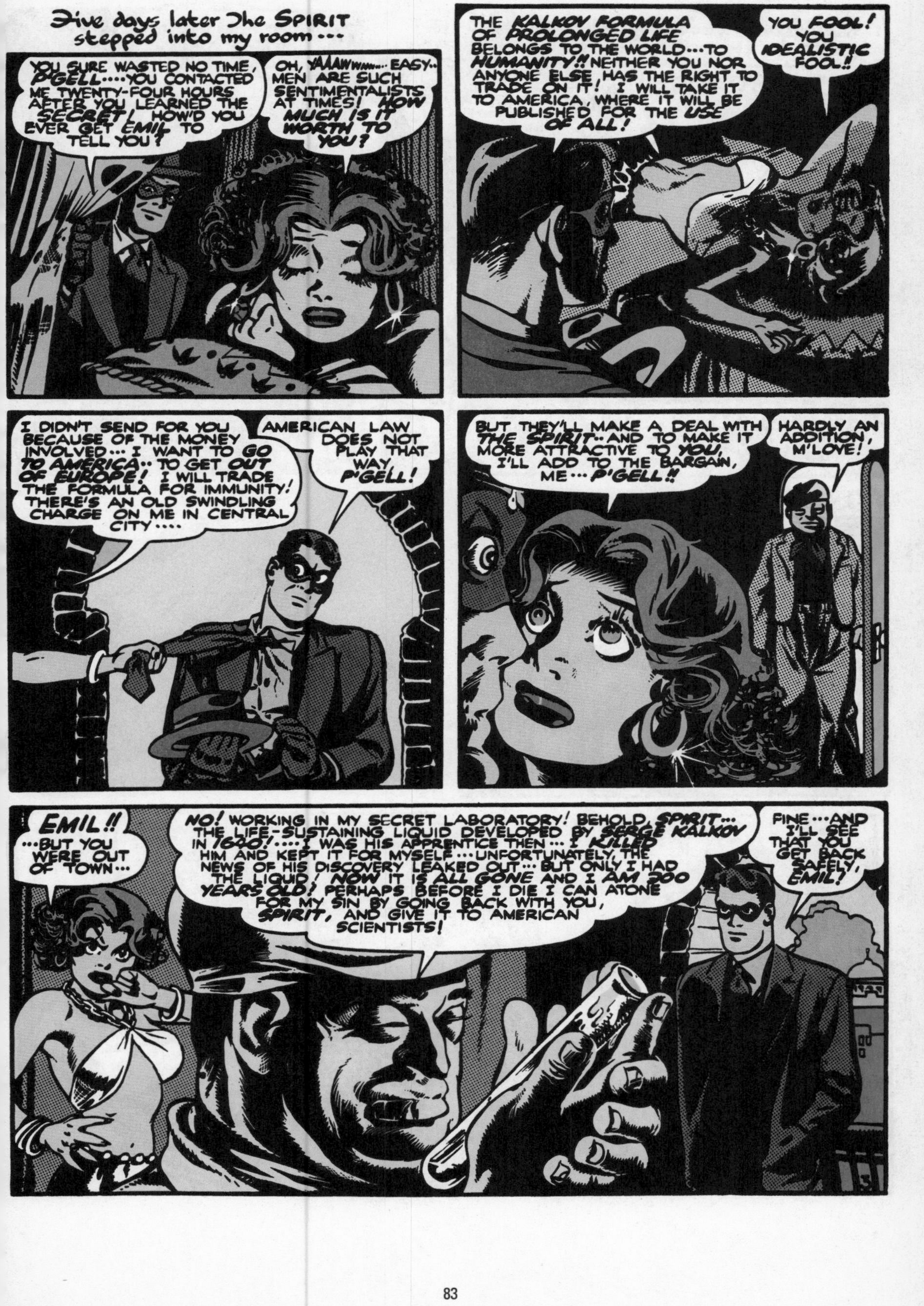
Five days later The Spirit stepped into my room...
YOU SURE WASTED NO TIME, P'GELL.... YOU CONTACTED ME TWENTY-FOUR HOURS AFTER YOU LEARNED THE SECRET! HOW'D YOU EVER GET EMIL TO TELL YOU?
OH, YAAAWWW.... EASY.. MEN ARE SUCH SENTIMENTALISTS AT TIMES! HOW MUCH IS IT WORTH TO YOU?
THE KALKOV FORMULA OF PROLONGED LIFE BELONGS TO THE WORLD... TO HUMANITY!! NEITHER YOU NOR ANYONE ELSE HAS THE RIGHT TO TRADE ON IT! I WILL TAKE IT TO AMERICA, WHERE IT WILL BE PUBLISHED FOR THE USE OF ALL!
YOU FOOL! YOU IDEALISTIC FOOL!!
I DIDN'T SEND FOR YOU BECAUSE OF THE MONEY INVOLVED... I WANT TO GO TO AMERICA.. TO GET OUT OF EUROPE! I WILL TRADE THE FORMULA FOR IMMUNITY! THERE'S AN OLD SWINDLING CHARGE ON ME IN CENTRAL CITY....
AMERICAN LAW DOES NOT PLAY THAT WAY P'GELL!
BUT THEY'LL MAKE A DEAL WITH THE SPIRIT.. AND TO MAKE IT MORE ATTRACTIVE TO YOU, I'LL ADD TO THE BARGAIN, ME... P'GELL!!
HARDLY AN ADDITION, M'LOVE!
EMIL!! ...BUT YOU WERE OUT OF TOWN...
NO! WORKING IN MY SECRET LABORATORY! BEHOLD, SPIRIT... THE LIFE-SUSTAINING LIQUID DEVELOPED BY SERGE KALKOV IN 1640!.... I WAS HIS APPRENTICE THEN... I KILLED HIM AND KEPT IT FOR MYSELF... UNFORTUNATELY, THE NEWS OF HIS DISCOVERY LEAKED OUT... BUT ONLY I HAD THE LIQUID! NOW IT IS ALL GONE AND I AM 300 YEARS OLD! PERHAPS BEFORE I DIE I CAN ATONE FOR MY SIN BY GOING BACK WITH YOU, SPIRIT, AND GIVE IT TO AMERICAN SCIENTISTS!
FINE... AND I'LL SEE THAT YOU GET BACK SAFELY, EMIL!

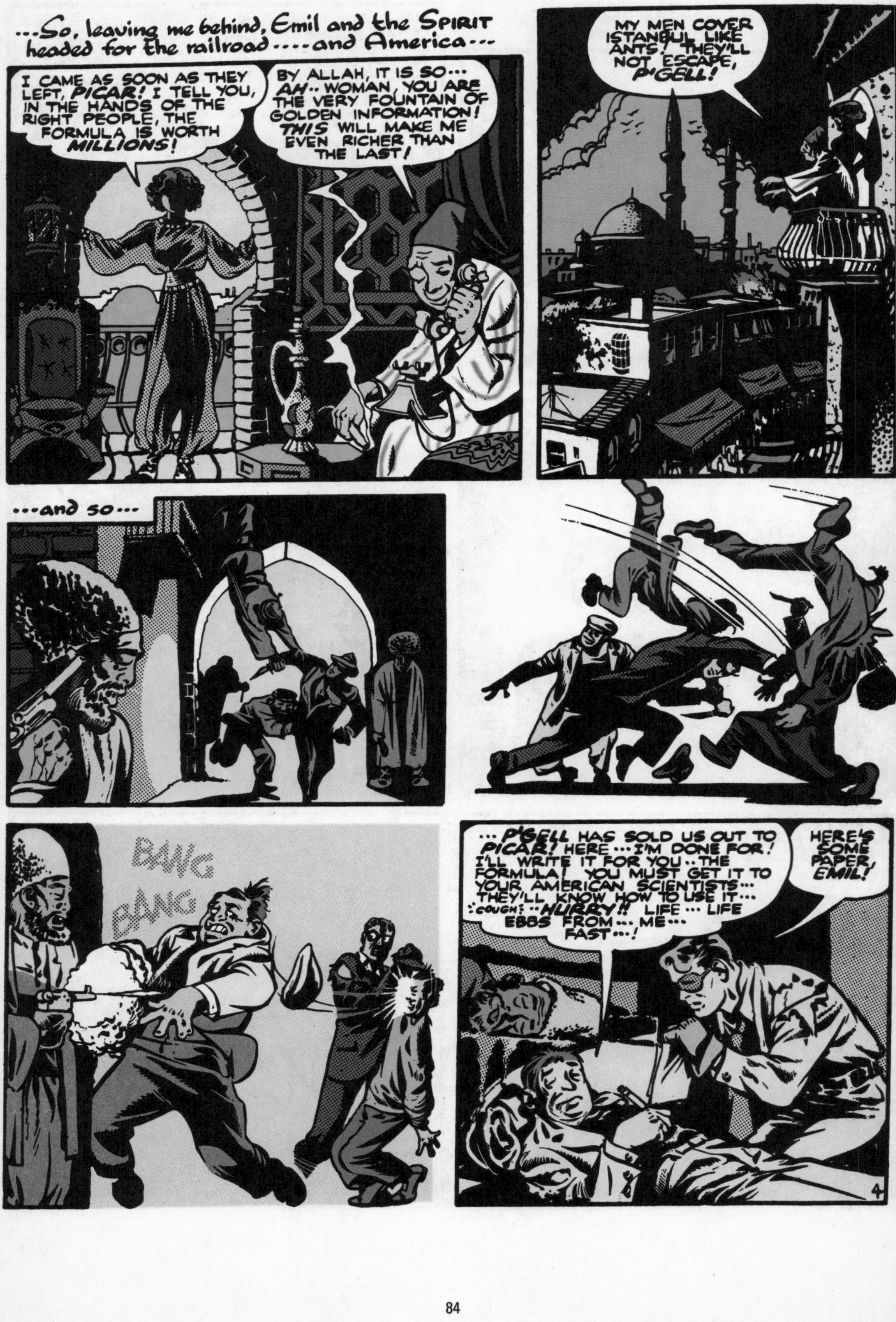
...So, leaving me behind, Emil and the SPIRIT headed for the railroad ....and America...
I CAME AS SOON AS THEY LEFT, PICAR! I TELL YOU, IN THE HANDS OF THE RIGHT PEOPLE, THE FORMULA IS WORTH MILLIONS!
BY ALLAH, IT IS SO... AH.. WOMAN, YOU ARE THE VERY FOUNTAIN OF GOLDEN INFORMATION! THIS WILL MAKE ME EVEN RICHER THAN THE LAST!
MY MEN COVER ISTANBUL LIKE ANTS! THEY'LL NOT ESCAPE, P'GELL!
...and so...
BANG
BANG
... P'GELL HAS SOLD US OUT TO PICAR! HERE ... I'M DONE FOR! I'LL WRITE IT FOR YOU .. THE FORMULA! YOU MUST GET IT TO YOUR AMERICAN SCIENTISTS... THEY'LL KNOW HOW TO USE IT... :COUGH: .. HURRY!! LIFE ... LIFE EBBS FROM... ME... FAST...!
HERE'S SOME PAPER, EMIL!
4

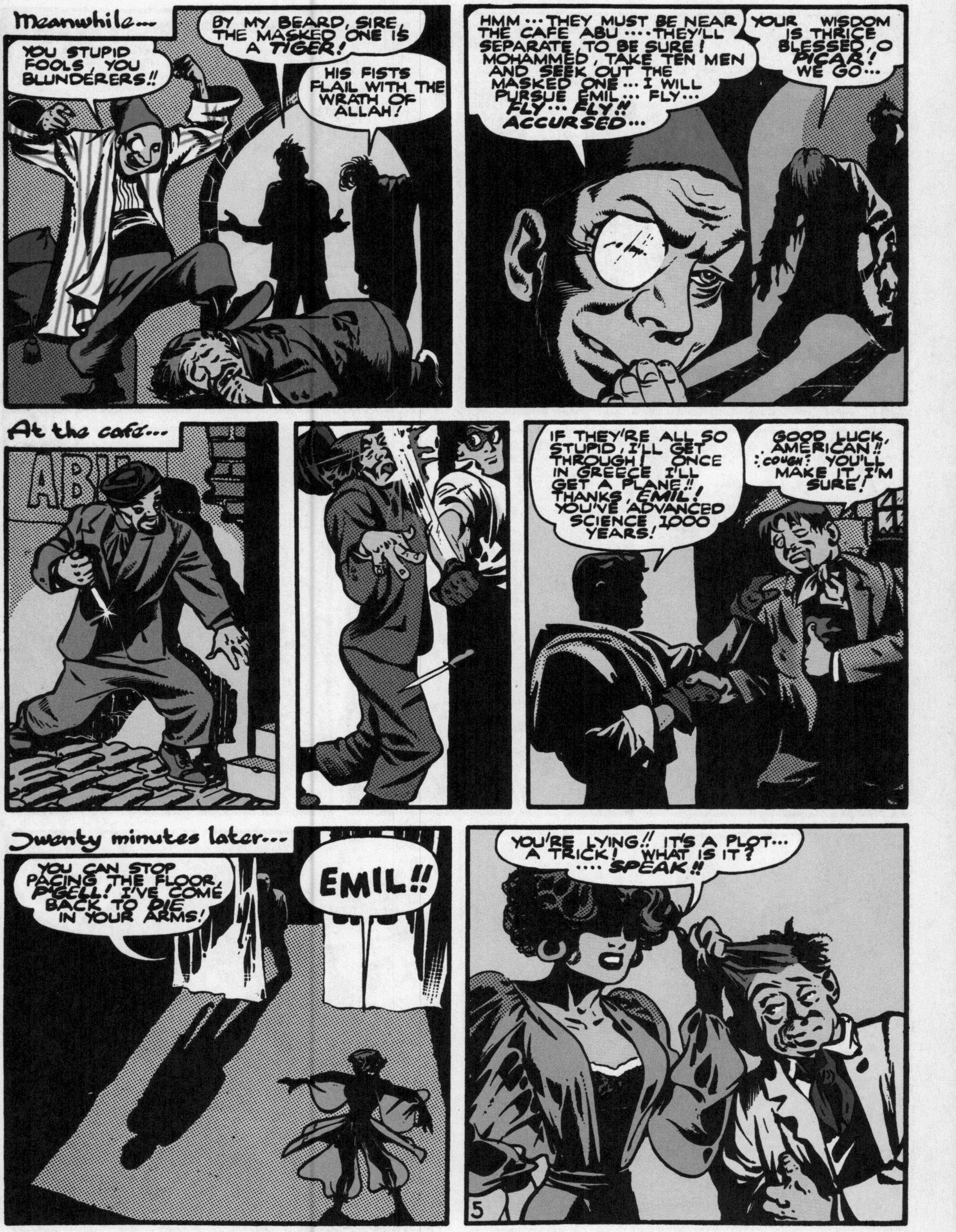
Meanwhile...
YOU STUPID FOOLS, YOU BLUNDERERS!!
BY MY BEARD, SIRE, THE MASKED ONE IS A TIGER!
HIS FISTS FLAIL WITH THE WRATH OF ALLAH!
HMM ... THEY MUST BE NEAR THE CAFE ABU .... THEY'LL SEPARATE, TO BE SURE! MOHAMMED, TAKE TEN MEN AND SEEK OUT THE MASKED ONE ... I WILL PURSUE EMIL ... FLY ... FLY ... FLY!! ACCURSED ...
YOUR WISDOM IS THRICE BLESSED, O PICAR! WE GO ...
At the cafe...
IF THEY'RE ALL SO STUPID, I'LL GET THROUGH! ONCE IN GREECE I'LL GET A PLANE!! THANKS, EMIL! YOU'VE ADVANCED SCIENCE 1000 YEARS!
GOOD LUCK, AMERICAN!! :COUGH: YOU'LL MAKE IT, I'M SURE!
Twenty minutes later...
YOU CAN STOP PACING THE FLOOR, PIGELL! I'VE COME BACK TO DIE IN YOUR ARMS!
EMIL!!
YOU'RE LYING!! IT'S A PLOT... A TRICK! WHAT IS IT? .... SPEAK!!
5

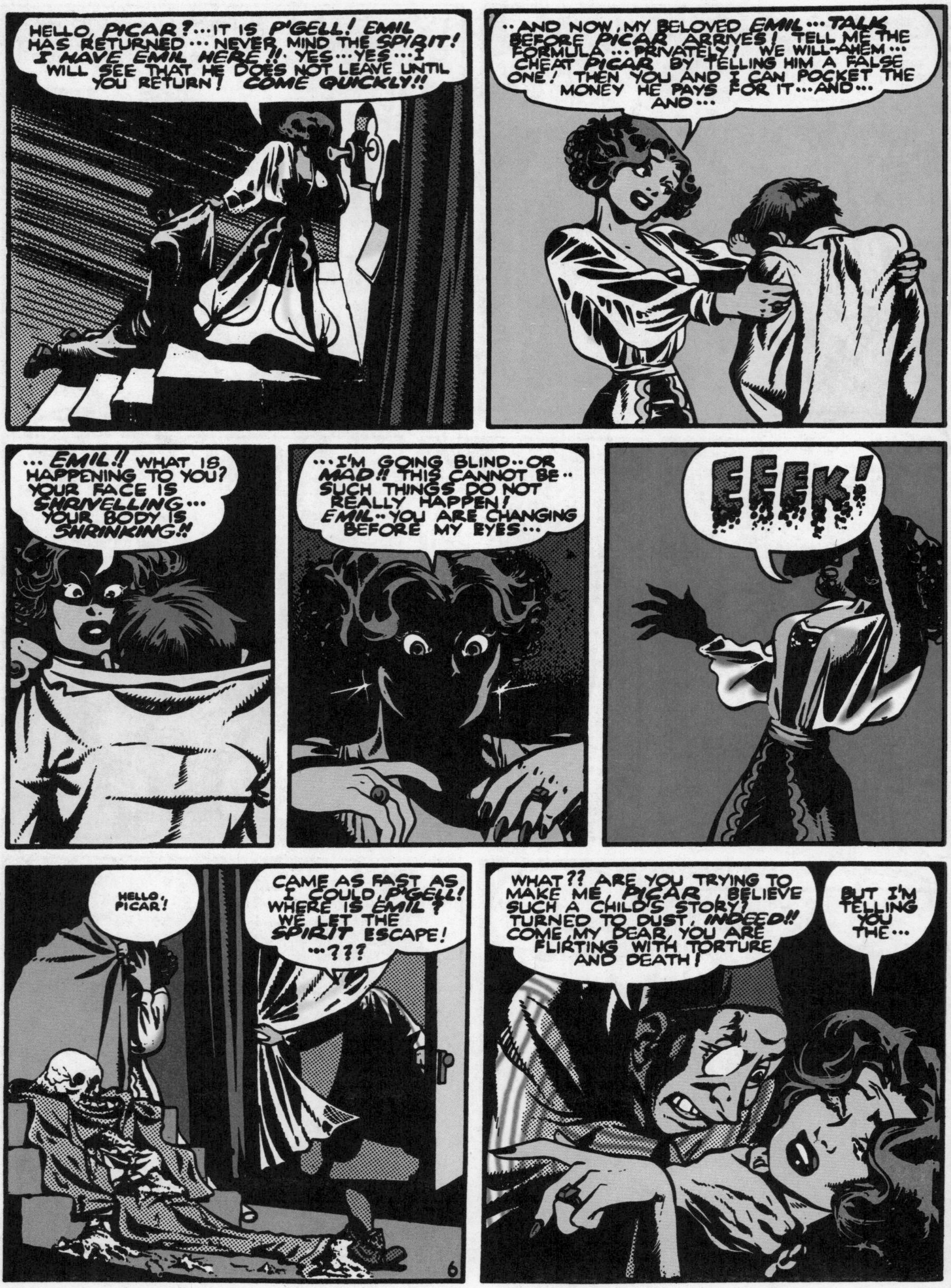
HELLO, PICAR?...IT IS P'GELL! EMIL HAS RETURNED... NEVER MIND THE SPIRIT! I HAVE EMIL HERE!! YES...YES...I WILL SEE THAT HE DOES NOT LEAVE UNTIL YOU RETURN! COME QUICKLY!!
..AND NOW, MY BELOVED EMIL...TALK BEFORE PICAR ARRIVES! TELL ME THE FORMULA... PRIVATELY! WE WILL-AHEM... CHEAT PICAR BY TELLING HIM A FALSE ONE! THEN YOU AND I CAN POCKET THE MONEY HE PAYS FOR IT...AND... AND...
...EMIL!! WHAT IS HAPPENING TO YOU? YOUR FACE IS SHRIVELLING... YOUR BODY IS SHRINKING!!
...I'M GOING BLIND..OR MAD!! THIS CANNOT BE.. SUCH THINGS DO NOT REALLY HAPPEN! EMIL..YOU ARE CHANGING BEFORE MY EYES...
EEEK!
HELLO, PICAR!
CAME AS FAST AS I COULD, P'GELL! WHERE IS EMIL? WE LET THE SPIRIT ESCAPE! ...???
6
WHAT?? ARE YOU TRYING TO MAKE ME, PICAR, BELIEVE SUCH A CHILD'S STORY! TURNED TO DUST, INDEED!! COME MY DEAR, YOU ARE FLIRTING WITH TORTURE AND DEATH!
BUT I'M TELLING YOU THE...

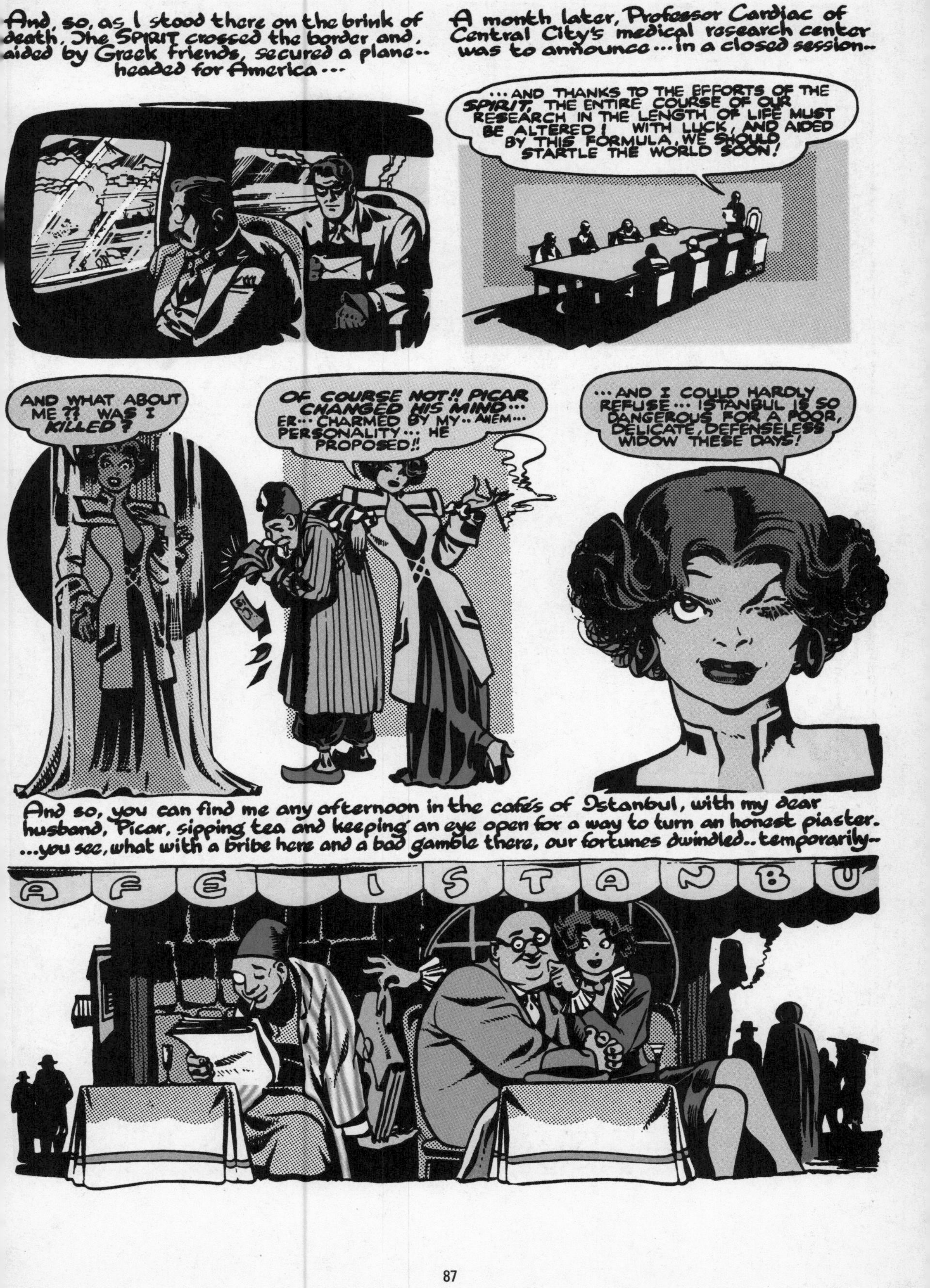
And, so, as I stood there on the brink of death, The SPIRIT crossed the border and, aided by Greek friends, secured a plane.. headed for America...
A month later, Professor Cardiac of Central City's medical research center was to announce... in a closed session..
...AND THANKS TO THE EFFORTS OF THE SPIRIT, THE ENTIRE COURSE OF OUR RESEARCH IN THE LENGTH OF LIFE MUST BE ALTERED! WITH LUCK, AND AIDED BY THIS FORMULA, WE SHOULD STARTLE THE WORLD SOON!
AND WHAT ABOUT ME?? WAS I KILLED?
OF COURSE NOT!! PICAR CHANGED HIS MIND... ER... CHARMED BY MY.. AHEM... PERSONALITY... HE PROPOSED!!
...AND I COULD HARDLY REFUSE... ISTANBUL IS SO DANGEROUS FOR A POOR, DELICATE, DEFENSELESS WIDOW THESE DAYS!
And so, you can find me any afternoon in the cafés of Istanbul, with my dear husband, Picar, sipping tea and keeping an eye open for a way to turn an honest piaster. ...you see, what with a bribe here and a bad gamble there, our fortunes dwindled.. temporarily..
AFE ISTANBU

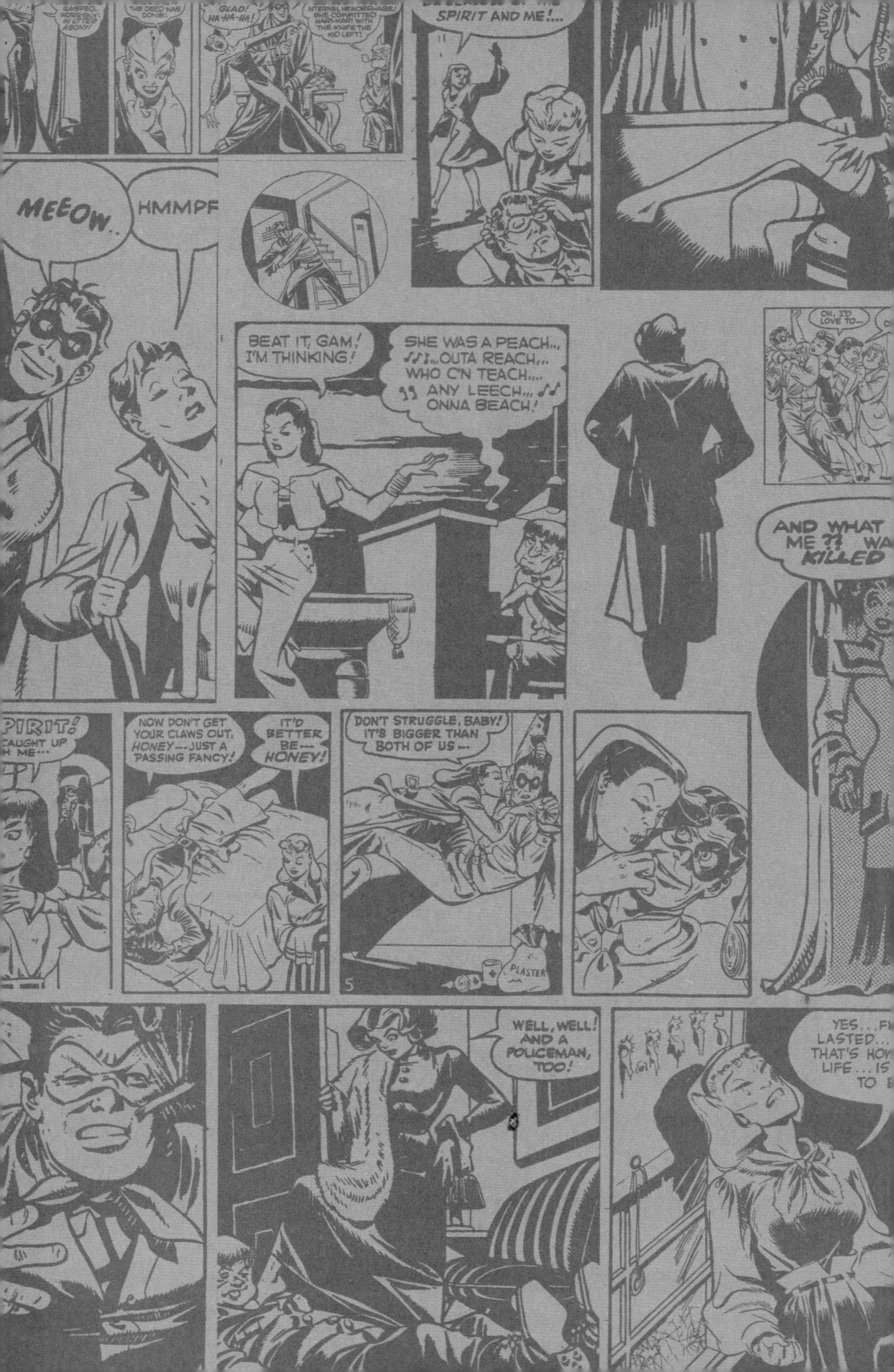
GASPED... HORRIBLY IN UTTER AGONY!
THE DEED WAS DONE!
GLAD! HA-HA-HA!
INTERNAL HEMORRHAGE! SHE COMMITTED HARI-KARI WITH THE KNIFE THE KID LEFT!
SPIRIT AND ME!...
MEEOW..
HMMPF
OH, I'D LOVE TO...
BEAT IT, GAM! I'M THINKING!
SHE WAS A PEACH... ♪♪♪...OUTA REACH... WHO C'N TEACH... ♪♪ ANY LEECH... ♪♪ ONNA BEACH!
AND WHAT ME ?? WA KILLED
SPIRIT! CAUGHT UP H ME...
NOW DON'T GET YOUR CLAWS OUT, HONEY---JUST A PASSING FANCY!
IT'D BETTER BE--- HONEY!
DON'T STRUGGLE, BABY! IT'S BIGGER THAN BOTH OF US --
5
PLASTER
WELL, WELL! AND A POLICEMAN, TOO!
YES... F LASTED... THAT'S HO LIFE... IS TO

COMIC BOOK SECTION

CARAMBA!

ACTION Mystery ADVENTURE

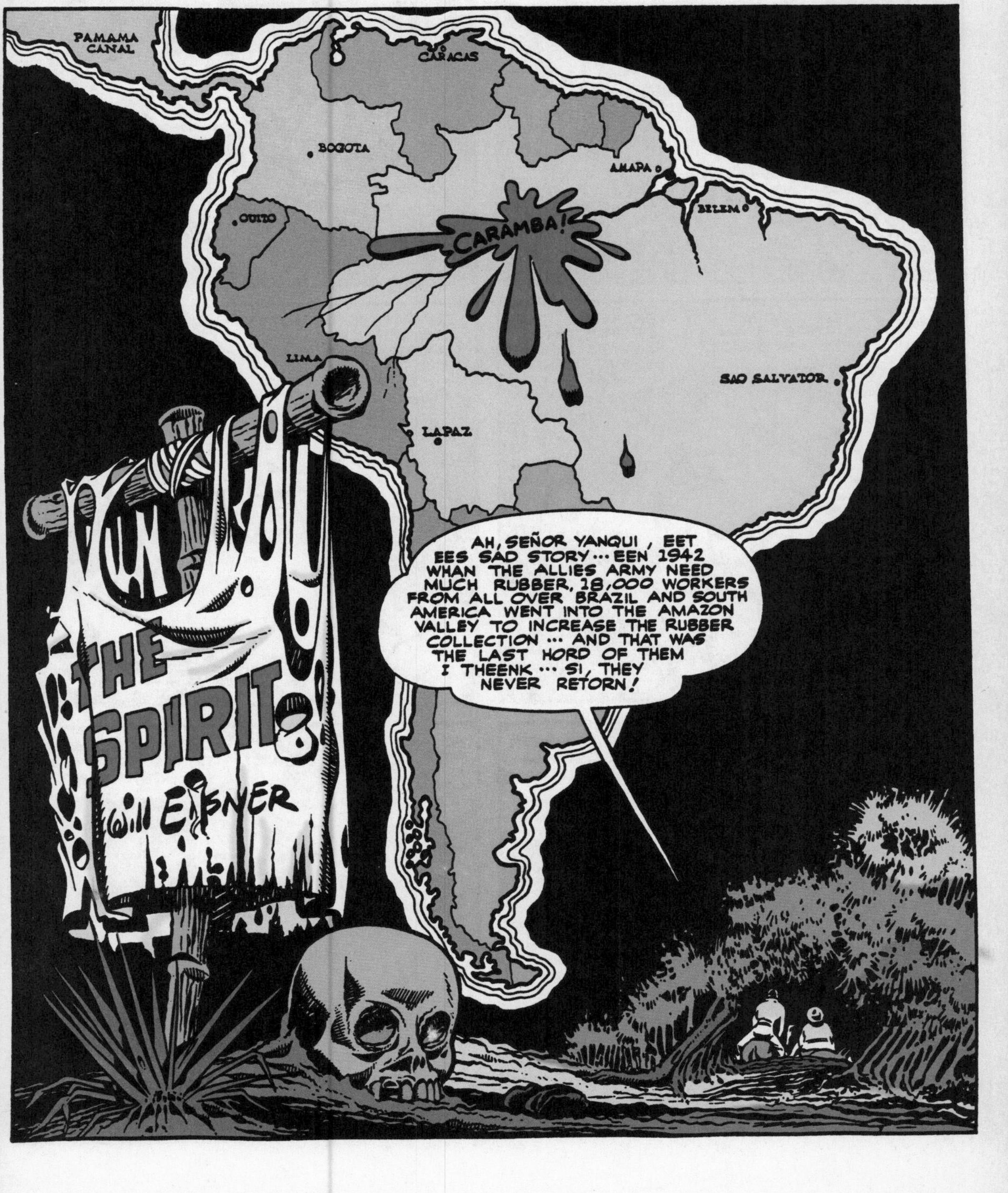

PAMAMA CANAL
CARACAS
BOGOTA
AMAPA
BELEM
QUITO
CARAMBA!
LIMA
SAO SALVATOR
LAPAZ
THE SPIRIT
Will Eisner
AH, SEÑOR YANQUI, EET EES SAD STORY... EEN 1942 WHAN THE ALLIES ARMY NEED MUCH RUBBER, 18,000 WORKERS FROM ALL OVER BRAZIL AND SOUTH AMERICA WENT INTO THE AMAZON VALLEY TO INCREASE THE RUBBER COLLECTION ... AND THAT WAS THE LAST HORD OF THEM I THEENK ... SI, THEY NEVER RETORN!

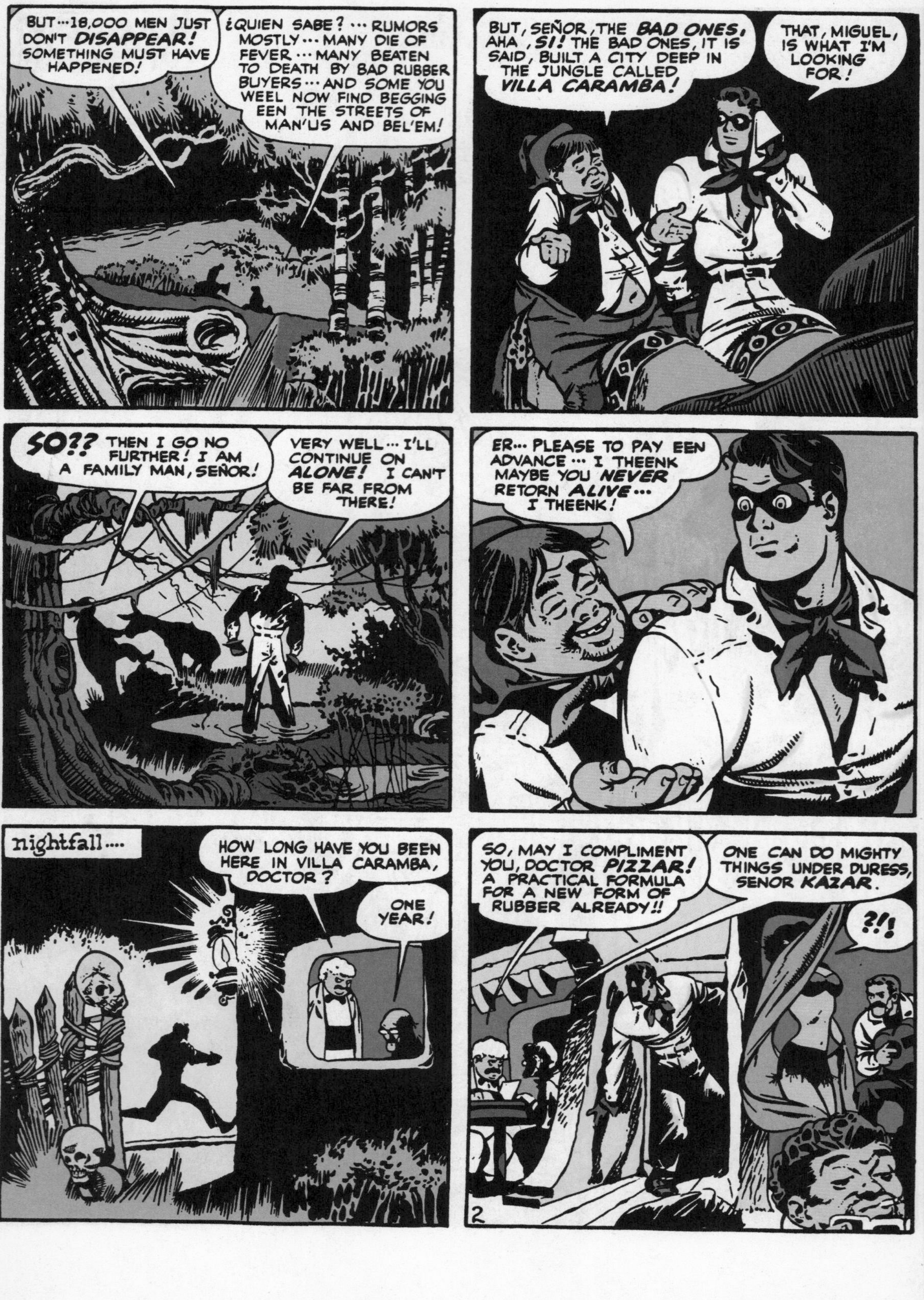

BUT···18,000 MEN JUST DON'T DISAPPEAR! SOMETHING MUST HAVE HAPPENED!
¿QUIEN SABE? ··· RUMORS MOSTLY··· MANY DIE OF FEVER··· MANY BEATEN TO DEATH BY BAD RUBBER BUYERS··· AND SOME YOU WEEL NOW FIND BEGGING EEN THE STREETS OF MAN'US AND BEL'EM!
BUT, SEÑOR, THE BAD ONES, AHA, SI! THE BAD ONES, IT IS SAID, BUILT A CITY DEEP IN THE JUNGLE CALLED VILLA CARAMBA!
THAT, MIGUEL, IS WHAT I'M LOOKING FOR!
SO?? THEN I GO NO FURTHER! I AM A FAMILY MAN, SEÑOR!
VERY WELL··· I'LL CONTINUE ON ALONE! I CAN'T BE FAR FROM THERE!
ER··· PLEASE TO PAY EEN ADVANCE··· I THEENK MAYBE YOU NEVER RETORN ALIVE··· I THEENK!
nightfall....
HOW LONG HAVE YOU BEEN HERE IN VILLA CARAMBA, DOCTOR?
ONE YEAR!
SO, MAY I COMPLIMENT YOU, DOCTOR PIZZAR! A PRACTICAL FORMULA FOR A NEW FORM OF RUBBER ALREADY!!
ONE CAN DO MIGHTY THINGS UNDER DURESS, SENOR KAZAR.
?!!
2

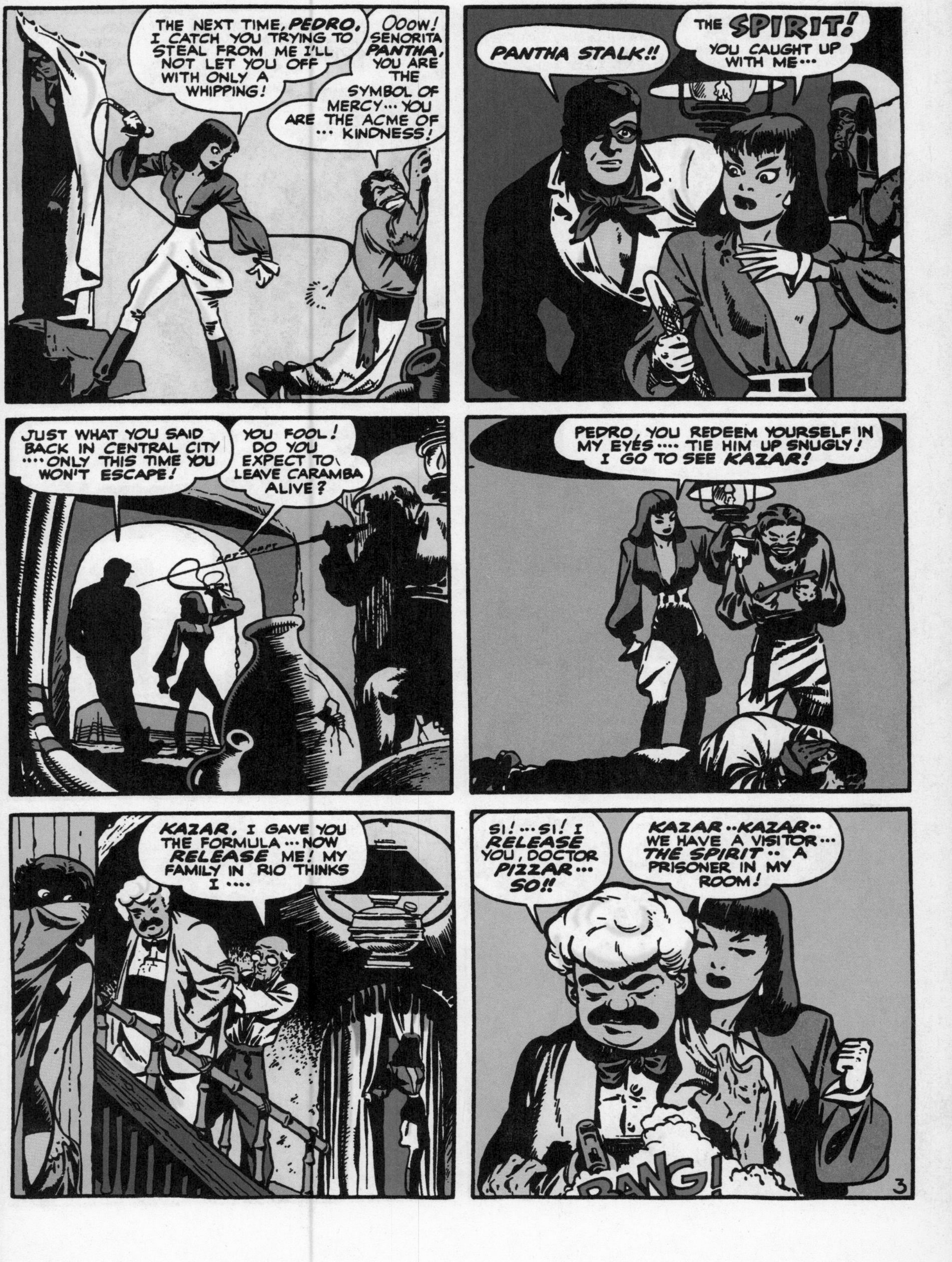
THE NEXT TIME, PEDRO, I CATCH YOU TRYING TO STEAL FROM ME I'LL NOT LET YOU OFF WITH ONLY A WHIPPING!
OOOW! SENORITA PANTHA, YOU ARE THE SYMBOL OF MERCY... YOU ARE THE ACME OF ... KINDNESS!
PANTHA STALK!!
THE SPIRIT! YOU CAUGHT UP WITH ME...
JUST WHAT YOU SAID BACK IN CENTRAL CITY ....ONLY THIS TIME YOU WON'T ESCAPE!
YOU FOOL! DO YOU EXPECT TO LEAVE CARAMBA ALIVE?
PEDRO, YOU REDEEM YOURSELF IN MY EYES.... TIE HIM UP SNUGLY! I GO TO SEE KAZAR!
KAZAR, I GAVE YOU THE FORMULA ... NOW RELEASE ME! MY FAMILY IN RIO THINKS I ....
SI! ...SI! I RELEASE YOU, DOCTOR PIZZAR... SO!!
KAZAR..KAZAR.. WE HAVE A VISITOR... THE SPIRIT.. A PRISONER IN MY ROOM!
BANG!
3

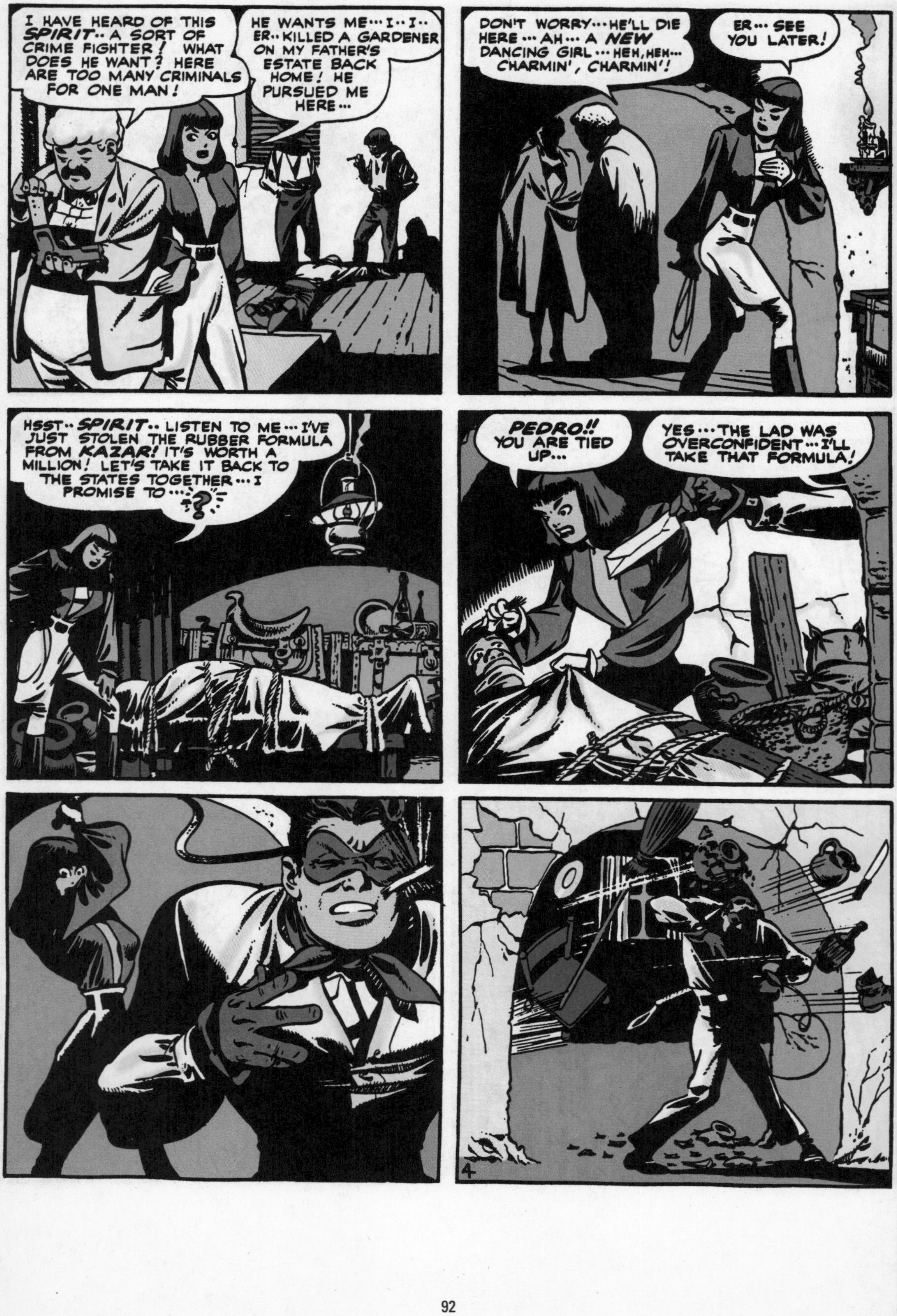
I HAVE HEARD OF THIS SPIRIT.. A SORT OF CRIME FIGHTER! WHAT DOES HE WANT? HERE ARE TOO MANY CRIMINALS FOR ONE MAN!
HE WANTS ME... I.. I.. ER.. KILLED A GARDENER ON MY FATHER'S ESTATE BACK HOME! HE PURSUED ME HERE...
DON'T WORRY... HE'LL DIE HERE... AH... A NEW DANCING GIRL... HEH, HEH... CHARMIN', CHARMIN'!
ER... SEE YOU LATER!
HSST.. SPIRIT.. LISTEN TO ME... I'VE JUST STOLEN THE RUBBER FORMULA FROM KAZAR! IT'S WORTH A MILLION! LET'S TAKE IT BACK TO THE STATES TOGETHER... I PROMISE TO...?
PEDRO!! YOU ARE TIED UP...
YES... THE LAD WAS OVERCONFIDENT... I'LL TAKE THAT FORMULA!
4

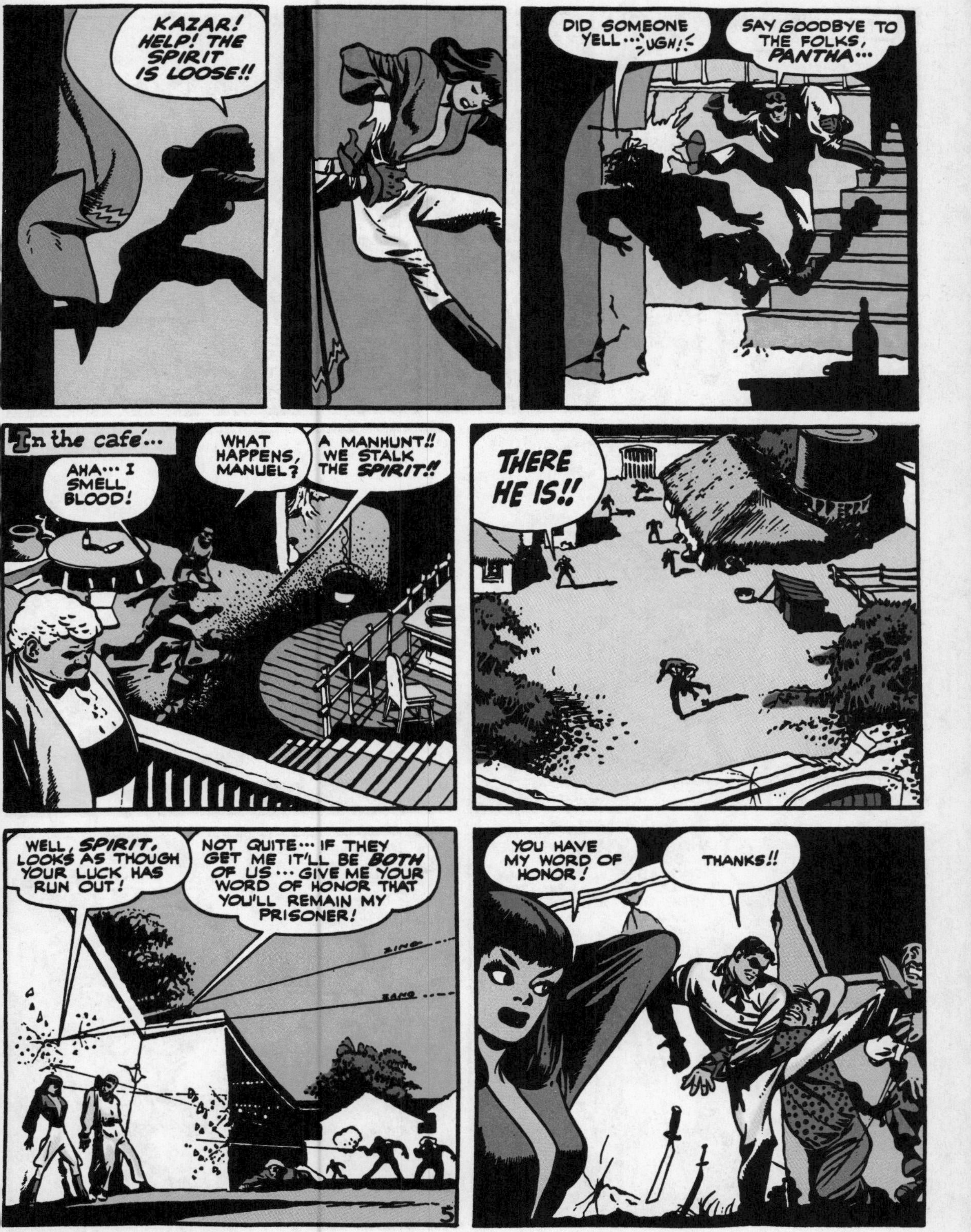
KAZAR! HELP! THE SPIRIT IS LOOSE!!
DID SOMEONE YELL... UGH!
SAY GOODBYE TO THE FOLKS, PANTHA...
In the café...
AHA... I SMELL BLOOD!
WHAT HAPPENS, MANUEL?
A MANHUNT!! WE STALK THE SPIRIT!!
THERE HE IS!!
WELL, SPIRIT, LOOKS AS THOUGH YOUR LUCK HAS RUN OUT!
NOT QUITE... IF THEY GET ME IT'LL BE BOTH OF US... GIVE ME YOUR WORD OF HONOR THAT YOU'LL REMAIN MY PRISONER!
ZING
ZANG
5
YOU HAVE MY WORD OF HONOR!
THANKS!!

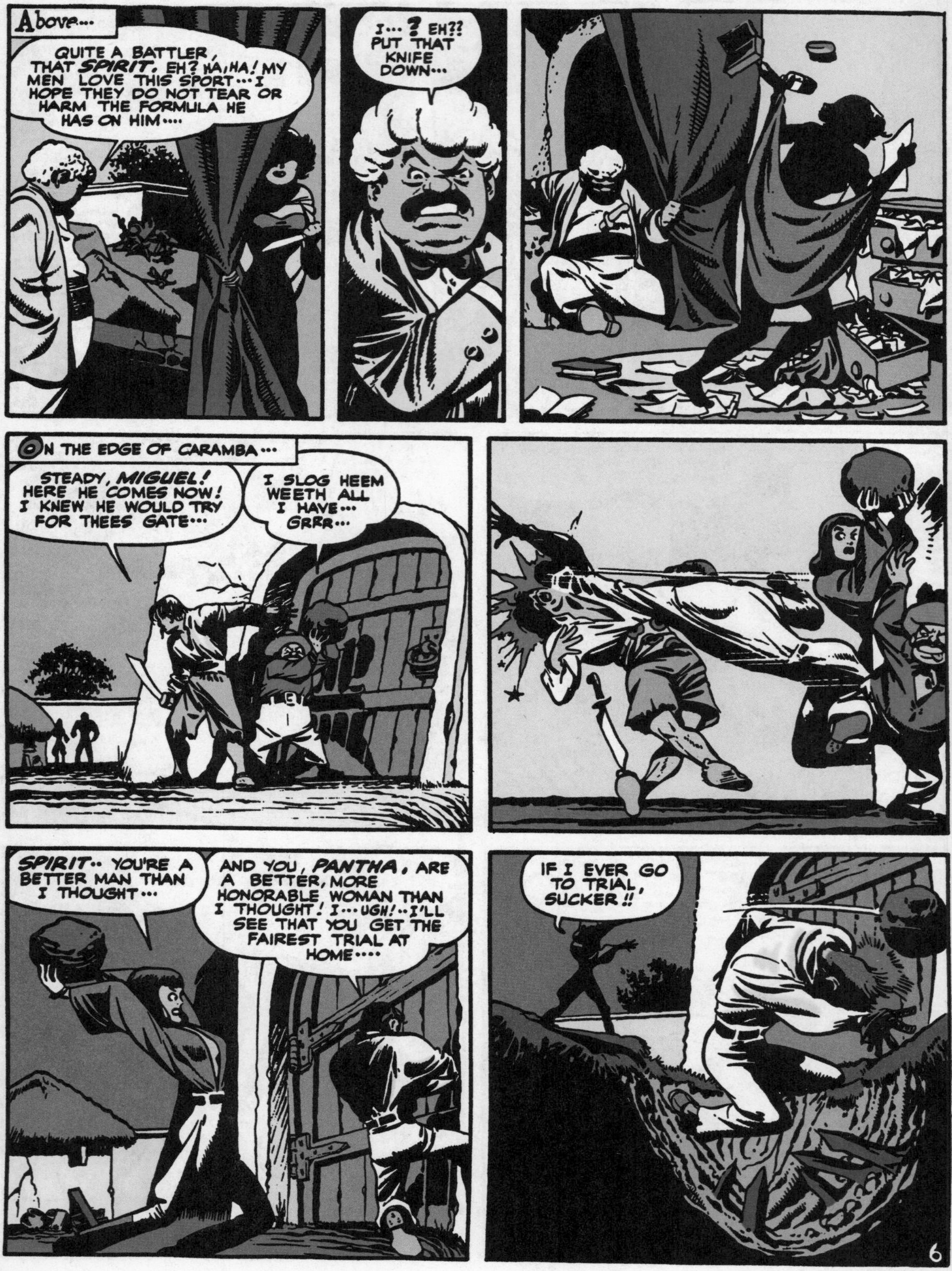

Above...
QUITE A BATTLER, THAT SPIRIT. EH? HA, HA! MY MEN LOVE THIS SPORT... I HOPE THEY DO NOT TEAR OR HARM THE FORMULA HE HAS ON HIM....
I... ? EH?? PUT THAT KNIFE DOWN...
ON THE EDGE OF CARAMBA...
STEADY, MIGUEL! HERE HE COMES NOW! I KNEW HE WOULD TRY FOR THEES GATE...
I SLOG HEEM WEETH ALL I HAVE... GRRR...
SPIRIT.. YOU'RE A BETTER MAN THAN I THOUGHT...
AND YOU, PANTHA, ARE A BETTER, MORE HONORABLE WOMAN THAN I THOUGHT! I... UGH!.. I'LL SEE THAT YOU GET THE FAIREST TRIAL AT HOME....
IF I EVER GO TO TRIAL, SUCKER!!
6

HOLD OFF, BOYS! I'VE GOT THE FORMULA... THE SPIRIT IS LYING AT THE BOTTOM OF THE COUGAR PIT....
THEN WE FEENISH HEEM... PRONTO!
STOP!
GIVE ME THAT FORMULA, PANTHA!
THE DANCING GORL.... @#!!@##!#!
BANG
BANG
P'GELL!! YOU HERE? COUGH! I'LL TAKE THAT FORMULA!
NO!! YOU MIGHT HAVE OUT-SMARTED ME IN ISTANBUL, BUT THIS TIME I'VE WORKED TOO HARD... I'VE SHOT THEM AND I'LL SHOOT YOU....
BESIDES YOU'RE IN BAD SHAPE... YOU OUTFOUGHT 50 MEN...
TSK...TSK! PASSED OUT...OH, BROTHER, WHAT A MAN!! IF ONLY YOU WERE A CROOK, WHAT A TEAM WE'D MAKE!
A WEEK LATER... RIO DE JANEIRO....
OOOOH... HOW DID I GET HERE??
HA.. THAT'S WHAT WE'D LIKE TO KNOW!
YOU WERE FOUND ON THE HOSPITAL STEPS THIS MORNING! YOU WERE SEEN WITH A LADY ABOUT DAWN!
WHO WAS THAT LADY THEY SAW YOU WITH LAST NIGHT?
OH, THAT WAS NO LADY... THAT WAS P'GELL!! YUK, YUK, YUK!!

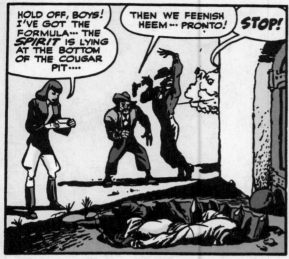

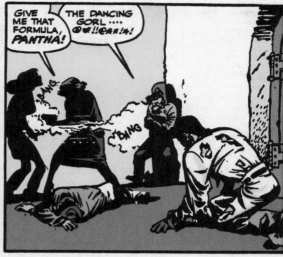

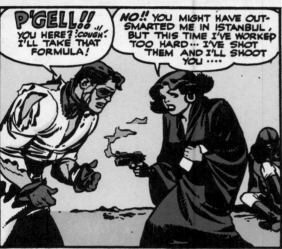

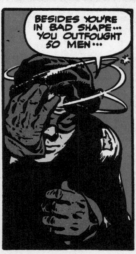

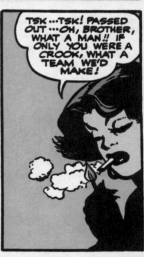

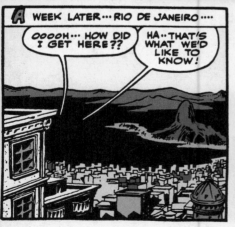

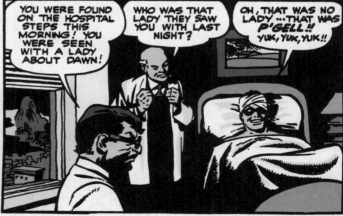

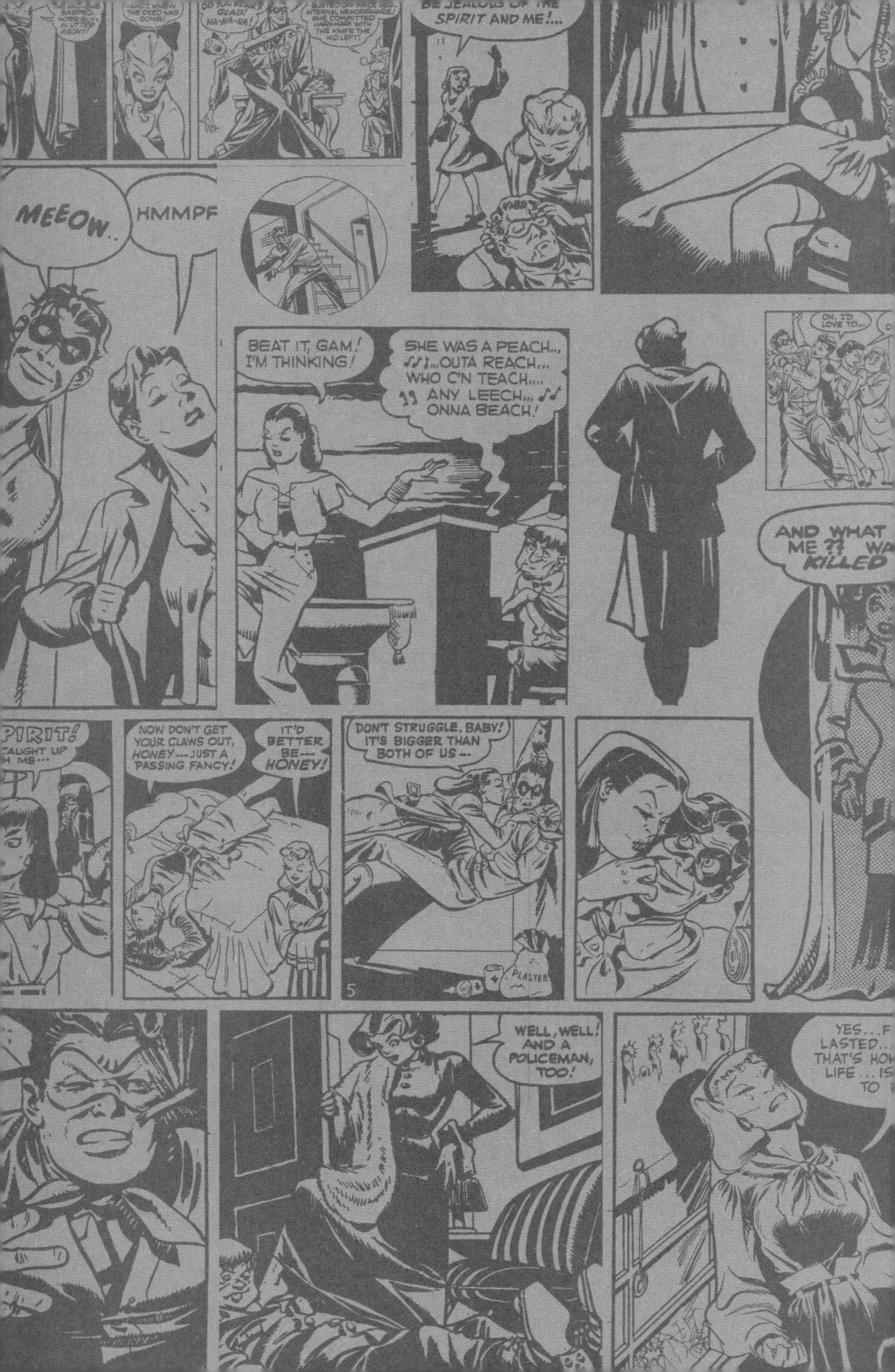
GASPED... HORRIBLY, IN UTTER AGONY!
—AND I KNEW THE DEED WAS DONE!
GLAD! HA-HA-HA!
INTERNAL HEMORRHAGE! SHE COMMITTED HARI-KARI WITH THE KNIFE THE KID LEFT!
SPIRIT AND ME!...
MEEOW..
HMMPF
BEAT IT, GAM! I'M THINKING!
SHE WAS A PEACH... ♪♪♪...OUTA REACH... WHO C'N TEACH.... ♪♪ ANY LEECH... ♪♪ ONNA BEACH!
OH, I'D LOVE TO...
NOW DON'T GET YOUR CLAWS OUT, HONEY --- JUST A PASSING FANCY!
IT'D BETTER BE--- HONEY!
DON'T STRUGGLE, BABY! IT'S BIGGER THAN BOTH OF US --
PLASTER
5
WELL, WELL! AND A POLICEMAN, TOO!

THE PORTIER FORTUNE

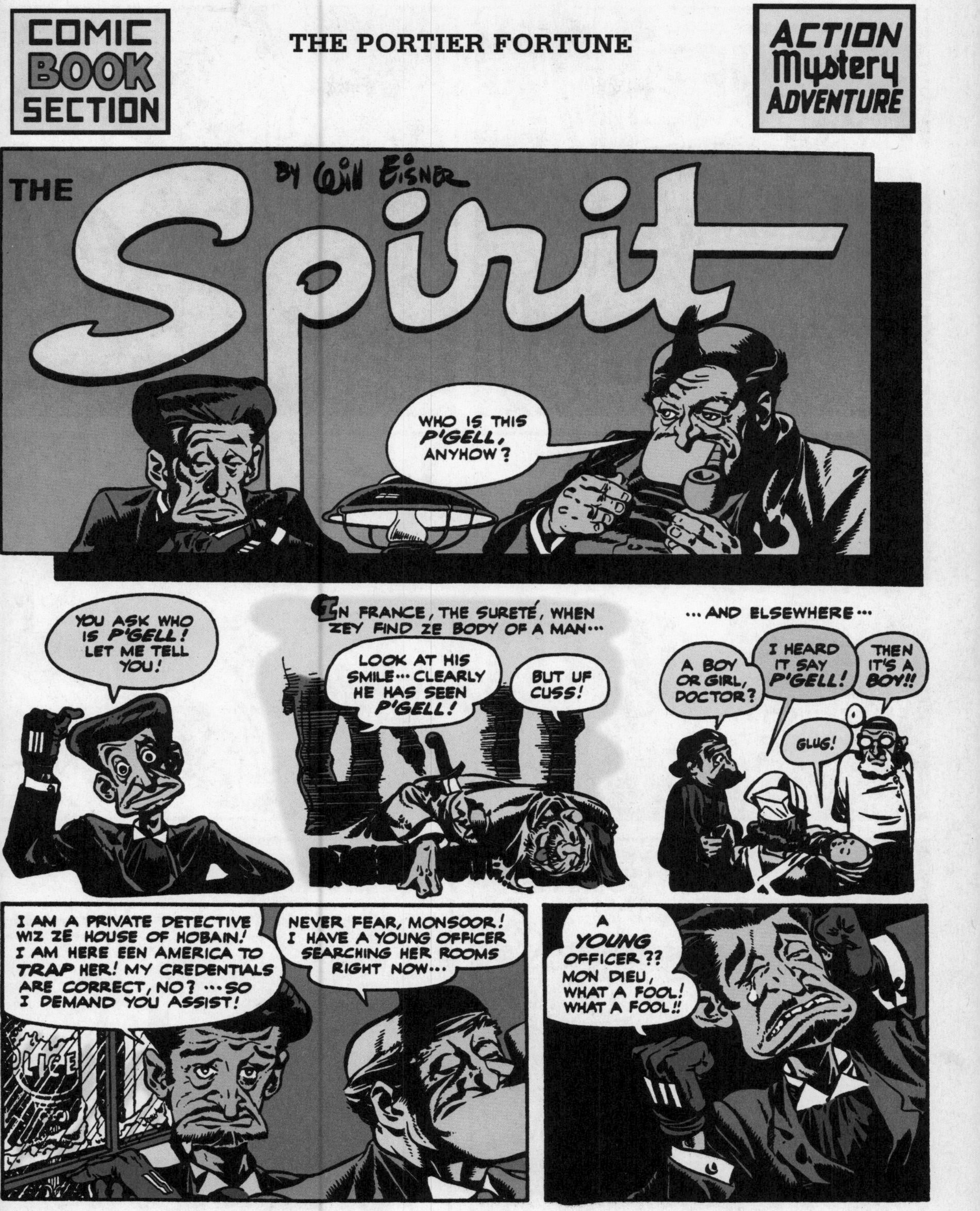
COMIC BOOK SECTION
ACTION Mystery ADVENTURE
THE Spirit
BY Will Eisner
WHO IS THIS P'GELL, ANYHOW?
YOU ASK WHO IS P'GELL! LET ME TELL YOU!
IN FRANCE, THE SURETÉ, WHEN ZEY FIND ZE BODY OF A MAN...
LOOK AT HIS SMILE... CLEARLY HE HAS SEEN P'GELL!
BUT UF CUSS!
...AND ELSEWHERE...
A BOY OR GIRL, DOCTOR?
I HEARD IT SAY P'GELL!
THEN IT'S A BOY!!
GLUG!
I AM A PRIVATE DETECTIVE WIZ ZE HOUSE OF HOBAIN! I AM HERE EEN AMERICA TO TRAP HER! MY CREDENTIALS ARE CORRECT, NO? ...SO I DEMAND YOU ASSIST!
NEVER FEAR, MONSOOR! I HAVE A YOUNG OFFICER SEARCHING HER ROOMS RIGHT NOW...
A YOUNG OFFICER?? MON DIEU, WHAT A FOOL! WHAT A FOOL!!

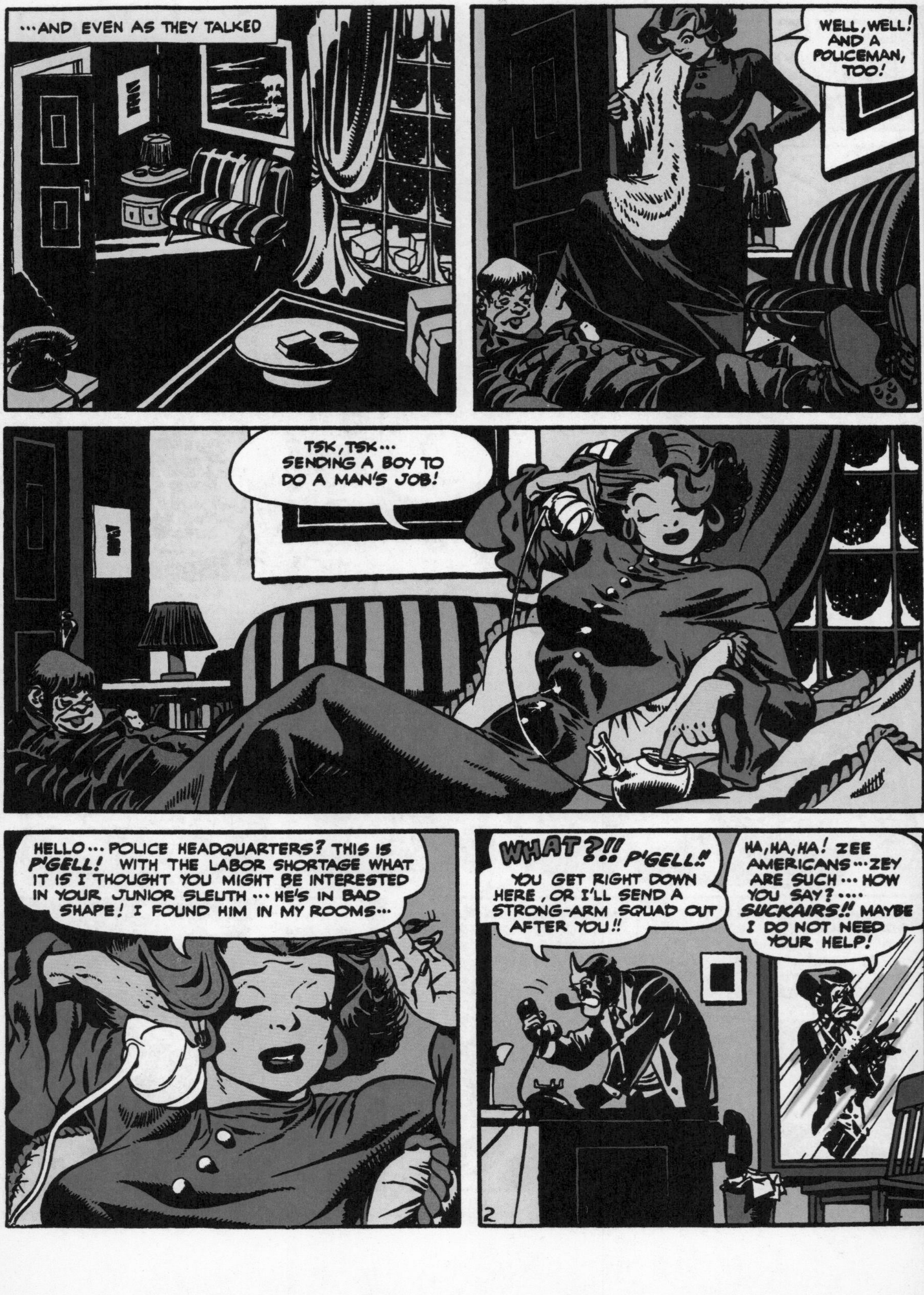
...AND EVEN AS THEY TALKED
WELL, WELL! AND A POLICEMAN, TOO!
TSK, TSK... SENDING A BOY TO DO A MAN'S JOB!
HELLO... POLICE HEADQUARTERS? THIS IS P'GELL! WITH THE LABOR SHORTAGE WHAT IT IS I THOUGHT YOU MIGHT BE INTERESTED IN YOUR JUNIOR SLEUTH... HE'S IN BAD SHAPE! I FOUND HIM IN MY ROOMS...
WHAT?!! P'GELL!! YOU GET RIGHT DOWN HERE, OR I'LL SEND A STRONG-ARM SQUAD OUT AFTER YOU!!
HA, HA, HA! ZEE AMERICANS... ZEY ARE SUCH... HOW YOU SAY?.... SUCKAIRS!! MAYBE I DO NOT NEED YOUR HELP!
2

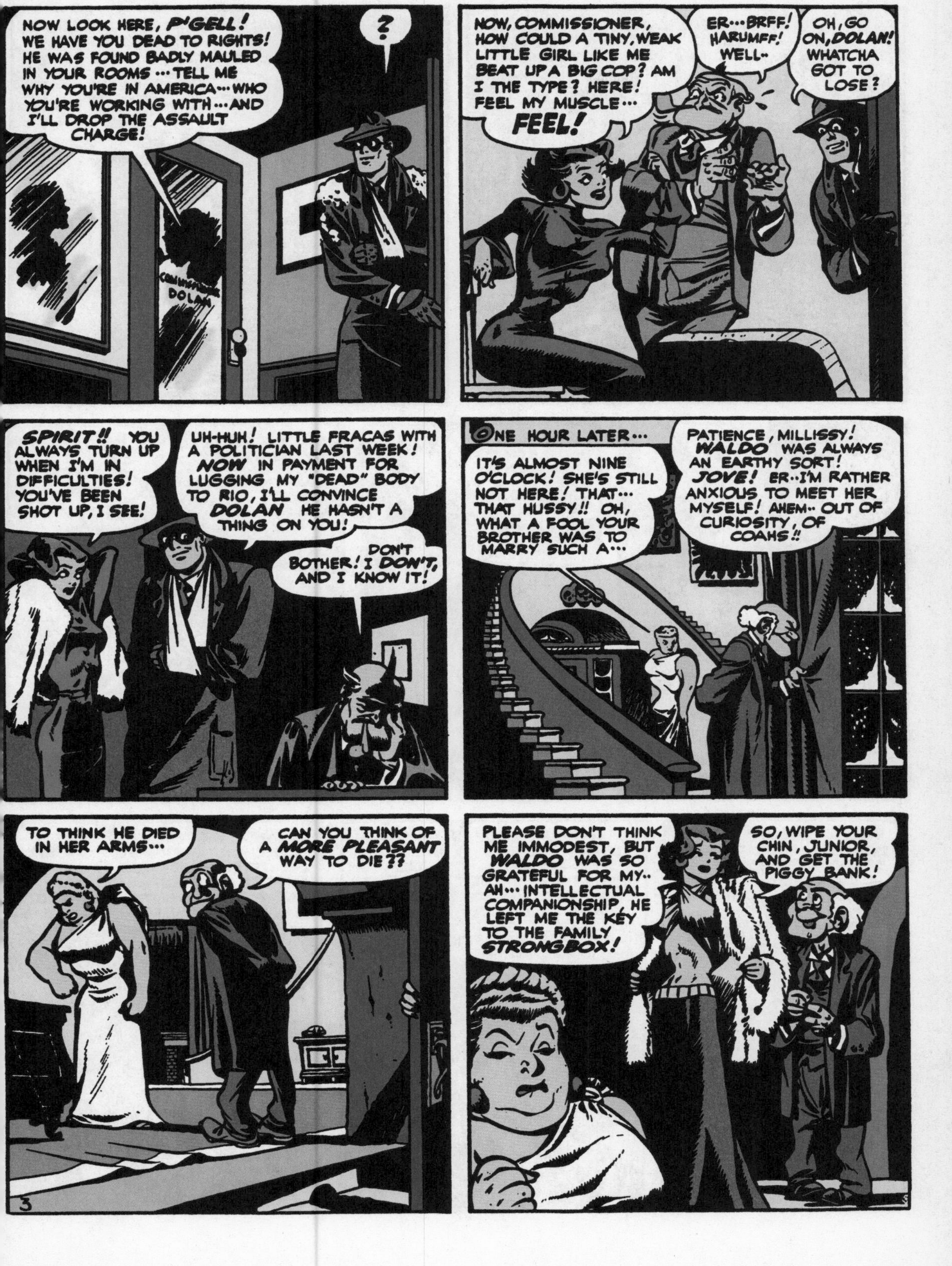
NOW LOOK HERE, P'GELL! WE HAVE YOU DEAD TO RIGHTS! HE WAS FOUND BADLY MAULED IN YOUR ROOMS ... TELL ME WHY YOU'RE IN AMERICA... WHO YOU'RE WORKING WITH ... AND I'LL DROP THE ASSAULT CHARGE!
?
NOW, COMMISSIONER, HOW COULD A TINY, WEAK LITTLE GIRL LIKE ME BEAT UP A BIG COP? AM I THE TYPE? HERE! FEEL MY MUSCLE... FEEL!
ER...BRFF! HARUMFF! WELL..
OH, GO ON, DOLAN! WHATCHA GOT TO LOSE?
SPIRIT!! YOU ALWAYS TURN UP WHEN I'M IN DIFFICULTIES! YOU'VE BEEN SHOT UP, I SEE!
UH-HUH! LITTLE FRACAS WITH A POLITICIAN LAST WEEK! NOW IN PAYMENT FOR LUGGING MY "DEAD" BODY TO RIO, I'LL CONVINCE DOLAN HE HASN'T A THING ON YOU!
DON'T BOTHER! I DON'T, AND I KNOW IT!
ONE HOUR LATER...
IT'S ALMOST NINE O'CLOCK! SHE'S STILL NOT HERE! THAT... THAT HUSSY!! OH, WHAT A FOOL YOUR BROTHER WAS TO MARRY SUCH A...
PATIENCE, MILLISSY! WALDO WAS ALWAYS AN EARTHY SORT! JOVE! ER..I'M RATHER ANXIOUS TO MEET HER MYSELF! AHEM.. OUT OF CURIOSITY, OF COAHS!!
TO THINK HE DIED IN HER ARMS...
CAN YOU THINK OF A MORE PLEASANT WAY TO DIE??
PLEASE DON'T THINK ME IMMODEST, BUT WALDO WAS SO GRATEFUL FOR MY.. AH... INTELLECTUAL COMPANIONSHIP, HE LEFT ME THE KEY TO THE FAMILY STRONGBOX!
SO, WIPE YOUR CHIN, JUNIOR, AND GET THE PIGGY BANK!

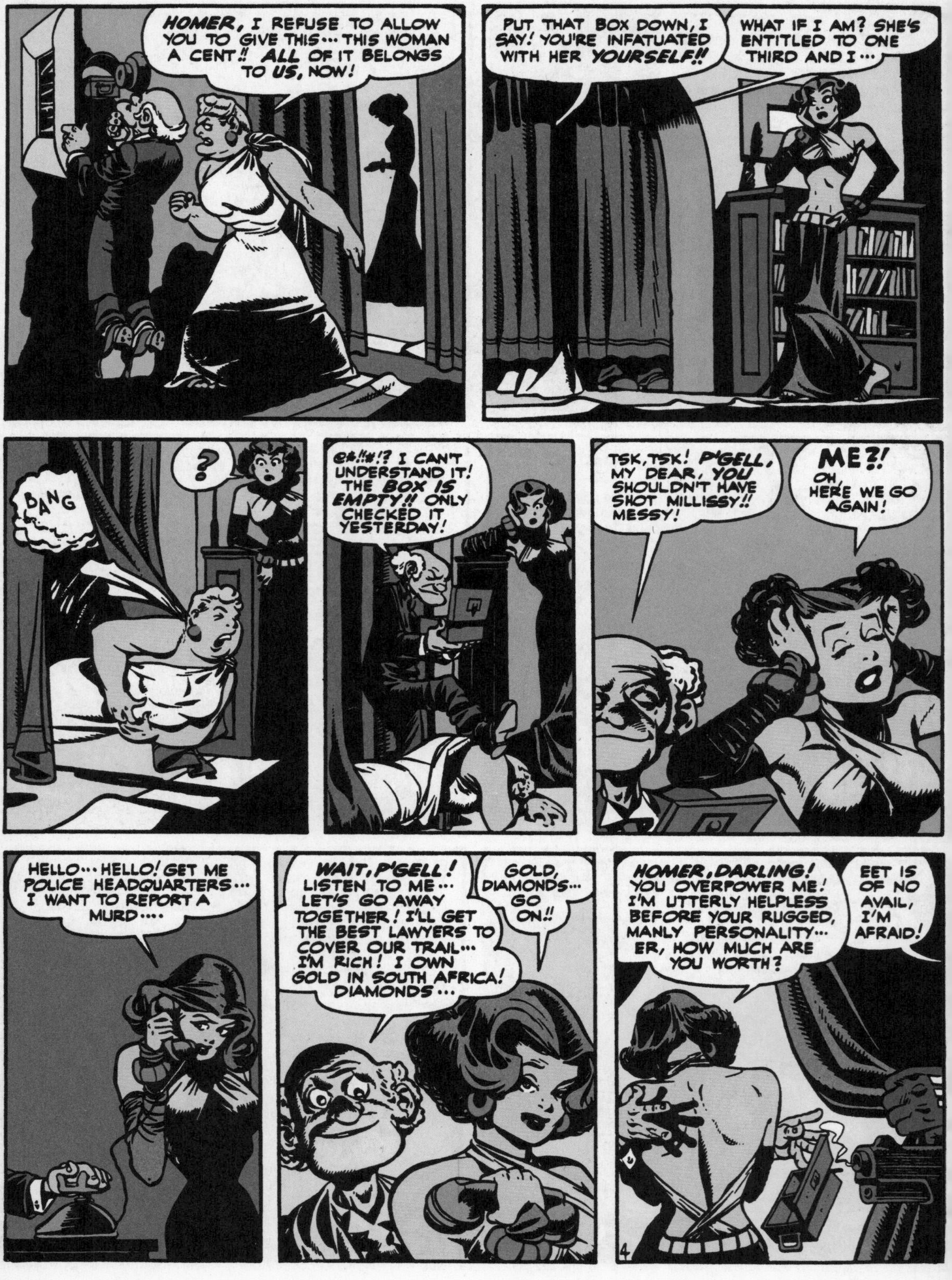
HOMER, I REFUSE TO ALLOW YOU TO GIVE THIS... THIS WOMAN A CENT!! ALL OF IT BELONGS TO US, NOW!
PUT THAT BOX DOWN, I SAY! YOU'RE INFATUATED WITH HER YOURSELF!!
WHAT IF I AM? SHE'S ENTITLED TO ONE THIRD AND I...
BANG
?
@#!!#!? I CAN'T UNDERSTAND IT! THE BOX IS EMPTY!! ONLY CHECKED IT YESTERDAY!
TSK, TSK! P'GELL, MY DEAR, YOU SHOULDN'T HAVE SHOT MILLISSY!! MESSY!
ME?! OH, HERE WE GO AGAIN!
HELLO... HELLO! GET ME POLICE HEADQUARTERS... I WANT TO REPORT A MURD....
WAIT, P'GELL! LISTEN TO ME... LET'S GO AWAY TOGETHER! I'LL GET THE BEST LAWYERS TO COVER OUR TRAIL... I'M RICH! I OWN GOLD IN SOUTH AFRICA! DIAMONDS...
GOLD, DIAMONDS... GO ON!!
HOMER, DARLING! YOU OVERPOWER ME! I'M UTTERLY HELPLESS BEFORE YOUR RUGGED, MANLY PERSONALITY... ER, HOW MUCH ARE YOU WORTH?
EET IS OF NO AVAIL, I'M AFRAID!

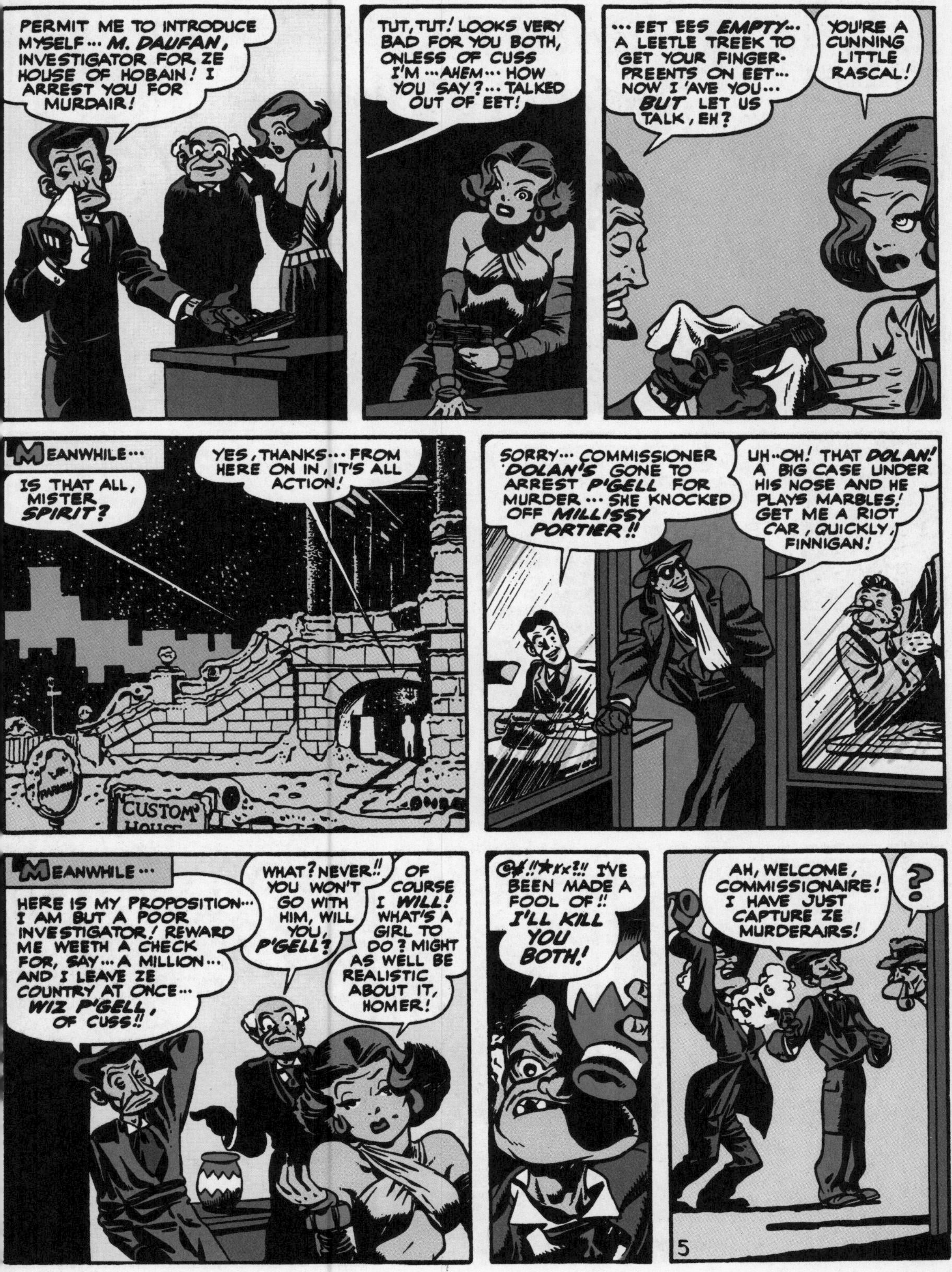

PERMIT ME TO INTRODUCE MYSELF... M. DAUFAN, INVESTIGATOR FOR ZE HOUSE OF HOBAIN! I ARREST YOU FOR MURDAIR!
TUT, TUT! LOOKS VERY BAD FOR YOU BOTH, ONLESS OF CUSS I'M ...AHEM... HOW YOU SAY?... TALKED OUT OF EET!
...EET EES EMPTY... A LEETLE TREEK TO GET YOUR FINGER-PREENTS ON EET... NOW I 'AVE YOU... BUT LET US TALK, EH?
YOU'RE A CUNNING LITTLE RASCAL!
MEANWHILE...
IS THAT ALL, MISTER SPIRIT?
YES, THANKS... FROM HERE ON IN, IT'S ALL ACTION!
CUSTOM
SORRY... COMMISSIONER DOLAN'S GONE TO ARREST P'GELL FOR MURDER... SHE KNOCKED OFF MILLISSY PORTIER!!
UH-OH! THAT DOLAN! A BIG CASE UNDER HIS NOSE AND HE PLAYS MARBLES! GET ME A RIOT CAR, QUICKLY, FINNIGAN!
MEANWHILE...
HERE IS MY PROPOSITION... I AM BUT A POOR INVESTIGATOR! REWARD ME WEETH A CHECK FOR, SAY... A MILLION... AND I LEAVE ZE COUNTRY AT ONCE... WIZ P'GELL, OF CUSS!!
WHAT? NEVER!! YOU WON'T GO WITH HIM, WILL YOU, P'GELL?
OF COURSE I WILL! WHAT'S A GIRL TO DO? MIGHT AS WELL BE REALISTIC ABOUT IT, HOMER!
@#!!★xx?!! I'VE BEEN MADE A FOOL OF!! I'LL KILL YOU BOTH!
AH, WELCOME, COMMISSIONAIRE! I HAVE JUST CAPTURE ZE MURDERAIRS!
?
BANG
5

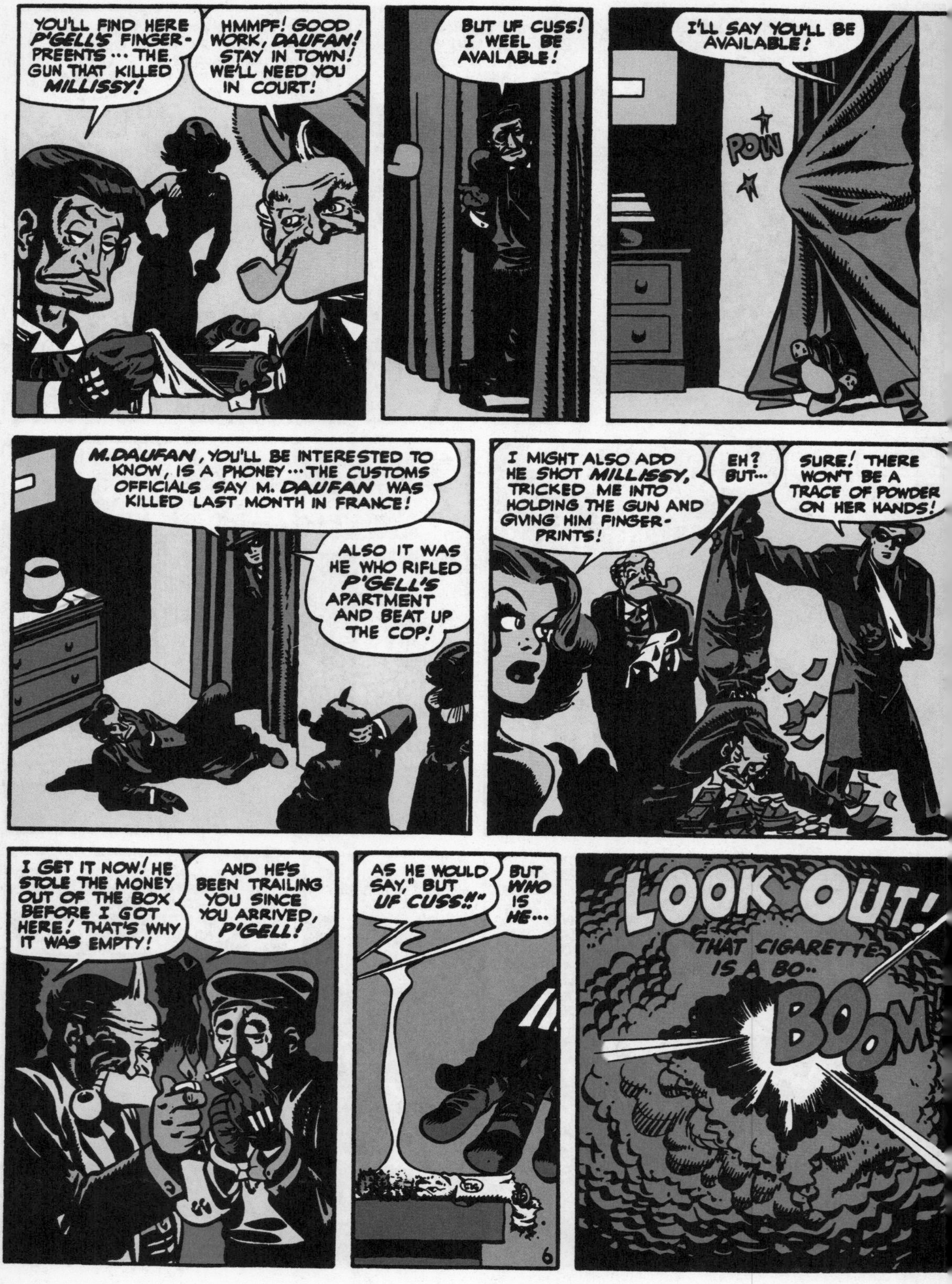
YOU'LL FIND HERE P'GELL'S FINGER-PREENTS... THE. GUN THAT KILLED MILLISSY!
HMMPF! GOOD WORK, DAUFAN! STAY IN TOWN! WE'LL NEED YOU IN COURT!
BUT UF CUSS! I WEEL BE AVAILABLE!
I'LL SAY YOU'LL BE AVAILABLE!
POW
M. DAUFAN, YOU'LL BE INTERESTED TO KNOW, IS A PHONEY... THE CUSTOMS OFFICIALS SAY M. DAUFAN WAS KILLED LAST MONTH IN FRANCE!
ALSO IT WAS HE WHO RIFLED P'GELL'S APARTMENT AND BEAT UP THE COP!
I MIGHT ALSO ADD HE SHOT MILLISSY, TRICKED ME INTO HOLDING THE GUN AND GIVING HIM FINGER-PRINTS!
EH? BUT...
SURE! THERE WON'T BE A TRACE OF POWDER ON HER HANDS!
I GET IT NOW! HE STOLE THE MONEY OUT OF THE BOX BEFORE I GOT HERE! THAT'S WHY IT WAS EMPTY!
AND HE'S BEEN TRAILING YOU SINCE YOU ARRIVED, P'GELL!
AS HE WOULD SAY," BUT UF CUSS!!"
BUT WHO IS HE...
6
LOOK OUT!
THAT CIGARETTE IS A BO..
BOOM

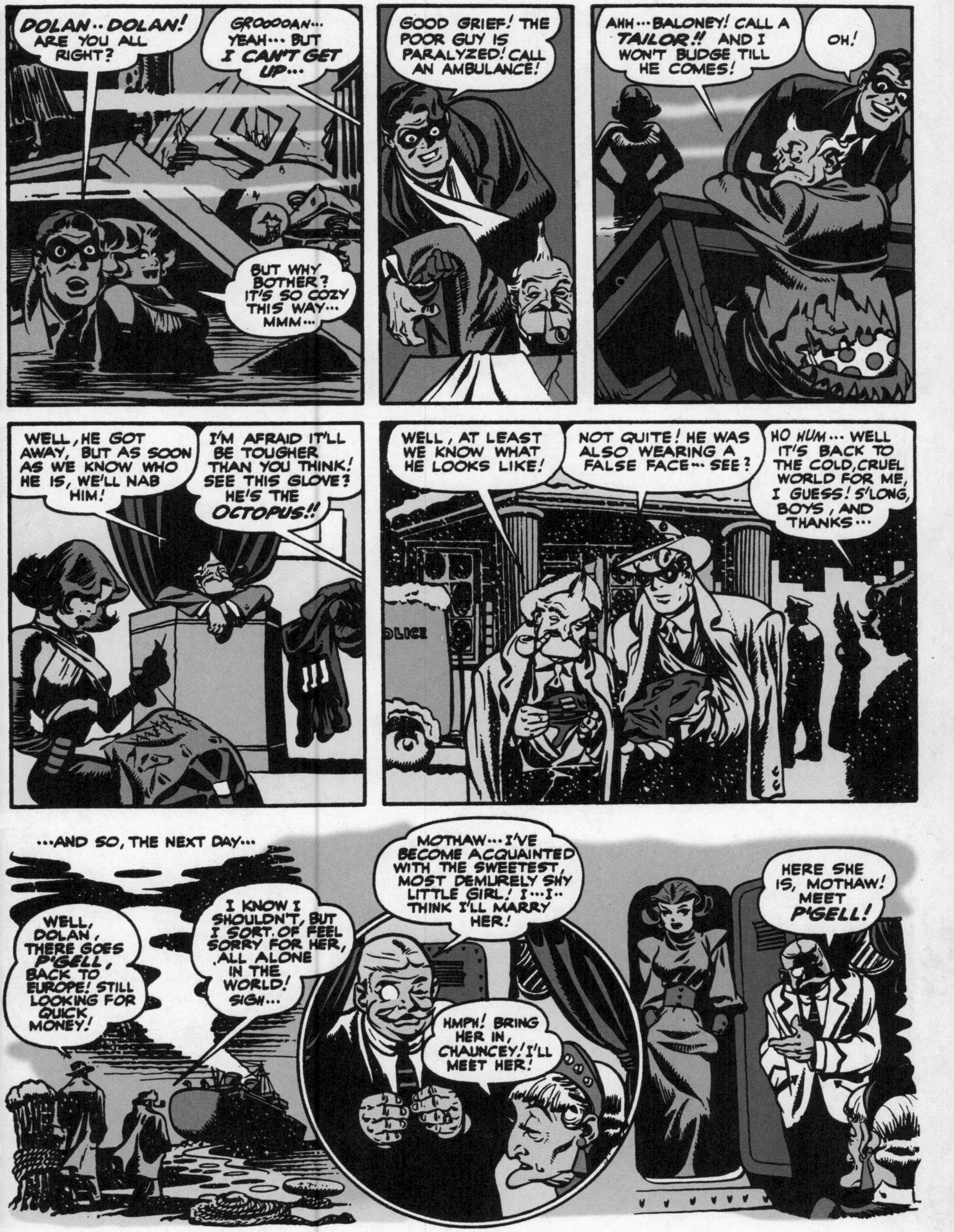
DOLAN..DOLAN! ARE YOU ALL RIGHT?
GROOOOAN... YEAH... BUT I CAN'T GET UP...
BUT WHY BOTHER? IT'S SO COZY THIS WAY... MMM...
GOOD GRIEF! THE POOR GUY IS PARALYZED! CALL AN AMBULANCE!
AHH...BALONEY! CALL A TAILOR!! AND I WON'T BUDGE TILL HE COMES!
OH!
WELL, HE GOT AWAY, BUT AS SOON AS WE KNOW WHO HE IS, WE'LL NAB HIM!
I'M AFRAID IT'LL BE TOUGHER THAN YOU THINK! SEE THIS GLOVE? HE'S THE OCTOPUS!!
WELL, AT LEAST WE KNOW WHAT HE LOOKS LIKE!
NOT QUITE! HE WAS ALSO WEARING A FALSE FACE... SEE?
HO HUM... WELL IT'S BACK TO THE COLD, CRUEL WORLD FOR ME, I GUESS! S'LONG, BOYS, AND THANKS...
POLICE
...AND SO, THE NEXT DAY...
WELL, DOLAN, THERE GOES P'GELL, BACK TO EUROPE! STILL LOOKING FOR QUICK MONEY!
I KNOW I SHOULDN'T, BUT I SORT OF FEEL SORRY FOR HER, ALL ALONE IN THE WORLD! SIGH...
MOTHAW... I'VE BECOME ACQUAINTED WITH THE SWEETEST, MOST DEMURELY SHY LITTLE GIRL! I...I.. THINK I'LL MARRY HER!
HMPH! BRING HER IN, CHAUNCEY! I'LL MEET HER!
HERE SHE IS, MOTHAW! MEET P'GELL!

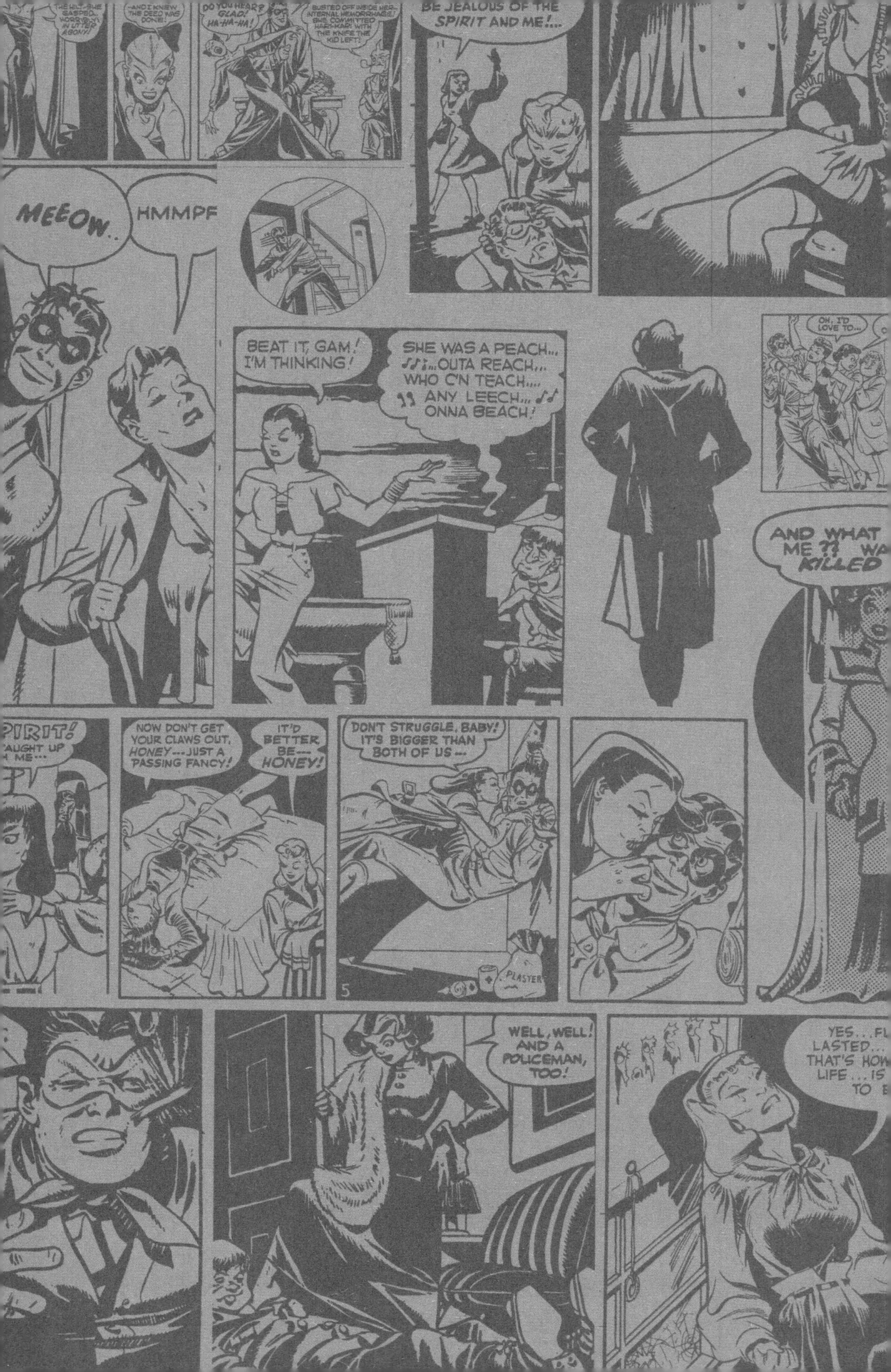

THE HILT–SHE GASPED, HORRIBLY, IN UTTER AGONY!
–AND I KNEW THE DEED WAS DONE!
DO YOU HEAR? GLAD! HA-HA-HA!
BUSTED OFF INSIDE HER– INTERNAL HEMORRHAGE! SHE COMMITTED HARI-KARI WITH THE KNIFE THE KID LEFT!
BE JEALOUS OF THE SPIRIT AND ME!...
MEEOW..
HMMPF
BEAT IT, GAM! I'M THINKING!
SHE WAS A PEACH... ...OUTA REACH... WHO C'N TEACH.... ANY LEECH... ONNA BEACH!
OH, I'D LOVE TO...
AND WHAT ME ?? KILLED
NOW DON'T GET YOUR CLAWS OUT, HONEY---JUST A PASSING FANCY!
IT'D BETTER BE--- HONEY!
DON'T STRUGGLE, BABY! IT'S BIGGER THAN BOTH OF US--
PLASTER
5
WELL, WELL! AND A POLICEMAN, TOO!

COMIC BOOK SECTION

SAREE

ACTION Mystery ADVENTURE

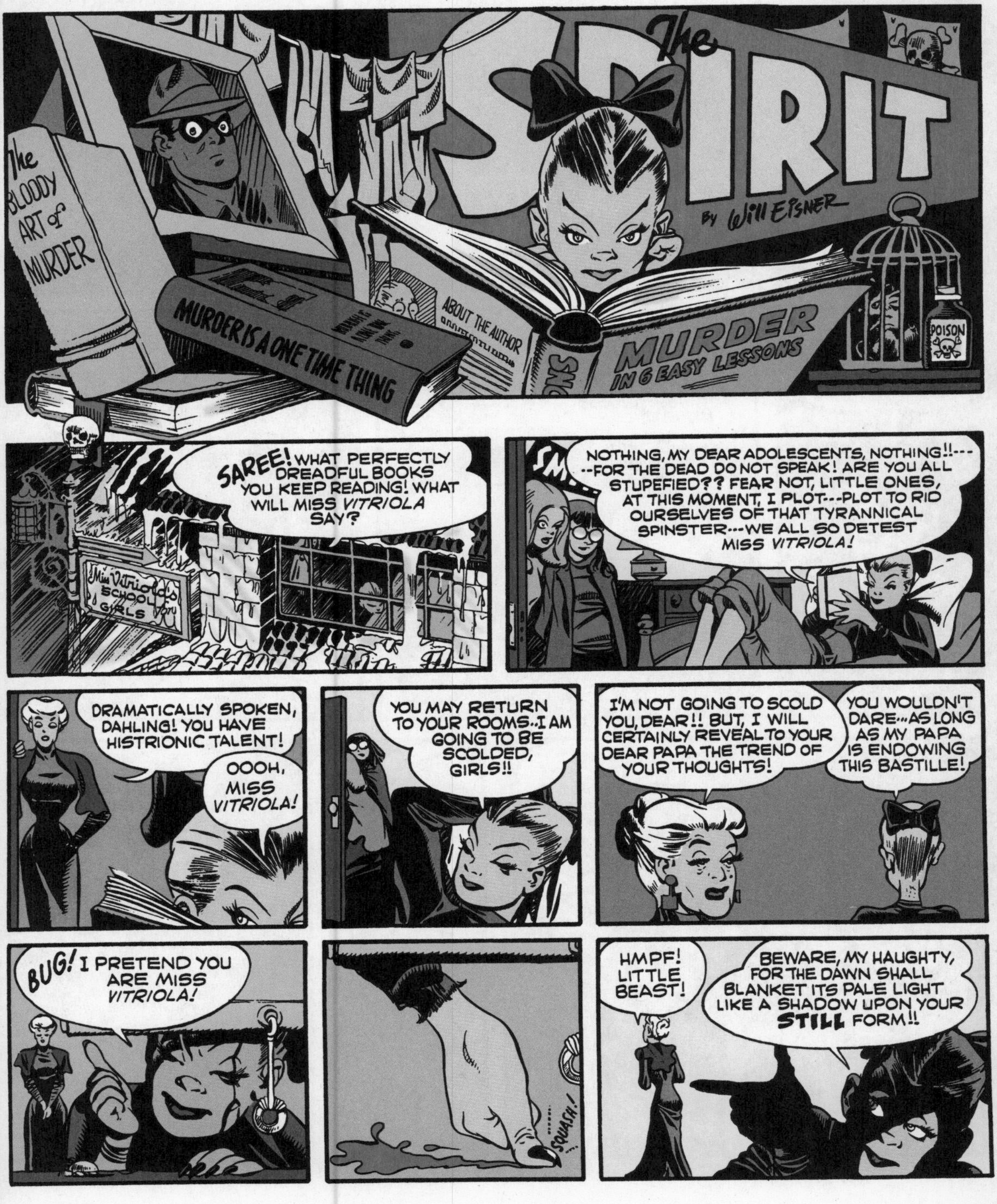

The SPIRIT
BY Will Eisner
The BLOODY ART of MURDER
MURDER IS A ONE TIME THING
ABOUT THE AUTHOR
MURDER IN 6 EASY LESSONS
POISON
SAREE! WHAT PERFECTLY DREADFUL BOOKS YOU KEEP READING! WHAT WILL MISS VITRIOLA SAY?
Miss Vitriola's SCHOOL for Young GIRLS
NOTHING, MY DEAR ADOLESCENTS, NOTHING!!--- --FOR THE DEAD DO NOT SPEAK! ARE YOU ALL STUPEFIED?? FEAR NOT, LITTLE ONES, AT THIS MOMENT, I PLOT---PLOT TO RID OURSELVES OF THAT TYRANNICAL SPINSTER---WE ALL SO DETEST MISS VITRIOLA!
DRAMATICALLY SPOKEN, DAHLING! YOU HAVE HISTRIONIC TALENT!
OOOH, MISS VITRIOLA!
YOU MAY RETURN TO YOUR ROOMS..I AM GOING TO BE SCOLDED, GIRLS!!
I'M NOT GOING TO SCOLD YOU, DEAR!! BUT, I WILL CERTAINLY REVEAL TO YOUR DEAR PAPA THE TREND OF YOUR THOUGHTS!
YOU WOULDN'T DARE...AS LONG AS MY PAPA IS ENDOWING THIS BASTILLE!
BUG! I PRETEND YOU ARE MISS VITRIOLA!
SQUASH!
HMPF! LITTLE BEAST!
BEWARE, MY HAUGHTY, FOR THE DAWN SHALL BLANKET ITS PALE LIGHT LIKE A SHADOW UPON YOUR STILL FORM!!

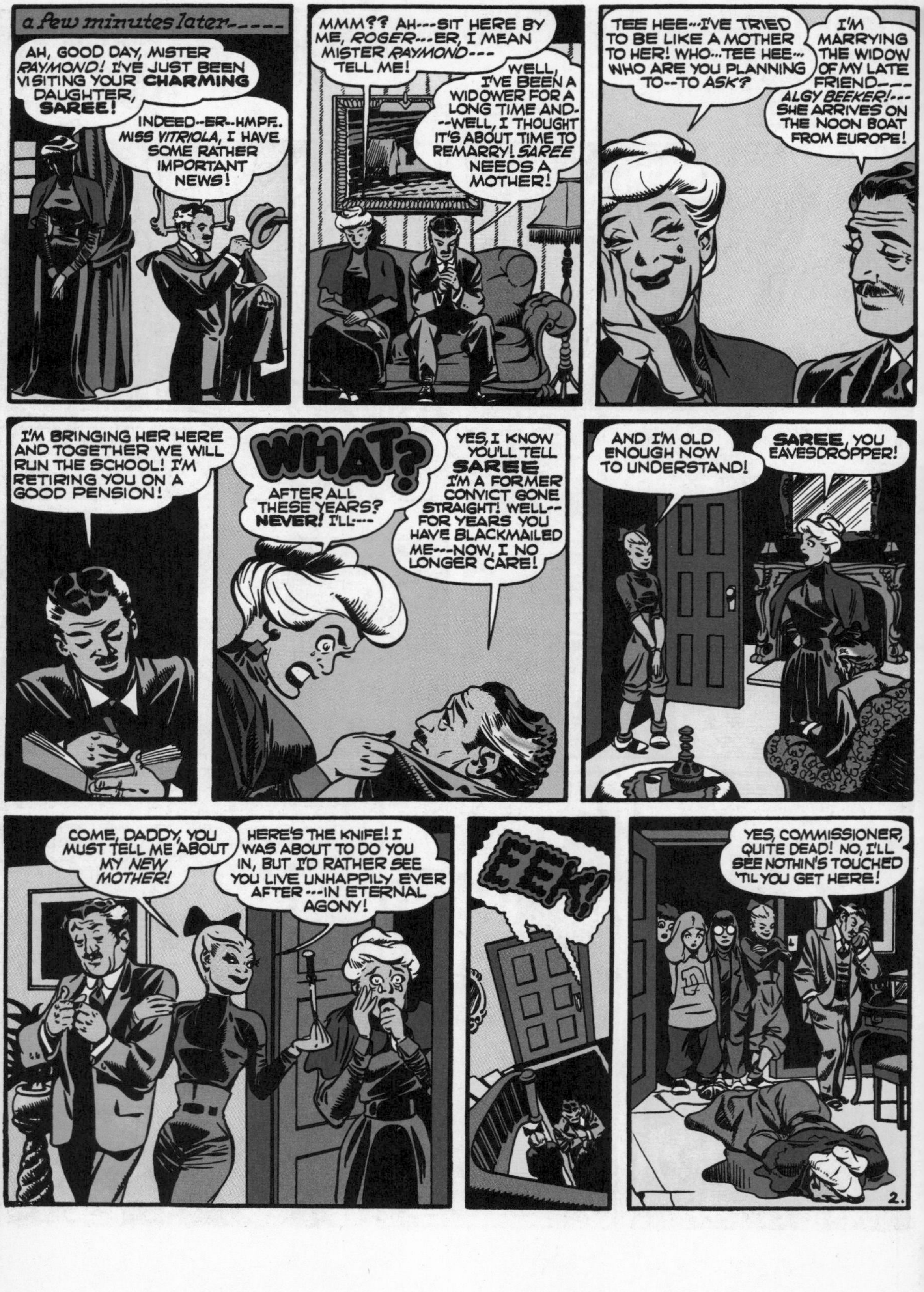

a few minutes later----
AH, GOOD DAY, MISTER RAYMOND! I'VE JUST BEEN VISITING YOUR CHARMING DAUGHTER, SAREE!
INDEED--ER--HMPF.. MISS VITRIOLA, I HAVE SOME RATHER IMPORTANT NEWS!
MMM?? AH---SIT HERE BY ME, ROGER---ER, I MEAN MISTER RAYMOND--- TELL ME!
WELL, I'VE BEEN A WIDOWER FOR A LONG TIME AND---WELL, I THOUGHT IT'S ABOUT TIME TO REMARRY! SAREE NEEDS A MOTHER!
TEE HEE--I'VE TRIED TO BE LIKE A MOTHER TO HER! WHO...TEE HEE... WHO ARE YOU PLANNING TO--TO ASK?
I'M MARRYING THE WIDOW OF MY LATE FRIEND--- ALGY BEEKER!--- SHE ARRIVES ON THE NOON BOAT FROM EUROPE!
I'M BRINGING HER HERE AND TOGETHER WE WILL RUN THE SCHOOL! I'M RETIRING YOU ON A GOOD PENSION!
WHAT? AFTER ALL THESE YEARS? NEVER! I'LL---
YES, I KNOW YOU'LL TELL SAREE I'M A FORMER CONVICT GONE STRAIGHT! WELL-- FOR YEARS YOU HAVE BLACKMAILED ME---NOW, I NO LONGER CARE!
AND I'M OLD ENOUGH NOW TO UNDERSTAND!
SAREE, YOU EAVESDROPPER!
COME, DADDY, YOU MUST TELL ME ABOUT MY NEW MOTHER!
HERE'S THE KNIFE! I WAS ABOUT TO DO YOU IN, BUT I'D RATHER SEE YOU LIVE UNHAPPILY EVER AFTER ---IN ETERNAL AGONY!
EEK!
YES, COMMISSIONER, QUITE DEAD! NO, I'LL SEE NOTHIN'S TOUCHED 'TIL YOU GET HERE!
2.

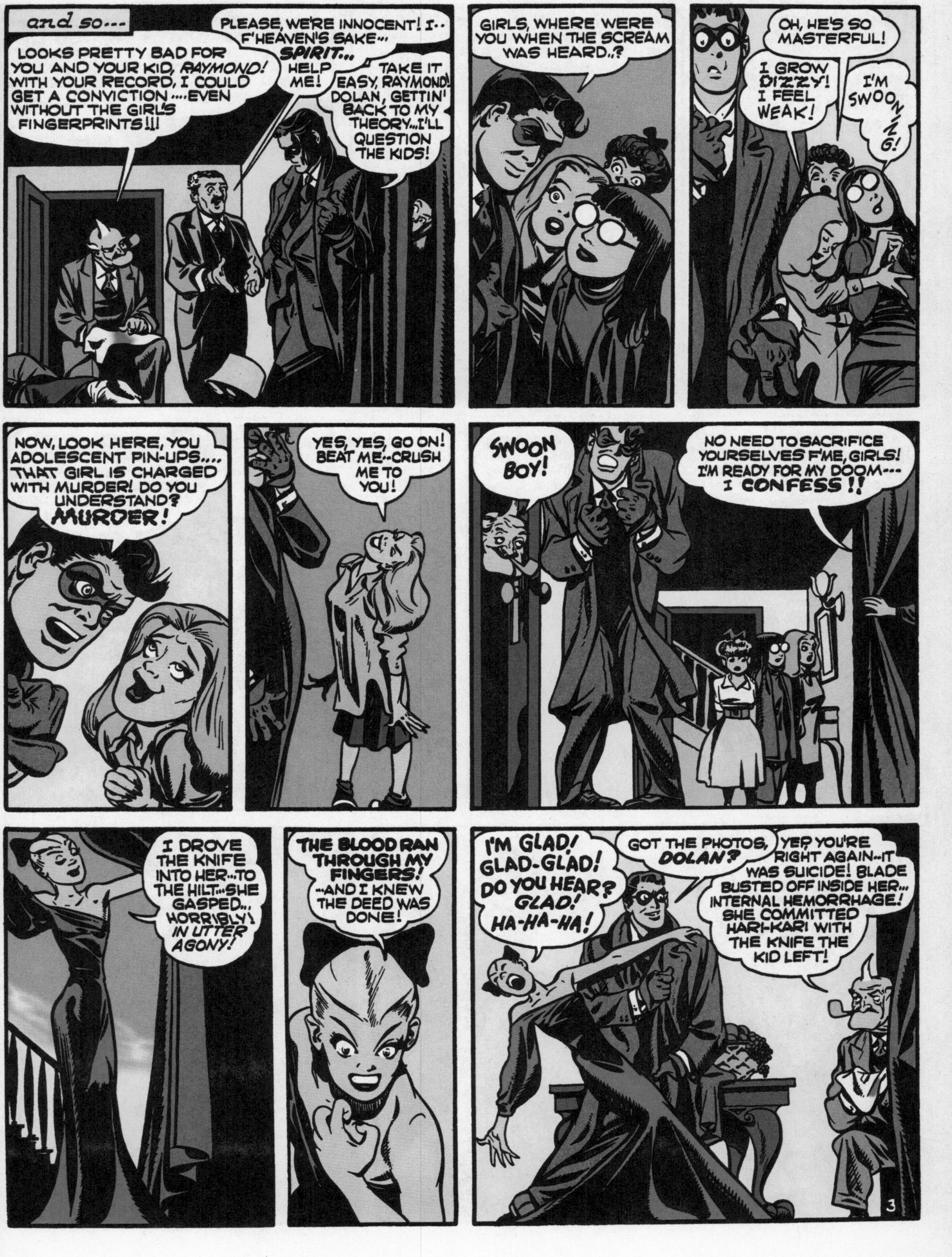
and so...
LOOKS PRETTY BAD FOR YOU AND YOUR KID, RAYMOND! WITH YOUR RECORD, I COULD GET A CONVICTION ....EVEN WITHOUT THE GIRL'S FINGERPRINTS!!!
PLEASE, WE'RE INNOCENT! I.. F'HEAVEN'S SAKE... SPIRIT... HELP ME!
TAKE IT EASY, RAYMOND! DOLAN, GETTIN' BACK TO MY THEORY...I'LL QUESTION THE KIDS!
GIRLS, WHERE WERE YOU WHEN THE SCREAM WAS HEARD..?
OH, HE'S SO MASTERFUL!
I GROW DIZZY! I FEEL WEAK!
I'M SWOONING!
NOW, LOOK HERE, YOU ADOLESCENT PIN-UPS.... THAT GIRL IS CHARGED WITH MURDER! DO YOU UNDERSTAND? MURDER!
YES, YES, GO ON! BEAT ME--CRUSH ME TO YOU!
SWOON BOY!
NO NEED TO SACRIFICE YOURSELVES F'ME, GIRLS! I'M READY FOR MY DOOM--- I CONFESS!!
I DROVE THE KNIFE INTO HER...TO THE HILT...SHE GASPED... HORRIBLY! IN UTTER AGONY!
THE BLOOD RAN THROUGH MY FINGERS! --AND I KNEW THE DEED WAS DONE!
I'M GLAD! GLAD-GLAD! DO YOU HEAR? GLAD! HA-HA-HA!
GOT THE PHOTOS, DOLAN?
YEP, YOU'RE RIGHT AGAIN--IT WAS SUICIDE! BLADE BUSTED OFF INSIDE HER... INTERNAL HEMORRHAGE! SHE COMMITTED HARI-KARI WITH THE KNIFE THE KID LEFT!
3

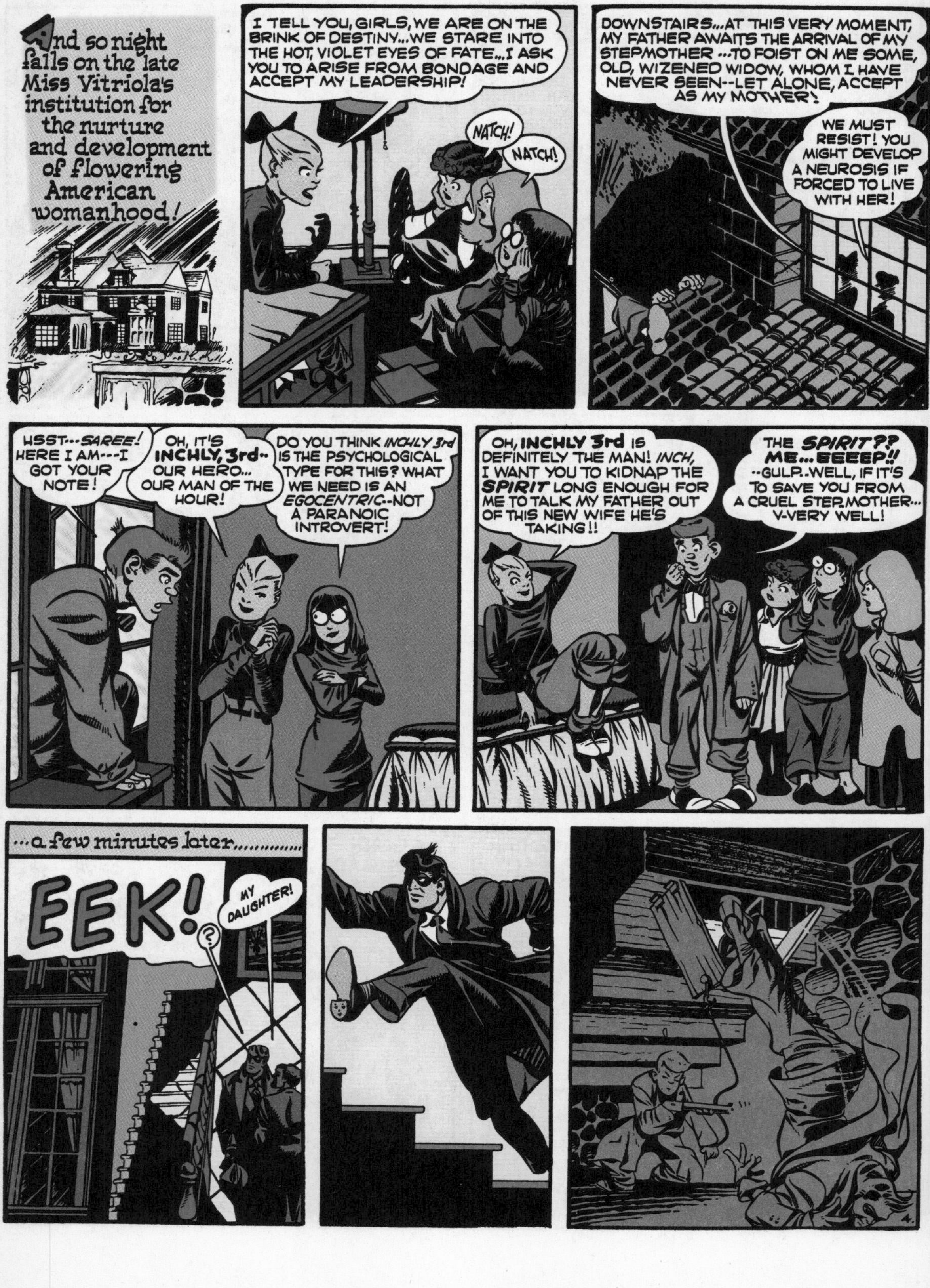
And so night falls on the late Miss Vitriola's institution for the nurture and development of flowering American womanhood!
I TELL YOU, GIRLS, WE ARE ON THE BRINK OF DESTINY...WE STARE INTO THE HOT, VIOLET EYES OF FATE...I ASK YOU TO ARISE FROM BONDAGE AND ACCEPT MY LEADERSHIP!
NATCH!
NATCH!
DOWNSTAIRS...AT THIS VERY MOMENT, MY FATHER AWAITS THE ARRIVAL OF MY STEPMOTHER ...TO FOIST ON ME SOME, OLD, WIZENED WIDOW, WHOM I HAVE NEVER SEEN--LET ALONE, ACCEPT AS MY MOTHER!
WE MUST RESIST! YOU MIGHT DEVELOP A NEUROSIS IF FORCED TO LIVE WITH HER!
HSST---SAREE! HERE I AM---I GOT YOUR NOTE!
OH, IT'S INCHLY, 3rd-- OUR HERO... OUR MAN OF THE HOUR!
DO YOU THINK INCHLY 3rd IS THE PSYCHOLOGICAL TYPE FOR THIS? WHAT WE NEED IS AN EGOCENTRIC--NOT A PARANOIC INTROVERT!
OH, INCHLY 3rd IS DEFINITELY THE MAN! INCH, I WANT YOU TO KIDNAP THE SPIRIT LONG ENOUGH FOR ME TO TALK MY FATHER OUT OF THIS NEW WIFE HE'S TAKING!!
THE SPIRIT?? ME...EEEEP!! --GULP..WELL, IF IT'S TO SAVE YOU FROM A CRUEL STEP-MOTHER... V-VERY WELL!
...a few minutes later.............
EEK!
?
MY DAUGHTER!
4.

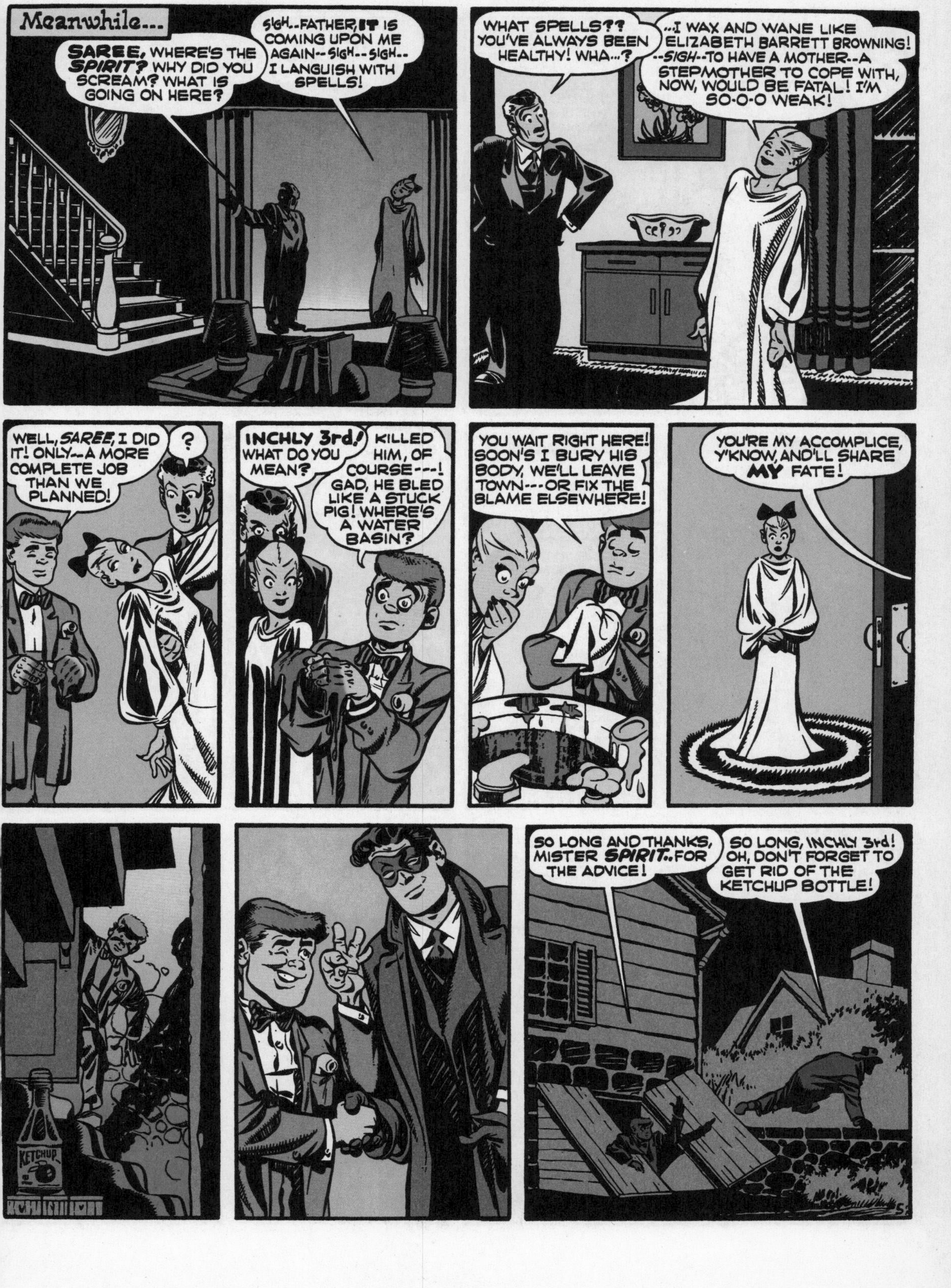
Meanwhile...
SAREE, WHERE'S THE SPIRIT? WHY DID YOU SCREAM? WHAT IS GOING ON HERE?
SIGH..FATHER, IT IS COMING UPON ME AGAIN--SIGH--SIGH.. I LANGUISH WITH SPELLS!
WHAT SPELLS?? YOU'VE ALWAYS BEEN HEALTHY! WHA...?
..I WAX AND WANE LIKE ELIZABETH BARRETT BROWNING! --SIGH--TO HAVE A MOTHER--A STEPMOTHER TO COPE WITH, NOW, WOULD BE FATAL! I'M SO-O-O WEAK!
WELL, SAREE, I DID IT! ONLY--A MORE COMPLETE JOB THAN WE PLANNED!
?
INCHLY 3rd! WHAT DO YOU MEAN?
KILLED HIM, OF COURSE---! GAD, HE BLED LIKE A STUCK PIG! WHERE'S A WATER BASIN?
YOU WAIT RIGHT HERE! SOON'S I BURY HIS BODY, WE'LL LEAVE TOWN---OR FIX THE BLAME ELSEWHERE!
YOU'RE MY ACCOMPLICE, Y'KNOW, AND'LL SHARE MY FATE!
KETCHUP
SO LONG AND THANKS, MISTER SPIRIT..FOR THE ADVICE!
SO LONG, INCHLY 3rd! OH, DON'T FORGET TO GET RID OF THE KETCHUP BOTTLE!

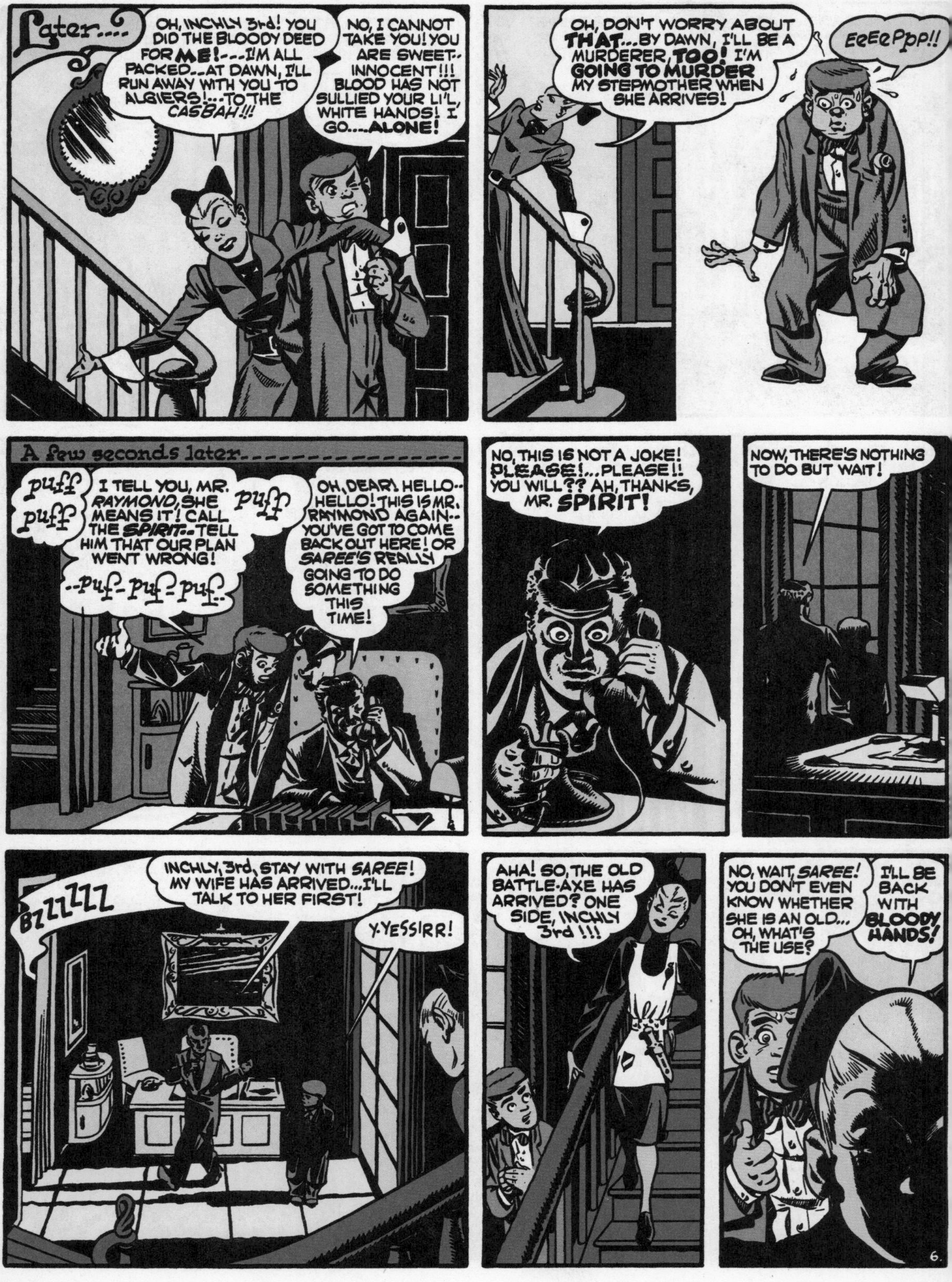
Later....
OH, INCHLY 3rd! YOU DID THE BLOODY DEED FOR ME!--I'M ALL PACKED--AT DAWN, I'LL RUN AWAY WITH YOU TO ALGIERS!...TO THE CASBAH!!!
NO, I CANNOT TAKE YOU! YOU ARE SWEET-INNOCENT!!! BLOOD HAS NOT SULLIED YOUR LI'L, WHITE HANDS! I GO....ALONE!
OH, DON'T WORRY ABOUT THAT...BY DAWN, I'LL BE A MURDERER, TOO! I'M GOING TO MURDER MY STEPMOTHER WHEN SHE ARRIVES!
EEEEPPP!!
A few seconds later..............
puff puff
I TELL YOU, MR. RAYMOND, SHE MEANS IT! CALL THE SPIRIT--TELL HIM THAT OUR PLAN WENT WRONG!
puff
--puf-puf-puf-
OH, DEAR! HELLO-- HELLO! THIS IS MR. RAYMOND AGAIN-- YOU'VE GOT TO COME BACK OUT HERE! OR SAREE'S REALLY GOING TO DO SOMETHING THIS TIME!
NO, THIS IS NOT A JOKE! PLEASE!...PLEASE!! YOU WILL?? AH, THANKS, MR. SPIRIT!
NOW, THERE'S NOTHING TO DO BUT WAIT!
BZZZZZZ
INCHLY, 3rd, STAY WITH SAREE! MY WIFE HAS ARRIVED...I'LL TALK TO HER FIRST!
Y-YESSIRR!
AHA! SO, THE OLD BATTLE-AXE HAS ARRIVED? ONE SIDE, INCHLY 3rd!!!
NO, WAIT, SAREE! YOU DON'T EVEN KNOW WHETHER SHE IS AN OLD... OH, WHAT'S THE USE?
I'LL BE BACK WITH BLOODY HANDS!
6.

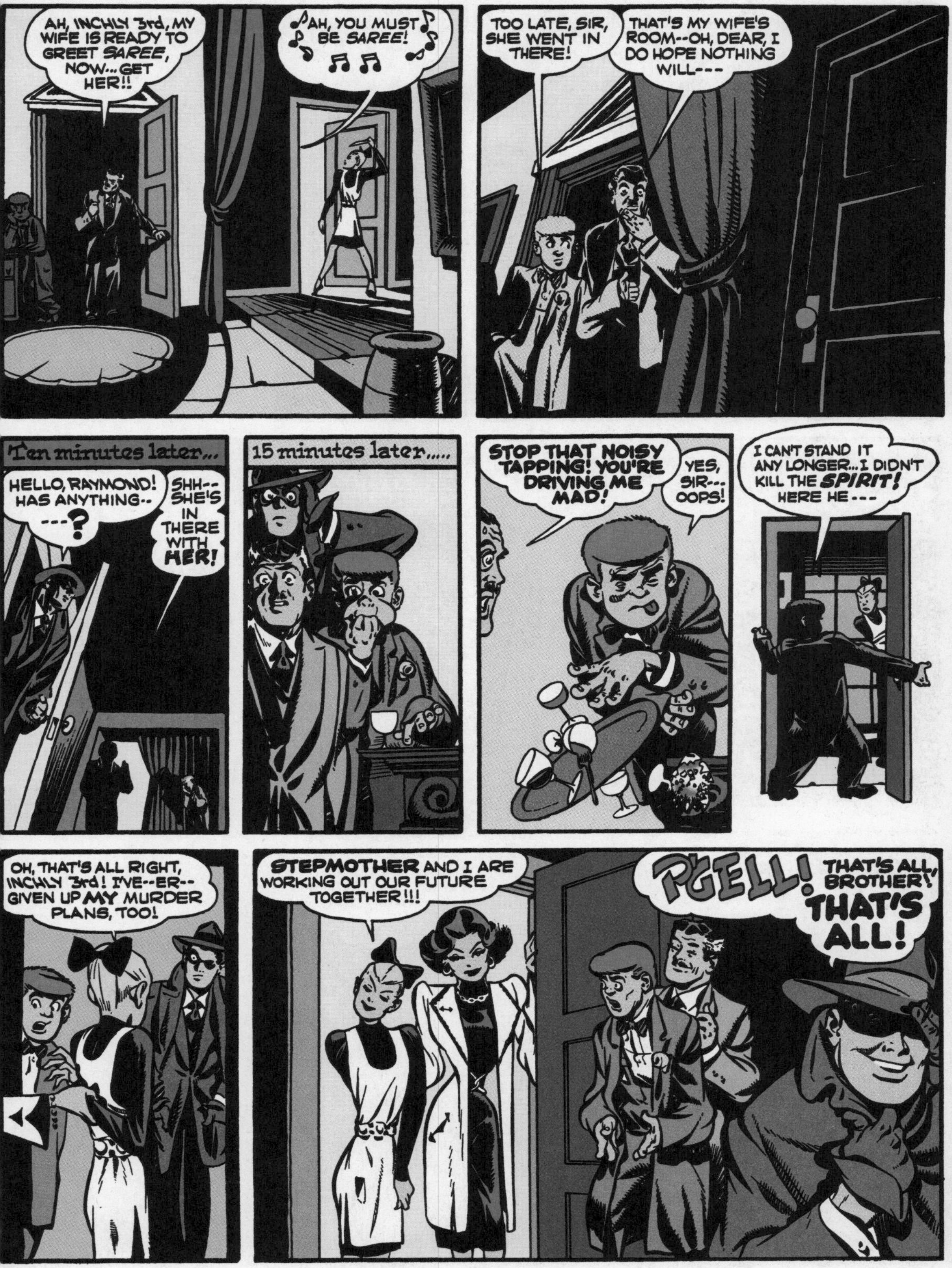
AH, INCHLY 3rd, MY WIFE IS READY TO GREET SAREE, NOW... GET HER!!
AH, YOU MUST BE SAREE!
TOO LATE, SIR, SHE WENT IN THERE!
THAT'S MY WIFE'S ROOM--OH, DEAR, I DO HOPE NOTHING WILL---
Ten minutes later...
HELLO, RAYMOND! HAS ANYTHING-- ---?
SHH-- SHE'S IN THERE WITH HER!
15 minutes later.....
STOP THAT NOISY TAPPING! YOU'RE DRIVING ME MAD!
YES, SIR--- OOPS!
I CAN'T STAND IT ANY LONGER... I DIDN'T KILL THE SPIRIT! HERE HE ---
OH, THAT'S ALL RIGHT, INCHLY 3rd! I'VE--ER-- GIVEN UP MY MURDER PLANS, TOO!
STEPMOTHER AND I ARE WORKING OUT OUR FUTURE TOGETHER!!!
P'GELL!
THAT'S ALL, BROTHER! THAT'S ALL!

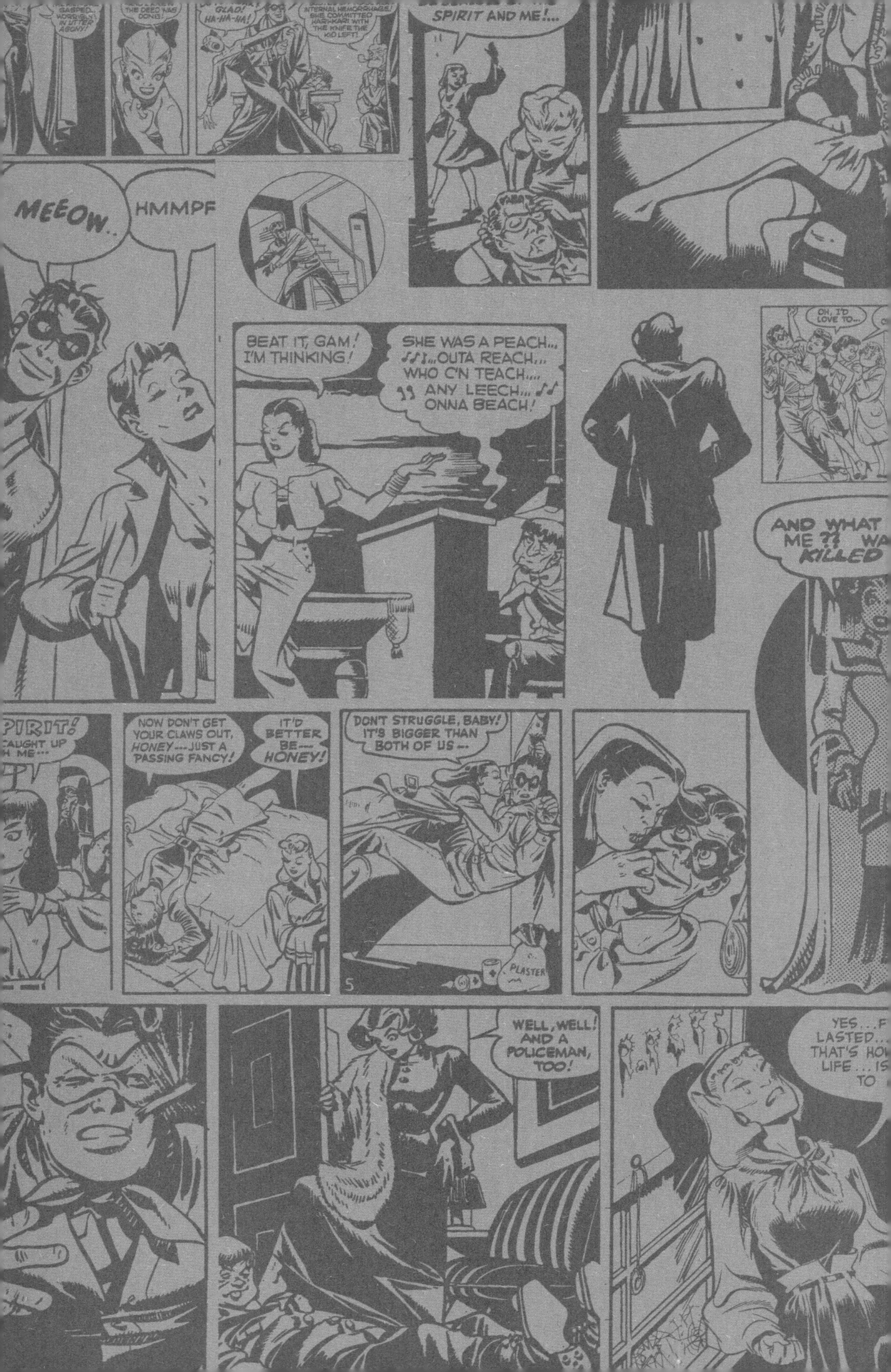
GASPED... IN UTTER AGONY!
THE DEED WAS DONE!
GLAD! HA-HA-HA!
INTERNAL HEMORRHAGE! SHE COMMITTED HARI-KARI WITH THE KNIFE THE KID LEFT!
SPIRIT AND ME!...
MEEOW..
HMMPF
BEAT IT, GAM! I'M THINKING!
SHE WAS A PEACH... ♪♪♪...OUTA REACH... WHO C'N TEACH.... ♪♪ ANY LEECH... ♪♪ ONNA BEACH!
OH, I'D LOVE TO...
AND WHAT ME ?? WA KILLED
SPIRIT! CAUGHT UP H ME...
NOW DON'T GET YOUR CLAWS OUT, HONEY---JUST A PASSING FANCY!
IT'D BETTER BE-- HONEY!
DON'T STRUGGLE, BABY! IT'S BIGGER THAN BOTH OF US --
PLASTER
5
WELL, WELL! AND A POLICEMAN, TOO!
YES... F LASTED... THAT'S HO LIFE... IS TO

THE SCHOOL FOR GIRLS

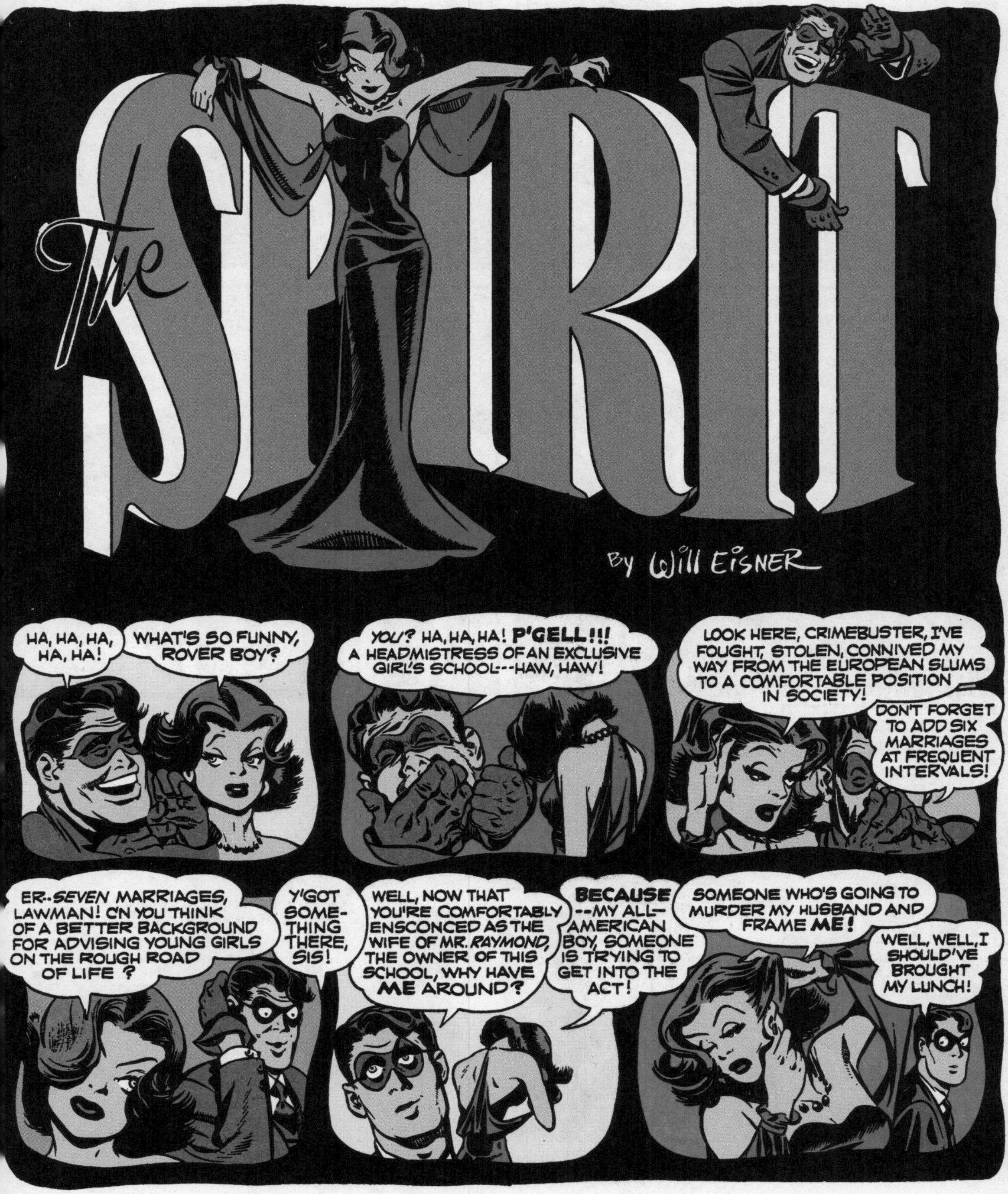
The SPIRIT
BY Will EISNER
HA, HA, HA, HA, HA!
WHAT'S SO FUNNY, ROVER BOY?
YOU? HA, HA, HA! P'GELL!!! A HEADMISTRESS OF AN EXCLUSIVE GIRL'S SCHOOL--HAW, HAW!
LOOK HERE, CRIMEBUSTER, I'VE FOUGHT, STOLEN, CONNIVED MY WAY FROM THE EUROPEAN SLUMS TO A COMFORTABLE POSITION IN SOCIETY!
DON'T FORGET TO ADD SIX MARRIAGES AT FREQUENT INTERVALS!
ER..SEVEN MARRIAGES, LAWMAN! C'N YOU THINK OF A BETTER BACKGROUND FOR ADVISING YOUNG GIRLS ON THE ROUGH ROAD OF LIFE ?
Y'GOT SOME-THING THERE, SIS!
WELL, NOW THAT YOU'RE COMFORTABLY ENSCONCED AS THE WIFE OF MR. RAYMOND, THE OWNER OF THIS SCHOOL, WHY HAVE ME AROUND?
BECAUSE --MY ALL-AMERICAN BOY, SOMEONE IS TRYING TO GET INTO THE ACT!
SOMEONE WHO'S GOING TO MURDER MY HUSBAND AND FRAME ME!
WELL, WELL, I SHOULD'VE BROUGHT MY LUNCH!

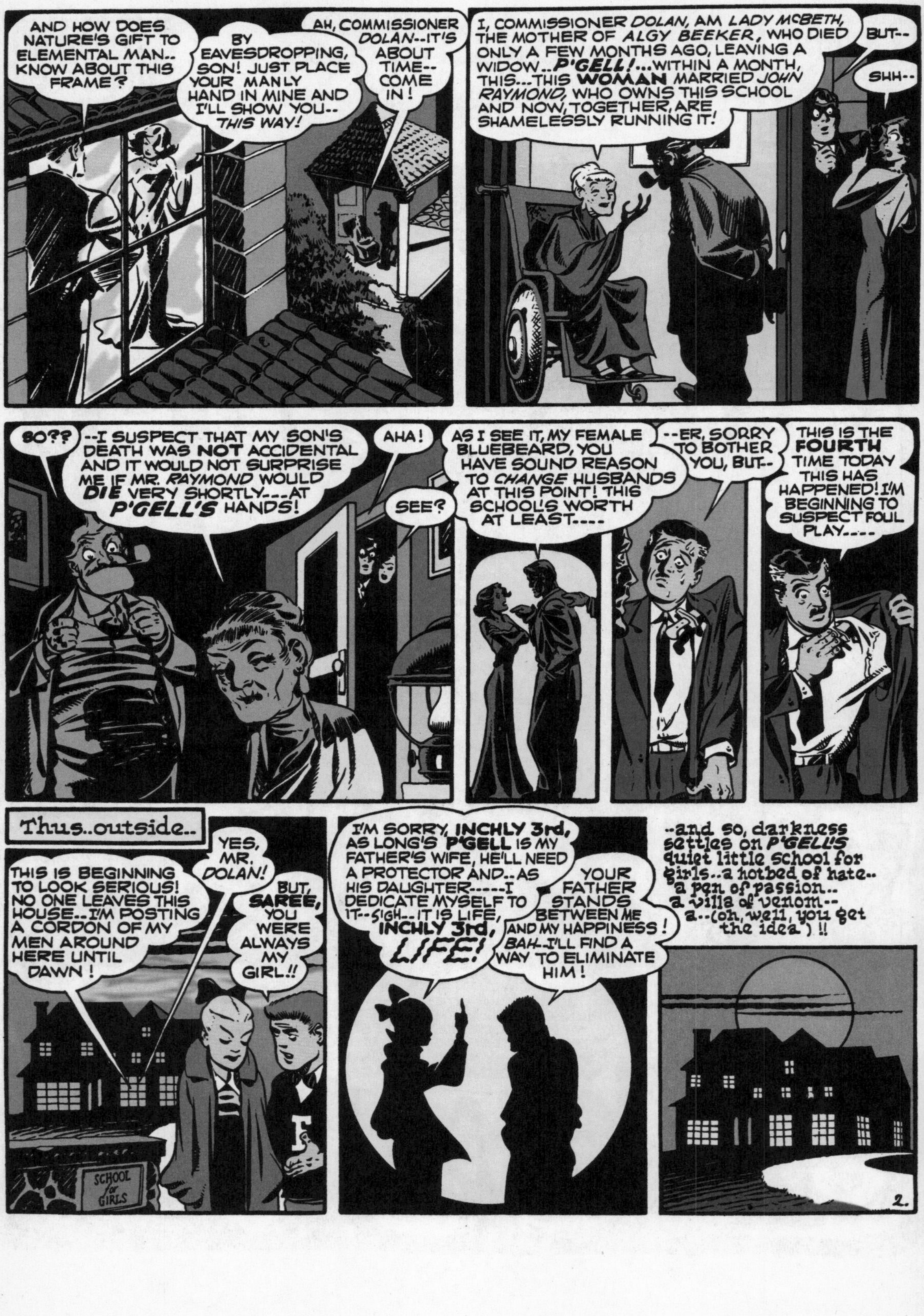

AND HOW DOES NATURE'S GIFT TO ELEMENTAL MAN.. KNOW ABOUT THIS FRAME?
BY EAVESDROPPING, SON! JUST PLACE YOUR MANLY HAND IN MINE AND I'LL SHOW YOU-- THIS WAY!
AH, COMMISSIONER DOLAN--IT'S ABOUT TIME-- COME IN!
I, COMMISSIONER DOLAN, AM LADY McBETH, THE MOTHER OF ALGY BEEKER, WHO DIED ONLY A FEW MONTHS AGO, LEAVING A WIDOW..P'GELL!...WITHIN A MONTH, THIS...THIS WOMAN MARRIED JOHN RAYMOND, WHO OWNS THIS SCHOOL AND NOW, TOGETHER, ARE SHAMELESSLY RUNNING IT!
BUT--
SHH--
SO??
--I SUSPECT THAT MY SON'S DEATH WAS NOT ACCIDENTAL AND IT WOULD NOT SURPRISE ME IF MR. RAYMOND WOULD DIE VERY SHORTLY---AT P'GELL'S HANDS!
AHA!
SEE?
AS I SEE IT, MY FEMALE BLUEBEARD, YOU HAVE SOUND REASON TO CHANGE HUSBANDS AT THIS POINT! THIS SCHOOL'S WORTH AT LEAST----
--ER, SORRY TO BOTHER YOU, BUT--
THIS IS THE FOURTH TIME TODAY THIS HAS HAPPENED! I'M BEGINNING TO SUSPECT FOUL PLAY----
Thus..outside..
THIS IS BEGINNING TO LOOK SERIOUS! NO ONE LEAVES THIS HOUSE..I'M POSTING A CORDON OF MY MEN AROUND HERE UNTIL DAWN!
YES, MR. DOLAN!
BUT, SAREE, YOU WERE ALWAYS MY GIRL!!
SCHOOL for GIRLS
I'M SORRY, INCHLY 3rd, AS LONG'S P'GELL IS MY FATHER'S WIFE, HE'LL NEED A PROTECTOR AND..AS HIS DAUGHTER-----I DEDICATE MYSELF TO IT--SIGH--IT IS LIFE, INCHLY 3rd, LIFE!
YOUR FATHER STANDS BETWEEN ME AND MY HAPPINESS! BAH--I'LL FIND A WAY TO ELIMINATE HIM!
--and so, darkness settles on P'GELL'S quiet little school for girls..a hotbed of hate.. a pen of passion.. a villa of venom-- a--(oh, well, you get the idea) !!
2.

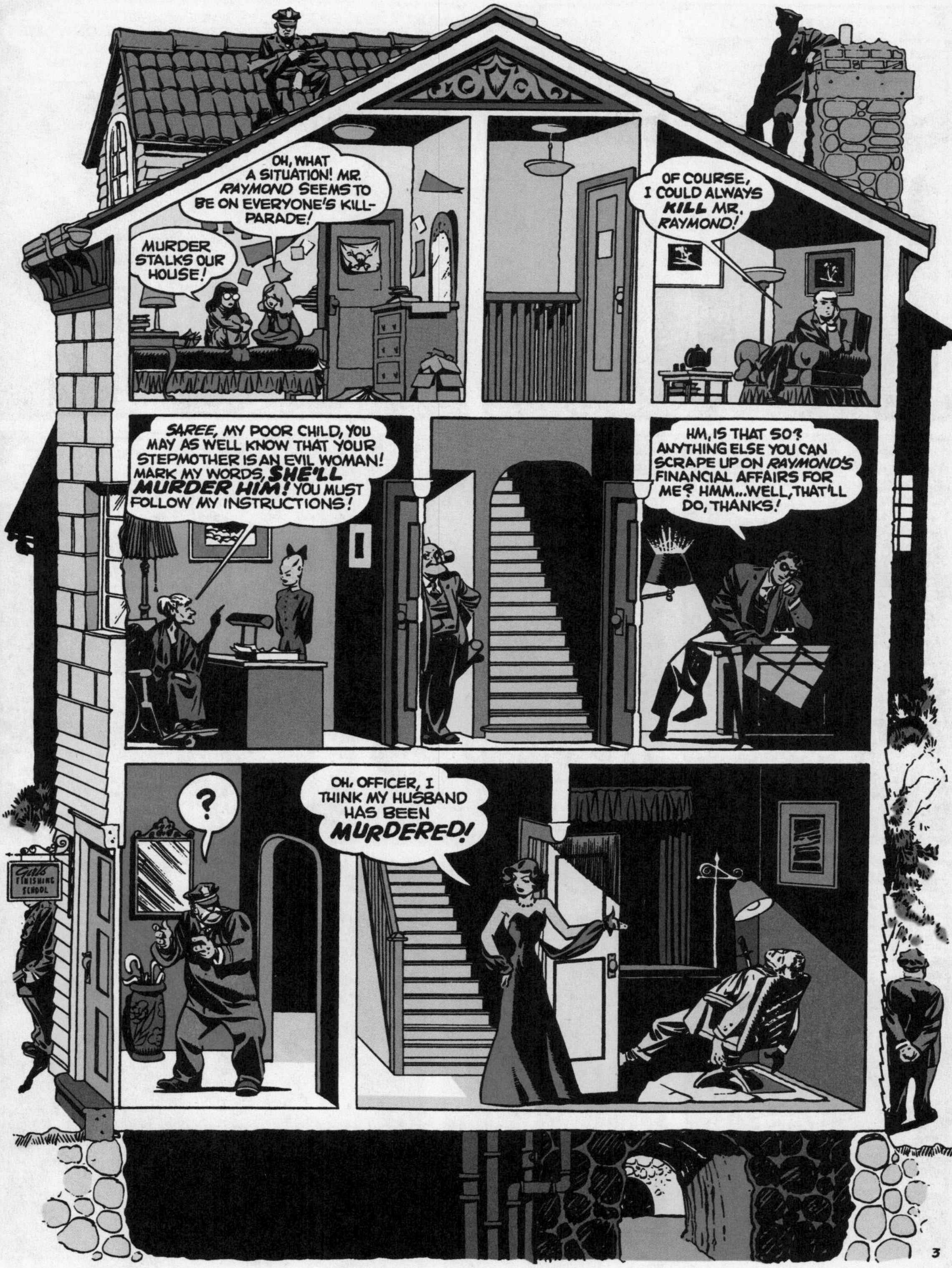
OH, WHAT A SITUATION! MR. RAYMOND SEEMS TO BE ON EVERYONE'S KILL-PARADE!
MURDER STALKS OUR HOUSE!
OF COURSE, I COULD ALWAYS KILL MR. RAYMOND!
SAREE, MY POOR CHILD, YOU MAY AS WELL KNOW THAT YOUR STEPMOTHER IS AN EVIL WOMAN! MARK MY WORDS, SHE'LL MURDER HIM! YOU MUST FOLLOW MY INSTRUCTIONS!
HM, IS THAT SO? ANYTHING ELSE YOU CAN SCRAPE UP ON RAYMOND'S FINANCIAL AFFAIRS FOR ME? HMM...WELL, THAT'LL DO, THANKS!
?
OH, OFFICER, I THINK MY HUSBAND HAS BEEN MURDERED!
GIRLS FINISHING SCHOOL
3

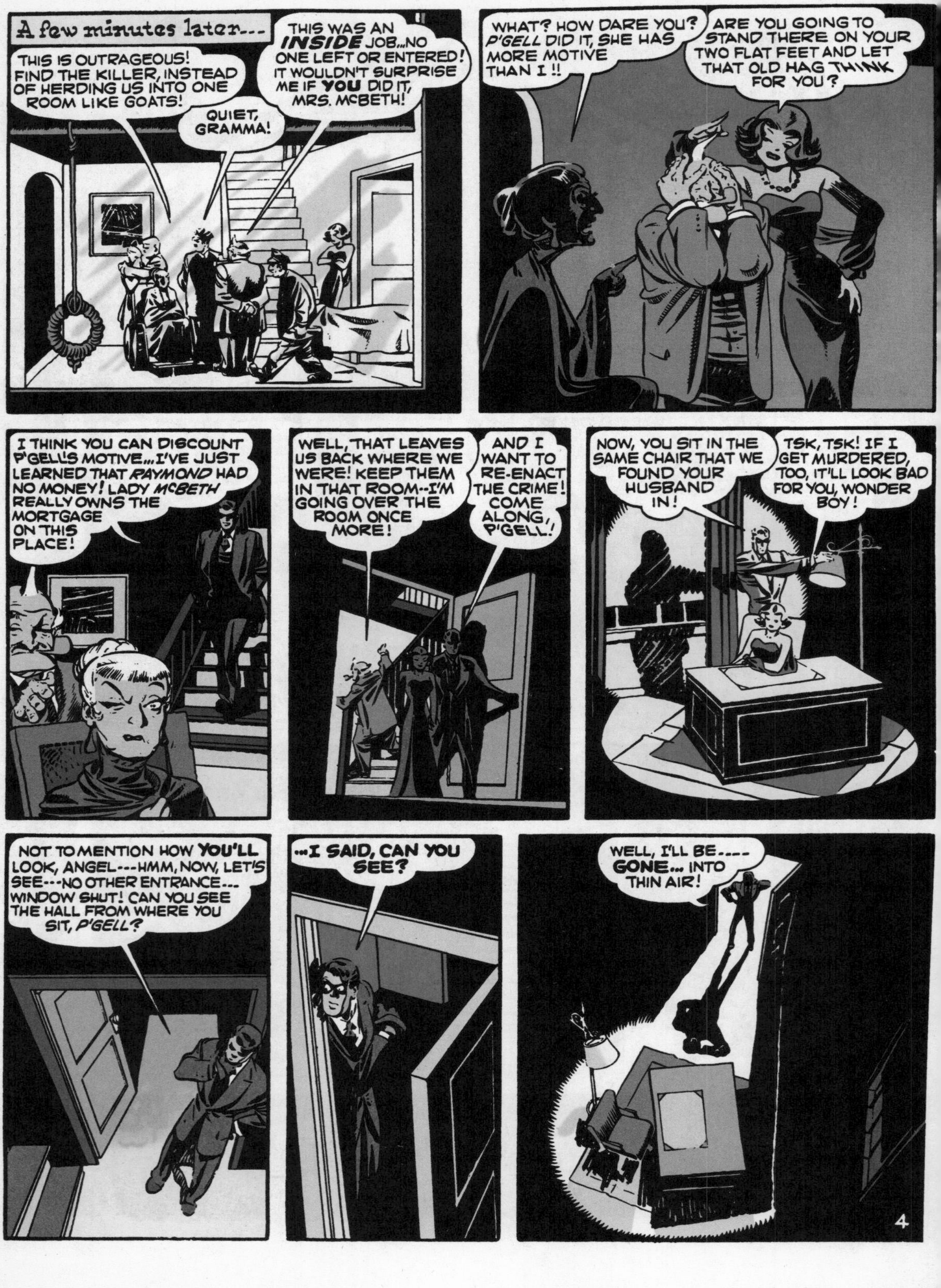
A few minutes later...
THIS IS OUTRAGEOUS! FIND THE KILLER, INSTEAD OF HERDING US INTO ONE ROOM LIKE GOATS!
QUIET, GRAMMA!
THIS WAS AN INSIDE JOB...NO ONE LEFT OR ENTERED! IT WOULDN'T SURPRISE ME IF YOU DID IT, MRS. McBETH!
WHAT? HOW DARE YOU? P'GELL DID IT, SHE HAS MORE MOTIVE THAN I !!
ARE YOU GOING TO STAND THERE ON YOUR TWO FLAT FEET AND LET THAT OLD HAG THINK FOR YOU?
I THINK YOU CAN DISCOUNT P'GELL'S MOTIVE...I'VE JUST LEARNED THAT RAYMOND HAD NO MONEY! LADY McBETH REALLY OWNS THE MORTGAGE ON THIS PLACE!
WELL, THAT LEAVES US BACK WHERE WE WERE! KEEP THEM IN THAT ROOM--I'M GOING OVER THE ROOM ONCE MORE!
AND I WANT TO RE-ENACT THE CRIME! COME ALONG, P'GELL!
NOW, YOU SIT IN THE SAME CHAIR THAT WE FOUND YOUR HUSBAND IN!
TSK, TSK! IF I GET MURDERED, TOO, IT'LL LOOK BAD FOR YOU, WONDER BOY!
NOT TO MENTION HOW YOU'LL LOOK, ANGEL---HMM, NOW, LET'S SEE---NO OTHER ENTRANCE... WINDOW SHUT! CAN YOU SEE THE HALL FROM WHERE YOU SIT, P'GELL?
...I SAID, CAN YOU SEE?
WELL, I'LL BE.... GONE... INTO THIN AIR!
4

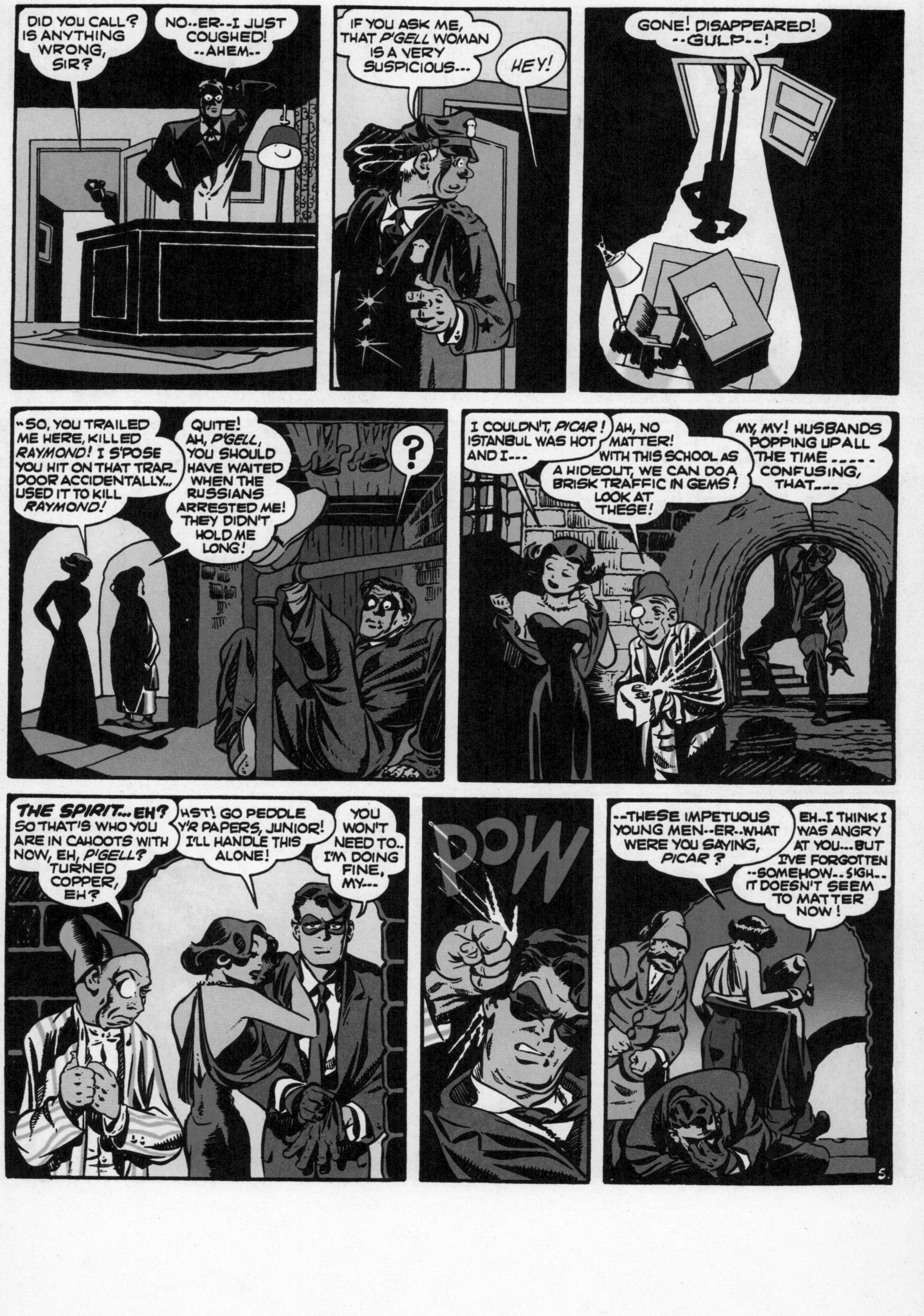
DID YOU CALL? IS ANYTHING WRONG, SIR?
NO..ER--I JUST COUGHED! --AHEM--
IF YOU ASK ME, THAT P'GELL WOMAN IS A VERY SUSPICIOUS...
HEY!
GONE! DISAPPEARED! --GULP--!
"SO, YOU TRAILED ME HERE, KILLED RAYMOND! I S'POSE YOU HIT ON THAT TRAP-DOOR ACCIDENTALLY... USED IT TO KILL RAYMOND!
QUITE! AH, P'GELL, YOU SHOULD HAVE WAITED WHEN THE RUSSIANS ARRESTED ME! THEY DIDN'T HOLD ME LONG!
?
I COULDN'T, PICAR! ISTANBUL WAS HOT AND I---
AH, NO MATTER! WITH THIS SCHOOL AS A HIDEOUT, WE CAN DO A BRISK TRAFFIC IN GEMS! LOOK AT THESE!
MY, MY! HUSBANDS POPPING UP ALL THE TIME ----- CONFUSING, THAT---
THE SPIRIT... EH? SO THAT'S WHO YOU ARE IN CAHOOTS WITH NOW, EH, P'GELL? TURNED COPPER, EH?
HST! GO PEDDLE Y'R PAPERS, JUNIOR! I'LL HANDLE THIS ALONE!
YOU WON'T NEED TO.. I'M DOING FINE, MY---
POW
--THESE IMPETUOUS YOUNG MEN--ER--WHAT WERE YOU SAYING, PICAR?
EH..I THINK I WAS ANGRY AT YOU... BUT I'VE FORGOTTEN --SOMEHOW.. SIGH.. IT DOESN'T SEEM TO MATTER NOW!
5.

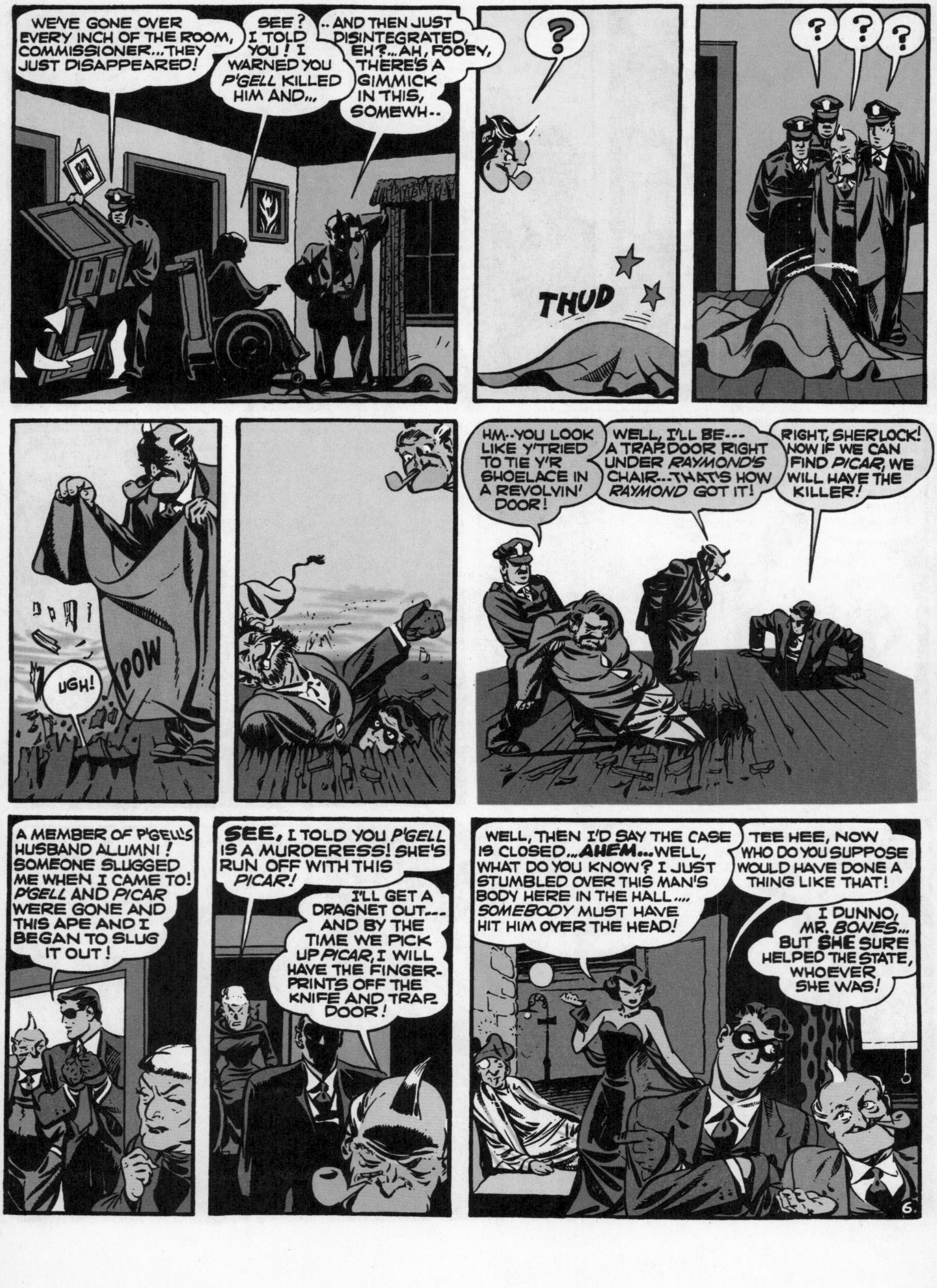
WE'VE GONE OVER EVERY INCH OF THE ROOM, COMMISSIONER... THEY JUST DISAPPEARED!
SEE? I TOLD YOU! I WARNED YOU P'GELL KILLED HIM AND...
..AND THEN JUST DISINTEGRATED, EH?...AH, FOOEY, THERE'S A GIMMICK IN THIS, SOMEWH..
?
THUD
? ? ?
UGH!
POW
HM..YOU LOOK LIKE Y'TRIED TO TIE Y'R SHOELACE IN A REVOLVIN' DOOR!
WELL, I'LL BE... A TRAP DOOR RIGHT UNDER RAYMOND'S CHAIR...THAT'S HOW RAYMOND GOT IT!
RIGHT, SHERLOCK! NOW IF WE CAN FIND PICAR, WE WILL HAVE THE KILLER!
A MEMBER OF P'GELL'S HUSBAND ALUMNI! SOMEONE SLUGGED ME WHEN I CAME TO! P'GELL AND PICAR WERE GONE AND THIS APE AND I BEGAN TO SLUG IT OUT!
SEE, I TOLD YOU P'GELL IS A MURDERESS! SHE'S RUN OFF WITH THIS PICAR!
I'LL GET A DRAGNET OUT... AND BY THE TIME WE PICK UP PICAR, I WILL HAVE THE FINGER-PRINTS OFF THE KNIFE AND TRAP DOOR!
WELL, THEN I'D SAY THE CASE IS CLOSED...AHEM...WELL, WHAT DO YOU KNOW? I JUST STUMBLED OVER THIS MAN'S BODY HERE IN THE HALL.... SOMEBODY MUST HAVE HIT HIM OVER THE HEAD!
TEE HEE, NOW WHO DO YOU SUPPOSE WOULD HAVE DONE A THING LIKE THAT!
I DUNNO, MR. BONES... BUT SHE SURE HELPED THE STATE, WHOEVER SHE WAS!
6.

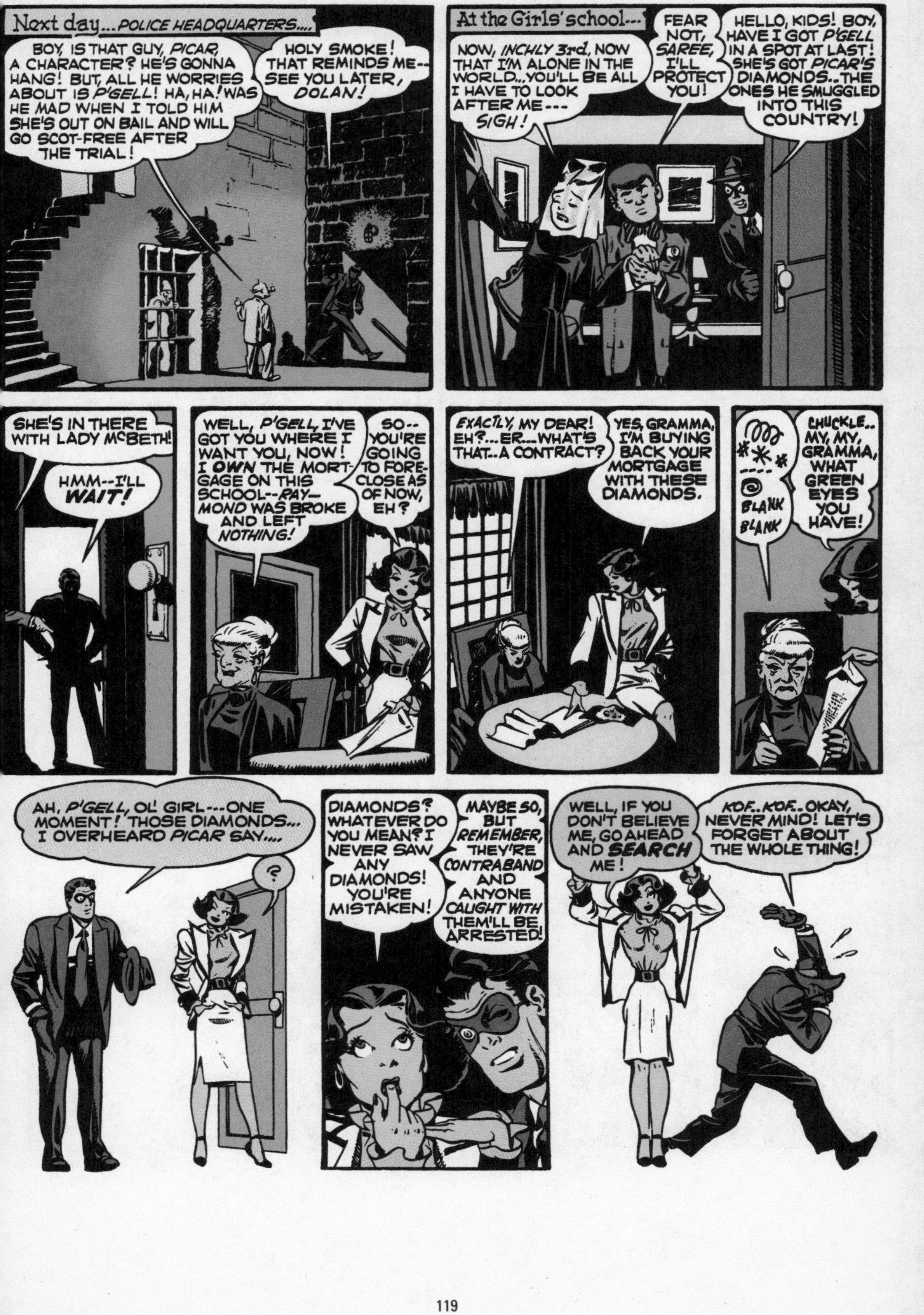
Next day... POLICE HEADQUARTERS....
BOY, IS THAT GUY, PICAR, A CHARACTER? HE'S GONNA HANG! BUT, ALL HE WORRIES ABOUT IS P'GELL! HA, HA! WAS HE MAD WHEN I TOLD HIM SHE'S OUT ON BAIL AND WILL GO SCOT-FREE AFTER THE TRIAL!
HOLY SMOKE! THAT REMINDS ME-- SEE YOU LATER, DOLAN!
At the Girls' school---
NOW, INCHLY 3rd, NOW THAT I'M ALONE IN THE WORLD... YOU'LL BE ALL I HAVE TO LOOK AFTER ME--- SIGH!
FEAR NOT, SAREE, I'LL PROTECT YOU!
HELLO, KIDS! BOY, HAVE I GOT P'GELL IN A SPOT AT LAST! SHE'S GOT PICAR'S DIAMONDS.. THE ONES HE SMUGGLED INTO THIS COUNTRY!
SHE'S IN THERE WITH LADY McBETH!
HMM--I'LL WAIT!
WELL, P'GELL, I'VE GOT YOU WHERE I WANT YOU, NOW! I OWN THE MORTGAGE ON THIS SCHOOL--RAYMOND WAS BROKE AND LEFT NOTHING!
SO-- YOU'RE GOING TO FORECLOSE AS OF NOW, EH?
EXACTLY, MY DEAR! EH?... ER... WHAT'S THAT.. A CONTRACT?
YES, GRAMMA, I'M BUYING BACK YOUR MORTGAGE WITH THESE DIAMONDS.
BLANK BLANK
CHUCKLE.. MY, MY, GRAMMA, WHAT GREEN EYES YOU HAVE!
AH, P'GELL, OL' GIRL---ONE MOMENT! THOSE DIAMONDS... I OVERHEARD PICAR SAY....
?
DIAMONDS? WHATEVER DO YOU MEAN? I NEVER SAW ANY DIAMONDS! YOU'RE MISTAKEN!
MAYBE SO, BUT REMEMBER, THEY'RE CONTRABAND AND ANYONE CAUGHT WITH THEM'LL BE ARRESTED!
WELL, IF YOU DON'T BELIEVE ME, GO AHEAD AND SEARCH ME!
KOF.. KOF.. OKAY, NEVER MIND! LET'S FORGET ABOUT THE WHOLE THING!

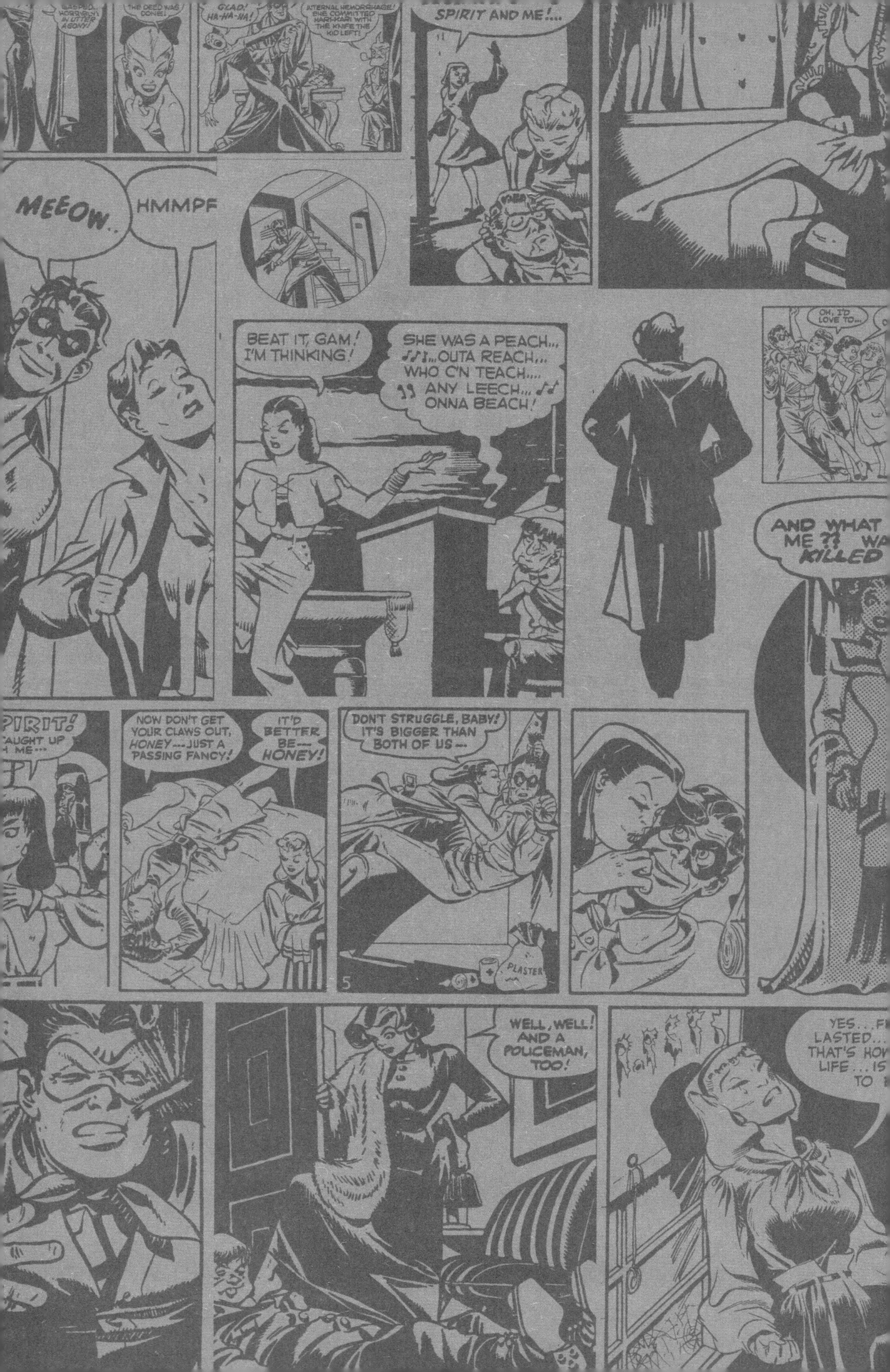
GASPED... HORRIBLY! IN UTTER AGONY!
THE DEED WAS DONE!
GLAD! HA-HA-HA!
ATERNAL HEMORRHAGE! SHE COMMITTED HARI-KARI WITH THE KNIFE THE KID LEFT!
SPIRIT AND ME!...
MEEOW..
HMMPF
BEAT IT, GAM! I'M THINKING!
SHE WAS A PEACH... ...OUTA REACH... WHO C'N TEACH.... ANY LEECH... ONNA BEACH!
OH, I'D LOVE TO...
AND WHAT ME ?? WA KILLED
SPIRIT! CAUGHT UP H ME---
NOW DON'T GET YOUR CLAWS OUT, HONEY---JUST A PASSING FANCY!
IT'D BETTER BE--- HONEY!
DON'T STRUGGLE, BABY! IT'S BIGGER THAN BOTH OF US---
5
PLASTER
WELL, WELL! AND A POLICEMAN, TOO!
YES...F LASTED... THAT'S HOW LIFE...IS TO

COMIC BOOK SECTION

SILKEN FLOSS, M.D.

ACTION Mystery ADVENTURE

The Spirit
Will Eisner
GAD!! WHAT SKILL!
WHAT CONSUMMATE COOLNESS!
AN ARTIST WITH NERVES OF STEEL!
THAT DR. FLOSS IS NOT HUMAN!
EXIT
UGH!
SCALPEL!
DR. QUAVER HAS FAINTED!
HERE..I'LL HELP IN HIS PLACE!
BAH!... ONE WOULD THINK THIS IS HIS FIRST OPERATION!
QUICKLY! YOUR ARM... HE NEEDS A TRANSFUSION.. CHECK YOUR BLOOD TYPE FIRST!
O.K.
...THERE!! IT'S FINISHED!
HE'S BREATHING NORMALLY AGAIN!
AMAZING SKILL!
BRAVO!
BRAVO, DR. FLOSS!
THANK YOU, GENTLEMEN!
© WILL EISNER
SOME COFFEE, SIR? Y'GAVE LOTS OF BLOOD!
OH, HE DOESN'T NEED IT! HE'S BUILT LIKE AN OX! COME IN HERE, SPIRIT, I WANT TO TALK TO YOU!

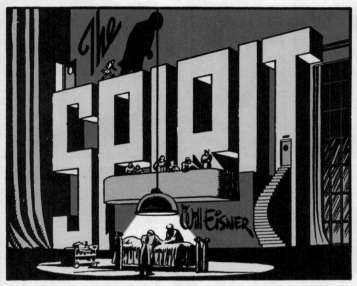

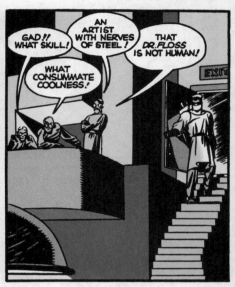

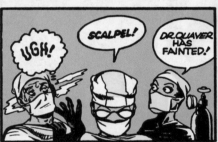

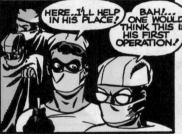

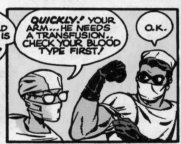

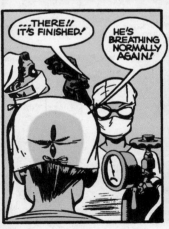

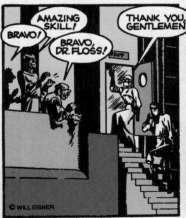

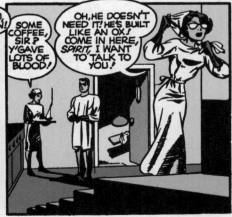

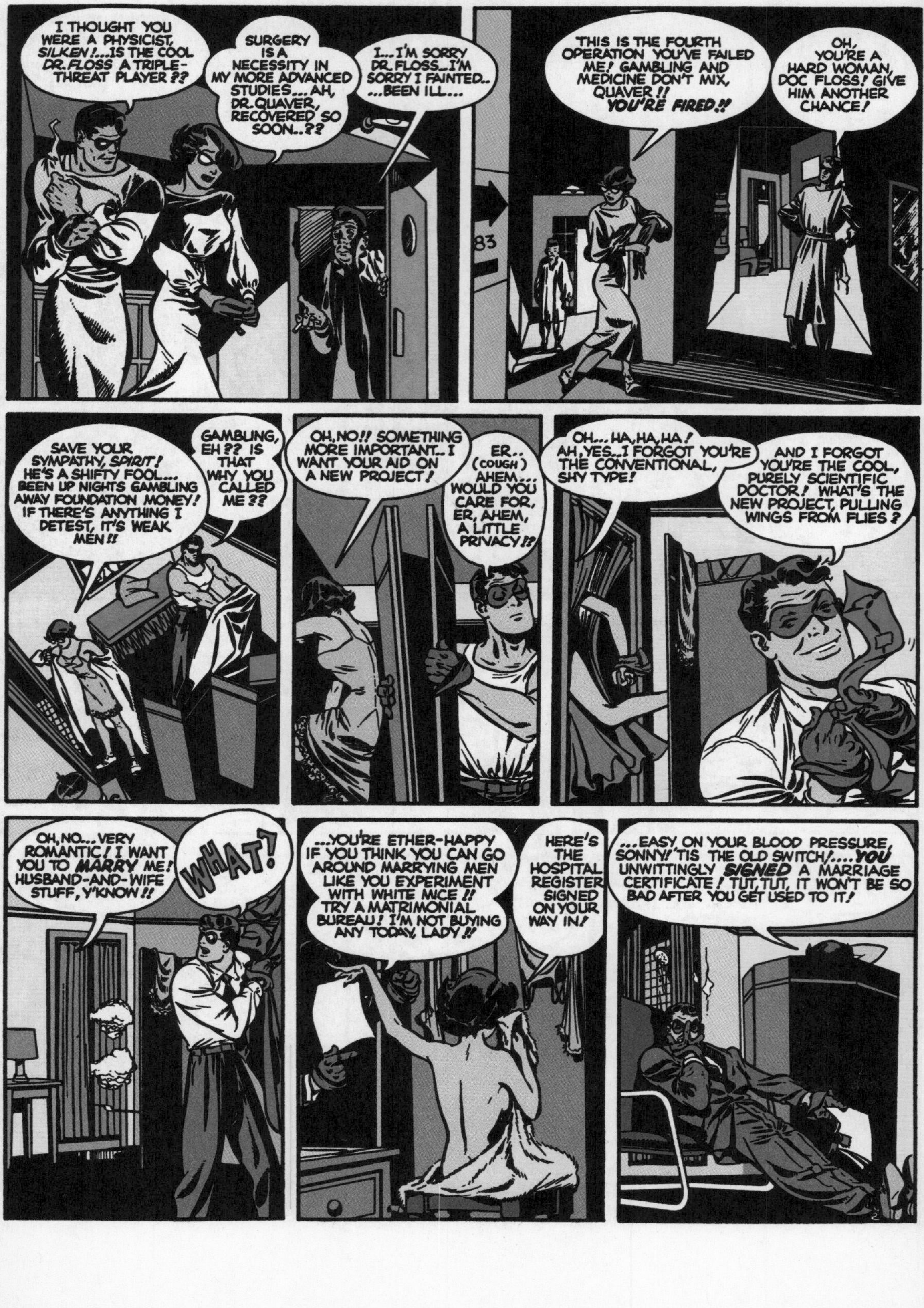
I THOUGHT YOU WERE A PHYSICIST, SILKEN!...IS THE COOL DR. FLOSS A TRIPLE-THREAT PLAYER ??
SURGERY IS A NECESSITY IN MY MORE ADVANCED STUDIES... AH, DR. QUAVER, RECOVERED SO SOON..??
I...I'M SORRY DR. FLOSS...I'M SORRY I FAINTED.. ...BEEN ILL...
THIS IS THE FOURTH OPERATION YOU'VE FAILED ME! GAMBLING AND MEDICINE DON'T MIX, QUAVER !! YOU'RE FIRED !!
OH, YOU'RE A HARD WOMAN, DOC FLOSS! GIVE HIM ANOTHER CHANCE!
SAVE YOUR SYMPATHY, SPIRIT! HE'S A SHIFTY FOOL... BEEN UP NIGHTS GAMBLING AWAY FOUNDATION MONEY! IF THERE'S ANYTHING I DETEST, IT'S WEAK MEN !!
GAMBLING, EH ?? IS THAT WHY YOU CALLED ME ??
OH, NO !! SOMETHING MORE IMPORTANT...I WANT YOUR AID ON A NEW PROJECT!
ER.. (COUGH) AHEM... WOULD YOU CARE FOR, ER, AHEM, A LITTLE PRIVACY !?
OH... HA, HA, HA! AH, YES...I FORGOT YOU'RE THE CONVENTIONAL, SHY TYPE!
AND I FORGOT YOU'RE THE COOL, PURELY SCIENTIFIC DOCTOR! WHAT'S THE NEW PROJECT, PULLING WINGS FROM FLIES ?
OH, NO... VERY ROMANTIC! I WANT YOU TO MARRY ME! HUSBAND-AND-WIFE STUFF, Y'KNOW !!
WHAT?
...YOU'RE ETHER-HAPPY IF YOU THINK YOU CAN GO AROUND MARRYING MEN LIKE YOU EXPERIMENT WITH WHITE MICE !! TRY A MATRIMONIAL BUREAU! I'M NOT BUYING ANY TODAY, LADY !!
HERE'S THE HOSPITAL REGISTER SIGNED ON YOUR WAY IN!
...EASY ON YOUR BLOOD PRESSURE, SONNY! 'TIS THE OLD SWITCH!... YOU UNWITTINGLY SIGNED A MARRIAGE CERTIFICATE! TUT, TUT, IT WON'T BE SO BAD AFTER YOU GET USED TO IT!

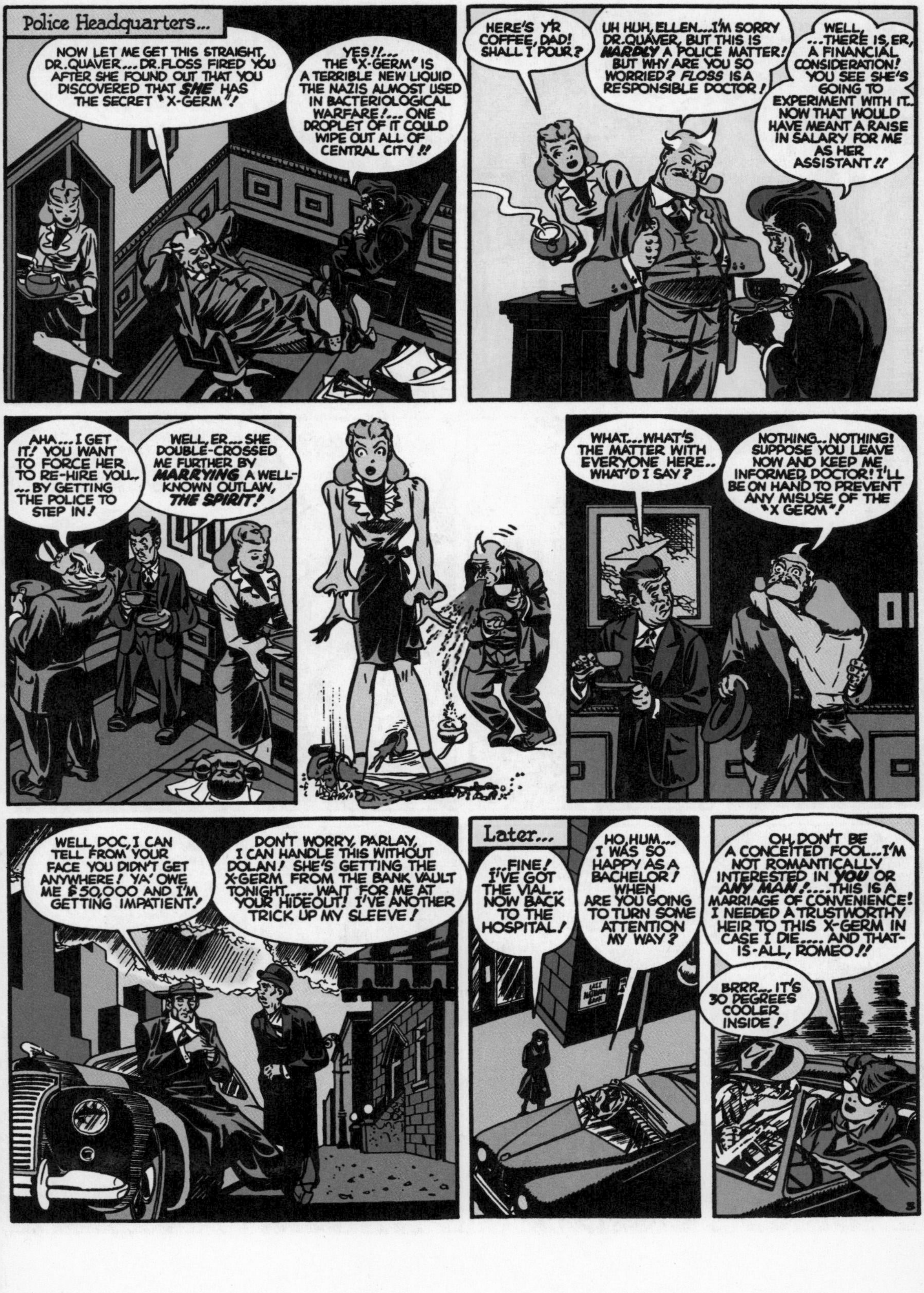
Police Headquarters...
NOW LET ME GET THIS STRAIGHT, DR. QUAVER... DR. FLOSS FIRED YOU AFTER SHE FOUND OUT THAT YOU DISCOVERED THAT SHE HAS THE SECRET "X-GERM"!
YES!!... THE "X-GERM" IS A TERRIBLE NEW LIQUID THE NAZIS ALMOST USED IN BACTERIOLOGICAL WARFARE!... ONE DROPLET OF IT COULD WIPE OUT ALL OF CENTRAL CITY!!
HERE'S Y'R COFFEE, DAD! SHALL I POUR?
UH HUH, ELLEN...I'M SORRY DR. QUAVER, BUT THIS IS HARDLY A POLICE MATTER! BUT WHY ARE YOU SO WORRIED? FLOSS IS A RESPONSIBLE DOCTOR!
WELL, ...THERE IS, ER, A FINANCIAL CONSIDERATION! YOU SEE SHE'S GOING TO EXPERIMENT WITH IT... NOW THAT WOULD HAVE MEANT A RAISE IN SALARY FOR ME AS HER ASSISTANT!!
AHA... I GET IT! YOU WANT TO FORCE HER TO RE-HIRE YOU... ...BY GETTING THE POLICE TO STEP IN!
WELL, ER... SHE DOUBLE-CROSSED ME FURTHER BY MARRYING A WELL-KNOWN OUTLAW, THE SPIRIT!
WHAT...WHAT'S THE MATTER WITH EVERYONE HERE.. WHAT'D I SAY?
NOTHING.. NOTHING! SUPPOSE YOU LEAVE NOW AND KEEP ME INFORMED, DOCTOR! I'LL BE ON HAND TO PREVENT ANY MISUSE OF THE "X GERM"!
WELL, DOC, I CAN TELL FROM YOUR FACE YOU DIDN'T GET ANYWHERE! YA' OWE ME $50,000 AND I'M GETTING IMPATIENT!
DON'T WORRY, PARLAY, I CAN HANDLE THIS WITHOUT DOLAN! SHE'S GETTING THE X-GERM FROM THE BANK VAULT TONIGHT..... WAIT FOR ME AT YOUR HIDEOUT! I'VE ANOTHER TRICK UP MY SLEEVE!
Later...
...FINE! I'VE GOT THE VIAL... NOW BACK TO THE HOSPITAL!
HO, HUM... I WAS SO HAPPY AS A BACHELOR! WHEN ARE YOU GOING TO TURN SOME ATTENTION MY WAY?
OH, DON'T BE A CONCEITED FOOL...I'M NOT ROMANTICALLY INTERESTED IN YOU OR ANY MAN!....THIS IS A MARRIAGE OF CONVENIENCE! I NEEDED A TRUSTWORTHY HEIR TO THIS X-GERM IN CASE I DIE.... AND THAT-IS-ALL, ROMEO!!
BRRR... IT'S 30 DEGREES COOLER INSIDE!
3

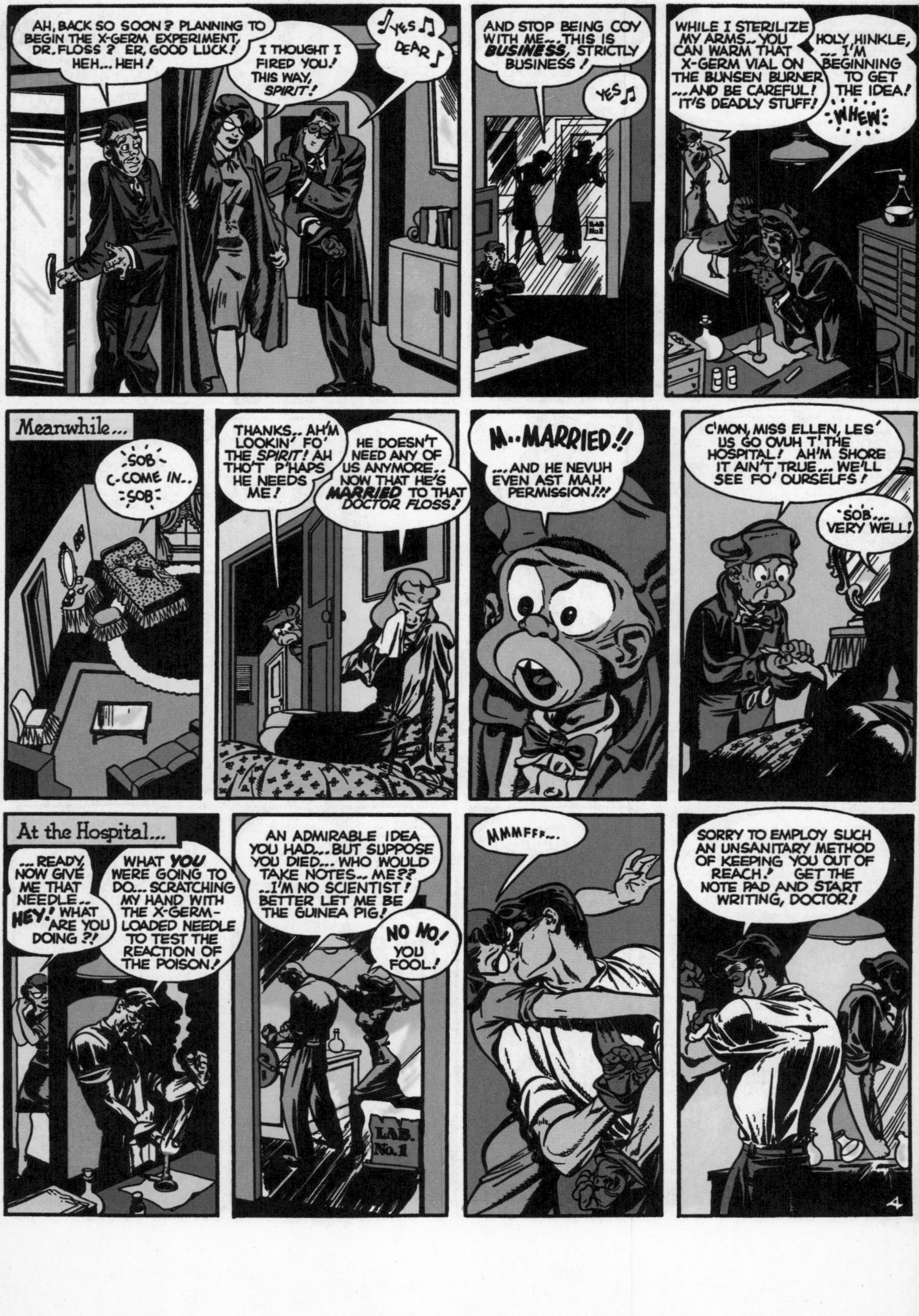

AH, BACK SO SOON? PLANNING TO BEGIN THE X-GERM EXPERIMENT, DR. FLOSS? ER, GOOD LUCK! HEH... HEH!
I THOUGHT I FIRED YOU! THIS WAY, SPIRIT!
YES DEAR
AND STOP BEING COY WITH ME... THIS IS BUSINESS, STRICTLY BUSINESS!
YES
WHILE I STERILIZE MY ARMS.. YOU CAN WARM THAT X-GERM VIAL ON THE BUNSEN BURNER ...AND BE CAREFUL! IT'S DEADLY STUFF!
HOLY HINKLE, ... I'M BEGINNING TO GET THE IDEA!
WHEW
Meanwhile...
SOB C-COME IN.. SOB
THANKS.. AH'M LOOKIN' FO' THE SPIRIT! AH THO'T P'HAPS HE NEEDS ME!
HE DOESN'T NEED ANY OF US ANYMORE.. NOW THAT HE'S MARRIED TO THAT DOCTOR FLOSS!
M..MARRIED!!
...AND HE NEVUH EVEN AST MAH PERMISSION!!!
C'MON, MISS ELLEN, LES' US GO OVUH T' THE HOSPITAL! AH'M SHORE IT AIN'T TRUE... WE'LL SEE FO' OURSELFS!
SOB... VERY WELL!
At the Hospital...
...READY, NOW GIVE ME THAT NEEDLE.. HEY! WHAT ARE YOU DOING?!
WHAT YOU WERE GOING TO DO... SCRATCHING MY HAND WITH THE X-GERM-LOADED NEEDLE TO TEST THE REACTION OF THE POISON!
AN ADMIRABLE IDEA YOU HAD... BUT SUPPOSE YOU DIED... WHO WOULD TAKE NOTES.. ME?? ..I'M NO SCIENTIST! BETTER LET ME BE THE GUINEA PIG!
NO NO! YOU FOOL!
LAB. No. 1
MMMFFF...
SORRY TO EMPLOY SUCH AN UNSANITARY METHOD OF KEEPING YOU OUT OF REACH! GET THE NOTE PAD AND START WRITING, DOCTOR!
4

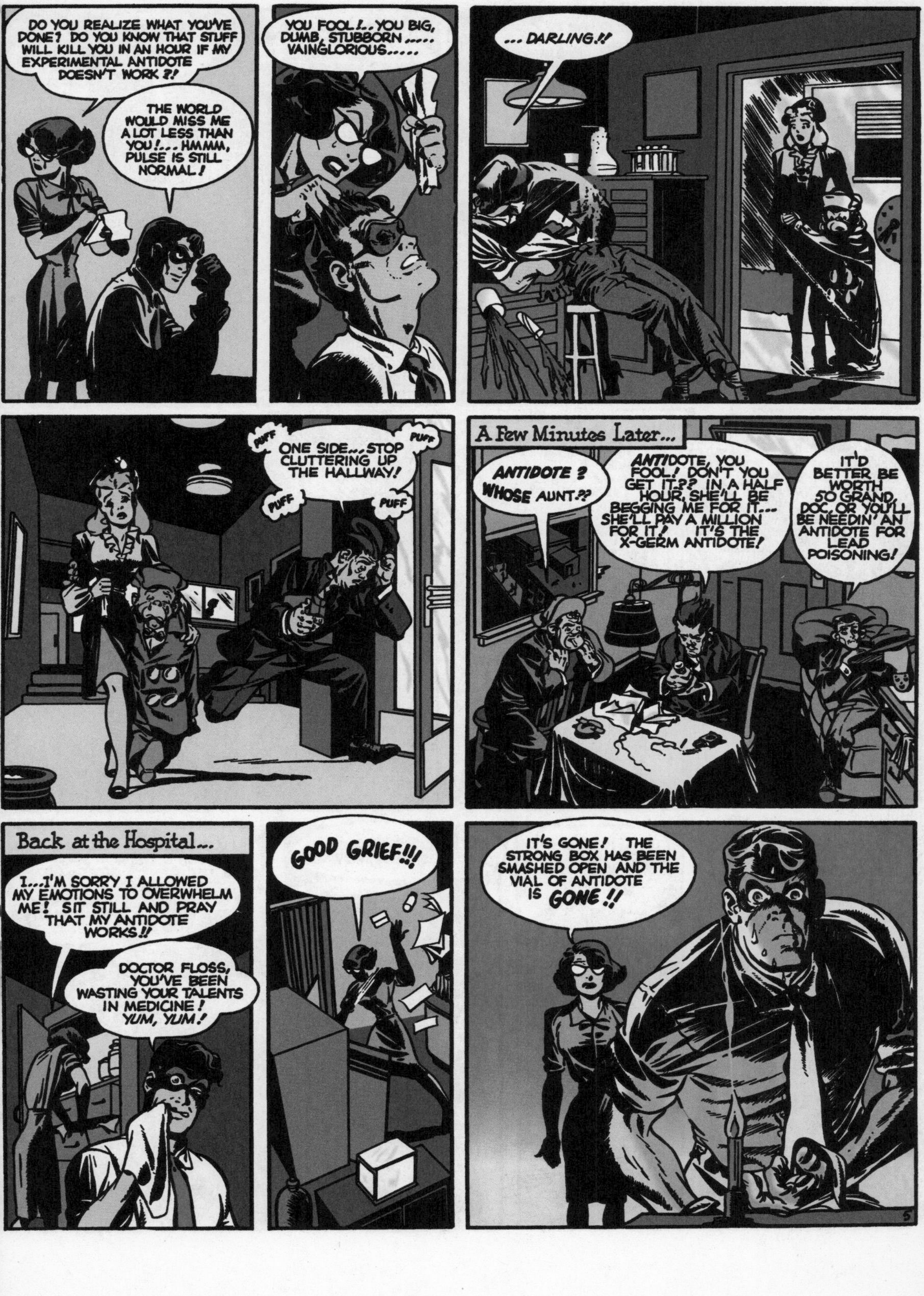

DO YOU REALIZE WHAT YOU'VE DONE? DO YOU KNOW THAT STUFF WILL KILL YOU IN AN HOUR IF MY EXPERIMENTAL ANTIDOTE DOESN'T WORK ?!
THE WORLD WOULD MISS ME A LOT LESS THAN YOU!... HMMM, PULSE IS STILL NORMAL!
YOU FOOL!.. YOU BIG, DUMB, STUBBORN..... VAINGLORIOUS.....
... DARLING.!!
PUFF
PUFF
ONE SIDE... STOP CLUTTERING UP THE HALLWAY!
PUFF
PUFF
A Few Minutes Later...
ANTIDOTE ? WHOSE AUNT.??
ANTIDOTE, YOU FOOL! DON'T YOU GET IT?? IN A HALF HOUR, SHE'LL BE BEGGING ME FOR IT... SHE'LL PAY A MILLION FOR IT! IT'S THE X-GERM ANTIDOTE!
IT'D BETTER BE WORTH 50 GRAND, DOC, OR YOU'LL BE NEEDIN' AN ANTIDOTE FOR LEAD POISONING!
Back at the Hospital...
I...I'M SORRY I ALLOWED MY EMOTIONS TO OVERWHELM ME! SIT STILL AND PRAY THAT MY ANTIDOTE WORKS!!
DOCTOR FLOSS, YOU'VE BEEN WASTING YOUR TALENTS IN MEDICINE! YUM, YUM!
GOOD GRIEF!!!
IT'S GONE! THE STRONG BOX HAS BEEN SMASHED OPEN AND THE VIAL OF ANTIDOTE IS GONE!!
5

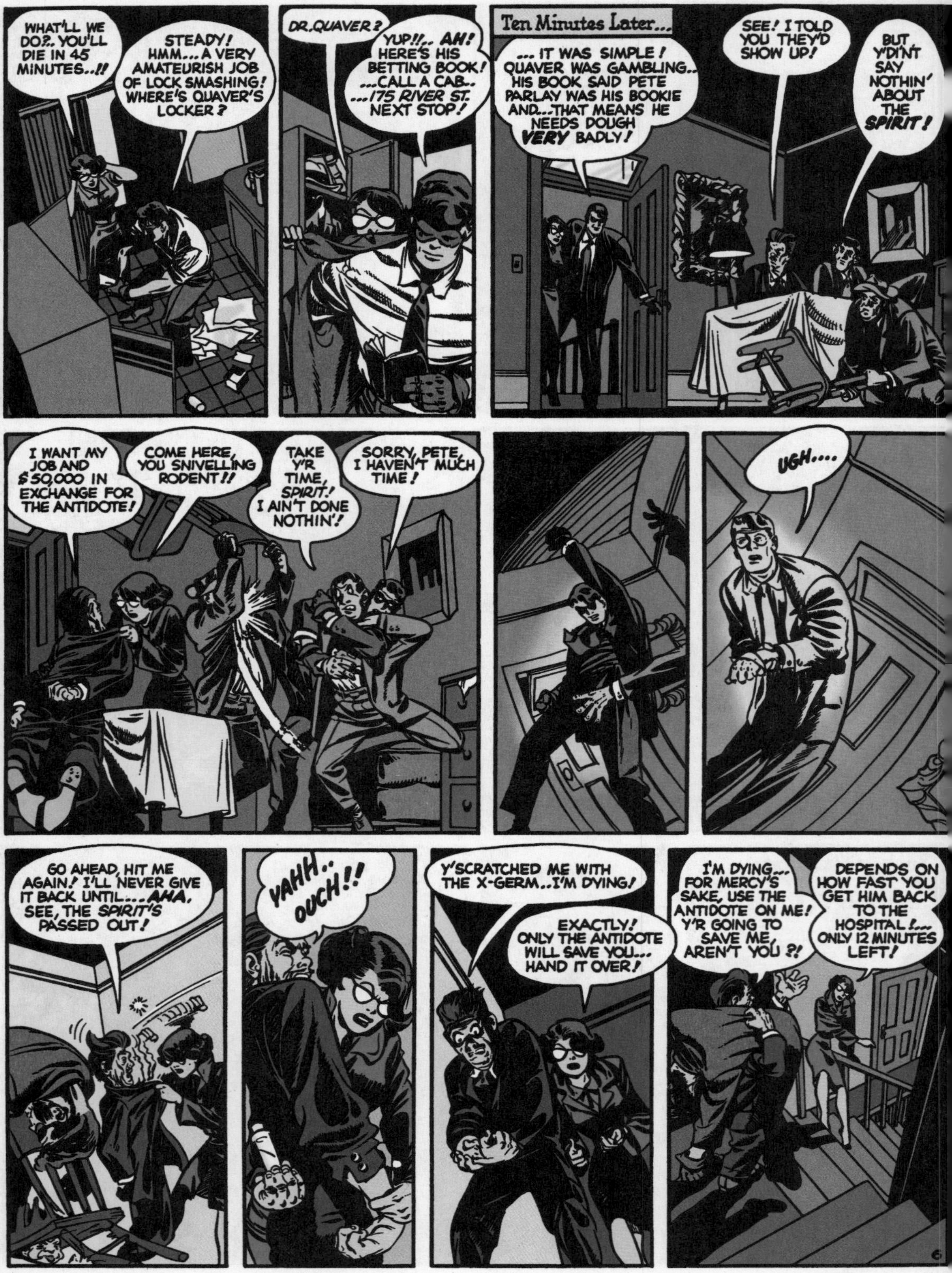
WHAT'LL WE DO?.. YOU'LL DIE IN 45 MINUTES..!!
STEADY! HMM... A VERY AMATEURISH JOB OF LOCK SMASHING! WHERE'S QUAVER'S LOCKER?
DR. QUAVER?
YUP!!.. AH! HERE'S HIS BETTING BOOK! ...CALL A CAB.. ...175 RIVER ST. NEXT STOP!
Ten Minutes Later...
... IT WAS SIMPLE! QUAVER WAS GAMBLING.. HIS BOOK SAID PETE PARLAY WAS HIS BOOKIE AND...THAT MEANS HE NEEDS DOUGH VERY BADLY!
SEE! I TOLD YOU THEY'D SHOW UP!
BUT Y'DIN'T SAY NOTHIN' ABOUT THE SPIRIT!
I WANT MY JOB AND $50,000 IN EXCHANGE FOR THE ANTIDOTE!
COME HERE, YOU SNIVELLING RODENT!!
TAKE Y'R TIME, SPIRIT! I AIN'T DONE NOTHIN'!
SORRY, PETE, I HAVEN'T MUCH TIME!
UGH....
GO AHEAD, HIT ME AGAIN! I'LL NEVER GIVE IT BACK UNTIL... AHA, SEE, THE SPIRIT'S PASSED OUT!
YAHH.. OUCH!!
Y'SCRATCHED ME WITH THE X-GERM..I'M DYING!
EXACTLY! ONLY THE ANTIDOTE WILL SAVE YOU... HAND IT OVER!
I'M DYING... FOR MERCY'S SAKE, USE THE ANTIDOTE ON ME! Y'R GOING TO SAVE ME, AREN'T YOU ?!
DEPENDS ON HOW FAST YOU GET HIM BACK TO THE HOSPITAL!... ONLY 12 MINUTES LEFT!
6

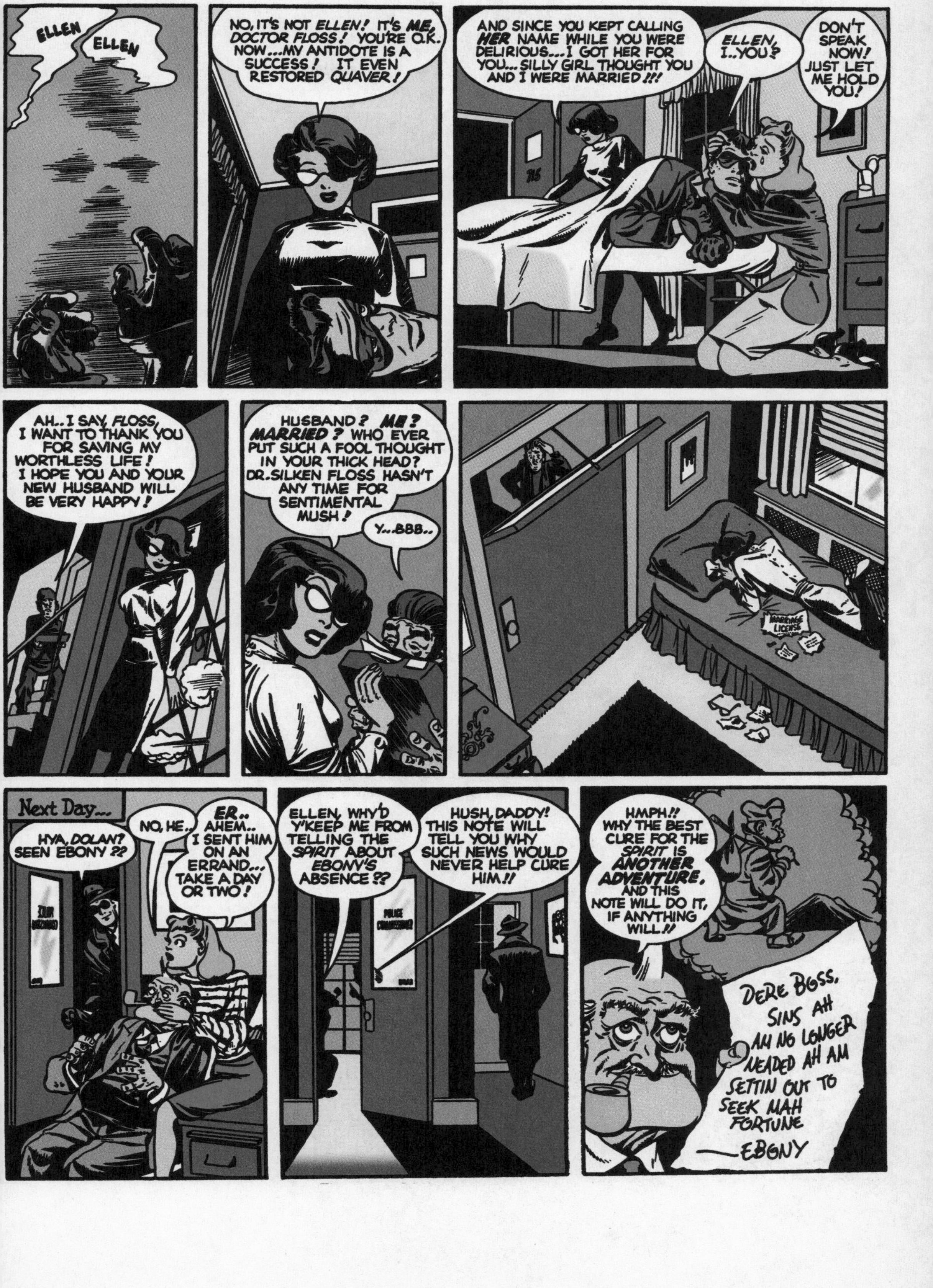
ELLEN
ELLEN
NO, IT'S NOT ELLEN! IT'S ME, DOCTOR FLOSS! YOU'RE O.K. NOW...MY ANTIDOTE IS A SUCCESS! IT EVEN RESTORED QUAVER!
AND SINCE YOU KEPT CALLING HER NAME WHILE YOU WERE DELIRIOUS...I GOT HER FOR YOU...SILLY GIRL THOUGHT YOU AND I WERE MARRIED!!!
ELLEN, I..YOU?
DON'T SPEAK NOW! JUST LET ME HOLD YOU!
AH..I SAY, FLOSS, I WANT TO THANK YOU FOR SAVING MY WORTHLESS LIFE! I HOPE YOU AND YOUR NEW HUSBAND WILL BE VERY HAPPY!
HUSBAND? ME? MARRIED? WHO EVER PUT SUCH A FOOL THOUGHT IN YOUR THICK HEAD? DR. SILKEN FLOSS HASN'T ANY TIME FOR SENTIMENTAL MUSH!
Y...BBB..
MARRIAGE LICENSE
Next Day...
HYA, DOLAN? SEEN EBONY??
NO, HE..
ER.. AHEM.. I SENT HIM ON AN ERRAND... TAKE A DAY OR TWO!
ELLEN, WHY'D Y'KEEP ME FROM TELLING THE SPIRIT ABOUT EBONY'S ABSENCE??
HUSH, DADDY! THIS NOTE WILL TELL YOU WHY SUCH NEWS WOULD NEVER HELP CURE HIM!!
HMPH!! WHY THE BEST CURE FOR THE SPIRIT IS ANOTHER ADVENTURE, AND THIS NOTE WILL DO IT, IF ANYTHING WILL!!
DERE BOSS, SINS AH AH NO LONGER NEADED AH AM SETTIN OUT TO SEEK MAH FORTUNE —EBONY

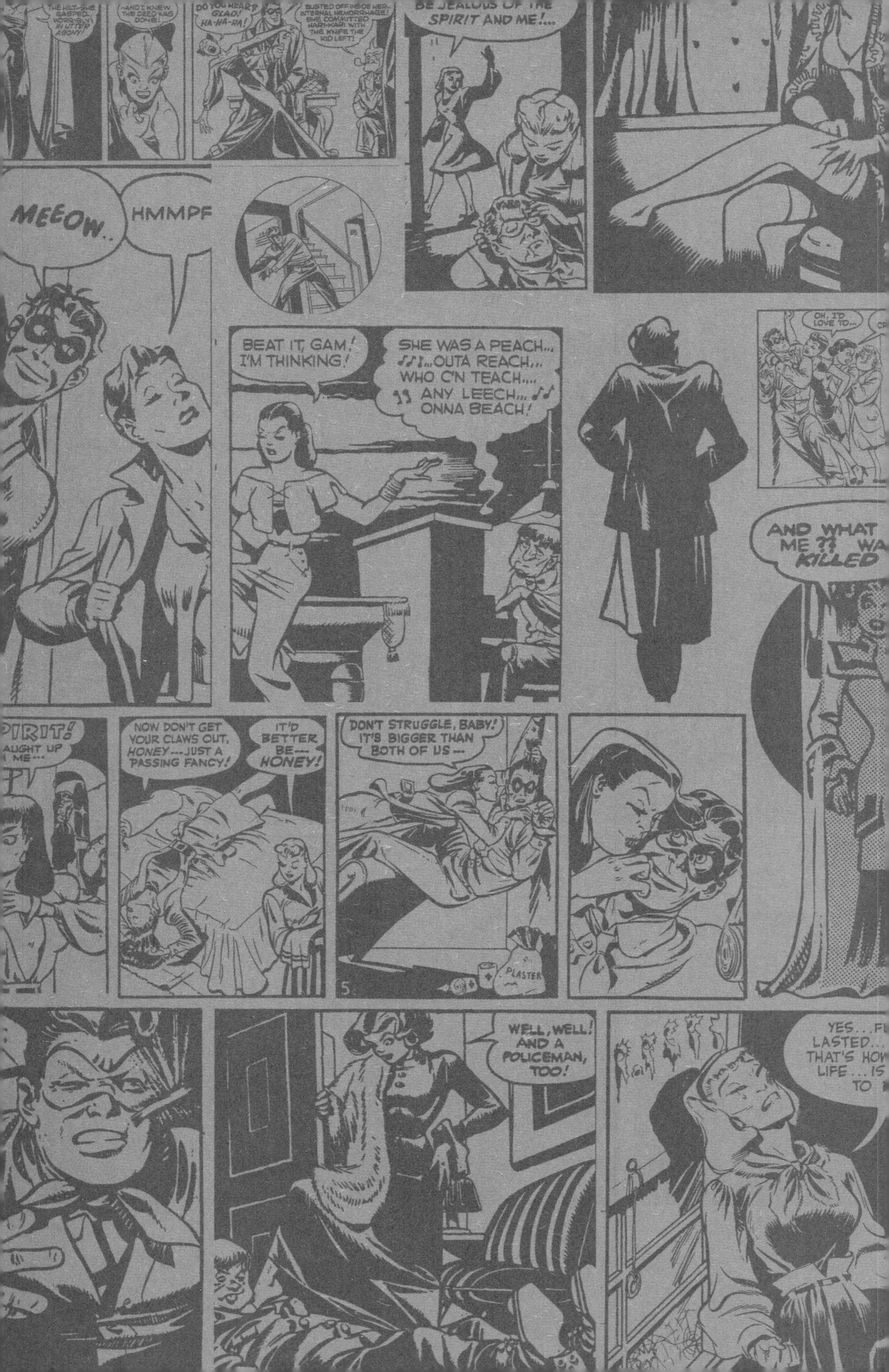
THE HILT—SHE GASPED.. HORRIBLY! IN UTTER AGONY!
—AND I KNEW THE DEED WAS DONE!
DO YOU HEAR? GLAD! HA-HA-HA!
BUSTED OFF INSIDE HER. INTERNAL HEMORRHAGE! SHE COMMITTED HARI-KARI WITH THE KNIFE THE KID LEFT!
SPIRIT AND ME!...
MEEOW..
HMMPF
BEAT IT, GAM! I'M THINKING!
SHE WAS A PEACH... ...OUTA REACH... WHO C'N TEACH.... ANY LEECH... ONNA BEACH!
OH, I'D LOVE TO...
AND WHAT ME ?? WA KILLED
NOW DON'T GET YOUR CLAWS OUT, HONEY---JUST A PASSING FANCY!
IT'D BETTER BE--- HONEY!
DON'T STRUGGLE, BABY! IT'S BIGGER THAN BOTH OF US---
PLASTER
WELL, WELL! AND A POLICEMAN, TOO!
YES... LASTED... THAT'S HOW LIFE... IS TO

APRIL FOOL

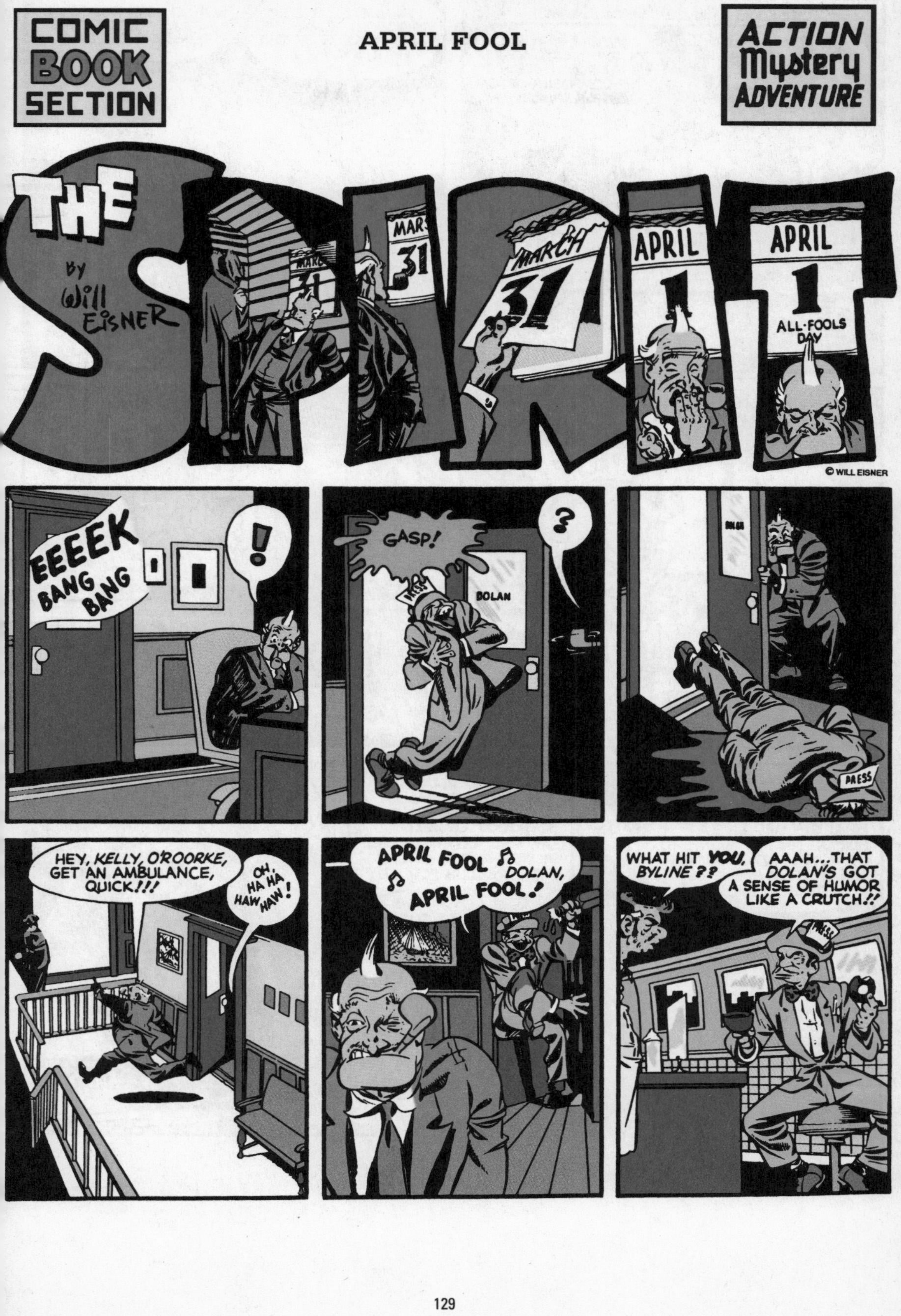

COMIC BOOK SECTION
ACTION Mystery ADVENTURE
THE SPIRIT
BY Will EISNER
MARS 31
MARCH 31
APRIL 1
APRIL 1 ALL·FOOLS DAY
© WILL EISNER
EEEEK BANG BANG
!
GASP!
PRESS
BOLAN
?
PRESS
HEY, KELLY, O'ROORKE, GET AN AMBULANCE, QUICK!!!
OH, HA HA HAW HAW!
APRIL FOOL DOLAN, APRIL FOOL!
WHAT HIT YOU, BYLINE ??
AAAH...THAT DOLAN'S GOT A SENSE OF HUMOR LIKE A CRUTCH!!
PRESS

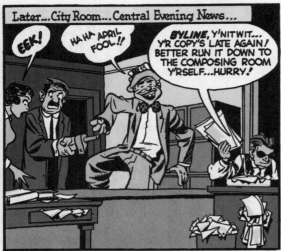

Later... City Room... Central Evening News...
EEK!
HA HA APRIL FOOL!!
BYLINE, Y'NITWIT... Y'R COPY'S LATE AGAIN! BETTER RUN IT DOWN TO THE COMPOSING ROOM Y'RSELF...HURRY!
PRESS
THANKS, I'LL RUSH IT THROUGH. HOW'S THE APRIL FOOL GAGS THIS YEAR, BYLINE?
NOT SO HOT! NOBODY'S GOT ANY SENSE OF HUMOR THESE DAYS!
OBITUARY
WELL, I WOULDN'T SAY THAT. ...DEPENDS ON HOW Y'LOOK AT IT.... JOKES IS STRICTLY PERSONAL!
PRESS
PRESS
WELL! WHAT D'YA KNOW? ROGER P. DEFICIT AND AVERY VAULT KILLED IN WHAT SEEMED LIKE A SUICIDE PACT AT MIDNIGHT. .... NOW I HADN'T NOTICED THAT ITEM IN THE DEATH NOTICES BEFORE!
REALLY ??
PRESS
I CAN'T UNDERSTAND IT! ...THEY WERE PALS AND PARTNERS SINCE BOYHOOD! OH, WELL ... SAY, WILL YOU DROP THESE STONE-PROOFS OFF AT THE CITY CLUB FOR ME?
SURE!
PRESS
HA HA HA HA HA HA HA !!!

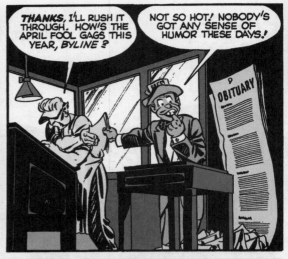

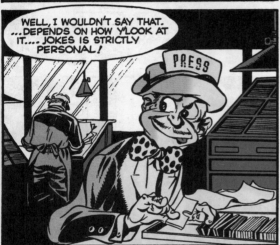

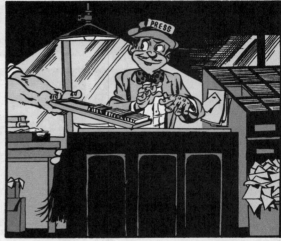

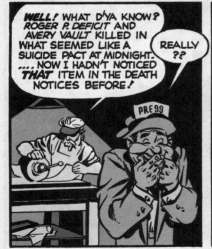

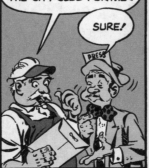

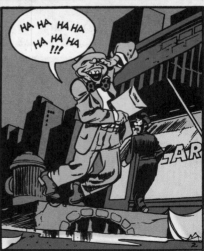

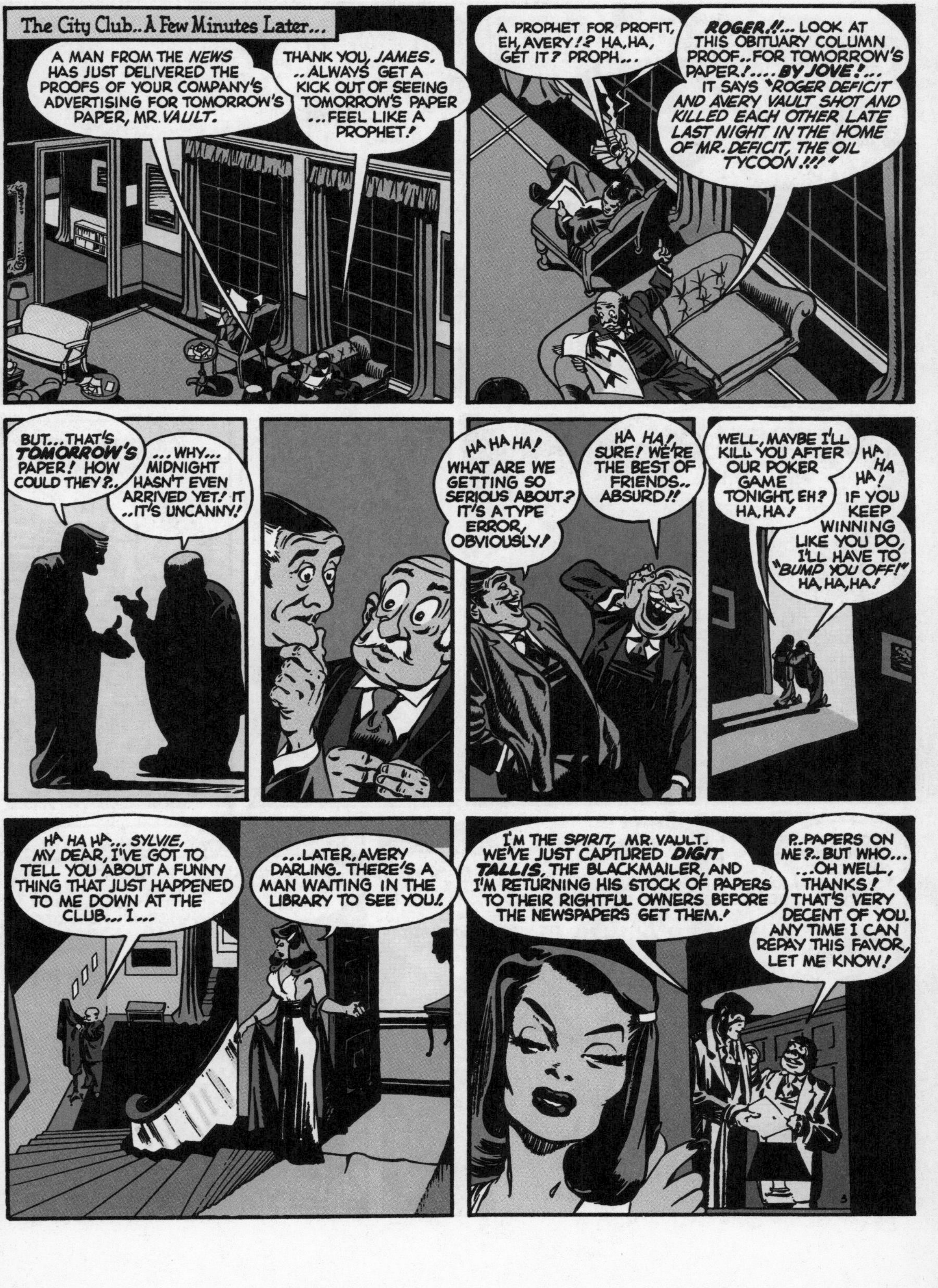
The City Club.. A Few Minutes Later...
A MAN FROM THE NEWS HAS JUST DELIVERED THE PROOFS OF YOUR COMPANY'S ADVERTISING FOR TOMORROW'S PAPER, MR. VAULT.
THANK YOU, JAMES. ..ALWAYS GET A KICK OUT OF SEEING TOMORROW'S PAPER ...FEEL LIKE A PROPHET!
A PROPHET FOR PROFIT, EH, AVERY!? HA, HA, GET IT? PROPH...
ROGER!!... LOOK AT THIS OBITUARY COLUMN PROOF..FOR TOMORROW'S PAPER!....BY JOVE!... IT SAYS "ROGER DEFICIT AND AVERY VAULT SHOT AND KILLED EACH OTHER LATE LAST NIGHT IN THE HOME OF MR. DEFICIT, THE OIL TYCOON!!!"
BUT...THAT'S TOMORROW'S PAPER! HOW COULD THEY?..
...WHY... MIDNIGHT HASN'T EVEN ARRIVED YET! IT ..IT'S UNCANNY!
HA HA HA! WHAT ARE WE GETTING SO SERIOUS ABOUT? IT'S A TYPE ERROR, OBVIOUSLY!
HA HA! SURE! WE'RE THE BEST OF FRIENDS.. ABSURD!!
WELL, MAYBE I'LL KILL YOU AFTER OUR POKER GAME TONIGHT, EH? HA, HA!
HA HA HA! IF YOU KEEP WINNING LIKE YOU DO, I'LL HAVE TO "BUMP YOU OFF!" HA, HA, HA!
HA HA HA... SYLVIE, MY DEAR, I'VE GOT TO TELL YOU ABOUT A FUNNY THING THAT JUST HAPPENED TO ME DOWN AT THE CLUB... I...
...LATER, AVERY DARLING. THERE'S A MAN WAITING IN THE LIBRARY TO SEE YOU!
I'M THE SPIRIT, MR. VAULT. WE'VE JUST CAPTURED DIGIT TALLIS, THE BLACKMAILER, AND I'M RETURNING HIS STOCK OF PAPERS TO THEIR RIGHTFUL OWNERS BEFORE THE NEWSPAPERS GET THEM.
P..PAPERS ON ME?.. BUT WHO... ...OH WELL, THANKS! THAT'S VERY DECENT OF YOU. ANY TIME I CAN REPAY THIS FAVOR, LET ME KNOW!
3

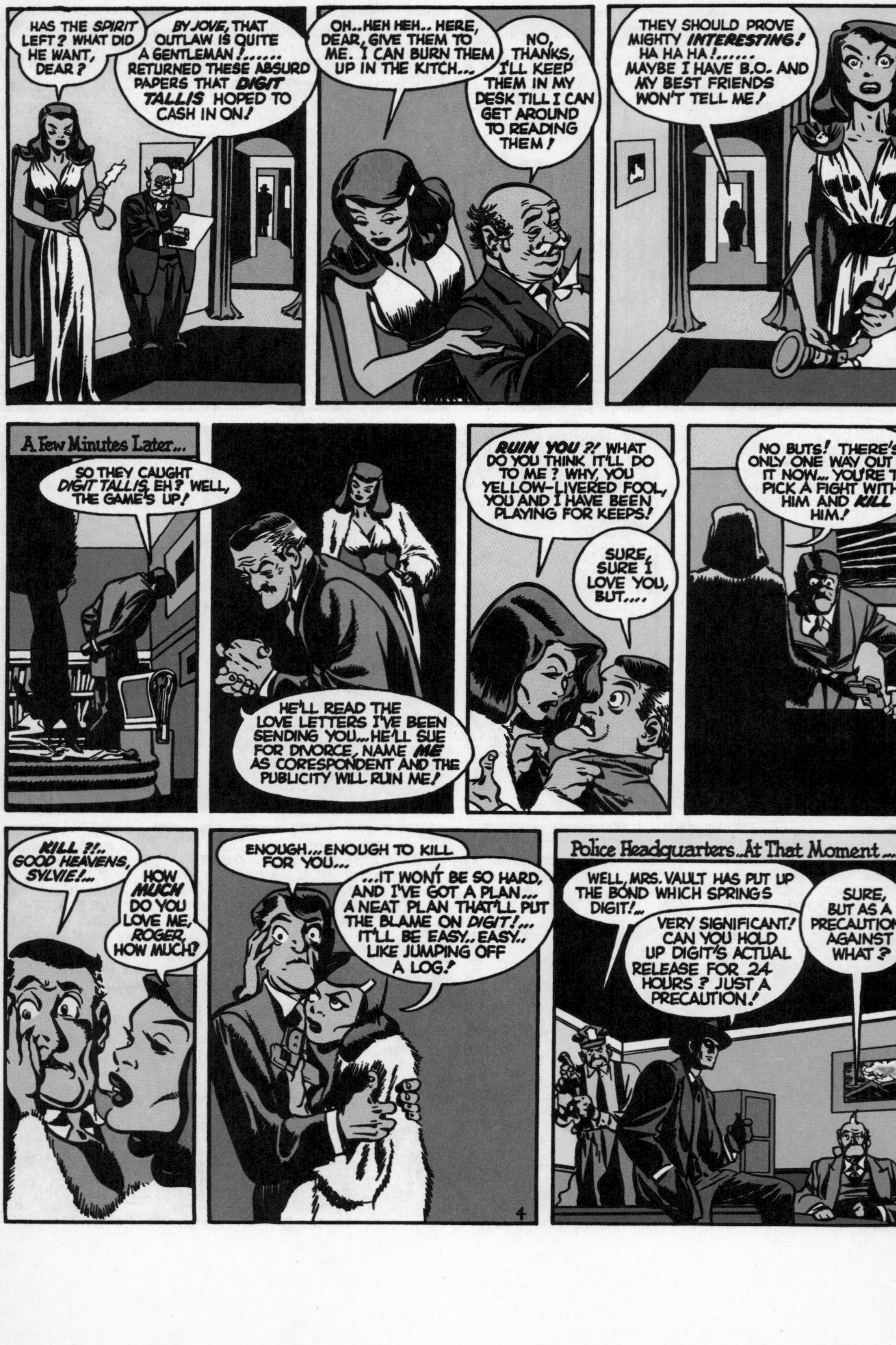

HAS THE SPIRIT LEFT? WHAT DID HE WANT, DEAR?
BY JOVE, THAT OUTLAW IS QUITE A GENTLEMAN!...... RETURNED THESE ABSURD PAPERS THAT DIGIT TALLIS HOPED TO CASH IN ON!
OH..HEH HEH.. HERE, DEAR, GIVE THEM TO ME. I CAN BURN THEM UP IN THE KITCH...
NO, THANKS, I'LL KEEP THEM IN MY DESK TILL I CAN GET AROUND TO READING THEM!
THEY SHOULD PROVE MIGHTY INTERESTING! HA HA HA!...... MAYBE I HAVE B.O. AND MY BEST FRIENDS WON'T TELL ME!
A Few Minutes Later...
SO THEY CAUGHT DIGIT TALLIS, EH? WELL, THE GAME'S UP!
HE'LL READ THE LOVE LETTERS I'VE BEEN SENDING YOU...HE'LL SUE FOR DIVORCE, NAME ME AS CORESPONDENT AND THE PUBLICITY WILL RUIN ME!
RUIN YOU?! WHAT DO YOU THINK IT'LL DO TO ME? WHY, YOU YELLOW-LIVERED FOOL, YOU AND I HAVE BEEN PLAYING FOR KEEPS!
SURE, SURE I LOVE YOU, BUT....
NO BUTS! THERE'S ONLY ONE WAY OUT OF IT NOW... YOU'RE TO PICK A FIGHT WITH HIM AND KILL HIM!
KILL?!.. GOOD HEAVENS, SYLVIE!...
HOW MUCH DO YOU LOVE ME, ROGER, HOW MUCH?
ENOUGH... ENOUGH TO KILL FOR YOU...
...IT WON'T BE SO HARD, AND I'VE GOT A PLAN... A NEAT PLAN THAT'LL PUT THE BLAME ON DIGIT!... IT'LL BE EASY.. EASY.. LIKE JUMPING OFF A LOG!
4
Police Headquarters..At That Moment....
WELL, MRS. VAULT HAS PUT UP THE BOND WHICH SPRINGS DIGIT!...
VERY SIGNIFICANT! CAN YOU HOLD UP DIGIT'S ACTUAL RELEASE FOR 24 HOURS? JUST A PRECAUTION!
SURE, BUT AS A PRECAUTION AGAINST WHAT?

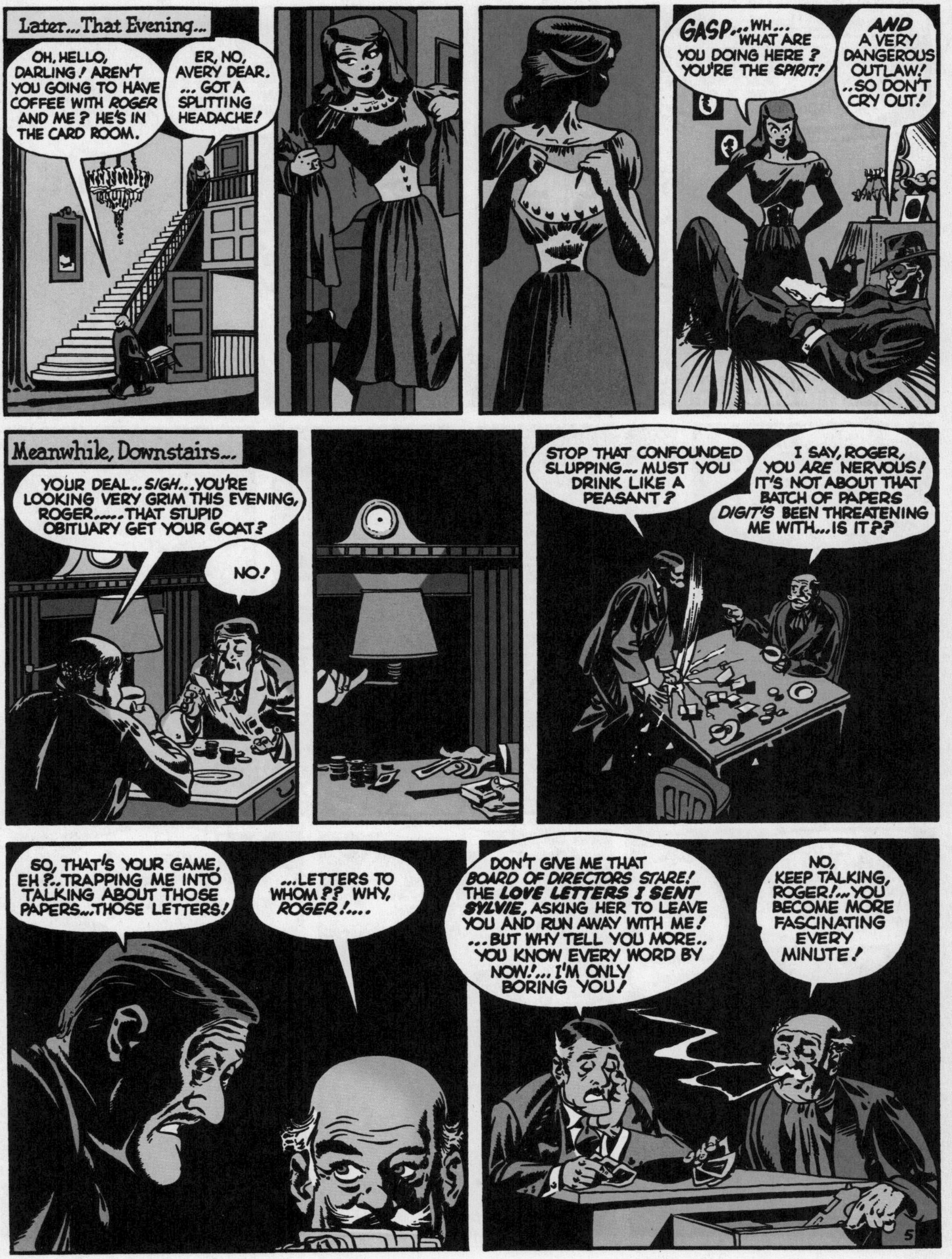
Later...That Evening...
OH, HELLO, DARLING! AREN'T YOU GOING TO HAVE COFFEE WITH ROGER AND ME? HE'S IN THE CARD ROOM.
ER, NO, AVERY DEAR. ...GOT A SPLITTING HEADACHE!
GASP...WH... WHAT ARE YOU DOING HERE? YOU'RE THE SPIRIT!
AND A VERY DANGEROUS OUTLAW! ..SO DON'T CRY OUT!
Meanwhile, Downstairs...
YOUR DEAL...SIGH...YOU'RE LOOKING VERY GRIM THIS EVENING, ROGER.....THAT STUPID OBITUARY GET YOUR GOAT?
NO!
STOP THAT CONFOUNDED SLUPPING... MUST YOU DRINK LIKE A PEASANT?
I SAY, ROGER, YOU ARE NERVOUS! IT'S NOT ABOUT THAT BATCH OF PAPERS DIGIT'S BEEN THREATENING ME WITH...IS IT??
SO, THAT'S YOUR GAME, EH?..TRAPPING ME INTO TALKING ABOUT THOSE PAPERS...THOSE LETTERS!
...LETTERS TO WHOM?? WHY, ROGER!....
DON'T GIVE ME THAT BOARD OF DIRECTORS STARE! THE LOVE LETTERS I SENT SYLVIE, ASKING HER TO LEAVE YOU AND RUN AWAY WITH ME! ...BUT WHY TELL YOU MORE.. YOU KNOW EVERY WORD BY NOW!...I'M ONLY BORING YOU!
NO, KEEP TALKING, ROGER!...YOU BECOME MORE FASCINATING EVERY MINUTE!
5

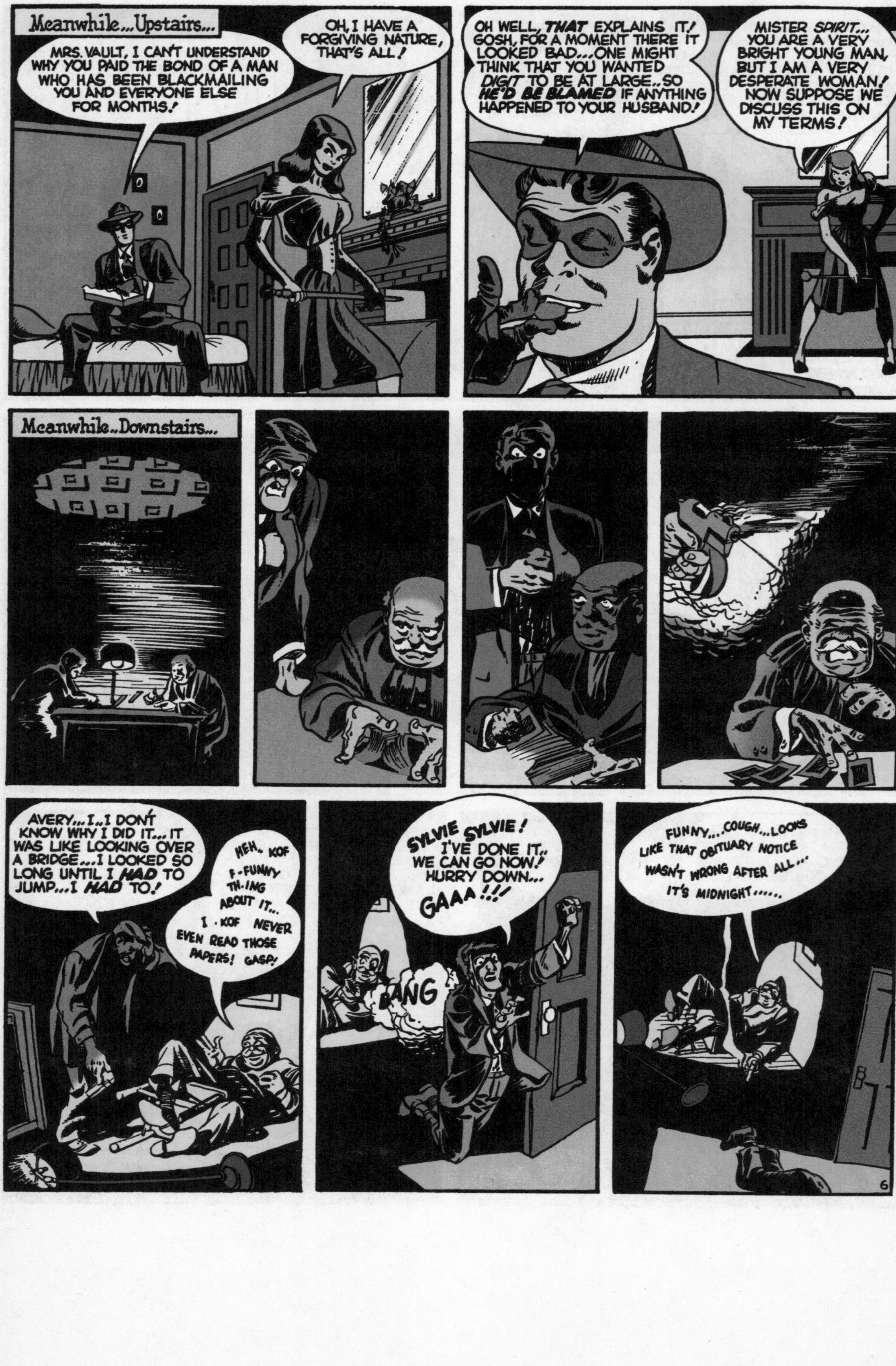

Meanwhile... Upstairs...
MRS. VAULT, I CAN'T UNDERSTAND WHY YOU PAID THE BOND OF A MAN WHO HAS BEEN BLACKMAILING YOU AND EVERYONE ELSE FOR MONTHS!
OH, I HAVE A FORGIVING NATURE, THAT'S ALL!
OH WELL, THAT EXPLAINS IT! GOSH, FOR A MOMENT THERE IT LOOKED BAD... ONE MIGHT THINK THAT YOU WANTED DIGIT TO BE AT LARGE.. SO HE'D BE BLAMED IF ANYTHING HAPPENED TO YOUR HUSBAND!
MISTER SPIRIT... YOU ARE A VERY BRIGHT YOUNG MAN, BUT I AM A VERY DESPERATE WOMAN! NOW SUPPOSE WE DISCUSS THIS ON MY TERMS!
Meanwhile.. Downstairs...
AVERY... I.. I DON'T KNOW WHY I DID IT... IT WAS LIKE LOOKING OVER A BRIDGE... I LOOKED SO LONG UNTIL I HAD TO JUMP... I HAD TO!
HEH.. KOF F-FUNNY TH-ING ABOUT IT..
I. KOF NEVER EVEN READ THOSE PAPERS! GASP!
SYLVIE SYLVIE! I'VE DONE IT.. WE CAN GO NOW! HURRY DOWN...
GAAA!!!
BANG
FUNNY... COUGH... LOOKS LIKE THAT OBITUARY NOTICE WASN'T WRONG AFTER ALL... IT'S MIDNIGHT......
6

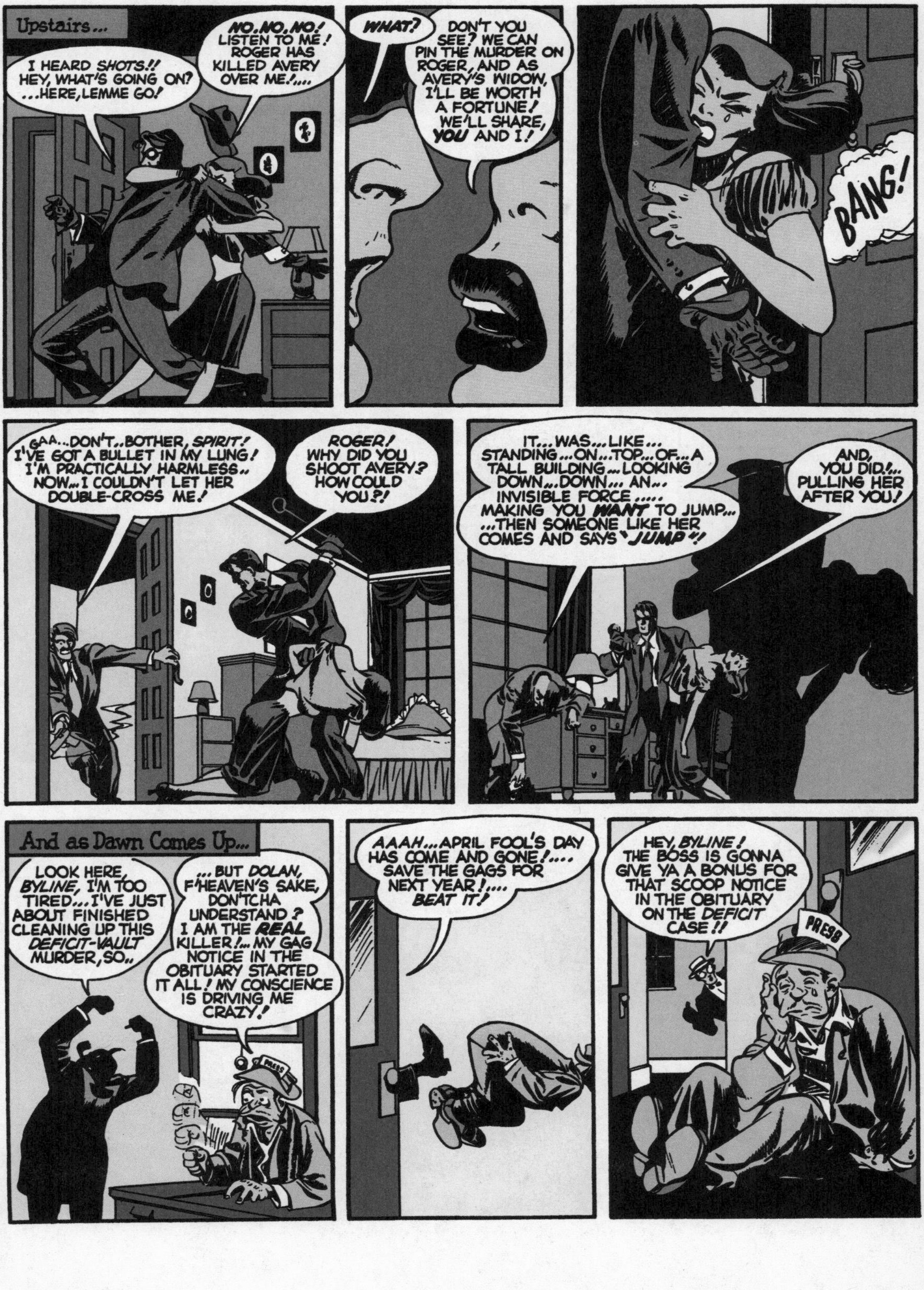
Upstairs...
I HEARD SHOTS!! HEY, WHAT'S GOING ON? ...HERE, LEMME GO!
NO. NO. NO! LISTEN TO ME! ROGER HAS KILLED AVERY OVER ME!...
WHAT?
DON'T YOU SEE? WE CAN PIN THE MURDER ON ROGER, AND AS AVERY'S WIDOW, I'LL BE WORTH A FORTUNE! WE'LL SHARE, YOU AND I!
BANG!
GAA...DON'T..BOTHER, SPIRIT! I'VE GOT A BULLET IN MY LUNG! I'M PRACTICALLY HARMLESS.. NOW... I COULDN'T LET HER DOUBLE-CROSS ME!
ROGER! WHY DID YOU SHOOT AVERY? HOW COULD YOU?!
IT...WAS...LIKE... STANDING...ON...TOP...OF...A TALL BUILDING...LOOKING DOWN...DOWN... AN... INVISIBLE FORCE..... MAKING YOU WANT TO JUMP... ...THEN SOMEONE LIKE HER COMES AND SAYS "JUMP"!
AND, YOU DID!... PULLING HER AFTER YOU!
And as Dawn Comes Up...
LOOK HERE, BYLINE, I'M TOO TIRED...I'VE JUST ABOUT FINISHED CLEANING UP THIS DEFICIT-VAULT MURDER, SO..
...BUT DOLAN, F'HEAVEN'S SAKE, DON'TCHA UNDERSTAND? I AM THE REAL KILLER!... MY GAG NOTICE IN THE OBITUARY STARTED IT ALL! MY CONSCIENCE IS DRIVING ME CRAZY!
AAAH...APRIL FOOL'S DAY HAS COME AND GONE!.... SAVE THE GAGS FOR NEXT YEAR!.... BEAT IT!
HEY, BYLINE! THE BOSS IS GONNA GIVE YA A BONUS FOR THAT SCOOP NOTICE IN THE OBITUARY ON THE DEFICIT CASE!!
PRESS

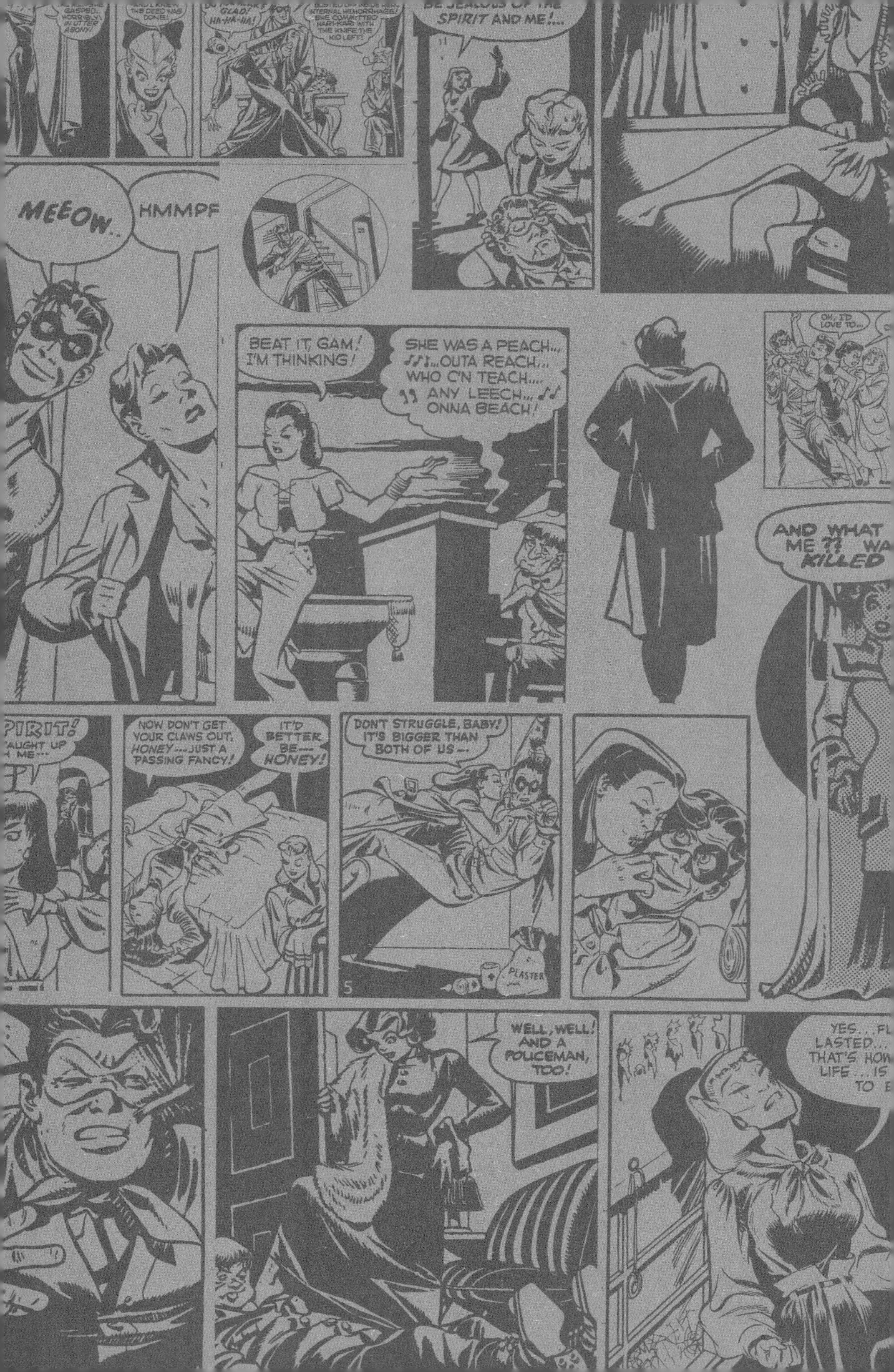
GASPED, HORRIBLY IN UTTER AGONY!
THE DEED WAS DONE!
GLAD! HA-HA-HA!
INTERNAL HEMORRHAGE! SHE COMMITTED HARI-KARI WITH THE KNIFE THE KID LEFT!
SPIRIT AND ME!...
MEEOW..
HMMPF
BEAT IT, GAM! I'M THINKING!
SHE WAS A PEACH... ...OUTA REACH... WHO C'N TEACH.... ANY LEECH... ONNA BEACH!
OH, I'D LOVE TO...
AND WHAT ME ?? KILLED
NOW DON'T GET YOUR CLAWS OUT, HONEY---JUST A PASSING FANCY!
IT'D BETTER BE--- HONEY!
DON'T STRUGGLE, BABY! IT'S BIGGER THAN BOTH OF US--
PLASTER
5
WELL, WELL! AND A POLICEMAN, TOO!
YES... LASTED... THAT'S HOW LIFE ... IS TO

COMIC BOOK SECTION

MONEY, MONEY

ACTION Mystery ADVENTURE

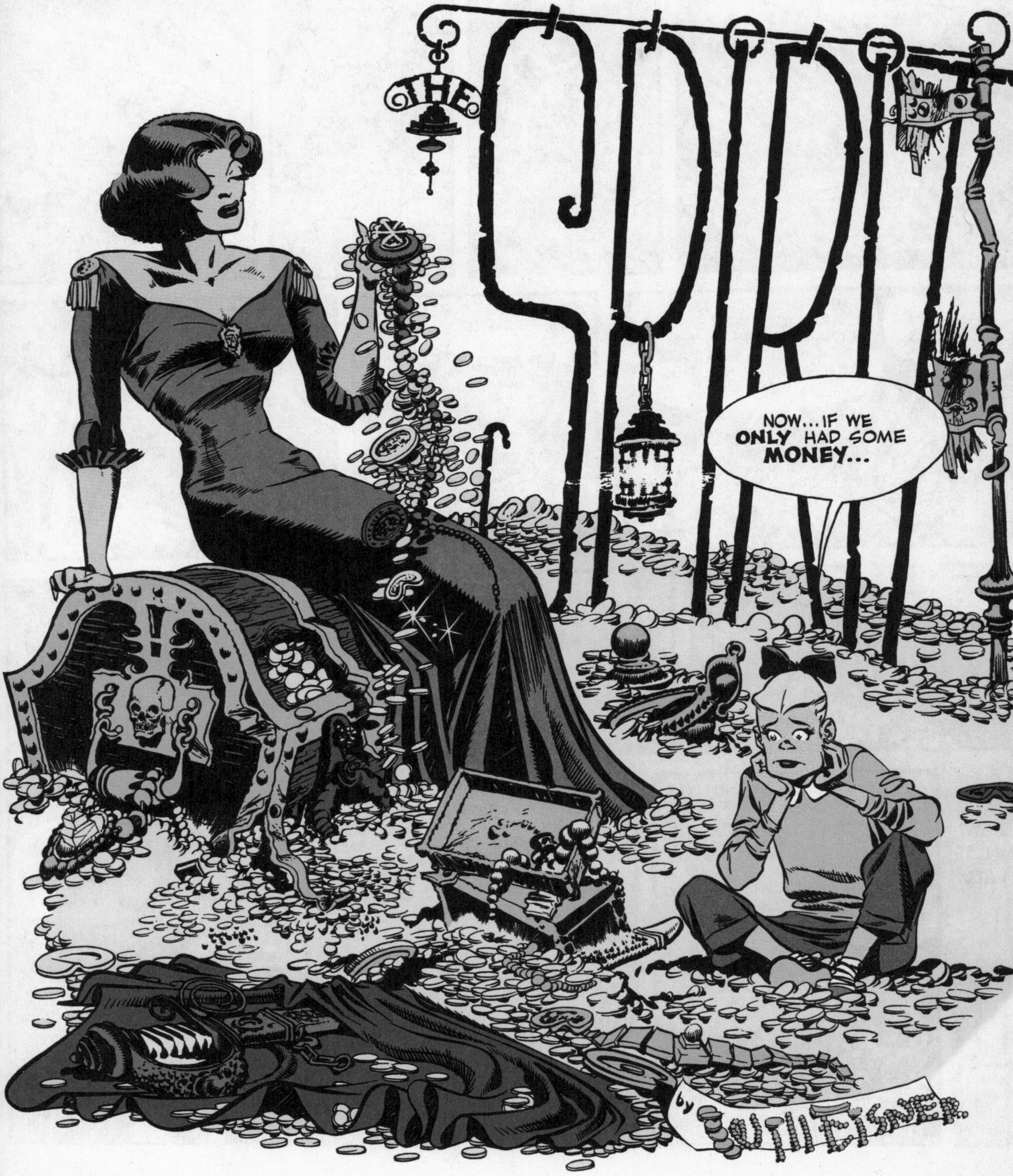
THE SPIRIT
NOW... IF WE ONLY HAD SOME MONEY...
by WILL EISNER

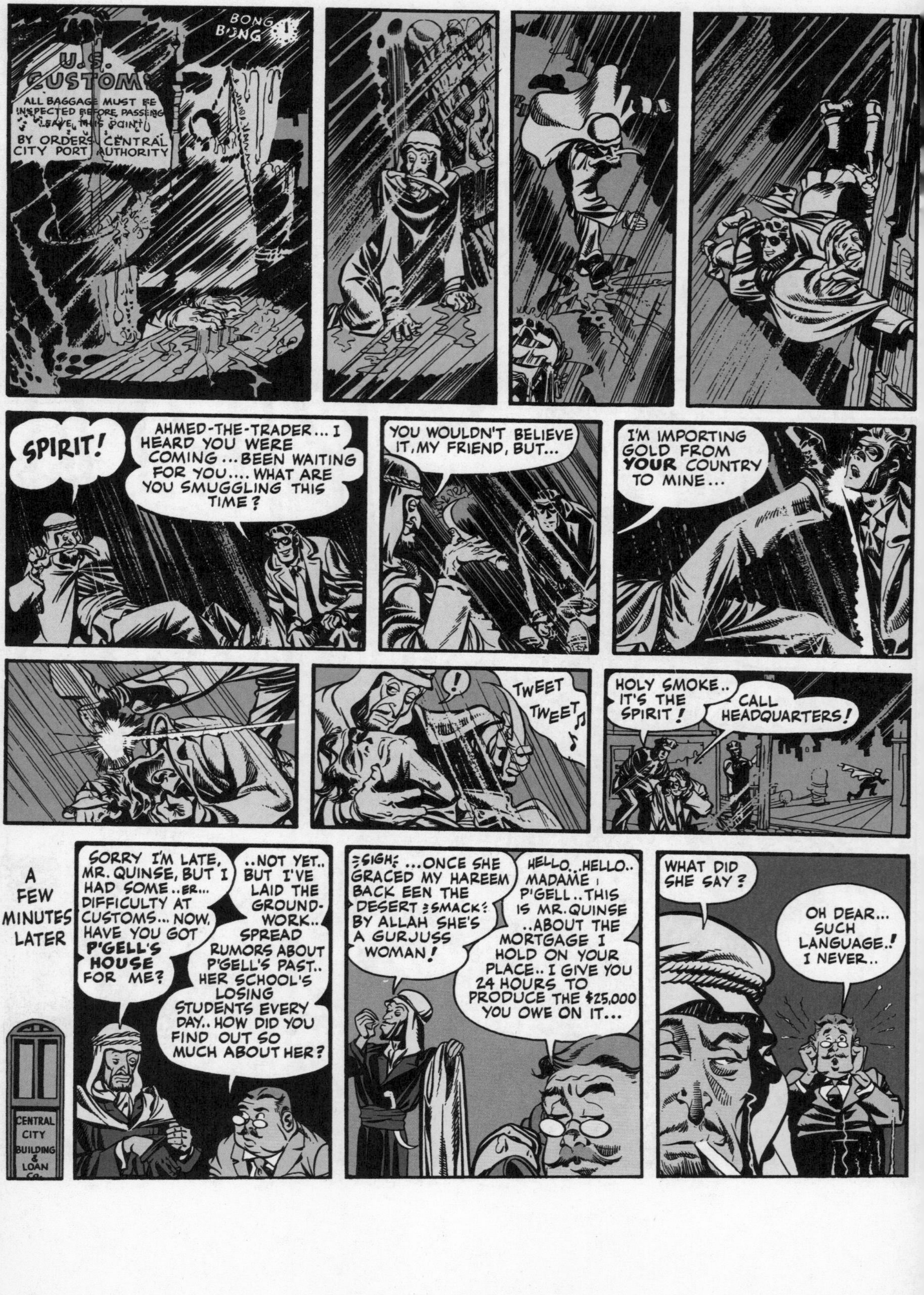

BONG BONG
U.S. CUSTOMS
ALL BAGGAGE MUST BE INSPECTED BEFORE PASSING LEAVE THIS POINT
BY ORDERS CENTRAL CITY PORT AUTHORITY
SPIRIT!
AHMED-THE-TRADER... I HEARD YOU WERE COMING ... BEEN WAITING FOR YOU.... WHAT ARE YOU SMUGGLING THIS TIME?
YOU WOULDN'T BELIEVE IT, MY FRIEND, BUT...
I'M IMPORTING GOLD FROM YOUR COUNTRY TO MINE...
!
TWEET TWEET
HOLY SMOKE.. IT'S THE SPIRIT!
CALL HEADQUARTERS!
A FEW MINUTES LATER
SORRY I'M LATE, MR. QUINSE, BUT I HAD SOME ..ER... DIFFICULTY AT CUSTOMS... NOW, HAVE YOU GOT P'GELL'S HOUSE FOR ME?
..NOT YET.. BUT I'VE LAID THE GROUND-WORK.. SPREAD RUMORS ABOUT P'GELL'S PAST.. HER SCHOOL'S LOSING STUDENTS EVERY DAY.. HOW DID YOU FIND OUT SO MUCH ABOUT HER?
CENTRAL CITY BUILDING & LOAN CO.
SIGH ...ONCE SHE GRACED MY HAREEM BACK EEN THE DESERT SMACK BY ALLAH SHE'S A GURJUSS WOMAN!
HELLO...HELLO.. MADAME P'GELL..THIS IS MR. QUINSE ..ABOUT THE MORTGAGE I HOLD ON YOUR PLACE.. I GIVE YOU 24 HOURS TO PRODUCE THE $25,000 YOU OWE ON IT...
WHAT DID SHE SAY?
OH DEAR... SUCH LANGUAGE.! I NEVER..

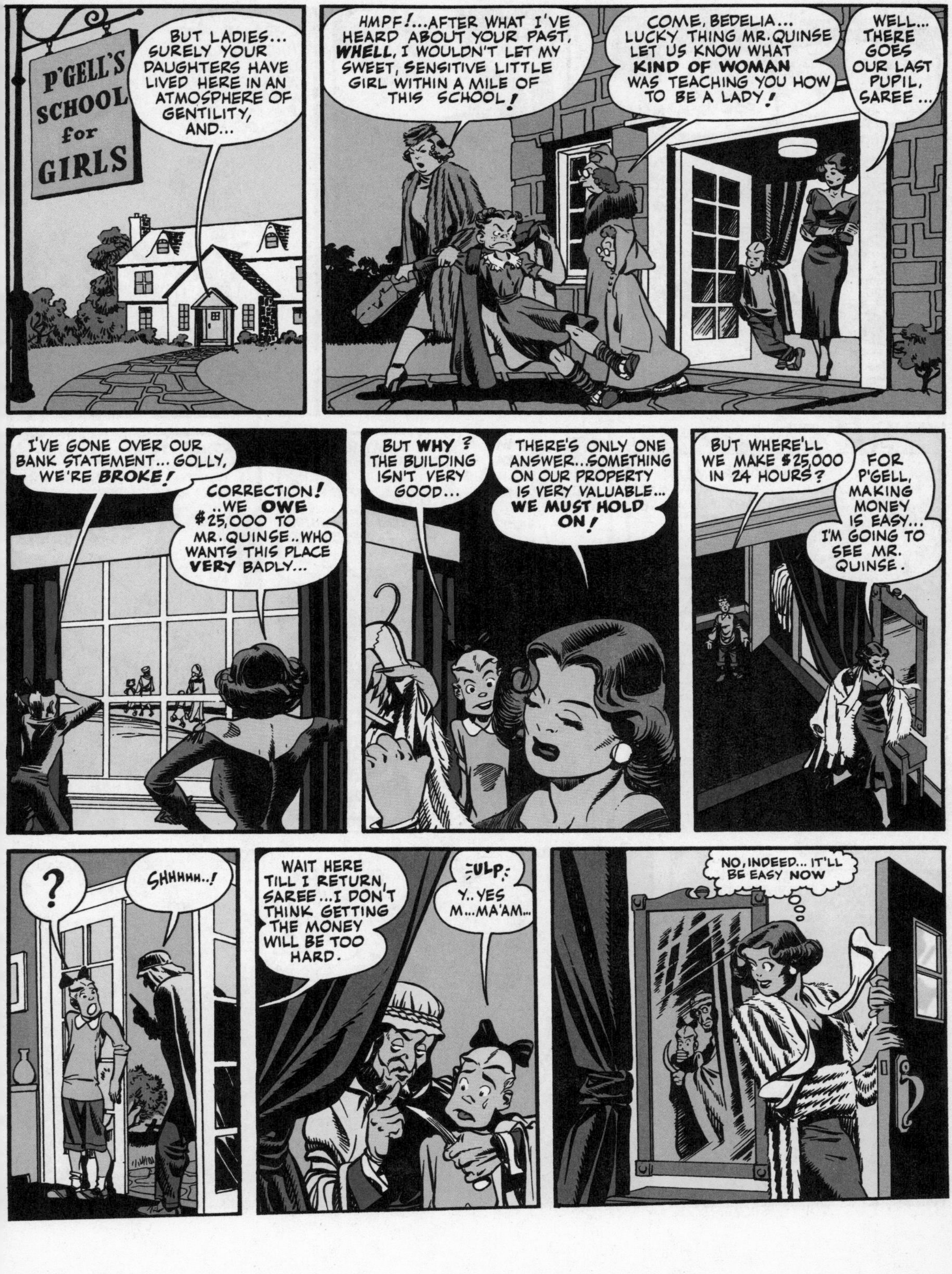
P'GELL'S SCHOOL for GIRLS
BUT LADIES... SURELY YOUR DAUGHTERS HAVE LIVED HERE IN AN ATMOSPHERE OF GENTILITY, AND...
HMPF!...AFTER WHAT I'VE HEARD ABOUT YOUR PAST, WHELL, I WOULDN'T LET MY SWEET, SENSITIVE LITTLE GIRL WITHIN A MILE OF THIS SCHOOL!
COME, BEDELIA... LUCKY THING MR. QUINSE LET US KNOW WHAT KIND OF WOMAN WAS TEACHING YOU HOW TO BE A LADY!
WELL... THERE GOES OUR LAST PUPIL, SAREE...
I'VE GONE OVER OUR BANK STATEMENT... GOLLY, WE'RE BROKE!
CORRECTION! ..WE OWE $25,000 TO MR. QUINSE..WHO WANTS THIS PLACE VERY BADLY...
BUT WHY? THE BUILDING ISN'T VERY GOOD...
THERE'S ONLY ONE ANSWER...SOMETHING ON OUR PROPERTY IS VERY VALUABLE... WE MUST HOLD ON!
BUT WHERE'LL WE MAKE $25,000 IN 24 HOURS?
FOR P'GELL, MAKING MONEY IS EASY... I'M GOING TO SEE MR. QUINSE.
?
SHHHHH..!
WAIT HERE TILL I RETURN, SAREE...I DON'T THINK GETTING THE MONEY WILL BE TOO HARD.
GULP
Y.. YES M...MA'AM...
NO, INDEED... IT'LL BE EASY NOW

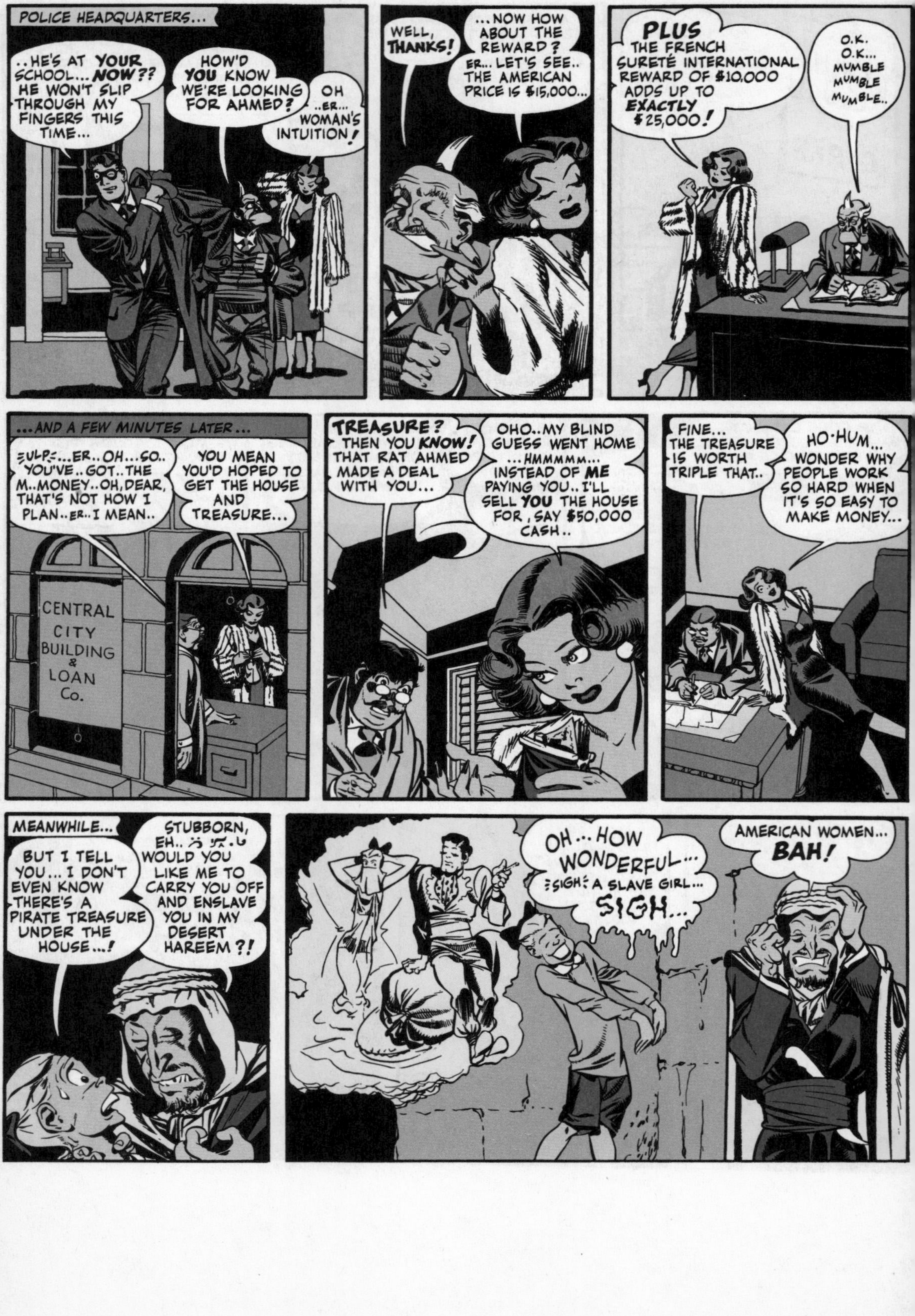
POLICE HEADQUARTERS...
..HE'S AT YOUR SCHOOL... NOW?? HE WON'T SLIP THROUGH MY FINGERS THIS TIME...
HOW'D YOU KNOW WE'RE LOOKING FOR AHMED?
OH ..ER... WOMAN'S INTUITION!
WELL, THANKS!
...NOW HOW ABOUT THE REWARD? ER... LET'S SEE.. THE AMERICAN PRICE IS $15,000...
PLUS THE FRENCH SURETÉ INTERNATIONAL REWARD OF $10,000 ADDS UP TO EXACTLY $25,000!
O.K. O.K... MUMBLE MUMBLE MUMBLE..
...AND A FEW MINUTES LATER...
ULP...ER..OH...SO.. YOU'VE..GOT..THE M..MONEY..OH, DEAR, THAT'S NOT HOW I PLAN..ER..I MEAN..
YOU MEAN YOU'D HOPED TO GET THE HOUSE AND TREASURE...
CENTRAL CITY BUILDING & LOAN Co.
TREASURE? THEN YOU KNOW! THAT RAT AHMED MADE A DEAL WITH YOU...
OHO..MY BLIND GUESS WENT HOME ...HMMMMM... INSTEAD OF ME PAYING YOU.. I'LL SELL YOU THE HOUSE FOR, SAY $50,000 CASH..
FINE... THE TREASURE IS WORTH TRIPLE THAT..
HO-HUM... WONDER WHY PEOPLE WORK SO HARD WHEN IT'S SO EASY TO MAKE MONEY...
MEANWHILE...
BUT I TELL YOU... I DON'T EVEN KNOW THERE'S A PIRATE TREASURE UNDER THE HOUSE...!
STUBBORN, EH.. WOULD YOU LIKE ME TO CARRY YOU OFF AND ENSLAVE YOU IN MY DESERT HAREEM?!
OH... HOW WONDERFUL... SIGH A SLAVE GIRL... SIGH...
AMERICAN WOMEN... BAH!

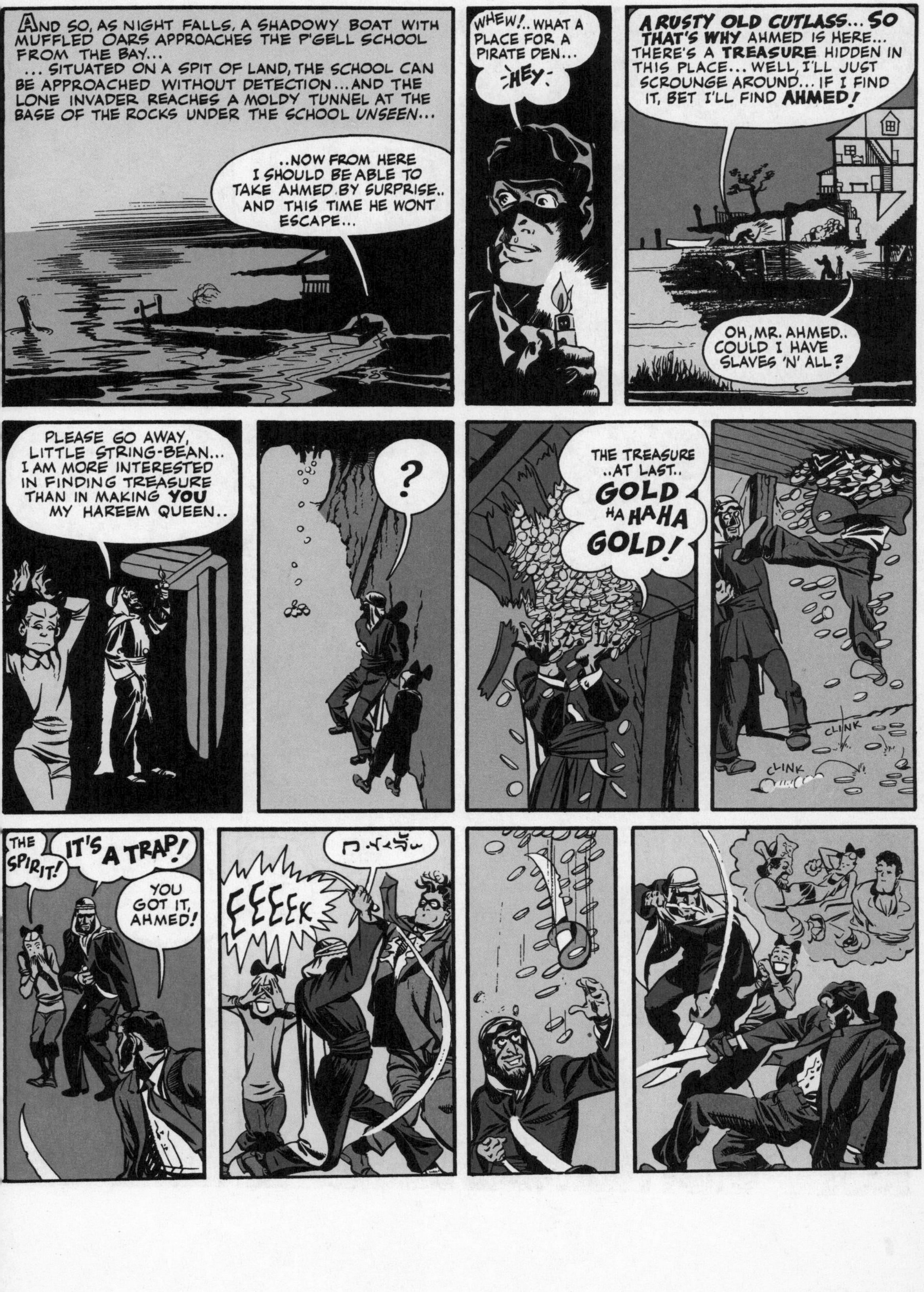
AND SO, AS NIGHT FALLS, A SHADOWY BOAT WITH MUFFLED OARS APPROACHES THE P'GELL SCHOOL FROM THE BAY...
... SITUATED ON A SPIT OF LAND, THE SCHOOL CAN BE APPROACHED WITHOUT DETECTION ... AND THE LONE INVADER REACHES A MOLDY TUNNEL AT THE BASE OF THE ROCKS UNDER THE SCHOOL UNSEEN...
..NOW FROM HERE I SHOULD BE ABLE TO TAKE AHMED BY SURPRISE.. AND THIS TIME HE WONT ESCAPE...
WHEW!.. WHAT A PLACE FOR A PIRATE DEN...
HEY
A RUSTY OLD CUTLASS... SO THAT'S WHY AHMED IS HERE... THERE'S A TREASURE HIDDEN IN THIS PLACE... WELL, I'LL JUST SCROUNGE AROUND... IF I FIND IT, BET I'LL FIND AHMED!
OH, MR. AHMED.. COULD I HAVE SLAVES 'N' ALL?
PLEASE GO AWAY, LITTLE STRING-BEAN... I AM MORE INTERESTED IN FINDING TREASURE THAN IN MAKING YOU MY HAREEM QUEEN..
?
THE TREASURE ..AT LAST.. GOLD HA HA HA GOLD!
CLINK
CLINK
THE SPIRIT!
IT'S A TRAP!
YOU GOT IT, AHMED!
EEEEK

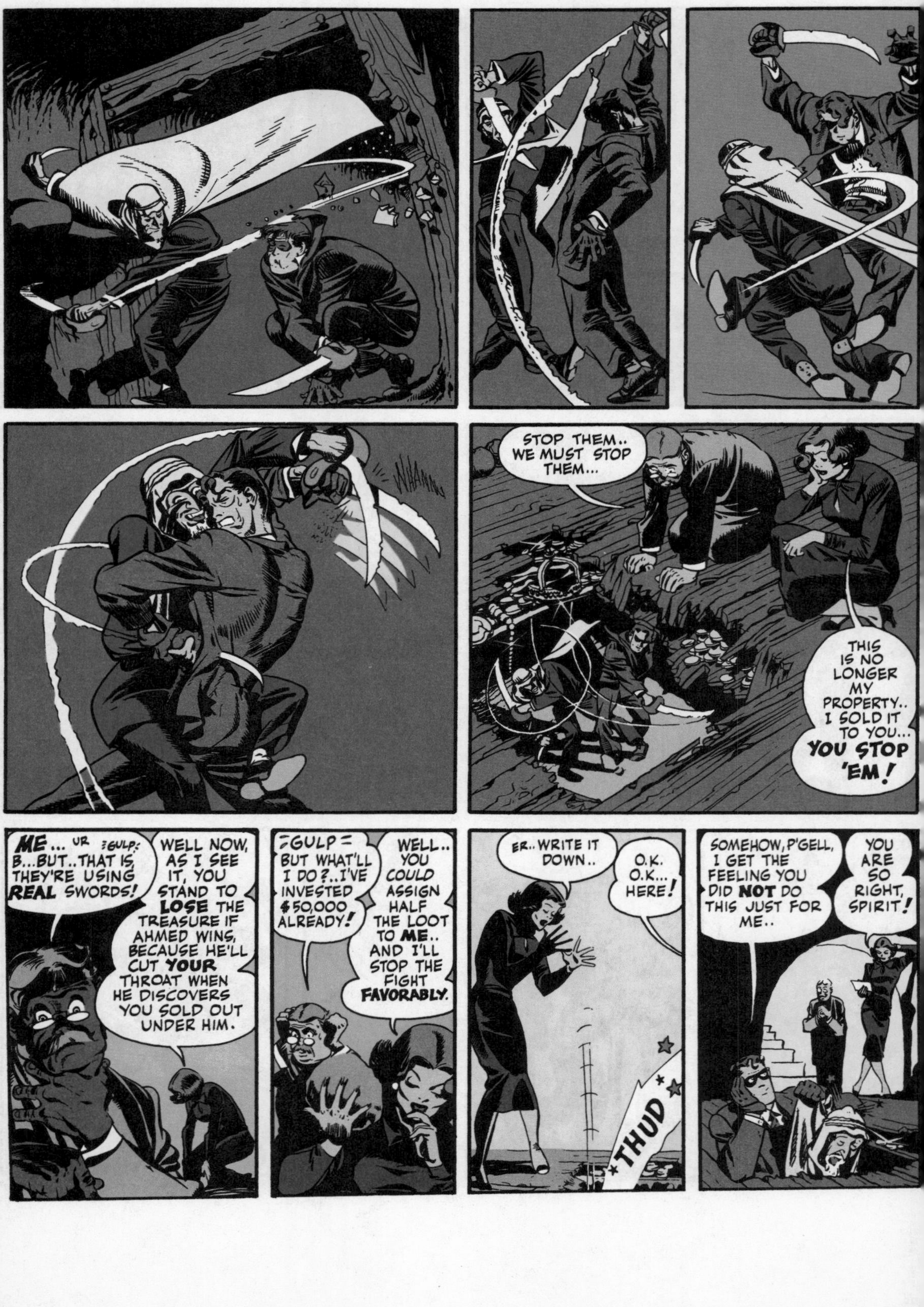
WHAMM
STOP THEM.. WE MUST STOP THEM...
THIS IS NO LONGER MY PROPERTY.. I SOLD IT TO YOU... YOU STOP 'EM!
ME... UR =GULP= B...BUT.. THAT IS, THEY'RE USING REAL SWORDS!
WELL NOW, AS I SEE IT, YOU STAND TO LOSE THE TREASURE IF AHMED WINS, BECAUSE HE'LL CUT YOUR THROAT WHEN HE DISCOVERS YOU SOLD OUT UNDER HIM.
=GULP= BUT WHAT'LL I DO?..I'VE INVESTED $50,000 ALREADY!
WELL.. YOU COULD ASSIGN HALF THE LOOT TO ME.. AND I'LL STOP THE FIGHT FAVORABLY.
ER.. WRITE IT DOWN..
O.K. O.K... HERE!
THUD
SOMEHOW, P'GELL, I GET THE FEELING YOU DID NOT DO THIS JUST FOR ME..
YOU ARE SO RIGHT, SPIRIT!

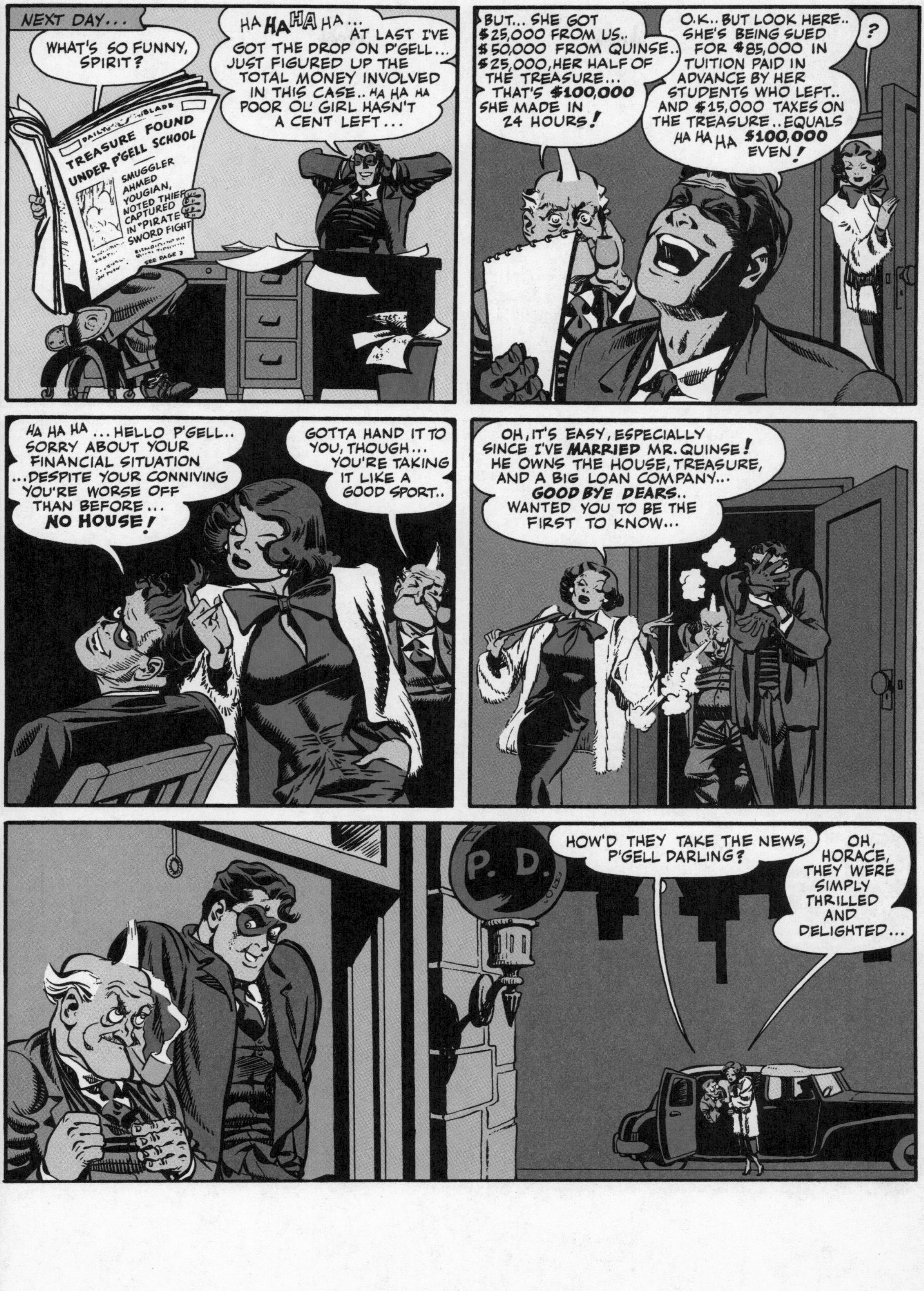
NEXT DAY...
WHAT'S SO FUNNY, SPIRIT?
HA HA HA HA... AT LAST I'VE GOT THE DROP ON P'GELL... JUST FIGURED UP THE TOTAL MONEY INVOLVED IN THIS CASE.. HA HA HA POOR OL' GIRL HASN'T A CENT LEFT...
TREASURE FOUND UNDER P'GELL SCHOOL
SMUGGLER AHMED YOUGIAN, NOTED THIEF CAPTURED IN "PIRATE SWORD FIGHT
SEE PAGE 3
BUT... SHE GOT $25,000 FROM US.. $50,000 FROM QUINSE.. $25,000, HER HALF OF THE TREASURE... THAT'S $100,000 SHE MADE IN 24 HOURS!
O.K.. BUT LOOK HERE.. SHE'S BEING SUED FOR $85,000 IN TUITION PAID IN ADVANCE BY HER STUDENTS WHO LEFT.. AND $15,000 TAXES ON THE TREASURE.. EQUALS HA HA HA $100,000 EVEN!
?
HA HA HA ... HELLO P'GELL.. SORRY ABOUT YOUR FINANCIAL SITUATION ...DESPITE YOUR CONNIVING YOU'RE WORSE OFF THAN BEFORE... NO HOUSE!
GOTTA HAND IT TO YOU, THOUGH... YOU'RE TAKING IT LIKE A GOOD SPORT..
OH, IT'S EASY, ESPECIALLY SINCE I'VE MARRIED MR. QUINSE! HE OWNS THE HOUSE, TREASURE, AND A BIG LOAN COMPANY... GOOD BYE DEARS.. WANTED YOU TO BE THE FIRST TO KNOW...
P. D.
HOW'D THEY TAKE THE NEWS, P'GELL DARLING?
OH, HORACE, THEY WERE SIMPLY THRILLED AND DELIGHTED...

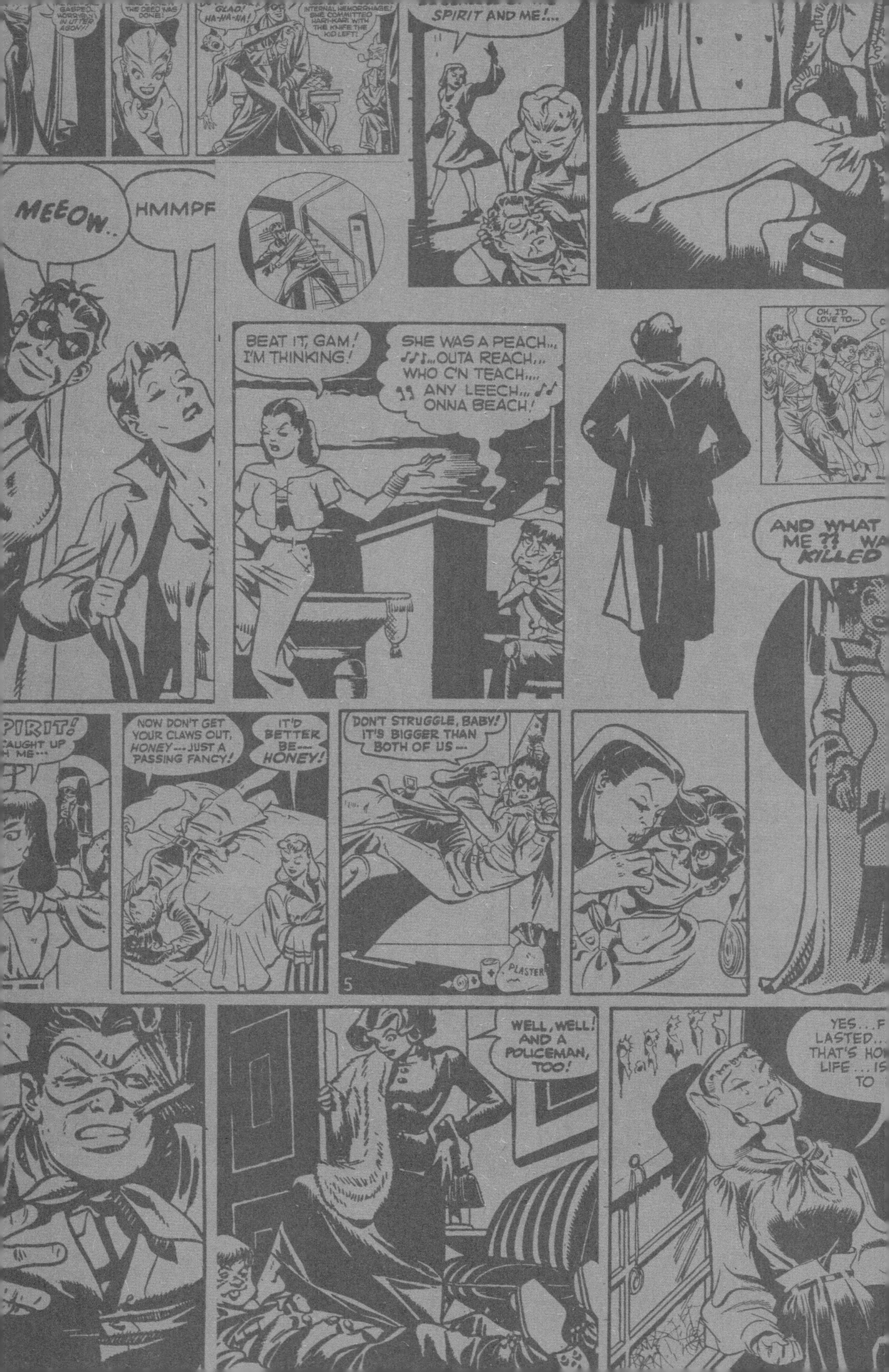

GASPED, HORRIBLY IN UTTER AGONY!
THE DEED WAS DONE!
GLAD! HA-HA-HA!
INTERNAL HEMORRHAGE! SHE COMMITTED HARI-KARI WITH THE KNIFE THE KID LEFT!
SPIRIT AND ME!...
MEEOW..
HMMPF
BEAT IT, GAM! I'M THINKING!
SHE WAS A PEACH... ♪♪♪...OUTA REACH... WHO C'N TEACH.... ANY LEECH... ♪♪ ONNA BEACH!
OH, I'D LOVE TO...
AND WHAT ME ?? WA KILLED
PIRIT! CAUGHT UP H ME...
NOW DON'T GET YOUR CLAWS OUT, HONEY --- JUST A PASSING FANCY!
IT'D BETTER BE--- HONEY!
DON'T STRUGGLE, BABY! IT'S BIGGER THAN BOTH OF US ---
5
PLASTER
WELL, WELL! AND A POLICEMAN, TOO!
YES... F LASTED... THAT'S HO LIFE... IS TO

COMIC BOOK SECTION

THE NAME IS POWDER

ACTION Mystery ADVENTURE

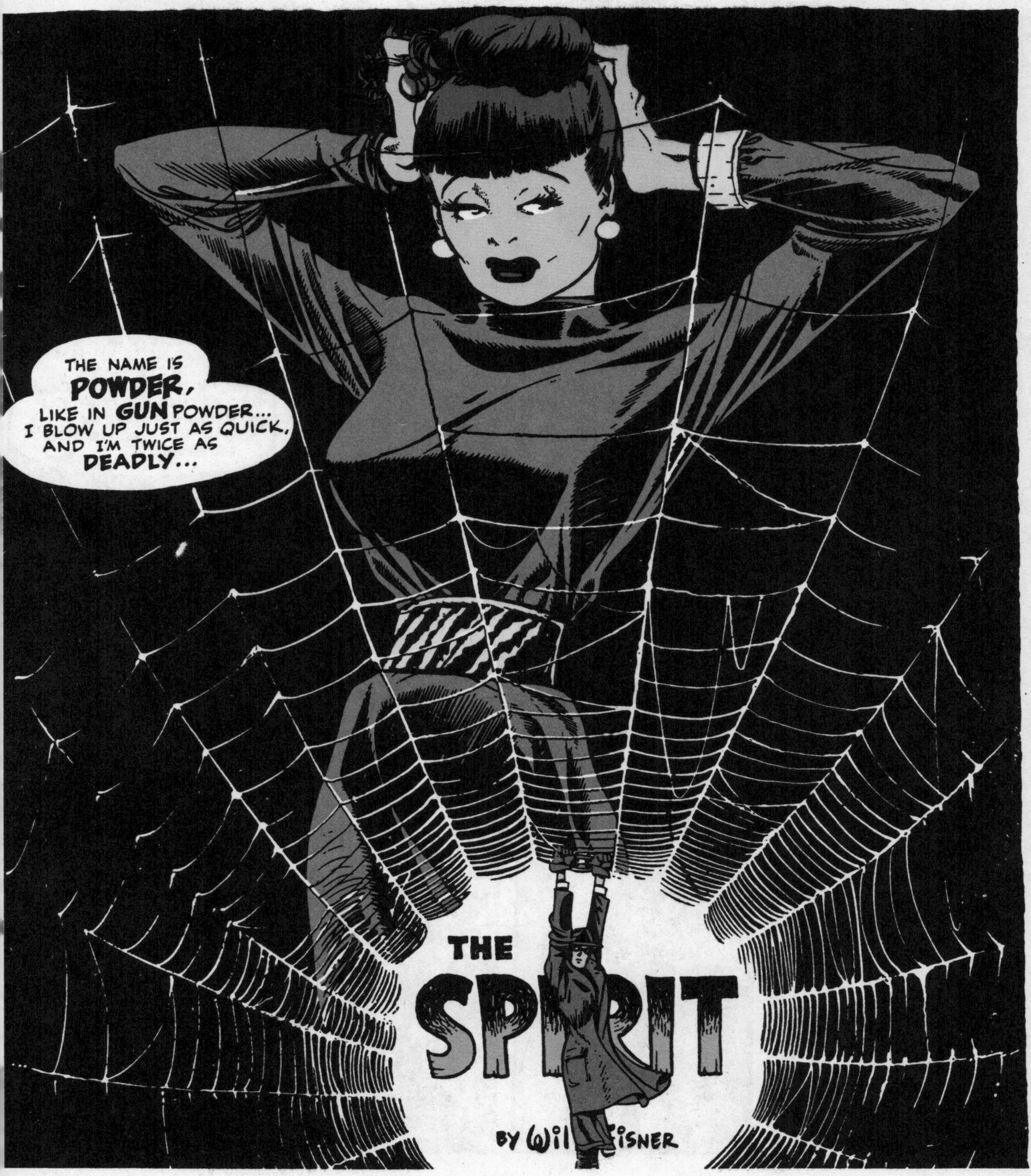

THE NAME IS POWDER, LIKE IN GUN POWDER... I BLOW UP JUST AS QUICK, AND I'M TWICE AS DEADLY...
THE SPIRIT

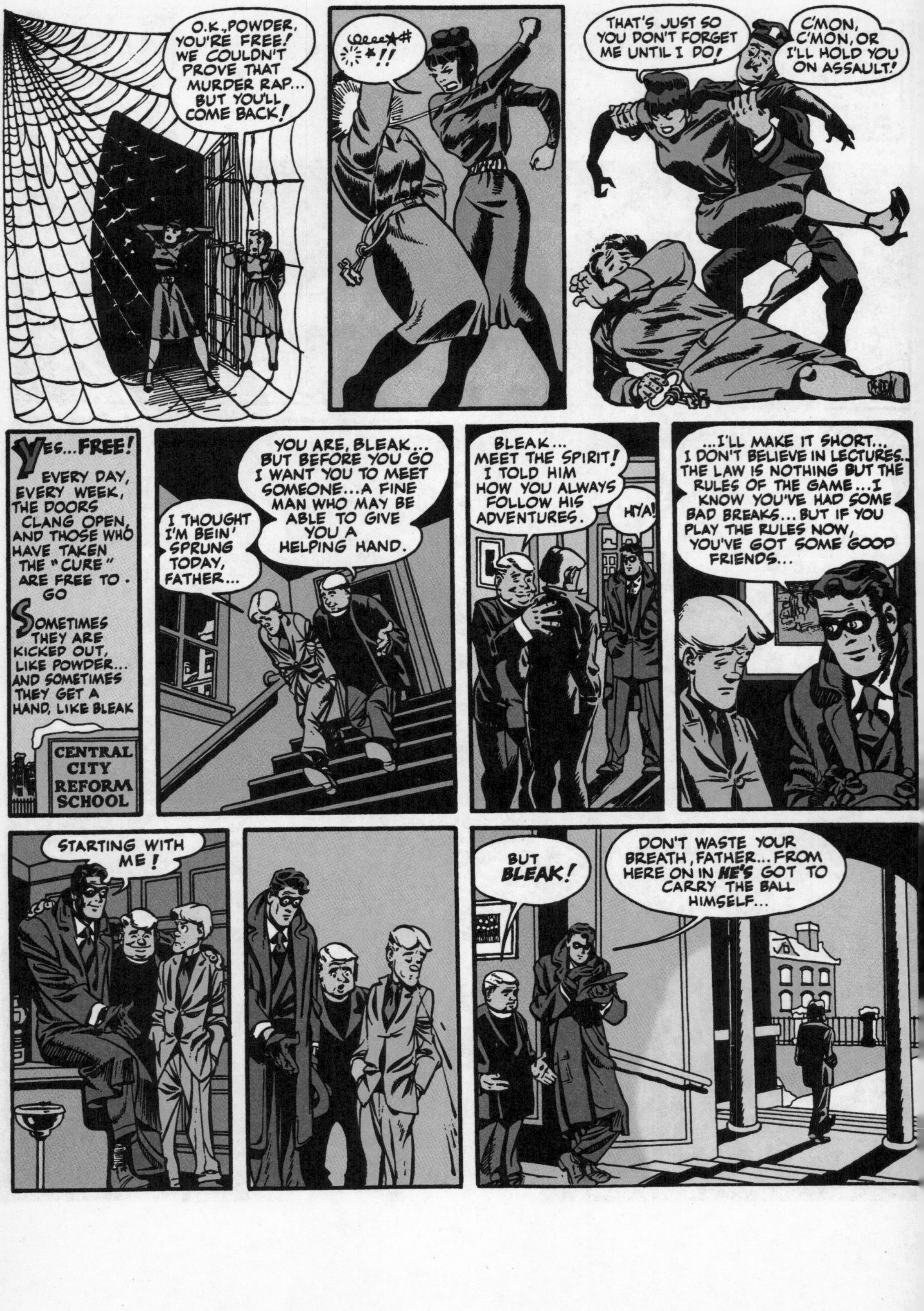
O.K., POWDER, YOU'RE FREE! WE COULDN'T PROVE THAT MURDER RAP... BUT YOU'LL COME BACK!
!!
THAT'S JUST SO YOU DON'T FORGET ME UNTIL I DO!
C'MON, C'MON, OR I'LL HOLD YOU ON ASSAULT!
YES... FREE! EVERY DAY, EVERY WEEK, THE DOORS CLANG OPEN, AND THOSE WHO HAVE TAKEN THE "CURE" ARE FREE TO GO
SOMETIMES THEY ARE KICKED OUT, LIKE POWDER... AND SOMETIMES THEY GET A HAND, LIKE BLEAK
CENTRAL CITY REFORM SCHOOL
I THOUGHT I'M BEIN' SPRUNG TODAY, FATHER...
YOU ARE, BLEAK... BUT BEFORE YOU GO I WANT YOU TO MEET SOMEONE... A FINE MAN WHO MAY BE ABLE TO GIVE YOU A HELPING HAND.
BLEAK... MEET THE SPIRIT! I TOLD HIM HOW YOU ALWAYS FOLLOW HIS ADVENTURES.
HIYA!
...I'LL MAKE IT SHORT... I DON'T BELIEVE IN LECTURES... THE LAW IS NOTHING BUT THE RULES OF THE GAME... I KNOW YOU'VE HAD SOME BAD BREAKS... BUT IF YOU PLAY THE RULES NOW, YOU'VE GOT SOME GOOD FRIENDS...
STARTING WITH ME!
BUT BLEAK!
DON'T WASTE YOUR BREATH, FATHER... FROM HERE ON IN HE'S GOT TO CARRY THE BALL HIMSELF...

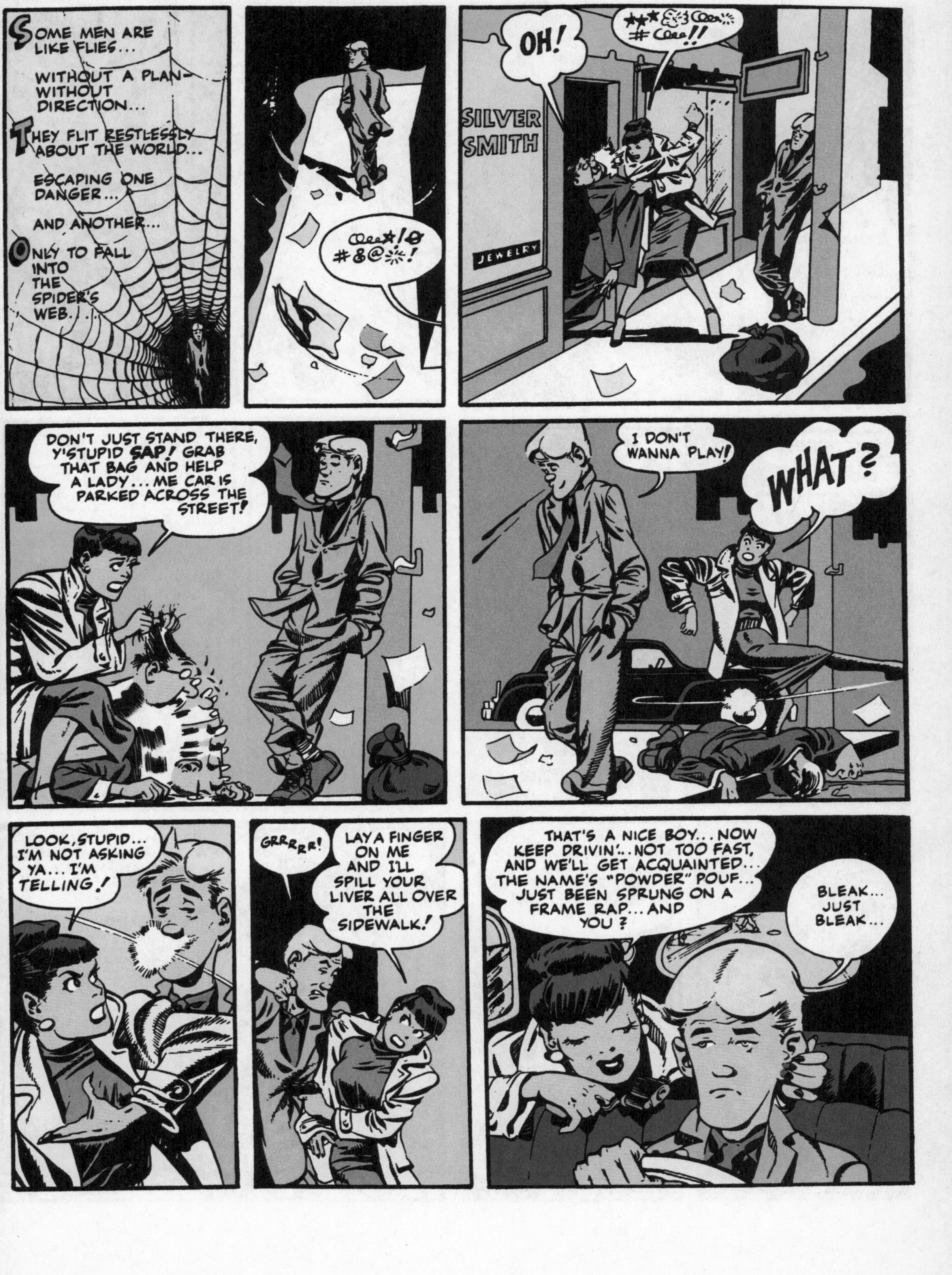

SOME MEN ARE LIKE FLIES...
WITHOUT A PLAN-WITHOUT DIRECTION...
THEY FLIT RESTLESSLY ABOUT THE WORLD...
ESCAPING ONE DANGER...
AND ANOTHER...
ONLY TO FALL INTO THE SPIDER'S WEB...
OH!
SILVER SMITH
JEWELRY
DON'T JUST STAND THERE, Y'STUPID SAP! GRAB THAT BAG AND HELP A LADY... ME CAR IS PARKED ACROSS THE STREET!
I DON'T WANNA PLAY!
WHAT?
LOOK, STUPID... I'M NOT ASKING YA... I'M TELLING!
GRRRRR!
LAY A FINGER ON ME AND I'LL SPILL YOUR LIVER ALL OVER THE SIDEWALK!
THAT'S A NICE BOY... NOW KEEP DRIVIN'... NOT TOO FAST, AND WE'LL GET ACQUAINTED... THE NAME'S "POWDER" POUF... JUST BEEN SPRUNG ON A FRAME RAP... AND YOU?
BLEAK... JUST BLEAK...

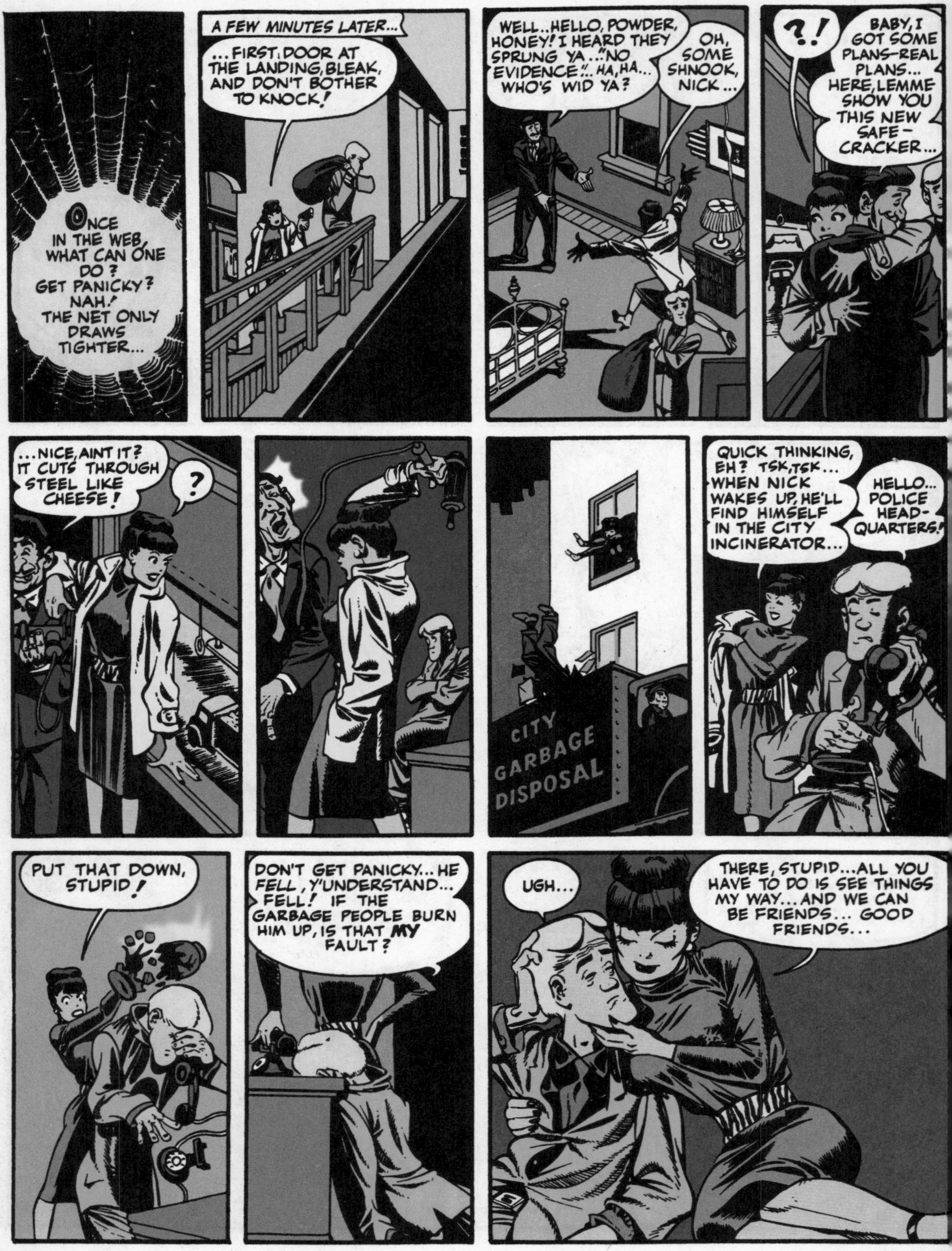

ONCE IN THE WEB, WHAT CAN ONE DO? GET PANICKY? NAH! THE NET ONLY DRAWS TIGHTER...
A FEW MINUTES LATER...
...FIRST DOOR AT THE LANDING, BLEAK, AND DON'T BOTHER TO KNOCK!
WELL..HELLO, POWDER, HONEY! I HEARD THEY SPRUNG YA..."NO EVIDENCE"..HA, HA... WHO'S WID YA?
OH, SOME SHNOOK, NICK...
?!
BABY, I GOT SOME PLANS-REAL PLANS... HERE, LEMME SHOW YOU THIS NEW SAFE-CRACKER...
...NICE, AINT IT? IT CUTS THROUGH STEEL LIKE CHEESE!
?
CITY GARBAGE DISPOSAL
QUICK THINKING, EH? TSK, TSK... WHEN NICK WAKES UP, HE'LL FIND HIMSELF IN THE CITY INCINERATOR...
HELLO... POLICE HEAD-QUARTERS!
PUT THAT DOWN, STUPID!
DON'T GET PANICKY... HE FELL, Y'UNDERSTAND... FELL! IF THE GARBAGE PEOPLE BURN HIM UP, IS THAT MY FAULT?
UGH...
THERE, STUPID...ALL YOU HAVE TO DO IS SEE THINGS MY WAY...AND WE CAN BE FRIENDS... GOOD FRIENDS...

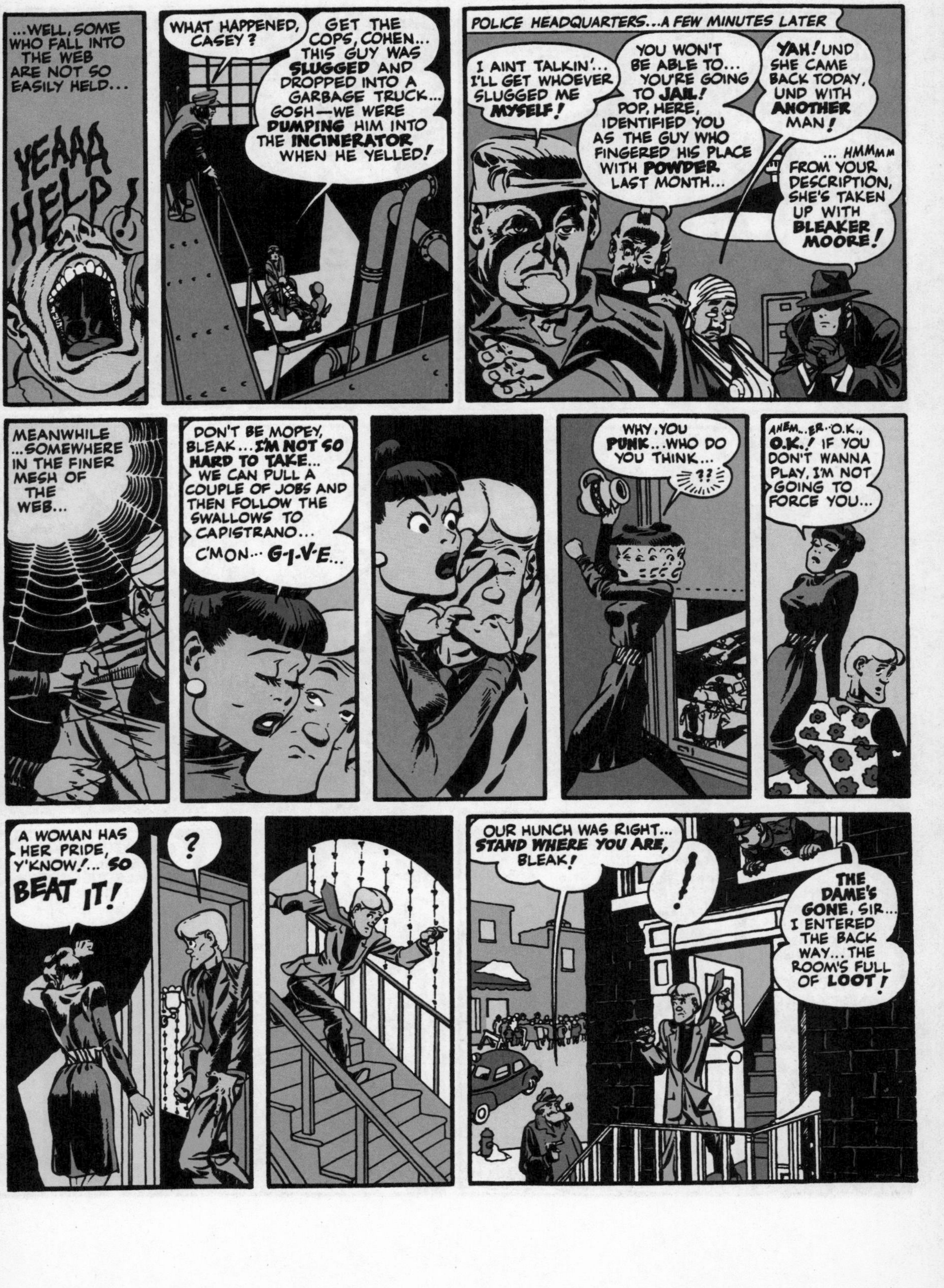
...WELL, SOME WHO FALL INTO THE WEB ARE NOT SO EASILY HELD...
YEAAA HELP!
WHAT HAPPENED, CASEY?
GET THE COPS, COHEN... THIS GUY WAS SLUGGED AND DROPPED INTO A GARBAGE TRUCK... GOSH—WE WERE DUMPING HIM INTO THE INCINERATOR WHEN HE YELLED!
POLICE HEADQUARTERS...A FEW MINUTES LATER
I AINT TALKIN'... I'LL GET WHOEVER SLUGGED ME MYSELF!
YOU WON'T BE ABLE TO... YOU'RE GOING TO JAIL! POP, HERE, IDENTIFIED YOU AS THE GUY WHO FINGERED HIS PLACE WITH POWDER LAST MONTH...
YAH! UND SHE CAME BACK TODAY, UND WITH ANOTHER MAN!
... HMMMM FROM YOUR DESCRIPTION, SHE'S TAKEN UP WITH BLEAKER MOORE!
MEANWHILE ...SOMEWHERE IN THE FINER MESH OF THE WEB...
DON'T BE MOPEY, BLEAK... I'M NOT SO HARD TO TAKE... WE CAN PULL A COUPLE OF JOBS AND THEN FOLLOW THE SWALLOWS TO CAPISTRANO... C'MON... G-I-V-E...
WHY, YOU PUNK...WHO DO YOU THINK...
??
AHEM...ER...O.K., O.K.! IF YOU DON'T WANNA PLAY, I'M NOT GOING TO FORCE YOU...
A WOMAN HAS HER PRIDE, Y'KNOW!... SO BEAT IT!
?
OUR HUNCH WAS RIGHT... STAND WHERE YOU ARE, BLEAK!
!
THE DAME'S GONE, SIR... I ENTERED THE BACK WAY... THE ROOM'S FULL OF LOOT!

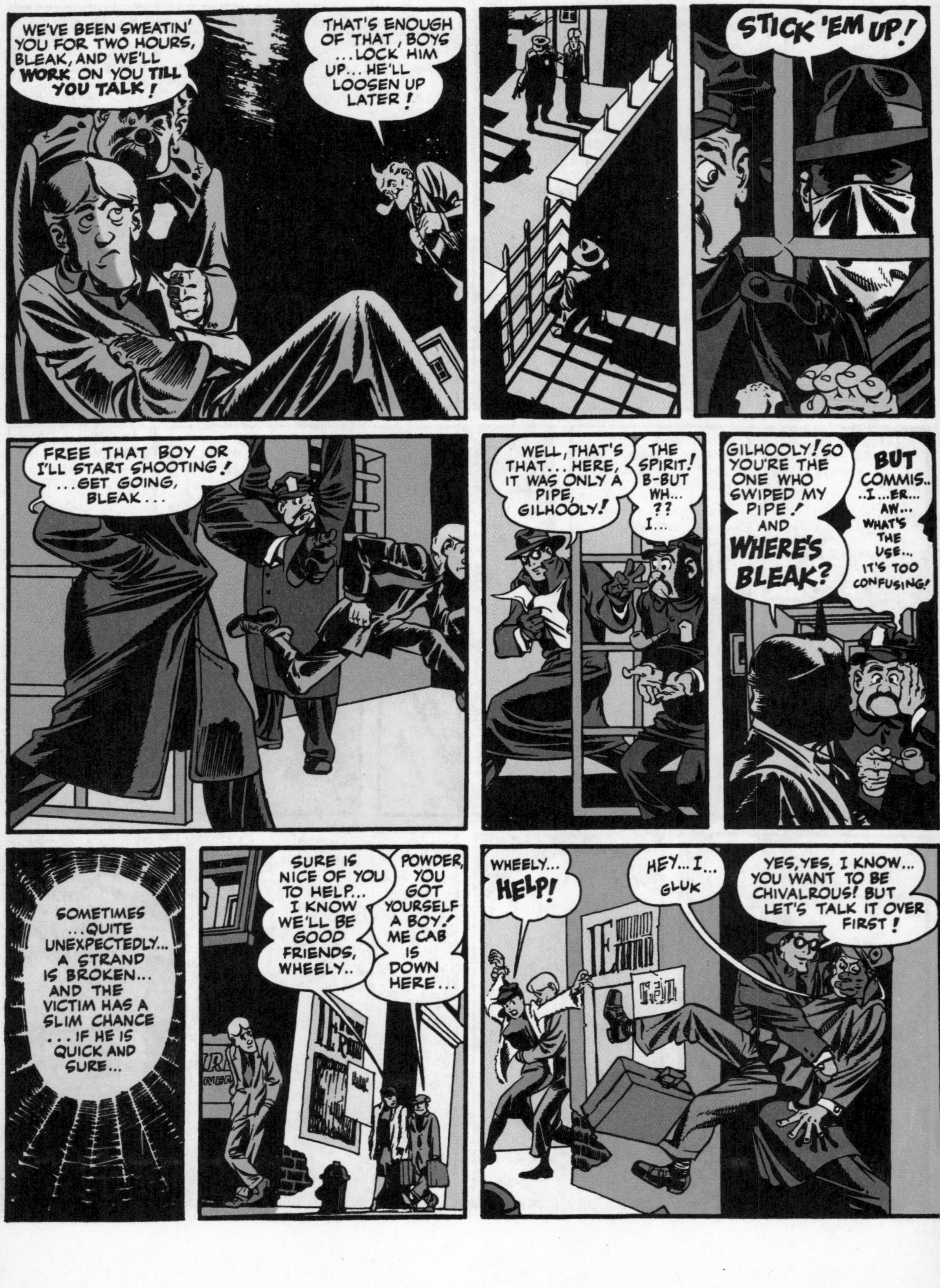
WE'VE BEEN SWEATIN' YOU FOR TWO HOURS, BLEAK, AND WE'LL WORK ON YOU TILL YOU TALK!
THAT'S ENOUGH OF THAT, BOYS ...LOCK HIM UP... HE'LL LOOSEN UP LATER!
STICK 'EM UP!
FREE THAT BOY OR I'LL START SHOOTING! ...GET GOING, BLEAK...
WELL, THAT'S THAT... HERE, IT WAS ONLY A PIPE, GILHOOLY!
THE SPIRIT! B-BUT WH... ?? I...
GILHOOLY! SO YOU'RE THE ONE WHO SWIPED MY PIPE! AND WHERE'S BLEAK?
BUT COMMIS.. ..I...ER... AW... WHAT'S THE USE... IT'S TOO CONFUSING!
SOMETIMES ...QUITE UNEXPECTEDLY... A STRAND IS BROKEN... AND THE VICTIM HAS A SLIM CHANCE ...IF HE IS QUICK AND SURE...
SURE IS NICE OF YOU TO HELP... I KNOW WE'LL BE GOOD FRIENDS, WHEELY..
POWDER, YOU GOT YOURSELF A BOY! ME CAB IS DOWN HERE...
WHEELY... HELP!
HEY... I... GLUK
YES, YES, I KNOW... YOU WANT TO BE CHIVALROUS! BUT LET'S TALK IT OVER FIRST!

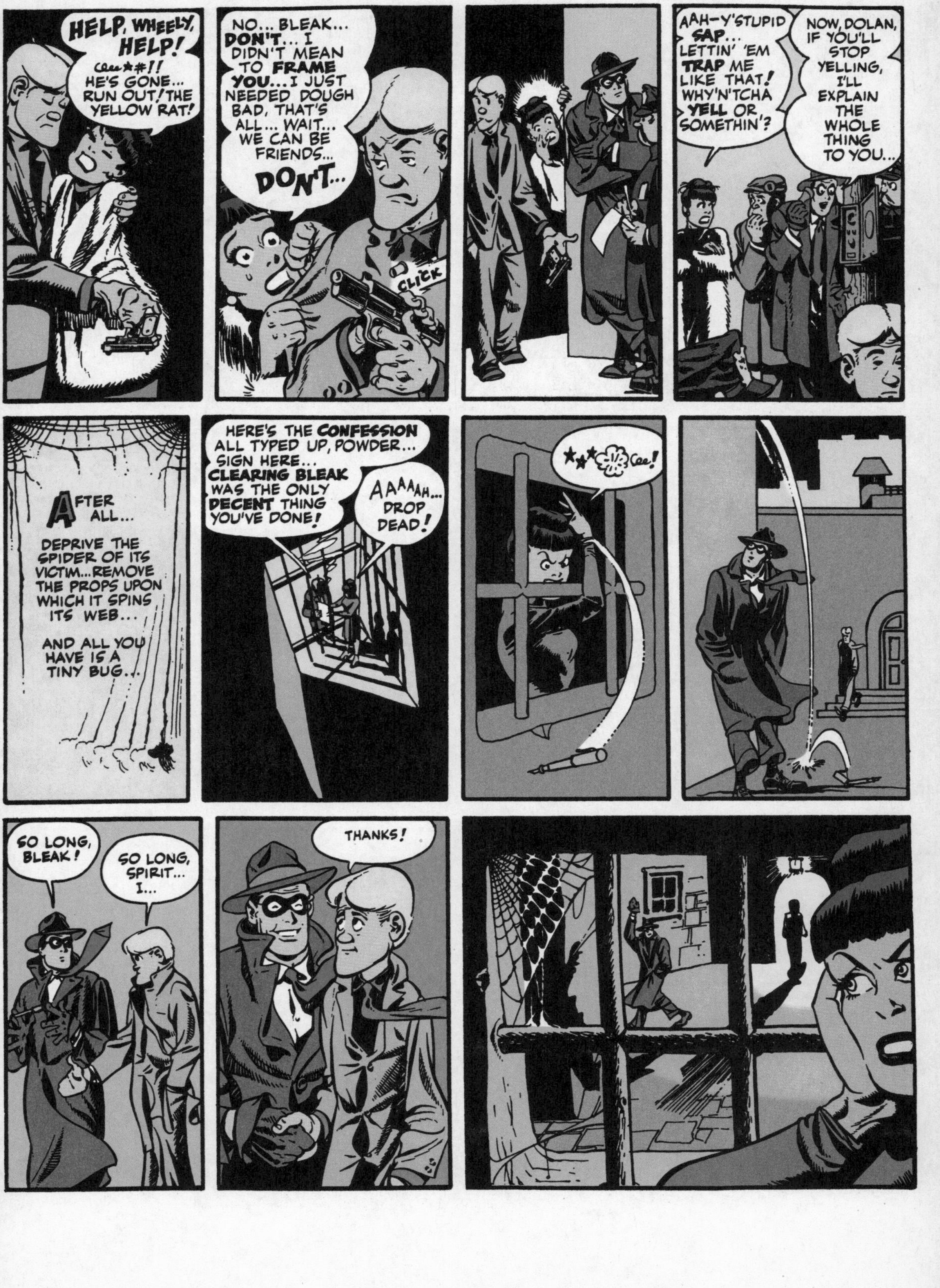
HELP, WHEELY, HELP!
Cee*#!! HE'S GONE... RUN OUT! THE YELLOW RAT!
NO... BLEAK... DON'T... I DIDN'T MEAN TO FRAME YOU... I JUST NEEDED DOUGH BAD, THAT'S ALL... WAIT... WE CAN BE FRIENDS...
DON'T...
CLICK
AAH-Y'STUPID SAP... LETTIN' 'EM TRAP ME LIKE THAT! WHY'N'TCHA YELL OR SOMETHIN'?
NOW, DOLAN, IF YOU'LL STOP YELLING, I'LL EXPLAIN THE WHOLE THING TO YOU...
AFTER ALL...
DEPRIVE THE SPIDER OF ITS VICTIM...REMOVE THE PROPS UPON WHICH IT SPINS ITS WEB...
AND ALL YOU HAVE IS A TINY BUG...
HERE'S THE CONFESSION ALL TYPED UP, POWDER... SIGN HERE... CLEARING BLEAK WAS THE ONLY DECENT THING YOU'VE DONE!
AAAAAH... DROP DEAD!
Cee!
SO LONG, BLEAK!
SO LONG, SPIRIT... I...
THANKS!

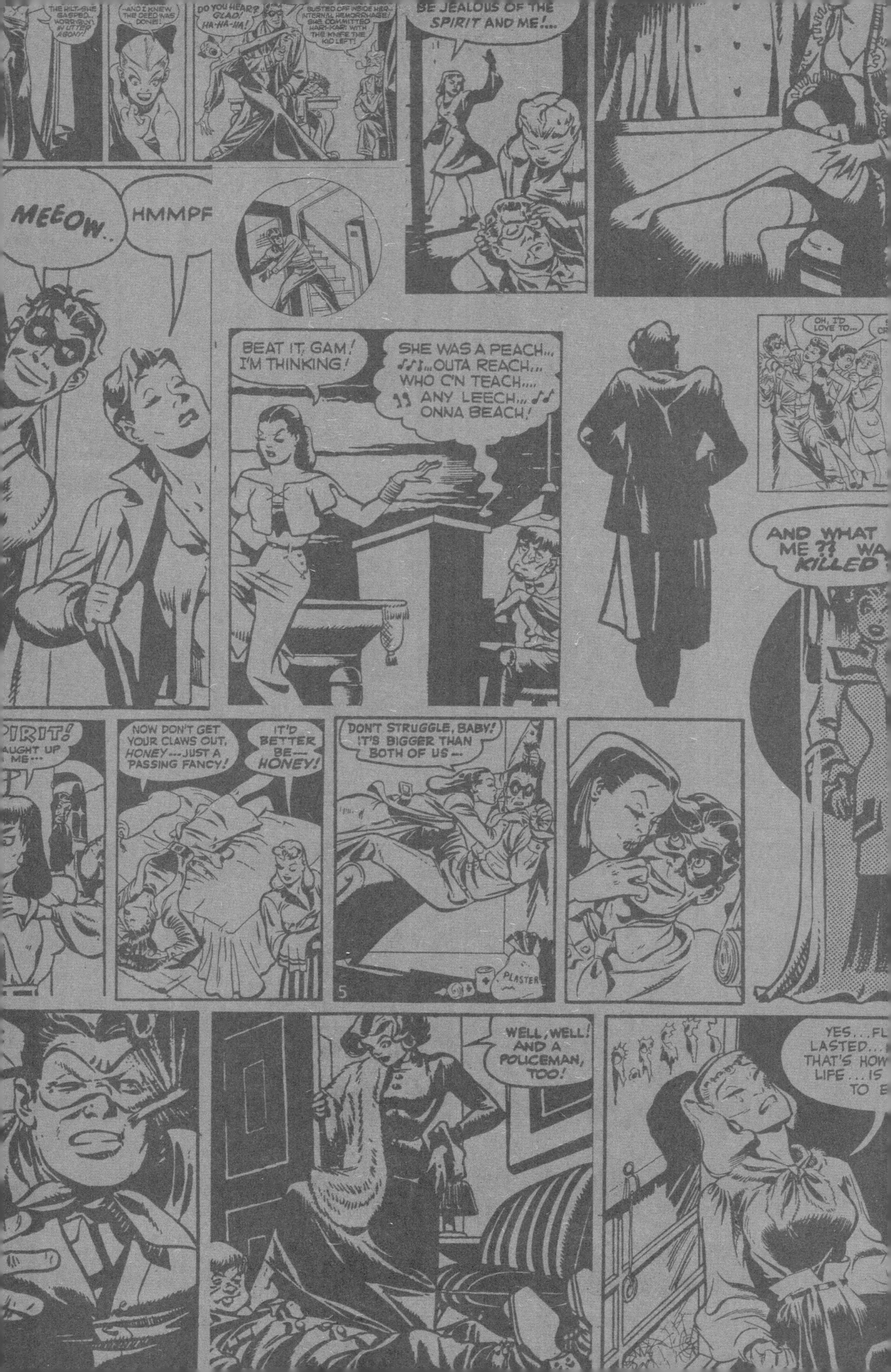

THE HILT–SHE GASPED, HORRIBLY, IN UTTER AGONY!
–AND I KNEW THE DEED WAS DONE!
DO YOU HEAR? GLAD! HA-HA-HA!
BUSTED OFF INSIDE HER... INTERNAL HEMORRHAGE! SHE COMMITTED HARI-KARI WITH THE KNIFE THE KID LEFT!
BE JEALOUS OF THE SPIRIT AND ME!...
MEEOW..
HMMPF
BEAT IT, GAM! I'M THINKING!
SHE WAS A PEACH... ♪♪♪...OUTA REACH... WHO C'N TEACH.... ANY LEECH... ♪♪ ONNA BEACH!
OH, I'D LOVE TO...
AND WHAT ME ?? KILLED
NOW DON'T GET YOUR CLAWS OUT, HONEY---JUST A PASSING FANCY!
IT'D BETTER BE— HONEY!
DON'T STRUGGLE, BABY! IT'S BIGGER THAN BOTH OF US—
PLASTER
WELL, WELL! AND A POLICEMAN, TOO!

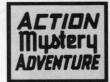

COMIC BOOK SECTION

WILD RICE

ACTION Mystery ADVENTURE

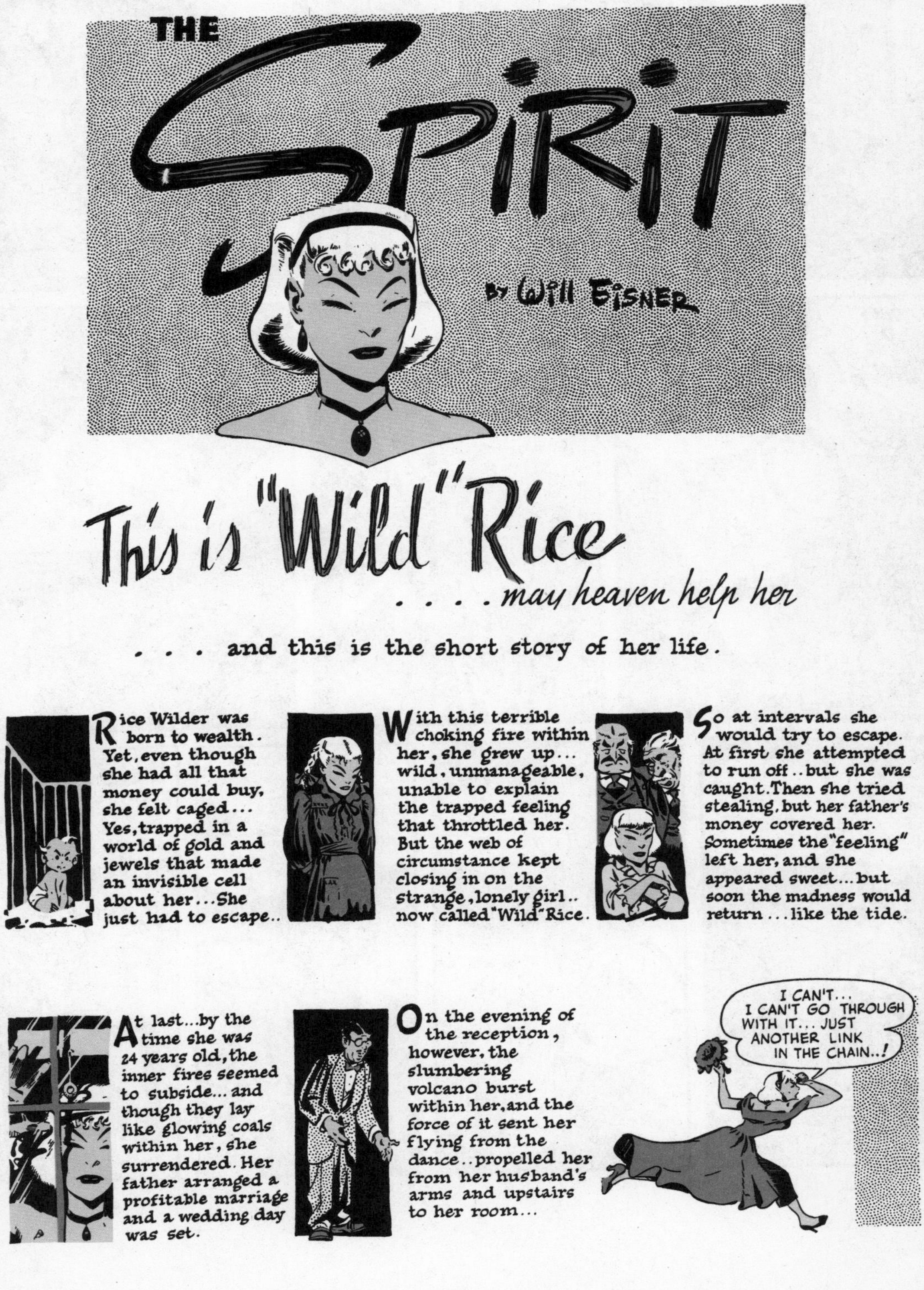

THE SPIRIT
BY WILL EISNER
This is "Wild" Rice
. . . . may heaven help her
. . . and this is the short story of her life.
Rice Wilder was born to wealth. Yet, even though she had all that money could buy, she felt caged... Yes, trapped in a world of gold and jewels that made an invisible cell about her... She just had to escape..
With this terrible choking fire within her, she grew up... wild, unmanageable, unable to explain the trapped feeling that throttled her. But the web of circumstance kept closing in on the strange, lonely girl.. now called "Wild" Rice.
So at intervals she would try to escape. At first she attempted to run off.. but she was caught. Then she tried stealing, but her father's money covered her. Sometimes the "feeling" left her, and she appeared sweet... but soon the madness would return... like the tide.
At last... by the time she was 24 years old, the inner fires seemed to subside... and though they lay like glowing coals within her, she surrendered. Her father arranged a profitable marriage and a wedding day was set.
On the evening of the reception, however, the slumbering volcano burst within her, and the force of it sent her flying from the dance.. propelled her from her husband's arms and upstairs to her room...
I CAN'T... I CAN'T GO THROUGH WITH IT... JUST ANOTHER LINK IN THE CHAIN..!

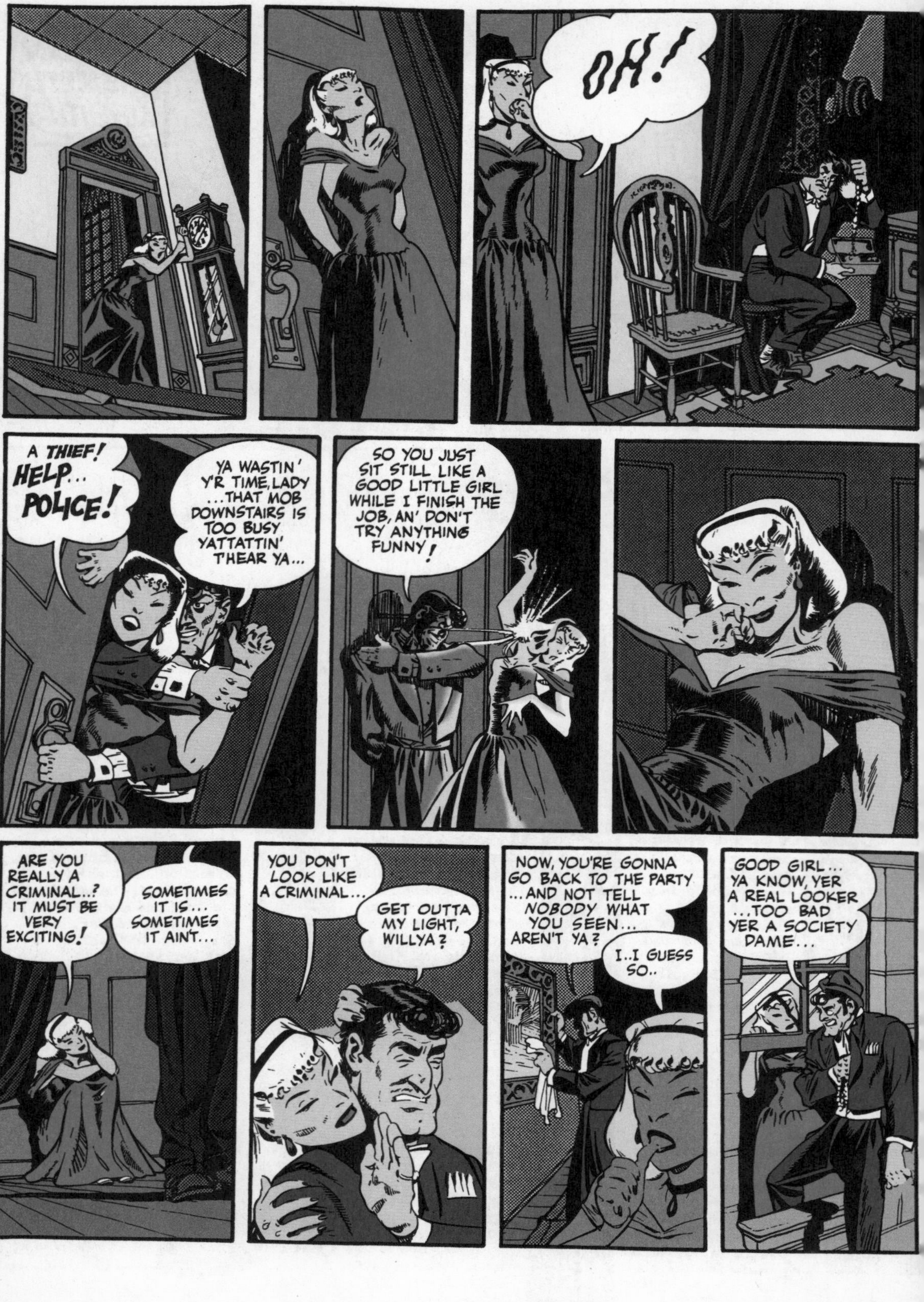
OH!
A THIEF! HELP... POLICE!
YA WASTIN' Y'R TIME, LADY ...THAT MOB DOWNSTAIRS IS TOO BUSY YATTATTIN' T'HEAR YA...
SO YOU JUST SIT STILL LIKE A GOOD LITTLE GIRL WHILE I FINISH THE JOB, AN' DON'T TRY ANYTHING FUNNY!
ARE YOU REALLY A CRIMINAL..? IT MUST BE VERY EXCITING!
SOMETIMES IT IS... SOMETIMES IT AIN'T...
YOU DON'T LOOK LIKE A CRIMINAL...
GET OUTTA MY LIGHT, WILLYA?
NOW, YOU'RE GONNA GO BACK TO THE PARTY ...AND NOT TELL NOBODY WHAT YOU SEEN... AREN'T YA?
I..I GUESS SO..
GOOD GIRL... YA KNOW, YER A REAL LOOKER ...TOO BAD YER A SOCIETY DAME...

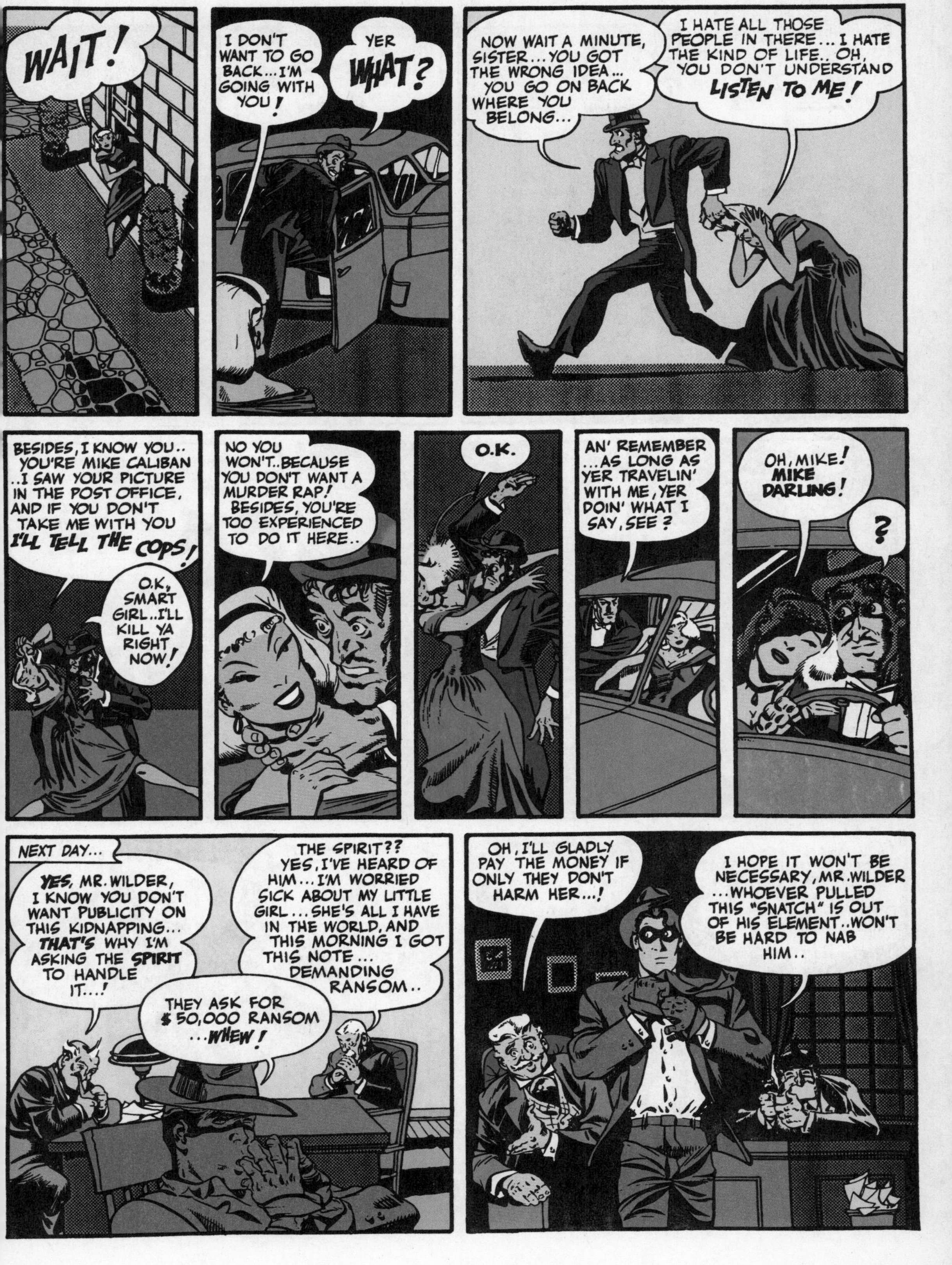
WAIT!
I DON'T WANT TO GO BACK... I'M GOING WITH YOU!
YER WHAT?
NOW WAIT A MINUTE, SISTER... YOU GOT THE WRONG IDEA... YOU GO ON BACK WHERE YOU BELONG...
I HATE ALL THOSE PEOPLE IN THERE... I HATE THE KIND OF LIFE.. OH, YOU DON'T UNDERSTAND LISTEN TO ME!
BESIDES, I KNOW YOU.. YOU'RE MIKE CALIBAN ..I SAW YOUR PICTURE IN THE POST OFFICE, AND IF YOU DON'T TAKE ME WITH YOU I'LL TELL THE COPS!
O.K., SMART GIRL..I'LL KILL YA RIGHT NOW!
NO YOU WON'T..BECAUSE YOU DON'T WANT A MURDER RAP! BESIDES, YOU'RE TOO EXPERIENCED TO DO IT HERE..
O.K.
AN' REMEMBER ...AS LONG AS YER TRAVELIN' WITH ME, YER DOIN' WHAT I SAY, SEE?
OH, MIKE! MIKE DARLING!
?
NEXT DAY...
YES, MR. WILDER, I KNOW YOU DON'T WANT PUBLICITY ON THIS KIDNAPPING... THAT'S WHY I'M ASKING THE SPIRIT TO HANDLE IT...!
THE SPIRIT?? YES, I'VE HEARD OF HIM... I'M WORRIED SICK ABOUT MY LITTLE GIRL... SHE'S ALL I HAVE IN THE WORLD, AND THIS MORNING I GOT THIS NOTE... DEMANDING RANSOM..
THEY ASK FOR $50,000 RANSOM ...WHEW!
OH, I'LL GLADLY PAY THE MONEY IF ONLY THEY DON'T HARM HER...!
I HOPE IT WON'T BE NECESSARY, MR. WILDER ...WHOEVER PULLED THIS "SNATCH" IS OUT OF HIS ELEMENT..WON'T BE HARD TO NAB HIM..

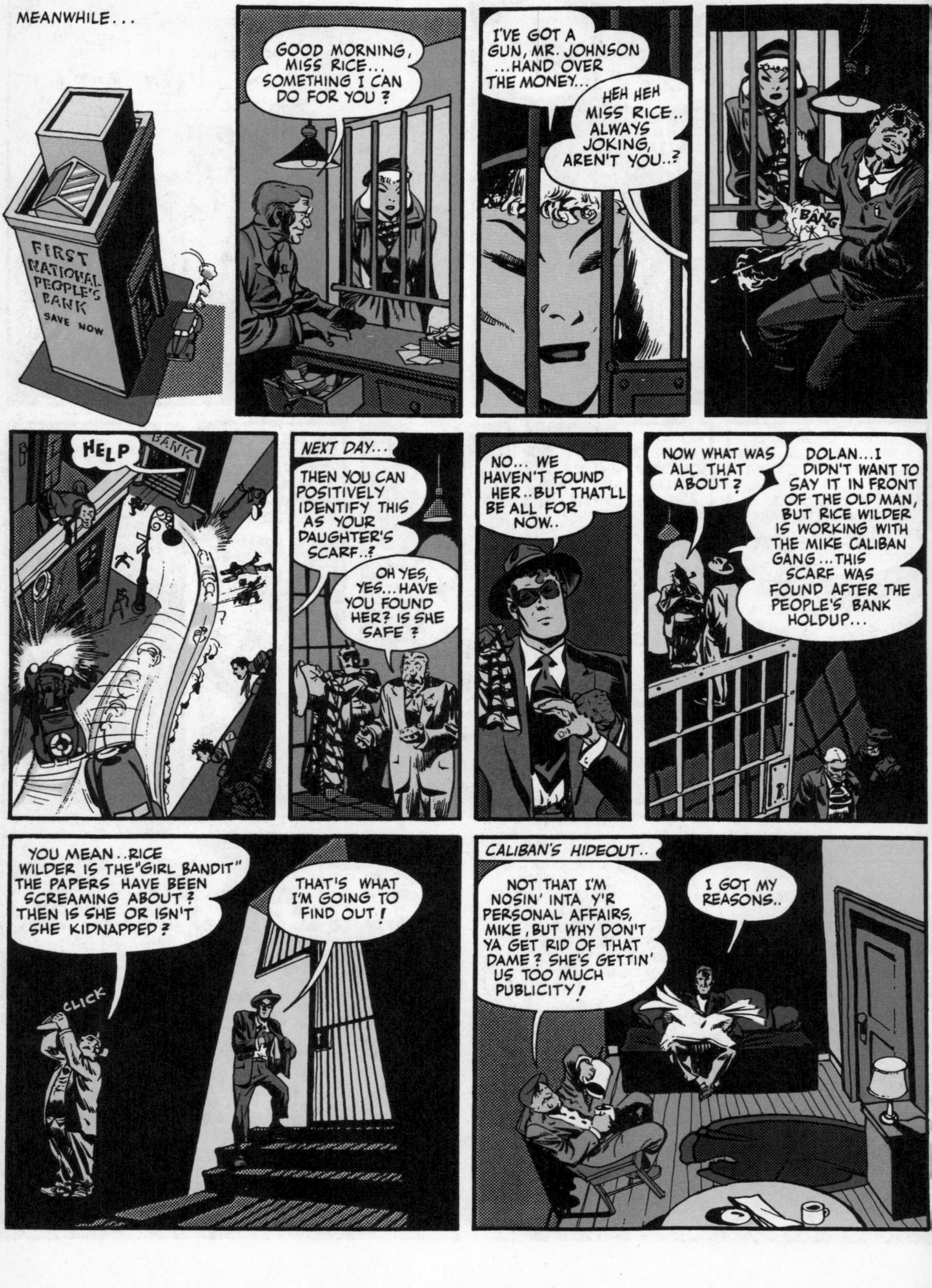
MEANWHILE...
FIRST NATIONAL PEOPLE'S BANK SAVE NOW
GOOD MORNING, MISS RICE... SOMETHING I CAN DO FOR YOU ?
I'VE GOT A GUN, MR. JOHNSON ...HAND OVER THE MONEY...
HEH HEH MISS RICE.. ALWAYS JOKING, AREN'T YOU..?
BANG
HELP
BANK
NEXT DAY...
THEN YOU CAN POSITIVELY IDENTIFY THIS AS YOUR DAUGHTER'S SCARF..?
OH YES, YES...HAVE YOU FOUND HER? IS SHE SAFE ?
NO... WE HAVEN'T FOUND HER..BUT THAT'LL BE ALL FOR NOW..
NOW WHAT WAS ALL THAT ABOUT ?
DOLAN...I DIDN'T WANT TO SAY IT IN FRONT OF THE OLD MAN, BUT RICE WILDER IS WORKING WITH THE MIKE CALIBAN GANG...THIS SCARF WAS FOUND AFTER THE PEOPLE'S BANK HOLDUP...
YOU MEAN..RICE WILDER IS THE "GIRL BANDIT" THE PAPERS HAVE BEEN SCREAMING ABOUT ? THEN IS SHE OR ISN'T SHE KIDNAPPED ?
CLICK
THAT'S WHAT I'M GOING TO FIND OUT !
CALIBAN'S HIDEOUT..
NOT THAT I'M NOSIN' INTA Y'R PERSONAL AFFAIRS, MIKE, BUT WHY DON'T YA GET RID OF THAT DAME ? SHE'S GETTIN' US TOO MUCH PUBLICITY !
I GOT MY REASONS..

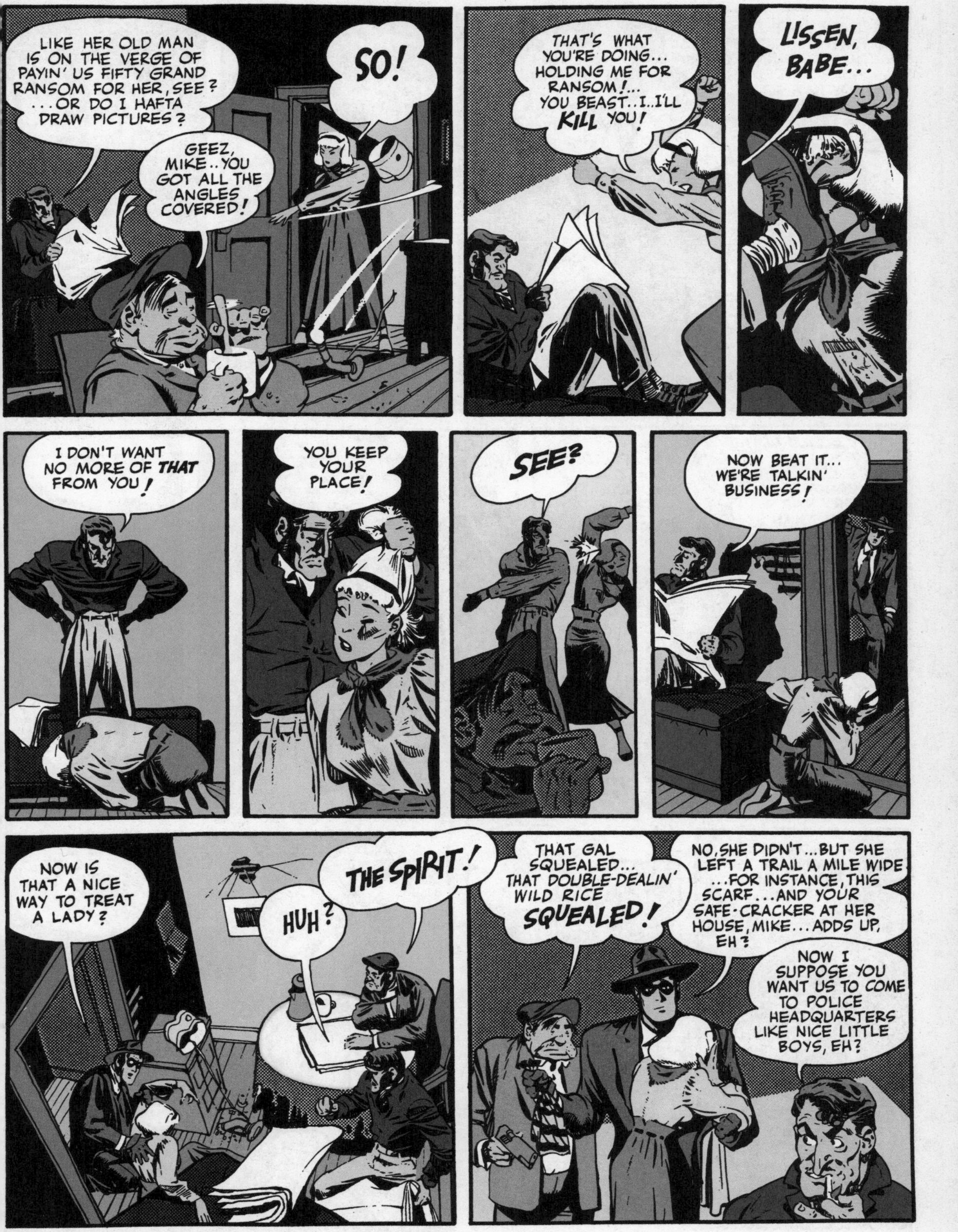
LIKE HER OLD MAN IS ON THE VERGE OF PAYIN' US FIFTY GRAND RANSOM FOR HER, SEE? ...OR DO I HAFTA DRAW PICTURES?
SO!
GEEZ, MIKE..YOU GOT ALL THE ANGLES COVERED!
THAT'S WHAT YOU'RE DOING... HOLDING ME FOR RANSOM!... YOU BEAST..I..I'LL KILL YOU!
LISSEN, BABE...
I DON'T WANT NO MORE OF THAT FROM YOU!
YOU KEEP YOUR PLACE!
SEE?
NOW BEAT IT... WE'RE TALKIN' BUSINESS!
NOW IS THAT A NICE WAY TO TREAT A LADY?
HUH?
THE SPIRIT!
THAT GAL SQUEALED... THAT DOUBLE-DEALIN' WILD RICE SQUEALED!
NO, SHE DIDN'T...BUT SHE LEFT A TRAIL A MILE WIDE ...FOR INSTANCE, THIS SCARF...AND YOUR SAFE-CRACKER AT HER HOUSE, MIKE...ADDS UP, EH?
NOW I SUPPOSE YOU WANT US TO COME TO POLICE HEADQUARTERS LIKE NICE LITTLE BOYS, EH?

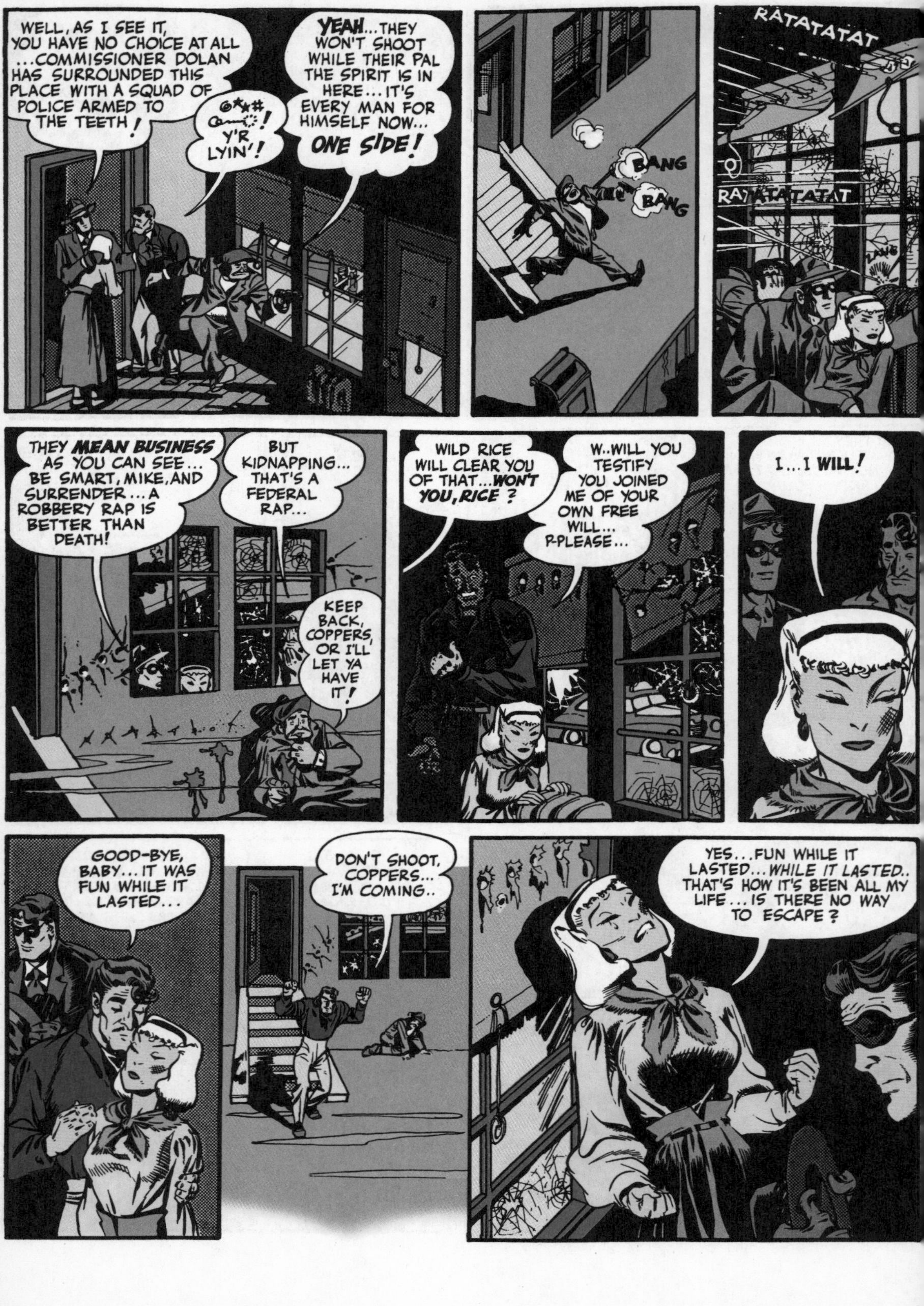

WELL, AS I SEE IT, YOU HAVE NO CHOICE AT ALL ...COMMISSIONER DOLAN HAS SURROUNDED THIS PLACE WITH A SQUAD OF POLICE ARMED TO THE TEETH!
Y'R LYIN'!
YEAH...THEY WON'T SHOOT WHILE THEIR PAL THE SPIRIT IS IN HERE...IT'S EVERY MAN FOR HIMSELF NOW... ONE SIDE!
BANG
BANG
RATATATAT
RATATATATAT
THEY MEAN BUSINESS AS YOU CAN SEE... BE SMART, MIKE, AND SURRENDER...A ROBBERY RAP IS BETTER THAN DEATH!
BUT KIDNAPPING... THAT'S A FEDERAL RAP...
KEEP BACK, COPPERS, OR I'LL LET YA HAVE IT!
WILD RICE WILL CLEAR YOU OF THAT...WON'T YOU, RICE?
W..WILL YOU TESTIFY YOU JOINED ME OF YOUR OWN FREE WILL... P-PLEASE...
I...I WILL!
GOOD-BYE, BABY...IT WAS FUN WHILE IT LASTED...
DON'T SHOOT, COPPERS... I'M COMING..
YES...FUN WHILE IT LASTED...WHILE IT LASTED.. THAT'S HOW IT'S BEEN ALL MY LIFE...IS THERE NO WAY TO ESCAPE?

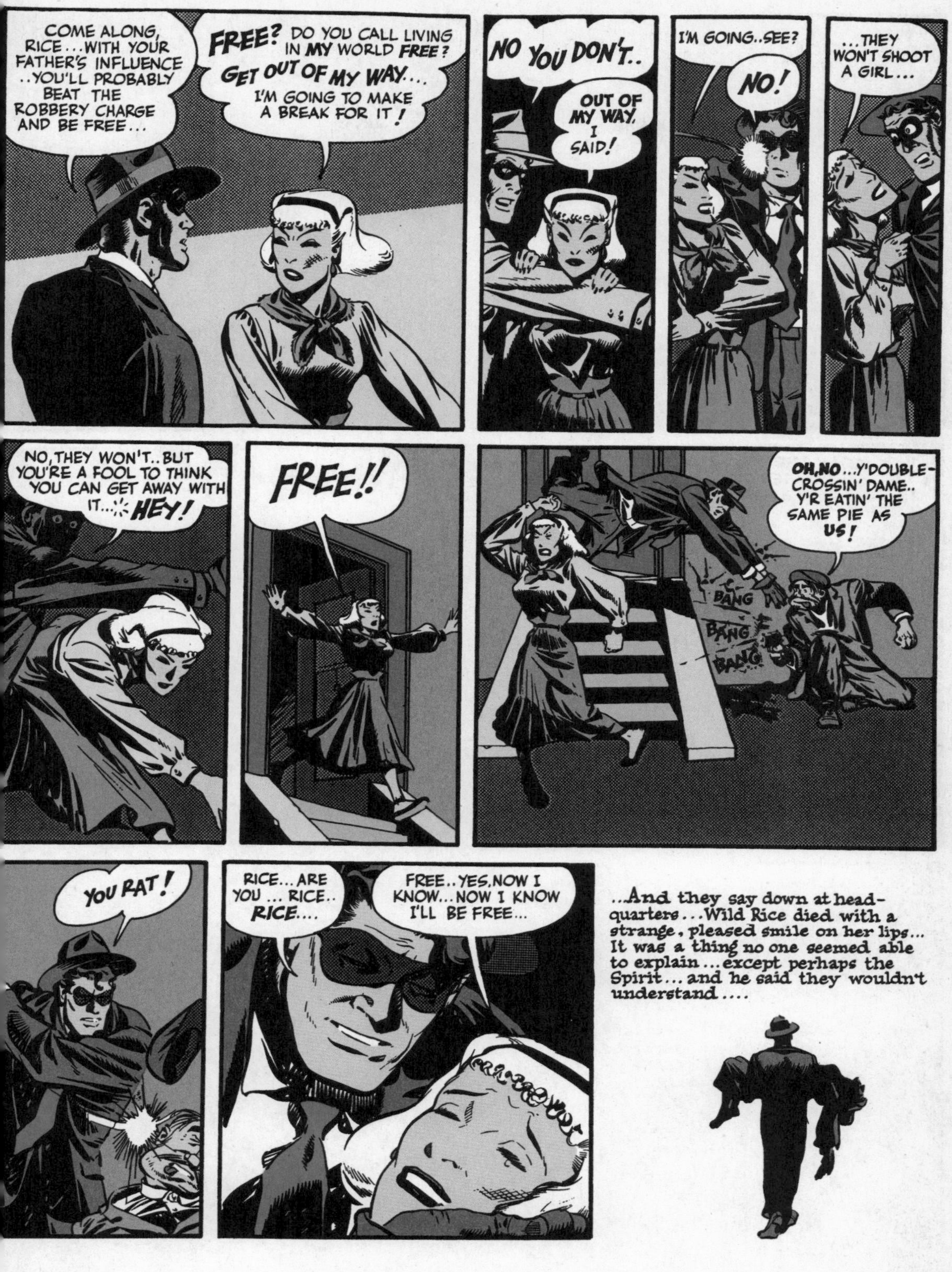
COME ALONG, RICE...WITH YOUR FATHER'S INFLUENCE ..YOU'LL PROBABLY BEAT THE ROBBERY CHARGE AND BE FREE...
FREE? DO YOU CALL LIVING IN MY WORLD FREE? GET OUT OF MY WAY.... I'M GOING TO MAKE A BREAK FOR IT!
NO YOU DON'T..
OUT OF MY WAY, I SAID!
I'M GOING..SEE?
NO!
...THEY WON'T SHOOT A GIRL...
NO, THEY WON'T..BUT YOU'RE A FOOL TO THINK YOU CAN GET AWAY WITH IT...HEY!
FREE!!
OH, NO...Y'DOUBLE-CROSSIN' DAME.. Y'R EATIN' THE SAME PIE AS US!
BANG
BANG
BANG
YOU RAT!
RICE...ARE YOU ... RICE.. RICE....
FREE..YES, NOW I KNOW...NOW I KNOW I'LL BE FREE...
...And they say down at headquarters...Wild Rice died with a strange, pleased smile on her lips... It was a thing no one seemed able to explain...except perhaps the Spirit...and he said they wouldn't understand....

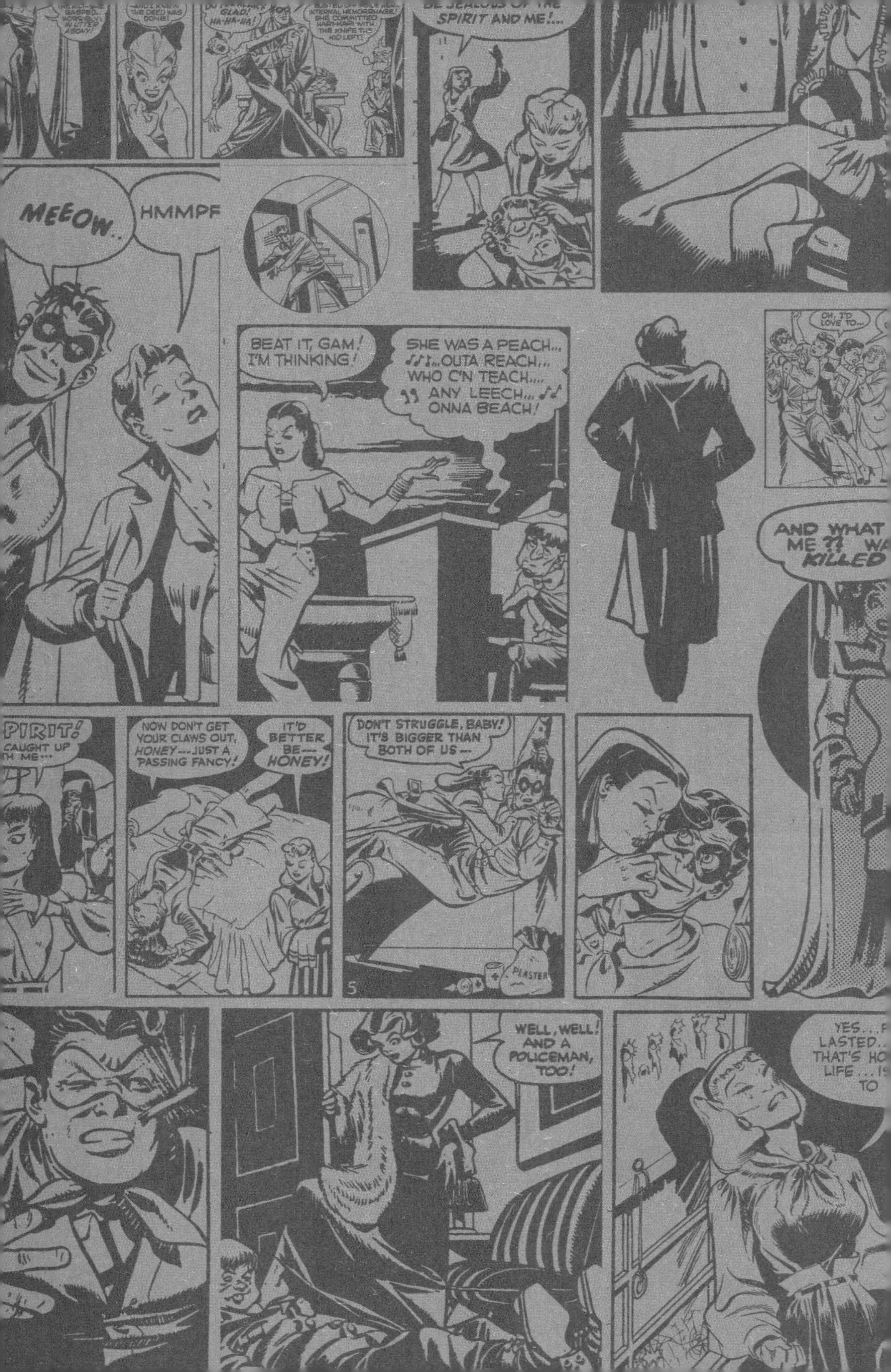

AND I KNEW THE DEED WAS DONE!
SPIRIT AND ME!...
MEEOW..
HMMPF
BEAT IT, GAM! I'M THINKING!
SHE WAS A PEACH... OUTA REACH... WHO C'N TEACH.... ANY LEECH... ONNA BEACH!
OH, I'D LOVE TO...
AND WHAT ME ?? WA KILLED
PIRIT! CAUGHT UP TH ME...
NOW DON'T GET YOUR CLAWS OUT, HONEY---JUST A PASSING FANCY!
IT'D BETTER BE--HONEY!
DON'T STRUGGLE, BABY! IT'S BIGGER THAN BOTH OF US---
PLASTER
5
WELL, WELL! AND A POLICEMAN, TOO!
YES... LASTED.. THAT'S HO LIFE... TO

COMIC BOOK SECTION

LORELEI ROX

ACTION Mystery ADVENTURE

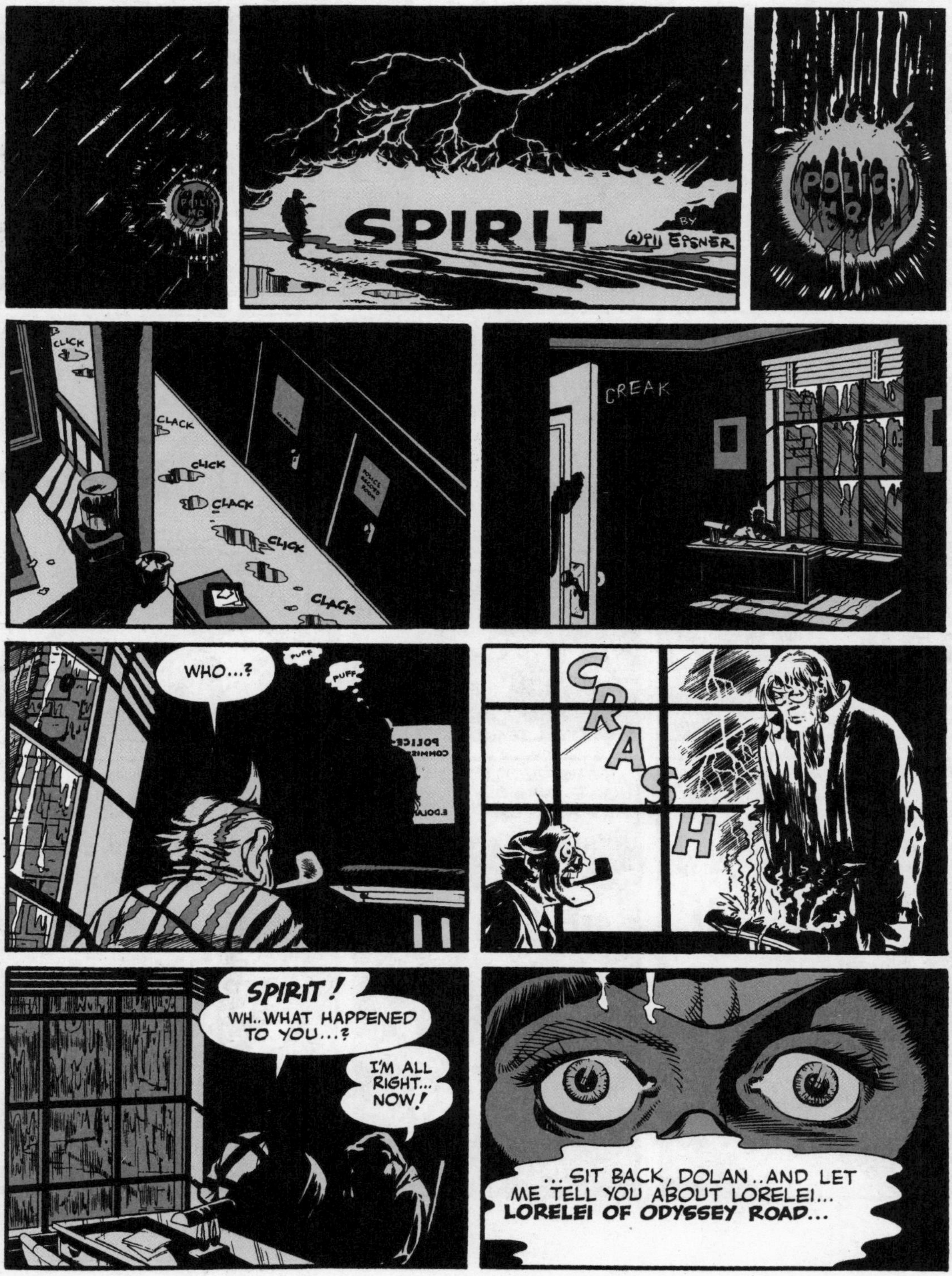
SPIRIT
BY WILL EISNER
CLICK
CLACK
CLICK
CLACK
CLICK
CLACK
CREAK
WHO...?
PUFF
PUFF
CRASH
SPIRIT! WH..WHAT HAPPENED TO YOU...?
I'M ALL RIGHT... NOW!
... SIT BACK, DOLAN .. AND LET ME TELL YOU ABOUT LORELEI... LORELEI OF ODYSSEY ROAD...

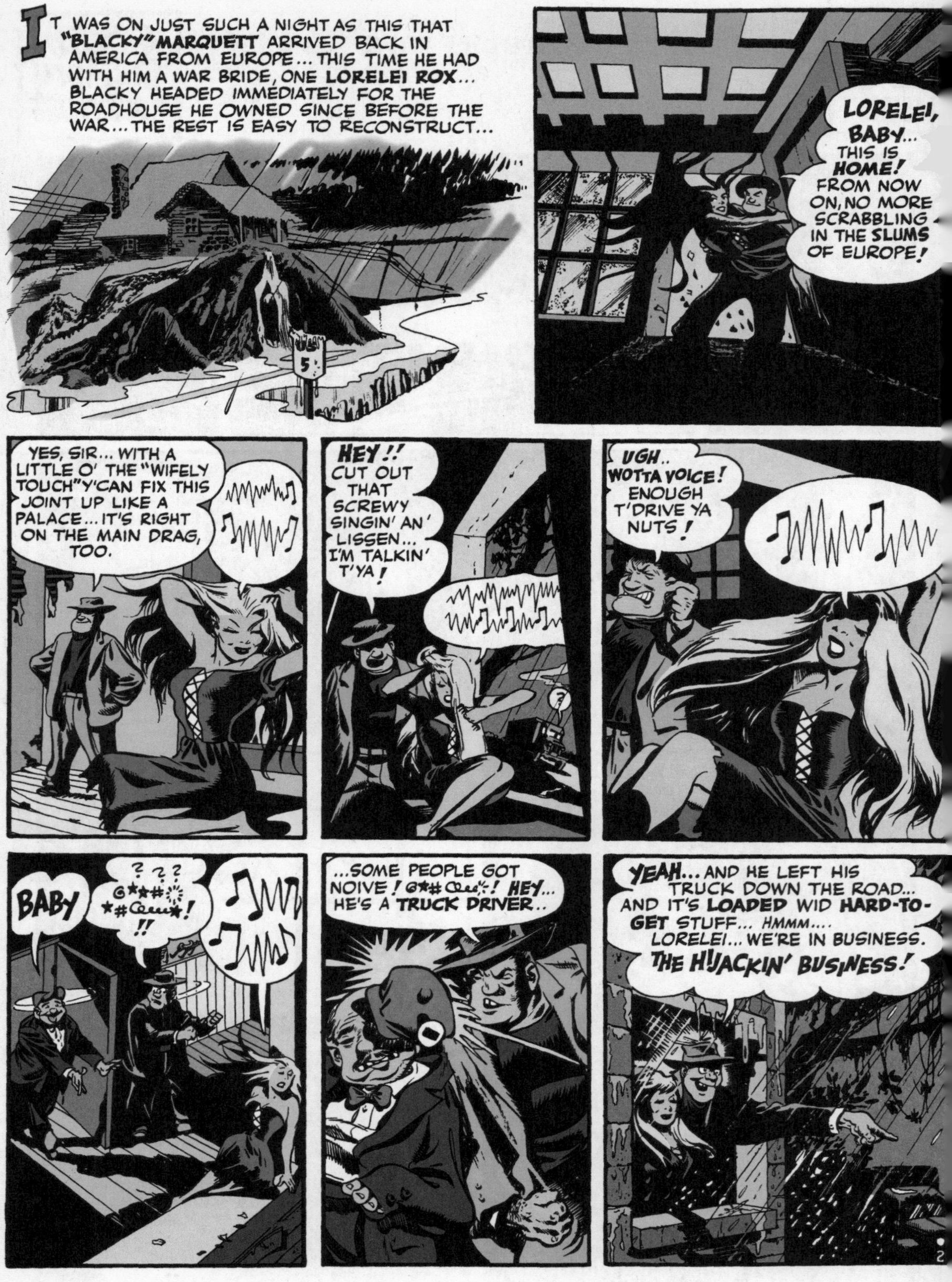

IT WAS ON JUST SUCH A NIGHT AS THIS THAT "BLACKY" MARQUETT ARRIVED BACK IN AMERICA FROM EUROPE... THIS TIME HE HAD WITH HIM A WAR BRIDE, ONE LORELEI ROX... BLACKY HEADED IMMEDIATELY FOR THE ROADHOUSE HE OWNED SINCE BEFORE THE WAR... THE REST IS EASY TO RECONSTRUCT...
5
LORELEI, BABY... THIS IS HOME! FROM NOW ON, NO MORE SCRABBLING IN THE SLUMS OF EUROPE!
YES, SIR... WITH A LITTLE O' THE "WIFELY TOUCH" Y'CAN FIX THIS JOINT UP LIKE A PALACE... IT'S RIGHT ON THE MAIN DRAG, TOO.
HEY!! CUT OUT THAT SCREWY SINGIN' AN' LISSEN... I'M TALKIN' T'YA!
?
UGH.. WOTTA VOICE! ENOUGH T'DRIVE YA NUTS!
BABY
? ? ? @*#*! *#@*! !!
...SOME PEOPLE GOT NOIVE! @*#@*! HEY... HE'S A TRUCK DRIVER..
YEAH... AND HE LEFT HIS TRUCK DOWN THE ROAD... AND IT'S LOADED WID HARD-TO-GET STUFF... HMMM.... LORELEI... WE'RE IN BUSINESS. THE HIJACKIN' BUSINESS!
2

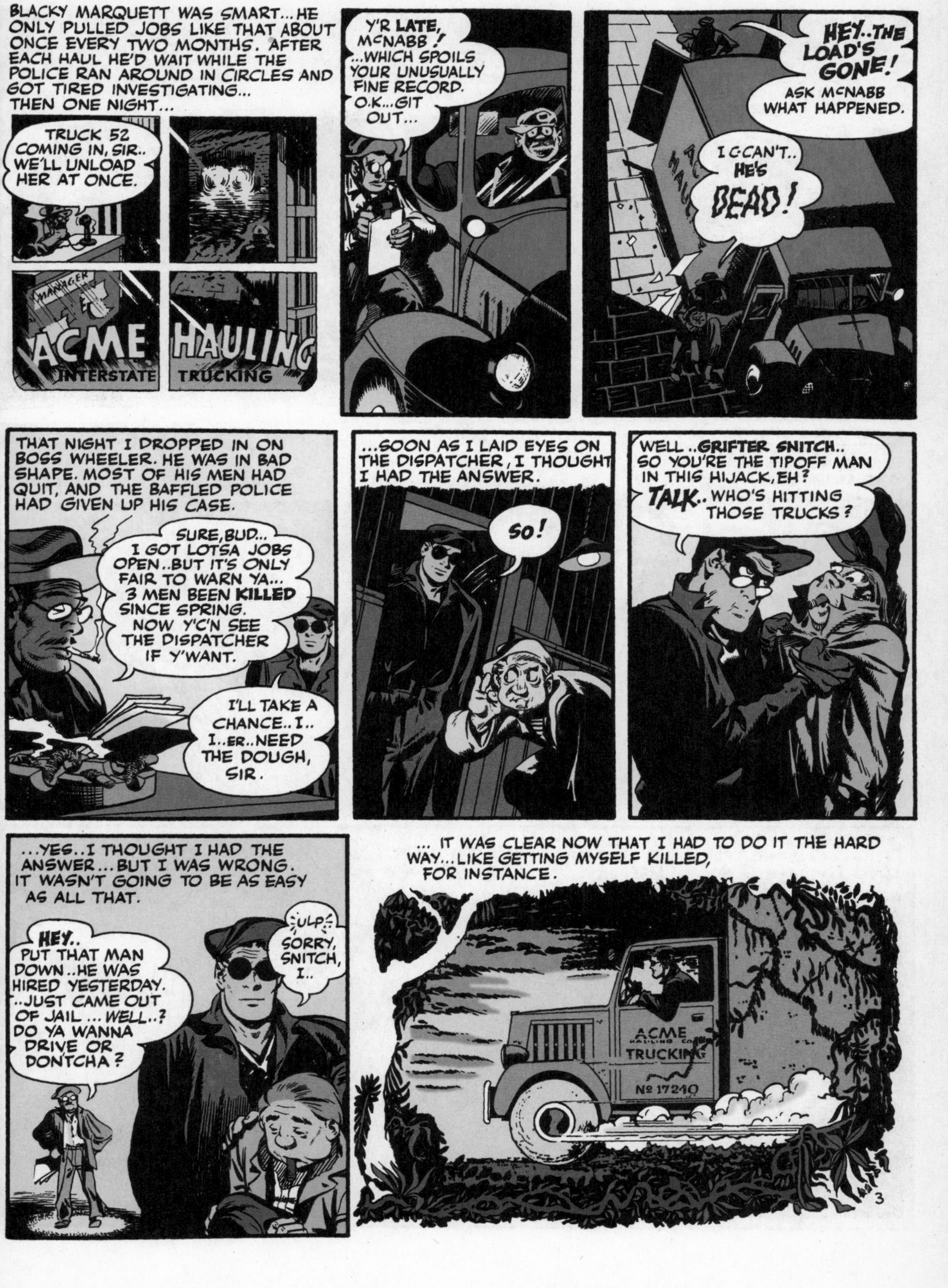
BLACKY MARQUETT WAS SMART...HE ONLY PULLED JOBS LIKE THAT ABOUT ONCE EVERY TWO MONTHS. AFTER EACH HAUL HE'D WAIT WHILE THE POLICE RAN AROUND IN CIRCLES AND GOT TIRED INVESTIGATING... THEN ONE NIGHT...
TRUCK 52 COMING IN, SIR.. WE'LL UNLOAD HER AT ONCE.
MANAGER
ACME HAULING
INTERSTATE TRUCKING
Y'R LATE, McNABB! ...WHICH SPOILS YOUR UNUSUALLY FINE RECORD. O.K...GIT OUT...
HEY..THE LOAD'S GONE! ASK McNABB WHAT HAPPENED.
I C-CAN'T.. HE'S DEAD!
THAT NIGHT I DROPPED IN ON BOSS WHEELER. HE WAS IN BAD SHAPE. MOST OF HIS MEN HAD QUIT, AND THE BAFFLED POLICE HAD GIVEN UP HIS CASE.
SURE, BUD... I GOT LOTSA JOBS OPEN..BUT IT'S ONLY FAIR TO WARN YA... 3 MEN BEEN KILLED SINCE SPRING. NOW Y'C'N SEE THE DISPATCHER IF Y'WANT.
I'LL TAKE A CHANCE..I.. I..ER..NEED THE DOUGH, SIR.
...SOON AS I LAID EYES ON THE DISPATCHER, I THOUGHT I HAD THE ANSWER.
SO!
WELL ..GRIFTER SNITCH.. SO YOU'RE THE TIPOFF MAN IN THIS HIJACK, EH? TALK.. WHO'S HITTING THOSE TRUCKS?
...YES..I THOUGHT I HAD THE ANSWER...BUT I WAS WRONG. IT WASN'T GOING TO BE AS EASY AS ALL THAT.
HEY.. PUT THAT MAN DOWN..HE WAS HIRED YESTERDAY. ..JUST CAME OUT OF JAIL ... WELL..? DO YA WANNA DRIVE OR DONTCHA?
ULP SORRY, SNITCH, I..
... IT WAS CLEAR NOW THAT I HAD TO DO IT THE HARD WAY...LIKE GETTING MYSELF KILLED, FOR INSTANCE.
ACME
TRUCKING
Nº 17240
3

CROSS-COUNTRY DRIVING IS A TOUGH JOB.. THE MONOTONY.. THE UNBROKEN HUM OF THE MOTOR.. ALL FORM A SORT OF HYPNOTIC INFLUENCE... ...SOON I FOUND MYSELF THINKING THAT NOTHING WAS GOING TO HAPPEN ON THIS RUN ...

THEN, AS I BEGAN THE LONG CLIMB UP ROUTE 5, THE HARMONIC VIBRATION NATURAL TO MOST TRUCKS ON HEAVY PULLS BEGAN TO DULL MY HEARING ...

AND SUDDENLY I BEGAN HEARING MUSIC... A STRANGE KIND OF MUSIC ...PITCHED HIGH..AND YET BLENDING WITH THE "SINGING" OF THE TIRES..

I KEPT SLOWING DOWN THE TRUCK SO THAT I MIGHT BETTER HEAR THE MUSIC ...

IT GOT **LOUDER**.......AND **LOUDER**

..AND IT SEEMED TO LIFT ME OUT OF MY TRUCK SEAT..

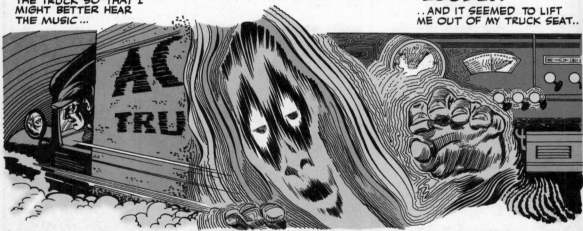

MY INSTINCTS WERE STILL DEPENDABLE.. ...I STOPPED THE TRUCK AND BRAKED IT.. BUT MY MIND...MY BRAIN..MY NERVES WERE VIBRATING LIKE PLUCKED VIOLIN STRINGS

I MOVED THROUGH SPACE ... OR WHAT SEEMED LIKE IT...THEN SUDDENLY...

WHAM

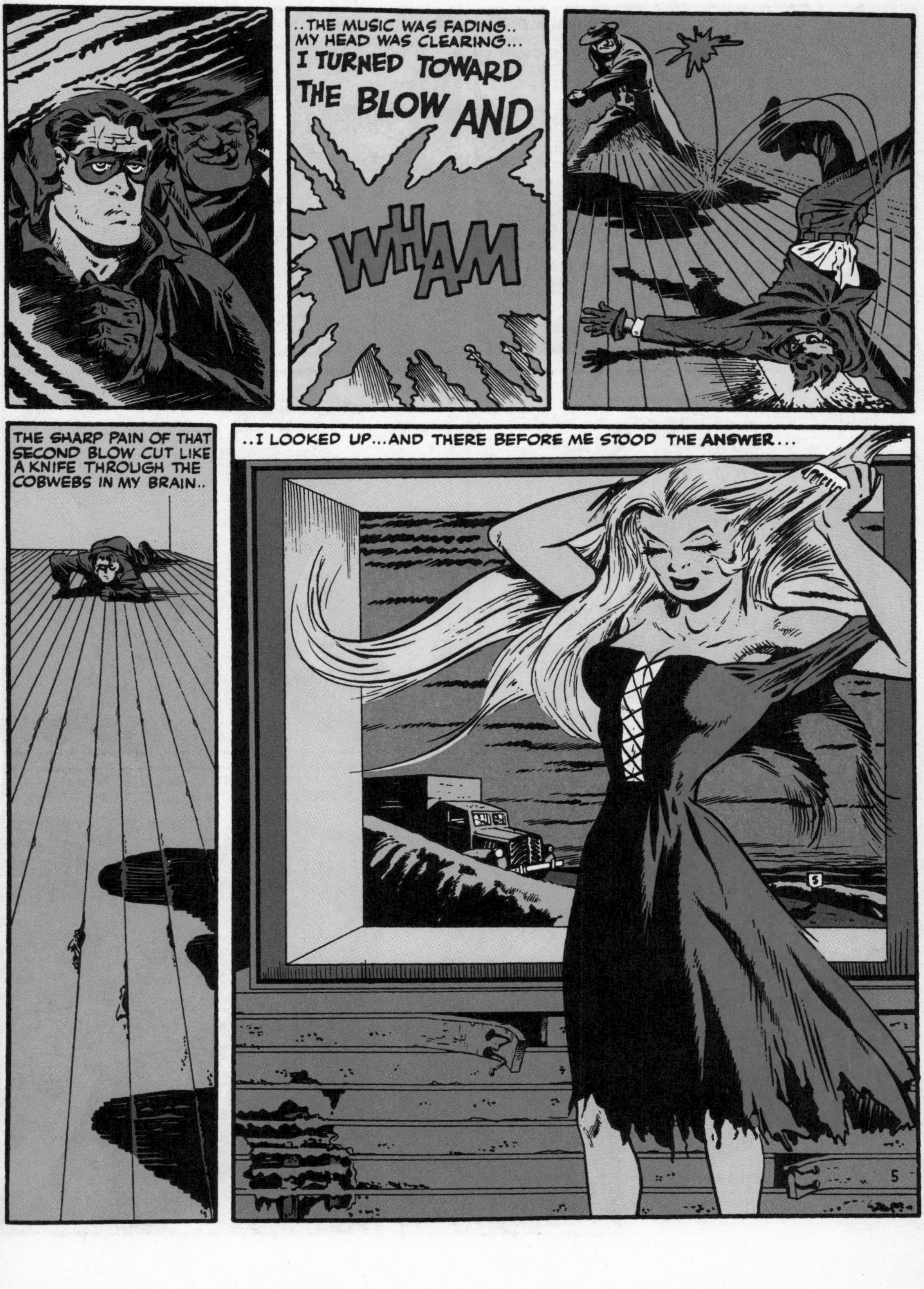
..THE MUSIC WAS FADING.. MY HEAD WAS CLEARING... I TURNED TOWARD THE BLOW AND
WHAM
THE SHARP PAIN OF THAT SECOND BLOW CUT LIKE A KNIFE THROUGH THE COBWEBS IN MY BRAIN..
..I LOOKED UP...AND THERE BEFORE ME STOOD THE ANSWER...
5

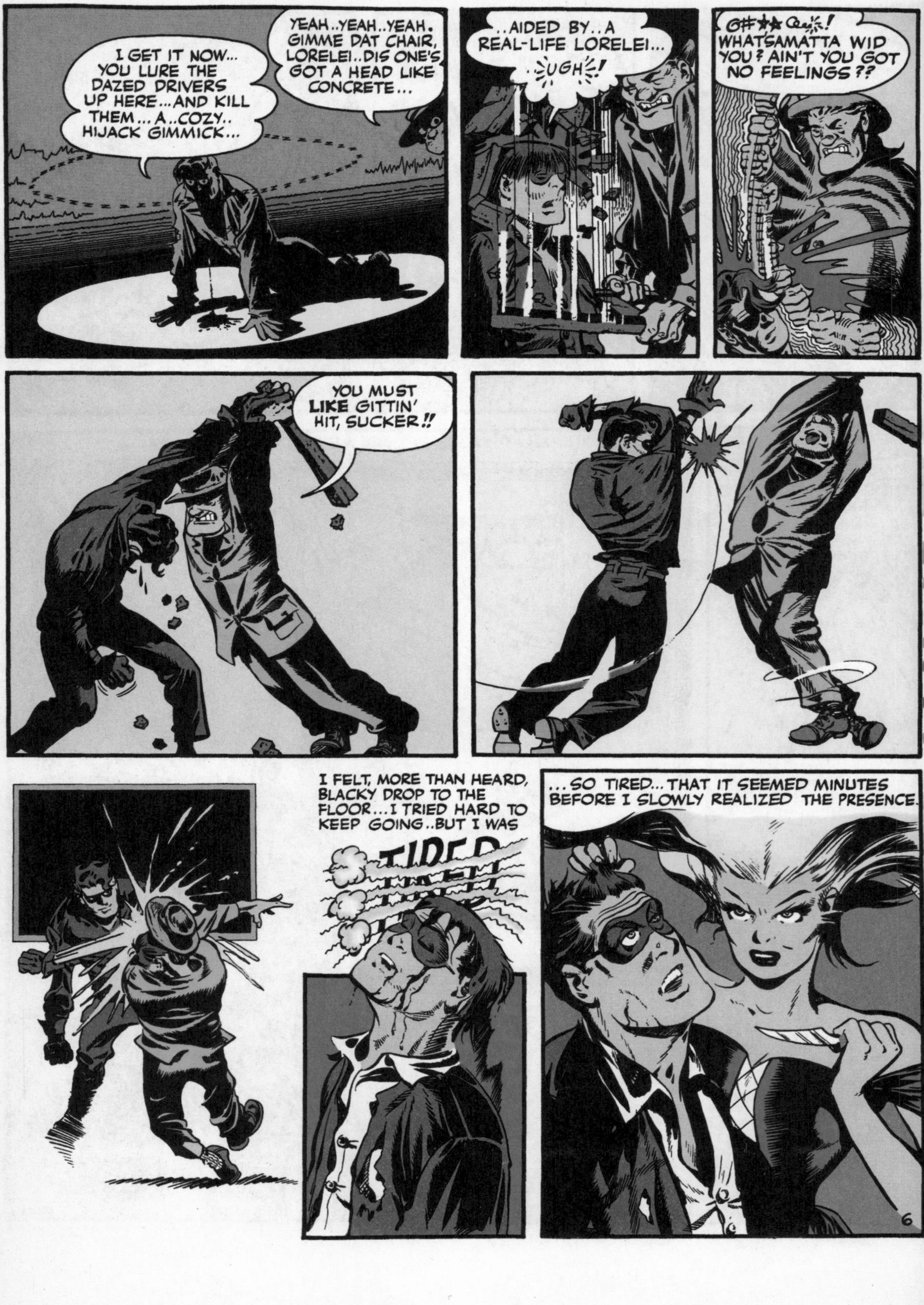
I GET IT NOW... YOU LURE THE DAZED DRIVERS UP HERE...AND KILL THEM... A..COZY.. HIJACK GIMMICK...
YEAH..YEAH..YEAH. GIMME DAT CHAIR, LORELEI..DIS ONE'S GOT A HEAD LIKE CONCRETE...
..AIDED BY..A REAL-LIFE LORELEI...
UGH!
WHATSAMATTA WID YOU? AIN'T YOU GOT NO FEELINGS??
YOU MUST LIKE GITTIN' HIT, SUCKER!!
I FELT, MORE THAN HEARD, BLACKY DROP TO THE FLOOR...I TRIED HARD TO KEEP GOING..BUT I WAS
TIRED
...SO TIRED...THAT IT SEEMED MINUTES BEFORE I SLOWLY REALIZED THE PRESENCE.
6

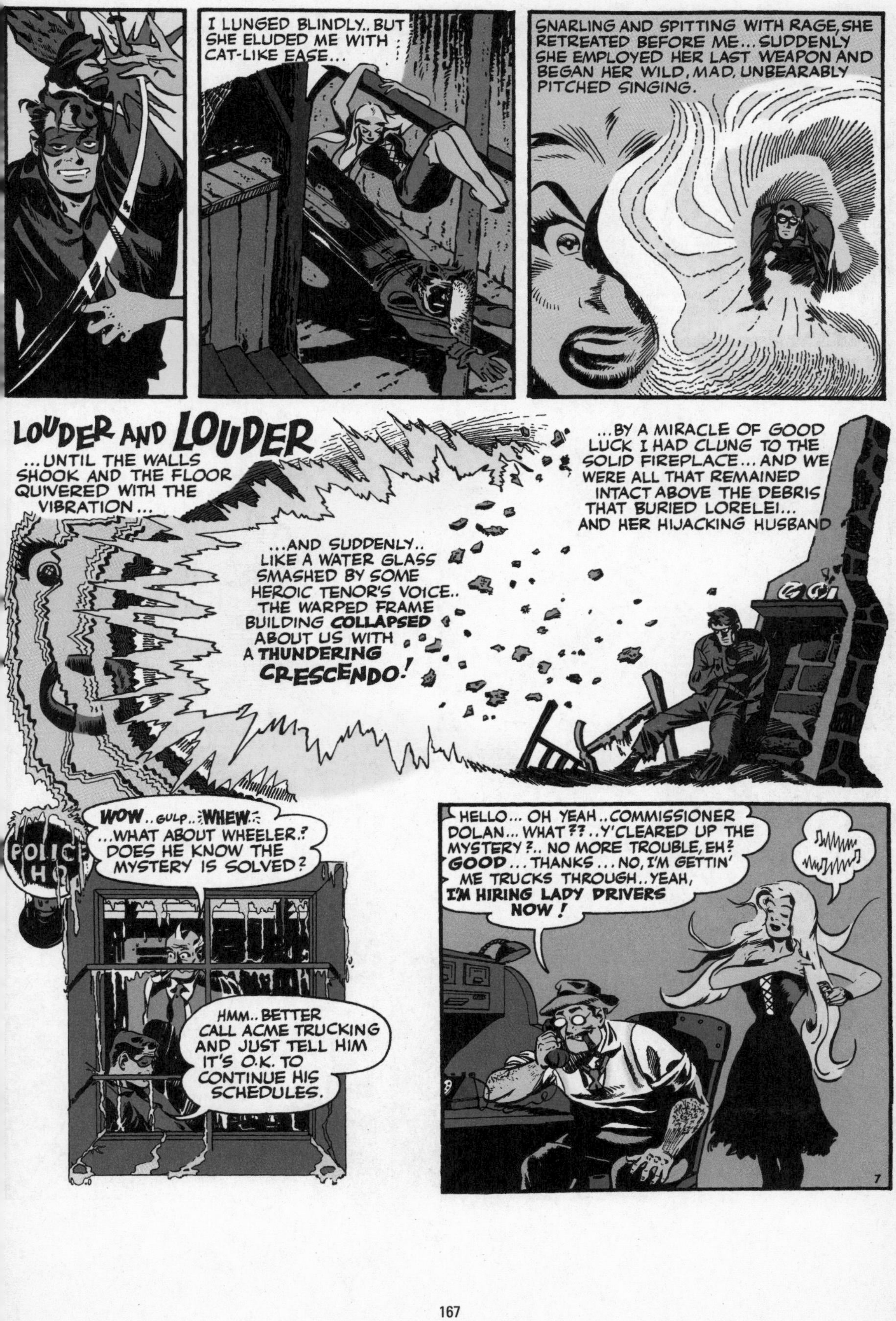

I LUNGED BLINDLY.. BUT SHE ELUDED ME WITH CAT-LIKE EASE...
SNARLING AND SPITTING WITH RAGE, SHE RETREATED BEFORE ME... SUDDENLY SHE EMPLOYED HER LAST WEAPON AND BEGAN HER WILD, MAD, UNBEARABLY PITCHED SINGING.
LOUDER AND LOUDER ...UNTIL THE WALLS SHOOK AND THE FLOOR QUIVERED WITH THE VIBRATION...
...AND SUDDENLY.. LIKE A WATER GLASS SMASHED BY SOME HEROIC TENOR'S VOICE.. THE WARPED FRAME BUILDING COLLAPSED ABOUT US WITH A THUNDERING CRESCENDO!
...BY A MIRACLE OF GOOD LUCK I HAD CLUNG TO THE SOLID FIREPLACE... AND WE WERE ALL THAT REMAINED INTACT ABOVE THE DEBRIS THAT BURIED LORELEI... AND HER HIJACKING HUSBAND
POLICE HQ
WOW.. GULP.. WHEW ...WHAT ABOUT WHEELER.? DOES HE KNOW THE MYSTERY IS SOLVED?
HMM.. BETTER CALL ACME TRUCKING AND JUST TELL HIM IT'S O.K. TO CONTINUE HIS SCHEDULES.
HELLO... OH YEAH.. COMMISSIONER DOLAN... WHAT??.. Y'CLEARED UP THE MYSTERY?.. NO MORE TROUBLE, EH? GOOD... THANKS... NO, I'M GETTIN' ME TRUCKS THROUGH.. YEAH, I'M HIRING LADY DRIVERS NOW!
7

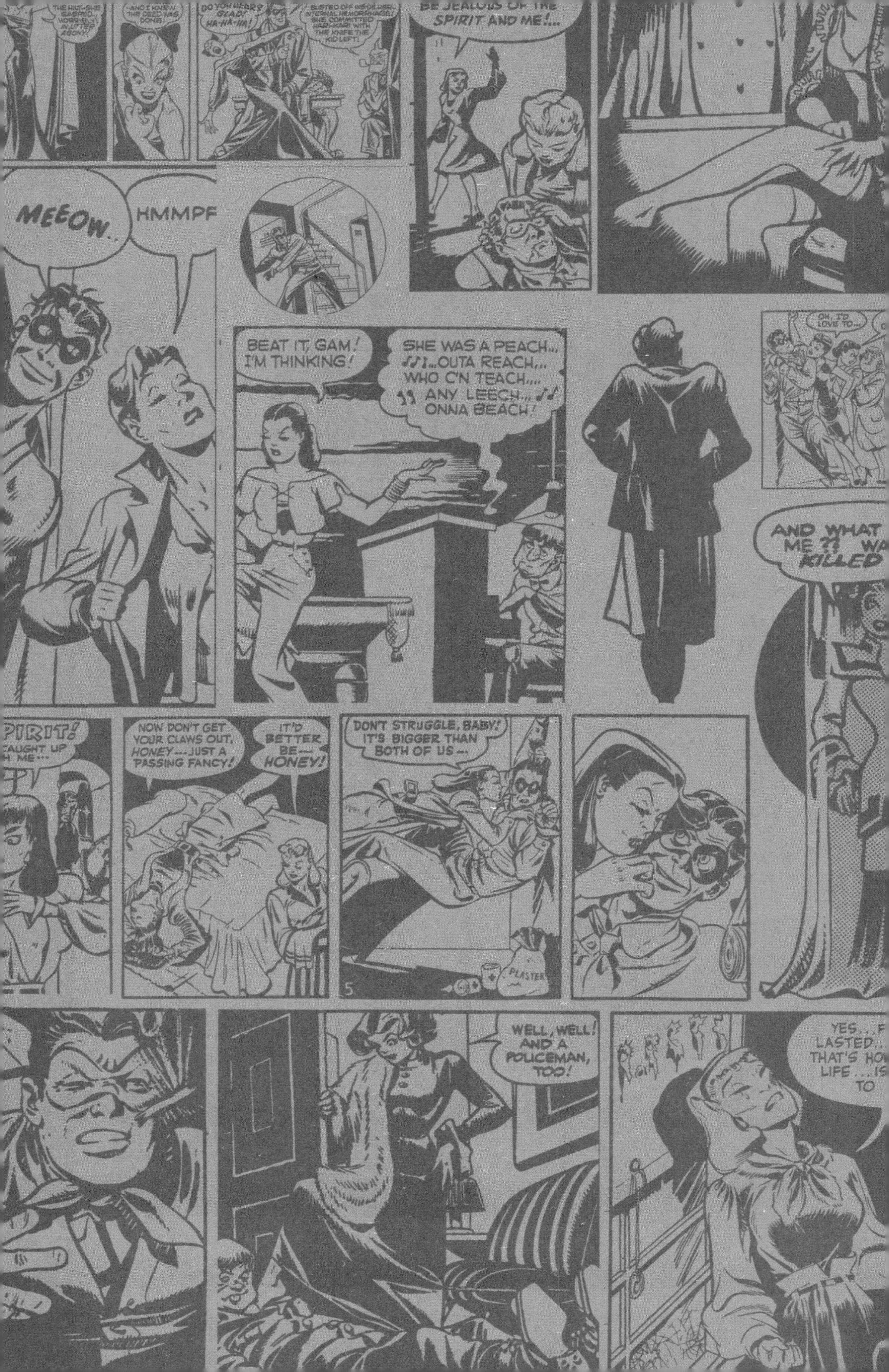

THE HILT–SHE GASPED.. HORRIBLY! IN UTTER AGONY!
–AND I KNEW THE DEED WAS DONE!
DO YOU HEAR? GLAD! HA-HA-HA!
BUSTED OFF INSIDE HER– INTERNAL HEMORRHAGE! SHE COMMITTED HARI-KARI WITH THE KNIFE THE KID LEFT!
SPIRIT AND ME!...
MEEOW..
HMMPF
OH, I'D LOVE TO...
BEAT IT, GAM! I'M THINKING!
SHE WAS A PEACH... ♪♪...OUTA REACH... WHO C'N TEACH.... ANY LEECH... ♪♪ ONNA BEACH!
NOW DON'T GET YOUR CLAWS OUT. HONEY---JUST A PASSING FANCY!
IT'D BETTER BE--- HONEY!
DON'T STRUGGLE, BABY! IT'S BIGGER THAN BOTH OF US--
PLASTER
5
WELL, WELL! AND A POLICEMAN, TOO!

COMIC BOOK SECTION

PLASTER OF PARIS

ACTION Mystery ADVENTURE

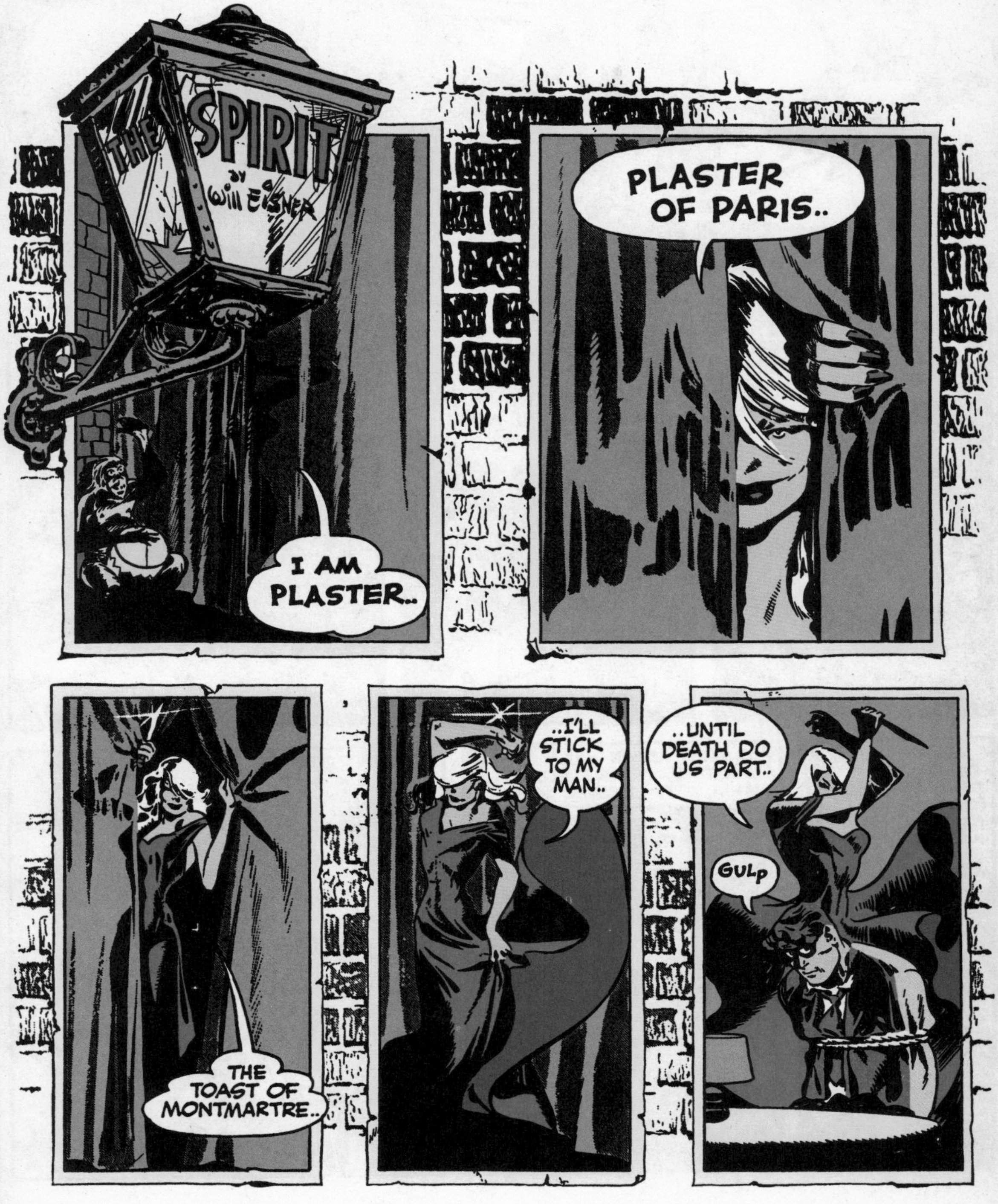
THE SPIRIT
BY Will Eisner
I AM PLASTER..
PLASTER OF PARIS..
THE TOAST OF MONTMARTRE..
..I'LL STICK TO MY MAN..
..UNTIL DEATH DO US PART..
GULP

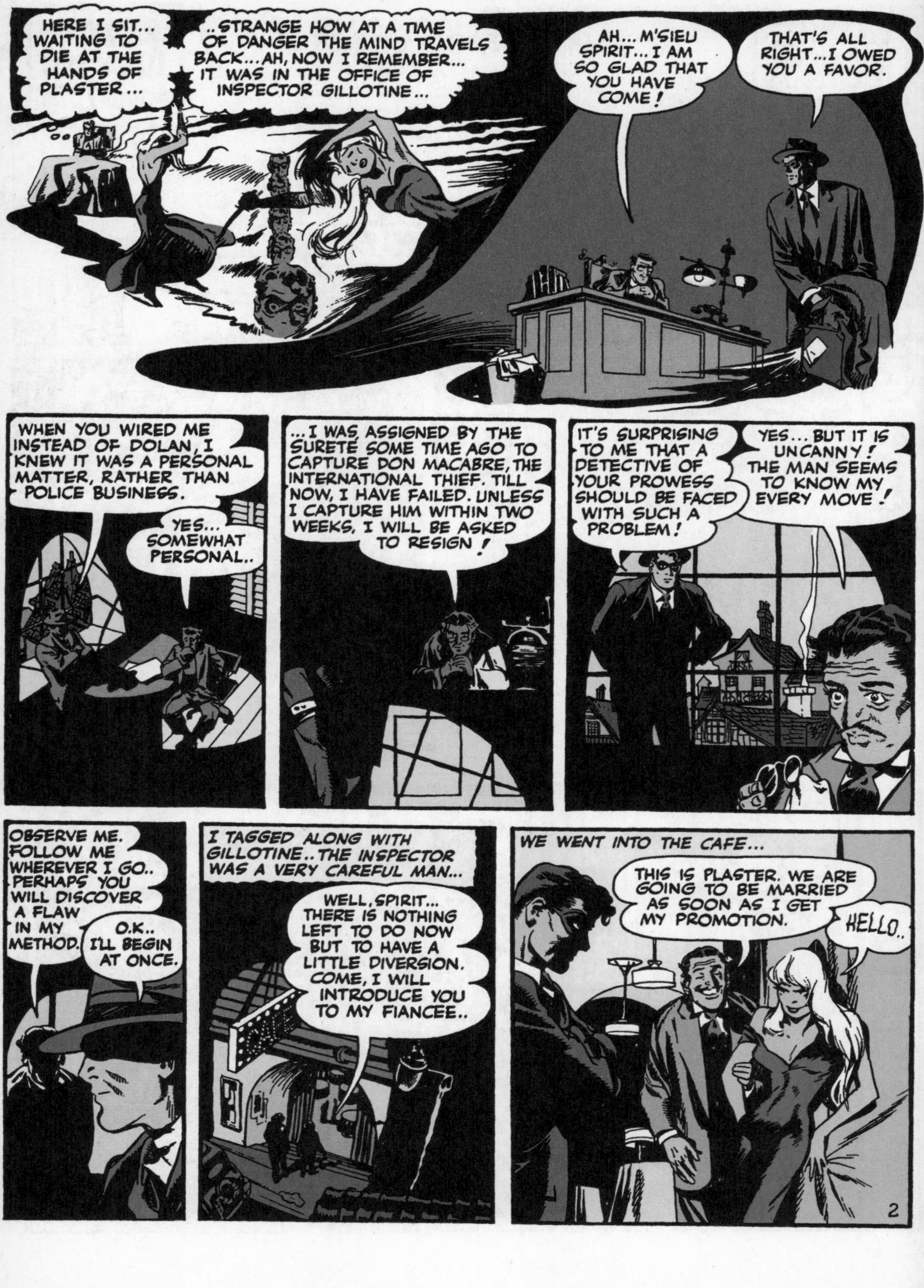
HERE I SIT... WAITING TO DIE AT THE HANDS OF PLASTER...
..STRANGE HOW AT A TIME OF DANGER THE MIND TRAVELS BACK...AH, NOW I REMEMBER... IT WAS IN THE OFFICE OF INSPECTOR GILLOTINE...
AH... M'SIEU SPIRIT... I AM SO GLAD THAT YOU HAVE COME!
THAT'S ALL RIGHT...I OWED YOU A FAVOR.
WHEN YOU WIRED ME INSTEAD OF DOLAN, I KNEW IT WAS A PERSONAL MATTER, RATHER THAN POLICE BUSINESS.
YES... SOMEWHAT PERSONAL..
...I WAS ASSIGNED BY THE SURETÉ SOME TIME AGO TO CAPTURE DON MACABRE, THE INTERNATIONAL THIEF. TILL NOW, I HAVE FAILED. UNLESS I CAPTURE HIM WITHIN TWO WEEKS, I WILL BE ASKED TO RESIGN!
IT'S SURPRISING TO ME THAT A DETECTIVE OF YOUR PROWESS SHOULD BE FACED WITH SUCH A PROBLEM!
YES... BUT IT IS UNCANNY! THE MAN SEEMS TO KNOW MY EVERY MOVE!
OBSERVE ME. FOLLOW ME WHEREVER I GO.. PERHAPS YOU WILL DISCOVER A FLAW IN MY METHOD.
O.K.. I'LL BEGIN AT ONCE.
I TAGGED ALONG WITH GILLOTINE..THE INSPECTOR WAS A VERY CAREFUL MAN...
WELL, SPIRIT... THERE IS NOTHING LEFT TO DO NOW BUT TO HAVE A LITTLE DIVERSION. COME, I WILL INTRODUCE YOU TO MY FIANCEE..
WE WENT INTO THE CAFE...
THIS IS PLASTER. WE ARE GOING TO BE MARRIED AS SOON AS I GET MY PROMOTION.
HELLO..
2

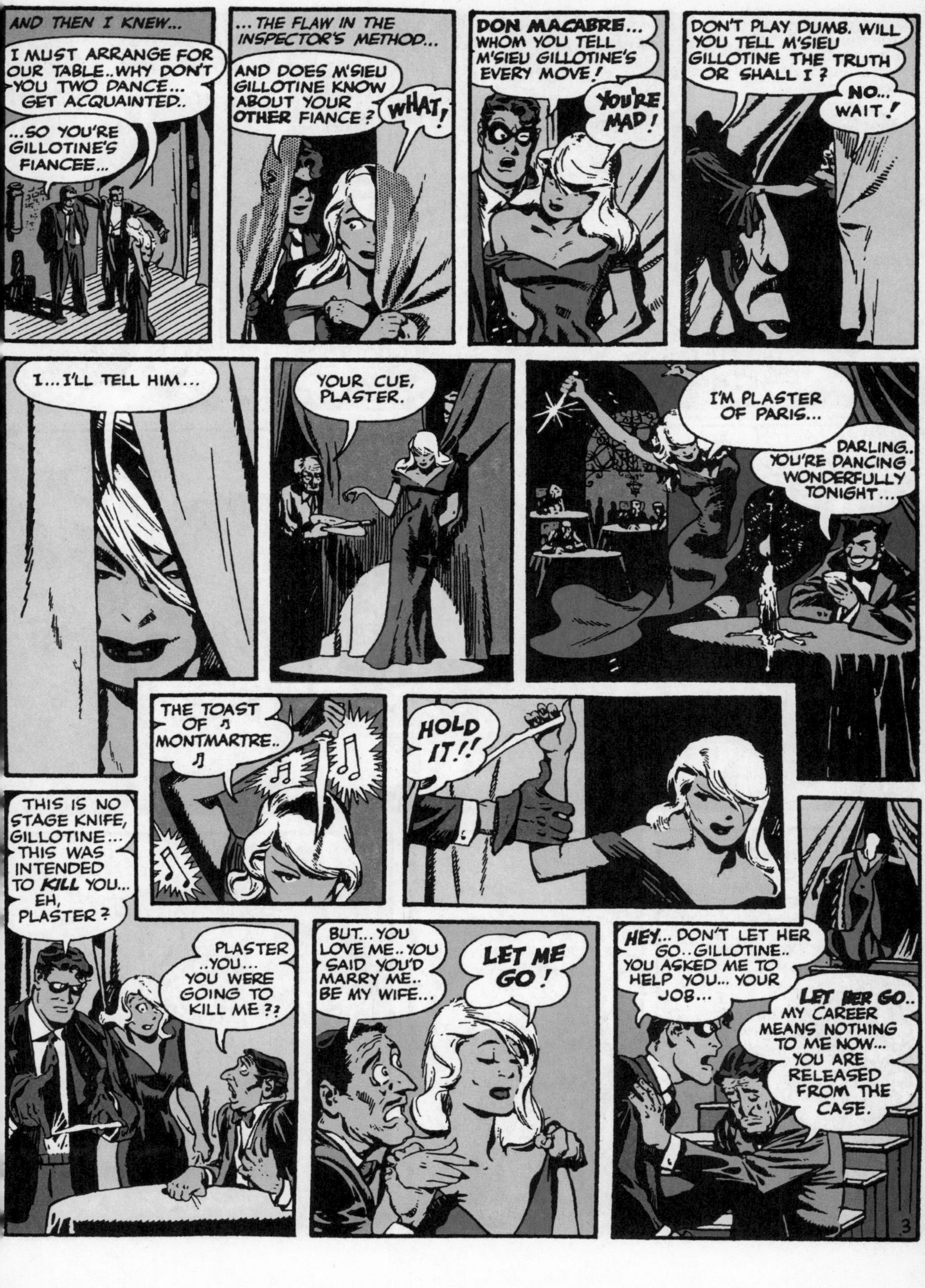
AND THEN I KNEW...
I MUST ARRANGE FOR OUR TABLE..WHY DON'T YOU TWO DANCE... GET ACQUAINTED..
...SO YOU'RE GILLOTINE'S FIANCEE...
...THE FLAW IN THE INSPECTOR'S METHOD...
AND DOES M'SIEU GILLOTINE KNOW ABOUT YOUR OTHER FIANCE?
WHAT!
DON MACABRE... WHOM YOU TELL M'SIEU GILLOTINE'S EVERY MOVE!
YOU'RE MAD!
DON'T PLAY DUMB. WILL YOU TELL M'SIEU GILLOTINE THE TRUTH OR SHALL I?
NO... WAIT!
I...I'LL TELL HIM...
YOUR CUE, PLASTER.
I'M PLASTER OF PARIS...
DARLING.. YOU'RE DANCING WONDERFULLY TONIGHT...
THE TOAST OF MONTMARTRE..
HOLD IT!!
THIS IS NO STAGE KNIFE, GILLOTINE... THIS WAS INTENDED TO KILL YOU... EH, PLASTER?
PLASTER ..YOU... YOU WERE GOING TO KILL ME??
BUT...YOU LOVE ME..YOU SAID YOU'D MARRY ME.. BE MY WIFE...
LET ME GO!
HEY... DON'T LET HER GO..GILLOTINE.. YOU ASKED ME TO HELP YOU... YOUR JOB...
LET HER GO.. MY CAREER MEANS NOTHING TO ME NOW... YOU ARE RELEASED FROM THE CASE.
3

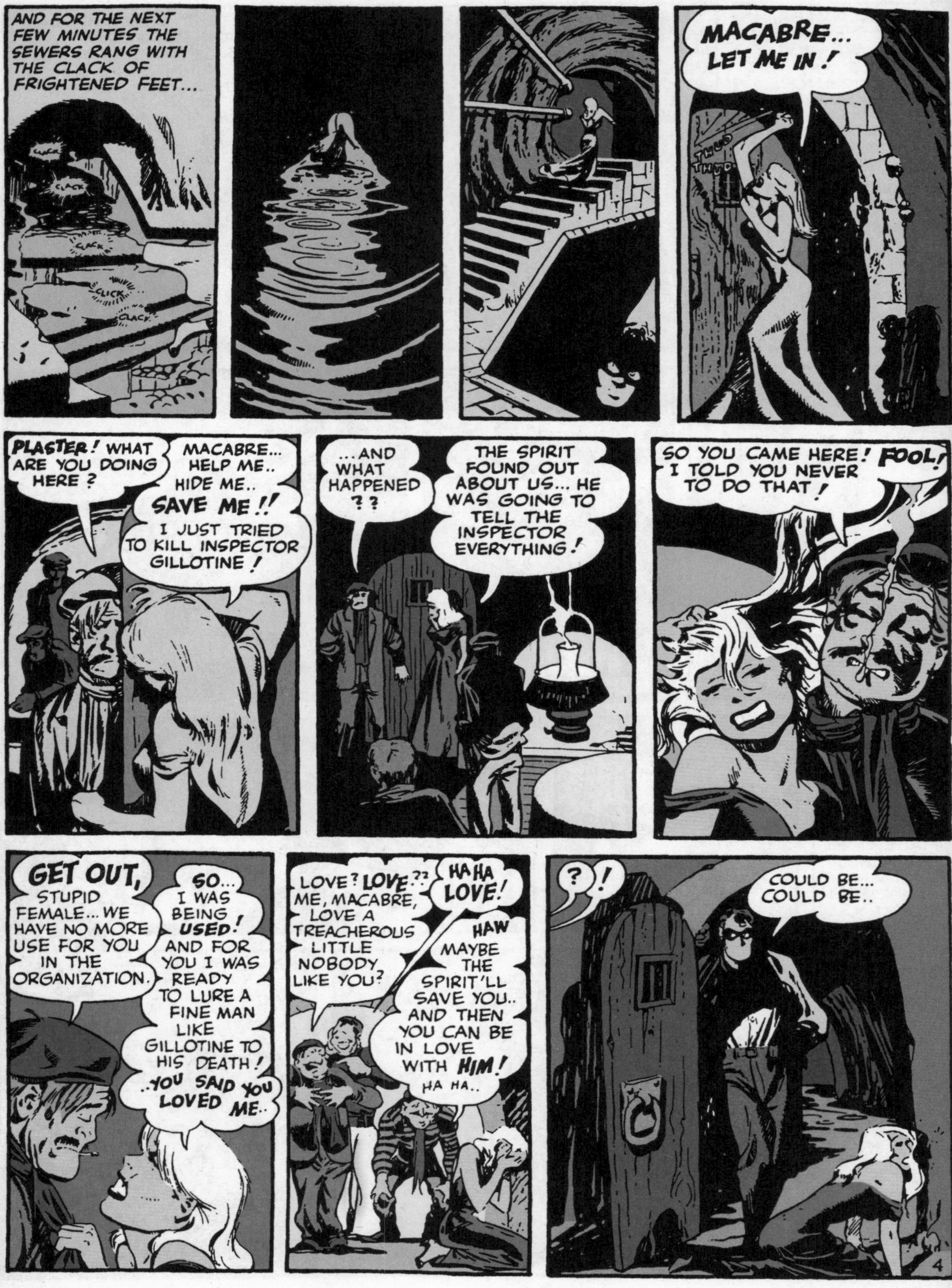
AND FOR THE NEXT FEW MINUTES THE SEWERS RANG WITH THE CLACK OF FRIGHTENED FEET...
CLACK
CLACK
CLACK
CLICK
CLACK
MACABRE... LET ME IN!
THUD THUD
PLASTER! WHAT ARE YOU DOING HERE?
MACABRE... HELP ME.. HIDE ME.. SAVE ME!!
I JUST TRIED TO KILL INSPECTOR GILLOTINE!
...AND WHAT HAPPENED ??
THE SPIRIT FOUND OUT ABOUT US... HE WAS GOING TO TELL THE INSPECTOR EVERYTHING!
SO YOU CAME HERE! FOOL! I TOLD YOU NEVER TO DO THAT!
GET OUT, STUPID FEMALE... WE HAVE NO MORE USE FOR YOU IN THE ORGANIZATION.
SO... I WAS BEING USED! AND FOR YOU I WAS READY TO LURE A FINE MAN LIKE GILLOTINE TO HIS DEATH!
..YOU SAID YOU LOVED ME..
LOVE? LOVE?? ME, MACABRE, LOVE A TREACHEROUS LITTLE NOBODY LIKE YOU?
HA HA LOVE!
HAW MAYBE THE SPIRIT'LL SAVE YOU.. AND THEN YOU CAN BE IN LOVE WITH HIM! HA HA..
?!
COULD BE... COULD BE..
4

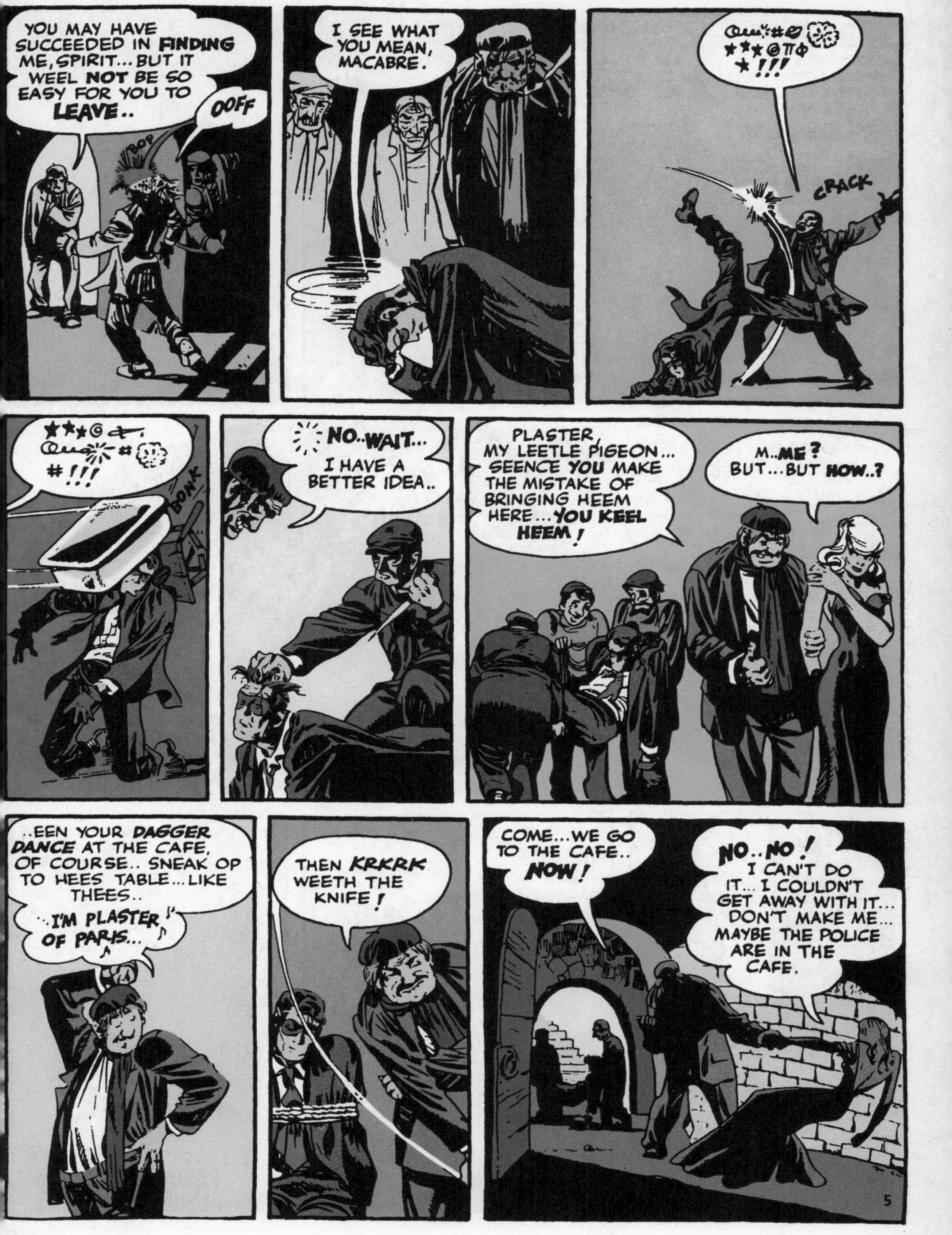
YOU MAY HAVE SUCCEEDED IN FINDING ME, SPIRIT... BUT IT WEEL NOT BE SO EASY FOR YOU TO LEAVE..
BOP
OOFF
I SEE WHAT YOU MEAN, MACABRE.
!!!
CRACK
!!!
BONK
NO..WAIT... I HAVE A BETTER IDEA..
PLASTER, MY LEETLE PIGEON... SEENCE YOU MAKE THE MISTAKE OF BRINGING HEEM HERE... YOU KEEL HEEM!
M..ME? BUT...BUT HOW..?
..EEN YOUR DAGGER DANCE AT THE CAFE, OF COURSE.. SNEAK OP TO HEES TABLE... LIKE THEES..
..I'M PLASTER OF PARIS...
THEN KRKRK WEETH THE KNIFE!
COME...WE GO TO THE CAFE.. NOW!
NO..NO! I CAN'T DO IT... I COULDN'T GET AWAY WITH IT... DON'T MAKE ME... MAYBE THE POLICE ARE IN THE CAFE.
5

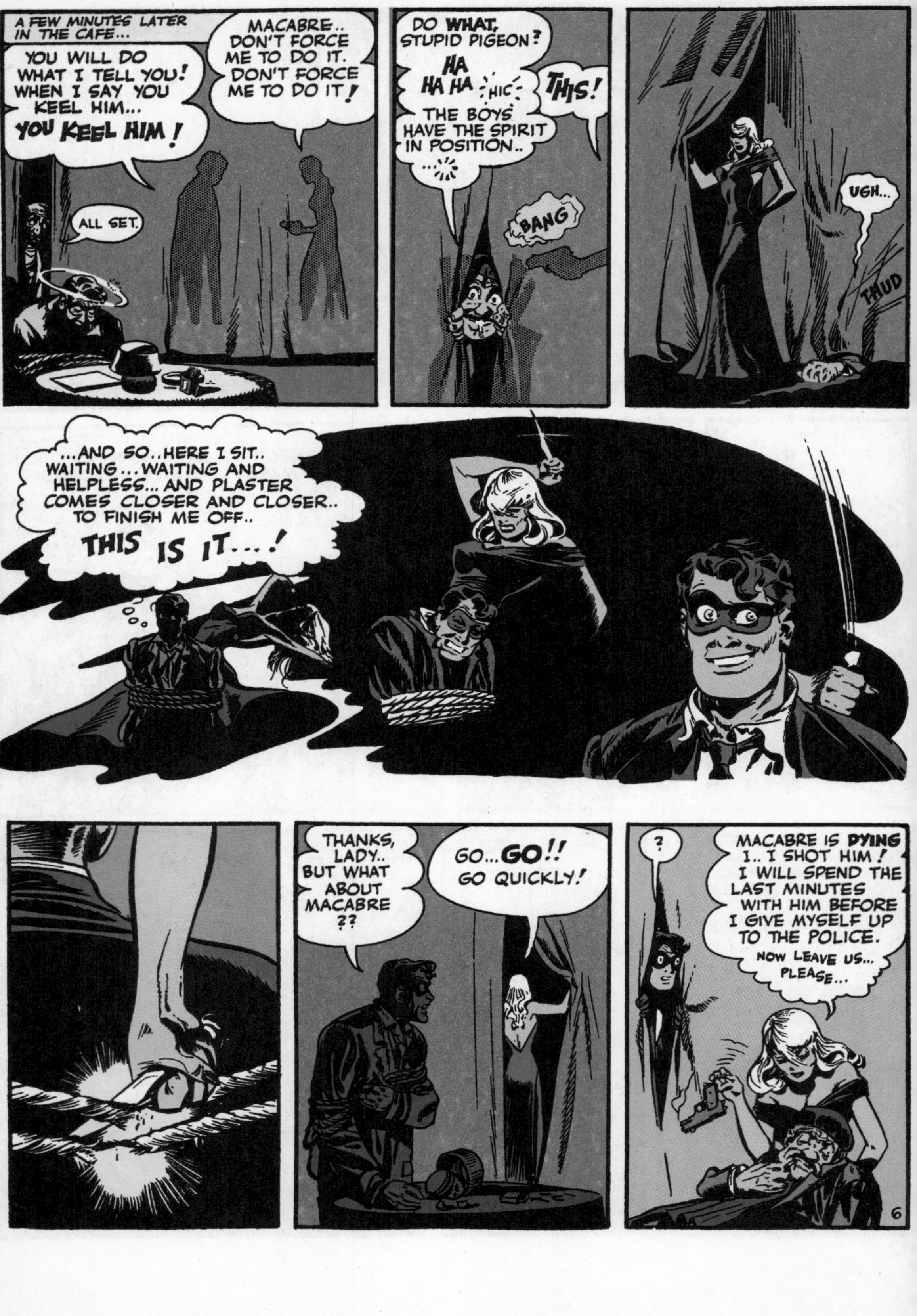
A FEW MINUTES LATER IN THE CAFE...
YOU WILL DO WHAT I TELL YOU! WHEN I SAY YOU KEEL HIM... YOU KEEL HIM!
MACABRE.. DON'T FORCE ME TO DO IT. DON'T FORCE ME TO DO IT!
ALL SET.
DO WHAT, STUPID PIGEON?
HA HA HA
HIC
THE BOYS HAVE THE SPIRIT IN POSITION..
THIS!
BANG
UGH...
THUD
...AND SO..HERE I SIT.. WAITING...WAITING AND HELPLESS...AND PLASTER COMES CLOSER AND CLOSER.. TO FINISH ME OFF..
THIS IS IT...!
THANKS, LADY.. BUT WHAT ABOUT MACABRE ??
GO...GO!! GO QUICKLY!
?
MACABRE IS DYING I.. I SHOT HIM! I WILL SPEND THE LAST MINUTES WITH HIM BEFORE I GIVE MYSELF UP TO THE POLICE.
NOW LEAVE US... PLEASE...
6

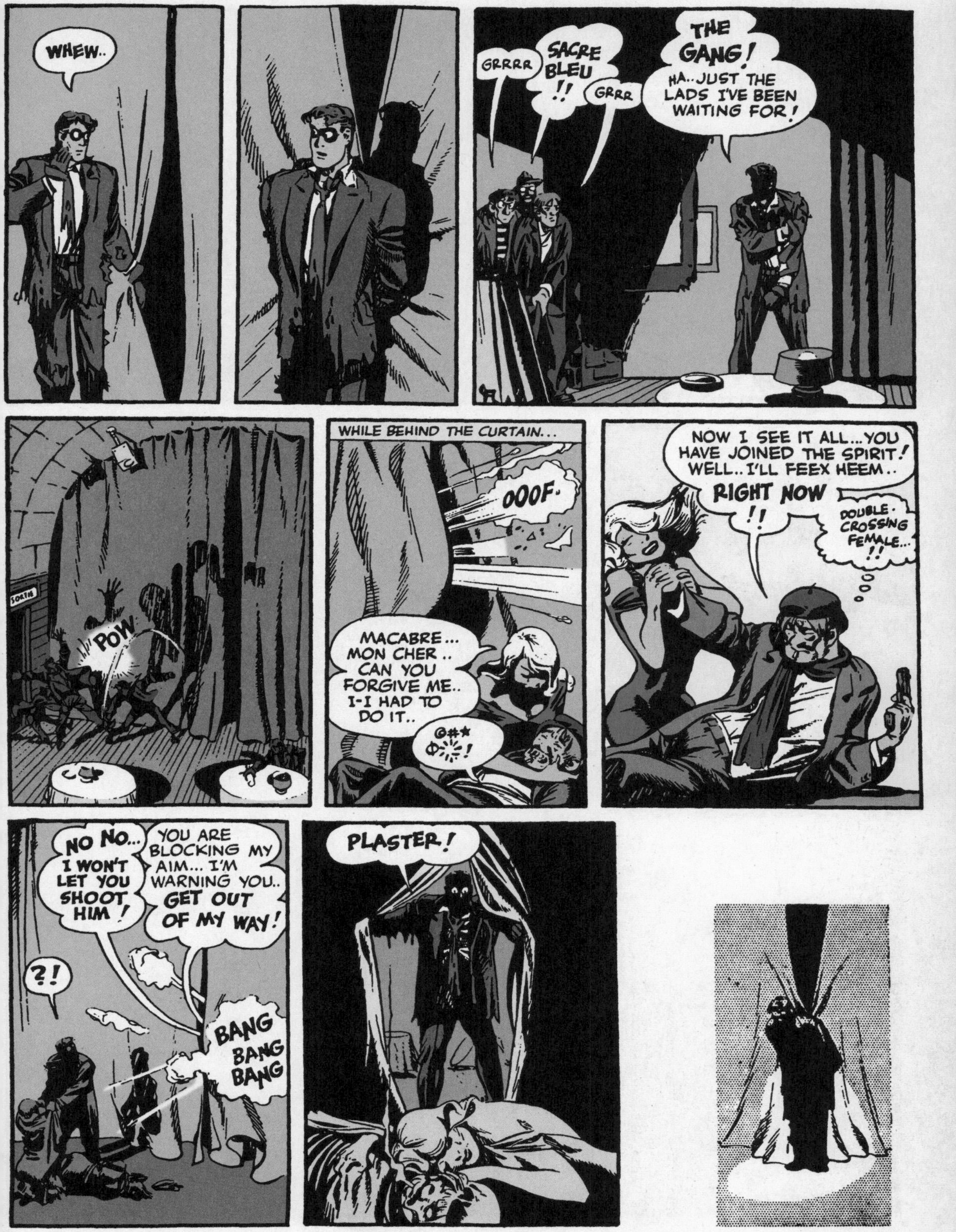

WHEW..
GRRRR
SACRE BLEU !!
GRRR
THE GANG! HA.. JUST THE LADS I'VE BEEN WAITING FOR!
POW
WHILE BEHIND THE CURTAIN...
OOOF
MACABRE... MON CHER.. CAN YOU FORGIVE ME.. I-I HAD TO DO IT..
@#* ¢!:-!
NOW I SEE IT ALL... YOU HAVE JOINED THE SPIRIT! WELL.. I'LL FEEX HEEM..
RIGHT NOW !!
DOUBLE-CROSSING FEMALE...!!
NO NO... I WON'T LET YOU SHOOT HIM!
YOU ARE BLOCKING MY AIM... I'M WARNING YOU.. GET OUT OF MY WAY!
?!
BANG BANG BANG
PLASTER!

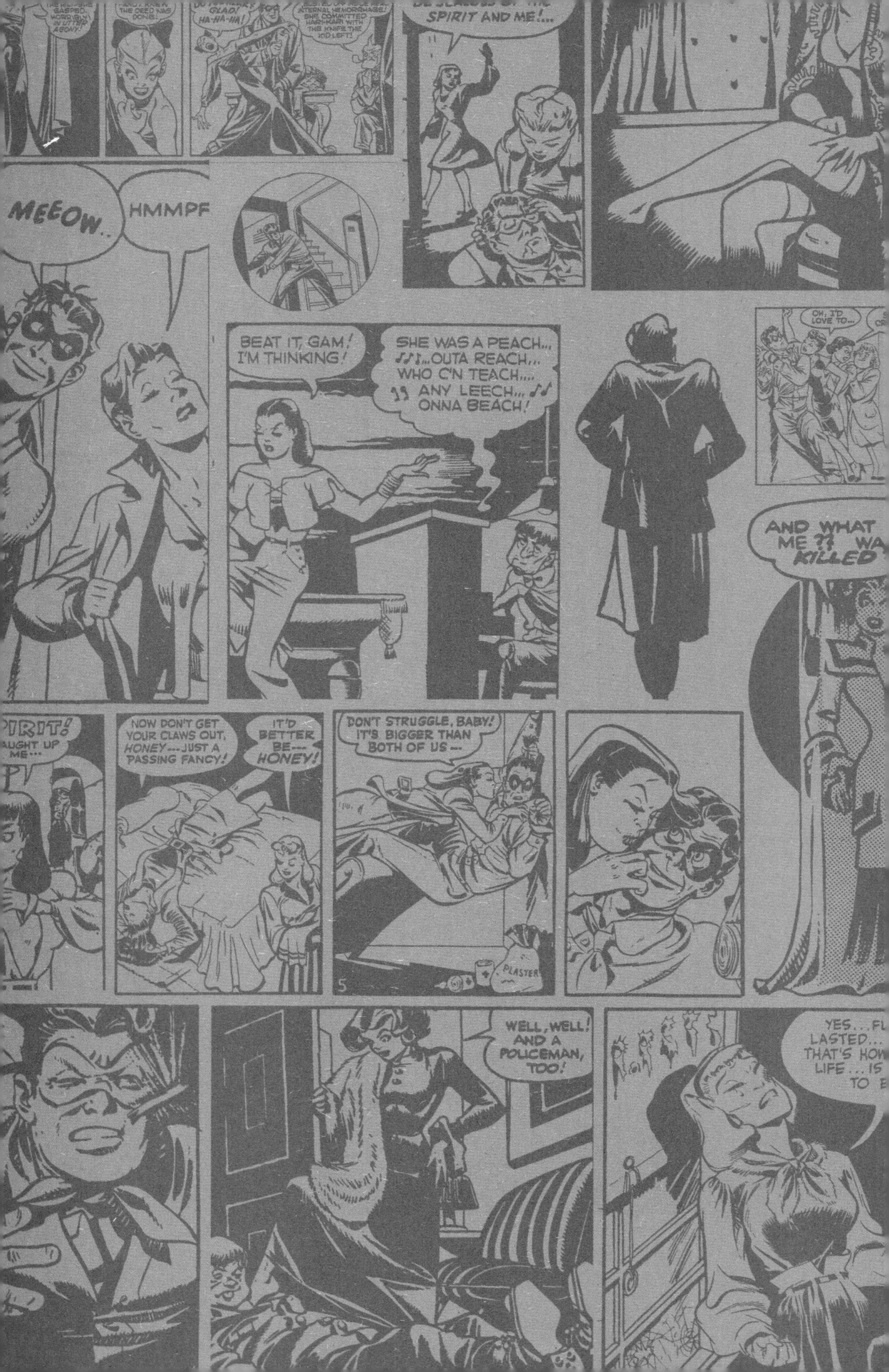
GASPED, HORRIBLY, IN UTTER AGONY!
THE DEED WAS DONE!
GLAD! HA-HA-HA!
INTERNAL HEMORRHAGE! SHE COMMITTED HARI-KARI WITH THE KNIFE THE KID LEFT!
SPIRIT AND ME!...
MEEOW..
HMMPF
BEAT IT, GAM! I'M THINKING!
SHE WAS A PEACH... ...OUTA REACH... WHO C'N TEACH.... ANY LEECH... ONNA BEACH!
OH, I'D LOVE TO...
AND WHAT ME ?? WA KILLED
NOW DON'T GET YOUR CLAWS OUT, HONEY--- JUST A PASSING FANCY!
IT'D BETTER BE--- HONEY!
DON'T STRUGGLE, BABY! IT'S BIGGER THAN BOTH OF US ---
PLASTER
WELL, WELL! AND A POLICEMAN, TOO!
YES... LASTED... THAT'S HOW LIFE... IS TO

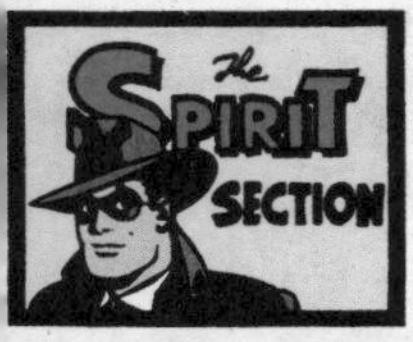

THORNE STRAND AND THE SPIRIT

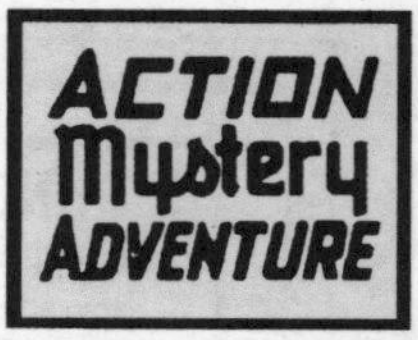

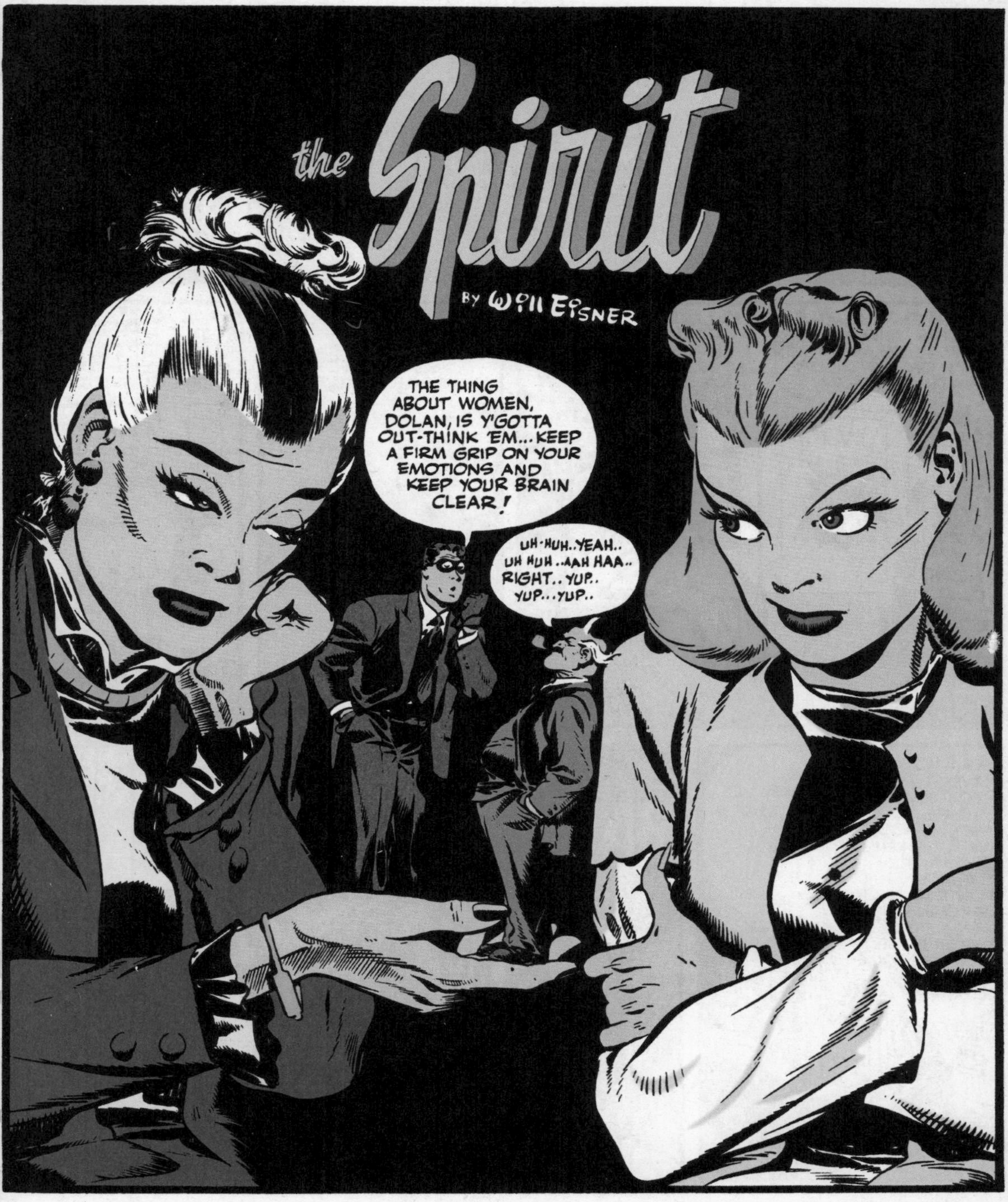

the Spirit
BY Will Eisner
THE THING ABOUT WOMEN, DOLAN, IS Y'GOTTA OUT-THINK 'EM... KEEP A FIRM GRIP ON YOUR EMOTIONS AND KEEP YOUR BRAIN CLEAR!
UH-HUH..YEAH.. UH HUH..AAH HAA.. RIGHT..YUP.. YUP...YUP..

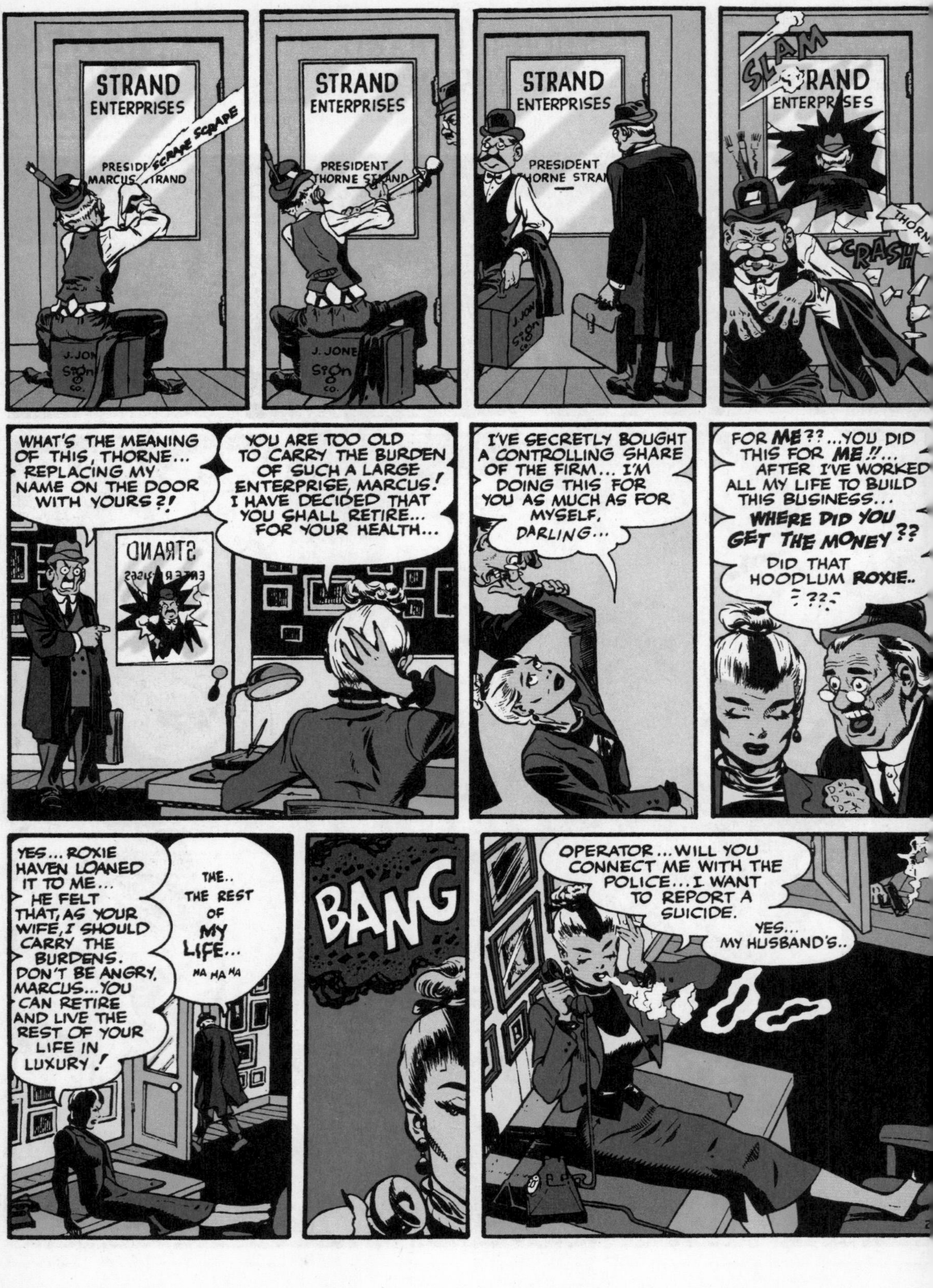
STRAND ENTERPRISES
PRESIDE MARCUS STRAND
SCRAPE SCRAPE
J. JON SIGN CO.
STRAND ENTERPRISES
PRESIDENT THORNE STRAND
J. JONE SIGN CO.
STRAND ENTERPRISES
PRESIDENT THORNE STRA
SLAM
CRASH
WHAT'S THE MEANING OF THIS, THORNE... REPLACING MY NAME ON THE DOOR WITH YOURS?!
YOU ARE TOO OLD TO CARRY THE BURDEN OF SUCH A LARGE ENTERPRISE, MARCUS! I HAVE DECIDED THAT YOU SHALL RETIRE... FOR YOUR HEALTH...
I'VE SECRETLY BOUGHT A CONTROLLING SHARE OF THE FIRM... I'M DOING THIS FOR YOU AS MUCH AS FOR MYSELF, DARLING...
FOR ME??... YOU DID THIS FOR ME!!... AFTER I'VE WORKED ALL MY LIFE TO BUILD THIS BUSINESS... WHERE DID YOU GET THE MONEY?? DID THAT HOODLUM ROXIE..
YES... ROXIE HAVEN LOANED IT TO ME... HE FELT THAT, AS YOUR WIFE, I SHOULD CARRY THE BURDENS. DON'T BE ANGRY, MARCUS... YOU CAN RETIRE AND LIVE THE REST OF YOUR LIFE IN LUXURY!
THE.. THE REST OF MY LIFE... HA HA HA
BANG
OPERATOR... WILL YOU CONNECT ME WITH THE POLICE... I WANT TO REPORT A SUICIDE.
YES... MY HUSBAND'S..

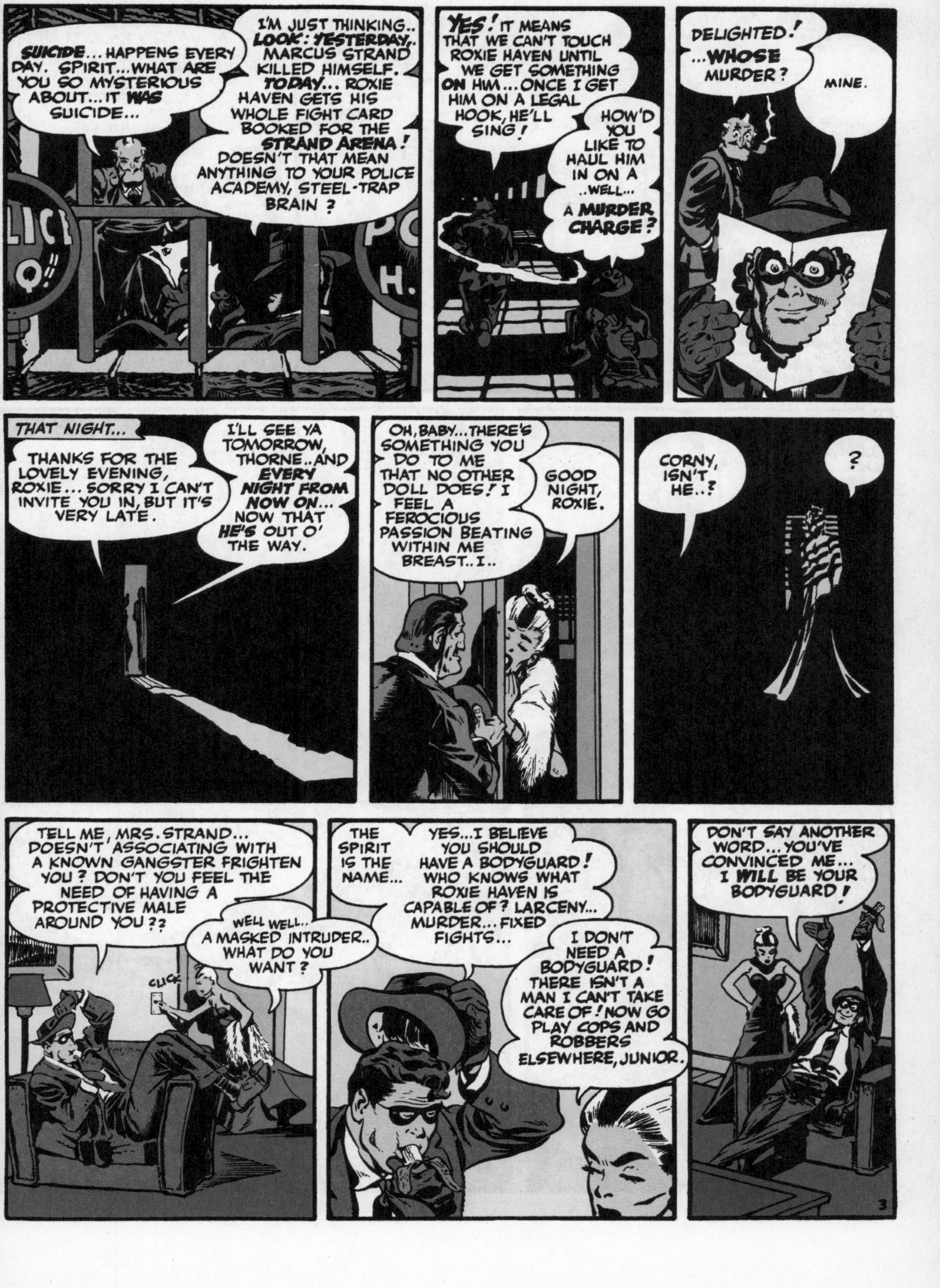
SUICIDE... HAPPENS EVERY DAY. SPIRIT...WHAT ARE YOU SO MYSTERIOUS ABOUT...IT WAS SUICIDE...
I'M JUST THINKING.. LOOK: YESTERDAY,. MARCUS STRAND KILLED HIMSELF. TODAY... ROXIE HAVEN GETS HIS WHOLE FIGHT CARD BOOKED FOR THE STRAND ARENA! DOESN'T THAT MEAN ANYTHING TO YOUR POLICE ACADEMY, STEEL-TRAP BRAIN?
YES! IT MEANS THAT WE CAN'T TOUCH ROXIE HAVEN UNTIL WE GET SOMETHING ON HIM...ONCE I GET HIM ON A LEGAL HOOK, HE'LL SING!
HOW'D YOU LIKE TO HAUL HIM IN ON A ..WELL... A MURDER CHARGE?
DELIGHTED! ...WHOSE MURDER?
MINE.
THAT NIGHT...
THANKS FOR THE LOVELY EVENING, ROXIE... SORRY I CAN'T INVITE YOU IN, BUT IT'S VERY LATE.
I'LL SEE YA TOMORROW, THORNE..AND EVERY NIGHT FROM NOW ON... NOW THAT HE'S OUT O' THE WAY.
OH, BABY...THERE'S SOMETHING YOU DO TO ME THAT NO OTHER DOLL DOES! I FEEL A FEROCIOUS PASSION BEATING WITHIN ME BREAST..I..
GOOD NIGHT, ROXIE.
CORNY, ISN'T HE..?
?
TELL ME, MRS. STRAND... DOESN'T ASSOCIATING WITH A KNOWN GANGSTER FRIGHTEN YOU? DON'T YOU FEEL THE NEED OF HAVING A PROTECTIVE MALE AROUND YOU??
CLICK
WELL WELL.. A MASKED INTRUDER.. WHAT DO YOU WANT?
THE SPIRIT IS THE NAME...
YES...I BELIEVE YOU SHOULD HAVE A BODYGUARD! WHO KNOWS WHAT ROXIE HAVEN IS CAPABLE OF? LARCENY... MURDER... FIXED FIGHTS...
I DON'T NEED A BODYGUARD! THERE ISN'T A MAN I CAN'T TAKE CARE OF! NOW GO PLAY COPS AND ROBBERS ELSEWHERE, JUNIOR.
DON'T SAY ANOTHER WORD... YOU'VE CONVINCED ME... I WILL BE YOUR BODYGUARD!
3

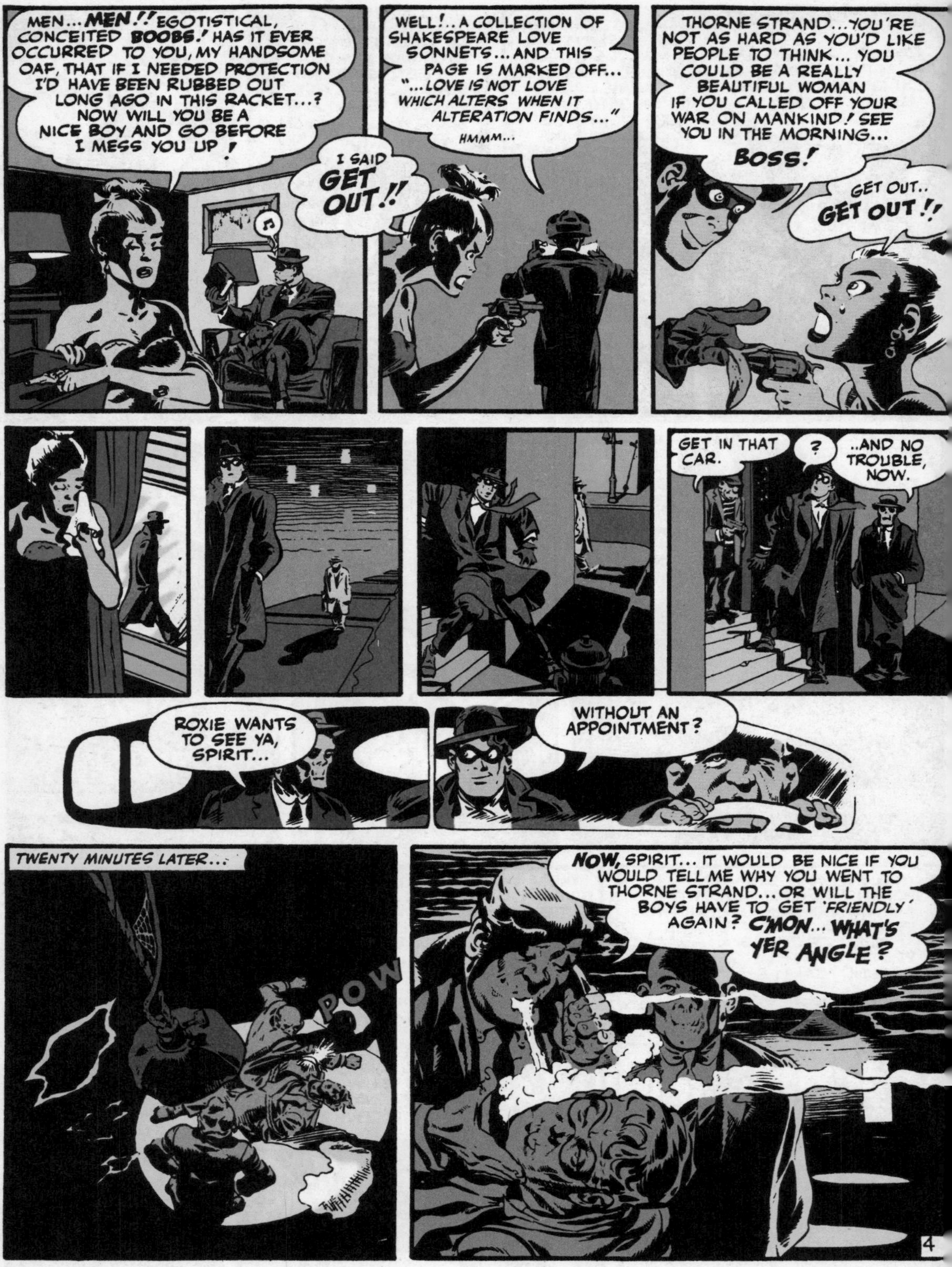
MEN... MEN!! EGOTISTICAL, CONCEITED BOOBS! HAS IT EVER OCCURRED TO YOU, MY HANDSOME OAF, THAT IF I NEEDED PROTECTION I'D HAVE BEEN RUBBED OUT LONG AGO IN THIS RACKET...? NOW WILL YOU BE A NICE BOY AND GO BEFORE I MESS YOU UP!
I SAID GET OUT!!
WELL!.. A COLLECTION OF SHAKESPEARE LOVE SONNETS... AND THIS PAGE IS MARKED OFF... "...LOVE IS NOT LOVE WHICH ALTERS WHEN IT ALTERATION FINDS..."
HMMM...
THORNE STRAND... YOU'RE NOT AS HARD AS YOU'D LIKE PEOPLE TO THINK... YOU COULD BE A REALLY BEAUTIFUL WOMAN IF YOU CALLED OFF YOUR WAR ON MANKIND! SEE YOU IN THE MORNING...
BOSS!
GET OUT.. GET OUT!!
GET IN THAT CAR.
?
..AND NO TROUBLE, NOW.
ROXIE WANTS TO SEE YA, SPIRIT...
WITHOUT AN APPOINTMENT?
TWENTY MINUTES LATER...
POW
NOW, SPIRIT... IT WOULD BE NICE IF YOU WOULD TELL ME WHY YOU WENT TO THORNE STRAND... OR WILL THE BOYS HAVE TO GET 'FRIENDLY' AGAIN? C'MON... WHAT'S YER ANGLE?
4

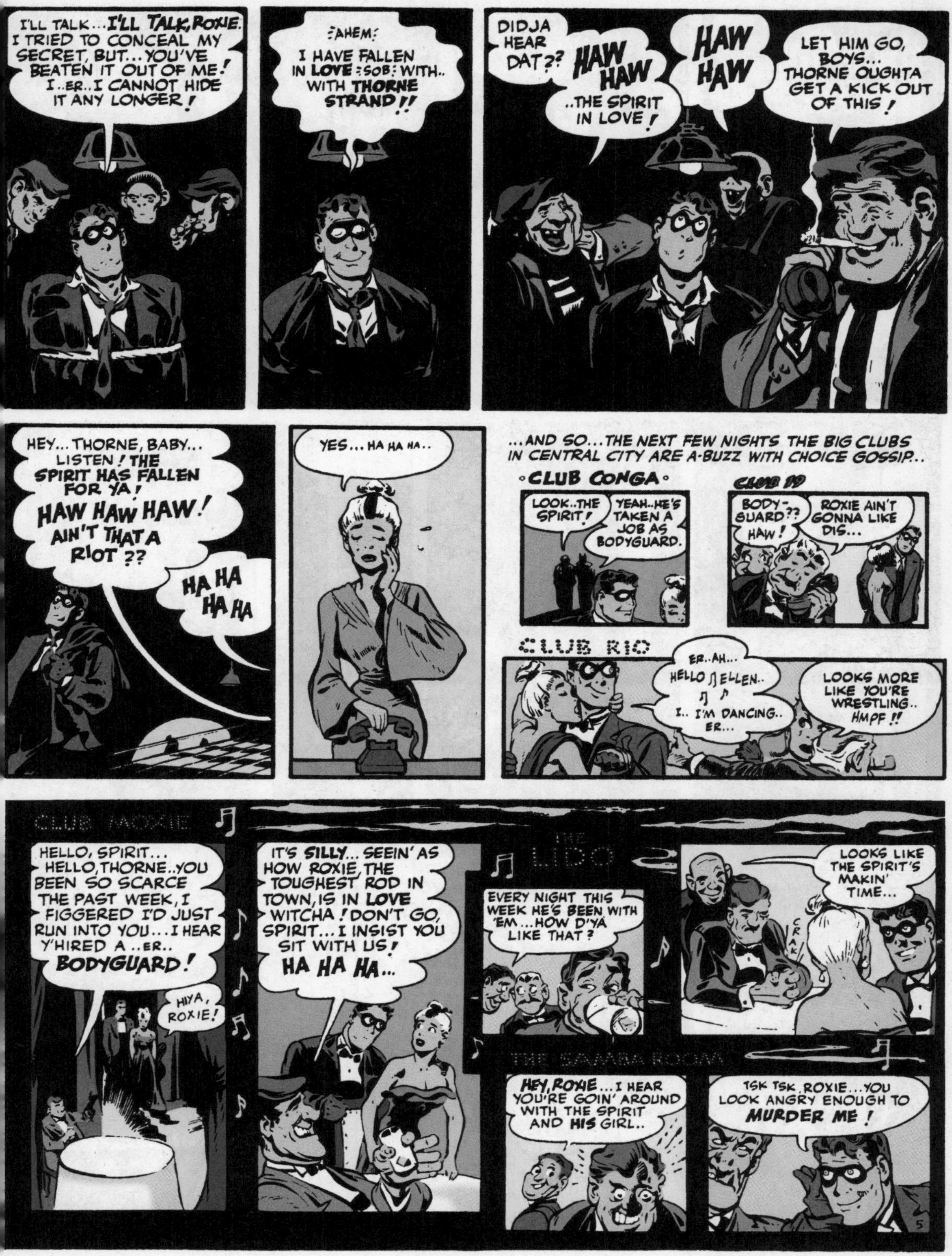
I'LL TALK... I'LL TALK, ROXIE. I TRIED TO CONCEAL MY SECRET, BUT... YOU'VE BEATEN IT OUT OF ME! I..ER..I CANNOT HIDE IT ANY LONGER!
:AHEM: I HAVE FALLEN IN LOVE :SOB: WITH.. WITH THORNE STRAND!!
DIDJA HEAR DAT??
HAW HAW
HAW HAW
..THE SPIRIT IN LOVE!
LET HIM GO, BOYS... THORNE OUGHTA GET A KICK OUT OF THIS!
HEY... THORNE, BABY... LISTEN! THE SPIRIT HAS FALLEN FOR YA! HAW HAW HAW! AIN'T THAT A RIOT??
HA HA HA HA
YES... HA HA HA..
...AND SO... THE NEXT FEW NIGHTS THE BIG CLUBS IN CENTRAL CITY ARE A-BUZZ WITH CHOICE GOSSIP..
CLUB CONGA
LOOK..THE SPIRIT!
YEAH..HE'S TAKEN A JOB AS BODYGUARD.
CLUB 19
BODY-GUARD?? HAW!
ROXIE AIN'T GONNA LIKE DIS...
CLUB RIO
ER..AH... HELLO ELLEN.. I.. I'M DANCING.. ER...
LOOKS MORE LIKE YOU'RE WRESTLING.. HMPF!!
HELLO, SPIRIT... HELLO, THORNE..YOU BEEN SO SCARCE THE PAST WEEK, I FIGGERED I'D JUST RUN INTO YOU... I HEAR Y'HIRED A ..ER.. BODYGUARD!
HIYA, ROXIE!
IT'S SILLY... SEEIN' AS HOW ROXIE, THE TOUGHEST ROD IN TOWN, IS IN LOVE WITCHA! DON'T GO, SPIRIT... I INSIST YOU SIT WITH US! HA HA HA...
THE LIDO
EVERY NIGHT THIS WEEK HE'S BEEN WITH 'EM...HOW D'YA LIKE THAT?
LOOKS LIKE THE SPIRIT'S MAKIN' TIME...
CRAK
THE SAMBA ROOM
HEY, ROXIE... I HEAR YOU'RE GOIN' AROUND WITH THE SPIRIT AND HIS GIRL..
TSK TSK, ROXIE... YOU LOOK ANGRY ENOUGH TO MURDER ME!
5

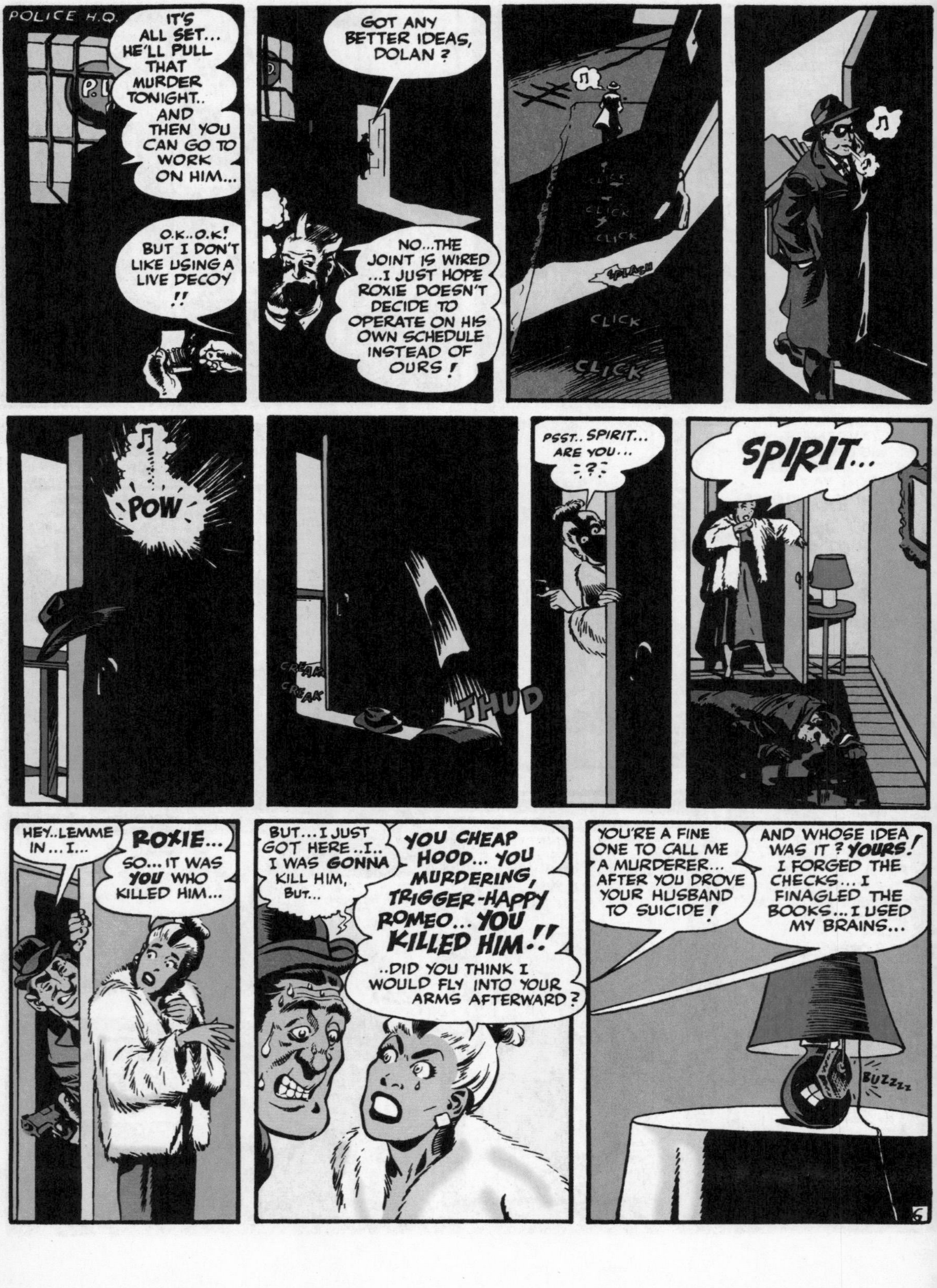
POLICE H.Q.
IT'S ALL SET... HE'LL PULL THAT MURDER TONIGHT.. AND THEN YOU CAN GO TO WORK ON HIM...
O.K..O.K! BUT I DON'T LIKE USING A LIVE DECOY !!
GOT ANY BETTER IDEAS, DOLAN ?
NO...THE JOINT IS WIRED ...I JUST HOPE ROXIE DOESN'T DECIDE TO OPERATE ON HIS OWN SCHEDULE INSTEAD OF OURS !
CLICK
CLICK
CLICK
SPLASH
CLICK
CLICK
POW
CREAK
CREAK
THUD
PSST.. SPIRIT... ARE YOU... ?
SPIRIT...
HEY..LEMME IN... I...
ROXIE... SO... IT WAS YOU WHO KILLED HIM...
BUT... I JUST GOT HERE..I.. I WAS GONNA KILL HIM, BUT...
YOU CHEAP HOOD... YOU MURDERING, TRIGGER-HAPPY ROMEO... YOU KILLED HIM!! ..DID YOU THINK I WOULD FLY INTO YOUR ARMS AFTERWARD ?
YOU'RE A FINE ONE TO CALL ME A MURDERER... AFTER YOU DROVE YOUR HUSBAND TO SUICIDE !
AND WHOSE IDEA WAS IT ? YOURS! I FORGED THE CHECKS... I FINAGLED THE BOOKS... I USED MY BRAINS...
BUZZzzz
6

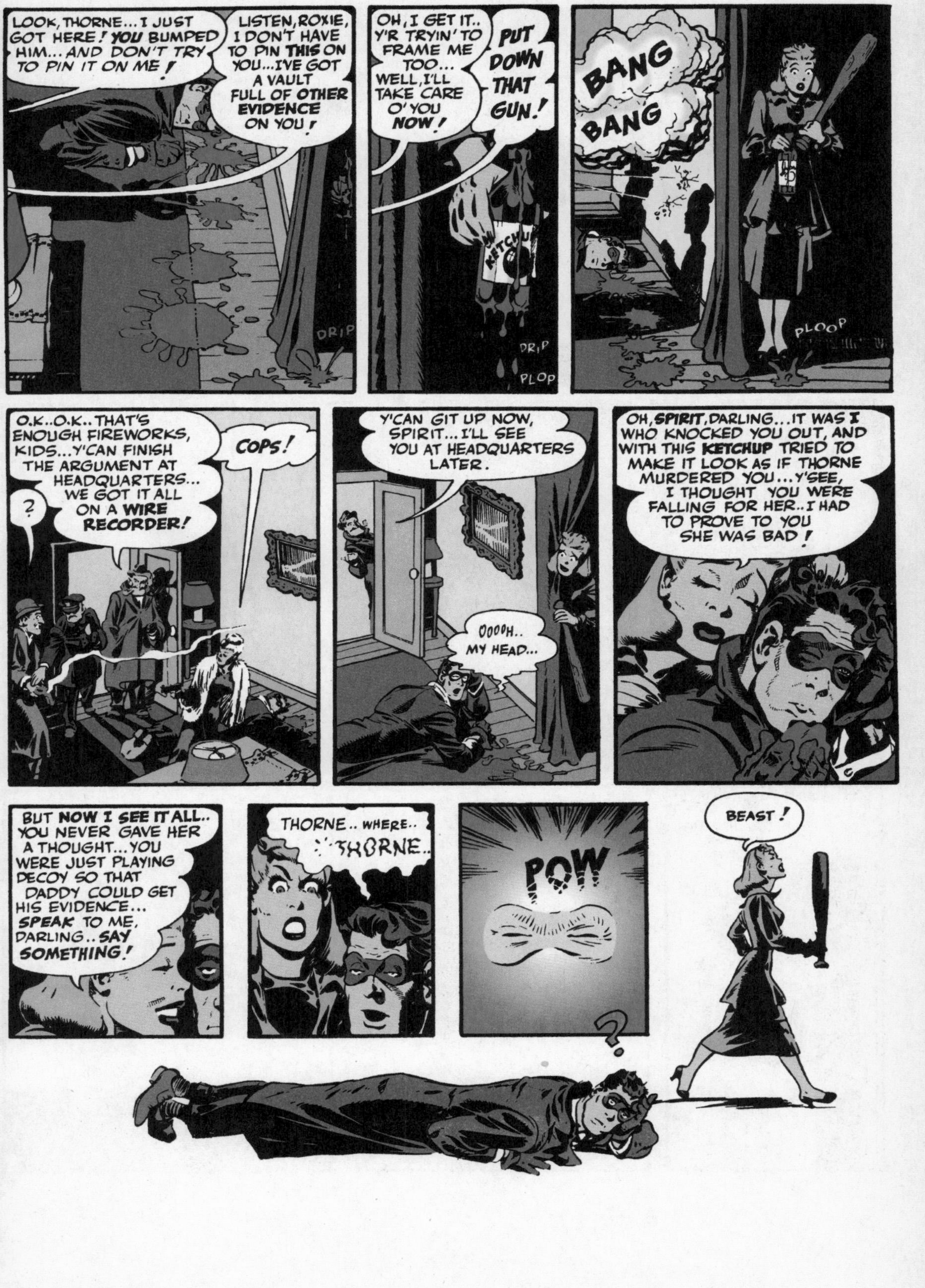
LOOK, THORNE... I JUST GOT HERE! YOU BUMPED HIM... AND DON'T TRY TO PIN IT ON ME!
LISTEN, ROXIE, I DON'T HAVE TO PIN THIS ON YOU... I'VE GOT A VAULT FULL OF OTHER EVIDENCE ON YOU!
DRIP
OH, I GET IT.. Y'R TRYIN' TO FRAME ME TOO... WELL, I'LL TAKE CARE O' YOU NOW!
PUT DOWN THAT GUN!
KETCHUP
DRIP
PLOP
BANG
BANG
PLOOP
O.K..O.K.. THAT'S ENOUGH FIREWORKS, KIDS... Y'CAN FINISH THE ARGUMENT AT HEADQUARTERS... WE GOT IT ALL ON A WIRE RECORDER!
?
COPS!
Y'CAN GIT UP NOW, SPIRIT... I'LL SEE YOU AT HEADQUARTERS LATER.
OOOOH.. MY HEAD...
OH, SPIRIT, DARLING... IT WAS I WHO KNOCKED YOU OUT, AND WITH THIS KETCHUP TRIED TO MAKE IT LOOK AS IF THORNE MURDERED YOU... Y'SEE, I THOUGHT YOU WERE FALLING FOR HER.. I HAD TO PROVE TO YOU SHE WAS BAD!
BUT NOW I SEE IT ALL.. YOU NEVER GAVE HER A THOUGHT... YOU WERE JUST PLAYING DECOY SO THAT DADDY COULD GET HIS EVIDENCE... SPEAK TO ME, DARLING.. SAY SOMETHING!
THORNE.. WHERE.. THORNE..
POW
BEAST!
?

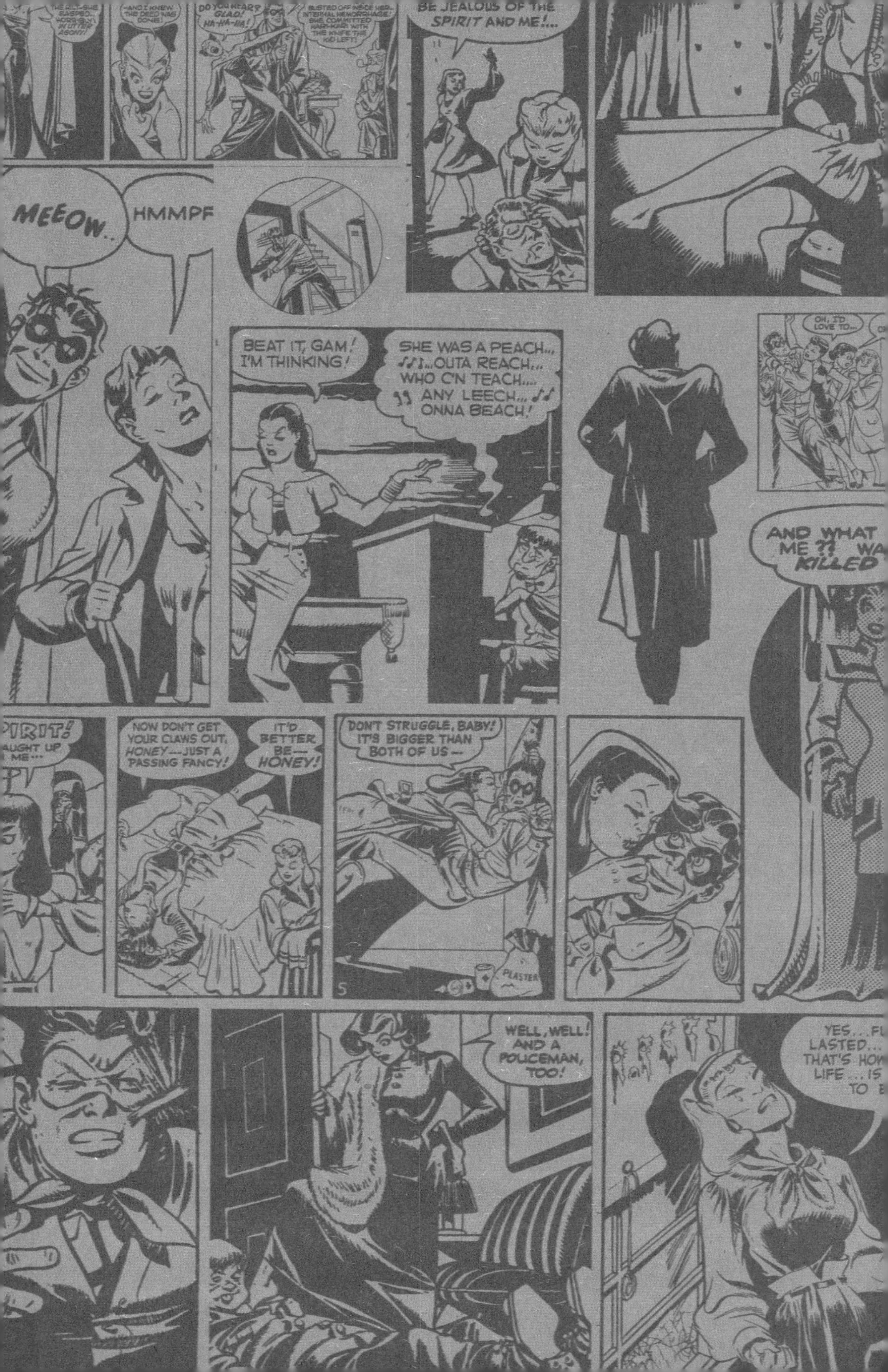
-AND I KNEW THE DEED WAS DONE!
DO YOU HEAR? GLAD! HA-HA-HA!
SHE COMMITTED HARI-KARI WITH THE KNIFE THE KID LEFT!
BE JEALOUS OF THE SPIRIT AND ME!...
MEEOW..
HMMPF
BEAT IT, GAM! I'M THINKING!
SHE WAS A PEACH... ...OUTA REACH... WHO C'N TEACH.... ANY LEECH... ONNA BEACH!
OH, I'D LOVE TO...
AND WHAT ME ?? WA KILLED
NOW DON'T GET YOUR CLAWS OUT, HONEY---JUST A PASSING FANCY!
IT'D BETTER BE--HONEY!
DON'T STRUGGLE, BABY! IT'S BIGGER THAN BOTH OF US--
PLASTER
WELL, WELL! AND A POLICEMAN, TOO!
YES...F LASTED... THAT'S HO LIFE...IS TO

DEATH OF AUTUMN MEWS

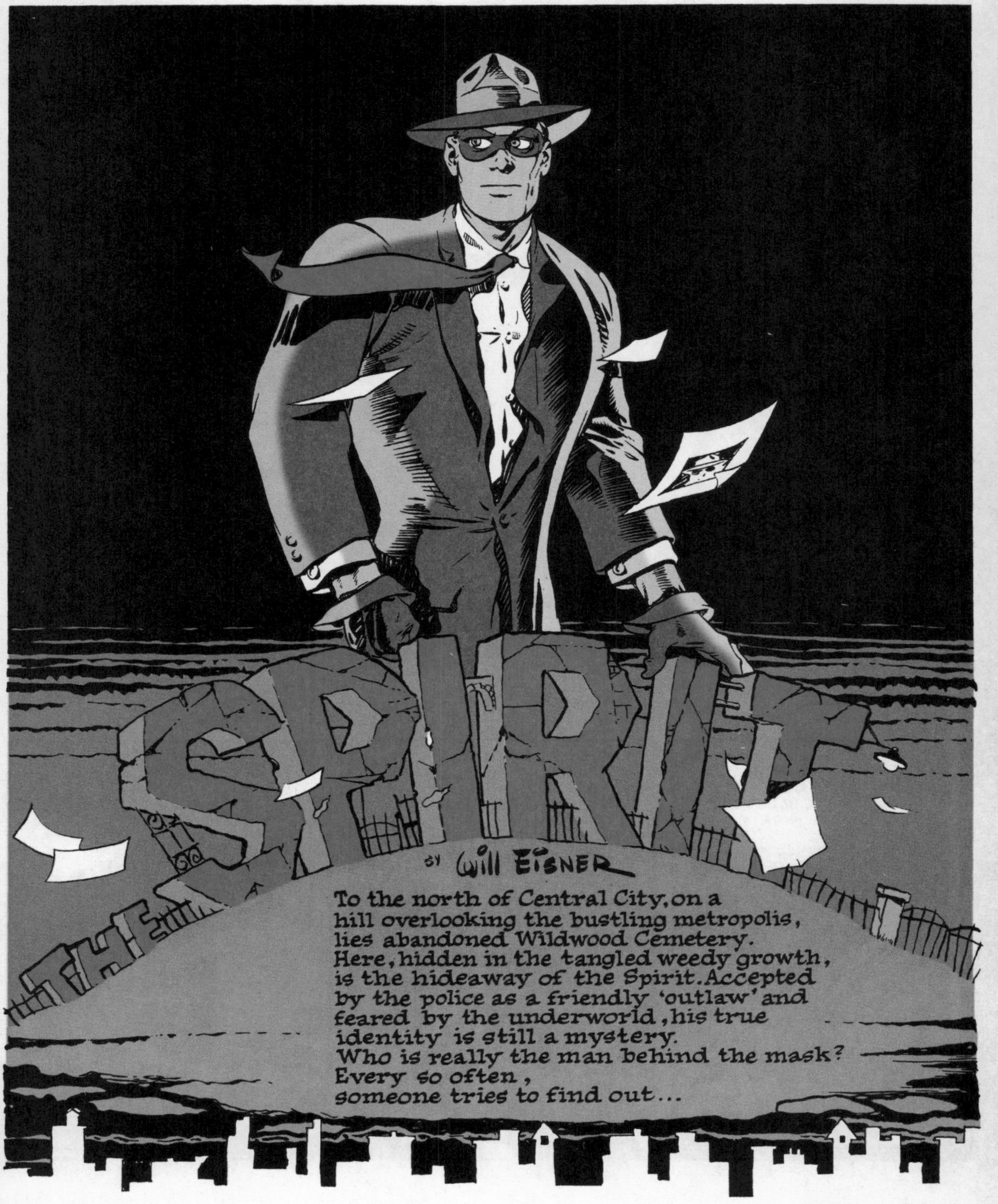
THE SPIRIT
BY WILL EISNER
To the north of Central City, on a hill overlooking the bustling metropolis, lies abandoned Wildwood Cemetery. Here, hidden in the tangled weedy growth, is the hideaway of the Spirit. Accepted by the police as a friendly 'outlaw' and feared by the underworld, his true identity is still a mystery. Who is really the man behind the mask? Every so often, someone tries to find out...

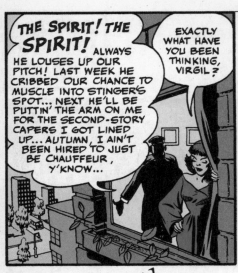

THE SPIRIT! THE SPIRIT! ALWAYS HE LOUSES UP OUR PITCH! LAST WEEK HE CRIBBED OUR CHANCE TO MUSCLE INTO STINGER'S SPOT... NEXT HE'LL BE PUTTIN' THE ARM ON ME FOR THE SECOND-STORY CAPERS I GOT LINED UP... AUTUMN, I AIN'T BEEN HIRED TO JUST BE CHAUFFEUR, Y'KNOW...

EXACTLY WHAT HAVE YOU BEEN THINKING, VIRGIL?

THIS!

YOU'RE A STUPID FOOL! YOU KNOW I WANT NO PART OF MURDER... BESIDES... THE SPIRIT ISN'T ONE TO BE "MUSCLED" OUT...

Y'GOT A BETTER WAY?

I'VE GOT A CLEANER WAY...

AND SO...

WILDWOOD CEMETERY

SIGH...

DENNY COLT 1940

Dear Sammy—
You do not know me, but I have secretly watched your career ever since you joined the Spirit. You're a greater detective than the Spirit... I need your confidential aid now. I'm in terrible trouble. Meet me at 8:30... Apt. 14A.. Royal Towe—
—Autumn Mew

WHAT'S THAT, SAMMY?

OH...ER.. NOTHING... JUST A CIRCULAR, SPIRIT...

I TELL YOU, DOLAN.. GET MORE OF YOUR COPS ON DUTY AT THE EGYPTIAN TAPESTRY EXHIBIT AT THE CENTRAL MUSEUM! SOMEBODY'S NOT GOING TO LET ALL THAT CLOTH JUST HANG THERE WITHOUT MAKING A ROBBERY ATTEMPT!!

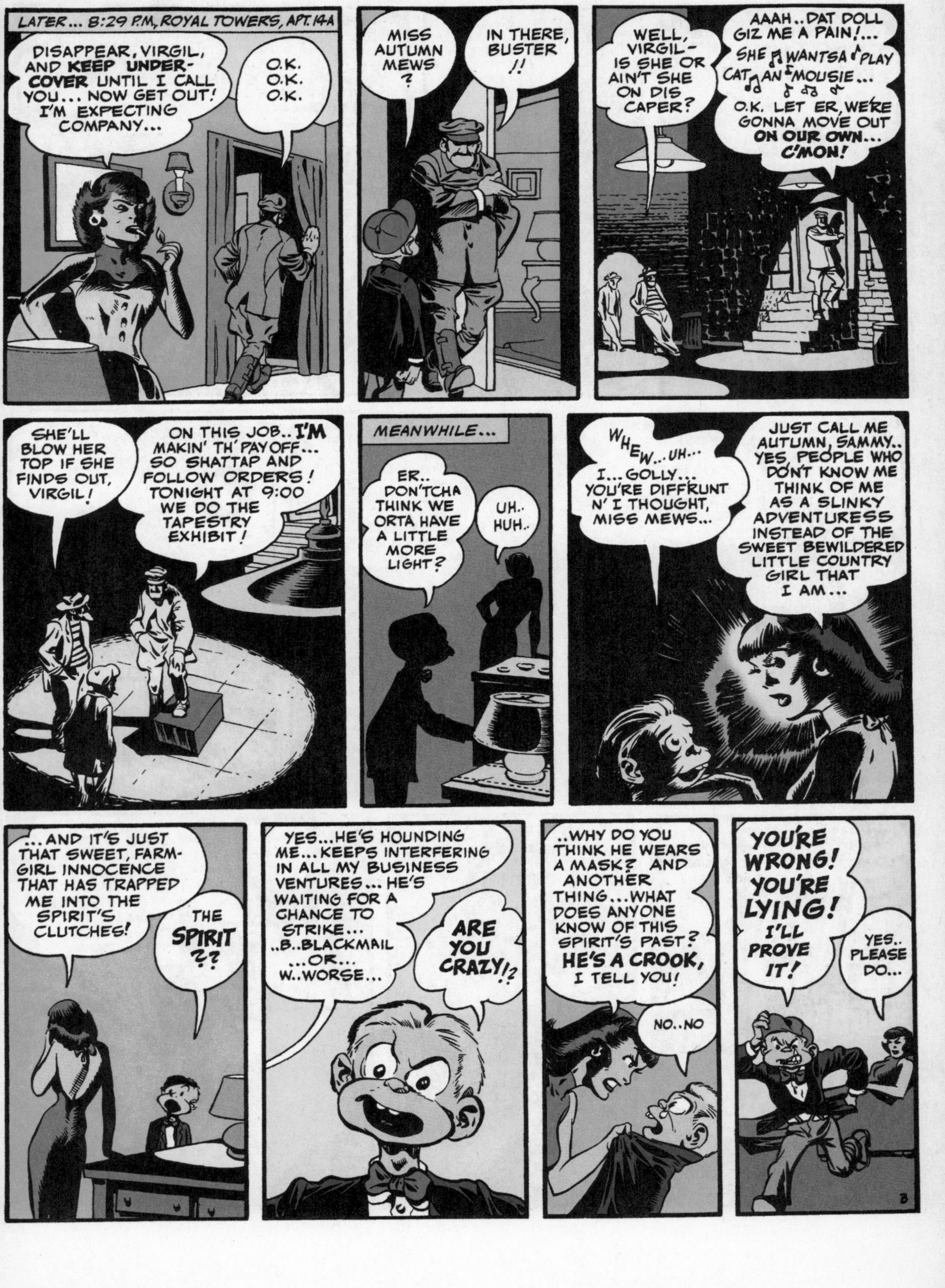
LATER... 8:29 P.M., ROYAL TOWERS, APT. 14A
DISAPPEAR, VIRGIL, AND **KEEP UNDER-COVER** UNTIL I CALL YOU... NOW GET OUT! I'M EXPECTING COMPANY...
O.K. O.K. O.K.
MISS AUTUMN MEWS ?
IN THERE, BUSTER !!
WELL, VIRGIL- IS SHE OR AIN'T SHE ON DIS CAPER?
AAAH.. DAT DOLL GIZ ME A PAIN!... SHE WANTSA PLAY CAT AN' MOUSIE... O.K. LET ER, WE'RE GONNA MOVE OUT **ON OUR OWN... C'MON!**
SHE'LL BLOW HER TOP IF SHE FINDS OUT, VIRGIL!
ON THIS JOB.. **I'M** MAKIN' TH' PAYOFF... SO SHATTAP AND FOLLOW ORDERS! TONIGHT AT 9:00 WE DO THE TAPESTRY EXHIBIT!
MEANWHILE...
ER.. DON'TCHA THINK WE ORTA HAVE A LITTLE MORE LIGHT?
UH.. HUH..
WHEW...UH... I...GOLLY... YOU'RE DIFF'RUNT N' I THOUGHT, MISS MEWS...
JUST CALL ME AUTUMN, SAMMY.. YES, PEOPLE WHO DON'T KNOW ME THINK OF ME AS A SLINKY ADVENTURESS INSTEAD OF THE SWEET BEWILDERED LITTLE COUNTRY GIRL THAT I AM...
...AND IT'S JUST THAT SWEET, FARM-GIRL INNOCENCE THAT HAS TRAPPED ME INTO THE SPIRIT'S CLUTCHES!
THE **SPIRIT** ??
YES...HE'S HOUNDING ME... KEEPS INTERFERING IN ALL MY BUSINESS VENTURES... HE'S WAITING FOR A CHANCE TO STRIKE... ..B..BLACKMAIL ...OR... W..WORSE...
ARE YOU CRAZY!?
..WHY DO YOU THINK HE WEARS A MASK? AND ANOTHER THING...WHAT DOES ANYONE KNOW OF THIS SPIRIT'S PAST? **HE'S A CROOK,** I TELL YOU!
NO..NO
YOU'RE WRONG! YOU'RE LYING! I'LL PROVE IT!
YES.. PLEASE DO...
3

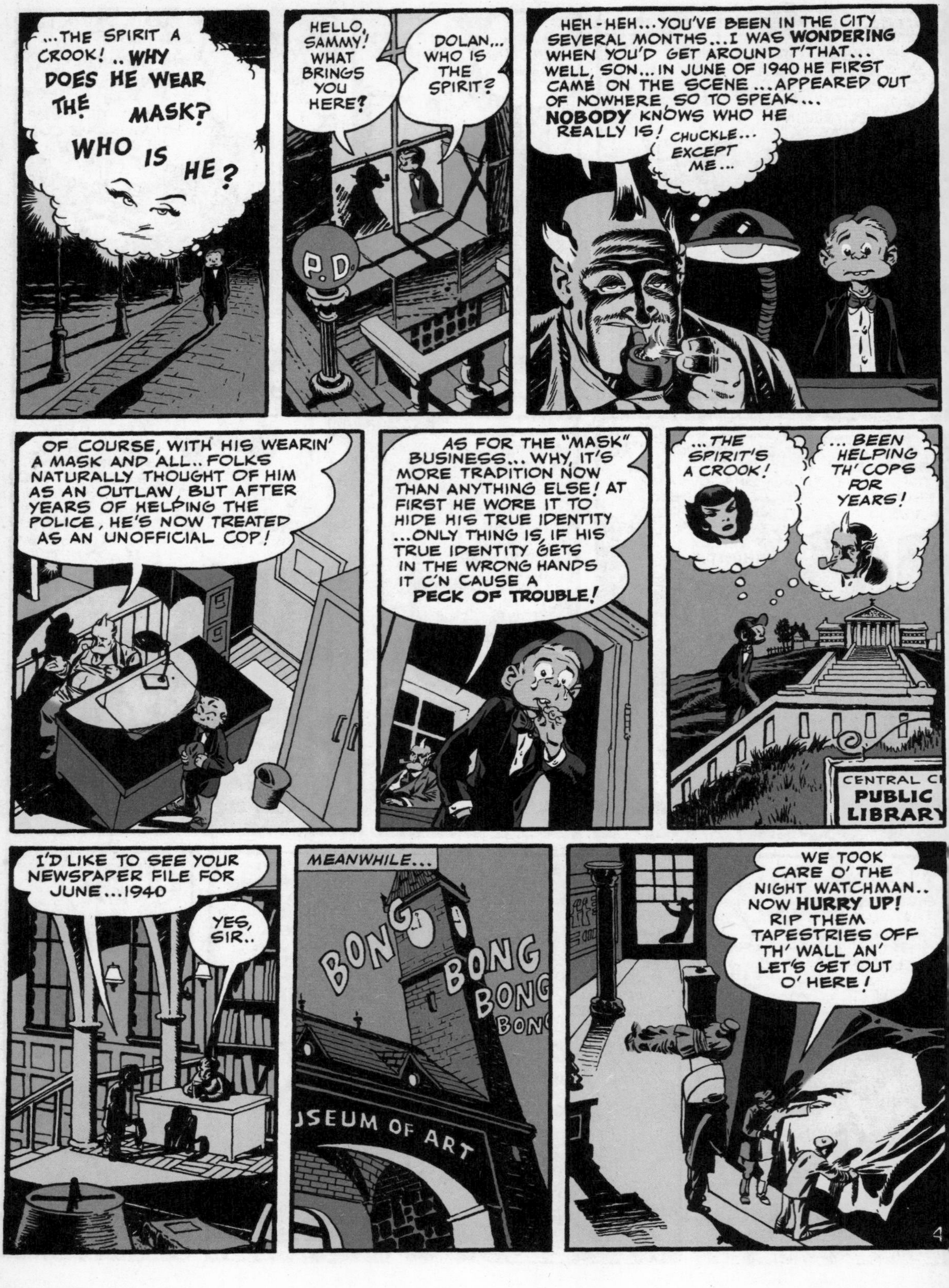
...THE SPIRIT A CROOK! ..WHY DOES HE WEAR THE MASK? WHO IS HE?
HELLO, SAMMY! WHAT BRINGS YOU HERE?
DOLAN... WHO IS THE SPIRIT?
P.D.
HEH-HEH... YOU'VE BEEN IN THE CITY SEVERAL MONTHS... I WAS WONDERING WHEN YOU'D GET AROUND T'THAT... WELL, SON... IN JUNE OF 1940 HE FIRST CAME ON THE SCENE... APPEARED OUT OF NOWHERE, SO TO SPEAK... NOBODY KNOWS WHO HE REALLY IS!
CHUCKLE... EXCEPT ME...
OF COURSE, WITH HIS WEARIN' A MASK AND ALL.. FOLKS NATURALLY THOUGHT OF HIM AS AN OUTLAW, BUT AFTER YEARS OF HELPING THE POLICE, HE'S NOW TREATED AS AN UNOFFICIAL COP!
AS FOR THE "MASK" BUSINESS... WHY, IT'S MORE TRADITION NOW THAN ANYTHING ELSE! AT FIRST HE WORE IT TO HIDE HIS TRUE IDENTITY ...ONLY THING IS, IF HIS TRUE IDENTITY GETS IN THE WRONG HANDS IT C'N CAUSE A PECK OF TROUBLE!
...THE SPIRIT'S A CROOK!
... BEEN HELPING TH' COPS FOR YEARS!
CENTRAL CI
PUBLIC LIBRARY
I'D LIKE TO SEE YOUR NEWSPAPER FILE FOR JUNE...1940
YES, SIR..
MEANWHILE...
BONG
BONG
BONG
BONG
USEUM OF ART
WE TOOK CARE O' THE NIGHT WATCHMAN.. NOW HURRY UP! RIP THEM TAPESTRIES OFF TH' WALL AN' LET'S GET OUT O' HERE!
4

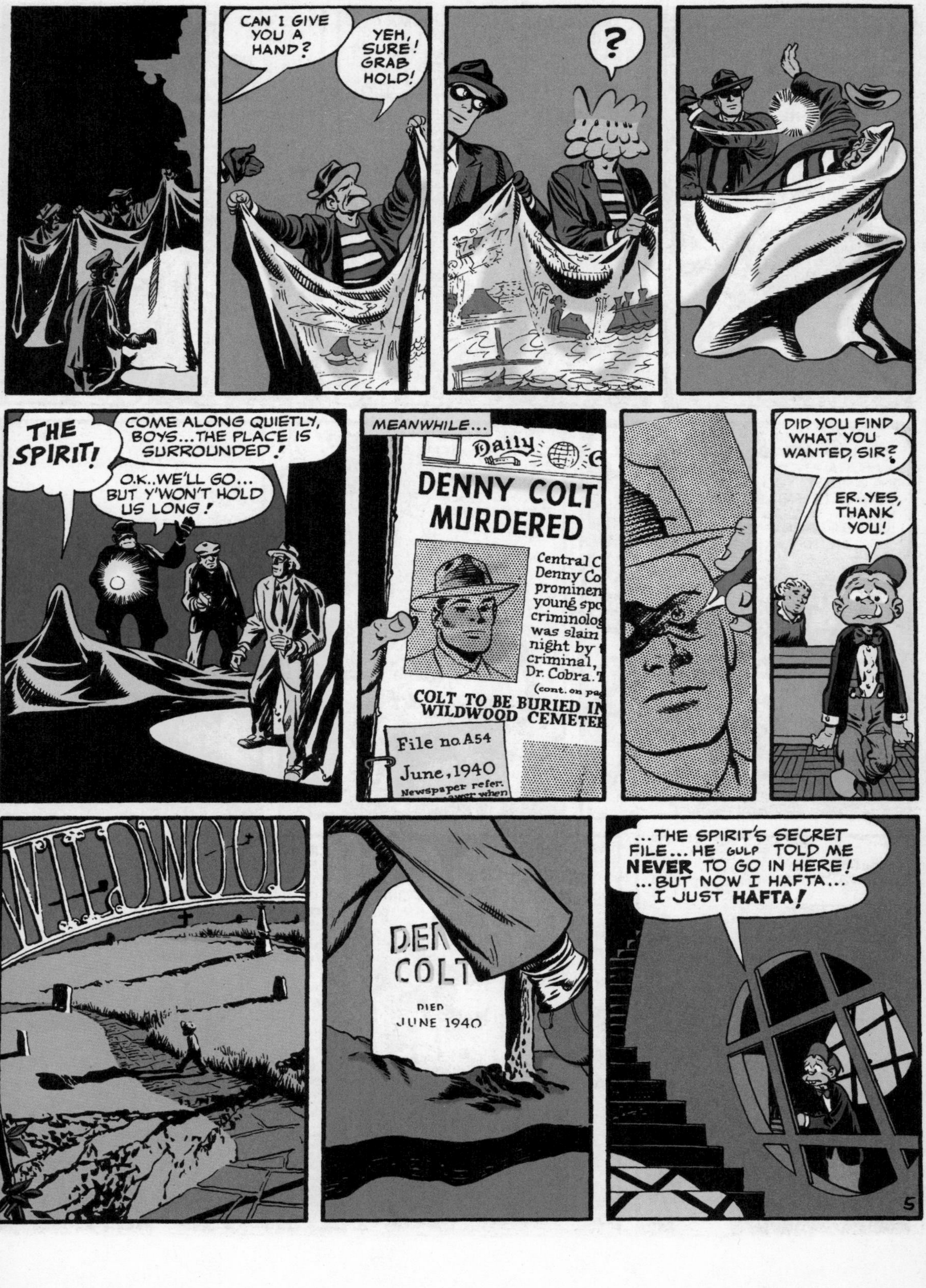
CAN I GIVE YOU A HAND?
YEH, SURE! GRAB HOLD!
?
THE SPIRIT!
COME ALONG QUIETLY, BOYS...THE PLACE IS SURROUNDED!
O.K..WE'LL GO... BUT Y'WON'T HOLD US LONG!
MEANWHILE...
Daily
DENNY COLT MURDERED
COLT TO BE BURIED IN WILDWOOD CEMETER
File no. A54
June, 1940
DID YOU FIND WHAT YOU WANTED, SIR?
ER..YES, THANK YOU!
WILDWOOD
DEN COLT
DIED JUNE 1940
...THE SPIRIT'S SECRET FILE... HE GULP TOLD ME NEVER TO GO IN HERE! ...BUT NOW I HAFTA... I JUST HAFTA!
5

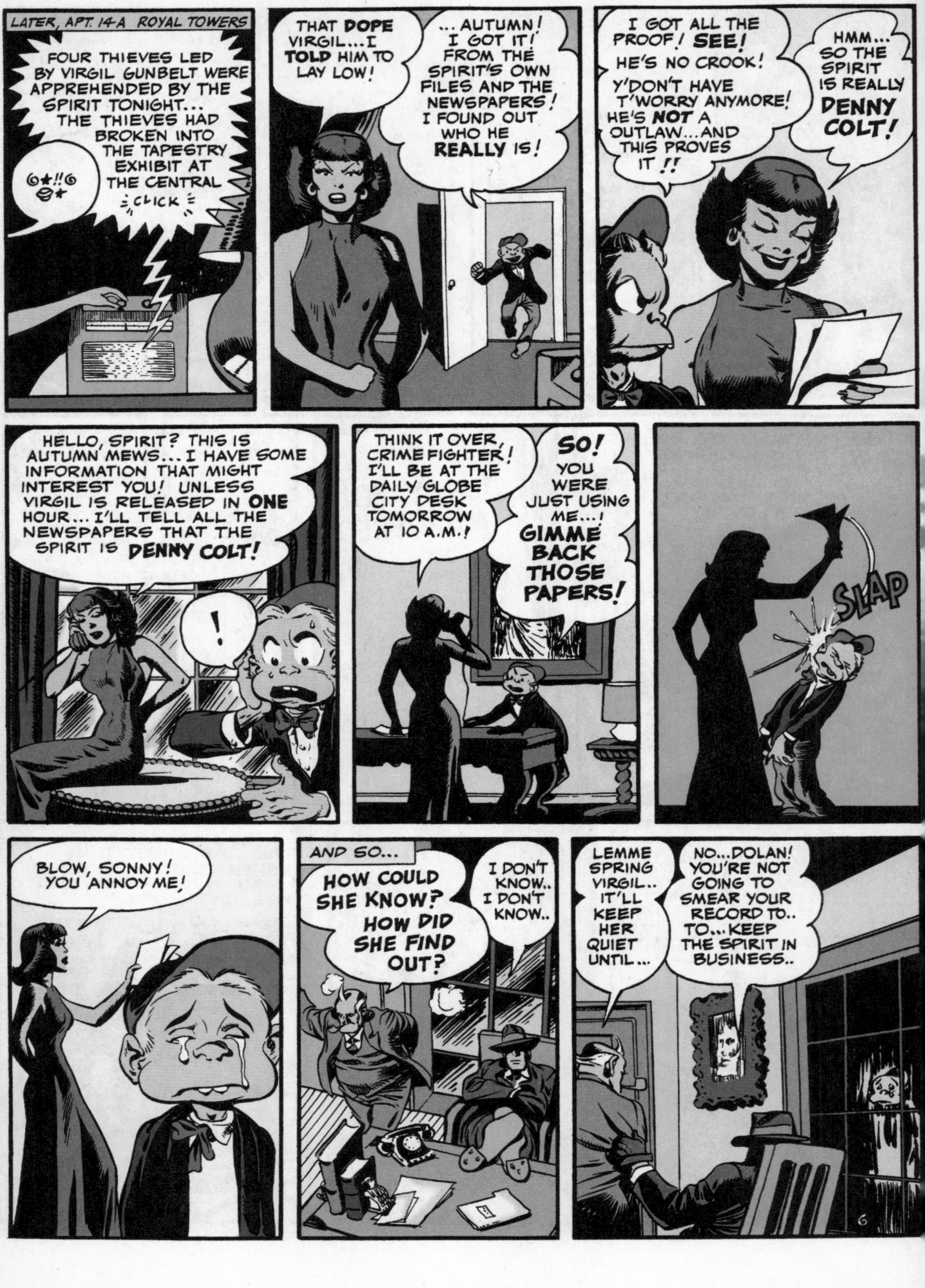
LATER, APT. 14-A ROYAL TOWERS
FOUR THIEVES LED BY VIRGIL GUNBELT WERE APPREHENDED BY THE SPIRIT TONIGHT... THE THIEVES HAD BROKEN INTO THE TAPESTRY EXHIBIT AT THE CENTRAL
CLICK
THAT DOPE VIRGIL...I TOLD HIM TO LAY LOW!
... AUTUMN! I GOT IT! FROM THE SPIRIT'S OWN FILES AND THE NEWSPAPERS! I FOUND OUT WHO HE REALLY IS!
I GOT ALL THE PROOF! SEE! HE'S NO CROOK! Y'DON'T HAVE T'WORRY ANYMORE! HE'S NOT A OUTLAW...AND THIS PROVES IT!!
HMM... SO THE SPIRIT IS REALLY DENNY COLT!
HELLO, SPIRIT? THIS IS AUTUMN MEWS... I HAVE SOME INFORMATION THAT MIGHT INTEREST YOU! UNLESS VIRGIL IS RELEASED IN ONE HOUR... I'LL TELL ALL THE NEWSPAPERS THAT THE SPIRIT IS DENNY COLT!
!
THINK IT OVER, CRIME FIGHTER! I'LL BE AT THE DAILY GLOBE CITY DESK TOMORROW AT 10 A.M.!
SO! YOU WERE JUST USING ME...! GIMME BACK THOSE PAPERS!
SLAP
BLOW, SONNY! YOU ANNOY ME!
AND SO...
HOW COULD SHE KNOW? HOW DID SHE FIND OUT?
I DON'T KNOW.. I DON'T KNOW..
LEMME SPRING VIRGIL.. IT'LL KEEP HER QUIET UNTIL...
NO...DOLAN! YOU'RE NOT GOING TO SMEAR YOUR RECORD TO.. TO... KEEP THE SPIRIT IN BUSINESS..
6

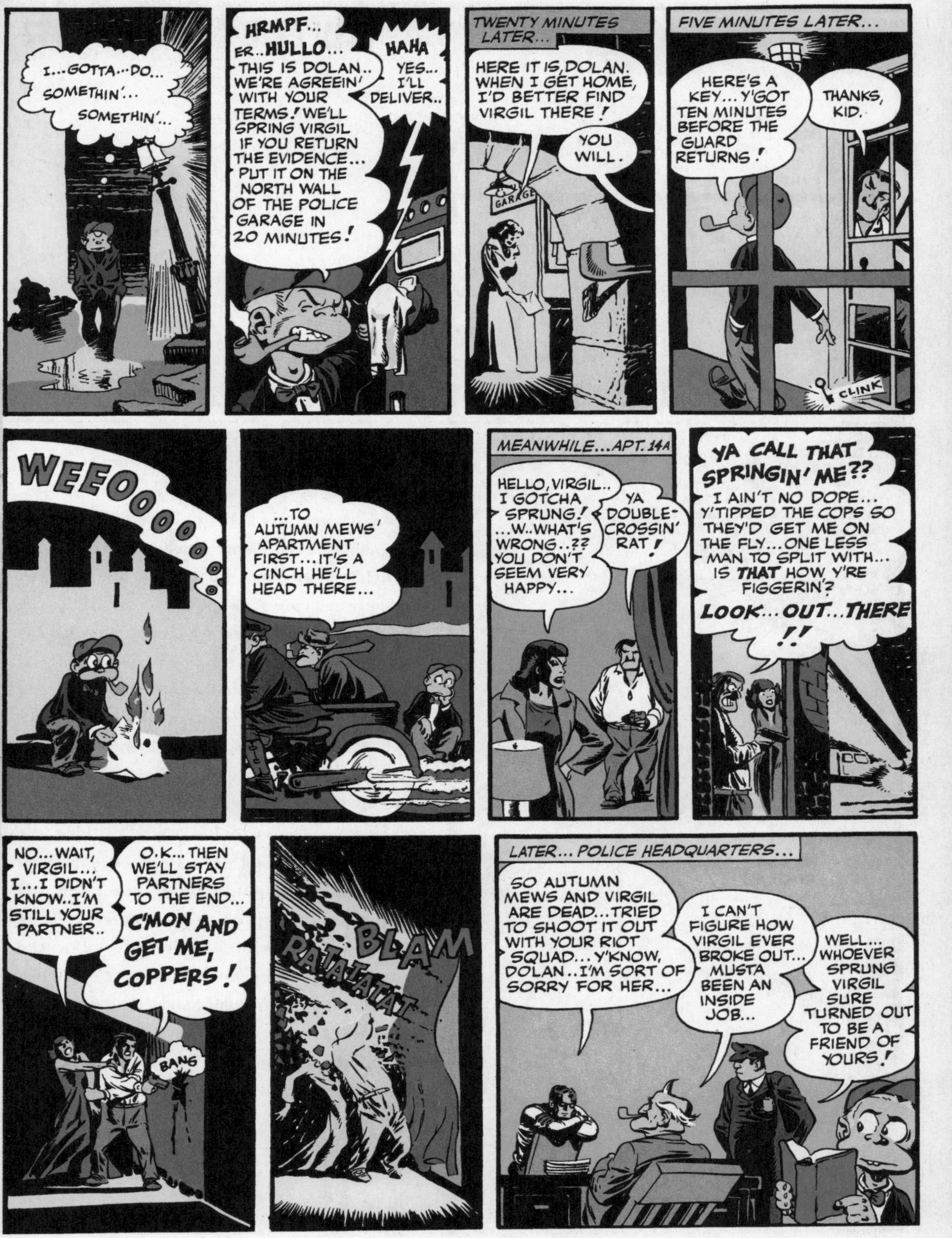
I...GOTTA...DO... SOMETHIN'... SOMETHIN'...
HRMPF...
ER..HULLO... THIS IS DOLAN.. WE'RE AGREEIN' WITH YOUR TERMS! WE'LL SPRING VIRGIL IF YOU RETURN THE EVIDENCE... PUT IT ON THE NORTH WALL OF THE POLICE GARAGE IN 20 MINUTES!
HAHA
YES... I'LL DELIVER..
TWENTY MINUTES LATER...
HERE IT IS, DOLAN. WHEN I GET HOME, I'D BETTER FIND VIRGIL THERE!
YOU WILL.
GARAGE
FIVE MINUTES LATER...
HERE'S A KEY... Y'GOT TEN MINUTES BEFORE THE GUARD RETURNS!
THANKS, KID.
CLINK
WEEOOOOOOO
...TO AUTUMN MEWS' APARTMENT FIRST... IT'S A CINCH HE'LL HEAD THERE...
MEANWHILE... APT. 14A
HELLO, VIRGIL.. I GOTCHA SPRUNG! ...W..WHAT'S WRONG..?? YOU DON'T SEEM VERY HAPPY...
YA DOUBLE-CROSSIN' RAT!
YA CALL THAT SPRINGIN' ME??
I AIN'T NO DOPE... Y'TIPPED THE COPS SO THEY'D GET ME ON THE FLY... ONE LESS MAN TO SPLIT WITH... IS THAT HOW Y'RE FIGGERIN'?
LOOK...OUT...THERE!!
NO...WAIT, VIRGIL... I...I DIDN'T KNOW..I'M STILL YOUR PARTNER..
O.K... THEN WE'LL STAY PARTNERS TO THE END... C'MON AND GET ME, COPPERS!
BANG
BLAM
RATATATATAT
LATER... POLICE HEADQUARTERS...
SO AUTUMN MEWS AND VIRGIL ARE DEAD... TRIED TO SHOOT IT OUT WITH YOUR RIOT SQUAD... Y'KNOW, DOLAN.. I'M SORT OF SORRY FOR HER...
I CAN'T FIGURE HOW VIRGIL EVER BROKE OUT... MUSTA BEEN AN INSIDE JOB...
WELL... WHOEVER SPRUNG VIRGIL SURE TURNED OUT TO BE A FRIEND OF YOURS!

WILL EISNER

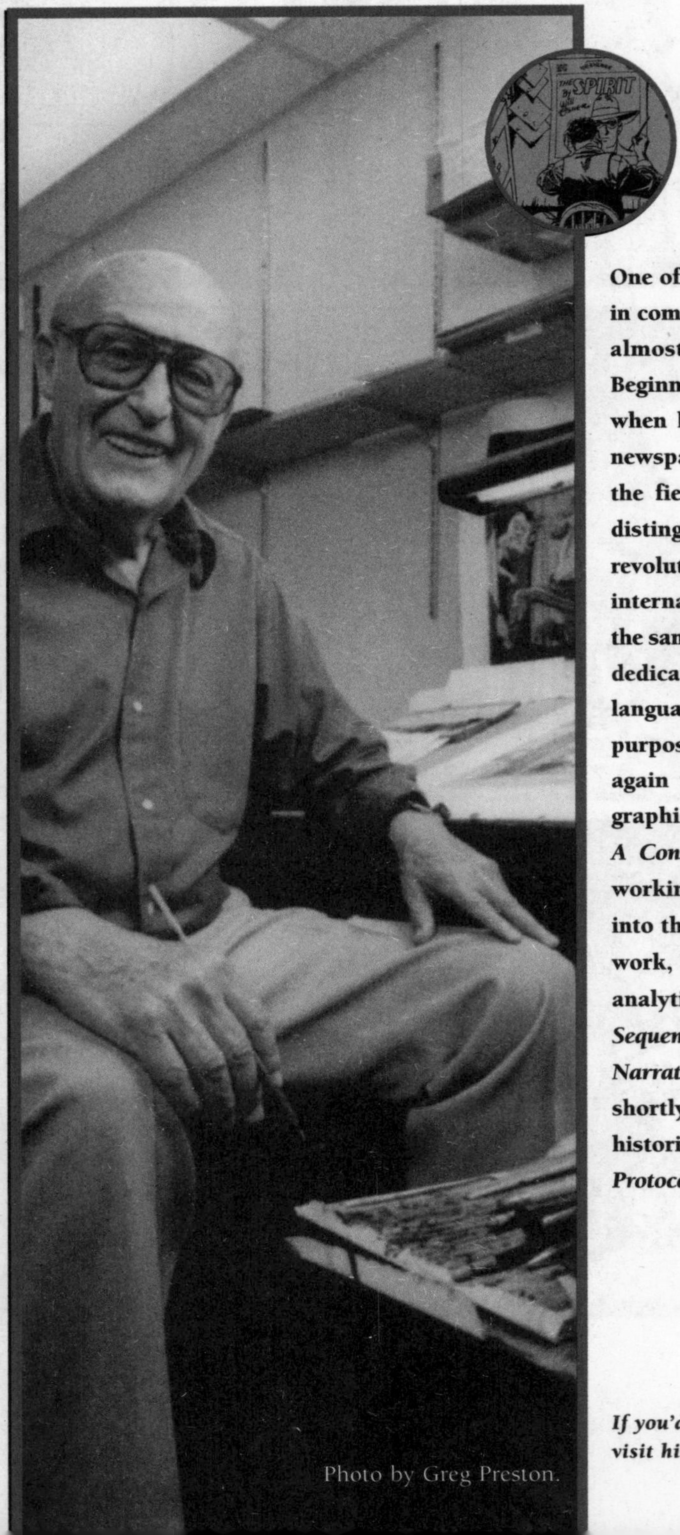

Photo by Greg Preston.

THE SPIRIT

One of the most celebrated creators ever to work in comics, Will Eisner crafted a legacy that spans almost the entire history of the medium. Beginning with his formative days in the 1930s, when he honed his skills on a series of weekly newspaper strips, Eisner consistently expanded the field's boundaries throughout his long and distinguished career. In the 1940s and 1950s, he revolutionized narrative sequential art with his internationally famed series *The Spirit* while at the same time creating an innovative new company dedicated to applying the accessibility of comics language towards educational and commercial purposes. He revolutionized the medium once again in the 1970s, creating the contemporary graphic novel form with his groundbreaking title *A Contract With God* — a form he continued working in throughout the 1980s and 1990s and into the new century. Beyond this purely creative work, Eisner also wrote and drew the influential analytical and instructional volumes *Comics and Sequential Art* and *Graphic Storytelling and Visual Narrative*. He passed away on January 3, 2005, shortly after completing his final work: the historical study *The Plot: The Secret Story of The Protocols of the Elders of Zion*.

If you'd like to learn more about Will Eisner, visit his website at www.willeisner.com.